Frommer's®

British Columbia & the Canadian Rockies

Here's what the critics say about Frommer's:

"Amazingly easy to use. Very portable, very complete."
—*Booklist*

♦

"The only mainstream guide to list specific prices. The Walter Cronkite of guidebooks—with all that implies."
—*Travel & Leisure*

♦

"Complete, concise, and filled with useful information."
—*New York Daily News*

♦

"Hotel information is close to encyclopedic."
—*Des Moines Sunday Register*

♦

"Detailed, accurate and easy-to-read information for all price ranges."
—*Glamour Magazine*

Other Great Guides for Your Trip:

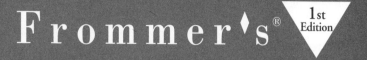

Frommer's®

1st Edition

British Columbia & the Canadian Rockies

by Bill McRae

with Shawn Blore

IDG Books Worldwide, Inc.
An International Data Group Company
Foster City, CA • Chicago, IL • Indianapolis, IN • New York, NY

ABOUT THE AUTHORS

Bill McRae was born and raised in rural eastern Montana, though he spent the better years of his youth attending university in Great Britain, France, and Canada. He has previously written about Montana and Utah for Moon Publications and about the Pacific Northwest and Seattle for Lonely Planet. He has also written for *National Geographic* and Microsoft Expedia, among others, and is a coauthor of *Frommer's Canada*. He makes his home in Portland, Oregon.

A native of California and resident by turns of Ottawa, Amsterdam, Moscow, and (for the past half-decade) Vancouver, **Shawn Blore** is an award-winning magazine writer and the best-selling author of *Vancouver: Secrets of the City*. He is also the author of *Frommer's Vancouver & Victoria* and a coauthor of *Frommer's Canada*.

IDG BOOKS WORLDWIDE, INC.

An International Data Group Company
919 E. Hillsdale Blvd.
Suite 400
Foster City, CA 94404

Find us online at **www.frommers.com**

ISBN 0-02-863628-7
ISSN 1524-1483

Editor: Leslie Shen
Production Editor: Carol Sheehan
Photo Editor: Richard Fox
Design by Michele Laseau
Staff Cartographers: John Decamillis, Elizabeth Puhl, Roberta Stockwell
Front cover photo: Emerald Lake, Yoho National Park
Back cover photo: Vancouver
Page creation: David Faust, Marie Kristine Parial-Leonardo, and Linda Quigley

SPECIAL SALES

For general information on IDG Books Worldwide's books in the U.S., please call our Consumer Customer Service department at 1-800-762-2974. For reseller information, including discounts, bulk sales, customized editions, and premium sales, please call our Reseller Customer Service department at 1-800-434-3422.

Manufactured in the United States of America

5 4 3 2 1

Contents

List of Maps

AN INVITATION TO THE READER

In researching this book, we discovered many wonderful places—hotels, restaurants, shops, and more. We're sure you'll find others. Please tell us about them, so we can share the information with your fellow travelers in upcoming editions. If you were disappointed with a recommendation, we'd love to know that, too. Please write to:

Frommer's British Columbia & the Canadian Rockies, 1st Edition
Frommer's Travel Guides
1633 Broadway
New York, NY 10019

AN ADDITIONAL NOTE

Please be advised that travel information is subject to change at any time—and this is especially true of prices. We therefore suggest that you write or call ahead for confirmation when making your travel plans. The authors, editors, and publisher cannot be held responsible for the experiences of readers while traveling. Your safety is important to us, however, so we encourage you to stay alert and be aware of your surroundings. Keep a close eye on cameras, purses, and wallets, all favorite targets of thieves and pickpockets.

WHAT THE SYMBOLS MEAN

✪ Frommer's Favorites

Our favorite places and experiences—outstanding for quality, value, or both.

The following abbreviations are used for credit cards:

AE	American Express	EURO	Eurocard
CB	Carte Blanche	JCB	Japan Credit Bank
DC	Diners Club	MC	MasterCard
DISC	Discover	V	Visa
ER	EnRoute		

FIND FROMMER'S ONLINE

www.frommers.com offers up-to-the-minute listings on almost 200 cities around the globe—including the latest bargains and candid, personal articles updated daily by Arthur Frommer himself. No other Web site offers such comprehensive and timely coverage of the world of travel.

The Best of British Columbia & the Canadian Rockies

British Columbia and the Canadian Rockies, which stretch across the provincial border into Alberta, are extravagantly scenic and quietly sophisticated. The diversity of landscapes is astounding: You'll travel from cactus-studded desert to soaring mountaintops and on to wilderness ocean beaches. You can visit traditional native Canadian villages, thread through market stalls in the largest Chinese community outside of Asia, and cheer on cowboys at an old-fashioned rodeo.

As for creature comforts, British Columbia and the Rockies are famed for their luxury hotels, rustic guest ranches, quiet inns, and B&Bs. And the food? With Alberta beef, Pacific salmon, and some of the world's most fertile farm and orchard land, these two provinces champion excellent regional cuisine.

Finally, there's no better place to get outdoors and enjoy yourself: These areas are flush with excellent ski resorts and golf courses, hiking is a near universal passion, and you'll find no better spot on earth to try your hand at adventure sports like sea kayaking, trail riding, or scuba diving.

This guide is chock-full of recommendations and tips to help you plan and enjoy your trip to western Canada; the following are some places and experiences you won't want to miss.

1 The Best Travel Experiences

- **Wandering Vancouver's West End:** Vancouver is one of the most cosmopolitan cities in the world, and wandering the streets, people watching, and sipping cappuccinos at street-side cafes can fill an entire weekend. Stroll up Robson Street with its busy boutique-shopping scene, turn down cafe-lined Denman Street, then stride into 1,000-acre Stanley Park, a gem of green space with old-growth cedars, miles of walkways, and the city's excellent aquarium. See chapter 3.
- **Taking Tea in Victoria:** Yeah, it's a little corny, but it's also fun—and delicious. Tea, scones, clotted cream—who said the British don't know good food? The afternoon tea at the Empress is world-renowned, a little stuffy, and very expensive; if that doesn't sound like fun to you, we'll show you other places where afternoon tea is more reasonably priced and a lot less formal. See chapter 4.

- **Ferrying through the Gulf Islands:** The Gulf Islands, a huddle of cliff-lined, forested islands between Vancouver Island and the British Columbia mainland, can only be reached via ferryboat. Hop from island to island, staying at excellent country inns and B&Bs; peddle the quiet farm roads on your bike, stopping to visit artists' studios or to quaff a pint in a cozy rural pub. The romantic getaway you've been dreaming of starts and ends right here on these idyllic islands. See chapter 5.

- **Traveling the Inside Passage:** The 15-hour Inside Passage ferry cruise aboard the MV *Queen of the North* takes you from Vancouver Island's Port Hardy along an otherwise inaccessible coastline north to Prince Rupert, near the southern tip of the Alaska Panhandle. Orcas swim past the ferry, bald eagles soar overhead, and the dramatic scenery—a narrow channel of water between a series of mountain islands and the craggy mainland—is utterly spectacular. See chapter 9.

- **Wine Tasting in the Okanagan Valley:** The Okanagan Valley in central British Columbia has some of the most arid climatic conditions in Canada, and with irrigation, grape varietals like merlot, cabernet sauvignon, and pinot noir flourish here. Vineyards line the edges of huge, glacier-dug lakes and clamber up the steep desert-valley walls. Visit wineries, taste delicious wines, go for a swim, play some golf, eat at excellent restaurants, and do it all again tomorrow. See chapter 11.

- **Golfing Southeastern British Columbia:** The upper reaches of the mighty Columbia River rise in a verdant, trenchlike valley, towered over by the 12,000-foot (3,658m) Canadian Rockies. Between Radium Hot Springs and Fairmont Hot Springs—a distance of just 20 miles (32km)—there are a dozen major golf courses. Nowhere else will you find such a variety of championship golf resorts in such a dramatically beautiful landscape. See chapter 12.

- **Skiing the Canadian Rockies:** You can hit all three ski areas in Banff National Park with a one-price ticket, using the frequent shuttle buses to ferry you and your skis from resort to resort. The skiing is superlative, the scenery astounding, and—best of all—you can stay at Banff's luxury hotels for a fraction of their astronomical summer rates. See chapter 14.

- **Riding Herd at a Guest Ranch:** The edge of the Great Plains nudges up to the face of the Canadian Rockies in Alberta, making this some of the most fertile and beautiful ranching country anywhere. For more than a century, ranches have welcomed guests to their rustic lodges and cabins, offering trail rides, cattle drives, evening barbecues, and barn dances that'll keep you entertained whether you're a greenhorn or an old hand. See chapter 14.

2 The Best Active Vacations

- **Hiking the West Coast Trail:** Hiking the entire length of the rugged 43-mile (69km) West Coast Trail, from Port Renfrew to Bamfield on Vancouver Island, takes 5 to 7 days, but it's truly the hike of a lifetime. This wilderness coastline, edged with old-growth forest and lined with cliffs, is utterly spectacular, and can be reached only on foot. If you're not up for it, consider a 7-mile (11km) day trip on the more easily accessible stretch just south of Bamfield. See chapter 6.

- **Scuba Diving off Vancouver Island:** According to no less an authority than Jacques Cousteau, the waters off Vancouver Island offer some of the best scuba diving in the world. Nanaimo and Port Hardy are popular departure points, with outfitters ready to drop you into the briny world of the wolf eel, yellow-edged cadlina, and the giant Pacific octopus. See chapters 6 and 7.

- **Kayaking Clayoquot Sound:** Paddle a kayak for 4 or 5 days through the waters of Clayoquot Sound on Vancouver Island's wilderness west coast, from the funky former fishing village of Tofino to a natural hot-springs bath near an ancient native village. Along the way, you'll see thousand-year-old trees and glaciers, whales and bald eagles. And if the pocketbook allows, you can stop in at one of two resorts that offer some of the best cuisine in the world. See chapter 6.
- **Salmon Fishing from Campbell River:** Even though salmon fishing is not what it once was, Campbell River is still the "Salmon Fishing Capital of the World." Join a daylong trip with an outfitter and fish the waters of Discovery Passage. Get ready to hook the Big One! Even if your trophy salmon gets away, you'll see plenty of wildlife: bald eagles, seals, even orcas and porpoises. See chapter 7.
- **Rafting the Chilko-Chilcotin-Fraser Rivers:** This 3-day white-water extravaganza flushes you from the slopes of the glaciered Coast Range down through shadowy canyons to the roiling waters of the mighty Fraser River, second only in North America to the Columbia River in power and size. A number of outfitters in Williams Lake offer river trips ranging from half-day thrill rides to multiday trips with catered camping. See chapter 10.
- **Canoeing Bowron Lakes Provincial Park:** Every summer, canoeists and kayakers set out to navigate a perfect 72-mile (120km) circle of six alpine lakes, with minimal portages in between. There are no roads or other signs of civilization beyond the launch point, except some well-placed cabins, campsites, and shelters set up and maintained by the provincial parks department. The full circuit is a 7-day trip, but the memories will last a lifetime. See chapter 10.
- **Mountain Biking the Kettle Valley Railway:** This rails-to-trails hiking-and-biking trail travels from Lake Okanagan up and over Okanagan Mountain, crossing 17 trestles and traversing two tunnels on its 108-mile (175km) route. The entire circuit, which takes from 3 to 5 days, provides lots of challenging grades and excellent scenery. See chapter 11.
- **Heli-Skiing near Golden:** Helicopters lift adventurous skiers to the tops of the Selkirk and Purcell mountains that rise just west of Golden, accessing acres of virgin powder far from the lift lines and crowds of traditional ski resorts. **CMH Heli-Skiing** (☎ **800/661-0252**) offers a variety of holidays, most based out of their private high-country lodges and reached only by helicopter. See chapter 12.
- **Cross-Country Skiing at Canmore:** The 1988 Olympic cross-country skiing events were held at Canmore, on the edge of Banff National Park. The routes at the Canmore Nordic Centre are now open to the public and offer 44 miles (70km) of world-class skiing. Canmore offers lots of moderately priced lodging, none finer than the **McNeill Heritage Inn** (☎ **877/MCNEILL**). See chapter 14.
- **Lodge-to-Lodge Trail Riding in Banff National Park:** See the park's backcountry without getting blisters on your feet. Instead, get saddle-sore as you ride horseback on a 3-day excursion, spending the nights in remote but comfortable mountain lodges. **Warner Guiding and Outfitting** (☎ **403/762-4551**) provides all meals and lodging, plus oats for Silver. See chapter 14.

3 The Best Nature & Wildlife Viewing

- **Tide Pools at Botanical Beach near Port Renfrew:** Waves have eroded potholes in the thrust of sandstone that juts into the Pacific at Botanical Beach, which remain water-filled when the waves ebb. Alive with starfish, sea anemones, hermit crabs, and hundreds of other sea creatures, these potholes are some of the best places on Vancouver Island to explore the rich intertidal zone. See chapter 5.

- **Bald Eagles near Victoria:** Just a few miles north of Victoria is one of the world's best bald eagle–spotting sites: Goldstream Provincial Park. Recent counts put the number of eagles wintering here at around 4,000. (January is the best month for viewing, though there are eagles here year-round.) See chapter 5.

- **Gray Whales at Pacific Rim National Park:** Few sights in nature match observing whales in the wild. March is the prime viewing time, as the whales migrate north from their winter home off Mexico. During March, both Tofino and Ucluelet celebrate the Pacific Rim Whale Festival; outfitters offer whale-watching trips out onto the Pacific. See chapter 6.

- **Orcas at Robson Bight:** From either the northeast shore of Vancouver Island or a whale-watching boat out of Telegraph Cove or Port MacNeill, watch orcas (killer whales) as they glide through the Johnstone Strait in search of salmon, and rub their tummies on the pebbly beaches at Robson Bight. See chapter 7.

- **Spawning Salmon at Adams River:** Every October, the Adams River fills with salmon, returning to their home water to spawn and die. While each autumn produces a large run of salmon, every fourth year (the next is 2002), an estimated 1.5 to 2 million sockeye salmon struggle upstream to spawn in the Adams River near Squilax. Roderick Haig-Brown Provincial Park has viewing platforms and interpretive programs. See chapter 10.

- **Songbirds and Waterfowl at the Columbia River Wetlands:** Between Golden and Windermere, the Columbia River flows through a valley filled with fluvial lakes, marshes, and streams—perfect habitat for hundreds of species, including moose and coyotes. Protected as a wildlife refuge, the wetlands are on the migratory flyway that links Central America to the Arctic; in spring and fall, the waterways fill with thousands of birds—over different 270 species. Outfitters in Golden and Invermere operate float trips through the wetlands. See chapter 12.

- **Elk in Banff National Park:** You won't need to mount an expedition to sight elk in Banff: They graze in the city parks and on people's front lawns. To see these animals in their own habitat, take the Fenlands Trail just west of Banff to Vermillion Lakes, another favorite grazing area. See chapter 14.

- **Black Bears in Waterton Lakes National Park:** There are black bears throughout the Canadian west, but chances are good you'll spot a bear or two along the entry road to Waterton Lakes National Park, where the open grasslands of the prairies directly abut the sheer faces of the Rocky Mountains (remember, bears are originally prairie animals). See chapter 14.

4 The Best Family-Vacation Experiences

- **The Beaches near Parksville and Qualicum Beach:** The sandy beaches near these towns warm in the summer sun, then heat the waters of Georgia Strait when the tides return. Some of the warmest ocean waters in the Pacific Northwest are here, making for good swimming and family vacations. See chapter 6.

- **The MV *Lady Rose* (☎ 800/663-7192):** This packet steamer delivers mail and merchandise to isolated marine communities along the otherwise inaccessible Alberni Inlet, the longest fjord on Vancouver Island's rugged west coast. Along the way, you may spot eagles, bears, and porpoises. The MV *Lady Rose* is large enough to be stable, yet small enough to make this daylong journey from Port Alberni to Bamfield and back seem like a real adventure. See chapter 6.

- **The Okanagan Lakes:** Sunny weather, sandy lake beaches, and miles of clean, clear water: If this sounds like the ideal family vacation, then head to the lake-filled Okanagan Valley. Osoyoos, Penticton, Kelowna, and Vernon all have dozens of family-friendly hotels, water-sports rentals, and lakeside parks and beaches. Mom and Dad can enjoy the golf and wineries as well. See chapter 11.
- **Fort Steele** (☎ 250/489-3351): In 1864, the frontier community of Fort Steele was a mining boomtown with a population of 4,000. Twenty years later, the town was practically abandoned, soon becoming a ghost town. Now a provincial heritage site, Fort Steele again bustles with life: The town has been largely rebuilt, other historic structures have been moved in, and daily activities with living-history actors give this town a real feel of the Old West. See chapter 12.
- **West Edmonton Mall** (☎ 800/661-8890): Okay, so it's a mall. But what a mall! Within its 5.2 million square feet are 800 stores and a mammoth enter-tainment center that contains a complete amusement park, roller coaster, bungee-jumping platform, and lake-sized swimming pool with real sand beach-es and rolling waves. You can also ice-skate, watch performing dolphins, ride a submarine, attend movies at 19 theaters—oh, and get your shopping done, too. See chapter 13.
- **The Kicking Horse River:** One of the best white-water rafting trips in the Rock-ies is on the Kicking Horse River near Golden. While it's the treacherous Class IV rapids that give the river its fame, there are also stretches gentle enough for the entire family. Better yet, most outfitters run simultaneous trips on both sec-tions of the river, so part of your brood can run the rapids while the other enjoys a leisurely float through lovely Rocky Mountain scenery. See chapter 14.

5 The Best Places to Rediscover Native Canadian Culture & History

- **Cowichan Native Village** (Duncan; ☎ 250/746-8119): North of Victoria, this facility contains a theater, carving shed, ceremonial clan house, restaurant, and art gallery, all dedicated to preserving traditional Cowichan history and culture. Try to visit when the tribe is preparing a traditional salmon bake. See chapter 5.
- **Kwagiulth Museum and Cultural Centre** (Quadra Island; ☎ 250/285-3733): To the native Indians along the Northwest coast, the potlatch was one of the most important ceremonies, involving the reenactment of clan myths and ritual gift giving. When Canadian officials banned the potlatch in the 1920s, the centuries-old costumes, masks, and artifacts of the Kwagiulth tribe on Quadra Island were confiscated and sent to museums in eastern Canada and England. When the items were repatriated in the early 1990s, the tribe built a handsome museum to showcase this incredible collection of native art. A must-see. See chapter 7.
- **Alert Bay** (off Vancouver Island): One of the best-preserved and still vibrant native villages in western Canada, Alert Bay is a short ferry ride from northern Vancouver Island. Totem poles face the waters, and cedar-pole longhouses are painted with traditional images and symbols. The **U'Mista Cultural Centre** (☎ 250/974-5403) contains a collection of carved wooden masks, baskets, and potlatch ceremonial objects. See chapter 7.
- **Gwaii Haanas National Park Reserve** (Queen Charlotte Islands): A UNESCO World Heritage Site and a Canadian National Park, this is the ancient homeland of the Haida people. Located on the storm-lashed Queen Charlottes, it isn't easy

or cheap to get to: You'll need to kayak, sail, or fly in on a floatplane. But once here, you'll get to visit the prehistoric village of Ninstints, abandoned hundreds of years ago and still shadowed by decaying totem poles. See chapter 9.

- **'Ksan Historical Village** (Hazelton): At the confluence of the Skeena and Bulkley rivers, the Gitksan people have lived for millennia, hunting and spearing salmon from the waters. On the site of an ancient village near present-day Hazelton, the Gitksan have built a pre-Contact village replica, complete with clan longhouses and totem poles. No ordinary tourist gimmick, the village houses a 4-year carving school, native-art gift shop, traditional-dance performance space, artists' studios, restaurant, and visitor center (☎ 250/842-5544). See chapter 9.

6 The Best Museums & Historical Sites

- **Museum of Anthropology** (Vancouver; ☎ 604/822-3825): Built to resemble a traditional longhouse, this splendid museum on the University of British Columbia campus contains one of the finest collections of Northwest native art in the world. Step around back to visit two traditional longhouses. See chapter 3.

- **Royal British Columbia Museum** (Victoria; ☎ 800/661-5411): The human and natural history of coastal British Columbia is the focus of this excellent museum. Visit a frontier main street, view lifelike dioramas of coastal ecosystems, and gaze at ancient artifacts of the First Nation people. Outside, gaze upward at the impressive collection of totem poles. See chapter 4.

- **The Museum at Campbell River** (Campbell River; ☎ 250/287-3103): The highlight of this regional museum is a multimedia presentation that retells a native Indian myth using carved ceremonial masks. Afterwards, explore the museum's extensive collection of contemporary aboriginal carving, then visit a fur trapper's cabin and see tools from a pioneer-era sawmill. See chapter 7.

- **North Pacific Cannery Museum** (Port Edward; ☎ 250/628-3538): Salmon canning was big business in northern B.C. in the early 20th century. Located on the waters of Inverness Passage, this isolated cannery built an entire working community of 1,200 people—complete with homes, churches, and stores—on boardwalks and piers. Now a national historic site, the mothballed factory is open for tours, and you can even spend a night at the old hotel. See chapter 9.

- **Fort St. James National Historic Site** (Vanderhoof; ☎ 250/996-7191): In summer, the rebuilt log Fort St. James trading post hums with activity, as actors play the roles of explorers, traders, and craftsmen. This open-air museum of frontier life is a replica of the first nonnative structure in British Columbia, constructed in 1806. See chapter 9.

- **Barkerville** (52 miles/83km east of Quesnel; ☎ 250/994-3302): Once the largest city west of Chicago and north of San Francisco—about 100,000 people passed through here during the 1860s—the gold-rush town of Barkerville is one of the best-preserved ghost towns in Canada. Now a provincial park, it comes to life in summer, when costumed "townspeople" go about their frontier way of life amid a completely restored late-Victorian pioneer town. See chapter 10.

- **Glenbow Museum** (Calgary; ☎ 403/268-4100): One of Canada's finest museums, the Glenbow has fascinating displays on the native and settlement history of the Canadian Great Plains, plus changing art shows and thematic exhibitions. The gift shop is a good place to find local crafts. See chapter 13.

- **Bar U Ranch National Historic Site** (Longview, Alberta; ☎ 403/395-2212): A working ranch established in the 1880s, the Bar U preserves the artifacts and lifestyles of Alberta's cattle-ranching past. This is still a real ranch: You might catch a rodeo one day, a calf branding the next. See chapter 13.

7 The Most Scenic Views

- **Vancouver from Cloud Nine** (☎ 604/687-0511): Situated on the top floor of the tallest building in Vancouver, towering 42 floors above the city, the restaurant/lounge Cloud Nine has 360° views that go on forever. See chapter 3.
- **Genoa Bay from the Deck of the Brigantine Inn** (Vancouver Island; ☎ 250/746-5422): A gentle bay on Vancouver Island's eastern shores, framed by mesa-like mountains and overlooking Salt Spring Island: This is one of the most enchanting views in all British Columbia. Order a drink at the Brigantine, watch the sun set, and enjoy the moment. See chapter 5.
- **Comox from the Otters Bistro** (Vancouver Island; ☎ 250/339-6150): Look across a busy marina and the glinting waters of Courtenay Bay to the jagged glaciered face of the mountains of Strathcona Provincial Park. The food at Otters Bistro ably lives up to the view. A beautiful place to reflect on the Canadian paradox: so much urbanity and so much wilderness, side by side. See chapter 6.
- **Calgary Tower** (☎ 403/266-7171): At 626 feet (191m), this is one landmark that you'll want to get on top of. From the windows of this revolving watchtower, you'll see the face of the Rocky Mountains to the west and the endless prairies to the east. If you like the view, stay for dinner or a drink. See chapter 13.
- **Flightseeing over Banff and Jasper National Parks:** Fly over some of the most dramatic landscapes in North America. **Alpenglow Aviation** (☎ 888/244-7117) offers flights along the Continental Divide in the Rockies, culminating with views of the Columbia Icefields, the world's largest nonpolar ice cap. See chapter 14.
- **Sulphur Mountain in Banff National Park:** Ride the gondola up to the top of Sulphur Mountain for tremendous views onto the cliff-faced mountains that frame Banff. Hike the ridge-top trails, have lunch in the coffeeshop, or run through an entire roll of film. See chapter 14.
- **Moraine Lake in Banff National Park:** Ten snow-clad peaks towering more than 10,000 feet (3,048m) rear up dramatically behind this tiny, eerily green lake. Rent a canoe and paddle to the mountains' base. See chapter 14.
- **Waterton Lakes from the Lounge at the Prince of Wales Hotel** (☎ 403/226-5551): There are lots of great views of the Canadian Rockies, but perhaps the most singular is the view from the Prince of Wales Hotel, high above Waterton Lake. With blue-green water stretching back between a series of rugged snowcapped peaks, the view is at once intimate and primeval. See chapter 14.

8 The Most Dramatic Drives

- **The Sea to Sky Highway:** Officially Highway 99, this drive is a lesson in geology. Starting in West Vancouver, the amazing route begins at sea level at Howe Sound and the Squamish Cliffs—sheer rock faces rising hundreds of feet—then up a narrowing fjord, climbing up to Whistler, at the crest of the rugged, glacier-clad Coast Mountains. Continue over the mountains and drop onto Lillooet. Here, on the dry side of the mountains, is an arid plateau trenched by the rushing Fraser River. See chapter 8.

- **The Sunshine Coast:** Highway 101 follows the mainland British Columbia coast from West Vancouver, crossing fjords and inlets three times on ferries on its way to Powell River. On the east side rise the soaring peaks of the Coast Mountains, while to the west lap the waters of the Georgia Strait, with the green bulk of Vancouver Island rising in the middle distance. From Powell River, you can cross over to Vancouver Island on the BC Ferries service to Comox. See chapter 8.
- **Hazelton to Hyder, Alaska:** This trip through the backcountry leads to two of the most isolated communities in North America. Highway 37 departs from the Yellowhead Highway near Hazelton, heading north through forests and climbing up to the Coast Range summit, an alpine wilderness choked with glaciers. The road then drops precipitously down to sea level at Stewart, British Columbia, and its cross-border neighbor, Hyder, Alaska. These twin towns are at the head of the Portland Canal, one of the longest fjords in the world. See chapter 9.
- **Williams Lake to Bella Coola:** Start at the ranching town of Williams Lake, and turn your car west toward the looming Coast Mountains. Highway 20 crosses the arid Fraser River plateau, famed for its traditional cattle ranches, until reaching the high country near Anaheim Lake. After edging through 5,000-foot (1,524m) Heckman Pass, the route descends what the locals simply call the Hill: a 20-mile stretch of road that drops from the pass to sea level with gradients of 18%. The road terminates at Bella Coola on the Pacific, where summer-only ferries depart for Port Hardy on northern Vancouver Island. See chapter 10.
- **The Icefields Parkway** (Hwy. 93 through Banff and Jasper national parks): This is one of the world's grandest and most beautiful mountain drives. Cruising along it is like a trip back to the ice ages. The parkway climbs past glacier-notched peaks to the Columbia Icefields, a sprawling cap of snow, ice, and glacier at the very crest of the Rockies. See chapter 14.

9 The Best Walks & Rambles

- **Vancouver's Stanley Park Seawall:** Stroll, jog, run, blade, bike, skate, ride—whatever your favorite mode of transport is, use it, but by all means get out here and explore this wonderful park. See chapter 3.
- **Victoria's Inner Harbour:** Watch the boats and aquatic wildlife come and go while walking along a pathway that winds past manicured gardens. The best stretch runs south from the Inner Harbour near the Government Buildings, past Undersea World and the Royal London Wax Museum. See chapter 4.
- **Strathcona Provincial Park:** Buttle Lake, which lies at the center of Strathcona Provincial Park, is the hub of several hiking trails that climb through old-growth forests to misty waterfalls and alpine meadows. Return to the trailhead, doff your hiking shorts, and skinny-dip in gem-blue Buttle Lake. See chapter 7.
- **Johnston Canyon in Banff National Park:** Just 15 miles west of Banff, Johnston Creek cuts a deep, very narrow canyon through limestone cliffs. The trail winds through tunnels, passes waterfalls, edges by shaded rock faces, and crosses the chasm on footbridges before reaching a series of iridescent pools, formed by springs that bubble up through highly colored rock. See chapter 14.
- **Plain of Six Glaciers Trail in Banff National Park:** From Chateau Lake Louise, a trail rambles along the edge of emerald-green Lake Louise, then climbs up to the base of Victoria Glacier. At a rustic teahouse, you can order a cup of tea and scones—each served up from a wood-fired stove—and gaze up at the rumpled face of the glacier. See chapter 14.

- **Maligne Canyon in Jasper National Park:** As the Maligne River cascades from its high mountain valley to its appointment with the Athabasca River, it carves a narrow, deep chasm in the underlying limestone. Spanned by six footbridges, the canyon is laced with hiking trails and interpretive sites. See chapter 14.

10 The Best Luxury Hotels & Resorts

- **Canadian-Pacific Hotel Vancouver** (Vancouver; ☎ 800/441-1414): Built by the Canadian Pacific Railway on the site of two previous Hotel Vancouvers, this landmark opened in 1929. The château-style exterior, the lobby, and even the guest rooms—now thoroughly restored—are built in a style and on a scale reminiscent of the great European railway hotels. See chapter 3.
- **The Empress** (Victoria; ☎ 800/441-1414): Architect Francis Rattenbury's masterpiece, the Empress has charmed princes (and their princesses), potentates, and movie moguls since 1908. If there's one hotel in Canada that represents a vision of bygone graciousness and class, this is it. See chapter 4.
- **Hastings House** (Salt Spring Island; ☎ 800/661-9255): This farm matured into a country manor and was then converted into a luxury inn. The manor house—a replica of a Sussex country home—is now an acclaimed restaurant, while other original buildings, including the barn and farmhouse, have been stylishly remade into opulent suites. You might feel like you've been transported to an idealized English estate, if it weren't for those wonderful views of the Pacific. See chapter 5.
- **Wickaninnish Inn** (Tofino; ☎ 800/333-4604): Standing stalwart in the forest above the sands of Chesterman Beach, this new log-stone-and-glass structure boasts incredible views over the Pacific and extremely comfortable luxury-level guest rooms. The dining room is equally superlative. See chapter 6.
- **Palliser Hotel** (Calgary; ☎ 800/441-1414): Calgary's landmark historic hotel, the Palliser is permeated with good breeding and high style. The magnificent lobby looks like an Edwardian gentlemen's club, while the guest rooms are large and luxurious. See chapter 13.
- **Hotel Macdonald** (Edmonton; ☎ 800/441-1414): When the Canadian Pacific bought and refurbished this landmark hotel in the 1980s, all of the charming period details were preserved, while the inner workings were modernized and brought up to snuff. The result is an elegant but still-friendly small hotel. From the kilted bellman to the gargoyles on the walls, this is a real class act. See chapter 13.
- **Rimrock Resort Hotel** (Banff; ☎ 800/661-1587): Banff is known for its scenery and its high prices; this is one of the few luxury hotels whose rates are actually justified. New and architecturally dramatic, it steps nine stories down a steep mountain slope. A fantastic marble lobby, great Italian restaurant, and handsomely appointed bedrooms complete the package. See chapter 14.
- **Chateau Lake Louise** (Lake Louise; ☎ 800/441-1414): First of all, there's the view: Across a tiny gem-green lake rise massive cliffs, shrouded in glacial ice. And then there's the hotel: Part hunting lodge, part palace, the Chateau is its own community, with sumptuous boutiques, sports-rental facilities, seven dining areas, a magnificent lobby, and beautifully furnished guest rooms. See chapter 14.
- **Post Hotel** (Lake Louise; ☎ 800/661-1586): Quietly gracious hospitality in a dramatic Canadian Rockies setting is the hallmark of this luxurious lodge. The

original log-built dining room and bar remain from the 1940s, now joined by a new hotel wing with extremely comfortable and beautifully furnished rooms. The "F" suites are the most desirable. See chapter 14.

11 The Best Bed-and-Breakfasts & Country Inns

- **West End Guest House** (Vancouver; ☎ 604/681-2889): Built in 1905 by two Vancouver photographers, this heritage home is filled with their work, along with an impressive collection of Victorian antiques. Fresh-baked brownies accompany evening turndown service, and the staff is thoroughly professional. See chapter 3.
- **Andersen House Bed & Breakfast** (Victoria; ☎ 250/388-4565): Your hosts outfit their venerable 1891 Queen Anne home in only the latest decor, from Raku sculptures to large cubist-inspired oil paintings and carved-wood African masks. Their taste is impeccable—the old place looks great. See chapter 4.
- **The Old Farmhouse B&B** (Salt Spring Island; ☎ 250/537-4113): The Old Farmhouse is an 1894 farmstead with a newly built guest house. The welcome you'll get here is as engaging and genuine as you'll ever receive, and the breakfasts are works of art—one of the hosts is a former professional chef. See chapter 5.
- **Oceanwood Country Inn** (Mayne Island; ☎ 250/539-5074): Overlooking Navy Channel, this inn offers top-notch lodgings and fine dining in one of the most extravagantly scenic locations on the west coast. Admirably, the inn maintains an array of prices that range from affordable and cozy garden-view rooms to luxury-level suites that open onto hot-tub decks and hundred-mile views. See chapter 5.
- **Sunset B&B** (Gabriola Island; ☎ 250/247-2032): A stylish modern home overlooking the ferry-churned waters of the Georgia Strait, the Sunset is the place for book and music lovers to enjoy an enchanting getaway. The rooms, especially the wood-paneled Wild Rose Suite, are wonderfully comfortable. See chapter 6.
- **Bahari B&B** (Qualicum Beach; ☎ 877/752-9278): This magnificent modern home is seriously Pacific Rim: The spectacular art and architecture of Bahari is half Asian, half contemporary North American. The rooms are extremely comfortable and beautifully outfitted with Pan-Pacific amenities and objects. One of the most stylish B&Bs in western Canada. See chapter 6.
- **Casa Rio Lakeside B&B** (Kelowna; ☎ 800/313-1033): If you're going to the Okanagan Valley to relax on the beaches, make this your B&B choice. Casa Rio has 150 feet (46m) of private lakeside beach, and it's far from the frenetic pace and traffic of downtown Kelowna. The three-story modern home is beautifully designed and decorated, the rooms very comfortable. See chapter 11.
- **The Cedars Inn** (Kelowna; ☎ 800/822-7100): A dream of a quaint English cottage, the Cedars is a handsome Arts and Crafts home in a quiet neighborhood, just a block from Lake Okanagan beaches. The inn has been beautifully restored and thoughtfully decorated to maintain its vintage charm, but updated to provide all the facilities you'd expect at a fine hotel. All this, and a pool! See chapter 11.
- **Mulvehill Creek Wilderness Inn and B&B** (Revelstoke; ☎ 877/837-8649): Equidistant to a waterfall and Arrow Lake, this remote inn in the forest has everything going for it: nicely decorated rooms with locally made pine furniture, a beautiful lounge with fireplace, decks to observe the hens and the garden (each

of which does its bit for breakfast), and gracious hosts who exemplify Swiss hospitality. Swimming, boating, fishing—it's all here. See chapter 12.

- **Union Bank Inn** (Edmonton; ☎ **780/423-3600**): Not quite a B&B, not quite a hotel, the absolutely charming Union Bank Inn is something in between. Right downtown, this marble-faced 1910 bank sat vacant for many years before being redeveloped as an inn and restaurant. Each bedroom was individually decorated by one of Edmonton's top interior designers. See chapter 13.
- **McNeill Heritage Inn** (Canmore; ☎ **877/MCNEILL**): This inn began its life in 1907 as the home of Canmore Mine's manager, and has passed through several lives since. Thankfully, the gracious building is now a beautifully restored B&B with spacious rooms and beautiful common areas. One of the best. See chapter 14.
- **Mountain Home Bed & Breakfast** (Banff; ☎ **403/762-3889**): All the comforts of home, plus commodious rooms and thoughtful hospitality. There are bigger and fancier places, but this is one of the best all-in-one B&B packages in the Rockies—and it's just steps from downtown Banff. See chapter 14.
- **Thea's House** (Banff; ☎ **403/762-2499**): A vision of stone, pine, and antique carpets, Thea's is a newly built bed-and-breakfast just 5 minutes from downtown Banff. "Elegant Alpine" is Thea's style, a cross between a log lodge and a vision out of *Architectural Digest.* Perfect for a romantic getaway. See chapter 14.

12 The Best Lodges, Wilderness Retreats & Log-Cabin Resorts

- **Tigh-Na-Mara Resort Hotel** (Parksville; ☎ **800/663-7373**): Comfortably rustic log cabins in a forest at beach's edge: Tigh-Na-Mara has been welcoming families for decades, and the new luxury log suites are just right for romantic getaways. See chapter 6.
- **Strathcona Park Lodge** (Strathcona Provincial Park; ☎ **250/286-3122**): A summer camp for the whole family is what you'll find at Strathcona Park Lodge, with rustic lakeside cabins and guided activities that range from sea kayaking and fishing to rock climbing and mountaineering. See chapter 7.
- **Emerald Lake Lodge** (Yoho National Park; ☎ **800/663-6336**): Location, location, location: Sumptuous lakeside cabins at the base of the Continental Divide make this a longtime favorite family-vacation spot. See chapter 14.
- **Deer Lodge** (Lake Louise; ☎ **800/661-1595**): There are grander and more famous places to stay at Lake Louise, but this lodge has charm and atmosphere to spare without the frantic pace of the nearby Chateau. See chapter 14.
- **Tekarra Lodge** (Jasper; ☎ **888/404-4540**): Quaint little cabins ring a central lodge building at this well-loved getaway. The cabins are atmospherically rustic; best of all, you're a mile distant from Jasper's busy town center. See chapter 14.
- **Becker's Chalets** (Jasper; ☎ **780/852-3779**): These very attractive new cabins are set right along the Athabasca River. Some units are as large as houses. Jasper's best restaurant is here as well. See chapter 14.
- **Overlander Mountain Lodge** (Jasper East; ☎ **780/866-2330**): Forget the wildly overpriced rooms in Jasper Townsite and stay here, just a quarter mile (0.4km) outside the park gates. Lovely new cabins plus a handsome older lodge with a good restaurant make this an in-the-know favorite. See chapter 14.

13 The Best Restaurants for Northwest Regional Cuisine

See "A Taste of British Columbia & the Canadian Rockies," in the appendix, for more information on the style of cuisine unique to this region.

- **Lumière** (Vancouver; ☎ 604/739-8185): From its early days, Lumière has been in the running for best restaurant in Vancouver. You won't be disappointed by the French-influenced Pacific Rim cuisine here. See chapter 3.
- **Blue Crab Bar and Grill** (Victoria; ☎ 250/480-1999): You might think that the food would have a hard time competing with the view at this restaurant in the Coast Hotel, but you'd be wrong. The creative chef serves up the freshest seafood, the presentation is beautiful, and the dishes are outstanding. See chapter 4.
- **Sooke Harbour House** (Sooke; ☎ 250/642-3421): This small country inn has one of the most noted restaurants in all of Canada. Fresh regional cuisine is the specialty, with an emphasis on local seafood. Views over the Strait of Juan de Fuca to Washington's mighty Olympic Mountains are spectacular. See chapter 5.
- **Rainbow Alley Restaurant and Gallery** (Smithers; ☎ 250/847-6121): Located a long ways from anywhere in scenic Smithers, the Rainbow Alley introduces a League of Nations approach to regional cuisine, with spicy highlights for local fish, produce, and meats. The restaurant doubles as an art gallery, creating a kind of gustatory and aesthetic synesthesia. See chapter 9.
- **de Montreuil** (Kelowna; ☎ 250/860-5508): Vivid and earthy flavors dominate at this popular and youthful hangout in the Okanagan Valley. Expect French finesse, exotic tastes, and regional ingredients such as pheasant, local foie gras, and fiddleheads. See chapter 11.
- **All Seasons Café** (Nelson; ☎ 250/352-0101): Innovative preparations and rich hearty flavors are the hallmarks of the cuisine at this superlative restaurant in a downtown Nelson heritage home. Food this stylish and up-to-date would pass muster anywhere. To find it in Nelson is astonishing. See chapter 12.
- **River Café** (Calgary; ☎ 403/261-7670): You'll walk through a quiet, tree-filled park on an island in the Bow River to reach this bustling place. At the restaurant's center, an immense wood-fired oven and grill produce smoky grilled meats and vegetables, all organically grown and freshly harvested. On warm evenings, picnickers loll in the grassy shade. See chapter 13.
- **Brava** (Calgary; ☎ 403/228-1854): A broad menu with lots of options for snacks or full-on meals makes this a great choice for casual diners. Located in Calgary's hottest neighborhood, Brava features Alberta beef and game dressed in exciting sauces and presented with dazzling architectural élan. See chapter 13.
- **Hardware Grill** (Edmonton; ☎ 780/423-0969): Although located in one of Edmonton's first hardware stores, there's nothing antique about the food at the Hardware Grill. A very broad selection of inventive appetizers makes it fun to snack your way through dinner. See chapter 13.
- **Sinclairs** (Canmore; ☎ 403/678-5370): Right downtown in Canmore, Sinclairs has some of the finest and most vibrantly flavored food in the Canadian Rockies. The menu reads like an adventure novel: exotic fruits and berries meet and wed homegrown produce and meats. See chapter 14.

14 The Best Festivals & Special Events

- **Vancouver's Three F Festivals:** The Folk, the Fringe, and the Film are the three F's in question. The Folk Fest brings folk and world-beat music to a waterfront stage in Jericho Park. The setting is gorgeous, the music great, and the crowd something else. Far more urban is the Fringe, a festival of new and original plays that takes place in the arty Commercial Drive area. The plays are wonderfully inventive; better yet, they're short and cheap. In October, the films of the world come to Vancouver. Serious film buffs buy a pass and see all 500 flicks (or as many as they can before their eyeballs fall out). See chapter 3.

- **Symphony of Fire** (Vancouver): This 4-night fireworks extravaganza takes place over English Bay in Vancouver. Three of the world's leading fireworks manufacturers are invited to represent their countries in competition against one another, setting their best displays to music. On the fourth night, all three companies launch their finales. See chapter 3.

- **Market in the Park** (Salt Spring Island): The little village of Ganges fills to bursting every Saturday morning, as local farmers, craftspeople, and flea marketers gather to talk, trade, and mill aimlessly. With all ages of hippies, sturdy housewives, fashion-conscious Eurotrash, and rich celebrities all mixed together, the event has the feel of a weird and benevolent ritual. See chapter 5.

- **World Championship Bathtub Race** (Nanaimo): Imagine guiding a clawfoot tub across the 36-mile Georgia Strait from Nanaimo to Vancouver: That's how this hilarious and goofily competitive boat race began. Nowadays, dozens of tubbers attempt the crossing as part of late July's weeklong Marine Festival, with street fairs, parades, and a ritual boat burning and fireworks display. See chapter 6.

- **Calgary Stampede:** In all of North America, there's nothing like the Calgary Stampede. Of course it's the world's largest rodeo, but it's also a series of concerts, an art show, an open-air casino, a carnival, a street dance—you name it, it's undoubtedly going on somewhere here. In July, all of Calgary is a party—and you're invited. See chapter 13.

- **Klondike Days** (Edmonton): Edmonton's big summer festival is July's Klondike Days, which commemorates the city's key role as a departure point to the Klondike goldfields in the Yukon. The Sourdough River Raft Race pits dozens of homemade boats against the strong currents of the North Saskatchewan River. The whole city gets decked out in its turn-of-the-20th-century finery for the street fairs, music events, parades, and general high jinks. See chapter 13.

2

Planning a Trip to British Columbia & the Canadian Rockies

This chapter can save you money, time, and headaches. Here's where you'll find travel know-how, including tips on when to visit, what documents you'll need, and where to look for more information. Planning ahead can make all the difference between a smooth trip and a bumpy ride.

1 The Regions in Brief

Canada's westernmost province, British Columbia, and the Canadian Rockies region, which stretches into the province of Alberta, are incredibly diverse, with many distinct regions that vary both in geography and culture. One thing's for sure: In a single trip, you'll never run out of places to visit.

Vancouver is one of the most beautiful and culturally cosmopolitan cities in the world. While there are certainly good museums and tourist sights, what we love most are the incredible mosaic of people and languages, the bustle of the streets, the mountains reaching down into the sea, and the wonderful food (Vancouver is surely one of the dining capitals of North America). When your thoughts turn to outdoor recreation, you'll find kayaking and canoeing just off your front step in False Creek and the Georgia Strait, and skiing up the road at **Whistler/Blackcomb Mountain Resorts,** one of the continent's greatest ski areas.

Vancouver Island is a world apart from busy urban Vancouver. At the island's southern tip is the British Columbia capital of **Victoria,** a small, charming city that makes a lot of fuss about its Merry Olde Englishness. In summer, the crowds can be off-putting, the sham Britishness intolerable. But in the off-season, Victoria is just a beautifully preserved frontier town in a magnificently scenic seaside location.

The rest of the mountainous island ranges from rural to wild. It would be easy to spend an entire vacation just on Vancouver Island, especially if you take a few days for **sea kayaking** on the island's wilderness west coast near **Tofino,** or off the east coast in the beautiful **Gulf Islands.** Or you can learn to **scuba dive:** No less an authority than Jacques Cousteau has claimed that the waters off Vancouver Island are some of the very best diving environments in the world. Vancouver Island is also home to dozens of First Nation Canadian bands. If you're shopping for native arts, or want to experience the culture of the Northwest Indians, this is the best single destination in western Canada.

From the northern tip of Vancouver Island, you can board a BC Ferries cruiser and take the 15-hour trip through the famed **Inside Passage** to Prince Rupert, a port town just shy of the Alaska Panhandle. Getting a glimpse of the dramatically scenic Inside Passage is what fuels the Alaska-to-Vancouver cruise-ship industry; by taking this route on BC Ferries, you'll save yourself thousands of dollars and catch the same views. From Prince Rupert, you can journey out to the mystical **Queen Charlotte Islands,** the ancient homeland of the Haida people, or turn inland and drive up the glacier-carved Skeena River valley to Prince George, on the Fraser River.

You can also reach the upper reaches of the Fraser River from Vancouver by following Highway 99 north past Whistler and Lillooet to the **Cariboo Country.** This route follows the historic Cariboo Trail, a gold-rush stage-coach road blazed in the 1860s. The road now leads through cattle- and horse-covered grasslands, past 19th-century ranches, and by lakes thick with trout. The gold rush started at **Barkerville,** which boomed to the size of a small city until the gold ran out. Today, it's one of the best-preserved ghost towns in North America. In addition to this great family destination, the Cariboo Country offers the province's best **guest ranches** and rustic lakeside **fishing resorts.**

The Thompson River meets the Fraser River south of Lillooet. This mighty river's southern fork has its headwaters in the **Shuswap Lakes,** a series of interconnected lakes that are favorites of houseboaters. You can rent a houseboat that sleeps up to 12, then chug around the lakes while fishing and exploring 600 miles (1,000km) of shoreline. The north fork Thompson River rises in the mountains of **Wells Gray Provincial Park,** one of British Columbia's neglected gems. Hiking and camping is as compelling as in the nearby Canadian Rockies, but without the overwhelming crowds.

One of the best summer family destinations in western Canada is the **Okanagan Valley.** Stretching from the U.S.–Canadian border nearly 120 miles (200km) north to Vernon, this arid canyon is filled with natural glacier-trenched lakes, which in summer become the playground for all manner of water sports. The summer heat is also good for wine grapes: This is the center for British Columbia's growing wine industry. Add to that a dozen golf courses and excellent lodging and dining in the cities of **Penticton** and **Kelowna,** and you've got the makings for an excellent family vacation.

The **Canadian Rockies** are among the most dramatically scenic destinations in the world. Unfortunately, this is hardly a secret—you'll find the entire area dripping with tourists in summer and early fall. **Banff** and **Jasper** national parks in Alberta are especially busy and wildly expensive; however, it's hard to find fault with the sheer beauty of these places. If you don't like the crowds and high prices, we cover several other options as well. The British Columbia side of the Rockies contains much less busy mountain parks, including **Yoho, Glacier,** and **Kootenay** national parks, and **Mount Robson Provincial Park. Waterton Lakes National Park,** which joins the United States's Glacier National Park, is another spectacular mountain retreat. You can also save money by staying outside the parks at Canmore and near Hinton, both in Alberta, or at Golden, British Columbia.

These considerations aside, spending several days in the Rockies should remain a part of any western Canadian itinerary. Despite the crowds, the town of **Banff** is

---

Insider Tip

The road trip between Calgary and Vancouver includes the most popular series of destinations in Canada. If you're planning to make this memorable journey, be sure to make lodging reservations as far in advance as possible.

British Columbia

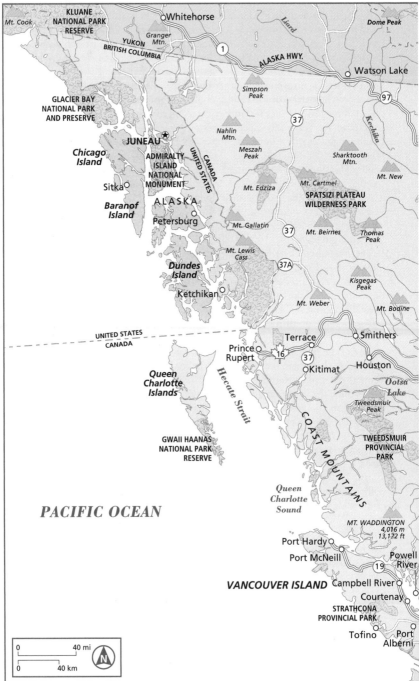

Mt. Cook

KLUANE NATIONAL PARK RESERVE

Whitehorse

Granger Mtn.

YUKON
BRITISH COLUMBIA

Liard

Dome Peak

1

ALASKA HWY.

Watson Lake

97

GLACIER BAY NATIONAL PARK AND PRESERVE

Simpson Peak

Kechika

37

JUNEAU

Chicago Island

ADMIRALTY ISLAND NATIONAL MONUMENT

Nahlin Mtn.

Meszah Peak

Sharktooth Mtn.

Mt. New

Sitka

CANADA
UNITED STATES

A L A S K A

Mt. Edziza

Mt. Cartmel

SPATSIZI PLATEAU WILDERNESS PARK

Baranof Island

Petersburg

Mt. Gallatin

37

Mt. Beirnes

Thomas Peak

Dundes Island

Mt. Lewis Cass

37A

Kisgegas Peak

Ketchikan

Mt. Weber

Mt. Bodine

UNITED STATES
CANADA

Terrace

Smithers

Prince Rupert

16

37

Houston

Queen Charlotte Islands

Hecate Strait

Kitimat

Ootsa Lake

Tweedsmuir Peak

GWAII HAANAS NATIONAL PARK RESERVE

C
O
A
S
T

M
O
U
N
T
A
I
N
S

TWEEDSMUIR PROVINCIAL PARK

Queen Charlotte Sound

PACIFIC OCEAN

MT. WADDINGTON
4,016 m
13,172 ft

Port Hardy

Powell River

Port McNeill

19

VANCOUVER ISLAND

Campbell River

Courtenay

STRATHCONA PROVINCIAL PARK

Tofino

Port Alberni

0   40 mi

0   40 km

N

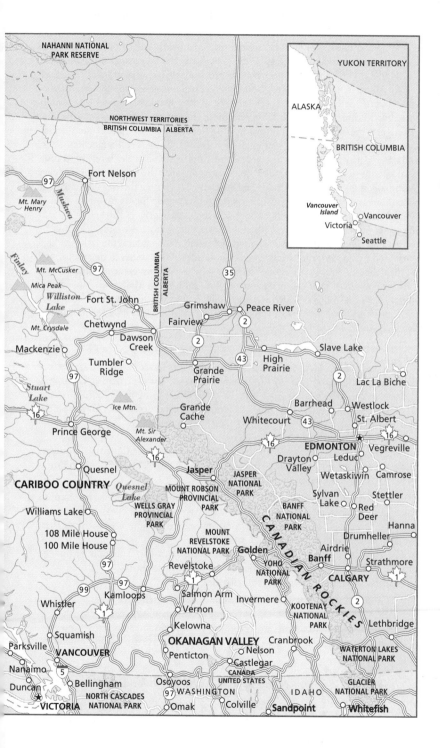

charming and filled with great hotels and fine restaurants; **Lake Louise** is a magical sight; and the **Icefields Parkway,** which joins Banff and Jasper parks, is completely spellbinding. Throughout this area, chances are good you'll see lots of **wildlife,** including the big mammals—like black bears, moose, bighorn sheep, mountain goat, and elk—that the parks are noted for. The parks all offer marvelous outdoor recreation, including **hiking, mountain biking, climbing,** and **skiing.**

Calgary, the city that oil built, is a friendly town on the foothills of the Rockies. One of the most prosperous cities in all of Canada, Calgary is still a ranchers' town, and the disparity between its role as a cow town and world oil center is one of its principal charms. The dichotomies are never more apparent than during the **Calgary Stampede,** the world's largest rodeo and an excuse for turning the city into one huge party. You can also thank Calgary's prosperity for its wonderful restaurant scene.

Edmonton, the capital of Alberta, sits high above the North Saskatchewan River at the center of a vast, farm-covered plain. This welcoming city has a wonderful historic district that's great for strolling, browsing, and eating. While Edmonton lacks the high spirits and urbane attitude of Calgary, it's no slouch when it comes to fine dining and excellent hotels. And if you enjoy shopping—or swimming, carnival rides, or performing dolphins—then you must visit the **West Edmonton Mall,** one of the world's largest shopping centers, with more than 800 stores and businesses. Like a cross between Disneyland, Las Vegas, and the Gap, West Ed Mall, as it's known, is unlike any mall you've ever seen.

2 Visitor Information

For advance information on British Columbia, contact **Tourism British Columbia,** Parliament Building, Victoria, BC, V8V 1X4 (☎ **800/663-6000** or 250/387-1642).

To request information on Alberta, contact **Alberta Economic Development and Tourism,** Commerce Place, 10155 102nd St., Edmonton, AB, T5J 4L6 (☎ **800/ 661-8888**).

For general information on Canada's national parks, contact **Canadian Heritage,** Publications Unit, Room 10H2, Hull, Québec, K1A 0M5 (☎ **819/994-6625;** fax 819/953-8770; www.parkscanada.pch.gc.ca).

ON THE WEB   Major sites like Yahoo (**www.yahoo.com**), Excite (**www.excite. com**), Lycos (**www.lycos.com**), and Infoseek (**www.infoseek.com**) contain subcategories on travel, country/regional information, and culture; search any of these for links to Web sites specializing in Canada.

The excellent all-Canada site at **www.travelcanada.ca** has thousands of links to official Web sites for destinations and activities across the country.

Here are some useful provincial and city sites:

- British Columbia: **www.discoverbc.com** or **www.travel.bc.ca**
- Alberta: **www.explorealberta.com** or **www.discoveralberta.com**
- Vancouver: **www.tourism-vancouver.org** (Discover Vancouver), **www.tourism-vancouver.org** (Tourism Vancouver), or **www.vancouverwow.com** (Vancouver-wow.com)
- Victoria: **www.city.victoria.bc.ca** (City of Victoria), **www.victoriabc.com** (Victoria BC), or **www.greatervictoria.com/tourist_information.htm** (Greater Victoria)
- Banff: **www.tourism.ede.org** (Banff/Lake Louise Tourism Bureau)
- Calgary: **www.visitor.calgaray.ab.ca** (Calgary Convention and Visitors Bureau)
- Edmonton: **www.tourism.ede.org** (Edmonton Tourism)

3 Entry Requirements & Customs

ENTRY REQUIREMENTS

Entry requirements for Canada have tightened in recent years. All visitors to Canada must be able to provide proof of citizenship. For U.S. citizens and permanent U.S. residents, a passport is not required, although it is the easiest and most convenient method of proving citizenship. If you don't have a passport, you'll need to carry other forms of proof of citizenship, such as a certificate of naturalization, a certificate of citizenship, a certificate of birth abroad with a photo ID, a birth certificate with photo ID, or a voter's registration card with photo ID or Social Security card. We recommend always carrying some form of photo ID. Although officers at border control are allowed to ask for these forms of identification, in most cases a U.S. driver's license is all that is asked for. Permanent U.S. residents who aren't U.S. citizens must have their Alien Registration Cards (green cards). If you plan to drive into Canada, be sure to bring your car's registration papers.

Citizens of most European countries and of former British colonies and certain other countries (Israel, Korea, and Japan, for instance) do not need visas, but must carry passports. Entry visas are required for citizens of more than 130 countries. Entry visas must be applied for and received from the Canadian embassy in your home country. For more information on entry requirements to Canada, check out **http://cicnet.ci.gc.ca/english/visit/index-visit.html**.

An important point: Any person under 18 must have a letter from a parent or guardian granting him or her permission to travel to Canada. The letter must state the traveler's name and the duration of the trip. It's essential that teenagers carry proof of identity, otherwise, their letter is useless at the border.

CUSTOMS

WHAT YOU CAN BRING IN   Customs regulations are very generous in most respects, but become pretty complicated when it comes to firearms, plants, meats, and pets. Fishing tackle poses no problems, but the bearer must possess a nonresident license for the province or territory where he or she plans to use it. You can bring in, free of duty, up to 50 cigars, 200 cigarettes, and 2 pounds of tobacco, providing you're over 18. You're also allowed 40 ounces of liquor or wine. Dogs, cats, and most other pets can enter Canada with their owners; you should have proof of rabies vaccinations within the last 36 months.

For more details concerning customs regulations, contact the **Customs and Revenue Agency,** Connaught Building, Sussex Drive, Ottawa, ON, K1A 0L5 (**www.ccra-adrc.gc.ca/**).

WHAT YOU CAN TAKE BACK HOME   Returning **U.S. citizens** who have been away for 48 hours or more are allowed to bring back, once every 30 days, $400 worth of merchandise duty-free. You'll be charged a flat rate of 10% duty on the next $1,000 worth of purchases. Be sure to have your receipts handy. On gifts, the duty-free limit is $100. You cannot bring fresh foodstuffs into the United States; tinned foods, however, are allowed. For more information, contact the **U.S. Customs Service,** 1301 Constitution Ave. (P.O. Box 7407), Washington, DC 20044 (☎ **202/927-6724**), and request the free pamphlet *Know Before You Go.* It's also available on the Web at **www.customs.gov/travel/travel.htm**.

U.K. citizens returning from Canada (or from the U.S.) have a customs allowance of: 200 cigarettes; 50 cigars; 250 grams of smoking tobacco; 2 liters of still table wine; 1 liter of spirits or strong liqueurs (over 22% volume); 2 liters of fortified wine, sparkling wine, or other liqueurs; 60 milliliters of perfume; 250 milliliters of toilet water; and £145 worth of all other goods, including gifts and souvenirs. People under 17 cannot have the tobacco or alcohol allowance. For more information, contact **HM Customs & Excise,** Passenger Enquiry Point, 2nd Floor Wayfarer House, Great South West Road, Feltham, Middlesex, TW14 8NP (☎ **0181/910-3744,** or 44/ 181-910-3744 from outside the U.K.; www.open.gov.uk).

The duty-free allowance in **Australia** is A$400 or, for those under 18, A$200. Upon returning to Australia, citizens can bring in 250 cigarettes or 250 grams of loose tobacco, plus 1,125 milliliters of alcohol. If you're returning with valuable goods you already own, such as foreign-made cameras, you should file form B263. A helpful brochure, available from Australian consulates or Customs offices, is *Know Before You Go.* For more information, contact **Australian Customs Services,** GPO Box 8, Sydney, NSW 2001 (☎ **02/9213-2000**).

The duty-free allowance for **New Zealand** is NZ$700. Citizens over 17 can bring in 200 cigarettes or 50 cigars or 250 grams of tobacco (or a combination of all three if their combined weight doesn't exceed 250g); plus 4.5 liters of wine and beer, or 1.125 liters of liquor. New Zealand currency does not carry import or export restrictions. Fill out a certificate of export, listing the valuables you are taking out of the country; that way, you can bring them back without paying duty. Most questions are answered in a free pamphlet available at New Zealand consulates and Customs offices: *New Zealand Customs Guide for Travellers, Notice No. 4.* For more information, contact **New Zealand Customs,** 50 Anzac Ave., P.O. Box 29, Auckland (☎ **09/ 359-6655**).

4 Money

CURRENCY Canadians use dollars and cents; the **Canadian dollar** is worth around 65¢ in U.S. money, give or take a couple of points' daily variation. You can bring in or take out any amount, but if you're importing or exporting sums of $5,000 or more, you must file a report of the transaction with U.S. Customs. Most tourist places in Canada will take U.S. cash, but for the best rate you should change your funds into Canadian currency.

The standard paper denominations are C$5, C$10, C$20, C$50, and C$100. Note that Canada has no $1 bills; single bucks come in brass coins bearing the picture of a loon—hence their nickname, the "loonie." There's also a two-toned $2 coin sometimes referred to as a "twoonie."

If you do spend American money at Canadian establishments, you should understand how the conversion is done. Often by the cash register there'll be a sign reading U.S. CURRENCY 25%. This 25% is the "premium," and it means that for every U.S. greenback you hand over, the cashier will see it as $1.25 in Canadian dollars. Thus, you'll get more for your money if you use Canadian currency instead.

TRAVELER'S CHECKS These days, traveler's checks seem less necessary than they once were; most cities and towns have 24-hour ATMs allowing you to withdraw cash as needed. Many banks, however, impose a fee every time you use a card at an ATM in a different city or bank. If you plan to withdraw money every day, you might be better off with traveler's checks—provided you don't mind showing ID every time you want to cash a check. When you cash U.S. dollar traveler's checks at banks, most will charge a $5 fee per transaction (not per check). Hotels, restaurants, and shops don't charge fees as a rule, but their exchange rates may be somewhat less favorable.

The Canadian Dollar & the U.S. Dollar

The prices cited in this guide are given first in Canadian dollars, then in U.S. dollars; amounts over $5 have been rounded to the nearest dollar. Note that the Canadian dollar is worth about 35% less than the American dollar but buys nearly as much. As we go to press, $1 U.S. is worth about $1.50 Canadian, which was the equivalency used to figure the prices in this guide.

Here's a brief table of equivalents:

C$	U.S.$	U.S.$	C$
1	0.65	1	1.50
5	3.25	5	7.50
10	6.50	10	15.00
20	13.00	20	30.00
50	32.50	50	75.00
80	52.00	80	120.00
100	65.00	100	150.00

You can get traveler's checks at almost any bank. **American Express** offers them in denominations of $10, $20, $50, $100, $500, and $1,000, and imposes a service charge of 1% to 4%. You can get American Express traveler's checks over the phone by calling ☎ **800/221-7282;** when using this number, AmEx Gold and Platinum cardholders are exempt from the 1% fee. AAA members can obtain checks without a fee at most AAA offices.

Visa offers traveler's checks at Citibank locations nationwide, as well as at several other banks. The service charge ranges from 1.5% to 2%; checks come in denominations of $20, $50, $100, $500, and $1,000. **MasterCard** also offers traveler's checks; call ☎ **800/223-9920** for a location near you.

Be sure to keep a record of the **serial numbers** of your traveler's checks (separately from the checks, of course) so you're ensured a refund if they're lost or stolen.

ATMs   You can usually get the best rate of exchange by using your bank card at ATMs. Besides getting the best commercial rate, it's convenient to not have to carry large amounts of cash or checks around.

ATMs are linked to a national network that most likely includes your bank at home. Both the **Cirrus** (☎ **800/424-7787;** www.mastercard.com/atm) and the **PLUS** (☎ **800/843-7587;** www.visa.com/atms) networks have automated ATM locators listing the banks in Canada that'll accept your card, or just search out any machine with your network's symbol emblazoned on it. You can also get a cash advance through Visa or MasterCard (contact the issuing bank to enable this feature and get a PIN), but note that the credit-card company will begin charging you interest immediately, and many have begun assessing a fee. American Express card cash advances are usually available only from AMEX offices.

CREDIT CARDS   Credit cards are invaluable when traveling—they're both a safe way to carry money and a convenient record of all your expenses. You can also get cash advances with your cards at any bank (though you'll start paying hefty interest the moment you receive the cash and won't receive frequent-flyer miles on an airline credit card). At most banks, you don't even need to go to a teller; you can get a cash advance at an ATM with your PIN.

Almost every credit-card company has an emergency toll-free number you can call if your wallet or purse is stolen. They may be able to wire you a cash advance off your credit card immediately, and in many places they can deliver an emergency card in a day or two. The issuing bank's number is usually on the back of the credit card (though that doesn't help you much if the card is stolen). Citicorp Visa's U.S. emergency number is ☎ **800/336-8472. American Express** cardholders and traveler's-check holders can call ☎ **800/221-7282. MasterCard** holders should call ☎ **800/307-7309.** The toll-free information directory at ☎ **800/555-1212** can provide other numbers for you.

WIRE SERVICES   If you find yourself out of money, a wire service can help you tap willing friends and family for funds. Through **MoneyGram,** 6200 S. Quebec St., P.O. Box 5118, Englewood, CO 80155 (☎ **800/945-2264**), you can get money sent to you in less than 10 minutes. Cash, Visa, and MasterCard are the only acceptable forms of payment. MoneyGram's fee is $20 for the first $200 and $30 for up to $400, with a sliding scale for larger sums.

A similar service is offered by **Western Union** (☎ **800/325-6000**), which accepts cash, Visa, MasterCard, and Discover. You can arrange for the service over the phone or in person at a Western Union office. A sliding scale begins at $15 for sums paid for by cash ($33 when paid by credit card) for the first $100.

5 When to Go

THE WEATHER   Canada west of the Rocky Mountains has generally mild and gray winters, with snow mostly at the higher elevations. Even though spring comes early—usually in March—gray Pacific clouds can linger through June. Dry summer weather is assured only after July 1; however, summerlike weather often continues through October. The Canadian Rockies are the spine of the North American continent, and are often socked in with cloud and rain throughout the summer. Plan to spend several days in the Rockies to assure that you'll catch at least some good weather. In winter, the Rockies fill with snow, but frequently the weather is not as cold as you'd expect. Chinook winds from the prairies can bring warm air systems, boosting temperatures up to early spring levels. On the prairies of Alberta, winters can be fiercely cold and windy. If you plan to travel across the prairies or through the Rockies in winter, be sure to have snow tires, chains, and plenty of warm clothing.

As a general rule, **spring** runs from mid-March to mid-May, **summer** from mid-May to mid-September, **fall** from mid-September to mid-November, and **winter** from mid-November to mid-March. Pick the season best suited to your tastes and temperament, and remember that your car should be winterized through March and that snow sometimes falls as late as April. September and October bring autumn foliage and great opportunities for photographers.

Evenings tend to be cool everywhere, particularly on or near water. In late spring and early summer, you'll need a supply of insect repellent if you're planning bush travel or camping.

With the huge size of the provinces, you naturally get considerable climate variations inside their borders. British Columbia shows the slightest changes: It rarely goes above the 70s in summer or drops below the 30s in winter.

FESTIVALS & SPECIAL EVENTS   Western Canada has some wonderfully unique festivals and events, from the Vancouver Folk Festival to the Nanaimo Bathtub Race to the rowdy Calgary Stampede. Each community's special events are listed in the following travel chapters. As the dates for events often change from year to year, it's a good idea to check the events calendar at each destination's Web site. These Web calendars are the easiest way to get the most up-to-date information.

6 The Active Vacation Planner

See the individual destination chapters for specific details on how and where to enjoy the activities below.

BIKING   Most of western Canada's highways are wide and well maintained, and thus well suited for long-distance bicycle touring. Most resort areas have ample supplies of rentals, so you don't have to worry about transporting your own (it's a good idea to call ahead and reserve a bike). You'll need to be in good shape to embark on a long bike trip and be able to deal with minor bike repairs.

While most hiking trails are closed to mountain bikes, other trails are developed specifically for backcountry biking. Ask at national-park and national-forest information centers for a map of mountain-bike trails.

Probably the most rewarding biking anywhere is in Banff and Jasper national parks. The wide and well-graded Icefields Parkway, running between the parks, is an eye-popping route that leads past soaring peaks and glaciers.

CANOEING & KAYAKING   Much of Canada was first explored by canoe, as low-lying lakes and rivers form vast waterway systems across the land. Canoes are still excellent for exploring the backcountry. Multiday canoe/camping trips through wilderness waterways make popular summer and early fall expeditions for small groups; you'll see lots of wildlife (especially mosquitoes) and keep as gentle a pace as you like. Generally speaking, the longer the trip, the more experience you should have with a canoe and with wilderness conditions (weather, wildlife, and chance of injury). The Bowron Lakes in the Cariboo Country make an excellent weeklong paddle through wilderness.

DIVING   An amazing array of colorful marine life flourishes amid the 2,000 shipwrecks that have become artificial reefs off the coast of British Columbia. Divers from around the world visit the area year-round to see the Pacific Northwest's unique underwater fauna and flora, and to swim among the ghostly remains of 19th-century whaling ships and 20th-century schooners.

The Pacific Rim National Park's Broken Group Islands is home to a multitude of sea life, while the waters off the park's West Coast Trail are known throughout the world as "the graveyard of the Pacific" for the hundreds of 19th- and 20th-century shipwrecks. Nanaimo and Campbell River, on Vancouver Island, are both centers for numerous dive outfitters.

FISHING   Angling is another sport enjoyed across western Canada. However, the famed salmon fisheries along the Pacific coasts face highly restricted catch limits in most areas, and outright bans on fishing in others. Not all salmon species on all rivers are threatened, though, and rules governing fishing change quickly, so check locally with fishing outfitters to find out if a season will open while you're visiting. Other species aren't so heavily restricted and probably make a better focus for a fishing-oriented vacation. Trout are found throughout the region, some reaching great size in the thousands of lakes in the British Columbia interior.

Fishing in Canada is regulated either by local government or by tribes, and appropriate licenses are necessary. Angling for some fish is regulated by season; in some areas, catch-and-release fishing is enforced. Be sure to check with local authorities before casting your line.

If you're looking for a great fishing vacation with top-notch service and accommodations, contact **Oak Bay Marine Group,** 1327 Beach Dr., Victoria, BC, V8S 2N4 (☎ 800/663-7090 or 250/598-3366; fax 250/598-1361; www.obmg.com; e-mail: obmg@pinc.com), which operates nine different fishing and adventure resorts along the British Columbian coast. Three of the resorts are on Vancouver Island; the other lodges and camps are found on remote islands and fjords along the north coast.

HIKING   Almost every national and provincial park in Canada is webbed with hiking trails, ranging from easy interpretive nature hikes to long-distance trails into the backcountry. Late summer and early fall are good times to plan a walking holiday, since spring comes late to much of Canada—trails in the high country may be snowbound until July.

Most parks have developed free hiking and trail information, as well as details on accessible trails for people with mobility concerns. Before setting out, be sure to request this information and buy a good map. If you're taking a long trip, evaluate your fitness and equipment before you leave; once in the backcountry, there's no way out except on foot, so make sure your boots fit and you understand the risks you're undertaking.

Though there are great trails and magnificent scenery across Canada, for many people the Canadian Rockies, with their abundance of parks and developed trail systems, provide the country's finest hiking.

HORSEBACK RIDING   Holidays on horseback have a long history in western Canada, and most outfitters and guest ranches offer a variety of options. Easiest are short rides that take a morning or an afternoon; you'll be given an easygoing horse and sufficient instruction to make you feel comfortable no matter what your previous riding ability. Longer pack trips take riders off into the backcountry on multiday guided expeditions, with lodging in tents or at rustic camps. These trips are best for those who don't mind roughing it: You'll probably go a day or two without showers or flush toilets and end up saddle sore and sunburned. While these trips are generally open to riders with varying degrees of experience, it's a good idea to spend some time on horseback before heading out: You get very sore if you haven't been in a saddle for a while. The Canadian Rockies in Alberta are filled with guest ranches offering a wide range of horseback activities.

SEA KAYAKING   Though it may seem like a newer sport, sea kayaking is an ancient activity: The Inuit have used hide-covered kayaks for centuries. New lightweight kayaks make it possible to transport these crafts to remote areas and explore previously inaccessible areas along sheltered coasts; kayaks are especially good for wildlife viewing.

Most coastal towns in British Columbia will have both kayak rentals and instruction, as well as guided trips. Handling a kayak isn't as easy as it looks, and you'll want to have plenty of experience in sheltered coves before heading out into the surf. Be sure to check the tide schedule and weather forecast before setting out, as well as what the coastal rock formations are. You'll need to be comfortable on the water and ready to get wet, as well as be a strong swimmer. One of the best places in the world to practice sea kayaking is in the sheltered bays, islands, and inlets along the coast of British Columbia.

SKIING   It's no wonder that Canada, a mountainous country with heavy snowfall, is one of the world's top ski destinations. If you've never skied before, you've got a basic choice between the speed and thrills of downhill skiing, or the more Zen-like pleasures of cross-country skiing. Both sports are open to all ages, though downhill skiing carries a higher price tag: A day on the slopes, with rental gear and lift ticket, can easily top C$90 (U.S.$59).

For **downhill skiing,** the Canadian Rockies and Whistler-Blackcomb resort near Vancouver are the primary destinations. The 1988 Winter Olympics were held at Nakiska, just outside Banff National Park, and the park itself is home to three other ski areas, including Lake Louise, the country's largest. If you're just learning to ski or are skiing with the family, then the easier slopes at Banff Mount Norquay are made to order. Readers of *Condé Nast Traveler* repeatedly award Whistler-Blackcomb the title of Best Ski Resort in North America. At all these ski areas, instruction, rentals, and day care are available, and there's world-class skiing at Banff, Lake Louise, and Whistler. The slopes are usually open from November through May.

Almost all downhill ski areas also offer groomed cross-country ski trails and rentals. Canmore Nordic Centre, in Canmore, Alberta, was the site of the 1988 Olympic cross-country competition, and is now open to the public.

WHITE-WATER RAFTING   Charging down a mountain river in a rubber raft is one of the most popular adventures for many people visiting Canada's western mountains. Trips range from daylong excursions, which demand little of a participant other than sitting tight, to long-distance trips through remote backcountry, where all members of the crew are expected to hoist a paddle through the rapids. Risk doesn't correspond to length of trip: Individual rapids and water conditions can make even a short trip a real adventure. On long trips, you'll be camping in tents and spending evenings by a campfire. Even on short trips, plan on getting wet; it's not unusual to get thrown out of a raft, so you should be comfortable in water and a good swimmer if you're floating an adventurous river (outfitters will always provide life jackets).

Jasper National Park is a major center for short yet thrilling white-water trips. Another excellent white-water destination is the Kicking Horse River near Golden, British Columbia.

7 Tips for Travelers with Special Needs

FOR TRAVELERS WITH DISABILITIES

For information on disability travel in British Columbia, contact the **BC Accessibility Advisor,** Accessibility Program, Ministry of Municipal Affairs, Box 9490 Stn. Prov. Govt., Victoria, BC, V8W 9N7 (☎ 250/387-7908). In Alberta, the **Canadian Paraplegic Association** (☎ 780/424-6312) can offer advice for mobility-challenged travelers. Both the official British Columbia and Alberta accommodations guides provide information about accessibility options at lodgings throughout western Canada.

A World of Options, a 658-page book of resources for travelers with disabilities, covers everything from biking trips to scuba outfitters. It costs $35 ($30 for members) and is available from **Mobility International USA,** P.O. Box 10767, Eugene, OR, 97440 (☎ 541/343-1284 voice and TDD; www.miusa.org). Annual membership for Mobility International is $35, which includes the quarterly newsletter *Over the Rainbow.*

In addition, **Twin Peaks Press,** P.O. Box 129, Vancouver, WA 98666 (☎ 360/694-2462), publishes travel-related books for people with disabilities.

You can join the **Society for the Advancement of Travel for the Handicapped (SATH),** 347 Fifth Ave., Suite 610, New York, NY 10016 (☎ 212/447-7284; fax 212/725-8253; www.sath.org), for $45 annually, $30 for seniors and students, to gain access to its vast network of connections in the travel industry. SATH provides information sheets on travel destinations and referrals to tour operators that specialize in traveling with disabilities. Its quarterly magazine, *Open World for Disability and Mature Travel,* is full of good information and resources. A year's subscription is $13 ($21 outside the U.S.).

FOR GAY & LESBIAN TRAVELERS

The larger cities of western Canada—Edmonton, Calgary, Victoria, and especially Vancouver—are generally gay tolerant, though you'll find less openly gay visibility and nonchalance here than in comparably sized U.S. cities. Each of these cities has a number of gay bars and gay-owned businesses, as well as a small gay newspaper. In smaller cities and towns throughout the region, gay and lesbian travelers are advised to be more cautious about overt displays of affection.

The **International Gay & Lesbian Travel Association** (IGLTA; ☎ 800/ 448-8550 or 954/776-2626; fax 954/776-3303; www.iglta.org) links travelers up with the appropriate gay-friendly service organization or tour specialist. With around 1,200 members, it offers quarterly newsletters, marketing mailings, and a membership directory that's updated quarterly. Membership is open to individuals for $150 yearly, plus a $100 administration fee for new members. Members are kept informed of gay and gay-friendly hoteliers, tour operators, and airline and cruise-line representatives. Contact the IGLTA for a list of its member agencies, who will be tied into IGLTA's information resources. Note that you do not need to be a member to use this service, and that the newsletter, travel information, and accommodations guide are available on the Web site at no charge.

There are also two good, biannual English-language gay guidebooks, both focused on gay men but including information for lesbians as well. You can get the **Spartacus International Gay Guide** or **Odysseus** from most gay and lesbian bookstores, or order them online from **Amazon.com.** Both lesbians and gays might want to pick up a copy of **Gay Travel A to Z** ($16). The **Ferrari Guides** (www.q-net.com) is yet another very good series of gay and lesbian guidebooks.

Out and About, 8 W. 19th St. #401, New York, NY 10011 (☎ 800/929-2268 or 212/645-6922), offers guidebooks and a monthly newsletter packed with good information on the global gay and lesbian scene. A year's subscription to the newsletter costs $49. **Our World,** 1104 North Nova Rd., Suite 251, Daytona Beach, FL 32117 (☎ 904/441-5367), is a slicker monthly magazine promoting and highlighting travel bargains and opportunities. Annual subscription rates are $35 in the United States, $45 outside the United States.

FOR SENIORS

Don't be shy about asking for discounts, but always carry some kind of identification, such as a driver's license, that shows your date of birth. Also, mention the fact that you're a senior citizen when you first make your travel reservations; many hotels offer senior discounts. In most cities, people over the age of 60 qualify for reduced admission to theaters, museums, and other attractions, as well as discounted fares on public transportation.

FOR FAMILIES

Several books on the market offer tips to help you travel with kids. Most concentrate on the United States, but two, **Family Travel** (Lanier Publishing International) and **How to Take Great Trips with Your Kids** (The Harvard Common Press), are full of good general advice that can apply to travel anywhere. Another reliable tome, with a worldwide focus, is **Adventuring with Children** (Foghorn Press).

Family Travel Times is published six times a year by TWYCH (Travel with Your Children; ☎ **888/822-4388** or 212/477-5524) and includes a weekly call-in service for subscribers. Subscriptions are $40 a year for quarterly editions. A free publication list and a sample issue are available by calling the above number.

FOR STUDENTS

The best resource for students is the **Council on International Educational Exchange,** or **CIEE** (www.ciee.org). It can set you up with an ID card (see below), and its travel branch, **Council Travel Service** (☎ **800/226-8624;** www.counciltravel. com), is the biggest student travel-agency operation in the world. It can get you discounts on plane tickets, rail passes, and the like. Ask for a list of CTS offices in major cities so you can keep the discounts flowing (and aid lines open) as you travel.

CIEE offers the student traveler's best friend, the **International Student Identity Card (ISIC),** available for U.S.$18. It's the only officially acceptable form of student identification, good for cut rates on rail passes, plane tickets, and more. It also provides you with basic health and life insurance and a 24-hour help line. If you're no longer a student but are still under 26, you can get a GO 25 card from the same organization; it gets you the insurance and some of the discounts, but not student admission prices in museums.

In Canada, **Travel CUTS,** 200 Ronson St., Suite 320, Toronto, ON, M9W 5Z9 (☎ **800/667-2887** or 416/614-2887; www.travelcuts.com), offers similar services.

FOR WOMEN TRAVELERS

Canada is one of the most polite and nonviolent places on earth, and most women will have no problems traveling here, either alone or with other women. A little common sense should prevent dangerous or uncomfortable situations. It's never a good idea to hitchhike alone, and walking alone late at night in cities isn't recommended. You may want to hook up with a buddy if you're planning on an extensive hiking or camping trip. A number of western Canadian outfitters offer women-only adventure tours.

Several Web sites offer women advice on how to travel safely and happily. The **Executive Woman's Travel Network** (**www.delta-air.com/womenexecs**) is the official women's travel site of Delta Air Lines; it offers tips on staying fit while traveling, eating well, finding special airfares, and dealing with many other travel issues. The excellent **WomanTraveler** (**www.womantraveler.com**) guide suggests places where women can stay and eat in various destinations. The site is authored by women and includes listings of woman-owned businesses such as hotels, hostels, and more.

8 Getting There

BY PLANE

THE MAJOR AIRLINES   Western Canada is linked with the United States, Europe, and Asia by frequent nonstop flights. Calgary and Vancouver are the major air hubs; regional airlines connect to smaller centers.

As this book goes to press, the Canadian government has given Air Canada tentative permission to buy and merge with Canadian Air. According to current plans, Canadian Air will continue to operate as a separate airline, and service to most Canadian Air destinations will continue, so in theory travelers should not notice great changes in service.

Air Canada (☎ 800/776-3000; www.aircanada.ca) has by far the most flights between the United States and Canada, but most major U.S. and Canadian carriers fly daily between major cities in Canada and the United States as well. These airlines include **American Airlines** (☎ 800/433-7300; www.americanair.com), **America West** (☎ 800/292-9378; www.americawest.com), **Canadian Airlines** (☎ 800/426-7000; www.cdnair.ca), **Continental** (☎ 800/525-0280; www.flycontinental.com), **Delta** (☎ 800/221-1212; www.delta-air.com), **Northwest** (☎ 800/447-4747; www.nwa.com), **United** (☎ 800/241-6522; www.ual.com), and **US Airways** (☎ 800/428-4322; www.usairways.com).

Air Canada offers nonstop service to Calgary from London and Frankfurt. Air Canada also links Edmonton and London with two flights a week, in summer only.

International airlines with nonstop service to/from Vancouver include **British Air** (☎ 800/247-9297; www.british-airways.com), **Lufthansa** (☎ 800/645-3880; www.lufthansa.com), and **KLM** (☎ 800/347-7747; www.klm-logistik.de). **Korean Air** (☎ 800/438-5000; www.koreanair.com), **Cathay Pacific** (☎ 800/233-2742; www.cathay-usa.com), and **Japan Air Lines** (☎ 800/525-3663; www.jal.co.jp) also fly into Vancouver. Additionally, Canadian Air and Air Canada offer international flights to and from Mexico, most cities in northern Europe, and many centers in Asia. **Canada 3000** (☎ 888/CAN-3000; www.Canada3000.com), one of Canada's new discount airlines, offers flights to and from Europe and Mexico at considerable discounts. Flights between Canada, Australia, and New Zealand usually connect through Honolulu or Los Angeles.

Another option is to fly into Seattle, Washington, just 2 hours south of Vancouver. Airfares are frequently less expensive to Seattle, and the difference in distance to destinations like the Okanagan, the Canadian Rockies, and Vancouver Island is negligible. Seattle has nonstop flights from London, Copenhagen, Frankfurt, Seoul, Tokyo, and Hong Kong, among others.

INTERNET DEALS   Not only can you buy your tickets directly through any airline's individual Web site—in fact, some airlines offer discounted Internet-only fares not available anywhere else—but the number of virtual travel agents on the Web has also exploded in recent years.

A good general place to start is **Arthur Frommer's Budget Travel Online** (**www.frommers.com**), home of *Arthur Frommer's Budget Travel* magazine and daily newsletter. Among the many virtual travel agents, the better-respected are **Travelocity** (**www.travelocity.com**), which also advertises last-minute deals; **Microsoft Expedia** (**www.expedia.com**), which will e-mail you weekly with the best fares for a chosen destination; and **Yahoo's Flifo Global** (**travel.yahoo.com/travel**), whose "Fare Beater" compares airlines to find the best going rate. **Preview Travel** (**www.reservations.com**) has a "Best Fare Finder" feature, which will search the Apollo computer reservations system for the three lowest fares for any route on any day of the year.

Great last-minute deals are available directly from many airlines through a free service called **E-Savers.** Sign up at the airline's Web site; then, each week, the airline e-mails you a list of discounted flights from the city or cities of your choice to any of a number of destinations. Usually, these are weekend getaway deals, leaving the upcoming Thursday to Saturday and returning the following Monday to Wednesday. On Wednesdays, the sites of **Air Canada** (**www.aircanada.ca**) and **Canadian Airlines** (**www.cdnair.ca**) offer highly discounted flights for the following weekend. For Air Canada, register at its Web Specials page; you'll then receive an e-mail every Wednesday listing available discounts. There's no need to register for the Canadian Airlines site, which posts its specials on Wednesday morning.

If the thought of all that surfing and comparison shopping gives you a headache, head right for **Smarter Living** (**www.smarterliving.com**). Sign up for its newsletter

Flying for Less: How to Find the Best Airfare

- **Take advantage of APEX fares.** Advance-purchase booking or APEX fares are often the key to getting the lowest fare. You generally must be willing to make your plans and buy your tickets as far ahead as possible: The **21-day APEX** is seconded only by the **14-day APEX,** with a stay of 7 to 30 days. Since the number of seats allocated to APEX fares is sometimes less than 25% of plane capacity, the early bird gets the low-cost seat. There's often a surcharge for flying on a weekend, and cancellation and refund policies can be strict.

- **Watch for sales.** You'll almost never see them during July and August or the Thanksgiving or Christmas holiday seasons, but at other times you can get great deals. If you already hold a ticket when a sale breaks, it may even pay to exchange it, which usually incurs a $50 to $75 charge.

- **Ask if you can get a cheaper fare by staying an extra day or flying mid-week.** If your schedule is flexible, you can definitely save money this way. Many airlines won't volunteer this information.

- **Be aware that consolidators (aka bucket shops) are good places to find low fares.** They buy seats in bulk from airlines and sell them to the public at prices below even the airlines' discounted rates. Their small boxed ads usually run in the Sunday travel section of the newspaper. **Council Travel** (☎ **800/ 226-8624;** www.counciltravel.com) and **STA Travel** (☎ **800/781-4040;** www.sta.travel.com) cater especially to young travelers, but their bargain prices are available to all ages. **Travel Bargains** (☎ **800/AIR-FARE;** www. 1800airfare.com) was once owned by TWA but now offers the deepest discounts on many other airlines, with a 4-day advance purchase. Other consolidators are **1-800-FLY-CHEAP** (www.1800flycheap.com); **TFI Tours International** (☎ **800/745-8000** or 212/736-1140), a clearinghouse for unused seats; and "rebators" like **Travel Avenue** (☎ **800/333-3335** or 312/ 876-1116) and the **Smart Traveller** (☎ **800/448-3338** in the U.S., or 305/ 448-3338; www.smarttraveller@juno.com), which rebate part of their commissions to you.

- **Book a seat on a charter flight.** Most charter operators advertise and sell their seats through travel agents. Check the ticket restrictions first, however: You may be asked to buy a tour package, pay in advance, be amenable if the departure day is changed, pay a service charge, fly on an airline you're not familiar with (unusual), and pay harsh penalties if you cancel (but be understanding if the charter doesn't fill up and is canceled up to 10 days before departure). Summer charters fill up more quickly than others and are almost sure to fly, but if you decide on a charter, seriously consider cancellation and baggage insurance.

- **Search for deals on the Web.** It's possible to get some great deals on airfare, hotels, and car rentals via the Internet. See above for details on getting the most from the Web.

service to get a weekly customized e-mail summarizing the discount fares available from your departure city. Smarter Living tracks more than 15 airlines, so it's a worth-while time-saver.

You can now "bid" for tickets at auction at **Priceline.com:** You type in the price you want to pay, then wait to see if any airline is willing to fly you for that rate.

BY CAR & FERRY

Hopping across the border by car is no problem, since there are nearly two dozen border crossings between the United States and the provinces of Alberta and British Columbia. You can also choose to take a car ferry to Vancouver Island and enter western Canada in style. Ferries link Port Angeles, Seattle, and Anacortes, Washington, with port facilities in the Victoria area; see chapter 4 for more information. Be sure to bring your car's registration papers.

BY BUS

Greyhound Canada (☎ **800/878-1290;** www.greyhound.ca) operates the major intercity bus system in Canada, with frequent cross-border links to cities in the United States northern tier. You can use Greyhound's reservation system to make arrangements on smaller local carriers (such as Brewster and Laidlaw) as well.

BY TRAIN

Amtrak serves the East Coast with four main routes into Canada, and one in the Midwest from Chicago. These trains all link up with the transcontinental VIA rail system that will take you west to Alberta and British Columbia. On the West Coast, the *Mt. Baker* runs between Seattle and Vancouver, British Columbia; the round-trip fare is U.S.$36.

In addition to these direct routes, connecting services are available from other major cities along the border. Call **Amtrak** (☎ **800/USA-RAIL**) for details. Remember that prices don't include meals; you can buy food on the train or carry your own.

PACKAGE TOURS & ESCORTED TOURS

Tour packages are divided into two main categories: escorted tours, which take care of all the details, and those package tours that simply give you a good price on the big-ticket items and leave you free to find your own way. Travelers who prefer not to drive and who don't relish the notion of getting from train or bus stations to hotels on their own might prefer an escorted tour. But if you're the kind of person who doesn't like to be herded around in a group and wants to be able to linger at various sights at your leisure, a bus tour will drive you to distraction. The independent tours offer much more flexibility, but require more effort on your part. The samples below will give you an idea of your choices.

FULLY ESCORTED TOURS **Collette Tours** offers a wide variety of trips by bus, including several in the Rockies. Ask for its *USA and Canada* brochure by contacting **Collette Tours,** 162 Middle St., Pawtucket, RI 02860 (☎ **800/340-5158;** www. collettetours.com).

If your destination is the Canadian Rockies, contact **Brewster Transportation** (☎ **800/661-1152;** www.brewster.ca) for tours in the west. Some packages include stays at guest ranches, hikes across glaciers, and white-water rafting trips.

INDEPENDENT PACKAGES **Air Canada** offers an array of package deals specially tailored to trim the costs of your vacation. Collectively, these packages come under the title "Air Canada's Canada." This term covers a whole series of travel bargains, ranging from city packages to fly/drive tours, escorted tours, motor-home travel, ski holidays, and Arctic adventures. For details, call ☎ **800/776-3000** and ask for the brochure, or visit the Web site at **www.aircanada.ca**.

Canadian Airlines operates an array of package tours in conjunction with World of Vacations, including a number of fly/rail packages. Contact **World of Vacations,** 3507 Frontage Rd., Suite 100, Tampa, FL 33607 (☎ **800/237-0190;** www. worldofvacations.com).

9 Getting Around

Western Canada is a land of immense distances, so transportation from point A to point B will take up a major part of your travel budget as well as your timetable.

BY PLANE

Canada has two major transcontinental airlines: **Air Canada** (☎ 800/776-3000; www.aircanada.ca) and **Canadian Airlines** (☎ 800/426-7000; www.cdnair.ca), which at press time are in the process of merging. However, according to announced plans, both airlines will continue to operate as separate entities with little change to current coverage and service.

Within Canada, Air Canada operates daily service between 18 major cities, and its schedules dovetail with a string of allied connector carriers like Air BC to serve scores of smaller Canadian towns. Fares vary widely depending on day of the week and seat availability.

BY CAR

Canada has scores of rental-car companies, including **Hertz** (☎ 800/654-3131; www.hertz.com), **Avis** (☎ 800/331-1212; www.avis.com), **Dollar** (☎ 800/ 800-4000; www.dollar.com), **Thrifty** (☎ 800/367-2277), and **Budget** (☎ 800/ 527-0700; www.budgetrentacar.com). Nevertheless, rental vehicles tend to get scarce during the high season, from around mid-May through summer. It's a good idea to reserve a car as far in advance as possible.

The biggest and most thoroughly Canadian car-rental agency is **Tilden Interrent,** with 400 locations coast to coast and affiliates both in the United States and throughout the world. To book a Tilden car or get additional information while in the States, contact **National Car Rental** (☎ 800/CAR-RENT). In Canada, contact the local branches listed in this book or Tilden Interrent headquarters at 250 Bloor St. E., Suite 1300, Toronto, ON, M4W 1E6 (☎ 800/387-4747).

Tilden rentals offer a **Roadside Assistance Program.** If you lock yourself out of your car or have an accident, breakdown, dead battery, flat tire, or dry gas tank, you can call ☎ **800/268-9711,** available 24 hours, and get an immediate response for roadside help anywhere in Canada.

Members of the **American Automobile Association (AAA)** should remember to bring their membership cards, as the Canadian Automobile Association (CAA) extends privileges to them in Canada.

GASOLINE   As in the United States, the trend in Canada is toward self-service stations, and in some areas you may have difficulty finding the full-service kind. Though

Sample Distances between Major Cities

- From **Vancouver** to: Seattle, 141 miles (227km); Calgary, 604 miles (975km); Edmonton, 718 miles (1,159km)
- From **Victoria** to: Toronto, 2,911 miles (4,687km)
- From **Calgary** to: Edmonton, 182 miles (294km); Montréal, 2,299 miles (3,700km)

The *Rocky Mountaineer:* One of the World's Great Train Trips

It's billed as the "Most Spectacular Train Trip in the World," and it may very well be. Operated by the privately owned Great Canadian Railtour Company, this sleek blue-and-white train winds past foaming waterfalls, ancient glaciers, towering snowcapped peaks, and roaring mountain streams. The *Rocky Mountaineer* gives you the option of traveling either east from Vancouver, traveling west from Jasper or Calgary, or taking a round-trip. The journey, which entails 2 days on the train and 1 night in a hotel, lets you see the Rocky Mountains as you never would behind the wheel of a car.

The train operates from late May through October, entirely in daylight hours. For information and bookings, contact the **Great Canadian Railtour Company,** Suite 104, 340 Brooksbank Ave., North Vancouver, BC, V7J 2C1 (☎ **800/ 665-7245;** www.rockymountaineer.com).

Canada (specifically Alberta) is a major oil producer, gasoline isn't particularly cheap. Gas sells by the liter and pumps at around 55¢ to 60¢ per liter ($2.20 to $2.40 per gal.); prices vary slightly from region to region. Filling the tank of a medium-size car will cost you roughly C$30 (U.S.$20).

DRIVING RULES　Canadian driving rules are similar to regulations in the United States. Wearing seat belts is compulsory (and enforced) in all provinces, for all passengers. Children under 5 must be in child restraints. Motorcyclists must wear helmets. It's legal to turn right at a red light after you've come to a full stop. Throughout the country, pedestrians have the right-of-way and crosswalks are sacrosanct. The speed limit on the express routes (limited-access highways) ranges from 100 kilometers per hour (62 m.p.h.) to 110 kilometers per hour (68 m.p.h.).

BY TRAIN

Most of Canada's passenger rail traffic is carried by the government-owned **VIA Rail** (☎ 800/561-3949; www.viarail.ca). You can traverse the continent very comfortably in sleeping cars, parlor coaches, bedrooms, and roomettes. Virtually all of Canada's major cities (save Calgary) are connected by rail, though service is less frequent than it used to be. Some luxury trains, like the *Canadian,* boast dome cars with panoramic picture windows, hot showers, and elegant dining cars.

If you buy a **Canrailpass,** which costs C$589 (U.S.$383) in high season and C$379 (U.S.$247) in low season, you'll get 12 days of unlimited travel in one 30-day period throughout the VIA national network. Seniors 60 and over and students receive a 10% discount on all fares. Fares for children up to 11 are half the adult rate.

Fast Facts: British Columbia & the Canadian Rockies

American Express　American Express has offices in the cities of Vancouver, Victoria, Calgary, and Edmonton; see the regional chapters that follow for addresses and phone numbers. To report lost or stolen traveler's checks, call ☎ 800/221-7282.

Car Rentals   See "Getting Around," earlier in this chapter.

Climate   See "When to Go," earlier in this chapter.

Driving Rules   See "Getting Around," earlier in this chapter.

Drugstores   See "Pharmacies," below.

Electricity   Canada uses the same electrical current as does the United States, 110 to 115 volts, 60 cycles.

Embassies & Consulates   All embassies are in Ottawa, the national capital; the **U.S. embassy** is at 100 Wellington St., Ottawa, ON, K1P 5T1 (☎ **613/ 238-4470**).

You'll find **U.S. consulates** in Alberta at Room 1050, 615 Macleod Trail SE, Calgary, AB, T2G 4T8 (☎ **403/266-8962**), and in British Columbia at 1095 W. Pender St., Vancouver, BC, V6E 2Y4 (☎ **604/685-4311**).

There's a **British consulate general** at 777 Bay St., Toronto (☎ **416/ 593-1267**), and an **Australian consulate general** at 175 Bloor St. E., Toronto (☎ **416/323-1155**).

Emergencies   In life-threatening situations, call ☎ **911.**

Holidays   National holidays are celebrated throughout the country; all government facilities and banks are closed, but some department stores and a scattering of smaller shops stay open. If the holiday falls on a weekend, the following Monday is observed.

Canadian national holidays include New Year's Day, Good Friday, Easter Monday, Victoria Day (in mid- to late May, the weekend before U.S. Memorial Day), Canada Day (July 1), Labour Day (first Mon in Sept), Thanksgiving (in mid-Oct), Remembrance Day (Nov 11), Christmas Day, and Boxing Day (Dec 26).

British Columbia and Alberta also celebrate a provincial holiday (called British Columbia or Alberta Day), usually on the first Monday of August.

In addition, you may run into other provincial holidays, festivals, and special events. You'll find the best of these listed in chapter 1 as well as in each regional or city chapter.

Liquor Laws   The minimum drinking age in Canada is 19. Laws regarding beer, wine, and liquor vary from province to province. In neither British Columbia nor Alberta can you buy wine or beer in a grocery store.

In British Columbia, spirits are sold only in government liquor stores, which keep very restricted hours and charge extortionate prices. Beer and wine are sold in state-controlled liquor stores and smaller independent stores.

Alberta has recently relaxed its liquor laws somewhat, and has privatized its liquor sales to the public. You still need to go to liquor stores for all forms of alcohol, including beer and wine, but there are a lot more stores than before, and they keep much longer hours.

Mail   At press time, it costs 46¢ to send a first-class letter or postcard within Canada and 55¢ to send a first-class letter or postcard from Canada to the United States. First-class airmail service to other countries is 95¢ for the first 20 grams. Rates go up frequently; delivery time is unaccountably slow between Canada and the States: Expect a letter from Calgary to take a week to reach Seattle.

Maps   Both provincial tourist offices produce excellent and up-to-date road maps, which you should request when you call to ask for information. The

Alberta map is free, while the British Columbia map costs C$3 (U.S.$1.95). See section 2, "Visitor Information," for both offices' contact information.

Pets   Your pets can accompany you on your vacation to Canada. All you need to prove is that your dog or cat has had its rabies shots in the last 36 months.

Pharmacies   Drugstores and pharmacies are found throughout western Canada. In fact, many prescription-only drugs in the United States are available over the counter in Canada, and pharmacists are more likely to offer casual medical advice than their counterparts in the States. If you're not feeling well, a trip to see a pharmacist might save you a trip to the doctor.

Smoking   Smoking in restaurants and public places is more prevalent in Canada than in many places in the United States, but less so than in Europe. Most restaurants will have no-smoking sections; hotels will have no-smoking rooms.

Taxes   In January 1991, the Canadian government imposed the **goods and service tax (GST),** a 7% federal tax on virtually all goods and services. Some hotels and shops include the GST in their prices, while others add it on separately.

Additionally, British Columbia levies another 7% sales tax on purchases and services. Alberta has no provincial sales tax, just the federal 7% GST.

Thanks to a government provision designed to encourage tourism, you can **reclaim the GST** portion of your hotel bills and the price of goods you've purchased in Canada—in due course. The minimum GST rebate is C$7 (the tax on C$100) and the claim must be filed within a year of purchase. You must submit all your original receipts (which will be returned) with an application form. Receipts from several trips during the same year may be submitted together. Claims of less than $500 can be made at certain designated duty-free shops at international airports and border crossings. Or you can mail the forms to **Revenue Canada,** Customs and Excise, Visitors' Rebate Program, Ottawa, ON, K1A 1J5. You can get the forms in some of the larger hotels, in some duty-free shops, or by phoning ☎ **613/991-3346** outside Canada or 800/66-VISIT in Canada.

The rebate does not apply to car rentals or restaurant meals. The GST is not levied on airline tickets to Canada purchased in the United States.

Telephone   The Canadian phone system is exactly the same as the system in the United States. Canadian phone numbers have 10 digits: The first three numbers are the area code, which corresponds to a state, province, or division thereof, plus a seven-digit local number. To call a number within the same locality, usually all you have to dial is the seven-digit local number. If you're making a long-distance call (out of the area or province), you need to precede the local number with "1" plus the area code.

For **directory assistance,** dial ☎ **411.** If that doesn't work, dial 1 + area code + 555-1212. Many public phones are set up to accept phone cards, which are readily available at drugstores, tobacco shops, and other shops.

Time Zone   Most of British Columbia is in the Pacific time zone, which is 8 hours earlier than Greenwich mean time. A sliver of British Columbia, stretching from Golden down to Cranbrook, is on mountain time, an hour later than the rest of the province. All of Alberta is in the mountain time zone. Each year, on the first Sunday in April, daylight saving time comes into effect in both provinces; clocks are advanced by 1 hour. On the last Sunday in October, Canada reverts to standard time.

Tipping   The rules for tipping in Canada parallel those in the United States. For good service in a restaurant, tip 15% to 20%. Tip hairdressers or taxi drivers 10%. Bellhops get C$1 (U.S.65¢) per bag for luggage taken to your room; for valets who fetch your car, a C$2 (U.S.$1.30) tip should suffice.

Water   The water in Canada is legendary for its purity. You can drink water directly from the tap anywhere in the country. Bottled water is also widely available.

3

Vancouver

by Shawn Blore

If you really want to understand Vancouver, stand at the edge of the Inner Harbour (the prow of the Canada Place pavilion makes a good vantage point) and look up: past the floatplanes taking off over Stanley Park, around the container terminals, over the tony waterfront high-rises, and then up the steep green slopes of the north-shore mountains to the twin snowy peaks of the Lions. All this—well, 90% of it anyway—is the result of a unique collaboration between God and the Canadian Pacific Railway (CPR).

It was the Almighty—or Nature, depending on your point of view—who raised up the coast range and then sent a glacier slicing along its foot, simultaneously carving out a deep trench and piling up a tall moraine of rock and sand. When the ice retreated, water from the Pacific flowed in and the moraine became a peninsula, flanked on one side by a deep natural harbor and on the other by a river of glacial meltwater. Some 10,000 years later, a CPR surveyor came by and decided he'd found the perfect spot for the railway's new Pacific terminus. He kept quiet until the company had bought up most of the land around town; then the railway moved in and set up shop. The city of Vancouver was born.

The resulting boom was pretty small. Though the port did a good business shipping out grain, and sawmills and salmon canneries sprang up, the city was too far from the rest of North America for any serious manufacturing. Vancouver became a town of sailors, lumberjacks, and fishers—until the 1980s, when it decided to host Expo '86, a stunning success. The world came to visit, including many people from the emerging tiger economies of Hong Kong, Taiwan, and Malaysia who moved here permanently. On the Fraser River delta, the bedroom community of Richmond became a city, with a population more than half Chinese. In older neighborhoods, prices went ballistic, doubling and tripling overnight. And on the rail-yard-turned-Expo site, 40 new high-rise condo towers began going up.

Unlike previous immigrants, these newcomers didn't worry about finding work; they made their own, founding financial-services, software, engineering, and architectural-consulting businesses. A film industry sprang up as well. Vancouver became a city of Jags, Beemers, cell phones, and shining residential towers. The newcomers brought with them a love of dining out, so the steak house and the ubiquitous Chinese-Canadian diner gave way to a thousand little places offering sushi and Szechuan, tapas and bami, and, inevitably, fusion.

Working indoors, Vancouverites fell in love with the nearby opportunities for outdoor activities: mountain biking, windsurfing, kayaking, rock climbing, parasailing, snowboarding, and back-country skiing. Once they mastered all these, they began experimenting with new sports, and strange summer-winter combinations were born: skiing-kayaking, mountain biking–snowboarding, and snowshoe-paragliding.

Splints and scrapes aside, folks seem happy with the new state of affairs—and the rest of the world seems to agree. *Outside* magazine voted Vancouver one of the 10 best cities in the world to live in. *Condé Nast Traveler* called it one of the 10 best cities to visit. And the World Council of Cities ranked it second only to Geneva for quality of life. Heady stuff, particularly for a spot that less than 20 years ago was derided as the world's biggest mill town. But then again, God—and the Canadian Pacific Railway—works in mysterious ways.

1 Orientation

ARRIVING

BY PLANE   Direct service between major U.S. cities and Vancouver is provided by **Air Canada** (☎ 800/661-3936), **Canadian Airlines** (☎ 800/363-7530), **American Airlines** (☎ 800/433-7300), **Continental Airlines** (☎ 800/231-0856), **Northwest Airlines** (☎ 800/447-4747), and **United Airlines** (☎ 800/241-6522).

Vancouver International Airport is 8 miles (13km) south of downtown on uninhabited Sea Island. A massive expansion of this facility was completed in 1997. To pay for these improvements, the airport authority imposes an **international departure surcharge** of C$15 (U.S.$10) per person for international travelers outside North America, C$10 (U.S.$7) for passengers traveling within North America (including Hawaii and Mexico), and C$5 (U.S.$3.25) for passengers departing on flights within British Columbia or the Yukon. There's no surcharge on arrival. **Tourist information kiosks** (☎ 604/276-6101), on Levels 2 and 3 of the Main and International terminals, are open daily from 6:30am to 11:30pm.

Both short- and long-term **parking** (☎ 604/276-6106) are available. **Courtesy buses** go to airport hotels, and a **shuttle bus** links the Main and International terminals to the South Terminal, where smaller and private aircraft land. Drivers heading into Vancouver take the Arthur Laing Bridge, which leads directly to Granville Street, the most direct route to downtown.

The **YVR Airporter** (☎ 604/946-8866) provides service to downtown Vancouver's major hotels. It leaves from Level 2 of the Main Terminal every 15 minutes daily from 6:30am to 10:30pm, and every 30 minutes from 10:30pm on, with a final run at 12:15am. The 30-minute ride whisks you up the delta through central Vancouver before taking the Granville Street Bridge into downtown. The one-way fare is C$10 (U.S.$7) for adults, C$8 (U.S.$5) for seniors, and C$5 (U.S.$3.25) for children. Bus service back to the airport leaves from selected downtown hotels.

Getting to and from the airport via public transit is a pain. The buses are slow, and you have to transfer at least once to get downtown. The hassle probably isn't worth the savings, but **bus no. 100** stops at both terminals. At the Granville/West 71st Street stop, get off and transfer to **no. 8** to downtown Vancouver. BC Transit fares are C$1.50 (U.S.$1) during off-peak hours and C$2.25 (U.S.$1.45) Monday through Friday until 6:30pm. Transfers are free within a 90-minute period.

The average **taxi** fare from the airport to downtown is about C$25 (U.S.$16), plus tip. Most major **car-rental firms** have airport counters and shuttles. Make advance reservations for fast check-in and guaranteed availability.

Greater Vancouver

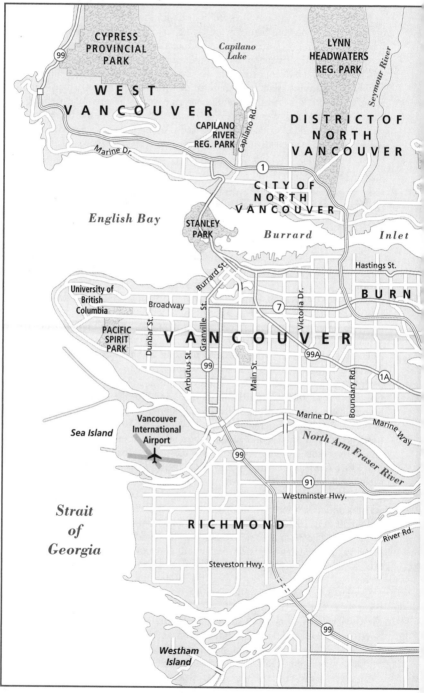

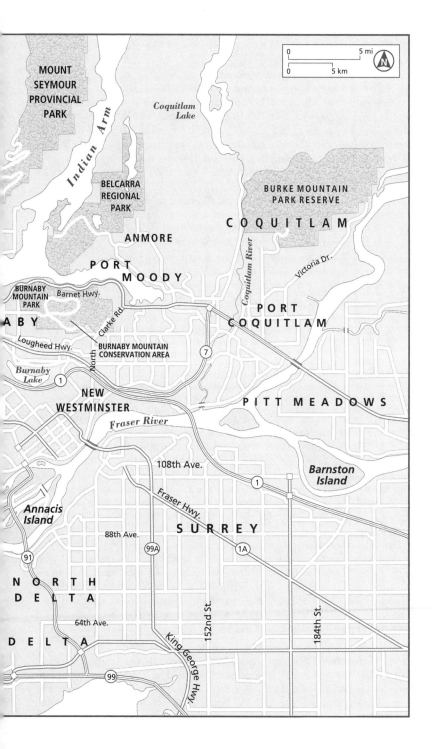

BY TRAIN   Vancouver is the western terminus of **VIA Rail,** 1150 Station St. (☎ 800/561-8630), Canada's intercity passenger train system. Other western Canadian stops along VIA's transcontinental route include Edmonton, Regina, and Winnipeg (but not Calgary). **Amtrak** (☎ 800/872-7245) offers daily service between Seattle and Vancouver (U.S.$36 round-trip); the VIA and Amtrak systems meet in Winnipeg as well. Non-U.S. and non-Canadian travelers can buy a 15- to 30-day **USA Railpass** for U.S.$340 to U.S.$425 peak or U.S.$229 to U.S.$339 off-peak. You can use the pass for rail connections to Vancouver. **BC Rail,** 1311 W. First St., North Vancouver (☎ 604/631-3500), also connects Vancouver to other cities in the province, including Whistler. The trip to Whistler is 2¹/₂ hours one-way; a one-way ticket, including breakfast or dinner, is C$31 (U.S.$20) for adults.

The main Vancouver rail station, **Pacific Central Station,** is at 1150 Station St., near Main Street and Terminal Avenue just south of Chinatown. From here, you can reach downtown Vancouver by cab for about C$5 (U.S.$3.25). A block from the station is the **SkyTrain's Main Street Station,** within minutes of downtown. The Granville and Waterfront stations are two and four stops away, respectively. A one-zone SkyTrain ticket, which covers the city of Vancouver, is C$1.50 (U.S.$1).

BY BUS   Greyhound Bus Lines (☎ 604/482-8747) and **Pacific Coach Lines** (☎ 604/662-8074) have terminals at the **Pacific Central Station,** 1150 Station St. Greyhound Canada's **Canada Pass** offers 10, 20, or 40 days of unlimited travel for C$246 to C$449 (U.S.$160 to U.S.$292). Pacific Coach Lines provides service between Vancouver and Victoria at C$26 (U.S.$17) one-way, including ferry. **Quick Coach Lines** (☎ 604/940-4428) connects Vancouver to the Seattle-Tacoma International Airport. The bus leaves from Vancouver's Sandman Inn, 180 W. Georgia St., makes pickups at most major hotels, and stops at the Vancouver International Airport. The 4-hour ride costs C$39 (U.S.$25) one-way, C$70 (U.S.$46) round-trip.

BY CAR   From Seattle, the 140-mile (224km) drive along **U.S. Interstate 5** takes about 2¹/₂ hours. The road changes into **Highway 99** when you cross the border. You'll drive through the cities of White Rock, Delta, and Richmond; pass under the Fraser River through the George Massey Tunnel; and cross the Oak Street Bridge. The highway ends here and becomes Oak Street, a busy urban thoroughfare. Turn left onto 70th Avenue (a small sign suspended above the left lane at the intersection of Oak Street and 70th Avenue reads CITY CENTRE). Six blocks later, turn right onto Granville Street, which heads directly into downtown Vancouver on the Granville Street Bridge.

Trans-Canada Highway 1 is a limited-access freeway running all the way to Vancouver's eastern boundary, where it crosses the Second Narrows Bridge to North Vancouver. When coming on Highway 1 from the east, exit at Cassiar Street and turn left at the first light onto Hastings Street (Hwy. 7A), adjacent to Exhibition Park. Follow Hastings Street 4 miles (6.5km) into downtown. When coming to Vancouver from Whistler or parts north, take Exit 13 (the sign says TAYLOR WAY, BRIDGE TO VANCOUVER) and cross the Lions Gate Bridge into Vancouver's West End.

BY SHIP & FERRY   The **Canada Place** cruise-ship terminal at the base of Burrard Street (☎ 604/665-9085) is a city landmark. Topped by five eye-catching white Teflon sails, Canada Place Pier juts out into the Burrard Inlet and is at the edge of the downtown financial district. Many ships dock here and at the nearby Ballantyne Pier to board passengers headed for Alaska via British Columbia's Inside Passage. Buses and taxis greet new arrivals, but you can also easily walk to many major hotels.

Special Events & Festivals

At the New Year's Day **Polar Bear Swim** at English Bay Beach, thousands of hardy citizens show up in elaborate costumes to take a dip in the icy waters. On the second Sunday in January, the **Annual Bald Eagle Count** kicks off at the **Brackendale Art Gallery** (☎ 604/898-3333). The **Chinese New Year** is celebrated in January or February with 2 weeks of firecrackers, dancing dragon parades, and other festivities. March's **International Wine Festival** features the latest vintages, while April's **Vancouver Sun Run** is Canada's biggest 10k race, featuring 17,000 runners and walkers who start and finish at B.C. Place Stadium.

The June **International Children's Festival** in Vanier Park (☎ 640/708-5655) features plays and music. The **VanDusen Flower and Garden Show** (☎ 604/878-9274) is the city's premier flora gala. The late-June **Alcan Dragon Boat Festival** brings more than 150 local and international teams racing huge dragon boats. Four stages of music, dance, and Chinese acrobatics also take place as part of the events at the **Plaza of Nations** (☎ 604/688-2382).

During the July **DuMaurier International Jazz Festival** (☎ 604/872-5200), more than 800 jazz and blues musicians perform at venues around town. Running from July through September, the **Bard on the Beach Shakespeare Festival,** in Vanier Park (☎ 604/739-0559), presents Shakespeare's plays in a tent overlooking English Bay. On **Canada Day,** July 1, Canada Place Pier hosts a celebration including music, dance, and a fireworks display. The second or third weekend in July brings the ✪ **Vancouver Folk Music Festival** (☎ 604/602-9798) at Jericho Beach Park. During the ✪ **Benson & Hedges Symphony of Fire,** three international fireworks companies compete for a coveted title by launching their best displays, which are programmed to explode in time to music over English Bay Beach. Don't miss the grand finale on the fourth night.

From mid-August to Labour Day, the **Pacific National Exhibition** (☎ 604/253-2311) offers everything from big-name entertainment to a demolition derby, livestock demonstrations, fashion shows, and North America's finest all-wooden roller coaster. On Labour Day weekend, the **Molson Indy** (☎ 604/684-4639) roars around the streets of False Creek, attracting more than 500,000 spectators. Later in September, Vancouver's ✪ **Fringe Festival** (☎ 604/257-0350) highlights the best of the city's independent theater.

Every October, the ✪ **Vancouver International Film Festival** (☎ 604/685-0260) features 250 new works, revivals, and retrospectives, representing filmmakers from 40 countries. All December, the **Christmas Carol Ship Parade** lights up the harbor, as cruise ships decorated with colorful lights sail around English Bay, while onboard guests sip cider and sing Christmas carols.

BC Ferries (☎ 888/223-3779; www.bcferries.bc.ca) has three routes between Vancouver and Vancouver Island. The one-way fare is C$9 (U.S.$6) for adults, C$4.25 (U.S.$2.75) for children, and C$29 (U.S.$19) per car. The most direct route to Victoria is via the **Tsawwassen–Swartz Bay ferry,** which runs daily every 2 hours from 7am to 9pm. The Tsawwassen terminal is 12 miles (19km) south of Vancouver. Take Highway 17 from Tsawwassen until it merges with Highway 99 just before the

George Massey Tunnel, then follow the directions to Vancouver given in "By Car," above. The **Mid-Island Express** operates between Tsawwassen and Duke Point, south of Nanaimo. The 2-hour crossing runs six times daily from 5:30am to 11pm. The **Horseshoe Bay–Nanaimo ferry** has eight daily sailings, leaving Horseshoe Bay near West Vancouver and arriving 95 minutes later in Nanaimo. To reach Vancouver from Horseshoe Bay, take the Trans-Canada Highway (Hwys. 1 and 99) east and take Exit 13 (Taylor Way) to the Lions Gate Bridge and downtown Vancouver's West End.

VISITOR INFORMATION

The **Vancouver Tourist Info Centre,** 200 Burrard St. (☎ **604/683-2000;** www. tourism-vancouver.org), is your best bet for information on Vancouver and the North Shore. From May to Labour Day, it's open daily from 8am to 6pm; the rest of the year, Monday through Friday from 8:30am to 5:30pm and Saturday from 9am to 5pm. For information on the rest of the province, contact **Super Natural British Columbia** (☎ **800/663-6000** or 604/663-6000; www.iias.com/travel or www. snbc-res.com).

Some of the best Web sites are **Tourism BC** (www.tourism-bc.ca), **Super Natural British Columbia** (www.iias.com/travel or www.snbc-res.com), **Tourism Vancouver** (www.tourism-vancouver.org), **Environment Canada** (www.weatheroffice.com), **BC Transit** (http://transitbc.com or www.cmbuslink.com), **BC Ferries** (www.bcferries. com), and *Vancouver* magazine (www.vanmag.com).

CITY LAYOUT

Think of Vancouver's downtown peninsula as being like an upraised thumb on the mitten-shaped Vancouver mainland. Stanley Park, the West End, Yaletown, and Vancouver's business-and-financial center are on the "thumb," bordered to the west by English Bay, to the north by Burrard Inlet, and to the south by False Creek. The mainland part of the city, the "mitten," is mostly residential, with a sprinkling of businesses along main arteries.

On the downtown peninsula are four key east-west streets. **Robson Street** starts at B.C. Place Stadium on Beatty Street, flows through the West End's shopping district, and ends at Stanley Park's Lost Lagoon on Lagoon Drive. **Georgia Street**—far more efficient for drivers than pedestrian-oriented Robson—runs from the Georgia Viaduct on downtown's east edge through the city's commercial core and Stanley Park and over the Lion's Gate Bridge to the North Shore. Three blocks north of Georgia is **Hastings Street,** which begins in the West End, runs east through downtown, and skirts Gastown's southern border as it heads east to the Trans-Canada Highway. **Davie Street** starts at Pacific Boulevard near the Cambie Street Bridge, travels through Yaletown into the West End's more residential shopping district, and ends at English Bay Beach.

Three north-south downtown streets will get you everywhere you want to go in and out of downtown. Two blocks east of Stanley Park is **Denman Street,** which runs from West Georgia Street at Coal Harbour to Beach Avenue at English Bay Beach. This main West End thoroughfare is where locals go to dine out. It's also the shortest north-south route between the two ends of the Stanley Park Seawall. Eight blocks east is **Burrard Street,** which starts near the Canada Place Pier, runs south through downtown, crosses the Burrard Street Bridge, and then forks. One branch, still **Burrard Street,** continues south and intersects **West 4th Avenue** and **Broadway** before terminating at **West 16th Avenue** on the borders of Shaughnessy. The other branch becomes **Cornwall Avenue,** which heads west through Kitsilano, changing its name two more times to **Point Grey Road** and then **Northwest Marine Drive** before entering the University of British Columbia campus.

Finding an Address

In many Vancouver addresses, the suite or room number precedes the building number. For instance, 100-1250 Robson St. is Suite 100 at 1250 Robson St. In downtown Vancouver, Chinatown's **Carrall Street** is the east-west axis from which streets are numbered and designated. Westward, numbers increase progressively to Stanley Park; eastward, numbers increase heading toward Commercial Drive. For example, 400 West Pender would be about 4 blocks from Carrall Street heading toward downtown; 400 East Pender would be 4 blocks on the opposite side of Carrall Street. Off the peninsula, the system works the same, but **Ontario Street** is the east-west axis. All east-west roads are avenues (like 4th Avenue), while streets (Main Street) run exclusively north-south.

Granville Street starts near the Waterfront Station on Burrard Inlet and runs the entire length of downtown, crosses the Granville Bridge to Vancouver's West Side, and continues south across the breadth of the city before crossing the Arthur Laing Bridge to **Vancouver International Airport.**

On the mainland portion of Vancouver, the east-west roads are numbered from 1st Avenue at the downtown bridges to 77th Avenue by the banks of the Fraser River. By far the most important east-west route is **Broadway** (formerly 9th Avenue), which starts a few blocks from the University of British Columbia and extends across the length of the city to the border with neighboring Burnaby, where it becomes the Lougheed Highway. In Kitsilano, **West 4th Avenue** is also a major east-west shopping-and-commercial corridor. Intersecting with Broadway at various points are a number of important north-south commercial streets, each of which defines a particular neighborhood. The most significant are (west to east) **Macdonald Street** in Kitsilano, then **Granville Street, Cambie Street, Main Street,** and **Commercial Drive.**

The tourist information center (see "Visitor Information," above) and most hotels can provide you with detailed downtown maps. A good all-around metropolitan area map is the ***Rand McNally Vancouver* city map,** available for C$3 (U.S.$1.95) at the Vancouver Airport Tourism Centre kiosk. Also good is the Canadian Automobile Association (CAA) map, free to both AAA and CAA members and available at AAA offices across North America. **International Travel Maps and Books,** 552 Seymour St. (☎ **604/687-3320**), has the city's most extensive selection of Vancouver and British Columbia maps and specialty guidebooks.

Neighborhoods in Brief

When figuring out what's where in Vancouver, keep in mind this is a city where property is king and where the word *west* has such positive connotations, folks have gone to great lengths to associate it with their particular patch of real estate. Thus there's the **West End,** the **West Side,** and **West Vancouver,** which improbably enough is located immediately beside **North Vancouver.** The West End is a high-rise residential neighborhood on the downtown peninsula. The West Side is half of Vancouver, from Ontario Street west to the University of British Columbia. (The more working-class **East Side** covers the city's mainland portion, from Ontario Street east to Boundary Road.) Tony West Vancouver is a city unto itself on the far side of Burrard Inlet. Together with its more middle-class neighbor North Vancouver, it forms an area called the **North Shore.**

Downtown   Vancouver's commercial-and-office core runs from Nelson Street north to the harbor, with Homer Street as the eastern edge and a more ragged boundary running roughly along Burrard Street forming the western border. The prime office space is on or near Georgia Street. Hotels are mostly in the northern third of downtown, clustered thickly near the water's edge; restaurants are sprinkled throughout. Walking is a good bet for getting around, day and night. Unlike in many other cities, lots of people live in and around the central business district, so the area is always populated.

The West End   A fascinating neighborhood of high-rise condos mixed with Edwardian homes, the West End has within its borders all the necessities of life: great cafes and nightclubs, many and varied bookshops, and some of the city's best restaurants. The Pacific Ocean laps against the West End on two sides, in the form of Burrard Inlet to the north and English Bay to the south, while on the western edge spreads Stanley Park. Burrard Street forms the West End's eastern border.

Gastown   The city's oldest section, Gastown was named after Vancouver's first settler, Jack Deighton, nicknamed "Gassy" thanks to his longwinded habits of speech. It was rebuilt in brick after the 1886 fire wiped out the original wooden city. Gastown's cobblestone streets and late-Victorian architecture make it well worth a visit, despite an infestation of curio shops and souvenir stands. It lies east of downtown, in the 6 square blocks between Water and Hastings streets and Cambie and Columbia streets.

Chinatown   South of Hastings Street, between Gore and Carrall streets to the east and west and Keefer Street to the south, Vancouver's Chinatown isn't large but is intense. Fishmongers call out their wares in Cantonese; customers hunt for dried sea horse at a traditional apothecary; and, inside any of a dozen restaurants, you'll find an entire extended family consuming half a dozen plates of succulent Cantonese cooking.

Yaletown   The former warehouse district, below Granville Street and above Pacific Boulevard, from Davie Street over to Smithe, has long since been converted to an area of lofts, clubs, restaurants, high-end furniture shops, and a fledgling multimedia biz. In recent years, the neighborhood has finally come into its own.

Granville Island   On a peninsula on False Creek, this former industrial site is now a fun mix of urban markets, artisan workshops, theaters, cafes, parks, and restaurants.

Kitsilano   In the '60s, this was Canada's Haight-Ashbury, a slightly seedy enclave of coffeehouses, head shops, and hippies. Today, Kits is one of Vancouver's most sought-after neighborhoods, with a mix of affordable apartments and heritage homes, funky shops, great restaurants, and pleasant, walkable streets. And then there's Kits beach. Roughly speaking, Alma Street and Burrard Street form Kitsilano's east and west boundaries, with West 16th Avenue to the south and the ocean to the north.

Richmond   Twenty years ago, Richmond was mostly farmland, with a bit of sleepy suburb. Now it has become Asia West, an agglomeration of malls geared to new (read: rich, educated, and successful) Chinese immigrants. Places like the Aberdeen Mall and the Yao Han Centre will make you feel as if you've just stepped into Singapore.

Commercial Drive   Every immigrant group that ever passed through the city has left its mark on "The Drive." Combine those influences with the indigenous culture of left-wing activism and ongoing yuppification, and the result is a peculiar but endearing mix: the Italian cafe next to the Marxist bookstore across from the vegetarian deli.

Punjabi Market   Most of the businesses catering to the city's Punjabi population are found on a 4-block stretch of Main Street, from 48th to 52nd avenues. During business hours, the fragrant scent of spices wafts out from food stalls.

The North Shore (North Vancouver & West Vancouver)   The most impressive thing about the North Shore is its mountain range. Huge and wild, the mountains are responsible for much of Vancouver's reputation for compelling physical beauty. The cities themselves, however, aren't without their charms. West Vancouver offers some fine waterfront restaurants, particularly in the Dundarave area. North Vancouver's Lonsdale Quay Market—where the SeaBus docks—makes a pleasant outing.

2 Getting Around

BY PUBLIC TRANSPORTATION   The **Translink/BC Transit** (☎ **604/ 521-0400;** www.cmbuslink.com) system includes electric buses, SeaBus catamaran ferries, and the magnetic-rail SkyTrain. It's an ecologically friendly, highly reliable, and inexpensive system that allows you to get everywhere, including the beaches and ski slopes. Regular service on the main routes runs daily from 5am to 2am, with less frequent "Owl" service operating on several routes until 4:20am.

Schedules and routes are available at the Tourist Info Centres, at many major hotels, online, and on buses. Pick up a copy of ***Discover Vancouver on Transit*** at the Info Centre (see "Visitor Information," above). This publication gives transit routes for many city neighborhoods, landmarks, and attractions.

Fares are the same for the bus, SeaBus, and SkyTrain. A one-way, all-zone fare is C$1.50 (U.S.$1) after 6:30pm weekdays and all day weekends and holidays. Weekdays before 6:30pm, a one-zone fare (covering all Vancouver) is C$1.50 (U.S.$1), a two-zone fare (required to travel to North Vancouver, Burnaby, or Richmond) is C$2.25 (U.S.$1.45), and a three-zone fare (for travel to Surrey) is C$3 (U.S.$1.95). Free transfers are good for 90 minutes for travel in any direction and for the SkyTrain and SeaBus. **DayPasses,** good any time for unlimited travel on all public transit, are C$6 (U.S.$3.90) for adults and C$4 (U.S.$2.60) for seniors, students, and children. Tickets and passes are available at Tourist Info Centres, SeaBus terminals, convenience stores, drugstores, credit unions, and other outlets displaying the "FareDealer" symbol.

The **SkyTrain** is a magnetic-rail train servicing 20 stations along its 35-minute trip from downtown Vancouver east to Surrey through Burnaby and New Westminster. The **SeaBus** catamaran ferries take passengers and cyclists on a scenic 12-minute commute between downtown's Waterfront Station and North Vancouver's Lonsdale Quay. Monday through Friday, the SeaBus runs every 15 minutes from 6:15am to 6:30pm, then every 30 minutes until 1am. SeaBuses depart on Saturdays every half hour from 6:30am to 12:30pm, then every 15 minutes to 7:15pm, then every half hour to 1am. On Sundays and holidays, the SeaBus runs every half hour from 8:30am to 11pm.

BY TAXI   Cab fares are quite reasonable, starting at C$2.30 (U.S.$1.50) and increasing at a rate of C$1.25 (U.S.80¢) per kilometer, plus C30¢ (U.S.20¢) per

Key Bus Routes

Keep these routes in mind as you tour the city by bus: **no. 5** (Robson Street), **no. 22** (Kitsilano Beach to downtown), **no. 50** (Granville Island), **nos. 35** and **135** (to Stanley Park bus loop), **no. 240** (North Vancouver), **no. 250** (West Vancouver–Horseshoe Bay), and **nos. 4** and **10** (UBC to Exhibition Park via Granville Street downtown). In summer, the Vancouver Parks Board operates a bus route through Stanley Park.

minute at stoplights. Within the downtown area, you can expect to travel for less than C$6 (U.S.$3.90). The typical fare from downtown to the airport is C$25 (U.S.$16).

Taxis are easy to find in front of major hotels, but flagging one down on the street can be tricky, as most drivers are usually on radio calls. If you call for a taxi, it usually arrives faster than if you go outside and hail one. Call **Black Top** (☎ 604/731-1111), **Yellow Cab** (☎ 604/681-1111), or **MacLure's** (☎ 604/731-9211). **AirLimo** (☎ 604/273-1331) offers flat-rate stretch limousine service; it charges C$29 (U.S.$19) per trip to the airport (not per person), plus tax and tip, and accepts all major credit cards.

BY CAR Vancouver's driving laws are similar to those in many parts of the United States; see "Getting Around" in chapter 2 for details. (The only exception is the flashing green light, which isn't a left-turn signal but a sign to proceed with caution.) Gas is sold by the liter, averaging around C60¢ (U.S.40¢). Remember that a gallon of gas is about C$2.70 (U.S.$1.75). Speeds and distances are posted in kilometers.

You won't need a car to see the city, but you may want one to explore the environs. If you're over 25 and have a major credit card, you can rent a vehicle from **Avis,** 757 Hornby St. (☎ 800/879-2847 or 604/606-2847); **Budget,** 450 W. Georgia St. (☎ 800/527-0700, 800/268-8900, or 604/668-7000); **Enterprise,** 585 Smithe St. (☎ 800/736-8222 or 604/688-5500); **Hertz Canada,** 1128 Seymour St. (☎ 800/263-0600 or 604/688-2411); **National/Tilden,** 1130 W. Georgia St. (☎ 800/387-4747 or 604/685-6111); or **Thrifty,** 1015 Burrard St. or 1400 Robson St. (☎ 800/367-2277 or 604/606-1666). These firms all have counters and shuttle service at the airport as well.

All major downtown hotels have guest **parking;** rates vary from free to C$20 (U.S.$13) per day. There's public parking at **Robson Square** (enter at Smithe and Howe streets), the **Pacific Centre** (Howe and Dunsmuir streets), and **The Bay** department store (Richards near Dunsmuir Street). You'll also find **parking lots** at Thurlow and Georgia, Thurlow and Alberni, and Robson and Seymour streets.

Metered **street parking** isn't impossible to come by, but it may take a trip or three around the block to find a spot. Rules are posted on the street and are strictly enforced. Unmetered parking on side streets is often subject to neighborhood residency requirements; check the signs. If your car is towed or if you need a towing service, call **Unitow** (☎ 604/251-1255) or **Busters** (☎ 604/685-8181).

Members of the American Automobile Association (AAA) can get assistance from the **Canadian Automobile Association (CAA),** 999 W. Broadway (☎ 604/268-5600, or 604/293-2222 for road service).

BY BICYCLE Vancouver is decidedly bicycle-friendly. There are plenty of bike-rental places along Robson Street and Denman Street near Stanley Park. Bike routes are designated throughout the city; paved paths crisscross though parks and along beaches. Helmets are mandatory, and riding on sidewalks is illegal except on designated paths.

Cycling BC (☎ 604/737-3034) accommodates cyclists on the SkyTrain and buses by providing "Bike & Ride" lockers at all "Park & Ride" parking lots. The department also dispenses loads of information about events, bike touring, and bicycle insurance. Many downtown parking lots and garages also have no-fee bike racks.

You can take a bike on the SeaBus for free. All West Vancouver blue buses (including the bus to the Horseshoe Bay ferry terminal) can carry two bikes on a first-come, first-served basis. In Vancouver, only a limited number of suburban routes allow bikes on the bus, and space is limited. Bikes aren't allowed on the SkyTrain or in the George Massey Tunnel, but a tunnel shuttle can transport you across the Fraser; it operates four times daily from mid-May through September, and on weekends only from May 1 to Victoria Day (the third weekend of May).

BY FERRY   Crossing False Creek to Vanier Park or Granville Island on a blue mini-ferry is both cheap and fun. The **Aquabus** docks at the foot of Howe Street. It takes you either to Granville Island's public market or east along False Creek to Science World and Stamps Landing. The **Granville Island Ferry** docks at Sunset Beach below the Burrard Street Bridge and the Aquatic Centre, and goes to Granville Island and Vanier Park. Ferries to Granville Island leave every 5 minutes from 7am to 10pm; those to Vanier Park leave every 15 minutes from 10am to 8pm. One-way fare on all routes is C$1.75 (U.S.$1.15) for adults and C75¢ (U.S.60¢) for seniors and children.

Fast Facts: Vancouver

American Express   The office is at 1040 W. Georgia St. (☎ **604/669-2813**); open Monday to Friday from 8:30am to 5:30pm, Saturday from 10am to 4pm.

Area Codes   The area code for the city of Vancouver and the rest of the British Columbia lower mainland is **604.** The area code for all of Vancouver Island, including Victoria and most of British Columbia, is **250.**

Business Hours   Banks are open Monday through Thursday from 10am to 5pm, Friday from 10am to 6pm. Some banks are also open Saturday. Office hours are Monday through Friday from 9am to 5pm. Stores are generally open Monday through Saturday from 10am to 6pm. Last call at bars and lounges is 2am.

Consulates   The U.S. Consulate is at 1095 W. Pender St. (☎ **604/685-4311**). The British Consulate is at 800-1111 Melville St. (☎ **604/683-4421**). The Australian Consulate is at 1225-888 Dunsmuir St. (☎ **604/684-1177**). Check the Yellow Pages for other countries.

Dentist   Most major hotels have a dentist on call. The **Vancouver Centre Dental Clinic,** Vancouver Centre Mall, 11-650 W. Georgia St. (☎ **604/682-1601**), is another option. The clinic is open Monday through Saturday with varying hours, usually between 8:30am and 6pm; you must make an appointment.

Doctor   Most hotels have a doctor on call. Drop-in clinics can be found at the **Vancouver Medical Clinics,** Bentall Centre, 1055 Dunsmuir St. (☎ **604/683-8138**), open Monday through Friday from 8am to 5pm; and **Carepoint Medical Centre,** 1175 Denman St. (☎ **604/681-5338**), open daily from 9am to 9pm.

Drugstores   See "Pharmacies," below.

Emergencies   Dial ☎ **911** for fire, police, ambulance, and poison control.

Hospitals   St. Paul's Hospital, 1081 Burrard St. (☎ **604/682-2344**), is the closest to downtown and the West End. On the West Side is **Vancouver General Hospital Health and Sciences Centre,** 855 W. 12th Ave. (☎ **604/875-4111**). In North Vancouver is **Lions Gate Hospital,** 231 E. 15th St. (☎ **604/988-3131**).

Internet Access   There's free Internet access at the **Vancouver Public Library Central Branch,** 350 W. Georgia St. (☎ **604/331-4000**). **Dakoda's Internet Cafe,** 1602 Yew St. (☎ **604/731-5616**), is a small, pleasant cafe in the pub/restaurant zone across from Kits Beach. **Webster's Internet Cafe,** 340 Robson St. (☎ **604/915-9327**), is across from the main public library.

Liquor Laws   The legal drinking age is 19. Spirits are sold only in government liquor stores, but you can buy beer and wine from specially licensed, privately owned stores. There are 22 LCBC (Liquor Control of British Columbia) stores in Vancouver, open Monday through Saturday. Call the **Liquor Distribution Branch** (☎ **604/252-3000**) for location details.

Newspapers/Magazines   The two local papers are the *Vancouver Sun* and the *Province*. The *Georgia Straight,* a free weekly entertainment paper, comes out on Thursday. The monthly *Vancouver* magazine covers the city's cultural scene.

Pharmacies   Shopper's Drug Mart, 1125 Davie St. (☎ **604/685-6445**), is open 24 hours. Several Safeway supermarkets have late-night pharmacies; the one at the corner of Robson and Denman streets is open until midnight.

Police   The Vancouver City Police can be reached at ☎ **604/717-3535.**

Post Office   The **main post office,** 349 W. Georgia St., at Homer Street, is open Monday through Friday from 8am to 5:30pm. Postal outlets are located in souvenir stores and drugstores displaying the red-and-white Canada Post emblem.

Safety   Overall, Vancouver is a safe city; violent-crime rates are quite low. However, property crimes do occur with troubling frequency. The Downtown East Side, between Gastown and Chinatown, should be avoided at night.

Taxes   Hotel rooms are subject to a 10% tax. The provincial sales tax (PST) is 7% (excluding food, restaurant meals, and children's clothing). For specific questions, call the **B.C. Consumer Taxation Branch** (☎ **604/660-4500**). Most goods and services are subject to a 7% federal goods and services tax (GST). You can get a refund on short-stay accommodations and all shopping purchases that total at least C$100 (U.S.$65) (this refund does not apply to car rentals, parking, restaurant meals, room service, tobacco, or alcohol). Hotels and the Info Centre can give you application forms. Be sure to save your receipts. For details on the GST, call ☎ **800/561-6990.**

Time Zone   Vancouver is in the Pacific time zone, as are Seattle and San Francisco. Daylight saving time applies from April through October.

3 Accommodations

The past few years have seen a lot of activity in the Vancouver hotel business. Lots of new rooms have opened up, many in the moderate-to-budget range. Most of the hotels are located in the downtown and Yaletown areas or in the West End.

In general, high season runs from June 15 to mid-September, during which time reservations are highly recommended. Shoulder seasons last from May 1 to June 15 and from mid-September through October. Note that quoted prices below don't include the 10% provincial accommodations tax or the 7% goods and services tax (GST). Non-Canadian residents can get a GST rebate on short-stay accommodations by filling out the Tax Refund Application (see "Taxes" under "Fast Facts: Vancouver," above).

DOWNTOWN & YALETOWN

All downtown hotels are within 5 to 10 minutes' walking distance of shops, restaurants, and attractions. You can reach the downtown hotels by taking the SkyTrain to the Granville or Burrard stops. The Waterfront station is close to the Pan-Pacific and

A Helping Hand

If you arrive without a reservation or have trouble finding a room, call Super Natural British Columbia's **Discover British Columbia hot line** (☎ 800/663-6000) or **Tourism Vancouver's hot line** (☎ 604/683-2000), which both specialize in last-minute bookings for hotels, hostels, and B&Bs. If you prefer to stay in a B&B, the **Beachside Bed & Breakfast Registry** (☎ 800/563-3311 or 604/922-7773) can assist you. Rates average from C$120 to C$200 (U.S.$78 to U.S.$130) for a double, C$250 to C$350 (U.S.$163 to U.S.$228) for a luxury room.

Waterfront Centre hotels. The Stadium station is just a few blocks from the Georgian Court, Rosedale on Robson, and YWCA. The no. 1 or 5 buses will take you to the West End hotels; the no. 4 or 10 will get you to hotels near False Creek.

VERY EXPENSIVE

Another deluxe choice is the **Sutton Place Hotel,** 845 Burrard St. (☎ 800/961-7555 or 604/682-5511; fax 604/682-5513). Don't let the pink hospital-like exterior fool you: Everything inside is pure luxury. Rates run C$289 to C$419 (U.S.$188 to U.S.$272).

✪ **Metropolitan Hotel Vancouver.** 645 Howe St., Vancouver, BC, V6C 2Y9. ☎ 800/667-2300 or 604/687-1122. Fax 604/643-7267. www.metropolitan.com. 215 units. A/C MINIBAR TV TEL. May–Sept C$365 (U.S.$237) double Sun–Thurs, C$225 (U.S.$146) double Fri–Sat; Oct–Apr C$285 (U.S.$185) double. Year-round, C$30 (U.S.$20) extra per room/suite for Business Class; C$1,500 (U.S.$975) suite. Children 16 and under stay free in parents' room; those under 6 eat free in the restaurant when accompanied by a paying adult. AE, DC, MC, V. Underground valet parking C$18 (U.S.$12). Bus: 4, 7. Small pets accepted.

Between the financial district and downtown shopping areas, the Metropolitan underwent a C$4-million renovation in 1997, and the result is uncompromised luxury. Most units in the 18-story hotel have small balconies; all have stately dark-wood furnishings, queen beds, marble baths, fluffy robes, and in-room coffee. I recommend the studio suites, much roomier and only slightly more expensive. Each of the Business Class rooms and studio suites has a printer, fax, modem hookup, cordless speaker phone, and power strip. No-smoking rooms are available as well.

Diva at the Met is one of Vancouver's finest restaurants (see "Dining," below). Amenities include concierge, room service, dry cleaning, baby-sitting, secretarial services, courtesy car, business center, health club, pool, saunas, and sundeck.

✪ **Pan-Pacific Hotel Vancouver.** 300-999 Canada Place, Vancouver, BC, V6C 3B5. ☎ 800/937-1515 or 604/662-8111. Fax 604/685-8690. www.panpac.com. 506 units. A/C MINIBAR TV TEL. June–Oct C$359–C$419 (U.S.$233–U.S.$272) double, Nov–May C$219–C$259 double (U.S.$142–U.S.$168); year-round C$455–C$2,500 (U.S.$296–U.S.$1,625) suite. AE, DC, ER, JCB, MC, V. Valet parking C$23 (U.S.$15). Bus: 4, 7.

Apart from its natural surroundings, the city's most distinctive landmark is the Canada Place Pier, with its five white Teflon sails. The pier houses the Vancouver Trade and Convention Centre, the Alaska cruise-ship terminal, and this spectacular 23-story hotel. (If you're taking an Alaskan cruise, this and the Canadian-Pacific Waterfront Centre Hotel are the closest accommodations.) All of the modern guest rooms are spacious and comfortably furnished with soft colors, down duvets on the king-size beds, and elegant marble baths. Many of the rooms look out over the harbor and up to the mountains; they're some of the most spectacular hotel-rooms-with-a-view in town.

Downtown Vancouver

LEGEND
(*i*) Information
✉ Post Office

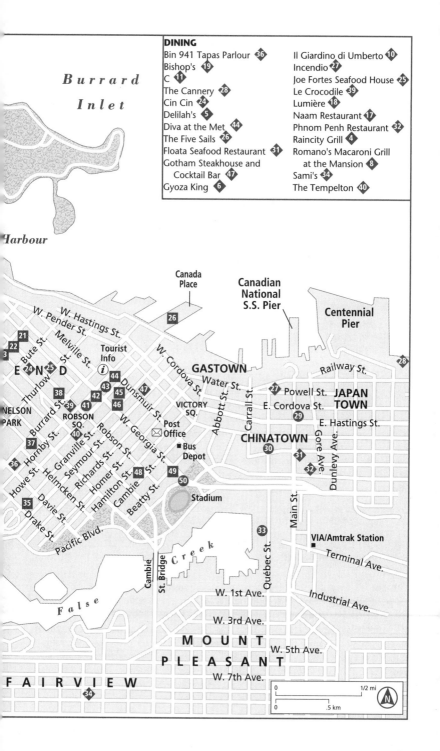

DINING

Bin 941 Tapas Parlour **36**
Bishop's **19**
C **11**
The Cannery **28**
Cin Cin **24**
Delilah's **5**
Diva at the Met **44**
The Five Sails **26**
Floata Seafood Restaurant **31**
Gotham Steakhouse and Cocktail Bar **47**
Gyoza King **6**

Il Giardino di Umberto **10**
Incendio **27**
Joe Fortes Seafood House **25**
Le Crocodile **39**
Lumière **18**
Naam Restaurant **17**
Phnom Penh Restaurant **32**
Raincity Grill **4**
Romano's Macaroni Grill at the Mansion **8**
Sami's **34**
The Tempelton **40**

Whether you stay here or not, the Five Sails restaurant is one of the city's best and worth a visit (see "Dining," below). Amenities include concierge, room service, valet, limo service, outdoor pool, and outstanding health club (extra C$10/U.S.$7 fee).

Sheraton Wall Centre Vancouver. 1088 Burrard St., Vancouver, BC, V6Z 2R9. ☎ **800/ 325-3535** or 604/331-1000. Fax 604/893-7200. www.sheratonwallcentre.com. 434 units. A/C MINIBAR TV TEL. C$400 (U.S.$260) double; C$450–C$500 (U.S.$293–U.S.$325) suite; C$1,500 (U.S.$975) loft penthouse. AE, DC, ER, MC, V. Free self-parking; valet parking C$17 (U.S.$11). Bus: 22.

The 35-story Wall Centre's two distinctive blue-gray glass towers are set on downtown's highest point. The rooms here are elegantly appointed with blond wood furnishings, luxury bathrooms, and down duvets and Egyptian cotton sheets. Every unit has stunning floor-to-ceiling windows that maximize the views. For an extra C$25 to C$40 (U.S.$16 to U.S.$26), you can upgrade to one of the 25th- or 26th-floor Crystal Club rooms, which offer added amenities as well as access to the bi-level Crystal Club lounge. No-smoking and wheelchair-accessible rooms are available.

Indigo features innovative West Coast cuisine. Amenities include concierge, room service, dry cleaning/laundry, massage, baby-sitting, secretarial services, business center, conference rooms, courtesy car, pool, health club, sauna, and salon.

EXPENSIVE

✪ Canadian-Pacific Hotel Vancouver. 900 W. Georgia St., Vancouver, BC, V6C 2W6. ☎ **800/441-1414** or 604/684-3131. Fax 604/662-1929. www.cphotels.ca. 579 units. A/C MINIBAR TV TEL. Low season from C$215 (U.S.$140) double, from C$300 (U.S.$195) suite; high season C$275–C$454 (U.S.$179–U.S.$295) double, C$360–C$640 (U.S.$234– U.S.$416) suite. AE, DC, DISC, MC, V. Parking C$18 (U.S.$12). Bus: 22.

With a C$50-million renovation completed in 1996, the grande dame of Vancouver's hotels has been restored beyond its former glory. The rooms are outfitted with marble baths and mahogany furnishings and offer city, harbor, and mountain views; 75% are equipped to accommodate the needs of business travelers, with speakerphones and dedicated fax and modem lines. The rooms on the Entree Gold floors include extras like a private concierge, continental breakfast, free local calls, and afternoon tea. Restaurants include the hot spot 900 West and Griffins. Amenities include concierge, room service, pool, health club, sauna, spa, valet/laundry, and high-end shops.

Crowne Plaza Hotel Georgia. 801 W. Georgia St., Vancouver, BC, V6C 1P7. ☎ **800/ 663-1111** or 604/682-5566. Fax 604/642-5579. www.hotelgeorgia.bc.ca. 313 units. A/C TV TEL. Jan–Apr C$209–C$269 (U.S.$136–U.S.$175) double; May–Oct C$299–C$399 (U.S.$194–U.S.$259) double; Nov–Dec C$219–C$279 (U.S.$142–U.S.$181) double. Children under 16 stay free in parents' room. AE, CB, DC, MC, V. Valet parking C$15 (U.S.$10). Bus: 4, 7.

This hotel has recently undergone major renovations to restore its 1920s glory. Guest rooms are outfitted with art-deco furniture, modem access, tea/coffeemakers, and two phone lines. The Club Level rooms are worth the C$30 (U.S.$20) surcharge, as they offer CD players, speakerphones, robes, and breakfast, as well as access to an executive lounge that serves afternoon hors d'ouevres and drinks and provides a workstation with a computer and office supplies. As Time Goes By serves three meals and afternoon tea. The Casablanca lounge, with leopard-skin wallpaper, is open for drinks and light lunches. There's also the funky Chameleon Lounge and the Georgia Street Bar and Grill. Amenities include concierge, room service, dry cleaning/laundry, health club, business center, conference rooms, and beauty salon.

Four Seasons Hotel. 791 W. Georgia St., Vancouver, BC, V6C 2T4. ☎ **800/332-3442** in the U.S., or 604/689-9333. Fax 604/684-4555. www.fshr.com. 385 units. A/C MINIBAR TV

TEL. C$285–C$440 (U.S.$185–U.S.$286) double; C$335–C$510 (U.S.$218–U.S.$332) junior suite; C$370–C$580 (U.S.$241–U.S.$377) executive suite. AE, DC, ER, MC, V. Parking C$20 (U.S.$13). Bus: 4, 7.

This modern 28-story palace sits atop the Pacific Centre's 200 retail stores a few blocks from the financial district, a particularly appealing location for both shoppers and businesspeople. The rooms are tastefully appointed with French provincial furniture and marble baths. They aren't large, however, so for more space, try a deluxe room on one of the building's corners, a deluxe Four Seasons room (with a separate sitting area), or a suite or junior suite. Wheelchair-accessible rooms are available.

Chartwell's serves an eclectic blend of continental, West Coast, and Asian dishes. More casual options are the Garden Terrace and the Terrace Bar. Amenities include concierge, room service, laundry/valet, and limo service; special menus, robes, and evening cookies and milk for kids; and a pool, weight room, saunas, and sundeck.

MODERATE

Best Western Downtown Vancouver. 718 Drake St. (at Granville St.), Vancouver, BC, V6Z 2W6. ☎ **888/669-9888** or 604/660-9888. Fax 604/669-3440. www.bestwestern downtown.com. 143 units. A/C TV TEL. C$139–C$209 (U.S.$90–U.S.$136) double; C$280–C$350 (U.S.$182–U.S.$228) penthouse. Rates include continental breakfast. AE, MC, V. Parking C$5 (U.S.$3.25). Bus: 4, 7.

The 12-story Best Western is a 5-block walk from the theater area at the south end of downtown. The hotel isn't overflowing with amenities, but the rooms are well furnished and the location is convenient. The 32 units with full kitchens are available for an extra C$20 to C$25 (U.S.$13 to U.S.$16). If you need a workspace, ask for one of the corporate rooms, which include a full-size desk and table. All rooms have voice mail, data ports, safes, irons and ironing boards, and hair dryers. Facilities include an exercise room, games area, sauna, Jacuzzi, sundeck, and laundry. A deluxe breakfast is served in the lounge in the lobby. Shuttle service to downtown is offered from 7am to 7pm.

Rosedale on Robson Suite Hotel. 838 Hamilton St. (at Robson St.), Vancouver, BC, V6B 6A2. ☎ **800/661-8870** or 604/689-8033. 275 units. A/C MINIBAR TV TEL. May–Oct C$215 (U.S.$140) 1-bedroom suite, C$265 (U.S.$172) 2-bedroom suite. Nov–Apr C$175 (U.S.$114) 1-bedroom suite, C$225 (U.S.$146) 2-bedroom suite. Extra adult C$20 (U.S.$13); kitchen utensils C$5 (U.S.$3.25). AE, DC, ER, JCB, MC, V. Parking C$8 (U.S.$5). Bus: 5.

Across from Library Square, the Rosedale has a tower capped by a 15-foot-tall (5m) rose emblem. The one- and two-bedroom suites each feature a separate living room, two TVs, and a full kitchenette with microwave, stove, oven, sink, and half-size fridge (dishes and cooking utensils available on request). The rooms are rather small, but ample bay windows and light-wood furnishings provide a feeling of spaciousness. The corner suites have more windows, while upper-floor suites boast furnished terraces and great city views. Guests on executive floors get robes, free local calls, daily newspaper, nightly turndown, in-room movies, Nintendo games, and modem and fax access. Rosie's is a New York–style deli, a rarity in this city filled with West Coast cuisine. Amenities include room service, concierge, pool, sauna, and exercise room.

INEXPENSIVE

✪ **YWCA Hotel/Residence.** 733 Beatty St., Vancouver, BC, V6B 2M4. ☎ **800/663-1424** or 604/895-5830. Fax 604/681-2550. 155 units (53 with bathroom). A/C TEL. C$64–C$84 (U.S.$42–U.S.$55) double without bathroom, C$98–C$130 (U.S.$64–U.S.$85) double with bathroom. Weekly, monthly, group, and off-season discounts available. AE, MC, V. Parking C$5 (U.S.$3.25). Bus: 5, 8.

Built in 1995, this attractive residence is an excellent choice for travelers on a budget. The rooms are simply furnished; some have TVs and all have minifridges. (There are a number of small grocery stores nearby, as well as a supermarket a 10-minute walk away.) Extras include three kitchens, TV lounges, coin-op laundry, and free access to the best gym in town at the nearby co-ed YWCA Fitness Centre.

THE WEST END
EXPENSIVE

Listel Vancouver. 1300 Robson St., Vancouver, BC, V6E 1C5. ☎ **800/663-5491** or 604/684-8461. Fax 604/684-8326. www.listel-vancouver.com. 130 units. A/C MINIBAR TV TEL. May–Sept C$240–C$300 (U.S.$156–U.S.$195) double, C$260–C$320 (U.S.$169–U.S.$208) suite; Oct–Apr C$150–C$190 (U.S.$98–U.S.$124) double, C$170–C$210 (U.S.$111–U.S.$137) suite. AE, DC, DISC, ER, JCB, MC, V. Parking C$14 (U.S.$9). Bus: 5.

This hotel boasts a killer location at the west end of the Robson Street shopping strip, and for the past couple of years, the owners have been putting a lot of effort into making the interior match the address. The rooms have been extensively remodeled and now feature top-quality bedding and cherry-wood furnishings, including little window seats that are perfect for reading or just relaxing. Particularly noteworthy are the 54 Gallery Rooms on the top two floors; each of these units is like a small art gallery, decorated with original works borrowed from the Buschlen Mowatt Gallery. They also feature Aveda toiletries and better views. The upper-floor rooms facing Robson Street are worth the price; each has views of the lively shopping strip as well as glimpses of the harbor and the mountains. The others face the alley and nearby apartment buildings. Soundproof windows eliminate traffic noise, which can get pretty loud on weekends.

Despite its sports-bar name, O'Doul's has been reinventing itself as a spot for fine dining. Amenities include concierge, room service, valet/laundry, secretarial services, pool, exercise room, meeting space, and access to a nearby health club.

✪ **Pacific Palisades Hotel.** 1277 Robson St., Vancouver, BC, V6E 1C4. ☎ **800/663-1815** or 604/688-0461. Fax 604/688-4374. www.pacificpalisadeshotel.com. 233 units. A/C MINIBAR TV TEL. May–Oct C$219 (U.S.$142) studio suite, C$269 (U.S.$175) executive suite; Nov 1–Dec 15 C$165 (U.S.$107) studio suite, C$205 (U.S.$133) executive suite; Dec 16–Apr C$165 (U.S.$107) studio suite, C$205 (U.S.$133) executive suite. Ask about extended stays. AE, DC, MC, V. Parking C$13 (U.S.$8). Bus: 5.

At press time, the Palisades had just been sold. The new management intends to leave things more or less the same, but given the place's popularity, a rate hike wouldn't be surprising. Standing on the crest of Robson, it was converted from two luxury apartment towers in 1991 and is popular with visiting film production companies who demand sterling service, privacy, spacious rooms, and great value. The well-appointed suites are divided into studio, executive, and penthouse levels, all with panoramic views and kitchenettes; most have private terraces as well. Full kitchens are C$10 (U.S.$7) extra. Amenities include concierge, room service, limo service, laundry/valet, business center, secretarial services, fitness center, sauna, pool, tanning room, and bike rentals.

MODERATE

✪ **Blue Horizon.** 1225 Robson St., Vancouver, BC, V6E 1C5. ☎ **800/663-1333** or 604/688-1411. Fax 604/688-4461. 214 units. A/C MINIBAR TV TEL. C$159–C$199 (U.S.$103–U.S.$129) double; C$279 (U.S.$181) suite. Off-season and senior discounts available. Children under 16 stay free in parents' room. Extra person C$15 (U.S.$10). AE, DC, MC, V. Parking C$8 (U.S.$5). Bus: 5.

This unmistakable blue-tiled 1960s high-rise capitalizes on one of Vancouver's best assets: the view. The guest rooms are spacious, and thanks to the hotel layout, every one is a corner unit, which maximizes light and window space. Each features a safe, voice mail, data port, tea/coffeemaker, iron and ironing board, sitting area, and balcony. There's no concierge or room service, but all units have a fridge or mini-bar. No-smoking and wheelchair-accessible rooms are available. Amenities include a pool, exercise equipment, laundry, baby-sitting, secretarial services, and conference rooms.

✪ **West End Guest House.** 1362 Haro St., Vancouver, BC, V6E 1G2. ☎ **604/681-2889.** Fax 604/688-8812. 7 units. TV TEL. C$145–C$225 (U.S.$94–U.S.$146) double. Rates include full breakfast. AE, MC, V. Free valet parking. Bus: 5.

This 1906 heritage home is a fine example of what the West End looked like until the early 1950s. Decorated with beautiful antiques and an amazing collection of old photos, this is a wonderful respite from the West End's hustle and bustle. The guest rooms provide the ultimate in bedtime luxury: feather mattresses and duvets; bathrobes; and your very own stuffed animal. Particularly indulgent is the Grand Queen Suite, an attic bedroom with skylights, a brass bed, a fireplace, a sitting area, and a clawfoot tub. Owner Evan Penner will pamper you with a scrumptious breakfast and afternoon drinks. Guests have access to the parlor, sundeck, stocked kitchen, and bikes.

INEXPENSIVE

Hostelling International Vancouver Downtown Hostel. 1114 Burnaby St. (at Thurlow St.), Vancouver, BC, V6E 1P1. ☎ **888/203-4302** or 604/684-4565. Fax 604/684-4540. www.hihostels.bc.ca. 239 beds in 4-person units; some double and triple units available. Beds C$20 (U.S.$13) IYHA members, C$24 (U.S.$16) nonmembers; doubles C$55 (U.S.$36) members, C$80 (U.S.$52) nonmembers; triples C$70 (U.S.$46) members, C$86 (U.S.$56) nonmembers. Annual adult membership C$27 (U.S.$18). MC, V. Limited free parking. Bus: 2, 5.

Housed in a converted nunnery, this modern hostel is a convenient base from which to explore downtown. The beach is a few blocks south, while downtown is a 10-minute walk north. Most beds are in quad dorms, with a limited number of doubles and triples and one wheelchair-accessible room available. Guests share common cooking facilities, a patio, and a game room. In summer, book well ahead. It's open 24 hours.

✪ **Sylvia Hotel.** 1154 Gilford St., Vancouver, BC, V6G 2P6. ☎ **604/681-9321.** Fax 604/ 682-3551. www.sylviahotel.com. 118 units. TV TEL. Oct–Mar C$75–C$100 (U.S.$49– U.S.$65) double, C$115–C$175 (U.S.$75–U.S.$114) suite; Apr–Sept C$75–C$125 (U.S.$49–U.S.$81) double, C$130–C$200 (U.S.$85–U.S.$130) suite. Children under 18 stay free in parents' room. AE, DC, MC, V. Parking C$5 (U.S.$3.25). Bus: 2, 5. Pets accepted.

The ivy-wreathed gray-stone Sylvia stands on the shores of English Bay a few blocks from Stanley Park. One of Vancouver's oldest hotels (built in 1912), it has in recent years become deservedly trendy. The room furnishings from the 1950s to the '70s are appropriately mismatched, and the views from the upper floors unparalleled. The suites, with full kitchens, are big enough for families. Sixteen rooms in the 12-year-old low-rise annex offer individual heating, but less atmosphere. Room service is available.

THE WEST SIDE

✪ **Granville Island Hotel.** 1253 Johnston St., Vancouver, BC, V6H 3R9. ☎ **800/ 663-1840** or 604/683-7373. Fax 604/683-3061. www.granvilleislandhotel.com. 54 units. A/C TV TEL. C$219 (U.S.$142) double. Off-season discounts available. AE, CB, DC, ER, MC, V. Parking C$6 (U.S.$3.90). Bus: 4, 10, 50.

Completely renovated in 1997, this modern hotel is at the east end of Granville Island. Surrounded by studios and galleries on one side and pleasure boats on the other, it enjoys a unique waterfront location near the public market. The rooms boast skylights and bathrooms with marble floors. The cozy lobby is attractively decorated with dark-wood paneling and stone floors. The Creek microbrewery restaurant has a harborside patio and a large stocked humidor. Amenities include concierge, room service, dry cleaning/laundry, massage, baby-sitting, secretarial services, and a health club with sauna and Jacuzzi; the staff can arrange boat charters at the marina.

Heritage Harbour Bed and Breakfast. 1838 Ogden Ave., Vancouver, BC, V6J 1A1. ☎ **604/736-0809.** Fax 604/736-0074. www.vancouver-bc.com/HeritageHarbour. E-mail: dhorner@direct.ca. 2 units. May 1–Oct 15 C$165 (U.S.$107) double; Oct 16–Apr 30 C$125 (U.S.$81) double. Rates include full breakfast. No credit cards. Free street parking. Bus: 22.

This B&B occupies a luxurious 1993 home in the upscale Kits Point neighborhood, within walking distance of Kits Beach and Vanier Park. The Garden Room is light and airy, with a high ceiling, fan, queen bed, and balcony. The Harbour Room is a bit smaller, but makes up for it with its small balcony with a fine view over English Bay. Guests share a library with oak panels, leather couches, and fireplace—the perfect room to spend a rainy day, browsing the shelves or watching a movie.

Hostelling International Vancouver Jericho Beach Hostel. 1515 Discovery St., Vancouver, BC, V6R 4K5. ☎ **888/203-4303** or 604/224-3208. Fax 604/224-4852. www. hihostels.bc.ca. 286 beds in 14 dorms; 10 family units. Wheelchair accessible. Dorms C$18 (U.S.$12) IYHA members, C$22 (U.S.$14) nonmembers; family units C$47–C$53 (U.S.$31–U.S.$34) IYHA members, C$56–C$62 (U.S.$36–U.S.$40) nonmembers. Annual adult membership C$27 (U.S.$18). Family and group memberships available. MC, V. Parking C$3 (U.S.$1.95). Bus: 4, 22. Children under 5 not accepted.

Housed in an old military barracks, this hostel is surrounded by an expansive lawn next to Jericho Beach. Individuals, families, and groups are welcome. The 10 private rooms can accommodate up to six each, and the dorm-style arrangements are well maintained. Linens are provided. Basic inexpensive food is served in the cafe from April through October. You also have the option of cooking for yourself in the hostel's kitchen.

THE NORTH SHORE

✪ **Beachside Bed & Breakfast.** 4208 Evergreen Ave., W. Vancouver, BC, V7V 1H1. ☎ **800/563-3311** or 604/922-7773. 3 units. C$150–C$250 (U.S.$98–U.S.$163) double. Extra person C$30 (U.S.$20). Rates include full breakfast. MC, V. Free parking. Bus: 250, 251, 252, 253.

Bouquets of fresh flowers in every room are a signature touch at this lovely Spanish-style waterfront home at the end of a quiet cul-de-sac. Its all-glass southern exposure affords a panoramic view of Vancouver, and the private beach is just steps from the door. You can watch the waves from the patio or outdoor Jacuzzi, or just spend the afternoon fishing and sailing. Your hosts are knowledgeable about local history and will direct you to Stanley Park, hiking, skiing, and other area highlights.

Lonsdale Quay Hotel. 123 Carrie Cates Court, N. Vancouver, BC, V6M 3K7. ☎ **800/ 836-6111** or 604/986-6111. Fax 604/986-8782. www.lonsdalequayhotel.bc.ca. E-mail: sales@lonsdalequayhotel.bc.ca. 83 units. A/C MINIBAR TV TEL. Low season C$140–C$165 (U.S.$91–U.S.$107) double or twin, C$250 (U.S.$163) harbor-view or waterfront executive suite; high season C$220–C$225 (U.S.$143–U.S.$146) double or twin, C$350 (U.S.$228) harbor-view or waterfront executive suite. Extra person C$25 (U.S.$16). Senior discount available. AE, CB, DC, DISC, ER, MC, V. Parking C$7 (U.S.$4.55), free on weekends and holidays. SeaBus: Lonsdale Quay.

This hotel is at the water's edge above the Lonsdale Quay Market at the SeaBus terminal. An escalator rises from the midst of the market's stalls to the front desk on the third floor. The rooms are simply and tastefully decorated, with coffeemakers and watercoolers but not the grand touches found in comparably priced downtown hotels. Nevertheless, you will find fabulous harbor and city views here, and you're only 15 minutes by car from the Grouse Mountain Ski Resort. Extras include the Waterfront Bistro, the Q Cafe, a whirlpool, and an exercise room. No-smoking rooms are available.

Mountainside Manor. 5909 Nancy Greene Way, N. Vancouver, BC, V7R 4W6. ☎ **604/ 990-9772.** Fax 604/985-8484. E-mail: mtnside@ibm.net. 4 units. TV. May–Oct C$95–C$155 (U.S.$62–U.S.$101) double; Nov–Apr C$85–C$135 (U.S.$55–U.S.$88) double. Off-season discounts available. Rates include breakfast. DC, MC, V. Free parking. SeaBus: Lonsdale Quay, then bus no. 241.

This is the closest lodging to both the ski slopes on Grouse Mountain and the 26-mile-long (42km) Baden-Powell hiking trail. High above the city on a tree-covered ridge and nestled in a peaceful alpine setting, this spectacular modern home offers a magnificent view of the Coast Mountains and the Burrard Inlet from both the guest rooms and the outdoor hot tub. The Panorama Room has a queen bed, rosewood furniture, and Jacuzzi with separate shower. All units are stocked with fresh flowers and lots of amenities.

4 Dining

Vancouverites seem to dine out more than residents of any other Canadian city. Outstanding meals are available in all price ranges and in many ethnic cuisines—Chinese, Japanese, Greek, French, Italian, Spanish, Mongolian, Ethiopian, Vietnamese, even Canadian. But though Vancouverites have come to expect top quality, they still absolutely refuse to pay the same kind of top dollar forked over by diners in New York or San Francisco. Somehow, restaurateurs here have managed to square this circle. For discerning diners, Vancouver can be a steal.

The cuisine buzz words here are "West Coast." More and more restaurants are shifting to seasonal (even monthly) menus, giving their chefs greater freedom to apply creativity and innovation to the local produce, game, and seafood. The focus on freshness, flavor, and local ingredients makes this cuisine unique and unparalleled.

If you're downtown, you can walk to restaurants in the West End and English Bay (west of downtown from Thurlow Street to Stanley Park), Gastown, or Chinatown. If you're willing to travel farther, venture to the West Side or West Vancouver. For something fun and casual, head east to a bistro on Main Street or Commercial Drive.

Note: See the "Downtown Vancouver" map (pp. 50–51) to locate most of the restaurants in this section.

DOWNTOWN & YALETOWN
EXPENSIVE

✪ **C.** 1600 Howe St. ☎ **604/681-1164.** Reservations recommended. Main courses C$15–C$32 (U.S.$10–U.S.$21). AE, DC, ER, JCB, MC, V. Daily 11:30am–11pm. Bus: 1, 2. SEAFOOD.

C wins top marks for the sheer indulgent quality with which it serves fish. C's taster box of appetizers includes salmon gravlax cured in Saskatoon-berry tea, artichoke carpaccio, abalone tempura, and grilled garlic squid. A variety of seafood main courses is available, but for the ultimate dining experience, let chef Robert Clark show off (he's dying to) and order the seven-course sampling menu. The highlight is a huge Alaskan scallop wrapped in octopus bacon! Wine pairings for each course are brought to you by Peter, a sommelier of exceptional knowledge. Savor the exquisite cuisine and watch as the sun goes down over yet another yacht gliding into the marina.

Diva at the Met. 645 Howe St. ☎ **604/602-7788.** Reservations recommended. Main courses C$12–C$18 (U.S.$8–U.S.$12) lunch, C$20–C$32 (U.S.$13–U.S.$21) dinner. AE, DC, JCB, MC, V. Daily 8:30am–11:30pm. Bus: 4, 7. PACIFIC NORTHWEST.

Since opening this place just a few years ago next to the revamped Metropolitan Hotel, chef Michael Noble has made a habit of walking off with city restaurant awards in categories like "Best West Coast" and "Most Creative Menu." His dishes extol the virtues of fresh seasonal ingredients combined with a light approach to spices and seasonings. Starters include house-smoked salmon with Québec foie gras, while main courses include halibut with black olive tapenade. Diva's tasting menu is also very popular, and its weekend brunches are among the best in town.

✪ **The Five Sails.** In the Pan-Pacific Hotel, 999 Canada Place Way. ☎ **604/891-2892.** Reservations recommended. Main courses C$21–C$38 (U.S.$14–U.S.$25); tasting menu C$34–C$45 (U.S.$22–U.S.$29). AE, DC, ER, JCB, MC, V. Sun–Fri 6–10pm, Sat 6–11pm. Sky-Train: Waterfront. WEST COAST.

The view from the Five Sails is spectacular, and so is the food. The hallmark of the Five Sails approach is top-quality ingredients given just enough preparation to bring out the finest flavors. Think dry-aged Angus beef done to perfection or a perfect steak of freshly caught Pacific salmon, lightly grilled and served with fresh potatoes. The wine selection lists slightly toward hard-to-find Cascadian bottles, which is all to the good.

Gotham Steakhouse and Cocktail Bar. 615 Seymour St. ☎ **604/605-8282.** Reservations recommended. Main courses C$27–C$42 (U.S.$18–U.S.$27). AE, MC, V. Mon–Fri 11:30am–2:30pm; daily 5–11pm (cocktail bar closes somewhat later). Bus: 4, 7. STEAK.

Vegetarians beware: This New York–style steak house serves USDA beef and little else but potatoes and a bit of fish flesh. The wine list is encyclopedic. And then there's the food. The deep-fried calamari appetizer is light and tasty. The sumo-size jumbo shrimp are served in a wonderful garlic-cream sauce. And the steaks are incredible: a porterhouse cut the size of a catcher's mitt; a petit filet mignon as tall as half a bread loaf. If you order yours medium rare, it'll come with a thin layer of broiling top and bottom, pink in the middle, and so tender that after that initial crunch of flavor, the meat melts on your tongue. The veggie side dishes are eminently forgettable.

Il Giardino di Umberto. 1382 Hornby St. ☎ **604/669-2422.** www.umberto.com. Reservations required. Main courses C$14–C$33 (U.S.$9–U.S.$21). AE, DC, ER, MC, V. Mon–Fri noon–2:30pm; daily 5:30–11pm. Bus: 1, 22. ITALIAN.

Decorated in burnt sienna with exposed wood beams, this restaurant re-creates the ambiance of an Italian seaside villa, down to the enclosed garden terrace for alfresco dining and Tuscan menu emphasizing pasta and game. Entrees include osso bucco Milanese with saffron risotto, tortellini with portobello mushrooms in truffle oil, and pheasant breast stuffed with wild mushrooms. After sampling the cuisine, more than a few devoted foodies have run off to enroll in Umberto's Tuscan cooking school.

✪ **Joe Fortes Seafood House.** 777 Thurlow St. (at Robson St.). ☎ **604/669-1940.** Reservations recommended. Main courses C$16–C$24 (U.S.$10–U.S.$16). AE, DC, DISC, ER, MC, V. Sun–Thurs 11:30am–11pm, Fri–Sat 11:30am–midnight. Bus: 5. SEAFOOD.

Named after the burly Caribbean seaman and popular local hero who became English Bay's first lifeguard in the early 1900s, Joe Fortes has been known for years as the place where the young and tan meet for mutual schmoozing over the oyster bar. Lately, under the direction of chef Brian Faulk, Joe's has grown into one of the city's best seafood fusion spots. The rooftop patio has its own bar and strategically placed gas heaters.

Le Crocodile. 100-909 Burrard St. ☎ **604/669-4298.** Reservations recommended. Main courses C$12–C$25 (U.S.$8–U.S.$16) lunch, C$18–C$28 (U.S.$12–U.S.$18) dinner. AE, DC, MC, V. Mon–Fri 11:30am–2pm; Mon–Thurs 5:30–10pm, Fri–Sat 5:30–10:30pm. Bus: 22. FRENCH.

On the ground floor of a redbrick condo tower a block south of Robson Street, you'll find this dining room with sassy yellow walls. This is French as de Gaulle would have had it—calf's liver, grilled pheasant breast with port-wine sauce, Dover sole with beurre blanc, and crème brûlée. The wine list doesn't deign to acknowledge grapes from outside the mother country, but the list of French vintages is vast.

MODERATE & INEXPENSIVE

Bin 941 Tapas Parlour. 941 Davie St. ☎ **604/683-1246.** Reservations not accepted. Main courses C$7–C$19 (U.S.$4.55–U.S.$12). AE, DC, MC, V. Daily 5:30pm–2am. Bus: 5, 4, 8. TAPAS.

At press time, Bin 941 was the latest in trendy tapas dining. True, the music's too loud, the room too small, and the menu unbelievably pretentious. However, the food that alights on the bar or ever-so-tiny tables is quite delicious, and like all tapas, a lot of fun to eat. Look especially for local seafood offerings such as scallops and tiger prawns in bonito butter sauce. Sharing is unavoidable in this sliver of a bistro—your food with your friends, your conversation with your neighbors, your jokes with the entire place.

The Tempelton. 1087 Granville St. ☎ **604/685-4612.** Main courses C$3.50–C$9 (U.S.$2.30–U.S.$6). MC, V. Sun–Mon 10am–10pm, Tues–Thurs 10am–midnight, Fri–Sat 10am–4am. Bus: 4, 7, 8, 10. AMERICAN.

It's a diner but not really a diner—more like a trendy retro interpretation of the diner, except that this place has been in continuous operation since 1934. True, back then the green Hamilton Beach milkshake makers were the height of modern and the staff likely didn't go in for nose and nipple rings, but other than that, what's changed? The food, for one. Hamburgers and fries aren't a staple anymore. Instead, expect chili, blackened chicken breast, or portobello-mushroom vegetarian burger. Saturday brunch is 10% off if you arrive in your pajamas—the staff members will already have theirs on.

THE WEST END

Cin Cin. 1154 Robson St. ☎ **604/688-7338.** www.cincin.net. Reservations recommended. Main courses C$12–C$35 (U.S.$8–U.S.$23). AE, DC, MC, V. Mon–Sat noon–2:30pm; daily 5–11pm. Bus: 5, 22. On-street parking. ITALIAN.

Cin Cin's dining room is built around an open kitchen that's centered around a huge alderwood-fired oven. Nice. But it's a penne toss whether to eat here, have a drink at the big bar, or duck out onto the heated terrace overlooking Robson Street and people-watch. Dishes range from elegant pastas and pizzas—capellini alla pomodoro, penne puttanesca, and pizza Margherita—to more substantial dishes like rosemary-marinated rack of lamb, sea bass crusted with porcini mushrooms, and smoked chicken breast. The wine list is extensive, as is the selection of wines by the glass.

✪ **Delilah's.** 1789 Comox St. ☎ **604/687-3424.** Limited reservations accepted for parties of 6 or more. Fixed-price menus C$21–C$34 (U.S.$14–U.S.$22). AE, DC, ER, MC, V. Daily 5:30pm–midnight. Bus: 5. CONTINENTAL.

The first order of business at Delilah's is ordering a martini—the restaurant's forte—from the two-page martini list. Then, to the sounds of campy tunes (Sinatra at the Sands, Petula Clark's "Downtown"), peruse the menu of some 20 dishes, listed vertically and divided into soups, salads, appetizers, and entrees. Order a small dinner and you get to tick off two courses (C$21/U.S.$14). Order a full dinner (C$34/U.S.$22) and tick off four courses, with dessert included in the price. The menu tends toward small portions and fresh seafood, which Delilah's does simply but well.

Gyoza King. 1508 Robson St. ☎ **604/669-8278.** Main courses C$6–C$13 (U.S.$3.90–U.S.$8). AE, DC, JCB, MC, V. Daily noon–2:30pm; Mon–Sat 5:30pm–2am, Sun 5:30pm–midnight. Bus: 5. JAPANESE.

Gyoza King features an entire menu of gyoza, succulent Japanese dumplings filled with prawns, pork, vegetables, and other combinations, as well as Japanese noodles and staples like *katsu-don* (pork cutlet over rice). This is the gathering spot for hordes of young Japanese visitors, probably because it's the closest thing to home cooking and there are many choices for less than C$10 (U.S.$7). Seating is divided among western-style tables, the bar, and the Japanese-style front table, reserved for larger groups if the restaurant is busy. The courteous staff is happy to answer any questions you may have.

✪ **Raincity Grill.** 1193 Denman St. ☎ **604/685-7337.** Reservations recommended. Main courses C$13–C$24 (U.S.$8–U.S.$16). AE, DC, ER, MC, V. Mon–Fri 11:30am–2:30pm, Sat–Sun brunch 10:30am–3pm; daily 5–10:30pm. Bus: 1, 5. WEST COAST.

Raincity's room is long and low and hugs the shoreline, the better to let the early-evening sun pour in. The restaurant excels in expertly sourced local ingredients done up West Coast style. That means appetizers of barbecued quail with sage and goat-cheese polenta, crispy jumbo spot prawns, and smoked steelhead salad as well as main courses of grilled Fraser Valley free-range chicken and fresh-caught spring salmon. And then there's the huge wine list, which focuses on British Columbia and the Pacific Northwest. Most varieties are available by the glass.

Romano's Macaroni Grill at the Mansion. 1523 Davie St. ☎ **604/689-4334.** Reservations recommended. Main courses C$8–C$16 (U.S.$5–U.S.$10); children's courses C$3.95–C$6 (U.S.$2.55–U.S.$3.90). AE, DC, MC, V. Daily 11:30am–10:30pm. Bus: 5. SOUTHERN ITALIAN.

Housed in a huge stone mansion built in the early 1900s, Romano's is fun and casual and perfect for families. The menu emphasizes southern Italian fare, and the pastas are definitely the favorites. This isn't high-concept cuisine; the food is simple, understandable, and consistently good. House wine is served in unlabeled bottles you pour yourself; you're then charged for only the amount you consume. Your kids will love the children's menu, which features lasagna and meat loaf as well as tasty pizzas, and the permissive staff members who burst into opera at the slightest provocation.

GASTOWN & CHINATOWN

The Cannery. 2205 Commissioner St., near Victoria Dr. ☎ **604/254-9606.** www.cannery seafood.com. Reservations recommended. Main courses C$17–C$27 (U.S.$11–U.S.$18). AE, DC, DISC, MC, V. Mon–Fri 11:30am–2:30pm; daily 5:30–10pm. Bus: 7 to Victoria Dr. From downtown, head east on Hastings St., turn left on Victoria Dr. (2 blocks past Commercial Dr.), then right on Commissioner St. SEAFOOD.

The Cannery is hidden away on the Vancouver waterfront, and at least some of the joy of eating here comes from simply finding the place. The building itself, loaded with old nets and seafaring memorabilia, chips in another hefty portion of the charm. And the view is one of the best in the city. So how about the food? It's good, solid, traditional seafood, often alder-grilled, with an ever-changing fresh sheet to complement the salmon and halibut basics. The wine list is stellar.

✪ **Floata Seafood Restaurant.** 400-180 Keefer St. ☎ **604/602-0368.** Reservations recommended. Main courses C$10–C$45 (U.S.$7–U.S.$29); dim sum C$2.50–C$3.75 (U.S.$1.65–U.S.$2.45). AE, DC, ER, JCB, MC, V. Daily 8am–10pm. Bus: 19, 22. CHINESE/ DIM SUM.

In classic Hong Kong style, Floata is on the third floor of a shopping plaza/parking garage. (Look for the bright red building a stone's throw from the Dr. Sun Yat-sen Garden.) Its dining area is nearly a full city block long. Dim sum is a traditional brunch/lunch buffet rolled out on numerous carts by friendly waitresses who stop at each table. Patrons make their selections of *shumai* and *hargow* (steamed dumplings), *dum bao* (buns filled with barbecued pork), roast pork, spring rolls, sausages rolled in sesame-crusted puff pastry, and other delicacies. Dinner dishes include shark-fin and bird's-nest soups, whole crisp sea bass in black-bean sauce, and crisp Peking duck.

Incendio. 103 Columbia St. ☎ **604/688-8694.** Main courses C$7–C$12 (U.S.$4.55– U.S.$8). AE, MC, V. Mon–Fri 11:30am–3pm and 5–10pm; Sat–Sun 5–11pm. Bus: 1, 8. PIZZA.

Incendio's 22 combinations of pizza are served on fresh, crispy crusts baked in an old wood-fired oven. The pastas are homemade, and you're encouraged to mix and match sauces and pastas—try the mussels with spinach fettuccine, capers, and tomatoes in lime butter. The wine list is decent, but the beer list is inspired. And now there's a patio. Sunday night features all-you-can-eat pizza for C$8 (U.S.$5).

Phnom Penh Restaurant. 244 E. Georgia St., near Main St. ☎ **604/682-5777.** Reservations recommended. Dishes C$4.50–C$11 (U.S.$2.95–U.S.$7). DC, MC, V. Wed–Mon 10am–9:30pm. Bus: 8, 19. CAMBODIAN/VIETNAMESE.

This family-run restaurant serves a mix of Vietnamese and Cambodian cuisine. Try the outstanding hot-and-sour soup, loaded with prawns and lemongrass; the delicious deep-fried garlic squid; and, for dessert, the exotic fruit-and-rice pudding. There's a second location at 955 Broadway, at Oak Street (☎ **604/734-8898**).

THE WEST SIDE

✪ **Bishop's.** 2183 W. 4th Ave. ☎ **604/738-2025.** www.settingsun.com/Bishops. Reservations required. Main courses C$24–C$30 (U.S.$16–U.S.$20). AE, DC, MC, V. Mon–Sat 5:30–11pm, Sun 5:30–10pm. Bus: 4, 7. FRENCH.

The atmosphere here features candlelight, white linen, and soft jazz. The service is impeccable and the food even better, with the menu changing three or four times a year. Recent dishes have included roast duck breast with sun-dried Okanagan Valley fruits, steamed smoked black cod with new potatoes and horseradish sabayon, and marinated sirloin of lamb with garlic mashed potatoes and a fresh mint, tomato, and balsamic vinegar reduction. If you have only one evening to dine in Vancouver, spend it here.

✪ **Lumière.** 2551 W. Broadway. ☎ **604/739-8185.** Reservations recommended. Main courses C$24–C$35 (U.S.$16–U.S.$23); vegetarian tasting menu C$55 (U.S.$36); chef's tasting menu C$70 (U.S.$46), accompanying flight of wines by the glass C$40 (U.S.$26). AE, DC, MC, V. Tues–Thurs and Sun 5:30–9:30pm; Fri–Sat 5:30–10:30pm. Bus: 9, 10. FRENCH.

The success of this fine-dining experiment in the heart of Kitsilano has turned chef Rob Feenie into a hot commodity. He now regularly jets off to New York to teach folks back east how to do it right. His preparation and presentation are immaculately French and his ingredients resolutely local, making for interesting surprises such as fresh ginger popping up in the veal or raspberries in the foie gras. Go for the tasting menu or vegetarian menu and let Feenie show you what French cuisine can be.

The Naam Restaurant. 2724 W. 4th Ave. ☎ **604/738-7151.** Reservations not accepted. Main courses C$3.95–C$8.25 (U.S.$2.55–U.S.$5.35). AE, ER, MC, V. Daily 24 hr. Bus: 4, 22. VEGETARIAN.

Back in the 1960s, when Kitsilano was Canada's hippie haven, the Naam was tie-dye central. Things have changed since, but this oldest of Vancouver's vegetarian/natural-foods restaurants retains a pleasantly granola feel. The decor is simple and welcoming; the brazenly healthy fare ranges from open-face tofu melts to Thai noodles and pita pizzas. The sesame spice fries are a Vancouver institution. *Tip:* Arrive well before you're actually hungry: The staff will invariably disappear on an extended search for personal fulfillment at some point during your meal.

Sami's. 986 W. Broadway. ☎ **604/736-8330.** Reservations not accepted. Main courses C$6–C$11 (U.S.$3.90–U.S.$7). AE, MC, V. Daily 11am–11pm. Bus: 9. INDIAN.

In the long and honorable history of South Asian food in Vancouver, there has never been a less promising location than this—a strip mall in the dull office corridor of West Broadway. But the food is fabulous, ranging from beef short ribs braised in cumin and ginger to seafood poached in coconut nectar. Restaurateur Sami Lalji decided he'd had it with the big time and wanted a fun, manageable spot where he could cook up the Indian/Western mix that is now his pride and joy. The result is a stunning success.

THE NORTH SHORE

✪ **The Beach House at Dundarave Pier.** 150 25th St., W. Vancouver. ☎ **604/922-1414.** Reservations recommended. Main courses C$12–C$16 (U.S.$8–U.S.$10) lunch, C$22–C$31 (U.S.$14–U.S.$20) dinner. AE, DC, ER, MC, V. Mon–Thurs 11:30am–3pm and 5–10pm; Fri–Sat 5–11pm; Sat–Sun brunch 11am–3pm. Light appetizers served Mon–Sat 3–5pm. WEST COAST.

Set in a dramatic waterfront location, every seat here boasts a panoramic view of English Bay. The cuisine is top quality—innovative but not so experimental it leaves the West Van burghers gasping for breath. Appetizers include soft-shell crab with salt-and-fire jelly and grilled portobellos with Okanagan Valley goat cheese. Entrees range from garlic-crusted rack of lamb with honey balsamic glaze to baked striped sea bass with basil mousse and rock prawns. The restaurant has an award-winning wine list.

✪ **The Salmon House on the Hill.** 2229 Folkstone Way, W. Vancouver. ☎ **604/926-3212.** www.salmonhouse.com. Reservations recommended for dinner. Main courses C$6–C$14 (U.S.$3.90–U.S.$9) lunch, C$14–C$24 (U.S.$9–U.S.$16) dinner. AE, DC, ER, MC, V. Mon–Sat 11:30am–2:30pm; Sun brunch 11am–2:30pm; daily 5:30–10pm. WEST COAST.

Perched high above West Vancouver, the Salmon House offers spectacular views. Chef Dan Atkinson's menu reflects his extensive research into local ingredients and First Nations cuisine. Entrees include Fraser Valley free-range chicken with roasted onion jus, and smoked West Coast black cod with wasabi cream and balsamic mustard-seed vinaigrette. The wine list earned an award of excellence from *Wine Spectator.*

5 Exploring the City

A city perched on the edge of a wilderness, Vancouver offers unmatched opportunities for exploring the outdoors: You can hike through old-growth forests, kayak an ocean fjord, and ski fresh powder, all within view of the city. Paradoxically, Vancouver is also intensely urban. There are sidewalk cafes to match Paris's and shopping streets to rival London's. The forest of downtown residential high-rises looks somewhat like

New York's, while the buzz in Chinatown is reminiscent of San Francisco's. Comparisons soon begin to pall, however, as you come to realize that Vancouver is entirely its own creation—a self-confident, sparklingly beautiful city, like no place else on earth.

Note: See the "Downtown Vancouver" map (pp. 50–51) to locate most of the sights in this section.

THE TOP ATTRACTIONS
DOWNTOWN & THE WEST END

B.C. Sports Hall of Fame and Museum. 777 Pacific Blvd. S. (B.C. Place Stadium, Gate A, Beatty and Robson sts.). ☎ **604/687-5520.** Admission C$6 (U.S.$3.90) adults, C$4 (U.S.$2.60) seniors and students, free for children under 5. Daily 10am–5pm. SkyTrain: Stadium. Bus: 15.

A great destination for kids with endless energy, the museum's Participation Gallery features interactive running, climbing, throwing, riding, rowing, and racing competitions where you can pit yourself against video-simulated competitors. There's also a climbing wall and pitching cages. For parents, the Hall of Champions and Builders Hall document the achievements of British Columbia's most lauded athletes.

Canadian Craft Museum. 639 Hornby St. ☎ **604/687-8266.** Admission C$5 (U.S.$3.25) adults, C$3 (U.S.$1.95) seniors and students, free for children under 12. Mon–Wed and Fri–Sat 10am–5pm, Thurs 10am–9pm, Sun and holidays noon–5pm. Closed Tues Sept–May. SkyTrain: Granville. Bus: 3.

Hidden behind the Cathedral Place building at the edge of a beautiful courtyard, the Canadian Craft Museum presents a vast collection of Canadian and international crafts in glass, wood, metal, clay, and fiber. Recent shows have included an impressive display of carved Chinese signature seals and calligraphy, local artist Bill Reid's gold and silver jewelry, and furniture created by Canada's best industrial designers.

✪ Vancouver Aquarium Marine Science Centre. Stanley Park. ☎ **604/659-FISH (3474).** www.vanaqua.org. Admission C$13 (U.S.$8) adults; C$11 (U.S.$7) seniors, students, and youths 13–18; C$9 (U.S.$6) children 4–12; C$43 (U.S.$28) families. June 23–Sept 4 daily 9:30am–7pm; Sept 5–June 22 daily 10am–5:30pm. Bus: 135; "Around the Park" shuttle bus June–Sept only. Parking C$5 (U.S.$3.25) summer, C$3 (U.S.$1.95) winter.

One of North America's largest and best aquaria, the Vancouver Aquarium houses more than 8,000 species, most in meticulously re-created environments, including the icy-blue Arctic Canada exhibit, the Amazon rain-forest gallery, and the Pacific Canada exhibit. On the Marine Mammal Deck are sea otters, sea lions, beluga whales, an orca (killer whale), and a Pacific white-sided dolphin. During regularly scheduled shows, the staff explains marine mammal behavior while working with these impressive creatures. In addition to tours, the aquarium has a regular program of special events, including behind-the-scenes tours, sleep-over programs for youths, and evening barbecues.

Vancouver Art Gallery. 750 Hornby St. ☎ **604/662-4719** or 604/662-4700. www.vanartgallery.bc.ca. Admission C$8 (U.S.$5) adults, C$6 (U.S.$3.90) seniors, C$4 (U.S.$2.60) students, C$25 (U.S.$16) families. Thurs 6–9pm by donation. Mon–Sun 10am–5:30pm, Thurs 10am–9pm, holidays noon–5pm. SkyTrain: Granville. Bus: 3.

The VAG is an excellent stop for anyone wanting to see what sets Canadian and West Coast art apart. You'll find an impressive collection of paintings by British Columbia native Emily Carr, as well as examples of a unique Canadian art style created during the 1920s by members of the "Group of Seven," who included Vancouver painter Fred Varley, and whose bold style was strongly influenced by dramatic Canadian landscapes. On the contemporary side, the VAG hosts rotating exhibits of sculpture, graphics, photography, and video art. Geared to younger audiences, the Annex Gallery features presentations of visually exciting educational exhibits.

GASTOWN & CHINATOWN

✪ **Dr. Sun Yat-sen Classical Garden.** 578 Carrall St. ☎ **604/689-7133.** C$7 (U.S.$4.55) adults, C$5 (U.S.$3.25) seniors, C$4 (U.S.$2.60) children and students. June 15–Sept 15 daily 9:30am–7pm; Sept 16–June 14 daily 10am–6pm. Bus: 4, 7.

The Classical Garden was built in Suzhou, China, around 1492 and relocated to Vancouver just in time for Expo '86. It was packed in 950 crates, and 52 artisans took nearly 10 years to completely reassemble it, replant it, and stock it with turtles and carp. This serenely beautiful garden is the only one of its kind in the western hemisphere.

✪ **Vancouver Centennial Police Museum.** 240 E. Cordova St. ☎ **604/665-3346.** www.city.vancouver.bc.ca/police/museum. Admission C$5 (U.S.$3.25) adults, C$3 (U.S.$1.95) students and seniors, free for children under 6. Year-round Mon–Fri 9am–3pm; May–Aug Sat 10am–3pm. Bus: 4, 7.

This is a bizarre, utterly delightful little museum, dedicated to memorializing some of the best crimes and crime-stoppers in the city's short but colorful history. Housed in the old Vancouver Coroner's Court—where actor Errol Flynn was autopsied after dropping dead in the arms of a 17-year-old girl—the museum features photos, text, and vintage equipment from the files and evidence room of Vancouver's finest.

THE WEST SIDE

✪ **Museum of Anthropology.** 6393 NW Marine Dr. ☎ **604/822-3825.** Admission C$6 (U.S.$3.90) adults, C$3.50 (U.S.$2.30) seniors and students, C$15 (U.S.$10) families, free for children under 6. Free Tues after 5pm. Mid-May to Sept Wed–Mon 10am–5pm, Tues 10am–9pm; Oct to mid-May Wed–Sun 11am–5pm, Tues 11am–9pm. Closed Dec 25–26. Bus: 4, 10.

This isn't just any old museum. In 1976, architect Arthur Erikson re-created a classic native post-and-beam structure out of modern concrete and glass to house one of the world's finest collections of West Coast native art. Haida artist Bill Reid's masterpiece, *Raven and the First Men,* is worth the price of admission alone. The huge carving in glowing yellow cedar depicts a Haida creation myth, in which Raven (the trickster) coaxes humanity out into the world. Some of Reid's creations in gold and silver are also on display. Don't forget to take a walk around the grounds behind the museum: Overlooking Point Grey are two longhouses and 10 hand-carved totem poles.

Pacific Space Centre. 1100 Chestnut St., in Vanier Park. ☎ **604/738-STAR.** www. pacific-space-centre.bc.ca. Admission C$12 (U.S.$8) adults, C$10 (U.S.$7) seniors and youths 11–16, C$8 (U.S.$5) children 5–10, C$4 (U.S.$2.60) children under 5; C$38 (U.S.$25) families (up to 5, maximum 2 adults). Extra family member C$8 (U.S.$5). Extra Virtual Voyages experiences C$4 (U.S.$2.60) each. Sept–June Tues–Sun 10am–5pm (to 8pm Fri); July–Aug Tues–Sun 10am–5pm (to 8pm Fri); holidays 10am–5pm. Closed Christmas. Bus: 22.

Housed in the same building as the Vancouver Museum (see below), the space center and observatory offer hands-on displays and exhibits that promise to delight both kids and amateur astronomy, space, science, and computer buffs. In the Virtual Voyages Simulator, you can go on a voyage to Mars or collide with an oncoming comet. In the interactive Cosmic Courtyard, you can look at an Apollo 17 manned-satellite engine, try your hand at designing a spacecraft, or maneuver a lunar robot.

✪ **Science World British Columbia.** 1455 Quebec St. ☎ **604/268-6363.** www. scienceworld.bc.ca. Admission C$12 (U.S.$8) adults; C$8 (U.S.$5) seniors, students, and children 4 and older. Combination tickets available for OMNIMAX film. Mon–Fri 10am–5pm, Sat–Sun 10am–6pm. SkyTrain: Main Street–Science World.

Science World is unmistakable—it's the big blinking geodesic dome on the eastern end of False Creek. At this hands-on scientific discovery center, you and your kids can light up a plasma ball, walk through a 1,700-square-foot (158m^2) maze, lose your shadow, walk through the interior of a camera, create a cyclone, blow square bubbles, and watch a zucchini explode as it's charged with 80,000 volts. In the OMNIMAX Theatre—a huge projecting screen equipped with surround sound—you'll feel as though you're taking a death-defying flight through the Grand Canyon.

✪ **Vancouver Maritime Museum.** 1905 Ogden Ave., in Vanier Park. ☎ **604/257-8300.** www.vmm.bc.ca. Admission C$6 (U.S.$3.90) adults, C$3 (U.S.$1.95) seniors and students, C$14 (U.S.$9) families, free for children under 6. Daily 10am–5pm; closed Tues Sept to mid-May. Bus: 22, then walk 4 blocks north on Cypress St. Boat: False Creek Ferries dock at Heritage Harbour.

This museum houses the RCMP Arctic patrol vessel *St. Roch,* the first ship to traverse its way back and forth through the Northwest Passage. Tours of the *St. Roch* are particularly popular with children—they get to clamber around the boat poking and prodding stuff. The other half of the museum holds intricate ship models, antique wood and brass fittings, maps, prints, and a number of permanent exhibits such as "Pirates!," a treasure chest of an exhibit filled with pirate lore, artifacts, a Jolly Roger, pieces of eight, and a miniature ship where kids can dress up and play pirate for the day.

Vancouver Museum. 1100 Chestnut St., in Vanier Park. ☎ **604/736-4431.** www. vanmuseum.bc.ca. Admission C$9 (U.S.$6) adults, C$6 (U.S.$3.90) youths. Group rates available. Daily 10am–5pm; closed Mon Sept–June. Bus: 22, then walk 3 blocks south on Cornwall Ave. Boat: Granville Island Ferry to Heritage Harbour.

Opened in 1894, this museum is dedicated to the city's history, from its days as a native settlement and European outpost to its early-20th-century maturation into a modern urban center. The exhibits let you walk through the steerage deck of a 19th-century passenger ship, peek into a Hudson's Bay Company frontier trading post, and take a seat in an 1880s Canadian-Pacific Railway passenger car. Re-creations of Victorian and Edwardian rooms show how early Vancouverites decorated their homes.

THE NORTH SHORE

Capilano Suspension Bridge & Park. 3735 Capilano Rd., N. Vancouver. ☎ **604/ 985-7474.** www.capbridge.com. Admission C$11 (U.S.$7) adults, C$9 (U.S.$6) seniors, C$6 (U.S.$3.90) students, C$3.25 (U.S.$2.10) children 6–12, free for children under 6. Discounted admission in winter. May–Sept daily 8:30am–dusk; Oct–Apr daily 9am–5pm. Closed Dec 25. Bus: 246 from downtown Vancouver, 236 from Lonsdale Quay SeaBus terminal.

Vancouver's first and oldest tourist trap (built in 1889), this attraction still works, mostly because there's still something inherently thrilling about standing on a narrow, shaking walkway, 230 feet (70m) above the canyon floor, held up by nothing but a pair of miserable cables. In addition to the bridge, there's a carving center where native carvers show their skill, a natural-history exhibit, two restaurants, and a gift shop.

Grouse Mountain Resort. 6400 Nancy Greene Way, N. Vancouver. ☎ **604/984-0661.** www.grousemountain. SkyRide C$17 (U.S.$11) adults, C$15 (U.S.$10) seniors, C$11 (U.S.$7) youths, C$6 (U.S.$3.90) children 6–12, free for children under 6. SkyRide free with advance Grouse Nest restaurant reservation. Daily 10am–10pm. SeaBus: Lonsdale Quay, then transfer to bus no. 236.

Once a small local ski hill, Grouse has been developing into a year-round recreation park, offering impressive views and easy access to the North Shore mountains. Only a

20-minute drive from downtown, the SkyRide gondola transports you to the mountain's 3,700-foot (1,128m) summit in about 10 minutes. At the top is a bar, restaurant, large-screen theater, ski and snowboard area, hiking and snowshoeing trails, skating pond, children's snow park, interpretive forest trails, logger sports show, helicopter tours, mountain-bike trails, and native feast house. Some of these are free with your SkyRide ticket, most aren't, but the view is free—and it's one of the best around.

PARKS & GARDENS

See also **Dr. Sun Yat-sen Classical Garden** in "The Top Attractions," above. For general information about Vancouver's parks, call ☎ 604/257-8400.

✪ **Stanley Park** is a 1,000-acre rain forest near the busy West End, filled with towering cedar trees, lagoons, trails, lawns, and gardens. It houses the Vancouver Aquarium, a petting zoo, restaurants, snack bars, cricket greens, a pool, a miniature railway, and a water park. It also boasts abundant wildlife and amazing marine views.

On the West Side, **Queen Elizabeth Park,** at Cambie Street and West 33rd Avenue, sits atop a 500-foot-high (152m) extinct volcano and is the highest urban vantage point south of downtown, offering panoramic views and manicured gardens. The **Bloedel Conservatory** (☎ 604/257-8570), next to the park's huge sunken garden, houses a tropical rain forest with more than 100 species as well as free-flying birds. Nearby is the 55-acre **VanDusen Botanical Garden,** 5251 Oak St., at 37th Avenue (☎ 604/878-9274), with lawns, lakes, Elizabethan hedge mazes, and sculptures.

On the University of British Columbia campus, the **UBC Botanical Garden,** 6250 Stadium Rd., Gate 8 (☎ 604/822-9666), has 70 acres of formal plantings. Nearby is the traditional Japanese **Nitobe Memorial Garden,** 6565 NW Marine Dr., Gate 4 (☎ 604/822-6038). Out near UBC, **Pacific Spirit Park** (also called the **Endowment Lands**) consists of 1,885 acres of temperate rain forest, marshes, and beaches; it includes 22 miles (35km) of trails for hiking, riding, and mountain biking.

Across the Lions Gate Bridge are six provincial parks that delight outdoor enthusiasts. The **Capilano River Regional Park,** 4500 Capilano Rd. (☎ 604/666-1790), surrounds the Capilano Suspension Bridge. Hikers can follow the river for 4¹/₂ miles (7km) to the Burrard Inlet and the Lions Gate Bridge, or about a mile upstream to **Cleveland Dam,** the launching point for white-water kayakers and canoeists. The **Capilano Salmon Hatchery,** on Capilano Road (☎ 604/666-1790), is on the river's east bank about a quarter-mile below the Cleveland Dam.

Five miles (8km) west of the Lions Gate Bridge on Marine Drive West is **Lighthouse Park.** This 185-acre rugged-terrain forest has 8 miles (13km) of trails. One path leads to the **Point Atkinson Lighthouse,** overlooking the Strait of Georgia. For information on other West Vancouver parks, call ☎ 604/925-7200.

ESPECIALLY FOR KIDS

Pick up a copy of the free monthly newspaper *West Coast Families* (☎ 604/689-1331). Its "Fun in the City" centerfold and events calendar list everything currently going on, including IMAX and OMNIMAX shows and free kids' programs.

Stanley Park's **Children's Farm** (☎ 604/257-8530) has peacocks, rabbits, calves, donkeys, and Shetland ponies. Next to the petting zoo is the popular **Miniature Railway** (☎ 604/257-8531), which runs on a circuit through the woods. Also in the park, the **Vancouver Aquarium** has sea otters, sea lions, whales, and numerous other marine creatures (see "The Top Attractions," above).

Right in town, budding scientists can get their hands into everything at **Science World**. And at the **Vancouver Maritime Museum,** kids can dress up like a pirate or naval captain, or board the RCMP icebreaker *St. Roch* (see "The Top Attractions," above, for both). **Granville Island's Kids Only Market,** 1496 Cartwright St. (☎ **604/689-8447**), offers playrooms and shops filled with toys, books, clothes, and food. Kids will love taking the Aquabus or Granville Island Ferry to get here.

Across Burrard Inlet on the North Shore, **Maplewood Farm,** 405 Seymour River Place, North Vancouver (☎ **604/929-5610**), has more than 200 barnyard animals living on its 5-acre farm, open daily year-round. About 45 minutes east of the city, the lush 120-acre **Greater Vancouver Zoological Center,** 5048 264th St., Aldergrove (☎ **604/856-6825**), has lions, tigers, elephants, giraffes, zebras, hippos, and camels.

Athletic kids can work up a sweat at the **B.C. Sports Hall of Fame and Museum** (see "The Top Attractions," above). At **Granville Island's Water Park and Adventure Playground,** 1496 Cartwright St., kids can let loose with water guns or frolic on the water slides. Open daily in summer; free admission. Changing facilities are nearby at the False Creek Community Center (☎ **604/257-8195**). Open in summer, **Splash-down Park,** 4799 Nu Lelum Way, Tsawwassen (☎ **604/943-2251**), is a 3-minute drive from the Tsawwassen ferry terminal, just south of Vancouver. With water slides, a giant hot tub, a pool, and a picnic area, it's a great escape for kids of all ages.

6 Outdoor Pursuits

Just about every imaginable sport has a world-class outlet within the city limits. Downhill and cross-country skiing, snowshoeing, sea kayaking, fly-fishing, diving, hiking, paragliding, and mountain biking are just a few of the options.

BEACHES   A great place for viewing sunsets, **English Bay Beach** is at the end of Davie Street off Denman Street and Beach Avenue. South of English Bay near the Burrard Street Bridge and the Vancouver Aquatic Centre is **Sunset Beach.** On **Stanley Park's** western rim, **Second Beach** is a quick stroll north from English Bay Beach. A playground, snack bar, and heated freshwater pool make it popular with families. Farther along the seawall is secluded **Third Beach,** north of Stanley Park Drive.

At **Kitsilano Beach,** along Ogden Street, a heated saltwater pool is open in summer. Farther west along Point Grey Road is **Jericho Beach,** followed by **Locarno Beach** and **Spanish Banks.** Below UBC's Museum of Anthropology, **Wreck Beach** is Vancouver's immensely popular nude beach. At the northern foot of the Lions Gate Bridge, **Ambleside Park** is a popular North Shore spot.

BIKING   Helmets are legally required for cyclists, both off-road and on. Marked bicycle lanes traverse Vancouver, including the cross-town Off-Broadway route, the Adanac route, and the Ontario route. One of the city's most scenic cycle paths has been extended and now runs all the way from Canada Place Pier to Pacific Spirit Park. Maps are available at most bike shops and rental outlets.

Mountain bikers love the cross-country ski trails on **Hollyburn Mountain** in Cypress Provincial Park. Mount Seymour's steep **Good Samaritan Trail** connects to the Baden-Powell Trail and the Bridle Path near Mount Seymour Road. Closer to downtown, **Pacific Spirit Park** and **Burnaby Mountain** offer excellent beginner and intermediate off-road trails.

Rentals run around C$4 (U.S.$2.60) per hour for a one-speed "Cruiser" to C$10 (U.S.$7) for a top-of-the-line bike, or C$15 to C$40 (U.S.$10 to U.S.$26) per day. Bikes, helmets, and child trailers are available at **Spokes Bicycle Rentals & Espresso Bar,** 1798 W. Georgia St. (☎ **604/688-5141**). **Bayshore Bicycle and Rollerblade**

Rentals, 745 Denman St. (☎ **604/688-2453**), and 1601 W. Georgia St. (☎ **604/ 689-5071**), rents mountain bikes, bike carriers, tandems, city bikes, and kids' bikes.

BOATING   You can find rentals of 15- to 17-foot powerboats for as little as a few hours or up to several weeks at **Stanley Park Boat Rentals Ltd.,** Coal Harbour Marina (☎ **604/682-6257**). **Granville Island Boat Rentals, Ltd.,** 1696 Duranleau St., Granville Island (☎ **604/682-6287**), features hourly, daily, and weekly rentals of 15- to 19-foot speedboats and also offers sportfishing, cruising, and sightseeing charters. Rates on all of the above begin at around C$30 (U.S.$20) per hour and C$135 (U.S.$88) per day. **Delta Charters,** 3500 Cessna Dr., Richmond (☎ **800/ 661-7762** or 604/273-4211), has weekly and monthly rates for 32- to 58-foot powered craft. Prices begin around C$1,400 (U.S.$910) per week for a boat that sleeps four.

CANOEING & KAYAKING   Both placid, urban False Creek and the incredibly beautiful 18⁴/₅-mile (30km) North Vancouver fjord known as Indian Arm have launching points you can reach by car or bus. Rentals range from C$7 (U.S.$4.55) per hour to C$32 (U.S.$21) per day for kayaks, and about C$25 (U.S.$16) per day for canoes. Customized tours range from C$70 to C$110 (U.S.$46 to U.S.$72) per person.

   Adventure Fitness, 1510 Duranleau St. on Granville Island (☎ **604/687-1528**), offers lessons and rentals. In North Vancouver, **Deep Cove Canoe and Kayak Rentals,** Deep Cove (☎ **604/929-2268**), is an easy starting point for those planning an Indian Arm run. It offers hourly and daily rentals of canoes and kayaks as well as lessons and tours. **Lotus Land Tours,** 2005-1251 Cardero St. (☎ **800/528-3531** or 604/684-4922), runs guided kayak tours on Indian Arm for C$130 (U.S.$85).

DIVING   British Columbia's underwater scenery is stunning, but the water is chilly. Most local divers use dry suits. Cates Park in Deep Cove, Whytecliff Park and Porteau Cover near Horseshoe Bay, and Lighthouse Park are nearby dive spots. The **Diving Locker,** 2745 W. 4th Ave. (☎ **604/736-2681**), rents equipment and offers courses and free advice. Rentals cost around C$50 (U.S.$33) per day or C$63 (U.S.$41) with a second tank included; hiring a dive master to accompany you costs about C$60 (U.S.$39) per dive; a seat on a weekend dive boat runs about C$69 (U.S.$45) per dive.

ECOTOURS   **Rockwood Adventures,** 1330 Fulton Ave. (☎ **604/926-7705**), offers guided hikes of the north-shore rain forest, complete with a trained naturalist and a gourmet lunch. Tours, which cost C$75 (U.S.$49), cover Capilano Canyon, Bowen Island, or Lighthouse Park. Pickups are at major hotels downtown.

FISHING   Five species of salmon, rainbow and Dolly Varden trout, steelhead, and even sturgeon abound in the local waters. The *Vancouver Sun* prints a daily **fishing report** that details which fish are in season and where they can be found.

   To fish, you need a nonresident saltwater or freshwater license. **Hanson's Fishing Outfitters,** 102-580 Hornby St. (☎ **604/684-8988** or 604/684-8998), and **Granville Island Boat Rentals,** 1696 Duranleau St. (☎ **604/682-6287**), are outstanding outfitters and great sources for tackle and licenses. Licenses for freshwater fishing are C$16 (U.S.$10) for 1 day or C$32 (U.S.$21) for 8 days. Saltwater fishing licenses are C$8 (U.S.$5) for 1 day, C$20 (U.S.$13) for 3 days, and C$39 (U.S.$25) for 5 days.

GOLF   The **University Golf Club,** 5185 University Blvd. (☎ **604/224-1818**), is a great 6,560-yard, par-71 course with a clubhouse, pro shop, locker rooms, sports lounge, and parking lot. Or call **A-1 Last Minute Golf Hotline** (☎ **800/684-6344**

or 604/878-1833) for discounts and short-notice tee times at 30 Vancouver-area courses.

HIKING   Good trail maps are available from the **Greater Vancouver Regional Parks District** (☎ 604/432-6350) and from **International Travel Maps and Books,** 552 Seymour St. (☎ 604/687-3320), which also stocks guidebooks and topo maps. If you're looking for a challenge without the time commitment, hike the aptly named **Grouse Grind** from the bottom of Grouse Mountain to the top, then buy a one-way ticket down on the Grouse Mountain SkyRide gondola (C$5/U.S.$3.25).

Lynn Canyon Park, Lynn Headwaters Regional Park, Capilano River Regional Park, Mount Seymour Provincial Park, Pacific Spirit Park, and Cypress Provincial Park have good easy-to-challenging trails that wind through stands of Douglas fir and cedar. Pay attention to the trail warnings posted at the parks; some have bear habitats.

ICE-SKATING   From November to early April, **Robson Square** has free skating on a rink directly under Robson Street between Howe and Hornby streets. The rink at **West End Community Centre,** 870 Denman St. (☎ 604/257-8333), is open October through March. The **Ice Sports Centre,** 6501 Sprott, Burnaby (☎ 604/291-0626), the Vancouver Canucks' official practice facility, has eight rinks open year-round.

IN-LINE SKATING   You'll find locals rolling along beach paths, streets, park paths, and promenades. If you didn't bring your own blades, try **Bayshore Bicycle and Rollerblade Rentals,** 745 Denman St. (☎ 604/688-2453). Rentals generally run C$5 (U.S.$3.25) per hour, with a 2-hour minimum, or C$15 (U.S.$10) per day.

JOGGING   You'll find fellow runners traversing Stanley Park's **Seawall Promenade,** where the scenery is spectacular and cars aren't allowed.

RAFTING   Reo Rafting (☎ 800/736-7238; www.reorafting.com) offers guided white-water trips on the Nahatlatch River, a 2¹/₂-hour drive from Vancouver. One-day packages including breakfast, lunch, gear, and 4 to 5 hours on the river start at C$99 (U.S.$64). Multiday trips and group packages are also available.

SAILING   **Cooper Boating Center,** 1620 Duranleau St. (☎ 604/687-4110), offers cruises, rentals, and instruction on 21- to 46-foot boats. Prices vary from C$150 (U.S.$98) for a 3-hour lesson to C$4,000 (U.S.$2,600) or more for a week charter.

SKIING & SNOWBOARDING   It seldom snows in the city's downtown and central areas, but Vancouverites can ski at three resorts in the North Shore Mountains.

The **Grouse Mountain Resort,** 6400 Nancy Greene Way, North Vancouver (☎ 604/984-0661, or 604/986-6262 for snow report), has four lifts, two tows, two T-bars, and 22 alpine runs, plus a half pipe for snowboarders. Lift tickets cost C$29 (U.S.$19) for adults, C$22 (U.S.$14) for youths 13 to 18, and C$16 (U.S.$10) for children.

Mount Seymour Provincial Park, 1700 Mt. Seymour Rd., North Vancouver (☎ 604/986-2261, or 604/986-3999 for snow report), has the area's highest base elevation, four chairs, and a tow. Lift tickets are C$18 (U.S.$12) for adults and children.

Cypress Bowl, 1610 Mt. Seymour Rd. (☎ 604/926-5612, or 604/926-6007 for snow report), has the area's biggest vertical drop (1,750 ft./533m), challenging ski and snowboard runs, and 10 miles (16km) of cross-country trails. Lift tickets are C$35 (U.S.$23) for adults, C$29 (U.S.$19) for ages 13 to 18, C$17 (U.S.$11) for ages 5 to 12, and C$2 (U.S.$1.30) for kids under 5.

SWIMMING   The midsummer saltwater temperature rarely exceeds 65°F (18°C). Some swimmers opt for fresh- and saltwater pools at city beaches (see "Beaches," above). Indoor pools include the **Vancouver Aquatic Centre,** 1050 Beach Ave. (☎ 604/665-3424); **YWCA fitness center,** 535 Hornby St. (☎ 604/895-5777); and **UBC's Aquatic Centre,** 2075 Westbrook Mall (☎ 604/822-4521).

TENNIS   Vancouver has 180 outdoor hard courts available on a first-come, first-served basis from 8am to dusk (1-hr. limit). With the exception of the Beach Avenue courts, which charge a nominal fee, all city courts are free. **Stanley Park** has four courts near Lost Lagoon and 17 courts near the Beach Avenue entrance; **Queen Elizabeth Park** and **Kitsilano Beach Park** also have courts.

You can play at night at the **Langara Campus** of Vancouver Community College, West 49th Avenue between Main and Cambie streets. The **UBC Coast Club,** on Thunderbird Boulevard (☎ 604/822-2505), has 10 outdoor and 4 indoor courts.

WILDLIFE WATCHING   In winter, thousands of bald eagles line the banks of **Indian Arm fjord** and the **Squamish, Cheakamus,** and **Mamquam** rivers to feed on spawning salmon. The annual summer salmon runs attract more than bald eagles. Tourists also flock to coastal streams and rivers to watch the waters turn red with leaping coho and sockeye. The salmon are plentiful at the **Capilano Salmon Hatchery** (see "Parks & Gardens," above) and **Goldstream Provincial Park** (see chapter 5).

Along the Fraser River delta, more than 250 bird species migrate to or inhabit the **George C. Reifel Sanctuary's** wetland reserve. Nearby **Richmond Nature Park** has educational displays and a boardwalk-encircled duck pond. **Stanley Park** and **Pacific Spirit Park** are both home to a heron rookery. Ravens, dozens of species of waterfowl, raccoons, skunks, beavers, and even coyotes are also full-time residents.

WINDSURFING   Windsurfing isn't allowed at the mouth of False Creek near Granville Island, but you can bring a board to Jericho and English Bay beaches or rent one here. Equipment sales, rentals, and instruction can be found at **Windsure Windsurfing School,** 1300 Discovery St., at Jericho Beach (☎ 604/224-0615).

7 Shopping

Robson Street is the spot for high-end fashion. Vancouver's old money heads to the 10-block stretch of **Granville Street** from 6th to 16th avenues for classic fashions, housewares, and furniture. **Water Street** in Gastown features antiques, First Nations art, and funky retro shops. **Main Street** from 19th to 27th avenues means antiques, and lots of 'em. **Granville Island,** a rehabilitated industrial site beneath the Granville Street Bridge, is one of the best places to pick up seafood, as well as crafts and gifts.

ANTIQUES   The **Vancouver Antique Centre,** 422 Richards St. (☎ 604/669-7444), has everything from china and jewelry to military objects. **Uno Langmann Ltd.,** 2117 Granville St. (☎ 604/736-8825), caters to upscale shoppers.

BOOKS   Locally owned **Duthie Books,** 2239 W. 4th Ave., Kitsilano (☎ 604/732-5344), has been in business since 1957. Pleasant **Chapters,** 788 Robson St. (☎ 604/682-4066), has little nooks and comfy benches.

DEPARTMENT STORES & SHOPPING MALLS   Ever since the establishment of its trading posts in the 1670s, **The Bay (Hudson's Bay Company),** 674 Granville St. (☎ 604/681-6211), has built its reputation on quality goods. You can still buy a Hudson's Bay woolen point blanket, but you'll also find wares from Tommy Hilfiger and DKNY. The 200-shop **Pacific Centre Mall,** 700 W. Georgia St. (☎ 604/688-7236), contains Godiva, Crabtree & Evelyn, and Eddie Bauer. For upscale boutiques like Armani, try the **Sinclair Centre,** 757 W. Hastings St. (☎ 604/659-1009).

FASHION   Designer outlets include **Chanel,** 103-755 Burrard St. (☎ 604/682-0522); **Salvatore Ferragamo,** 918 Robson St. (☎ 604/669-4495); **Gianni Versace,** 757 W. Hastings St. (☎ 604/683-1131); and **Polo/Ralph Lauren,** the Landing, 375 Water St. (☎ 604/682-7656). For something uniquely West Coast, **Dorothy Grant,** 250-757 W. Hastings St. (☎ 604/681-0201), offers exquisite First Nations designs.

FOOD & WINE   **Murchie's Tea & Coffee,** 970 Robson St. (☎ **604/669-0783**), is a Vancouver institution. The **Lobsterman,** 1807 Mast Tower Rd. (☎ **604/687-4531**), is one of the best spots for salmon and other seafood, which can be packed for air travel. **Marquis Wine Cellars,** 1034 Davie St. (☎ **604/684-0445** or 604/685-2246), carries British Columbian and international wines.

JEWELRY   Since 1879, **Henry Birk & Sons Ltd.,** 698 W. Hastings St. (☎ **604/669-3333**), has designed and created beautiful jewelry and watches. On Granville Island, **The Raven and the Bear,** 1528 Duranleau St. (☎ **604/669-3990**), is a great spot to shop for West Coast native jewelry.

NATIVE ART   **Images for a Canadian Heritage,** 164 Water St. (☎ **604/685-7046**), is a government-licensed First Nations gallery. The **Leona Lattimer Gallery,** 1590 W. 2nd Ave. (☎ **604/732-4556**), presents museum-quality masks, totem poles, and jewelry, at more affordable prices than galleries downtown.

SPORTING GOODS   Everything you'll ever need for the outdoors is at **Mountain Equipment Co-op,** 130 W. Broadway (☎ **604/872-7858**).

8 Vancouver After Dark

Check out the weekly *Georgia Straight, Vancouver* magazine, or *Xtra! West,* the gay/lesbian tabloid. The **Vancouver Cultural Alliance Arts Hotline** (☎ **604/684-2787**) and Web site (**www.culturenet.ca/vca**) are great sources for the performing arts. **Ticketmaster** (☎ **604/280-3311**) has 40 outlets in the greater Vancouver area.

Three major Vancouver theaters regularly host touring performances: the **Queen Elizabeth Theatre,** 600 Hamilton St., and the **Vancouver Playhouse,** which share a number (☎ **604/665-3050**) and Web site (**www.city.vancouver.bc.ca/theatres**); and the **Orpheum Theatre,** 801 Granville St. (☎ **604/665-3050**).

In a converted early 1900s church, the **Vancouver East Cultural Centre** (the "Cultch" to locals), 1895 Venables St. (☎ **604/254-9578;** www.thedrive.net/vecc), hosts avant-garde theater productions, children's programs, and art exhibits.

THE PERFORMING ARTS

THEATER   Every summer brings an outdoor Shakespeare series called **Bard on the Beach,** in Vanier Park (☎ **604/737-0625**). You can also bring a picnic to Stanley Park and watch **Theatre Under the Stars** (☎ **604/687-0174**), which features popular musicals and light comedies. ✪ **Vancouver's Fringe Festival** (☎ **604/257-0350;** www.vancouverfringe.com) offers more than 500 innovative shows each September, all costing under C$10 (U.S.$7). The **Arts Club Theatre Company** (☎ **604/687-1644;** www.culturenet.ca/vca/artscl.htm) performs at the **Granville Island Stage** at the Arts Club Theatre, 1585 Johnston St., and the **Stanley Theatre,** 2750 Granville St.

OPERA   The **Vancouver Opera,** 500-845 Cambie St. (☎ **604/683-0222**), alternates between obscure or new works and older, more popular favorites.

CLASSICAL MUSIC   The extremely active **Vancouver Symphony,** 601 Smithe St. (☎ **604/876-3434**), presents a number of series: great classical works, ethnic works, pop and show tunes, and music geared toward children. The traveling summer concert series takes the orchestra from White Rock to the top of Whistler Mountain.

DANCE   Fans of modern and original dance should visit in July, when the **Dancing on the Edge Festival** (☎ 604/689-0691) presents 60 to 80 original pieces. **Ballet British Columbia,** 502-68 Water St. (☎ 604/732-5003), presents innovative works. For information on other companies, call the **Dance Centre** (☎ 604/606-6400).

THE CLUB SCENE

In June, the **du Maurier International Jazz Festival** (☎ 604/872-5200) takes over a number of venues and outdoor locations around town. The July ✪ **Vancouver Folk Festival** (☎ 604/602-9798) takes place on the beach at Jericho Park. The **Coastal Jazz and Blues Society,** 316 W. 6th Ave. (☎ 604/872-5200), has information on current and upcoming events throughout the year.

The functional **Starfish Room,** 1055 Homer St. (☎ 604/682-4171), hosts bands varying from jazz to lounge, funk, even punk. For folk, the **WISE Hall,** 1882 Adanac (☎ 604/254-5858), is the place to be. And for blues, go to the smoky old **Yale Hotel,** 1300 Granville St. (☎ 604/681-9253).

If you wanna dance, head to Gastown's **The Purple Onion,** 15 Water St. (☎ 604/602-9442). Vancouver's purest hip-hop house joint is **Sonar,** 66 Water St. (☎ 604/683-6695), named one of the world's top 20 clubs by Britain's *Ministry* magazine.

BARS, PUBS & LOUNGES

Fred's Tavern, 1006 Granville St. (☎ 604/605-4350), features a steady stream of simulcast sports, but for some reason the beautiful young crowd is mostly interested in each other. **Steamworks Pub & Brewery,** 375 Water St. (☎ 604/689-2739), offers a dozen in-house beers. View junkies will think they've died and gone to heaven at the rotating ✪ **Cloud Nine,** 1400 Robson St., on the 42nd floor of the Empire Landmark Hotel (☎ 604/687-0511). Finally, you won't find a better martini than at decadent ✪ **Delilah's,** 1789 Comox St. (☎ 604/687-3424); see "Dining," above.

GAY & LESBIAN BARS

The **Gay & Lesbian Centre,** 2-1170 Bute St. (☎ 604/684-6869), has information on current hot spots, or you can pick up a copy of *Xtra West!,* available in most cafes. **Celebrities,** 1022 Davie St. (☎ 604/689-3180), is the West End's largest gay dance club, with a cover of C$4 to C$7 (U.S.$2.60 to U.S.$4.55). The **Dufferin Pub,** 900 Seymour St. (☎ 604/683-4251), is home to the city's glitziest drag show. The **Odyssey,** 1251 Howe St. (☎ 604/689-5256), is the hippest gay/mixed dance bar in town, with a cover of C$3 to C$5 (U.S.$1.95 to U.S.$3.25). The **Heritage House Hotel,** 455 Abbott St. (☎ 604/685-7777), is home to two gay bars, **Charlie's Lounge** and the slightly seedy **Chuck's Pub,** and one lesbian locale, the **Lotus Cabaret.**

CASINOS

There's no alcohol and no floor shows, but you haven't really lived until you've done some serious gambling with a room full of Far Eastern big shots trying to re-create the huge night they had in Happy Valley or Macau. At the **Gateway Casino,** 611 Main St., 3rd floor (☎ 604/688-9412), you can play pai gow poker, blackjack, roulette, and let it ride. It's open from noon to 2am. Similar games are on offer at the **Great Canadian Casino,** 1133 W. Hastings St. (☎ 604/682-8145), and the **Royal Diamond Casino,** 750 Pacific Blvd., in the Plaza of Nations (☎ 604/685-2340).

Victoria 4

by Shawn Blore

There's more to British Columbia than Vancouver's urban bustle. In fact, the other Vancouver—Vancouver Island—is 90 minutes from the city by ferry. At the southeastern tip of Vancouver Island is the province's capital, Victoria, right across the Strait of Juan de Fuca from Washington State's snowcapped Olympic peninsula. It's 45 miles (72km) south of the 49th parallel, which is the border between most of Canada and the contiguous United States.

Victoria is the island's largest city and one of the most popular destinations in Canada. *Condé Nast Traveler* regularly rates Victoria as one of the most romantic places in the world, and its location is certainly superb: The regal Empress hotel and the city's downtown face the Inner Harbour, busy with ferries, sailboats, and passenger ships. Flanking downtown across the harbor are the domed Parliament Buildings. The streets of Victoria's old downtown area are lined with inviting shops selling British woolens, Northwest native art, outdoor gear, and souvenirs. If you're not into shopping, you'll at least enjoy the lovely period architecture; at night especially, when most buildings are outlined with strings of lights, the effect is enchanting.

Many people come to Victoria expecting to find a kind of Olde English theme park; certainly that's the city's reputation and the point of much of the hype generated by the tourist industry. Victoria is very charming and eminently worthy of a visit; however, its Englishness is nowadays a fairly thin veneer laid on for the tourists.

Victoria also makes the ideal place to begin exploring the rest of Vancouver Island, which stretches more than 280 miles (450km) from Victoria to the northwest tip of Cape Scott (see chapters 5 through 7 for coverage of the rest of the island).

1 Orientation

ARRIVING

BY PLANE **Air Canada** (☎ 800/661-3936) and **Canadian Airlines** (☎ 800/363-7530) offer direct connections from Seattle, Vancouver, and other western cities. Provincial commuter airlines, including floatplanes that land in Victoria's Inner Harbour, and helicopters, service the city as well. These include **Air BC** (☎ 800/663-3721 or 604/688-5515), **Harbour Air** (☎ 604/688-1277), **Pacific Spirit Air** (☎ 800/665-2359), **Kenmore Air** (☎ 800/543-9595), and **Helijet Airways** (☎ 250/382-6222 in Victoria, or 604/273-1414 in Vancouver).

The **Victoria International Airport** (☎ 250/953-7500) is near the Sidney ferry terminal, 16 miles (25.5km) north of Victoria off the Patricia Bay Highway (Hwy. 17).

The Patricia Bay Highway (Hwy. 17) heads south to downtown Victoria on Douglas Street. The **airport bus service,** operated by AKAL Airport (☎ 250/386-2526), makes the trip into town in about half an hour. Buses leave every 30 minutes from 4:30am to midnight; the fare is C$13 (U.S.$8) one-way, C$23 (U.S.$15) round-trip. A limited number of hotel courtesy buses also serve the airport.

A cab ride from the airport into downtown costs about C$40 (U.S.$26), plus tip. **Empress Cabs** and **Blue Bird Cabs** (see "Getting Around," below) make airport runs.

Several **car-rental agencies** have desks at the airport. These include **Avis** (☎ 800/387-4747 or 250/656-6033), **Hertz** (☎ 800/263-0600 or 250/656-2312), and **Tilden** (☎ 800/879-2847 or 250/656-2541). During peak seasons, make reservations a few days in advance.

BY TRAIN & BUS   The **E&N Station,** 450 Pandora Ave., is near the Johnson Street Bridge. The **Victoria Bus Depot** is at 710 Douglas St.

BY FERRY   **BC Ferries** (☎ 888/724-5223 in B.C., or 604/444-2890; www.bcferries.bc.ca) operates an extensive year-round network of car and passenger ferries that link Vancouver Island and the Gulf Islands to one another and to the British Columbia mainland. Victoria has car-ferry connections from Vancouver via Tsawwassen, and from Seattle and Port Angeles, Washington.

Washington State Ferries (☎ 800/843-3779 in Wash., 206/464-6400 in the rest of the U.S., or 250/381-1551 in Canada; www.wsdot.wa.gov/ferries) has daily ferry service from Anacortes, in northwest Washington, to Sidney, just north of Victoria. One-way fares for a car and driver cost around U.S.$41 in high season.

The year-round passenger ferries *Victoria Clipper* and *Victoria Clipper II* (☎ 800/888-2535 or 206/448-5000) depart from Seattle's Pier 69; adult round-trip tickets range from U.S.$58 to U.S.$66. The same company offers a summer-only car ferry.

From Port Angeles, Washington, the year-round (except for a 2-week maintenance break in Jan) car ferry Black Ball *Coho* (☎ 360/457-4491) offers service to Victoria for U.S.$7 per foot passenger, U.S.$30 per vehicle. In summer, foot passengers and bicyclists can hop on the *Victoria Express* (☎ 800/633-1589 or 360/452-8088).

In summer only, the daily *Victoria Star* (☎ 800/443-4552) passenger ferry travels between Bellingham and Victoria via the San Juan Islands.

VISITOR INFORMATION

On the Inner Harbour's wharf, across from the Empress hotel, the **Tourism Victoria Visitor Info Centre,** 812 Wharf St. (☎ 250/953-2033; www.tourismvictoria.bc.ca or www.travel.victoria.bc.ca), is a great source of information. You can stop by or call the **reservations hot line** (☎ 800/663-3883 or 250/953-2022) for last-minute bookings at hotels, inns, and B&Bs. The center is open daily, September through April from 9am to 5pm, May and June from 9am to 8pm, and July and August from 9am to 9pm.

CITY LAYOUT

Victoria was born at the edge of the Inner Harbour in the 1840s, and grew outward from here. The areas of most interest to visitors, including **downtown** and **Old Town,** lie along the eastern edge of the **Inner Harbour.** (North of the Johnson Street Bridge is the **Upper Harbour,** which is almost entirely industrial.) A little further east, the **Ross Bay** and **Oak Bay** residential areas around Dallas Road and Beach Drive reach the beaches along the open waters of the Strait of Juan de Fuca.

Victoria's central landmark is the **Empress hotel,** on Government Street, right across from the Inner Harbour wharf. If you turn your back to the hotel, downtown and Old Town are on your right, while the provincial **Legislative Buildings** and the **Royal B.C. Museum** are on your immediate left. Next to them is the dock for the **Seattle–Port Angeles ferries** and, beyond that, the residential community of **James Bay.**

MAIN ARTERIES & STREETS   Three main north-south arteries intersect just about every destination you might want to find in Victoria. **Government Street** goes through Victoria's main downtown shopping and dining district. Wharf Street, which edges the harbor, merges with Government Street at the Empress hotel. **Douglas Street,** parallel to Government Street, is the main business thoroughfare as well as the road to Nanaimo and the rest of the island; it's also Trans-Canada Highway 1. The "Mile 0" marker sits at the intersection of Douglas and Dallas roads. Also running parallel to Government and Douglas streets is **Blanshard Street** (Hwy. 17), the route to Saanich Peninsula, including the Sidney-Vancouver ferry terminal, and Butchart Gardens.

Important east-west streets include the following: **Johnson Street** lies at the northern end of downtown and the Old Town, where the old E&N Rail station sits opposite Swans Hotel at the corner of Wharf Street. The Johnson Street Bridge is the demarcation line between the Upper Harbour and the Inner Harbour. **Belleville Street** is the Inner Harbour's southern edge. The Legislative Buildings and the ferry terminal are both here. Belleville Street loops around westward toward Victoria Harbour before heading south, becoming Dallas Road. **Dallas Road** follows the water's edge past residential areas and beaches before it winds northward up to Oak Bay.

FINDING AN ADDRESS   Victoria addresses are written like those in Vancouver: The suite or room number precedes the building number. For instance, 100–1250 Government St. refers to suite 100 at 1250 Government St. Victoria's streets are numbered from the city's southwest corner and increase in increments of 100 per block as you go north and east (1000 Douglas St., for example, is 2 blocks north of 800 Douglas St.). Fort Street starts its 500 block at Wharf Street.

STREET MAPS   Free street maps are available at the **Tourism Victoria Visitor Info Centre** (see "Visitor Information," above). The best map of the surrounding area is the *BC Provincial Parks* map of Vancouver Island, also available at the Info Centre.

Neighborhoods in Brief

Downtown & Old Town   This has been the city's social and commercial center since the mid-1800s. Filled with museums, heritage buildings, and restaurants, it's also the area most popular with visitors, as it reflects its fascinating Barbary Coast–style history (which includes rum smuggling, opium manufacturing, gold prospecting, whaling, and trading). The two neighborhoods are usually listed together because it's difficult to say where one leaves off and the other begins. The Old Town consists of the pre-1900 commercial sections of the city that grew up around View and Government streets. Roughly speaking, it extends from Fort Street north to Pandora, and from Wharf Street east to Douglas. Downtown is everything outside of that, from the Inner Harbour to Quadra Street in the east, and from Belleville Street in the south up to Herald Street at the northern edge of downtown.

Chinatown   Victoria's Chinatown is tiny (2 square blocks) but venerable. In fact, it's the oldest Chinese community in North America. Its many interesting historic sites include **Fan Tan Alley,** Canada's narrowest commercial street, where legal opium man-ufacturing took place in the hidden courtyard buildings.

James Bay, Ross Bay & Oak Bay   When Victoria was a busy port and trading post, the local aristocracy—merchant princes and their merchant princess daughters, for the most part—would retire to homes in these neighborhoods to escape the noise and hustle-bustle in the city center below. Today, they remain beautiful residential communities. Golf courses, marinas, and a few cozy inns edge the waters, where you can stroll the beaches or go for a dip if you don't mind a slight chill.

2 Getting Around

Strolling along the Inner Harbour's pedestrian walkways and streets can be very pleas-ant. The terrain is predominantly flat, and with few exceptions, Victoria's points of interest are accessible in less than 30 minutes on foot.

BY BUS   The **Victoria Regional Transit System (BC Transit),** 520 Gorge Rd. (☎ 250/382-6161), operates 40 bus routes through greater Victoria and the nearby towns of Sooke and Sidney. You can take the bus to Butchart Gardens and the Vancouver ferry terminal at Sidney. Regular service runs from 6am to midnight.

Schedules and routes are available at the Tourism Victoria Visitor Info Centre (see "Visitor Information," above), where you can pick up a copy of the *Victoria Rider's Guide* or *Discover Vancouver on Transit: Including Victoria.* These publications provide transit routes for many of the city's neighborhoods, landmarks, and attractions.

Popular Victoria bus routes include **no. 2** (Oak Bay), **no. 5** (downtown, James Bay, Beacon Hill Park), **no. 14** (Victoria Art Gallery, Craigdarroch Castle, University of Victoria), **no. 25** (Anne Hathaway's Thatched Cottage), **no. 61** (Sooke), **no. 70** (Sidney, Swartz Bay), and **no. 75** (Butchart Gardens).

One-way, single-zone fares are C$1.75 (U.S.$1.15) for adults, C$1.10 (U.S.70¢) for seniors and children; two zones are C$2.50 (U.S.$1.65) and C$1.75 (U.S.$1.15), respectively. Transfers are good for travel in one direction only with no stopovers.

A **DayPass,** which costs C$6 (U.S.$3.90) for adults, C$4 (U.S.$2.60) for seniors and children, is available at the Tourism Victoria Visitor Info Centre, convenience stores, and outlets displaying the "FareDealer" symbol.

Special Events & Festivals

So many flowers bloom in February that the city holds an annual **Flower Count** (☎ 250/383-7191). In April, Victoria hosts the **TerrifVic Dixieland Jazz Party** (☎ 250/953-2011), with bands from around the world playing swing, Dixieland, honky-tonk, and fusion. In May, thousands of yachts sail into the harbor during the **Swiftsure Yacht Race** (☎ 250/953-2033). June's **Jazz Fest International** (☎ 250/388-4423) brings international jazz, swing, fusion, and improv artists. The **Folkfest,** a free 8-day world-beat music festival, takes place at the end of June.

The provincial capital celebrates **Canada Day** (July 1) with music, food, and fireworks centered around the Inner Harbour. The August **First Peoples Festival** (☎ 250/384-3211) highlights the culture and heritage of the Pacific Northwest First Nations tribes. In November, the **Great Canadian Beer Festival** (☎ 250/952-0360) features samples from the province's best microbreweries. And Victoria rings in the New Year with **First Night** (☎ 250/380-1211), a family-oriented New Year's Eve celebration with free performances at many downtown venues.

BY FERRY   Crossing the Inner, Upper, and Victoria harbors on one of the blue 12-passenger **Victoria Harbour Ferries** (☎ 250/708-0201) is both cheap and fun. Identical to Vancouver's False Creek Ferries, these boats have big windows all the way around and look like they're straight out of a cartoon. In late spring, summer, and early fall, the ferries to the Empress hotel, Coast Harborside Hotel, and Ocean Pointe Resort Hotel run about every 15 minutes from 9am to 9pm. During the off-season, the ferries operate on sunny weekends from 11am to 6pm. The cost is C$3 (U.S.$1.95) for adults and C$1.50 (U.S.$1) for children. Instead of just taking the ferry for a short hop across, try the 45-minute harbor tour for C$12 (U.S.$8) adults and C$6 (U.S.$3.90) children, or the 50-minute Gorge tour for C$14 (U.S.$9) adults and C$7 (U.S.$4.55) children.

BY CAR   The downtown area is easily explored on foot. If you're planning out-of-town activities, however, rent a car in town or bring your own. Note that traffic can be heavy and parking scarce; if you have a city-bound agenda, make sure your hotel has parking. Gas is sold by the liter, averaging around C60¢ (U.S.40¢). That may seem inexpensive until you consider that a gallon of gas costs about C$2.70 (U.S.$1.75). Speeds and distances are posted in kilometers.

Car-rental agencies include **ABC,** 2507 Government St. (☎ 800/464-6464 or 250/388-3153); **Avis,** 1001 Douglas St. (☎ **800/879-2847** or 250/386-8468); **Budget,** 757 Douglas St. (☎ **800/268-8900** or 250/253-5300); **Hertz Canada,** 102-907 Fort St. (☎ **800/263-0600** or 250/388-4411); and **Tilden International,** 767 Douglas St. (☎ **800/387-4747** or 250/386-1213). Rentals are C$25 to C$45 (U.S.$16 to U.S.$29).

Metered **street parking** is hard to come by in the downtown area, and rules are strictly enforced. Unmetered parking on side streets is rare.

Major downtown hotels offer guest parking; rates vary from free to C$20 (U.S.$13) per day. There are parking lots at **View Street** between Douglas and Blanshard streets; **Johnson Street** off Blanshard Street; **Yates Street** north of Bastion Square; and **the Bay** on Fisgard at Blanshard Street.

See "Getting Around" in chapter 2 for details on Canada's driving rules. Note that the flashing green light isn't a left-turn signal but a sign to proceed with caution. Some of the best places on the island can be reached only via gravel logging roads, on which logging trucks have absolute right-of-way. If you're on a logging road and you see a truck coming from either direction, pull over and stop to let it pass.

Members of the American Automobile Association (AAA) can get assistance from the **Canadian Automobile Association (CAA)** by calling ☎ **800/222-4357.**

BY BICYCLE & SCOOTER   Biking is the easiest way to get around the downtown and beach areas. There are bike lanes throughout the city and paved paths along parks and beaches. Helmets are mandatory. Riding on sidewalks is illegal, except where bike paths are indicated.

At **Budget,** 757 Douglas St. (☎ **250/953-5300**), you can rent bikes for C$6 (U.S.$3.90) per hour or C$20 (U.S.$13) per day, and scooters for C$12 (U.S.$8) per hour or C$45 (U.S.$29) per day. Those who would like to bike but are worried about the hills (or just feeling lazy) can rent an electric-powered bike or scooter from **Electric Bike Rentals,** 65 Market Sq., 560 Johnson St. (☎ **250/381-2223**).

BY TAXI   Within the downtown area, you can expect to travel for less than C$6 (U.S.$3.90), plus tip. It's best to call for a cab; drivers don't always stop on city streets for flag-downs, especially when it's raining. Try **Empress Cabs** (☎ **250/381-2222**) or **Blue Bird Cabs** (☎ **250/382-8294**).

Fast Facts: Victoria

American Express   The office is at 1203 Douglas St. (☎ 250/385-8731); open Monday to Friday from 8:30am to 5:30pm, Saturday from 10am to 4pm.

Area Code   The telephone area code for all of Vancouver Island, including Victoria and most of British Columbia, is **250.**

Business Hours   Victoria banks are open Monday through Thursday from 10am to 3pm, Friday from 10am to 6pm. Stores are open Monday through Saturday from 10am to 6pm. Many stores are also open on Sundays in summer. Last call at the city's bars and cocktail lounges is 2am.

Currency Exchange   The best exchange rates in town can be found at banks and by using ATMs. **Royal Bank,** 1079 Douglas St., is in the heart of downtown.

Dentist   Most major hotels have a dentist on call. **Cresta Dental Centre,** 3170 Tillicum Rd., at Burnside Street (☎ 250/384-7711), in the Tillicum Mall, is open Monday from 8am to 5pm, Tuesday through Friday from 8am to 9pm, Saturday from 9am to 5pm, and Sunday from noon to 5pm.

Doctor   Hotels usually have a doctor on call. **James Bay Treatment Center,** 100-230 Menzies St. (☎ 250/388-9934), a medical facility, is open Monday through Friday from 9am to 6pm, Saturday and holidays from 10am to 4pm.

Drugstores   See "Pharmacies," below.

Emergencies   Dial ☎ 911 for fire, police, ambulance, and poison control.

Hospitals   Local hospitals include **Royal Jubilee Hospital,** 1900 Fort St. (☎ 250/370-8000, or 250/370-8212 for emergencies), and **Victoria General Hospital,** 1 Hospital Way (☎ 250/727-4212, or 250/727-4181 for emergencies).

Internet Access   Try **Victoria Cyber Cafe,** 1414-B Douglas St. (☎ 250/995-0175).

Newspapers   The morning *Times Colonist* comes out daily. The weekly entertainment paper *Monday* magazine comes out, believe it or not, on Thursday.

Pharmacies   **Shopper's Drug Mart,** 1222 Douglas St. (☎ 250/384-0544), is open Monday through Friday from 7am to 8pm, Saturday from 9am to 7pm, and Sunday from 9am to 6pm. **McGill and Orne,** 649 Broad St., at Fort (☎ 250/384-1195), is open Monday through Friday from 9am to 6pm, Saturday from 9am to 6pm, and Sunday from noon to 4pm.

Police   The Victoria City Police can be reached by calling ☎ 250/995-7654.

Post Office   The **main post office** is at 714 Yates St. (☎ 250/595-2552). There are also postal outlets in Shopper's Drug Mart (see "Pharmacies," above).

Safety   Crime rates are quite low in Victoria, but transients panhandle throughout the downtown and Old Town areas. The most common crimes are property crimes, which are usually preventable with a few commonsense precautions like not leaving items in plain sight when you park your car.

Taxes   Hotel rooms are subject to a 10% tax. The provincial sales tax (PST) is 7% (excluding food, restaurant meals, and children's clothing). For specific questions, call the **B.C. Consumer Taxation Branch** (☎ 604/660-4500). Most goods and services are subject to a 7% federal goods and services tax (GST). You can get a refund on short-stay accommodations and all shopping purchases that total at least C$100 (U.S.$65) (this refund does not apply to car rentals, parking, restaurant meals, room service, tobacco, or alcohol). Hotels and the Info Centres can give you application forms. Be sure to save your receipts. For details on the GST, call ☎ **800/561-6990.**

Time Zone   Victoria is in the Pacific time zone, as are Seattle and San Francisco. Daylight saving time applies from April through October.

Useful Telephone Numbers   Emergency numbers include: Royal Canadian Mounted Police (☎ **250/380-6261**), Emotional Crisis Centre (☎ **250/386-6323**), and Poison Control Centre (☎ **250/595-9211**). For lost property, call the Victoria City Police (see "Police," above).

Weather   Call ☎ **250/656-3978** for weather updates.

3 Accommodations

Victoria has been welcoming folks from out of town for well nigh 100 years now, so it knows how to do it with style. There's a wide choice of fine accommodations in all price ranges, most of them in Old Town or around the Inner Harbour. All are in, or within walking distance of, the downtown core. A half-hour drive east or west takes you to Sooke and Malahat—wonderful hideaways, offering more peace and solitude.

If you're looking a B&B, try **Beachside Bed & Breakfast Registry** (☎ **800/563-3311** or 604/922-7773), **Born Free Bed & Breakfast of BC** (☎ **800/488-1941** or 604/298-8815; www.vancouverbandb.bc.ca; e-mail: vancouverbandb@direct.ca),

---

Tips on Accommodations

Keep in mind the following tricks of the trade while looking for a place to lay your weary head:

- Quoted prices don't include the 10% provincial accommodations tax, nor the 7% goods and services tax (GST). Non-Canadian residents can get a GST rebate on short-stay accommodations by filling out the Tax Refund Application (see "Taxes" under "Fast Facts: Victoria," above).

- The prices listed below are the "rack rates"—the ones listed on the door and given out to the public. Always ask about discounts (AAA, corporate, whatever) or vacation packages, particularly in the October-to-April low season. In summer, the prices, like the desk clerks' faces, are set in stone. Which brings up the following point:

- Reservations are absolutely essential from May through September.

- If you arrive without a reservation, **Tourism Victoria** (☎ **800/663-3883** or 250/382-1131) can book rooms at hotels, inns, and B&Bs. It only deals with establishments that pay a fee to list with them—but fortunately, most do.

- Beware the incidentals. A parking charge of C$5 to C$10 (U.S.$3.25 to U.S.$7) per night has become commonplace in Victoria. Fair enough, perhaps, when you consider the parking situation, but the same can't be said for the C$1 (U.S.65¢) surcharge many hotels still tack on each time you make a local call. To avoid unpleasant surprises, ask beforehand what surcharges exist.

Canada-West Accommodations Bed & Breakfast Registry (☎ 800/561-3223 or 604/990-6730; www.b-b.com; e-mail: ellison@b-b.com), or **Town and Country Bed & Breakfast** (☎ **604/731-5942;** www.townandcountrybandb.bc.ca).

INNER HARBOUR
VERY EXPENSIVE

✪ **The Empress.** 721 Government St., Victoria, BC, V8W 1W5. ☎ **800/441-1414** or 250/384-8111. Fax 250/381-4334. www.cphotels.ca. 497 units. MINIBAR TV TEL. May–Oct C$295–C$490 (U.S.$192–U.S.$319) double; Nov–Apr C$200–C$395 (U.S.$130–U.S.$257) double. Year-round C$425–C$1,500 (U.S.$276–U.S.$975) suite. AE, CB, DC, DISC, ER, MC, V. Underground valet parking C$15 (U.S.$10). Bus: 5.

Francis Rattenbury's 1908 harborside creation is such a joy to look at, the folks at the Empress should probably charge just for the view. When you catch sight of the place, you'll know immediately that you absolutely must stay here. But before you throw down your credit card, there are some things you should know. First and foremost, with 90 different room configurations, not all units are created equal. Some of the deluxe rooms and all of the Entree Gold rooms are a dream (or a Merchant Ivory film): large beds, wide windows, high ceilings, and abundant natural light. The 36 Entree Gold rooms also include concierge, breakfast in the private lounge, and extras like CD players and TVs in the bathrooms. Many of the other rooms—despite a C$4-million renovation in 1996—are built to the "cozy" (read: small) standards of 1908—and the down duvets, ceiling fans, and minibars don't make them feel any bigger. If you can afford an Entree Gold or deluxe room, go for it. If not, you might be better off admiring the Empress from afar. Wheelchair-accessible rooms are available.

Dining choices include the Bengal Lounge, the Empress Dining Room, and Kipling's. The famous afternoon tea is served in the Palm Court and Lobby Lounge. Amenities include concierge, room service, dry cleaning/laundry, secretarial services, massage, shops, meeting space, car-rental desk, pool, health club, and sauna.

✪ **Ocean Pointe Resort.** 45 Songhees Rd., Victoria, BC, V9A 6T3. ☎ **800/667-4677** or 250/360-2999. Fax 250/360-1041. www.oprhotel.com. 284 units. A/C MINIBAR TV TEL. Apr 16–May 31 C$312–C$492 (U.S.$203–U.S.$320) double. June 1–Oct 11 C$412–C$628 (U.S.$268–U.S.$408) double; Oct 12–Apr 15 C$304–C$412 (U.S.$198–U.S.$268) double. Year-round C$399–C$595 (U.S.$259–U.S.$387) suite. Promotional rates available all seasons. Children under 17 stay free in parents' room. AE, DC, ER, MC, V. Underground valet parking C$9 (U.S.$6). Bus: 24 to Colville.

A luxurious modern establishment on the Inner Harbour's north shore, the OPR offers commanding views of downtown Victoria, the legislature, and the Empress. Other nice touches include the fancy toiletries, fluffy robes, hair dryers, and coffeemakers with Starbucks-quality coffee. In a city with a fetish for floral prints, the OPR's decor is refreshingly modern—polished woods and solid muted colors, and not a lot of cluttery bric-a-brac. The Inner Harbour rooms offer the best views, many with floor-to-ceiling windows. Units that face the Outer Harbour top that with floor-to-ceiling bay windows. Keep in mind that the OPR is a very large establishment with lots of rooms to fill—ask about seasonal promotional rates and you may well be pleasantly surprised to see the rack rate cut in half. Wheelchair-accessible rooms are available.

All three resort restaurants have fabulous views. Amenities include concierge, room service, dry cleaning/laundry, massage, baby-sitting, secretarial services, tennis and squash courts, pool, sundeck, and the best spa in town.

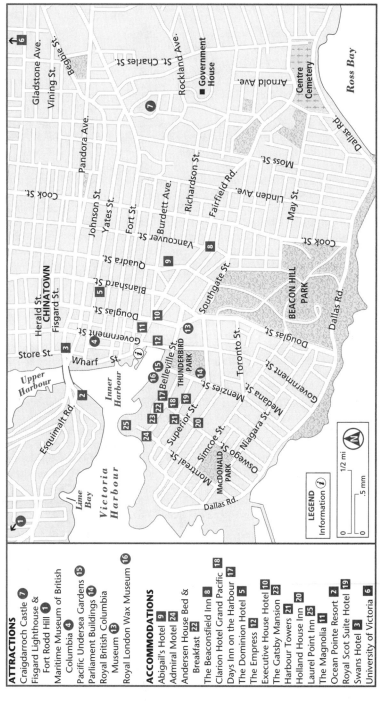

Victoria

ATTRACTIONS

Craigdarroch Castle **7**
Fisgard Lighthouse &
Fort Rodd Hill **1**
Maritime Museum of British
Columbia **4**
Pacific Undersea Gardens **15**
Parliament Buildings **14**
Royal British Columbia
Museum **13**
Royal London Wax Museum **16**

ACCOMMODATIONS

Abigail's Hotel **9**
Admiral Motel **24**
Andersen House Bed &
Breakfast **22**
The Beaconsfield Inn **8**
Clarion Hotel Grand Pacific **18**
Days Inn on the Harbour **17**
The Dominion Hotel **5**
The Empress **12**
Executive House Hotel **10**
The Gatsby Mansion **23**
Harbour Towers **21**
Holland House Inn **20**
Laurel Point Inn **25**
The Magnolia **11**
Ocean Pointe Resort **2**
Royal Scot Suite Hotel **19**
Swans Hotel **3**
University of Victoria **6**

EXPENSIVE

⭘ **Clarion Hotel Grand Pacific.** 450 Quebec St., Victoria, BC, V8V 1W5. ☎ **800/ 228-5151** or 250/386-0450. Fax 250/386-8779. www.hotelgrandpacific.com. 164 units. A/C MINIBAR TV TEL. July 1–Sept 15 C$199–C$299 (U.S.$129–U.S.$194) double, C$222– C$399 (U.S.$144–U.S.$259) suite; May 16–June 30 C$159–C$199 (U.S.$103–U.S.$129) double, C$182–C$399 (U.S.$118–U.S.$259) suite; Sept 16–May 15 C$109–C$159 (U.S.$71–U.S.$103) double, C$132–C$309 (U.S.$86–U.S.$201) suite. Off-season and weekend discounts. AE, DC, DISC, MC, V. Free parking. Bus: 30 to Superior and Oswego sts.

Overlooking the Inner Harbour, the Clarion gives off an indefinable sense of luxury. The standard rooms are elegant and comfortable. All units have balconies, with the best views overlooking the water. Business travelers will appreciate the desks and data ports. The spacious one-bedroom suites include extras such as cordless phones, robes, and makeup mirrors. Executive suites feature double Jacuzzis, fireplaces, three balconies, and wet bars. So successful has this eight-story property been since it opened in 1989, it's now expanding and cannibalizing its neighbors. The adjoining Quality Inn has been bought and will soon be demolished, enabling the Clarion to add another 160 rooms. Construction is expected to be completed in spring 2001. The dining room serves breakfast and dinner, while Trophies Lounge offers lighter fare. Amenities include concierge, room service, courtesy transportation, and an impressive fitness facility with a pool, aerobics classes, squash courts, and exercise equipment.

Harbour Towers. 345 Quebec St., Victoria, BC, V8V 1W4. ☎ **800/663-5896** or 250/ 385-2405. Fax 250/385-4453. 185 units. A/C MINIBAR TV TEL. Apr 16–May 31 C$238 (U.S.$155) double, C$278–C$500 (U.S.$181–U.S.$325) suite; June 1–Oct 15 C$249 (U.S.$162) double, C$358–C$600 (U.S.$233–U.S.$390) suite. Oct 16–Apr 15 C$178 (U.S.$116) double, C$218–C$550 (U.S.$142–U.S.$358) suite. Children under 16 stay free in parents' room. AE, CB, DC, ER, MC, V. Underground parking C$2 (U.S.$1.30). Bus: 30 to Superior and Oswego sts.

The decor in this 1975 tower retains a bit of that '70s feeling—check out the wall-to-wall shag—but given current trends, that may not be a bad thing. All rooms in this modern, 12-story hotel have floor-to-ceiling windows opening onto private balconies. (You can guarantee a harbor-view room by paying an extra C$15/U.S.$10.) All units come with hair dryers, ironing boards, coffeemakers, and voice mail. Royal Treatment rooms on the 11th floor include continental breakfast, upgraded amenities, free local calls, robes, and unobstructed views. No-smoking rooms are available. The restaurant has a menu heavily weighted towards seafood. Amenities include room service, courtesy van, baby-sitting, fitness center, pool, salon, and meeting space.

Holland House Inn. 595 Michigan St., Victoria, BC, V8V 1S7. ☎ **250/384-6644.** Fax 250/ 384-6117. www.hollandhouse.victoria.bc.ca. 14 units. TV TEL. May–Sept C$145–C$250 (U.S.$94–U.S.$163) double; Oct–Apr C$145–C$200 (U.S.$94–U.S.$130) double. Extra person C$35 (U.S.$23). Rates include full breakfast. AE, MC, V. Free parking. Bus: 5 to Superior and Government sts.

If your aim is a night spent in style, the Holland is definitely worth a visit. The elegant home provides all the amenities of a modern B&B in a classy, romantic setting. The rooms are tastefully and uniquely decorated. Some have wood-burning fireplaces, others balconies or Jacuzzis. A number of rooms have canopy beds and vaulted ceilings. TVs and phones are available for those who can't do without. Wheelchair-accessible rooms are available. After a scrumptious breakfast served in the conservatory, step outside and you're a block behind the Legislature and Royal B.C. Museum, just a 5-minute walk to the Inner Harbour. Not a bad way to start the day.

❂ **Laurel Point Inn.** 680 Montreal St., Victoria, BC, V8V 1Z8. ☎ **800/663-7667** or 250/386-8721. Fax 250/386-9547. www.laurelpoint.com. 200 units. A/C TV TEL. June 16–Oct 15 C$190 (U.S.$124) double, C$250 (U.S.$163) junior suite, C$375 (U.S.$244) bedroom suite, C$450 (U.S.$293) full suite; May 16–June 15 C$155 (U.S.$101) double, C$215 (U.S.$140) junior suite, C$350 (U.S.$228) bedroom suite, C$425 (U.S.$276) full suite; Oct 16–May 15 C$125 (U.S.$81) double, C$185 (U.S.$120) junior suite, C$255 (U.S.$166) bedroom suite, C$325 (U.S.$211) full suite. Seasonal discounts available. Children under 12 stay free in parents' room. AE, CB, ER, JCB, MC, V. Free parking. Bus: 30 to Montreal and Superior sts.

The Laurel's original owners were deeply enamored of Japan, so the hotel design and lobby reflect Japanese artistic principals—elegant simplicity and the subtle integration of light and water and stone. Wander past the little gurgling fountains up to your room, where a crisp cotton kimono has been laid out on the thick white duvet—something to slip into before steeping out onto a spacious private terrace, with a panoramic view of the harbor and hills beyond. The hotel consists of the original north wing and a new south wing; the latter is where you want to be. All the rooms here are suites, featuring blond wood with black marble accents, shoji-style sliding doors, stunning views, Asian art, and soaker tubs and floor-to-ceiling glassed-in showers. Thankfully, these studio-style junior suites cost only about 25% more than north-wing standard rooms. No-smoking and wheelchair-accessible rooms are available.

The Terrace Room serves meals in a glassed-in atrium by a Japanese garden; Cafe Laurel serves casual fare; and Cooke's Landing is the lounge. Amenities include concierge, room service, laundry, pool, sauna, exercise bikes, and meeting space.

MODERATE

❂ **Admiral Motel.** 257 Belleville St., Victoria, BC, V8V 1X3. ☎ and fax **250/388-6267.** www.admiral.bc.ca. 29 units. A/C TV TEL. May–Sept C$105–C$155 (U.S.$68–U.S.$101) double, C$115–C$165 (U.S.$75–U.S.$107) suite with kitchen or harbor-view rm.; Oct–Apr C$69–C$89 (U.S.$45–U.S.$58) double, C$79–C$99 (U.S.$51–U.S.$64) suite with kitchen or harbor-view rm. Extra person C$10 (U.S.$7). Rates include continental breakfast. Children under 12 stay free in parents' rm. Senior, weekly, and off-season discounts available. AE, ER, MC, V. Pets free. Free parking. Bus: 5 to Belleville and Government sts.

The three-story Admiral attracts young couples, families, seniors, and other travelers in search of a room with a harbor view at a price that doesn't break the bank. The rooms are pleasant and comfortably furnished, with balconies or terraces, coffeemakers, and small fridges. Full kitchen units are also available. Some rooms can sleep up to six. The owners are very friendly and can provide assistance with sightseeing. Extras include free use of bicycles, Internet access in the lobby, and a self-service laundry.

❂ **Andersen House Bed & Breakfast.** 301 Kingston St., Victoria, BC, V8V 1V5. ☎ **250/388-4565.** www.islandnet.com/~andersen. 5 units, 1 yacht. TV TEL. C$85–C$195 (U.S.$55–U.S.$127) double, C$235 (U.S.$153) yacht. Rates include gourmet breakfast. MC, V. Free parking on street. Bus: 30 to Superior and Oswego sts.

The 1891 Andersen House has the high ceilings, stained-glass windows, and ornate fireplaces typical of the Queen Anne style, but the art and decor are far more eclectic: hand-knotted Persian rugs, cubist-inspired paintings, and carved-wood African masks. Each room has a unique style: The sun-drenched Casablanca on the top floor is decorated with Persian rugs, a four-poster queen bed, and a lovely boxed window seat, while the ground-floor Garden studio has a two-person Jacuzzi and a fireplace. Each room has a private entrance and comes with CD player and CDs. If you're looking for something even more unconventional, try the *Mamita*, a 50-foot 1927 yacht moored in the Inner Harbour that provides double-bed accommodation in the teak wheelhouse.

Days Inn on the Harbour. 427 Belleville St., Victoria, BC, V8V 1X3. ☎ and fax **250/ 386-3451.** www.daysinnvictoria.com. 71 units. TV TEL. May–June C$125–C$155 (U.S.$81– U.S.$101); July–Sept C$163–C$193 (U.S.$106–U.S.$125); Oct–Apr C$95–C$125 (U.S.$62– U.S.$81). Units with kitchenette C$10 (U.S.$7) extra. Children under 12 stay free in parents' room. Off-season discounts available. AE, DC, MC, V. Free parking. Bus: 5 to Belleville and Government sts.

This newly refurbished hotel is across the street from the MV *Coho* ferry terminal on the edge of the Inner Harbour. It has a subtle nautical decor: The lobby contains a scale model of the 17th-century HMS *Royal Sovereign*, while the restaurant and lounge are named for the HMS *Swiftsure,* one of the last of the tall ships that served in the Pacific. Half of the rooms face the Inner Harbour; the other half have views of the nearby residential area. View rooms cost a little more, but it's worth it. All units are outfitted in floral prints and comfortable modern furnishings. The heated outdoor pool is open only in summer, but the hot tub is open year-round.

The Gatsby Mansion. 309 Belleville St., Victoria, BC, V8V 1X2. ☎ **250/388-9191.** Fax 250/920-5651. www.bctravel.com/gatsby.html. 20 units. TV TEL. C$135–C$275 (U.S.$88– U.S.$179) double. Rates include full breakfast. AE, DC, MC, V. Free parking. Bus: 5 to Belleville and Government sts.

Built in 1897, this white clapboard Victorian hotel, just across from the Seattle–Port Angeles ferry, has been faithfully restored to resemble a period museum, from the hand-painted ceramic-tiled fireplace to the rich wood paneling to the stained-glass windows and velvet tapestries. The atmosphere is that of a slightly dashing 1920s seaside resort. Rooms feature down duvets, fine linen, and lots of Victorian antiques. Some units boast views of the Inner Harbour, while others have private parlors.

✪ Royal Scot Suite Hotel. 425 Quebec St., Victoria, BC, V8V 1W7. ☎ **800/663-7515** or 250/388-5463. Fax 250/388-5452. www.royalscot.com. 178 units. TV TEL. June 1–Sept 30 C$129 (U.S.$84) double, C$149–C$299 (U.S.$97–U.S.$194) suite; Oct 1–May 31 C$99 (U.S.$64) double, C$135–C$155 (U.S.$88–U.S.$101) suite. Weekly, monthly, and off-season rates available. AE, MC, V. Free parking. Bus: 5 to Belleville and Government sts.

Just a block from the Inner Harbour, the Royal Scot provides excellent value for your money, attracting families in summer and retirees from the prairie provinces in winter. It used to be an apartment building, so the guest rooms are huge. All units have lots of closet space, full kitchens, sitting and dining areas, TVs, complimentary refreshments, and sofa beds. Decor runs to pastels, pinks, and florals (this is Victoria, after all). The restaurant serves three meals daily. Amenities include room service, laundry, free local calls, pool, sauna, revamped fitness area, and video arcade.

DOWNTOWN & OLD TOWN
EXPENSIVE

✪ Abigail's Hotel. 906 McClure St., Victoria, BC, V8V 3E7. ☎ **800/561-6565** or 250/388-5363. Fax 250/388-7787. www.abigailshotel.com. 22 units. TEL. C$199–C$329 (U.S.$129–U.S.$214) double. Rates include full breakfast. Winter discounts available. AE, MC, V. Free parking. Bus: 1.

In a Tudor mansion east of downtown, Abigail's began in the 1920s as a luxury apartment house before being converted into an elegant boutique hotel. Not all the rooms come with all the frills, but pampering is clearly an objective here. In the original building, some rooms are beautifully furnished with pedestal sinks and down comforters. One unit has a sundeck; others boast soaker tubs and fireplaces. The six Celebration Suites in the new Coach House are the apogee of indulgence. The gourmet breakfast may include French toast with chocolate and raspberries, or eggs with champagne and chive sauce. Amenities include concierge and dry cleaning.

The Beaconsfield Inn. 998 Humboldt St., Victoria, BC, V8V 2Z8. ☎ **250/384-4044.** Fax 250/721-2442. www.islandnet.com/beaconsfield. 9 units, 1 beach cottage. TEL. Jan–May and Oct–Dec C$125–C$225 (U.S.$81–U.S.$146) double, June and Sept C$150–C$295 (U.S.$98–U.S.$192) double, July–Aug C$200–C$350 (U.S.$130–U.S.$228) double. Cottage Nov 1–May 14 C$295 (U.S.$192), May 15–Oct 31 C$395 (U.S.$257), weekly rate C$1,600 (U.S.$1,040). Rates include full breakfast and afternoon tea/sherry. MC, V. Free parking. Bus: 1, 2.

Built in 1905 by Victoria's leading domestic architect, Samuel McClure, this elegantly restored Edwardian mansion now serves as a charming retreat much favored by newlyweds. Just 4 blocks from downtown, the inn boasts rich mahogany paneling, antique furnishings, and delicate stained-glass window trim. Upon arrival, guests find a half split of champagne, fresh flowers, and chocolate truffles awaiting them. Each lavishly decorated room is unique; some have fireplaces or skylights and French doors that open onto the garden. The spacious Emily Carr Suite features a Jacuzzi, fireplace, and, in the bathroom, a chandelier above the two-person shower. There are no TVs or phones in the rooms, and children, pets, and smoking are not permitted. The Beach Cottage, at the water's edge about 10 minutes away by car, is a wonderful alternative. It has two fireplaces, a two-person Jacuzzi, an outdoor hot tub, a kitchen, and a TV/VCR.

A gourmet breakfast is served in the sunroom or the dining room, while afternoon tea (tea, port, sherry, scones, crème fraîche, fruit, and cheese) is served in the library. Amenities include concierge and complimentary umbrellas.

✪ **The Magnolia.** 623 Courtney St., Victoria, BC, V8W 1B8. ☎ **877/624-6654** or 250/381-0999. Fax 250/381-0988. www.magnoliahotel.com. 68 units. MINIBAR TV TEL. Apr 16–May 31 C$159–C$199 double (U.S.$103–U.S.$129), C$259 (U.S.$168) suite; June 1–Oct 15 C$189–C$219 (U.S.$123–U.S.$142) double, C$319 (U.S.$207) suite; Oct 16–Apr 15 C$139–C$179 (U.S.$90–U.S.$116) double, C$239 (U.S.$155) suite. AE, ER, MC, V. Valet parking C$8 (U.S.$5). Bus: 5.

A brand-new boutique hotel in the center of Victoria, the Magnolia offers luxurious accommodations at reasonable prices. Guest rooms contain well-lit work desks, two phone lines, two-poster beds dressed in high-quality linen and down duvets, and walk-in showers and soaker tubs. Windows extend floor to ceiling, providing excellent views of the harbor from some rooms. Meals at the Capitol City Steakhouse seem to be hit or miss, not a surprising turn of events in a kitchen so new. One expects that things will settle down soon. A brewpub, Hugo's Lounge, offers good beer in a hip atmosphere. Amenities include concierge, room service, dry cleaning, and secretarial services.

MODERATE & INEXPENSIVE

The Dominion Hotel. 759 Yates St., Victoria, BC, V8W 1L6. ☎ **800/663-6101** or 250/384-4136. Fax 250/382-6416. www.dominion-hotel.com. 101 units. TV TEL. May–Sept C$119 (U.S.$77) double, C$179 (U.S.$116) suite; Oct–Apr C$45–C$50 (U.S.$29–U.S.$33) double, C$79–C$99 (U.S.$51–U.S.$64) suite. Children under 16 stay free in parents' rm. AE, CB, DC, MC, V. Parking C$5–C$10 (U.S.$3.25–U.S.$7) Bus: 10, 11, 14.

Victoria's oldest hotel, the Dominion opened in 1876 and recently underwent a C$7-million restoration. The public areas of this lovely family-oriented heritage property are decorated with rich woods, marble floors, and velvet upholstery on antique chairs. Guest rooms have more modern appointments, but maintain the flavor of times past with ceiling fans and brass lamps. There are dozens of types of rooms, all fully renovated in the past few years. The Lettuce Patch family-style restaurant serves three meals daily. Hunters, a mesquite-grill steak house, is open for lunch and dinner daily. Amenities include room service, laundry, health club, and steam rooms.

Executive House Hotel. 777 Douglas St., Victoria, BC, V8W 2B5. ☎ **800/663-7001** or 250/388-5111. Fax 250/385-1323. http://executivehouse.com. 179 units. TV TEL. C$99–C$195 (U.S.$64–U.S.$127) double, C$195–C$275 (U.S.$127–U.S.$179) suite, C$295–C$695 (U.S.$192–U.S.$452) penthouse rm. and suites. Extra person C$15 (U.S.$10). Children 16 and under stay free in parents' rm. Seasonal discounts of 10%–50%, depending on availability. AE, CB, DC, ER, MC, V. Parking C$2 (U.S.$1.30). Bus: 2.

You can't miss the 13-story, concrete Executive House, rising above the Empress on the east side of the old town; the 1960s-style architecture is unmistakably new world. Step inside, however, and the ambiance evokes London in the 1880s. Some suites come with a queen bed in the bedroom and a fold-out sofa, perfect for families. Other suites have double beds in both living room and bedroom, so business associates traveling together can economize. Furnishings are a bit fussy, but hey, it's 1880 after all. Up on the 17th floor, each of the penthouse-level suites has a Jacuzzi, fireplace, garden terrace, and full kitchen. Dining options include Bartholomew's pub, the more elegant Barkley's for steak and seafood, and Italian/Californian cuisine at the informal Caffe d'Amore. The full spa offers a steam room, tanning bed, massage, and herbal wraps.

✪ **Swans Hotel.** 506 Pandora Ave., Victoria, BC, V8W 1N6. ☎ **800/668-7926** or 250/361-3310. Fax 250/361-3491. www.islandnet.com/~swans. 29 suites. TV TEL. C$135–C$189 (U.S.$88–U.S.$123) suite. Off-season discounts available. AE, MC, V. Parking C$8 (U.S.$5). Bus: 23, 24.

Near the Johnson Street Bridge, this heritage property is one of Old Town's best-loved buildings. The suites are spacious; many are split-level, featuring open lofts and huge exposed beams. All have full kitchens, separate dining areas, living rooms, and queen beds. The two-bedroom suites have the feel of little town houses—they're great for families, accommodating up to six comfortably. Business travelers will appreciate the dual data ports. Furnishings throughout are new and contemporary; exceptional arrangements of fresh flowers add to the pleasant atmosphere. The fine-dining Fowl Fish Cafe is open daily for dinner. Other facilities include Swans Pub, Buckerfield's Brewery, and Millennium Jazz Club. Amenities include room service, laundry, access to a nearby health club, baby-sitting referrals, secretarial services, and video rentals.

✪ **Victoria International Youth Hostel.** 516 Yates St., Victoria, BC, V8W 1K8. ☎ **250/385-4511.** Fax 250/385-3232. www.hostels.bc.ca. 104 beds. C$16 (U.S.$10) International Youth Hostel members, C$20 (U.S.$13) nonmembers. MC, V. Street parking available. Bus: 70 from Swartz Bay ferry terminal.

The location is perfect—right in the heart of Old Town. In addition, this hostel has all the usual accoutrements, including two kitchens, a dining room, a TV lounge, a game room, a common room, a library, indoor bicycle lockup, 24-hour security, and laundry facilities. The dorms are on the large side (16 beds to a room) and strictly segregated by sex. There are also a couple of family rooms, as well as one wheelchair-accessible unit. An extensive ride board helps those in need of transportation, while the collection of outfitter and tour information rivals that of the local tourism office.

4 Dining

Though early Victoria settlers were intent on re-creating a little patch of the old country on their wild western island, the one thing they were never tempted to import was British cooking. Thankfully. Instead, each immigrant group imported its own cuisine;

now Victoria is a cornucopia of culinary styles. With more than 700 restaurants, there's something for every taste and wallet size. But with all this variety, the one thing visitors are unlikely to find is a lot of late-night dining. Victorians time their meal to the setting of the sun. Try for a seat at 7pm and the restaurant will be packed. Try at 9pm, and it'll be empty. Try at 10pm, and it'll be closed, especially on week-days. Reservations are strongly recommended for prime sunset seating during the peak summer season.

There's no provincial tax on restaurant meals in British Columbia, just the 7% federal goods and services tax (GST).

THE INNER HARBOUR

Barb's Place. 310 St. Lawrence St. ☎ **250/384-6515.** Reservations not accepted. Menu items C$2.25–C$9.25 (U.S.$1.45–U.S.$6). No credit cards. Daily 7am–sunset. FISH-AND-CHIPS.

The best chippie in town, Barb offers halibut and hand-hewn chips served in folded-newspaper pouches from a floating restaurant at Fisherman's Wharf. There are picnic tables to sit on, plus boats and seagulls and lots of other eye-candy to amuse the kids.

✪ **Blue Crab Bar and Grill.** In the Coast Hotel, 146 Kingston St. ☎ **250/480-1999.** Reservations recommended. Main courses C$16–C$30 (U.S.$10–U.S.$20). AE, DC, ER, MC, V. Daily 6:30am–10pm (dinner from 5pm). SEAFOOD.

Victoria's best seafood spot, the Blue Crab combines fresh ingredients, inventive recipes, and beautiful presentations with a killer view. The first order of business is to peruse the chalkboard of daily seafood specials. What's there is entirely depen-dent on what came in on the boats or floatplanes that day—salmon in season is a strong possibility, as are spotted prawns or crab. Occasionally, Salt Spring Island lambs also wander onto the board. The chefs are fond of unusual combinations, like sea bass with taro root, grapefruit, and blood orange. The service is deft, smart, and very obliging.

Pablo's Dining Lounge. 225 Quebec St. ☎ **250/388-4255.** Reservations recommended. Main courses C$14–C$29 (U.S.$9–U.S.$19). AE, MC, V. Daily 5pm to around 11pm. Bus: 30. CONTINENTAL.

Pablo's paella valenciana—saffron rice with a medley of meats, seafood, and vegetables—has been a local favorite for nearly 20 years. This intimate restaurant is in an Edwardian house near Laurel Point. Special dinners for two include rack of Salt Spring Island lamb and chateaubriand forestière (with mushrooms). Wednesdays through Saturdays, a guitarist plays a muted version of the Gypsy Kings while you sip Spanish coffee and nibble flambéed crepes and ice cream.

Pescatore's Fish House and Piano Bar. 614 Humboldt St. (across from the Empress). ☎ **250/920-4846.** Reservations recommended. Main courses C$11–C$20 (U.S.$7–U.S.$13). AE, DC, ER, MC, V. Daily 11am to around 11pm. SEAFOOD.

For a town surrounded by an ocean literally teeming with fish, Victoria is surprising-ly lacking in good seafood restaurants. Fortunately, there's Pescatore's. The food in this Italian-influenced restaurant floats somewhere between very good and excellent. The grand ceilings and the striking paintings by local artist Luis Merino set the ambiance, and the well-stocked oyster bar will grab your attention. Get past that, and you're in danger of getting caught by the lunch specials, including items such as prawns, crab cakes, and creamy seafood bisques. Come supper time, the menu expands to include scallops, trout, and salmon. There's also an excellent rack of lamb.

Tea for Two

So it's expensive and touristy. Go anyway. Far from a simple beverage, high tea is both a meal and a ritual. The pot is warmed, the boiling water is poured in over the tea leaves, and the sweet and subtle flavor will almost certainly put you off the lukewarm-water-and-tea-bag thing for life. While you sip, trays of cucumber, smoked salmon, or watercress sandwiches come by, along with scones, butter, and the freshest berry preserves. Pick up a cup and—pinkies out!—adopt a posture of unshakable confidence. *Note:* In summer, high tea becomes highly popular. Consider booking at least a week ahead.

The afternoon tea at the ✪ **Empress hotel,** 721 Government St. (☎ 250/384-8111), is undoubtedly the best in town, served in the Palm Court or in the Lobby Lounge, both of which are beautifully ornate and luxurious. For C$30 (U.S.$20) per person, the Empress will pamper and spoil you shamelessly.

An old villa on the Gorge waterway just outside downtown, **Point Ellice House,** 2616 Pleasant St. (☎ 250/380-6506), makes a fine destination for high tea, especially on a sunny day, when it's served out on the lawn for C$15 (U.S.$10). The best way to get here is to take a 5-minute ferry ride. In addition to enjoying the afternoon tea, you can tour the house, grounds, and gardens.

With impeccably maintained gardens as a backdrop, afternoon tea at the **Butchart Gardens Dining Room Restaurant,** 800 Benvenuto Ave. (☎ 250/652-4422), is a memorable experience. You can sit back and savor this fine tradition for C$25 (U.S.$16). (See "The Saanich Peninsula," in chapter 5.)

DOWNTOWN & OLD TOWN
EXPENSIVE

Camille's. 45 Bastion Sq. ☎ 250/381-3433. Reservations recommended. Main courses C$14–C$22 (U.S.$9–U.S.$14). AE, MC, V. Daily 5:30–10pm. WEST COAST.

The most romantic of Victoria's restaurants, Camille's is seductively tucked away in a little two-room enclave beneath the old Law Chambers. The decor contrasts white linen with century-old exposed brick, antique books, stained-glass lamps, and old wine bottles. The menu combines European dishes with a fetish for local ingredients. Seasonal choices include smoked-salmon pinwheels with avocado and horseradish cream. Fillet of salmon and delicate roast rack of lamb are two perennial specialties. The reasonable wine list comes with liner notes that are both amusing and informative. On Sunday evenings, wine tastings introduce you to the best selections from the cellar.

Il Terrazzo Ristorante. 555 Johnson St., off Waddington Alley. ☎ 250/361-0028. Reservations recommended. Main courses C$15–C$31 (U.S.$10–U.S.$20). AE, MC, V. Mon–Fri 11:30am–3:30pm, Sat 11:30am–3pm; daily 5–10:30pm. Bus: 5. NORTHERN ITALIAN.

A quick poll among Victorians as to their favorite Italian restaurant yields the unanimous answer: Il Terrazzo! This bustling, upbeat place's exposed-brick walls are decorated with colorful artwork and illuminated with wrought-iron candelabras. The courtyard is romantically furnished with flowers, marble tables, and wrought-iron chairs. The food, oh yes, is wonderful; pastas, risottos, seafood, and roast duck are just some of the comforting menu items. The Italian cuisine has a West Coast twist, meaning an emphasis on fresh produce and local seafood.

La Ville d'Is. 26 Bastion Sq. ☎ **250/388-9414.** Reservations recommended. Main courses C$17–C$29 (U.S.$11–U.S.$19). Mon–Sat 5–10pm. AE, DC, MC, V. FRENCH.

Possibly the most French restaurant in Victoria, La Ville d'Is specializes in cuisine from Brittany. The result is a perfect marriage of superb French cooking paired with some of British Columbia's best seafood and other fresh ingredients. The most popular item is the lobster soufflé. Monkfish, rabbit, and local salmon with Chablis sauce are just a few of the delicacies served with a charming French accent. The wine list includes Canadian and American wines as well as French favorites.

MODERATE

Bowman's Rib House. 825 Burdett Ave., at the Cherry Bank Hotel. ☎ **250/385-5380.** Reservations recommended. 3-course rib special C$13 (U.S.$8); main courses C$12–C$20 (U.S.$8–U.S.$13). AE, DC, MC, V. Daily 11:30am–2pm and 5–9pm. Bus: 5. RIBS.

Located in an 1897 landmark hotel, this has been Victoria's top rib house for more than 40 years. You won't find another place in town that serves up healthy portions at such a reasonable price. For kids, it's an opportunity to eat with your hands and get gooey. The staff serves up tangy racks of ribs accompanied by salad, potatoes, vegetables, and garlic bread to a family-oriented clientele.

Cafe Brio. 944 Fort St. ☎ **250/383-0009.** Reservations recommended. Main courses C$13–C$23 (U.S.$8–U.S.$15). AE, MC, V. Mon–Fri 11:30am–2pm; daily 5:30pm–closing. WEST COAST/ITALIAN.

Brio is a joint project between longtime city chef Sean Brennan and Tuscan restaurateur Sylvia Marcolini. The food, not surprisingly, has Italian influences, but the menu also reflects the seasons, the availability of local produce, and Brio's location on the edge of the Pacific. Dishes may include pan-fried halibut cheeks with beet risotto, or sea bass atop cider-braised cabbage. Located on Antique Row, the patio is great on summer days, while inside, the attractive room contains lots of Italian-themed bric-a-brac.

Da Tandoor. 1010 Fort St. ☎ **250/384-6333.** Reservations recommended. Main courses C$7–C$16 (U.S.$4.55–U.S.$10); combination dinners C$13–C$20 (U.S.$8–U.S.$13). MC, V. Daily 5–10:30pm. NORTHERN INDIAN.

Tandoori-baked chicken, seafood, and lamb are the house specialties at this elegant northern Indian restaurant. The extensive, well-prepared menu also includes masalas, vindaloos, goshts, and vegetarian dishes, as well as classic appetizers such as vegetable or meat samosas, pakoras, and papadums. If you get inspired to try some at home, the restaurant sells a wide variety of spices and chutneys.

✪ Herald Street Caffe. 546 Herald St. ☎ **250/381-1441.** Reservations required. Main courses C$11–C$20 (U.S.$7–U.S.$13). AE, ER, MC, V. Wed–Sat 11:30am–3pm; Sun brunch 10am–3pm; Sun–Wed 5:30–10:30pm, Thurs–Sat 5:30pm–midnight. Bus: 5. PASTA/WEST COAST.

At this casual bistro, young hip locals flock to the excellent Sunday brunch, where the poached eggs on fresh cheese scones (all breads are baked on the premises) is a wonderful twist on eggs Benedict. The lemon ricotta pancakes are fluffy and delicious, especially with the homemade marionberry butter. Located in a 19th-century heritage building, the dining room is filled with potted palms and floral arrangements. Works by local artists decorate the exposed-brick walls. However, it's the chef's own creations—fresh pastas, venison, or steamed mussels with prawns, ginger, lemongrass, and roasted cashews—that make the place so wonderful. The award-winning wine list highlights the province's best vintages.

Millos. 716 Burdett Ave. ☎ **250/382-4422** or 250/382-5544. Reservations recommended. Main courses C$9–C$25 (U.S.$6–U.S.$16). AE, DC, ER, MC, V. Mon–Sat 11:30am–4:30pm; daily 4:30–11pm. Bus: 5. GREEK.

Millos isn't hard to find—look for the blue-and-white windmill behind the Empress hotel or listen for the hand clapping and plate breaking as diners get into the swing of things. Flaming *saganaki* (a sharp cheese sautéed in olive oil and flambéed with Greek brandy), grilled halibut souvlaki, and succulent grilled salmon are just a few of the menu items at this lively five-level restaurant. Kids get their own menu. Folk dancers and belly dancers entertain on Friday and Saturday nights.

✪ **Pagliacci's.** 1011 Broad St. ☎ **250/386-1662.** Reservations not accepted. Main courses C$11–C$19 (U.S.$7–U.S.$12). AE, MC, V. Daily 11:30am–midnight (light menu 3–6pm). SOUTHERN ITALIAN.

Launched in 1979 by expatriate New Yorker Howie Siegal, Pagliacci's radiates an un-Victorian kind of big-city buzz. Diners ogle their neighbors' food and eavesdrop on conversations while Howie works the room, dispensing a word or two to long-lost friends, many of whom he's only just met. The cuisine comes from the south of Italy— veal Parmesan, tortellini, and 19 or 20 other à la carte pastas, many quite inventive and all made by hand. The service isn't blindingly fast, but when you're having this much fun, who cares? Grab some wine, munch on hot focaccia, and enjoy the atmosphere. Sunday through Wednesday nights, there's live jazz, swing, or blues.

Taj Mahal. 679 Herald St. (near Douglas St.). ☎ **250/383-4662.** Reservations recommended. Main courses C$12–C$18 (U.S.$8–U.S.$12). AE, CB, DC, MC, V. Daily 5–10pm. Bus: 4, 10, or 14 to Douglas St. INDIAN.

Domes and minarets trimmed in blue-and-gold tiles grace the exotic exterior of this restaurant. Inside, waitresses in saris greet you in this elaborate re-creation of a Punjab prince's palace. Entrees include fish in coconut sauce, Pacific prawn biriyani, tandooris, and an extensive selection of delectable vegetarian dishes. Beverages include fresh mango drinks, chai, and *kawa* (coffee with cinnamon, cardamom, and cloves).

INEXPENSIVE

Café Mexico. 1425 Store St. ☎ **250/386-1425.** Main courses C$6–C$14 (U.S.$3.90–U.S.$9). AE, DC, MC, V. Daily 11am–11pm. MEXICAN.

Bullfighting and Dos Equis posters decorate the walls of this Market Square cantina, where you can get all the usuals served with verve and big pitchers of sangria. The Vista del Mar (grilled flour tortilla topped with prawns and scallops in a wine-cream sauce and covered with melted cheese, avocado, and sour cream) is a favorite. If you're just looking for a light bite, nibble on nachos as Latin music plays in the background.

✪ **Don Mee Restaurant.** 538 Fisgard St. ☎ **250/383-1032.** Reservations not needed. Main courses C$4.95–C$10 (U.S.$3.20–U.S.$7); 4-course dinner for 2 C$17 (U.S.$11). AE, DC, MC, V. Mon–Fri 11am–2:30pm, Sat–Sun and holidays 10:30am–2:30pm; daily 5–11pm. Bus: 5. CANTONESE/SZECHUAN.

Since the 1920s, elegant Don Mee's has been serving up Victoria's best dim sum, chop suey, and chow mein, along with delectable Szechuan seafood dishes and Cantonese sizzling platters. You can't miss this second-story restaurant: A huge, neon Chinese lantern looms above the small doorway, and a 4-foot-tall gold-leaf laughing Buddha greets you at the entrance. If it's lunchtime, you'll find many of Victoria's Chinese-Canadian businessmen munching away. The dinner specials for two, three, or four people are particularly good deals if you want to sample lots of everything.

Pub Grub

Those in the mood for solid nourishment and a fun atmosphere should try one of the following brewpubs. The oldest in town, offering impressive food and views, is **Spinnaker's Brew Pub,** 308 Catherine St. (☎ **250/386-2739**), on the far side of the Inner Harbour. The **Harbour Canoe Club,** 450 Swift St. (☎ **250/ 361-1940**), just north of the Johnson Street Bridge, is a sunlit cathedral of a room, with good food and live music. Enjoy the best grub in the windproof glass patio at ✪ **Swans Pub,** 506 Pandora Ave. (☎ **250/361-3310**). One of the newest pubs is **Hugo's,** 625 Courtney St. (☎ **250/920-4844**), which has gotten good reviews for its food, though most are more impressed with the crowd and the bullet-riddled brick walls.

Re-bar. 50 Bastion Sq. ☎ **250/361-9223.** Main courses C$7–C$14 (U.S.$4.55–U.S.$9). AE, MC, V. Mon–Thurs and Sat 7:30am–8pm, Fri 7:30am–9pm, Sun 10am–3pm. Bus: 5. WEST COAST/VEGETARIAN.

Even if you're not hungry, it's worth dropping in for a juice blend—say, grapefruit, banana, melon, and pear combined with bee pollen or blue-green algae for added oomph. If you're hungry, then rejoice: Re-bar is the city's premier dispenser of vegetarian comfort food. Disturbingly wholesome as that may sound, Re-bar is not only tasty, but also fun, and a great spot to take the kids for breakfast. The room—in an 1890s heritage building—is funky; service is friendly and casual. Dishes include a vegetable-and-almond patty served with red onions and sprouts on a multigrain kaiser roll; quesadillas; omelets; and crisp salads with toasted pine nuts, feta, and sun-dried–tomato vinaigrette. The juices come in more than 80 different blends.

Sam's Deli. 805 Government St. ☎ **250/328-8424.** Main courses C$3.95–C$10 (U.S.$2.55–U.S.$7). MC, V. Daily 9am–7pm. DELI.

If you don't like lines, avoid the lunch hour, for Sam's is *the* lunchtime Victoria soup-and-sandwich spot. Sandwiches come in all tastes and sizes (mostly large), but the shrimp-and-avocado is the one to get. Sam's homemade soups are excellent, as is his chili. And it's but a hop, skip, and sandwich-laden lurch from the harbor—so unless it's raining, there's no excuse not to order to go.

✪ **Wah Lai Yuen.** 560 Fisgard St. ☎ **250/381-5355.** Main courses C$6–C$14 (U.S.$3.90–U.S.$9). No credit cards. Tues–Sat 10am–8:30pm, Sun 10am–7pm. CANTONESE.

Here, wonton is not your basic noodle dumpling soup—it's a brimming bowl of won-tons, sliced barbecued pork, black mushrooms, prawns, and bok choy in a clear, rich chicken stock. It's one of the many delights at this brightly lit, Formica-filled China-town diner, where you may find yourself sharing a large round table with a Chinese family. Favorite selections include hot-pot dishes such as chicken steamed with black mushrooms and ginger, and large baked buns filled with barbecued pork.

5 Exploring the City

Victoria's top draws are its waterfront—the beautiful viewscape created by the Empress hotel and the Parliament Buildings on the edge of the Inner Harbour—and its historic Old Town.

Note: See the "Victoria" map on p. 81 to locate most of the sights in this section.

THE TOP ATTRACTIONS

Aviation Museum. 1910 Norseman Rd., Sidney. ☎ **250/655-3300.** Admission C$4 (U.S.$2.60) adults, C$3 (U.S.$1.95) seniors, free for children under 12. Summer daily 10am–4pm; winter daily 11am–3pm. Closed Christmas. Bus: Airport.

This is a working museum inside a hangar at Victoria International Airport. Volunteers keep busy restoring vintage aircraft to add to the collection, which already includes World War II fighters and bombers, a 1929 Eastman Flying Boat, a Gibson Twin (built in Victoria in 1911), and much more.

◯ **Craigdarroch Castle.** 1050 Joan Crescent. ☎ **250/592-5323.** Admission C$8 (U.S.$5) adults, C$5 (U.S.$3.25) students, C$2 (U.S.$1.30) children 6–12, free for children under 6. Daily June 15–Aug 31 9am–7pm, Sept 1–June 14 10am–4:30pm. Bus: 11. Take Fort St. out of downtown, just past Pandora, and turn right on Joan Crescent.

What do you do when you're the richest man in British Columbia, when you've clawed, scraped, and bullied your way up from indentured servant to coal baron and merchant prince? You build a castle, of course, and show the other buggers what you're worth. Located in the highlands above Oak Bay, Robert Dunsmuir's home is a stunner. The 39-room, Highland-style castle is topped with stone turrets and chimneys, and filled with detailed woodwork, Persian carpets, stained glass, and artwork. The nonprofit society that runs Craigdarroch does an excellent job showcasing the castle. Visitors get a self-guided–tour booklet, and volunteer docents are happy to answer questions.

Fisgard Lighthouse National Historic Site & Fort Rodd Hill. 603 Fort Rodd Hill Rd. ☎ **250/478-5849.** http://parkscanada.pch.gc.ca. Admission C$3 (U.S.$1.95) adults, C$2.25 (U.S.$1.45) seniors, C$1.50 (U.S.$1) children 6–16, free for children under 6. Family discounts. Mar–Oct daily 10am–5:30pm, Nov–Feb daily 9am–4:30pm.

Perched on an outcrop of volcanic rock, the **Fisgard Lighthouse** has guided ships toward Victoria's sheltered harbor since 1873. The light no longer has a keeper (the beacon has long been automated), but the site itself has been restored to its 1873 appearance. Two floors' worth of exhibits in the light keeper's house narrate stories of the lighthouse and the terrible shipwrecks that gave this coastline its ominous moniker, "the graveyard of the Pacific." Adjoining the lighthouse, **Fort Rodd Hill** is a preserved 1890s coastal artillery fort that still sports searchlights, underground magazines, and its original guns. Check out audiovisual exhibits with the voices and faces of the men who served here, displays of artifacts, room re-creations, and videos of historic film footage.

Maritime Museum of British Columbia. 28 Bastion Sq. ☎ **250/385-4222.** http://mmbc.bc.ca. Admission C$5 (U.S.$3.25) adults, C$4 (U.S.$2.60) seniors, C$3 (U.S.$1.95) students, C$2 (U.S.$1.30) children 6–12, free for children under 6. Family discounts. Daily 9am–4:30pm. Closed Christmas. Bus: 5.

Housed in the former provincial courthouse, this museum is dedicated to recalling the province's rich maritime heritage. The displays do a good job illustrating maritime history, from the early explorers to the fur-trading and whaling era to the days of grand ocean liners and military conflict. There's also an impressive collection of ship models and paraphernalia—uniforms, weapons, gear—along with photographs and journals. Films are shown in the Vice Admiralty Theatre.

Pacific Undersea Gardens. 490 Belleville St. ☎ **250/382-5717.** Admission C$7 (U.S.$4.55) adults, C$6 (U.S.$3.90) seniors, C$5 (U.S.$3.25) children 5–11, free for children under 5. Family discounts. Daily May–Sept 9am–5pm, Oct–Apr 10am–5pm. Bus: 5, 27, 28, 30.

A gently sloping stairway leads down to this unique marine observatory's glass-enclosed viewing area, where visitors can observe the Inner Harbour's marine life up close. Some 5,000 creatures feed, play, and hunt in these protected waters. Sharks, wolf eels, poisonous stonefish, flowery sea anemones, starfish, and salmon are just a few of the organisms that make their homes in these waters. One of the star attractions is a remarkably photogenic octopus (reputedly the largest in captivity). Injured seals and orphaned seal pups are cared for in holding pens alongside the observatory.

Parliament Buildings (Provincial Legislature). 501 Belleville St. ☎ **250/387-3046.** www.parl-bldgs.gov.bc.ca. Free admission. Daily 9am–5pm. Free half-hour tours offered every 20 min. in summer, hourly in winter.

Designed by 25-year-old Francis Rattenbury, and built between 1893 and 1898 at a cost of nearly C$1 million, the Parliament Buildings (also called the Legislature) are an architectural gem. The tour comes across at times like an 8th-grade civics lesson, but it's worth it just to see the fine mosaics, marble, woodwork, and stained glass.

✪ Royal British Columbia Museum. 675 Belleville St. ☎ **800/661-5411** or 250/387-3701. http://rbcm1.gov.bc.ca. Admission C$7 (U.S.$4.55) adults; C$4 (U.S.$2.60) seniors, students, and children; C$18 (U.S.$12) families. Higher rates sometimes in effect for traveling exhibits. Daily 9am–5pm. Closed Christmas and New Year's Day. Bus: 5, 28, or 30.

One of the best regional museums in the world, the Royal B.C. features natural-history dioramas indistinguishable from the real thing, full-size re-creations of frontier towns and native longhouses, and a collection of native art and artifacts that will leave you gasping. The Natural History Gallery shows the coastal flora, fauna, and geography, from the Ice Age to the present; it includes dioramas of a seacoast, an underground ecology of giant bugs, and—particularly appealing to kids—a live tidal pool with sea stars and anemones. The Modern History Gallery presents the recent past, including re-creations of downtown and Chinatown. The First Peoples Gallery is an incredible showpiece of native art; it also houses a full-size re-creation of a longhouse. The IMAX theater shows a variety of movies. On the way out, stop by Thunderbird Park, where a cedar longhouse houses a workshop in which native carvers work on new totem poles.

Royal London Wax Museum. 470 Belleville St. ☎ **250/388-4461.** Admission C$8 (U.S.$5) adults, C$7 (U.S.$4.55) seniors, C$3 (U.S.$1.95) children. Daily 9am–7:30pm. Bus: 5, 27, 28, or 30.

On the Lookout: Victoria's Best Views

The best view of the Empress and the Parliament Buildings (the Legislature) comes from walking along the pedestrian path in front of the **Ocean Pointe Resort** south of the Johnson Street Bridge. The light is good early in the day. When the fishing fleets come in, head over to **Fisherman's Wharf** at St. Lawrence and Erie streets, where you can watch the activity as the fishermen unload their catches. Later on, take in the sunset from the **wharf along the eastern edge of the Inner Harbour** or from the **Parrot House Restaurant,** 740 Burdett Ave. (☎ **250/382-9258**).

Just south of downtown, you can see across the Strait of Juan de Fuca and the San Juan Islands to the Olympic Mountains from the **Ogden Point** breakwater, from the top of the hill in **Beacon Hill Park,** or from the path above the beach along **Dallas Road.** Further afield, **Fort Rodd Hill** and **Fisgard Lighthouse** offer equally good views of the mountains, as well as a view of the warships in Esquimalt Harbour.

See the same royal family you already get too much of on TV. See other, older royals of even less significance. See their family pets. All courtesy of Madame Tussaud's 200-year-old wax technology. The chamber of horrors rates well below a *Buffy the Vampire Slayer* episode on the scariness scale. Still not thrilled? The management seems to suspect as much—they've started taking liberties with their wax figures' figures. Look especially for the Princess Diana mannequin with the Pamela Anderson implants.

ARCHITECTURAL HIGHLIGHTS & HISTORIC HOMES

First a fortified trading post, then a gold-rush town, a naval base, and sleepy provincial capital, Victoria bears architectural witness to all these eras. The best of its buildings date to the years before World War I, when gold poured in from the Fraser and Klondike rivers, fueling a building boom responsible for most of the downtown.

Perhaps the most intriguing downtown edifice isn't a building at all, but a work of art. The walls of **Fort Victoria,** which once covered much of downtown, have been demarcated in the sidewalk with bricks bearing the names of original settlers and fur traders. Look in the sidewalk on Government Street at the corner of Fort Street.

Most of the retail establishments in Old Town are housed in 19th-century shipping warehouses that have been carefully restored. Visitors can take a **self-guided tour** of the buildings, most of which were erected between the 1870s and 1890s and whose history is recounted on outdoor plaques. Most of these buildings are between Douglas and Johnson streets from Wharf to Government streets. The most impressive one once contained shipping offices and warehouses; it's now the home of a 45-shop complex known as **Market Square,** 560 Johnson St./255 Market Sq. (☎ 250/386-2441).

✪ **Craigdarroch Castle,** 1050 Joan Crescent (☎ 250/592-5323), was built in the 1880s (see "The Top Attractions," above). It's filled with the opulent Victorian splendor one would expect to read about in a romance novel.

Dunsmuir's son, James, built his own palatial home, **Hatley Castle,** off Highway 14 in Colwood. The grounds of the castle, now home to **Royal Roads University,** feature extensive floral gardens and are open to the public free of charge (☎ 250/391-2511).

To get a taste of how upper-middle-class Victorians lived, visit the **Carr House,** 207 Government St. (☎ 250/383-5843), where the painter Emily Carr was born; and the **Helmcken House,** 675 Belleville St. (☎ 250/386-0021), the residence of a pioneer doctor who settled here in the 1850s. The doctor's house still contains his medicine chest and original British furnishings. **Craigflower Farmhouse,** 110 Island Hwy. (☎ 250/383-4621), in the View Royal district, was built in 1856 by a Scottish settler who brought many of his furnishings from the old country. All three houses are open in summer, Thursday through Monday from 11am to 5pm. Admission is C$3.25 (U.S.$2.10) for adults, C$2.25 (U.S.$1.45) for seniors and students, and C$1.25 (U.S.80¢) for children. A three-site discount pass is available.

The **Olde England Inn, Anne Hathaway's Thatched Cottage, and English Village,** 429 Lamson St. (☎ 250/388-4353), are a piece of Shakespearean England just a few minutes' drive (or a 40-min. stroll) from the Inner Harbour. Complete with an appropriately costumed staff, the village features replicas of famous English buildings, including the birthplace of William Shakespeare's wife, Anne Hathaway. Free tours are available. Admission is C$8 (U.S.$5) for adults, C$7 (U.S.$4.55) for seniors, and C$4.50 (U.S.$2.95) for children. Afternoon tea is served.

NEIGHBORHOODS OF NOTE

From the time the Hudson's Bay Company settled here in the mid-1800s, the **Old Town** was the center of the city's shipping, trading, and opium-manufacturing businesses. Market Square and the surrounding warehouses once brimmed with exports like furs and timber. Now part of the downtown core, this is still a terrific place to find British imports, souvenirs, and even outdoor equipment for modern-day adventurers.

Just a block north on Fisgard Street is the oldest **Chinatown** in North America, founded in 1863. Lined with restaurants, bakeries, and specialty shops, Chinatown is a wonderful spot to stop for dim sum or a full Hong Kong–style seafood dinner.

The **James Bay** area on the southern shores of the Inner Harbour is a quiet, middle-class residential community. As you walk through its tree-lined streets, you'll find many pristine older residences that have maintained their original Victorian flavor.

Beautiful communities such as **Ross Bay** and **Oak Bay** have a more modern West Coast appearance. You'll see luscious landscaped gardens, houses perched on hills overlooking the beaches, and private marinas filled with sailing craft.

Fernwood, northeast of downtown and Old Town, attracts Victoria's youth. Originally a 300-acre estate with a Tudor-style house (Fernwood Manor) at its center, it now has a run-down and rebuilt character that accounts for its charm.

PARKS & GARDENS

In addition to Butchart Gardens (see chapter 5, section 2), several city parks attract strollers and picnickers. The 154-acre **Beacon Hill Park** stretches from Southgate Street to Dallas Road between Douglas and Cook streets. Stands of indigenous Garry oaks (found only on Vancouver, Hornby, and Salt Spring islands) and manicured lawns are interspersed with floral gardens and ponds. Hike up Beacon Hill to get a clear view of the Strait of Georgia, Haro Strait, and Washington's Olympic Mountains. The children's farm (see below), aviary, tennis courts, lawn-bowling green, putting green, wading pool, playground, and picnic area make this a wonderful place for families.

Government House, the official residence of the lieutenant governor, is at 1401 Rockland Ave., in the Fairfield district. The house itself is closed to the public, but the formal gardens are well worth a wander.

Victoria has an indoor garden that first opened as a huge saltwater pool in 1925 (Olympic swimmer and *Tarzan* star Johnny Weismuller competed here) and was converted into a big-band dance hall during World War II. The **Crystal Garden,** 731 Douglas St. (☎ **250/953-8800**), is filled with rare and exotic tropical flora and fauna.

Just outside downtown, **Mount Douglas Park** offers great views of the area, several hiking trails, and—down at the waterline—a picnic and play area with a trail leading to a good walking beach.

ESPECIALLY FOR KIDS

Nature's the thing for kids in Victoria. At the **Beacon Hill Children's Farm,** Beacon Hill Park (☎ **250/381-2532**), kids can ride ponies, pet goats and rabbits, and cool off in the wading pool. It's open daily mid-March through September from 10am to 5pm. For a new take on this old concept, visit the **Victoria Butterfly Gardens** (see chapter 5, section 2). Closer to town and creepier than the Butterfly Gardens is the **Victoria Bug Zoo,** 1107 Wharf St. (☎ **250/384-BUGS**), home to praying mantises and giant African cockroaches, along with knowledgeable guides who can bring the bugs out and let the kids handle and touch them. Admission is C$6 (U.S.$3.90) for adults, C$4 (U.S.$2.60) for children 3 to 16. Kids also love the creatures at the **Pacific Undersea Gardens** and the displays at the **Royal British Columbia Museum** (see "The Top Attractions," above, for details on both).

ORGANIZED TOURS

BUS TOURS   **Gray Line of Victoria,** 700 Douglas St. (☎ **250/388-5248**), conducts daily tours of Victoria and Butchart Gardens. The 1¹/₂-hour "Grand City Tour" costs C$14 (U.S.$9) for adults and C$7 (U.S.$4.55) for children.

The same company operates a **trolley service** every 40 minutes from 9:30am to 5:30pm on a circuit of 35 hotels, attractions, shops, and restaurants. A day pass, which allows you to stop and reboard at the destinations of your choice throughout the day, costs C$7 (U.S.$4.55) for adults and C$4 (U.S.$2.60) for children.

SPECIALTY TOURS   For C$12 (U.S.$8), **Victoria Harbour Ferries,** 922 Old Esquimalt Rd. (☎ **250/708-0201**), offers a terrific 45-minute tour of the Inner and Outer harbors. The 12-person, fully enclosed ferries are adorably cartoonish. They generally operate from mid-March to mid-October depending on the weather.

To get a bird's-eye view of Victoria, take a 30-minute tour with **Harbour Air Seaplanes,** 1234 Wharf St. (☎ **250/361-6786**). Rates are C$72 (U.S.$47) per person. The bicycle-rickshaws operated by **Kabuki Kabs,** 15-950 Government St. (☎ **250/385-4243**), usually "park" in front of the Empress. Tours are C$60 (U.S.$39) per hour for a two-person cab and C$90 (U.S.$59) per hour for a four-person cab.

Tallyho Horse Drawn Tours, 2044 Milton St. (☎ **250/383-5067**), has conducted horse-drawn carriage tours since 1903. Excursions start at the corner of Belleville and Menzies streets; fares are C$14 (U.S.$9) for adults, C$12 (U.S.$8) for seniors, C$9 (U.S.$6) for students, and C$6 (U.S.$3.90) for children. Tours operate daily every 30 minutes from 9am to 10pm in summer (from 10am to 5:30pm in spring and fall).

6 Outdoor Pursuits

Pick up a copy of *Coast: The Outdoor Recreation Magazine* (☎ **604/267-1143**), available at many outfitters. It lists snow conditions, bike trails, climbing areas, competitions, races, and the like, as well as where to get services such as bike tune-ups.

Specialized rental outfitters are listed with each activity below. **Sports Rent,** 3084 Blanshard St. (☎ **250/385-7368**), is a general-equipment and water-sports rental outlet to keep in mind if you forget to pack something.

BEACHES   Because you're on the sunny side of western Canada, you can take advantage of the beaches in and around the area. Most popular is Oak Bay's **Willows Beach,** at Beach and Dalhousie roads along the Esplanade. The park, playground, and snack bar make it a great place to spend the day. **Gyro Beach Park,** Beach Road on Cadboro Bay, is another good spot for winding down. At the **Ross Bay Beaches,** below Beacon Hill Park, you can stroll or bike along the promenade at the water's edge.

Two inland lakes give you the option of swimming in freshwater. **Elk and Beaver Lake Regional Park,** on Patricia Bay Road, is 7 miles (11km) north of downtown Victoria; **Thetis Lake,** about 6 miles (9.5km) west, is where locals shed their clothes.

BIKING   This is one of the best ways to get around Victoria. The 8-mile (13km) **Scenic Marine Drive** bike path begins at Dallas Road and Douglas Street, at the base of Beacon Hill Park. The path follows the walkway along the beaches, winds up through the residential district on Beach Drive, and eventually heads south toward downtown on Oak Bay Avenue. The **Inner Harbour pedestrian path** has a lane for cyclists who want to take a leisurely ride around the city seawall. The new **Galloping Goose Trail** runs from Victoria west through Colwood and Sooke all the way up to

Leechtown. If you don't want to bike the whole thing, there are numerous places to park along the way, as well as several places where the trail intersects with public transit. Call **BC Transit** (☎ 250/382-6161) to find out which bus routes take bikes.

The **Greater Victoria Cycling Coalition,** which publishes a monthly newsletter entitled *Cycletherapy,* has a group ride and special-events hot line (☎ 250/480-5155). Bikes, helmets, locks, and child trailers are available by the hour or day at **Budget Car Rentals,** 727 Courtenay St., behind the Empress (☎ 250/953-5333). Rentals start at C$5 (U.S.$3.25) per hour, C$20 (U.S.$13) per day. The **Pacific Rim Bicycle Tour Company,** 950 Wharf St., inside the Marine Adventure Centre (☎ 250/881-0585), offers guided bike tours starting at C$29 (U.S.$19). **Electric Bike Rentals,** 65 Market Sq. (☎ 250/381-2233), rents electric-powered mountain bikes and scooters.

BOATING   There are a number of independent charter companies docked at the **Oak Bay Marina,** 1327 Beach Dr. (☎ 250/598-3369), including the **Horizon Yacht Centre** (☎ 250/595-2628), which offers sailboat charters, lessons, and navigational tips. The **Marine Adventure Centre** (☎ 250/995-2211), on the floatplane docks in the Inner Harbour, can arrange boat charters and more. Skippered charters in the area generally run about C$600 (U.S.$390) per day. Boat rentals average around C$125 (U.S.$81) for a couple of hours. If you're taking the wheel yourself, don't forget to check the **marine forecast** (☎ 250/656-7515) before casting off.

CANOEING & KAYAKING   ✪ **Ocean River Sports,** 1437 Store St. (☎ 250/381-4233), can equip you with everything from single kayak, double kayak, and canoe rentals to lifejackets and tents. Rental costs for a single kayak range from C$14 (U.S.$9) per hour to C$42 (U.S.$27) per day; weekly rates are also available. If you're a little tentative about renting a boat on your own, Ocean River also runs guided tours. The best ones take you to the sheltered waters near Sidney, in sight of the Gulf Islands. Tours start at C$55 (U.S.$36). Sundown tours are especially popular.

DIVING   The coastline of **Pacific Rim National Park** is known as "the graveyard of the Pacific." Submerged in the waters are dozens of 19th- and 20th-century shipwrecks and the marine life that has taken up residence in them. Underwater interpretive trails help identify what you'll see. Contact the **Ocean Centre,** 800 Cloverdale St. (☎ 250/475-2202), where head-to-toe equipment rental is C$60 (U.S.$39) for 2 days, and charters start at C$40 (U.S.$26) for 2 dives.

FISHING   Saltwater fishing's the thing out here, and unless you know a lot about fishing, it's probably best to take a guide. **Adam's Fishing Charters** (☎ 250/370-2326) and the **Marine Adventure Centre** (☎ 250/995-2211), both in Victoria, are good places to start (see also "Boating," above).

To fish, you need a nonresident saltwater or freshwater license. Licenses for freshwater fishing cost C$16 (U.S.$10) for 1 day. Saltwater fishing licenses cost C$6 (U.S.$3.90) for 1 day, plus a surcharge of C$6 (U.S.$3.90) for salmon fishing. **Robinson's Sporting Goods Ltd.,** 1307 Broad St. (☎ 250/385-3429), is a reliable source for information, recommendations, lures, licenses, and gear.

GOLF   The **Cedar Hill Municipal Golf Course,** 1400 Derby Rd. (☎ 250/595-3103), is an 18-hole public course 2 miles (3.3km) from downtown; greens fees are C$30 (U.S.$20). The **Cordova Bay Golf Course,** 5333 Cordova Bay Rd. (☎ 250/658-4075), is northeast of downtown. Designed by Bill Robinson, the 18-hole course features 66 sand traps and some tight fairways. Greens fees are C$45 (U.S.$29) Monday through Thursday and C$48 (U.S.$31) Friday through Sunday. One of the top courses in Canada, the 18-hole **Olympic View Golf Club,**

643 Latoria Rd. (☎ **250/474-3673;** www.sunnygolf.com/ov/ov.html), has 12 lakes and a pair of waterfalls. Facilities include shuttle service from downtown hotels, cart rentals, pro shop, dining room, and lounge. Greens fees are C$49 (U.S.$32) Monday through Thursday, C$55 (U.S.$36) Friday through Sunday and holidays. Call **A-1 Last Minute Golf** (☎ **800/684-6344** or 604/878-1833) for discounts and short-notice tee times at area courses.

HIKING   See chapter 5, section 5, for information on ✪ **Goldstream Provincial Park,** 30 minutes west of downtown and a tranquil site for a short hike.

Groups who want to learn more about the surrounding flora and fauna can book a naturalist-guided tour of the island's rain forests and seashore with **Coastal Connections Interpretive Nature Hikes** (☎ **250/480-9560**) or **Nature Calls** (☎ **877/ 361-HIKE**). Tours cost from C$60 to C$110 (U.S.$39 to U.S.$72).

WATER SPORTS   The **Crystal Pool & Fitness Centre,** 2275 Quadra St. (☎ **250/ 380-7946,** or 250/380-4636 for schedule), is Victoria's main aquatic facility. The lap pool, kids' pool, diving pool, sauna, whirlpool, and steam, weight, and aerobics rooms are open daily from 6am to midnight. Admission is C$4.20 (U.S.$2.75) for adults, C$3.15 (U.S.$2.05) for seniors and students, and C$2.10 (U.S.$1.35) for kids.

Beaver Lake, in Elk and Beaver Lake Regional Park, has lifeguards on duty as well as picnicking facilities. **All Fun Recreation Park,** 650 Hordon Rd. (☎ **250/ 474-4546** or 250/474-3184), operates a water-slide complex that's ideal for cooling off on hot days. It's open daily from 11am to 7pm in season. Full-day passes are C$16 (U.S.$10) for sliders over age 6 (nonsliders get in for C$6/U.S.$3.90); after 3pm, admission drops to C$12 (U.S.$8) for sliders and C$5 (U.S.$3.25) for nonsliders.

Windsurfers skim along the Inner Harbour and Elk Lake when the breezes are right. Though there are no specific facilities, French Beach, off Sooke Road on the way to Sooke Harbour, is a popular windsurfing spot. **Ocean Wind Water Sports Rentals,** 5411 Hamsterly Rd. (☎ **250/658-8171**), rents nearly every form of gear.

WHALE WATCHING   The waters surrounding the southern tip of Vancouver Island teem with orcas (killer whales), as well as harbor seals, sea lions, bald eagles, and porpoises. **Victoria Marine Adventures,** 950 Wharf (☎ **250/995-2211**), is just one of many outfits offering whale-watching tours in both Zodiacs and covered boats. Fares are C$75 (U.S.$49) for adults and C$49 (U.S.$32) for kids. From March through October, **Pride of Victoria Cruises,** Oak Bay Beach Hotel, 1175 Beach Dr. (☎ **250/592-3474**), offers daily whale-watching charters on a fully equipped 45-foot catamaran. Fares are C$79 (U.S.$51) for adults and C$39 (U.S.$25) for children.

7 Shopping

The **Government Street** promenade, from the Inner Harbour 5 blocks north to Yates Street, is a jungle of cheap souvenir shops, with a few hidden gems. Further north, the **Old Town** district and **Market Square,** 560 Johnson St. (☎ **250/386-2441**), feature a fascinating blend of heritage buildings and up-to-date shops. **Chinatown** is tiny but charmingly preserved, with a number of fine shops and quirky back alleys.

ANTIQUES   Victoria has long been known for its British antiques. Many of the best stores are on the east edge of downtown in **Antique Row,** Fort Street between Blanshard and Cook streets.

ART GALLERIES   The **Fran Willis Gallery,** 1619 Store St. (☎ **250/381-3422**), is one of Victoria's most beautiful display spaces, with contemporary oils and bronzes by local artists. Tucked away on Canada's narrowest commercial street, **Small Pressings Gallery and Paper,** 103–3 Fan Tan Alley (☎ **250/380-2479**), specializes in paper arts. At the gallery-cum-workshop ✪ **Starfish Glass Works,** 630 Yates St. (☎ **250/388-7827**), you can watch the ground-floor kiln from an open catwalk above. **Magpie Gift Studio,** 556 Fisgard St. (☎ **250/383-1880**), carries intricate Chinese decorative items, along with larger Asian antiques and elegant jewelry.

BOOKS   ✪ Munro's Book Store, 1108 Government St. (☎ **250/382-2464**), has a mile-high ceiling, wall murals, and more than 35,000 titles.

DEPARTMENT STORES & SHOPPING MALLS   The Bay (Hudson's Bay Company), 1701 Douglas St. (☎ **250/385-1311**), sells sports equipment, Hudson's Bay woolen point blankets, and fashions by Tommy Hilfiger and DKNY. The **Victoria Eaton Centre,** between Government and Douglas streets (☎ **250/382-7141**), is a modern shopping mall disguised as a block of heritage buildings.

FASHION   Voted best women's boutique year after year in *Monday* magazine, **Sunday's Snowflakes,** 1000 Douglas St. (☎ **250/381-4461**), features exclusively Canadian designers. Men can try **British Importers,** 1125 Government St. (☎ **250/386-1496**), which carries designers such as Hugo Boss. If there's a do-gooder lurking inside your inner consumer, go to **Carnaby Street,** 538 Yates St. (☎ **250/382-3747**), packed with handcrafted caftans, djebellas, and ethnic textiles, all from third-world co-ops and cottage industries. For quality retro from the '30s through the '50s, try **Still Life,** 551 Johnson St. (☎ **250/386-5655**).

FOOD & WINE   It's worth stepping into **Murchie's,** 1110 Government St. (☎ **250/383-3112**), just to suck up the coffee smell or sniff the specialty teas. The 97-year-old **Roger's Chocolates,** 913 Government St. (☎ **800/663-2220** or 250/384-7021), sells what it daringly calls "quite possibly the best chocolates in the world." The **Wine Barrel,** 644 Broughton St. (☎ **250/388-0606**), is a must-see for any wine lover.

JEWELRY   Ian MacDonald of **MacDonald Jewelry,** 618 View St. (☎ **250/382-4113**), designs all of his own jewelry. At the **Jade Tree,** 606 Humboldt St. (☎ **250/388-4326**), you'll find British Columbia jade crafted into unique items.

NATIVE ART   **Sasquatch Trading,** 1233 Government St. (☎ **250/386-9033**), carries basketry, beads, jewelry, and much fine carving. All of the coastal tribes are represented at the **Alcheringa Gallery,** 665 Fort St. (☎ **250/383-8224**). Presentation is museum quality, with prices to match. In business for 50 years, **Hill's Indian Crafts,** 1008 Government St. (☎ **250/385-3911**), features exquisite traditional native art, including wooden masks and carvings, silver jewelry, drums, and talking sticks.

SPORTING GOODS   **Ocean River Sports,** 1437 Store St. (☎ **250/381-4233**), is the place to go to arrange a sea-kayak tour or pick up outdoor equipment.

8 Victoria After Dark

Monday magazine (☎ **250/382-6188;** www.monday.com) covers everything going on in town. The **Community Arts Council of Greater Victoria,** 511–620 View St. (☎ **250/381-ARTS** or 250/381-2787), runs an events hot line. You can buy tickets and get schedules from the **Tourism Victoria Travel Visitor Centre,** 812 Wharf St. (☎ **800/663-3883** or 250/382-2127), open daily from 9am to 5pm (until 9pm in summer).

THE PERFORMING ARTS

The **Royal Theatre,** 805 Broughton St. (☎ **250/361-0820;** box office 250/386-6121), hosts concerts (including the Victoria Symphony), dance recitals, and

What was for many years known as the Dixieland Jazz Festival is now the **TerrifVic Jazz Party** (☎ 250/953-2011). Its expanded format now features swing, honky-tonk, fusion, some blues, and yes, Dixieland, for 5 days in late April. More progressive is the **International Jazz Fest** (☎ 250/388-4423), offering a range of styles from Cuban, salsa, and world beat to fusion and acid jazz, all from late June to early July. The **Victoria Jazz Society** (☎ 250/388-4423) runs a hot line listing jazz events throughout the year.

touring plays. The box office is at the **McPherson Playhouse,** 3 Centennial Sq., at Pandora Avenue and Government Street (☎ 250/386-6121), also home to the Pacific Opera and the Victoria Operatic Society.

THEATER   The nationally acclaimed **Belfry Theatre Society,** 1291 Gladstone St. (☎ 250/385-6815), stages productions in an intimate playhouse that was once a church. Based at the Fringe Theatre, 301-1205 Broad St. (☎ 888/FRINGE-2 or 250/383-2663), the **Intrepid Theatre Company** offers an eclectic mix of new and alternative theater. The **Fringe Festival** (☎ 888/FRINGE-2 or 250/383-2663), from late August to mid-September, features amazingly inventive plays. **Theatre Inconnu** (☎ 250/380-1284 or 250/360-0234) is known for its annual production of Victoria's **Shakespeare Festival,** which takes place in July and August.

OPERA   The **Pacific Opera Victoria,** 1316B Government St. (☎ 250/385-0222; box office 250/386-6121), presents productions during the months of October, February, and April. Tickets are available at the McPherson Playhouse and Opera box offices. The **Victoria Operatic Society,** 798 Fairview Rd. (☎ 250/381-1021), stages old-time musicals and other popular fare year-round at the McPherson Playhouse.

CLASSICAL MUSIC   The **Victoria Symphony Orchestra,** 846 Broughton St. (☎ 250/385-9771), kicks off its season in August with Symphony Splash, a free concert performed on a barge in the Inner Harbour. The **Victoria International Festival** is held in July and August. Concerts, ballet, and other events are presented at various locations. Call Tourism Victoria for details.

DANCE   Dance recitals and full-scale performances by local and international dance troupes are scheduled throughout the year. Call the **Community Arts Council of Greater Victoria** (☎ 250/381-ARTS or 250/381-2787) for information.

THE CLUB SCENE

Legends, 919 Douglas St. (☎ 250/383-7137), is a pop-music palace that books some hopping international bands. **Steamers,** 570 Yates St. (☎ 250/381-4340), is the city's premier blues bar. ✪ **Millennium Jazz Club,** 506 Pandora St., in the basement of Swans Pub (☎ 250/360-9098), offers swing on Thursday, disco on Friday, soul and R&B on Saturday, and salsa from time to time. **Hermann's Jazz Club,** 753 View St. (☎ 250/388-9166), offers straight-ahead jazz in a low-lit room with nice acoustics.

Most dance clubs are open Monday through Saturday until 2am and Sunday until midnight. The **Jet Lounge,** 751 View St. (☎ 250/920-7797), is a plush hangout for Victoria's small but oh-so-beautiful crowd of upscale Gen-Xers. DJs spin house, rave, and acid jazz. ✪ **Sweetwaters Niteclub,** 27-570 Store St. (☎ 250/383-7844), is an elegant singles spot for those in their late 20s to early 40s.

BARS, PUBS & LOUNGES

The ✪ **Harbour Canoe Club,** 450 Swift St. (☎ **250/361-1940**), is a pleasant spot to hoist a pint after a long day's sightseeing. Overlooking Victoria Harbour on the west side of the Songhees Point Development, **Spinnaker's Brew Pub,** 308 Catherine St. (☎ **250/386-BREW** or 250/386-2739), has one of the best views and some of the best beer in town. See "Pub Grub" under "Dining," above, for ✪ **Swans Pub,** 506 Pandora Ave. (☎ **250/361-3310**). A truly unique experience, the ✪ **Bengal Lounge,** in the Empress hotel at 721 Government St. (☎ **250/384-8111**), is one of the last outposts of the old empire, except the martinis are ice cold and jazz plays in the background. **Rick's Lounge,** in the Ocean Pointe Resort at 45 Songhees Rd. (☎ **250/360-2999**), is without a doubt the best place to watch as the last light of day fades.

GAY & LESBIAN BARS

The scene isn't large enough in Victoria for homosexuals to segregate by sex, so they all come to **Rumors,** 1325 Government St. (☎ **250/385-0566**), where they pack the dance floor on weekends. **Friends of Dorothy's Cafe,** 615 Johnson St. (☎ **250/381-2277**), has *The Wizard of Oz* playing continuously, which adds to the kitschy glam without—surprisingly enough—driving you over the rainbow. **BJ's Lounge,** 642 Johnson St. (☎ **250/388-0505**), has a full menu and lounge decor.

5 Southern Vancouver Island & the Gulf Islands

Stretching more than 280 miles (450km) from Victoria to the northwest tip of Cape Scott (that's nearly three times the size of New York's Long Island), Vancouver Island is one of the most scenic and fascinating destinations in Canada, a mountainous bulwark of deep-green forests, rocky fjords, and wave-battered headlands. For an area so easily accessible by car, the quantity and range of wildlife here is surprising: Bald eagles float above the shorelines, seals and sea lions slumber on rocky islets, and porpoises and orca whales cavort in narrow passes between islands. The hummingbird population is one of the densest in the world, and bears, cougars, moose, wolves, and elk haunt the woods.

The British Columbia capital, Victoria, is the ideal place to begin exploring the entire island; see chapter 4 for complete coverage of the city.

Duncan, the "City of Totem Poles" in the Cowichan Valley north of Victoria, reveals another facet of Vancouver Island culture. This lush green valley is the ancestral home of the Cowichan tribe, famed for crafting hand-knit sweaters; it also contains some of the island's best wineries.

Nestled just off the island's east coast lie the Gulf Islands. The fact that they are only reached by a confusing network of ferries just enhances their sense of remoteness and mystery. These mountainous, rock-faced islands exist in their own time and space: Part arty, counterculture enclave, part trophy-home exurb, and part old-fashioned farm and orchard territory, the Gulf Islands are full of contradictions and charm. The largest, Salt Spring Island, is a haven for artists who are attracted to its mild climate, slow pace, and pastoral landscapes.

Running down the spine of Vancouver Island is a lofty chain of mountains that functionally divide the island into west and east. In the west, which receives the full brunt of Pacific storms, vast rain forests grow along inaccessible, steep-sided fjords. Unsurprisingly, these forests have been the focus of conflict between the timber industry, which sees the virgin forest as a source of valuable building materials, and environmentalists, who consider it a unique habitat for rare and unusual plants and animals. The west coast is hard to get to: Paved roads provide access in only a few places, and boat charters, ferries, and floatplanes are the preferred means of transport.

The east side of Vancouver Island, and in particular the area from Nanaimo southward, is home to the vast majority of the island's population of 750,000. The climate here is drier and warmer than on the storm-tossed west coast—a benefit of the central mountains' rain shadow—and agriculture is a major industry. Tourism is also key to the local economy: The southeast portion of Vancouver Island has the warmest median temperatures in all of Canada, and tourists and retirees flood the area in search of warm temperatures and rain-free summer days.

While the Gulf Islands and the southern portions of Vancouver were long ago colonized by European settlers, the native First Nation people are very much a part of cultural and political life in the area. Historically, the Pacific coast of British Columbia was one of the greatest centers of art and culture in Native America, and this past is beautifully preserved in many museums and in several well-preserved villages. Modern-day First Nation artists are very active, and nearly every town and village will have native-art galleries and workshops filled with exquisitely stylized carvings, paintings, and sculpture.

This chapter covers the southern portion of Vancouver Island, along with the Gulf Islands. For central Vancouver Island, from Nanaimo to Courtenay/Comox and including the West Coast Trail and Pacific Rim National Park, see chapter 6. In chapter 7, we discuss the portion of Vancouver Island from the town of Campbell River northward, including Strathcona Provincial Park.

1 Essentials

GETTING THERE

BY PLANE   **Victoria** is the island's major air hub, with jet, commuter airplane, and floatplane service from Vancouver and Seattle. See chapter 4 for details.

Both standard commuter aircraft and floatplanes provide regularly scheduled service to a number of other island communities. Many towns have regular air service from **Vancouver International Airport.** All of the southern Gulf Islands, as well as many towns, can be reached by scheduled harbor-to-harbor floatplane service, either from Vancouver International's seaplane terminal or from downtown Vancouver's Coal Harbour terminal. In fact, it's easy to arrange a chartered floatplane for almost any destination along coastal Vancouver Island. Since floatplanes don't require airport facilities, even the most remote fishing camp can be as accessible as a major city.

Commercial airline service is provided by **Air BC** (☎ **800/776-3000** in the U.S., 800/663-3721 in B.C., or 250/360-9074), a division of Air Canada, and **Canadian Regional Airlines** (☎ **800/665-1177**), a division of Canadian Air.

Commuter seaplanes that serve Vancouver Island include **Harbour Seaplanes** (☎ 800/665-9308), **Pacific Spirit Air** (☎ 800/665-2359), **Air Rainbow** (☎ 604/681-0311), and **Baxter Aviation** (☎ 800/661-5599 or 250/754-1066).

BY FERRY   **BC Ferries** (☎ **888/724-5223** in B.C., or 604/444-2890; www.bcferries.bc.ca) operates an extensive year-round network of ferries that link Vancouver Island and the Gulf Islands to one another and to the British Columbia mainland. Major routes include the crossing from Tsawwassen to Swartz Bay and to Nanaimo, and from Horseshoe Bay (west of Vancouver) to Nanaimo. In summer, reservations should be made in advance. Sample fares are included in the regional sections that follow.

If you're traveling with a car on BC Ferries, you'll find that ticket prices add up quickly. You may want to leave the car on the mainland and travel by bus, taxi, or air.

Washington State Ferries (☎ **800/843-3779** in Wash., 206/464-6400 in the rest of the U.S., or 250/381-1551 in Canada; www.wsdot.wa.gov/ferries) has daily ferry service from Anacortes, in Washington, to Sidney, on Vancouver Island. One-way fares for a car and driver range from U.S.$25 in low season to U.S.$41 in high season.

Vancouver Island

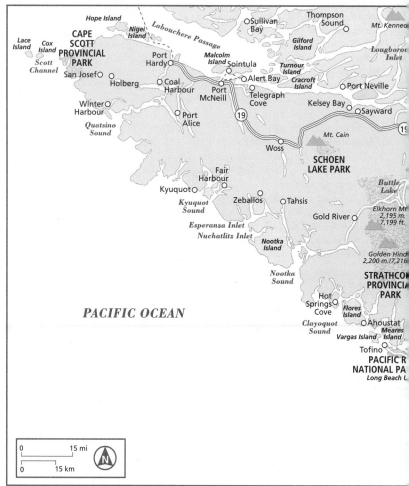

The year-round passenger ferries *Victoria Clipper* and *Victoria Clipper II* (☎ 800/888-2535 or 206/448-5000) depart from Seattle's Pier 69; adult round-trip tickets range from U.S.$58 to U.S.$66. The same company offers a summer-only car ferry.

From Port Angeles, Washington, the year-round (except for a 2-week maintenance break in Jan) car ferry Black Ball *Coho* (☎ 360/457-4491) offers service to Victoria for U.S.$7 per foot passenger, U.S.$30 per vehicle. In summer, foot passengers and bicyclists can hop on the *Victoria Express* (☎ 800/633-1589 or 360/452-8088).

In summer only, the daily *Victoria Star* (☎ 800/443-4552) passenger ferry travels between Bellingham and Victoria via the San Juan Islands.

BY BUS One of the easiest ways to get to and from Vancouver and Vancouver Island destinations is by bus. Conveniently, the bus will start its journey from a city center (like Vancouver), take you directly to the ferry dock and onto the ferry, and then

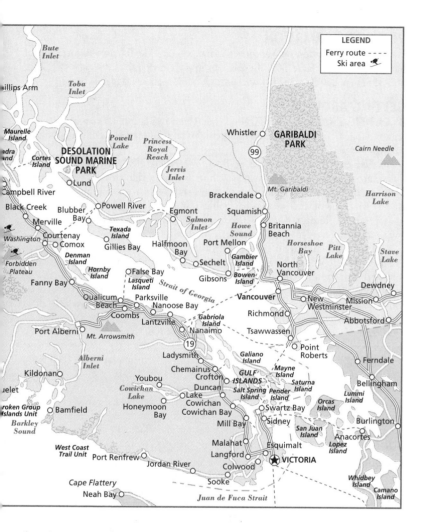

deposit you in another city center (Victoria or Nanaimo). A lot of the hassle of ferry travel is minimized, and the costs are usually lower than other alternatives. (If you're traveling to Vancouver on the VIA rail system, you'll find bus connections simple, as the bus and train share the same terminal.)

Pacific Coach Lines (☎ 800/661-1725 or 604/662-8074; www.pacificcoach. com) offers bus service between downtown Vancouver via BC Ferries to downtown Victoria. One-way fare is C$27 (U.S.$18) for adults, C$13 (U.S.$8) for children; in summer, there are more than a dozen departures daily.

Maverick Coach Tours provides service between Nanaimo and Vancouver; one-way transport is C$19 (U.S.$12). Reserve through Greyhound's network by calling ☎ 800/661-8747 or 604/482-8747. Information on these and other Canadian motor-coach services is available at Greyhound Canada's Web site, **www. greyhound.ca**.

VISITOR INFORMATION

For general information on Vancouver Island, contact the **Tourism Association of Vancouver Island,** Suite 302, 45 Bastion Sq., Victoria, BC, V8W 1J1 (☎ **250/ 382-3551;** fax 250/382-3523; www.islands.bc.ca; e-mail: tavi@islands.bc.ca).

GETTING AROUND

BY PUBLIC TRANSPORTATION   While Vancouver Island has an admirable system of public transport, getting to remote sights and destinations is difficult without your own vehicle.

BC Ferries (☎ **888/724-5223** in B.C., or 604/444-2890; www.bcferries.bc.ca) link Vancouver Island ports to many offshore islands, including the Southern Gulf Islands of Kuper and Thetis, as well as Gabriola and Denman and Hornby islands (see chapter 6). None of these islands has public transport, so once there you'll need to hoof it, hitch it, hire a taxi, or arrange for bicycle rentals. Most innkeepers will pick you up from the ferry if you've reserved in advance.

Another charming way to get around Vancouver Island is on the **E&N Railway** (☎ **800/561-8630** or 250/383-4324), a division of VIA Rail that makes a daily round-trip run from Victoria to Courtenay in period passenger cars. The *Malahat* train passes through some of the most beautiful landscapes on the east coast of Vancouver Island, taking about 4¹/₂ hours. Your ticket allows you to get on and off as many times as you'd like: You can stop at Chemainus, Nanaimo, Parksville, or Qualicum Beach and catch the return train back, or take the next day's train north. What's more, ticket prices are very reasonable, especially with 7-day advance purchase. A round-trip between Victoria and Courtenay can cost as little as C$46 (U.S.$30), plus tax. *Note:* The *Malahat* has no baggage car, and checked-baggage service is not available. The train does have a limited beverage-and-snack service.

Laidlaw Coach Lines (☎ **800/318-0818** or 250/385-4411; www.victoriatours. com) operates the island's intercity bus service, which runs along the main highway from Victoria to Port Hardy, and from Nanaimo to Tofino. The one-way fare from Victoria to Nanaimo is C$18 (U.S.$12), from Nanaimo to Tofino C$30 (U.S.$20).

BY CAR   The southern half of Vancouver Island is well served by paved highways. The trunk road between Victoria and Nanaimo is **Highway 1,** the Trans-Canada. This busy route alternates between four-lane expressway and congested two-lane highway, and requires patience and vigilance, especially during the busy summer months. North of Nanaimo, the major road north is **Highway 19,** which is largely a well-maintained two-lane highway, with expressway sections near Parksville and Qualicum Beach, and near Campbell River. The only other major paved road system on the island connects Parksville with Tofino, on the rugged west coast. Access to gasoline and car services is no problem, even in more remote north Vancouver Island.

Rental cars are readily available. Agencies include **Budget Car & Truck Rental** (☎ **800/268-8900** or 250/953-5300), **National Tilden Interrent** (☎ **800/ 387-4747** or 250/386-1213), and **Thrifty Car Rental** (☎ **800/367-2277** or 250/ 383-3659).

2 The Saanich Peninsula

Swartz Bay: 17 miles (27km) N of Victoria

A long finger of land that extends north from Victoria toward Sidney, the Saanich Peninsula is now largely given over to suburbs of Victoria. Flanked on one side by Saanich Inlet and on the other by the Georgia Strait, the peninsula is dominated by transportation: Highway 17 is the main vehicle route between Vancouver and Victoria via the Swartz Bay ferries; Washington State Ferries' service to the San Juan Islands and Anacortes departs from Sidney; and the Victoria airport is just west of Sidney. The Sidney harbor area is a pleasant stopover to or from the Swartz Bay ferries.

To get here from Victoria, take Blanchard Street north, which turns into Highway 17. For advance information, contact the **Saanich Peninsula Visitor Info Centre,** 10382 Patricia Bay Hwy. (Box 2014), Sidney, BC, V8L 3S3 (☎ **250/656-0525**).

✪ **Butchart Gardens.** 800 Benvenuto Ave., Brentwood Bay. ☎ **250/652-4422**, or 250/652-8222 for dining reservations. www.butchartgardens.com. Admission C$16 (U.S.$10) adults, C$8 (U.S.$5) youths 13–17, C$2 (U.S.$1.30) children 5–12. Off-season discounts available. AE, MC, V. Daily from 9am. Take Blanshard St. (Hwy. 17) north toward ferry terminal in Saanich; turn left on Keating Crossroads, which leads directly to the gardens—about 20 min. from downtown Victoria. Bus: 75.

These internationally acclaimed gardens were born after Robert Butchart exhausted the limestone quarry near his Tod Inlet home. His wife gradually landscaped the deserted eyesore into the resplendent Sunken Garden, opening it for public display in 1904. A Rose Garden, Italian Garden, and Japanese Garden were added later. Still in the family, the 50-acre gardens now display more than a million plants. As impressive as the numbers is the sheer perfection of each garden—not a blade out of place, each flower the same height, and all blooming at the same time. On summer evenings, the gardens are illuminated with softly colored lights. Musical entertainment is provided Monday through Saturday evenings from June through September. Saturday nights in July and August bring firework displays. A very good lunch, dinner, and afternoon tea are offered in the Dining Room Restaurant; casual fare is served in the Blue Poppy Restaurant. The gift shop sells seeds of some of the plants you'll see.

✪ **Victoria Butterfly Gardens.** 1461 Benvenuto Ave. (P.O. Box 190), Brentwood Bay. ☎ **250/652-3822.** www.victoriabc.com/attract/butterfly.htm. Admission C$8 (U.S.$5) adults, C$7 (U.S.$4.55) students and seniors, C$4.50 (U.S.$2.95) children 3–12, free for children under 3; C$25 (U.S.$16) families. Daily May–Oct 9:30am–5pm; Nov–Apr call in advance. Bus: 75.

A great spot for kids and nature buffs. Hundreds of exotic species flutter freely through this lush tropical greenhouse. Guests are provided with an identification chart and set free to roam around. The species present range from the tiny Central American Julia to the Southeast Asian Giant Atlas Moth (with a wingspan approaching a foot). Naturalists are on hand to explain butterfly biology, and there's even a display where you can see the beautiful creatures emerge from their cocoons.

3 The Gulf Islands

The ✪ **Gulf Islands** are a collection of several dozen mountainous islands that sprawl across the Strait of Georgia between the British Columbia mainland and Vancouver Island. While only a handful of the islands are served by regularly scheduled ferry service, this entire area is very popular with boaters, cyclists, kayakers, and sailboat enthusiasts, and with good reason. Lying in the rain shadow of Washington State's Olympic Mountains, the Gulf Islands have the most temperate climate in all of Canada, without the heavy rainfall that characterizes much of coastal British Columbia. In fact, the climate here is officially listed as semi-Mediterranean!

The Gulf Islands are the northern extension of Washington's San Juan Islands, and they share those islands' farming and seafaring past. Agriculture, especially sheep raising, is still a major industry. However, the past few decades have seen radical changes in traditional island life: The sheer beauty of the land- and seascapes, the balmy

The Gulf Islands

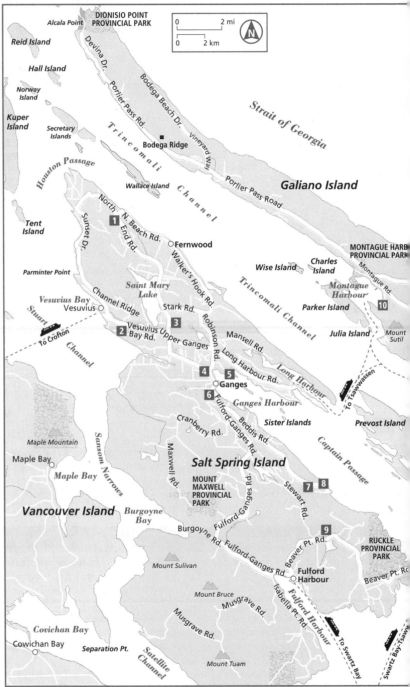

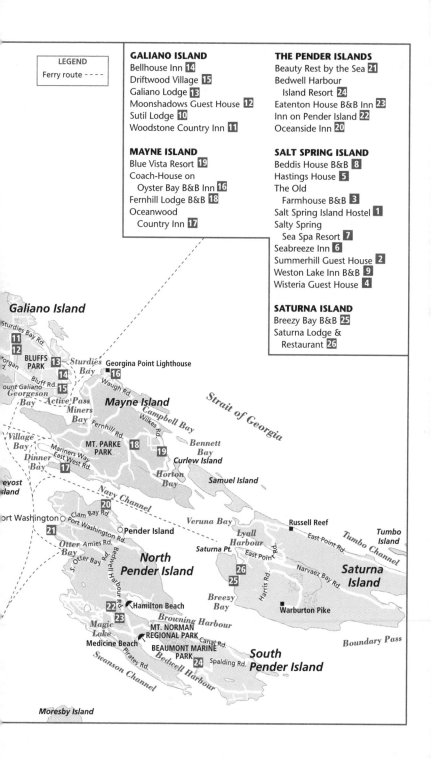

LEGEND

Ferry route - - - -

GALIANO ISLAND
Bellhouse Inn **14**
Driftwood Village **15**
Galiano Lodge **13**
Moonshadows Guest House **12**
Sutil Lodge **10**
Woodstone Country Inn **11**

MAYNE ISLAND
Blue Vista Resort **19**
Coach-House on
  Oyster Bay B&B Inn **16**
Fernhill Lodge B&B **18**
Oceanwood
  Country Inn **17**

THE PENDER ISLANDS
Beauty Rest by the Sea **21**
Bedwell Harbour
  Island Resort **24**
Eatenton House B&B Inn **23**
Inn on Pender Island **22**
Oceanside Inn **20**

SALT SPRING ISLAND
Beddis House B&B **8**
Hastings House **5**
The Old
  Farmhouse B&B **3**
Salt Spring Island Hostel **1**
Salty Spring
  Sea Spa Resort **7**
Seabreeze Inn **6**
Summerhill Guest House **2**
Weston Lake Inn B&B **9**
Wisteria Guest House **4**

SATURNA ISLAND
Breezy Bay B&B **25**
Saturna Lodge &
  Restaurant **26**

Galiano Island

Sturdies Bay Rd.
11
12
organ
d.
BLUFFS
PARK
13 Sturdies
Bay
Bluff Rd.
14
15
ount Galiano
Georgeson
Bay
Active Pass
Miners
Bay
Georgina Point Lighthouse
16
Waugh Rd.

Mayne Island
Campbell Bay
Wilkes Rd.
Fernhill Rd.
Village
Bay
Mariners Way
East West Rd.
Dinner
Bay
17
MT. PARKE
PARK
18
19
Bennett
Bay
Curlew Island

Strait of Georgia

evost
sland
Horton
Bay
Samuel Island

20
Navy Channel
Clam Bay Rd.
ort Washington
Port Washington Rd.
21
Pender Island
Veruna Bay
Lyall
Harbour
Saturna Pt.
Russell Reef
East Point Rd.
Tumbo
Island
Tumbo Channel

Otter
Bay
Amies Rd.
S. Otter Bay Rd.
Bedwell Harbour Rd.
*North
Pender Island*
East Point Rd.
Narvaez Bay Rd.
*Saturna
Island*

22 Hamilton Beach
23
Magic
Lake
Medicine Beach
Browning Harbour
MT. NORMAN
REGIONAL PARK
BEAUMONT MARINE
PARK
Canal Rd.
24 Spalding Rd.
Breezy
Bay
*South
Pender Island*
Harris Rd.
26
25
Warburton Pike
Boundary Pass

Pirates Rd.
Bedwell Harbour
Swanson Channel

Moresby Island

A Travel Tip for Families

If you're traveling with the kids, you'll find the Gulf Islands a fairly inhospitable place to find accommodations. Nearly all B&Bs have listed minimum ages for guests (usually 12 or 16), and there are only a few standard motels or cottage resorts where families are welcome. Note that for all accommodations, it's mandatory to make reservations well in advance, as the ferry system doesn't make it exactly easy to just drive on to the next town to find a place to stay.

---

climate, and relaxed "island-time" lifestyle have brought in a major influx of new residents. About 30 years ago, these islands were a major destination for Vietnam War–era draft evaders, many of whom married and set up homes, farms, and businesses here. The islands quickly developed a reputation as a countercultural hippie enclave, a reputation they still maintain—and still somewhat deserve, for the back-to-the-earth immigration continues. Even as one generation's radicals gray and become the islands' business class, younger generations of free spirits have come here to grow organic vegetables, explore an artistic urge, and hang out in the coffee shops.

The 1990s witnessed a parallel but different land-rush. High-tech moguls, Hollywood stars, and other wealthy refugees from urban centers—many of them Americans—have been moving to the islands in droves. Land prices have shot through the roof in recent years. The quality of facilities has also shot up: The islands now boast fine restaurants, elegant inns, and a multitude of galleries. In fact, the Gulf Islands are noted across Canada as a major center for crafts and arts.

The population influx is having some unexpected consequences. Groundwater is a precious commodity on these arid islands, and visitors may find that some inns will ask guests to monitor their water use. Water-rights conflicts are beginning to hit the courts. Adding to the problem is that saltwater aquifers underlie parts of the islands: A well of corrosive saltwater doesn't do anyone much good.

Despite the one-direction migration, the Gulf Islands remain a charming destination. The islands are still underdeveloped, and some of the best restaurants and accommodations are tucked away in forests down long roads. There's little in the way of organized activities here: no waterslides, theme parks, or major resorts; just incredible scenery, great biking and kayaking, lovely B&Bs and inns, and fine dining.

ESSENTIALS

GETTING THERE   By Ferry   Getting to the Gulf Islands is half the fun. **BC Ferries** (☎ **888/223-3779** or 604/444-2890; www.bcferries.bc.ca) operates three different ferry runs to the Gulf Islands, one from Tsawwassen on the British Columbia mainland, and from Swartz Bay and Crofton on Vancouver Island. While this may look like good public transportation on paper, the system is designed primarily to get commuters from their island homes to their jobs on the mainland or in Victoria. Getting from island to island is anything but straightforward, unless you want to travel with the commuters at 6am and 6pm. Be aware that the ferries that serve the islands are not particularly large; to insure that you actually make the one you want, arrive at least 15 minutes early (30 min. on summer weekends). You can make reservations on the service from Tsawwassen, but you can't reserve space on the other runs.

Ticket pricing is confusing. There are separate fares for passengers and vehicles, and vehicles over 20 feet long pay extra. Tickets from Vancouver Island (Crofton or Swartz Bay) are calculated as return fares. That is, you buy a ticket when you leave from Crofton or Swartz Bay, but if you return to these ports, you don't have to buy an additional ticket. However, all fares via Tsawwassen are one-way: You pay going and coming. To make it more puzzling, outward-bound fares from Tsawwassen are more expensive than the same journey inward-bound. There's a flat rate for all interisland travel. Sample peak-season fares: a car and two passengers from Swartz Bay to Salt Spring Island, C$31 (U.S.$20); a single foot passenger, C$6 (U.S.$3.90). The ferry terminals accept Visa and MasterCard in addition to cash and traveler's checks.

The actual ferry schedule is also confusing. Pick up a copy and give yourself plenty of time to study it. You can get to any of the major Gulf Islands from Swartz Bay or Tsawwassen, except Saturna Island, which is only accessible from Swartz Bay.

By Plane   A number of small commuter airlines offer regularly scheduled floatplane service from either Vancouver Harbour or Vancouver International Airport's Coal Harbour Terminal. One-way tickets to the islands usually cost C$60 to C$70 (U.S.$39 to U.S.$46), not a bad fare when you consider the time and hassle of the ferries. However, floatplanes are small and seats sell out quickly, so reserve ahead of time. For schedules and reservations, contact **Harbour Air** (☎ **800/665-0212** or 604/688-1277; www.harbour-air.com), **Seair** (☎ **800/447-3247** or 250/273-8900), or **Pacific Spirit Air** (☎ **800/665-2359** or 250/537-9359).

VISITOR INFORMATION   For general information on the Gulf Islands, contact **Tourism Association of Vancouver Island,** Suite 302, 45 Bastion Sq., Victoria, BC, V8W 1J1 (☎ **250/382-3551;** fax 250/382-3523; www.islands.bc.ca; e-mail: tavi@islands.bc.ca). Another good comprehensive Web site is **www.gulfislands.com**.

GETTING AROUND   Most innkeepers will pick up guests at either the ferry or floatplane terminals, if given sufficient notice. There's taxi service on most islands.

By Bicycle   Winding country roads and bucolic landscapes make the Gulf Islands a favorite destination for cyclists. Although the islands' road networks aren't exactly large, it can be great fun to bike the back roads, jump a ferry, and peddle to an outlying inn for lunch. Note that the narrow roads really fill up in summer, making them less than idyllic for cycling. Several parks have designated mountain-bike trails. Bikes can be taken onboard BC Ferries for a small surcharge, usually less than C$1.50 (U.S.$1), depending on the route. Bicycle rentals are available on most islands, and it's not unusual for inns and B&Bs to have bikes available for guests' use.

By Kayak   The Gulf Islands' lengthy and rugged coastline, plus their proximity to other more remote island groups, make them a good base for kayaking trips. A great many places in the Gulf Islands aren't accessible except by boat, and low-drawing kayaks are perfect for exploring shallow bays and rocky inlets, centers of marine life. Most of the islands have kayak outfitters; however—depending on their insurance coverage—not all outfitters will offer simple rentals apart from guided kayak tours. If you're an experienced kayaker and just want to rent a kayak and get out on the water, be sure to call ahead to make sure rentals are available at your destination.

A Helping Hand

Reserve rooms at B&Bs, lodges, resorts, and country inns in all price ranges, free of charge, through a centralized booking agency. **Canadian Gulf Islands Reservation Service** (☎ **888/539-2930** or 250/539-2930; www.gulfislandreservations.com; e-mail: reservations@gulfislands.com) is operated by Galiano Island natives. They've inspected all the participating lodgings and are therefore able to place you with exactly what you're looking for, whether that's a farm vacation, honeymoon suite, cozy B&B, or cottage on the beach.

SALT SPRING ISLAND

The largest of the Gulf Islands, Salt Spring is—to the outside world—a bucolic get-away filled with artists, sheep pastures, and cozy B&Bs. While this image is mostly true, Salt Spring is also a busy cultural crossroads: Movie stars, economy-minded retirees, high-tech telecommuters, and hippie farmers all rub shoulders here. Mercedes convertibles share the narrow roads with VW buses. The hilly terrain and deep forests afford equal privacy for all lifestyles, and that's the way the residents like it.

Salt Spring is divided geographically into three distinct lobes. In fact, the island looks as if it were once three separate islands that somehow got pushed together. Most of the population lives in the area around **Ganges** and **Vesuvius;** the rugged lower third of the island is the least developed. Although Salt Spring's configuration makes for a lot of coastline, there are very few beaches; instead, the island's underlying gran-ite forms headlands that drop straight into the sea.

GETTING THERE   Salt Spring Island is served by three different **BC Ferries** routes (☎ **888/724-5223** in B.C.). From Tsawwassen on the mainland, ferries depart twice daily for Long Harbour, on the island's northeast coast. If you're on Vancouver Island, you have a choice of the Vesuvius Bay–Crofton run or the crossing from Swartz Bay to Fulford Harbour.

Regularly scheduled floatplane service operates from Vancouver International Air-port and Vancouver's Inner Harbour seaplane terminal to Ganges Harbour. See "Essentials," above, for contact information.

VISITOR INFORMATION   The **Salt Spring Chamber of Commerce** operates a visitor information center at 121 Lower Ganges Rd., Salt Spring Island, BC, V8K 2T1 (☎ **250/537-5252;** www.saltspringisland.bc.ca; e-mail: chamber@saltspring.com).

GETTING AROUND   There is no public transport on Salt Spring, so if you don't have a car, you will need to rely on a bicycle or call **Silver Shadow Taxi** (☎ **250/537-3030**). If it fits into your schedule, a summer option for interisland transport is **Gulf Islands Water Taxi** (☎ **250/537-2510;** www.saltspring.com/watertaxi), which offers speedboat service between Salt Spring, Mayne, and Galiano islands on Wednesday and Saturday. The taxi leaves from Government Dock in Ganges Harbour. Reservations are highly recommended; bikes are transported free of charge.

EXPLORING THE ISLAND

With a year-round population of 10,000 residents, Salt Spring is served by three fer-ries, making it by far the easiest of the Gulf Islands to visit. Not coincidentally, Salt Spring also has the most facilities for visitors. The center of island life is **Ganges,** a lit-tle village with gas stations, grocery stores, banks, and galleries, all overlooking a busy pleasure-boat harbor. A wander around the town needn't take more than an hour—just follow the boardwalk to enjoy the harbor vistas—but you can easily spend most of a day poking around the art galleries, boutiques, and coffee shops.

In fact, many people visit Salt Spring expressly to see the galleries and studios of local artists and craftspeople: The island is famed across Canada as an artists' colony, and Ganges claims to be one of the top 10 small art towns in North America. Stop by the tourist office for a copy of the Studio Tour Map, which locates 35 artists—glassblowers, painters, ceramists, weavers, carvers, sculptors—around the island. As you're driving, just watch for the STUDIO sign with the blue sheep on it.

Pegasus Gallery, in Mouat's Mall, 1-104 Fulford Ganges Rd. (☎ **250/537-2421**), displays a mix of contemporary Canadian painting and sculpture as well as native carving and basketry. Just south of Ganges, **Ewart Gallery,** 175 Saltspring Way (☎ **250/537-2313**), offers paintings and sculpture from blue-chip Canadian artists.

The Mother of All Saturday Markets

A Salt Spring event not to be missed is ✪ **Market in the Park,** held every Saturday from 8am to 4pm (Apr through Oct) on the waterfront's Centennial Park. The market brings together a lively mix of craftspeople, farmers, musicians, bakers, and just about everyone else on the island who might plausibly be able to sell or buy something. It's great fun, and a good chance to shop for local products at fair prices. As you might guess, the people-watching possibilities are matchless. See "Exploring the Island," above, for other special Salt Spring events.

On Fridays from 5 to 9pm, 10 Ganges galleries remain open late for the **Gallery Walk.** From early July to mid-September, the Gulf Islands Community Arts Council presents **ArtCraft,** a fair featuring the work of more than 250 local artists, held at Mahon Hall, just north of Ganges at the corner of Park Drive and Lower Ganges Road.

BIKING   Although Salt Spring has the best network of paved roads, it's not the best island for cycling. With 10,000 inhabitants and ferries unleashing cars throughout the day, there's a lot more traffic here than you'd think. However, these same ferries—plus the **Gulf Islands Water Taxi** (see "Getting Around," above)—make Salt Spring a convenient base for cyclists. Besides the constant traffic, expect plenty of hills. For bike rentals, contact **Salt Spring Kayaking** (☎ **250/537-4664**), located on the Ganges Harbour docks.

HIKING   **Ruckle Provincial Park,** on the southeast corner of the island, is the largest park in the Gulf Islands. Five miles (8km) of trails wind through forests to rocky headlands where the tide-pool exploring is excellent; some trails are designated for mountain bikes. Ruckle Park is also the only public campground on Salt Spring.

KAYAKING   **Island Escapades,** 118 Natalie Lane (☎ **888/529-2567**), offers guided introductory lake trips starting at C$30 (U.S.$20), with guided 3-hour ocean tours at C$50 (U.S.$33). Island Escapades also offers paddle and mountaineering holidays. **Sea Otter Kayaking,** 1168 N. End Rd. (☎ **250/537-5678;** www.saltspring.com/kayaking), rents both kayaks and canoes, starting at C$20 (U.S.$13) an hour. Guided tours begin at C$35 (U.S.$23) for 2 hours.

WHERE TO STAY

The only **campground** on the island is at **Ruckle Provincial Park,** off Beaver Point Road (☎ **250/391-2300**). It has 70 walk-in-only sites for C$12 (U.S.$8). Hiking, kayaking, and mountain biking are all possible in the park.

   Salt Spring Island Hostel, 640 Cusheon Lake Rd. (☎ **250/537-4149**; www.beacom.com/ssihostel), offers 23 beds, plus the option of sleeping in a teepee or tree house. It's hard to get to without a car, though. Rates are about C$23 (U.S.$15).

Beddis House B&B. 131 Miles Ave., Salt Spring Island, BC, V8K 2E1. ☎ **250/537-1028.** Fax 250/537-9888. www.saltspring.com/beddishouse. E-mail: beddis@saltspring.com. 3 units. C$150–C$180 (U.S.$98–U.S.$117) double. Rates include breakfast and tea. MC, V. Closed Dec 15–Feb 1.

Both vintage and contemporary, this B&B combines the best of the old and the new. Perched above a strand of pebble beach, white-clapboard Beddis House was built as a farmhouse in 1900. The still-producing apple and plum orchards beside the home also date from that period, when much of this headland was devoted to sheep raising and farm production. The owners retained the old farmhouse as the dining room and parlor area, then built a new beachfront guest house—called the Coach House—in the style of the original farmhouse. Each of the spacious guest rooms has wonderful views, a private patio or balcony, a wood-burning stove, a private entrance, and access to multilevel decks, beautifully landscaped gardens, and manicured lawns.

✪ **Hastings House.** 160 Upper Ganges Rd., Salt Spring Island, BC, V8K 2S2. ☎ **800/661-9255** or 250/537-2362. Fax 250/537-5333. www.hastingshouse.com. E-mail: hasthouse@saltspring.com. 17 suites. C$400–C$500 (U.S.$260–U.S.$325) double. Rates include breakfast and tea. Off-season discounts available. AE, DC, ER, MC, V. Closed Jan–Feb. Children must be 16 or older.

This utterly charming inn is just east of Ganges, in a forested valley that drops directly onto Ganges Harbour. This spot was once the site of a Hudson's Bay Company trading post, and then a late-19th-century farm. In the 1930s, an English couple bought the farm and built an exact replica of a 16th-century Sussex estate, now known as the Manor House. At the end of the 20th century, new owners decided to open an exclusive small inn. Almost all of the original structures have been converted into beautifully furnished accommodations. The Manor House now serves as the restaurant and library, with two guest suites on the second floor. The 19th-century farmhouse contains two two-story suites, while the old trading post is now a two-room cottage suite. Architecturally most ingenious are the five suites in the old barn, which offer all of the modern luxuries you'd expect in a five-star hotel. All units are outfitted with original art, antiques, fireplaces, and down comforters; most have deep soaker tubs.

While the rooms are certainly full of character, what really sets Hastings House apart is its incredible 25-acre setting. Cheviot ewes trim the meadow grass, the gardens provide vegetables for the excellent restaurant (see "Where to Dine," below), and the old orchard bears sour cherries, apples, and pears. Idyllic only begins to describe this idealized English manor, popular with honeymooners. A member of the exclusive French hotel network Relais et Châteaux, Hastings House has a tremendous international reputation. Reserve 6 months in advance for summer visits.

✪ **The Old Farmhouse B&B.** 1077 N. End Rd., Salt Spring Island, BC, V8K 1L9. ☎ **250/537-4113.** Fax 250/537-4969. www.islandnet.com/~pixsell.bcbbd/1/1000182.html. E-mail: farmhouse@saltspring.com. 4 units. C$170 (U.S.$111) double. Rates include breakfast. MC, V. Children must be 10 or older.

One of the best-loved of all accommodations in the Gulf Islands, the Old Farmhouse B&B combines top-quality lodgings, great food, and two of the friendliest innkeepers you'll ever meet. The Old Farmhouse is in fact a Victorian-era homestead, built in 1894 amid 3 acres of meadows and orchards. The guest rooms are in a new, stylistically harmonious guest house adjoining the restored original farmhouse, which means that you get the charm of the old home as well as the comforts of a modern, spacious bedroom with new plumbing. Each room has a private bathroom and a balcony or patio; the decor incorporates just the right country touches—floral wallpaper, wainscoted walls—without lapsing into Laura Ashley excess. The extensive meadows are perfect for lolling with a book or playing a game of croquet.

However, the real heart and soul of the Old Farmhouse are its two proprietors, Karl and Gerti. Previously employed as a chef, Gerti whips out fresh-baked croissants and sticky currant buns as a precursor to the breakfast main course, which might be an unusual fruit omelet or an herb soufflé. *Note:* Smoking is not permitted.

Salty Spring Sea Spa Resort. 1460 N. Beach Rd., Salt Spring Island, BC, V8K 1J4. ☎ **800/665-0039** or 250/537-5087. Fax 250/537-2939. www.saltysprings.com. E-mail: saltyspring@saltspring.com. 12 chalets. C$189 (U.S.$123) 1-bedroom chalet for 2 persons. Extra person C$25 (U.S.$16) per night. AE, MC, V. 3-night minimum stay in summer. Packages available. Children must be 16 or older.

Salt Spring's notorious saltwater aquifers are put to good use at this ocean-side day spa and chalet development on the north end of the island. This brand-new center offers a variety of facials, revitalizing mineral baths utilizing the spa's salt spring water, and body treatments such as massage, aromatherapy, and wraps. Even if you're not into the spa scene, Salty Springs is worth considering for its new knotty-pine chalets, which face the busy waters of Trincomali Channel and overlook Wallace Island, now a marine park. Each well-designed, rustic-looking one- or two-bedroom unit has a full kitchen, picture windows, wood-burning fireplace, wide porch, and two tubs: one a therapeutic tub with jetted mineral water, the other a soaker tub. Guests have free access to bicycles, rowboats, and a game room. Smoking is not permitted.

Seabreeze Inn. 101 Bittancourt Rd., Salt Spring Island, BC, V8K 2K2. ☎ **800/434-4112** or 250/537-4145. Fax 250/537-4323. www.ferrytravel.com/seabreeze. E-mail: seabreeze@ saltspring.com. 28 units. TV TEL. C$79–C$89 (U.S.$51–U.S.$58) double. Kitchen unit C$10 (U.S.$7) extra. Extra person C$10 (U.S.$7). Rates include breakfast. Senior discounts, off-season rates, and weekly and monthly rates available. AE, DC, DISC, MC, V.

An excellent alternative to Salt Spring's expensive B&Bs, the Seabreeze is a well-maintained, attractive motel just south of Ganges. All rooms are very clean and nicely furnished, with extras such as fridges and coffeemakers. The kitchen units come with an electric cook-top, full-size fridge, and microwave. Guests can use a large deck area with grapevine-covered arbors, picnic tables, and a barbecue. The Seabreeze is perfect for families, cyclists, or those who don't need to be fussed over in a B&B.

Summerhill Guest House. 209 Chu-an Dr., Salt Spring Island, BC, V8K 1H9. ☎ **250/ 537-2727.** Fax 250/537-4301. www.bestinns.net./canada/bc/summerhill.html. E-mail: summerhill@saltspring.com. 3 units. C$100–C$125 (U.S.$65–U.S.$81) double. Rates include breakfast. MC, V. Children must be 15 or older.

With one of the finest views on Salt Spring Island, Summerhill has the feel of a true hideaway. Located atop a cliff overlooking Sansom Narrows and Vancouver Island, this modern structure was built in the 1970s, and was, according to the current innkeepers, a "very Brady Bunch kind of home." Strategic renovations turned the rambling home into an attractive lodging filled with natural light, intriguing colors, and quality furniture—the restrained up-to-date good taste of the decor here is a relief from the faux-country look usually dominant at B&Bs. Each room has a private bathroom, and two of them share a large deck. The gardens and the vista are what's really captivating here: The lawn slopes past banks of lavender to a rocky cliff, with incredible views of forested islands. Summerhill is a lovely, calming spot, and the service is both friendly and discrete. *Note:* Smoking is not permitted.

Weston Lake Inn B&B. 813 Beaver Point Rd., Salt Spring Island, BC, V8K 1X9. ☎ **888/ 820-7174** or 250/653-4311. Fax 250/653-4340. www.saltspring.com/westonlake. E-mail: westonlake@saltspring.com. 3 units. TV TEL. C$110–C$130 (U.S.$72–U.S.$85). MC, V. It's a little hard to find, so be sure to ask for directions when making reservations. The inn is close to Fulford Harbour, and is about half an hour south of Ganges. Children must be 14 or over.

Ask the locals on Salt Spring for B&B recommendations, and invariably one of the top suggestions is Weston Lake. The hosts are natives of this region, and their large, contemporary farmhouse inn captures more of the island's fun-loving-though-impassioned back-to-the-earth spirit than any other. The house sits above Weston Lake on 10 acres of gardens, orchards, and pastureland, which provide the ingredients for the inn's wonderful farm breakfasts. The comfortable guest rooms are filled with local art, island crafts, and the host's own embroidery. All units have private bathrooms and entrances. Guests share two common areas, one with a fireplace and TV/VCR. What makes this rural retreat such a gem is the effortless refinement and hospitality of the hosts, which infuses every element of the inn. Farm living doesn't get much better than this. *Note:* Smoking is not permitted.

Wisteria Guest House. 268 Park Dr., Salt Spring Island, BC, V8K 2S1. ☎ **250/537-5899.** www. pixsell.bc.ca.bb. E-mail: wisteria@saltspring.com. 7 units. From C$65 (U.S.$42) double. Rates include breakfast. Open in off-season for groups of 4 or more, by reservation only. Closed Nov 1–Mar 31. Children must be 10 or older.

This inn, tucked off a side street in Ganges, has an unusual pedigree: In its previous life, the rambling structure was a nursing home. Remodeled into a guest house, the Wisteria offers large rooms plus a stand-alone cottage at some of the most moderate prices on Salt Spring. The institutional aspect of the building has largely disappeared behind the pleasant furnishings and the handsome gardens, making this an excellent lodging choice for cyclists or other groups traveling together.

WHERE TO DINE

Bouzouki Greek Cafe. 2104-115 Fulford Ganges Rd., Grace Point Sq., Ganges. ☎ **250/537-4181.** Reservations recommended on weekends. Main courses C$8–C$18 (U.S.$5–U.S.$12). ER, MC, V. Daily 11am–3pm and 5–9pm. GREEK.

This little Greek cafe looks institutional—metal chairs and laminate tables—but the views over the harbor are lovely, and in summer, there's seating on a waterfront patio. The best news? The classic Greek food is both well prepared and moderately priced. Moussaka is C$14 (U.S.$9), while the lamb kleftiko is C$18 (U.S.$12).

Dare's To Be Different. 112 Hereford St. ☎ **250/537-0050.** Reservations not accepted. Main courses C$5–C$12 (U.S.$3.25–U.S.$8). MC, V. Daily 7am–9pm. VEGETARIAN.

This small vegetarian restaurant, in the dining rooms of an old home, is an offshoot of a health-food store. If you're careful about the food you eat, you'll value the organic, vegetarian, mostly local-grown ethos of this friendly cafe. And if you're weary of heavy, meat-laden meals, you'll be glad to see the lighter options on the large menu. Breakfasts—particularly the expansive omelets and spicy hash-browned potatoes—are especially good, and feature organic free-range eggs from Salt Spring Island. For lunch or dinner, try the vegetarian burger or savory Mexican pie.

✪ **Hastings House.** 160 Upper Ganges Rd. ☎ **250/537-2362.** Reservations required. Jacket required for men. Prix-fixe 5-course dinner C$70 (U.S.$46). AE, DC, MC, V. Summer dinner seating at 7:30pm, spring and fall at 7pm. PACIFIC NORTHWEST.

Easily the most elegant culinary experience on the island, the dining room at Hastings House combines old-world sophistication with the freshest of west-coast ingredients. Menus, which change daily, incorporate local produce and fish; many of the herbs and vegetables are grown on the grounds. The rose-covered Manor House—built in the 1930s to resemble a medieval English manse—is now the inn's restaurant and lounge area. The evening begins with cocktails served by the fireplace an hour before dinner. The meal includes an appetizer (perhaps ahi sashimi with black sesame seeds), an excellent soup, and a small fish course, such as gingered scallops with citrus cream. Guests have a choice of four main dishes: Salt Spring lamb is nearly always featured, as is local salmon or other seasonal fish. An inventive dessert concludes the meal.

   Dinner at the Hastings House is for many guests a special occasion. However, if the experience is too formal for your taste, request seating in The Snug, a pleasant room tucked below the main dining room. If you're an aspiring chef, you can also reserve a special table in the kitchen, where you can watch the cooks perform their magic.

✪ **House Piccolo.** 108 Hereford Ave., Ganges. ☎ **250/537-1844.** Reservations required. Main courses C$18–C$29 (U.S.$12–U.S.$19). AE, DC, MC, V. Daily 5–9pm. CONTINENTAL.

Located in a heritage home in Ganges, House Piccolo offers excellent à la carte dining and a good wine list in slightly formal surroundings. The Finnish origins of the chef/owner are reflected in the northern European accents on the restaurant's unusual menu, particularly the fish specials that feature the best of the local catch. Sole in sorrel sauce might be one night's special, while the seasonal menu features dishes such as grilled lamb chops with aioli.

Moby's Marine Pub. 124 Upper Ganges Rd. ☎ **250/537-5559.** Reservations not accepted. Main courses C$8–C$15 (U.S.$5–U.S.$10). AE, MC, V. Mon–Thurs 10am–midnight, Fri–Sat 11am–1pm, Sun 11am–midnight. PUB.

This large, airy, and pleasant pub offers the island's best entertainment and is the best place for a burger or light meal, accompanied by a pint of microbrewed beer. Located just east of Ganges, the dining room overlooks the harbor; in summer, a lively cocktail scene develops beneath the patio umbrellas on the waterfront deck. The menu offers the usual pub grub with twists—lamb burger with chutney, seafood fajitas. Live bands perform on Fridays and Saturdays, and Sunday Dinner Jazz is a tradition.

GALIANO ISLAND

Galiano is a long string bean of an island stretching along the Gulf Islands' eastern flank. On the map, Galiano looks like an attenuated sand spit; it is in fact quite mountainous, with rocky, cliff-faced shorelines and dense forests.

Galiano is the closest Gulf Island to Vancouver, and many of the properties here are the second homes of the city's elite. The rural yet genteel feel of the island is perfect for a romantic getaway or a relaxing break from the hassles of urban life. However, don't come to Galiano looking for high-octane nightlife or boutique shopping. There isn't much of a town on the island, just a few shops and galleries at Sturdies Bay. There are no banks or ATMs, either, though you will find a couple of stores, a pub, a gas station, and—most important—several unique eateries and many good inns.

GETTING THERE   **BC Ferries** (☎ **888/724-5223** in B.C.) serves Sturdies Bay from both Tsawwassen and Swartz Bay. Floatplanes serve Galiano Island from the docks at Monague Harbour. For contact information, see "Essentials," above.

VISITOR INFORMATION   For information on Galiano Island, contact **Galiano Island Tourist/Visitor Info,** 2590 Sturdies Bay Rd., Box 73, Galiano Island, BC, V0N 1P0 (☎ **250/539-2233;** www.galianoisland.com; e-mail: info@galianoisland.com).

GETTING AROUND   For taxi service, call **Go Galiano** (☎ **250/539-0202**).

EXPLORING THE ISLAND

Galiano is perhaps the most physically striking of the Gulf Islands, particularly the mountainous southern shores. Mount Sutil, Mount Galiano, and the exposed cliffs above Georgeson Bay (simply called the Bluffs) rise above sheep-filled meadows, shadowy forests, and fern-lined ravines. **Active Pass,** the narrow strait that separates Galiano from Mayne Island, is another scenic high spot: All of the pleasure-boat and ferry traffic between Vancouver and Victoria negotiates this turbulent, cliff-lined passage. Watch the bustle of the boats and ferries from **Bellhouse Provincial Park,** a picnicking area at the end of Jack Road. Or pack a picnic and head to **Montague Harbour Provincial Park,** a beautiful preserve of beach and forest.

Like Salt Spring Island, Galiano is also a center for artists and craftspeople. **Studio One Gallery,** in the Galiano Lodge in Sturdies Bay (☎ **250/539-2216**), displays the work of more than 30 Gulf Island painters and sculptors. Check out a selection of local and international crafts at **Ixchel,** with locations at both Montague Marina (☎ **250/539-9819**) and at 61 Georgeson Bay Rd. (☎ **250/539-3038**).

BIKING   The farther north you go on Galiano, the more remote the island becomes, making this a favorite of cyclists. While you won't have to worry too much about traffic on the 19-mile-long (30km) paved road that runs up the island's west side, there are enough steep ascents to keep your attention focused. Mountain bikers can follow unmaintained logging roads that skirt the eastern shores. Contact **Galiano Bicycle Rental,** 36 Burrill Rd. (☎ **250/539-9906**), for a full range of rental options.

HIKING   Several short hikes lead to Active Pass overlooks, including the trail to the top of 1,082-foot (330m) Mount Galiano and the cliff-edge path in Bluffs Park. Bodega Ridge is a park about two-thirds of the way up the island, with old-growth forest, wildflowers, and views of the distant Olympic and Cascade mountain ranges.

KAYAKING & BOATING   Home to otters, seals, and bald eagles, the gentle waters of Montague Harbour are a perfect kayaking destination. **Galiano Island Sea Kayaking** (☎ **888/539-2930**) at Sutil Lodge (see "Where to Stay," below), offers guided trips; a 2-hour wildlife-viewing paddle is C$19 (U.S.$12). If you want to really get away, consider one of the multiday kayak/camping trips from **Gulf Island Kayaking** (☎ **250/539-2442**). Both of the above also offer rental kayaks.

Another way to explore the bay and islands is with Galiano Island Sea Kayaking's catamaran cruises. The 4-hour sail cruise leaves from Montague Harbour Marina and travels across the bay to a remote uninhabited island, where your skipper prepares a gourmet meal. The cost, including picnic lunch or dinner, is C$39 (U.S.$25) for adults and C$29 (U.S.$19) for children under 12; it departs daily in summer.

WHERE TO STAY

The only **campground** is at **Montague Harbour Provincial Marine Park,** with 40 sites for C$10 (U.S.$7). It offers beach access, but no showers or flush toilets. Call ☎ **800/689-9025** for reservations, or 250/391-2300 for information.

Bellhouse Inn. 29 Farmhouse Rd., Galiano Island, BC, V0N 1P0. ☎ **800/970-7464** or 250/539-5667. Fax 250/539-5316. www.Monday.com/bellhouse. 6 units. Inn room C$135–C$175 (U.S.$88–U.S.$114) double, self-catering 2-bedroom cabin C$125 (U.S.$81). Extra person in cabin C$10 (U.S.$7). Inn rates include breakfast. MC, V. Children accepted in cabins; inn guests must be 16 or older.

If you're looking for historic charm and a wonderfully scenic location, the Bellhouse Inn is hard to beat. Built in 1890 as a farmhouse, this Galiano Island original sits in a grassy meadow above a private beach. The views of Mayne Island across boat-filled Active Pass are stunning, and pods of orcas sometimes swim up to frolic right in front of you. The 6 acres of grounds retain the feel of the old farm, with fruit trees lining the property and sheep grazing in the fields. Each inn guest room has a private bathroom; three units have private balconies. Guests share a lounge that overlooks the harbor; filled with vintage furniture and period art, this is a great spot to curl up with a book.

Bellhouse also offers two modern two-bedroom "cabins." These motel-like units have little of the charm of the original inn, but they do sleep up to six, offer full kitchens, and are available to families with young children.

Driftwood Village. 205 Bluff Rd. E., Galiano Island, BC, V0N 1P0. ☎ **888/240-1466** or 250/539-5457. www.driftwoodcottages.com. 11 cottages. TV. Studio C$98 (U.S.$64) double, 1-bedroom unit C$115 (U.S.$75), 2-bedroom unit C$135 (U.S.$88). Extra person C$5–C$15 (U.S.$3.25–U.S.$10). Rates include ferry pickup. MC, V. Pets accepted.

This venerable cottage resort is perfect for a laid-back vacation with the kids and pets in tow. The fully equipped cottages of differing vintages and styles are scattered around a 2-acre garden complete with ponds, flowers, and fruit trees. Each cottage has a full kitchen, private bathroom, and TV; most have fireplaces and private decks with views onto Sturdies Bay. The one- and two-bedroom cottages are effectively small, furnished houses, suitable for two to four people. All are decorated with a sense of artful thrift that will instantly bring back youthful memories of idealized lakeside cabins. The cottages share a deck area with hot tub, badminton court, and barbecues. Unlike most places in the islands, Driftwood Village welcomes both kids and pets.

Galiano Lodge. 134 Madrona Dr., Galiano Island, BC, V0N 1P0. ☎ **250/539-3388.** Fax 604/539-3338. 17 units. Motel room C$85 (U.S.$55) double, lodge room C$145–C$195 (U.S.$94–U.S.$127). Off-season and group rates available. Rates include breakfast. MC, V.

Galiano Lodge has quite a history. One of the original accommodations on the island, the lodge was a large stone-and-timber structure that for decades greeted ferry passengers as they arrived in Sturdies Bay. After a disastrous fire in the 1980s, the lodge was rebuilt as two structures, a large restaurant/bar complex beside an imposing new lodge of glass and native wood. The new Galiano Lodge was intended to be a true destination resort, but due to a series of financial missteps, it sat closed up for the better part of the 1990s. Finally reopened for business in 1999, the lodge offers some of the largest rooms and best views on Galiano; unique on the island, guests can simply leave the car at home and walk the 2 minutes from the ferry. Each room has a fireplace, sitting area, large patio or balcony, and Jacuzzi tub. One room is wheelchair-accessible. Also on the 3-acre property is a wing of older motel units; these aren't fancy, but are some of the least expensive, most accessible rooms on the island.

Moonshadows Guest House. 771 Georgeson Bay Rd., Galiano Island, BC, V0N 1P0. ☎ **888/666-6742** or 250/539-5544. Fax 250/539-5544. www.pixsell.bc.ca/bb/147.htm. E-mail: moonshadowsbb@bc.sympatico.ca. 3 units. C$100–C$135 (U.S.$65–U.S.$88) double. 2-night minimum stay. MC, V. Children must be 12 or older.

This classy, modern B&B stands at the edge of a copse of trees, overlooking a series of meadows and distant Mount Galiano. The architect-designed guest house combines the best elements of modern homes—a spacious and airy floor plan filled with flickering sunlight—with the rich stone-and-wood surfaces of a classic older inn. The large guest rooms are nicely decorated with quilts, wicker, and quality furniture. The room of choice is the Gardenside Suite, with a private deck and massive bathroom with a stationary bike, two-person soaker tub, and shower that measures 7 by 10 feet! Guests are invited to relax in the cozy living area, which has a stone fireplace and banks of windows overlooking a duck pond and pastures. The large deck has comfy chairs—perfect for an afternoon snooze—and a hot tub.

Sutil Lodge. 637 Southwind Rd., Montague Harbour, Galiano Island, BC, V0N 1P0. ☎ **250/539-2930.** Fax 250/539-5390. www.gulfislandreservations.com. E-mail: reservations@gulfislands.com. 7 units. C$75–C$95 (U.S.$49–U.S.$62) double. B&B packages and off-season rates available. Rates include use of canoes. MC, V.

Built in the 1920s as a fishing resort, Sutil Lodge's rustic character and gorgeous location set it apart from other places. If you're looking for a recreation-oriented lodging that's steeped in history and atmosphere, this might be it. Reached by a short drive down a country lane, the lodge sits at the edge of Montague Harbour on 20 acres of beach, woodland, and gardens. Guests can look out across the waters bobbing with sailboats, floatplanes, and kayaks. This view has long been admired: According to local custom, native peoples have met here for centuries to parley, trade, and hunt.

The venerable lodge looks like a sepia-toned memory of far simpler times. Simpler times also means that none of the snug rooms come with private bathrooms, though the lodge's laid-back atmosphere makes such old-fashioned ways seem gracious. The gardens produce many of the ingredients for the ample breakfasts. Sutil Lodge is a center for kayaking tours on beautiful Montague Harbour, offering rentals, guided tours, and cruises (see "Exploring the Island," above). *Note:* Smoking is not permitted.

✪ **Woodstone Country Inn.** 743 Georgeson Bay Rd., RR 1, Galiano Island, BC, V0N 1P0. ☎ **888/339-2022** or 250/539-2022. Fax 250/539-5198. www.gulfislands.com/woodstone. E-mail: woodstone@gulfislands.com. 12 units. C$99–C$185 (U.S.$64–U.S.$120) double. Rates include full breakfast and afternoon tea. Packages available. AE, ER, MC, V. Children must be 15 or older.

The quintessential small country inn, Woodstone is the most refined and comfortable place to stay on Galiano Island. The inn sits in a stand of fir trees overlooking a series of meadows, which serve as a de facto bird sanctuary. Gardens stair-step down from the front of the inn; from the deck, you can listen to the song of birds and frogs. The entire inn is decorated with restrained but hearty good taste: the owners' collection of folk art and sculpture from their world travels, including marvelous carvings from arctic Canada and southern Africa, plus many quality antiques. The guest rooms are large and beautifully furnished, with writing tables, upholstered chairs, and intriguing art. Gleaming bathrooms are fitted with hair dryers, soaker or Jacuzzi tubs, and luxury toiletries. All units have fireplaces, some have soaker tubs and sofa beds, and one room is wheelchair-accessible. All rooms on the main floor have small private patios.

The restaurant (see below) serves the island's finest cuisine. Spending a few days here is like staying at the home of a favorite friend, a friend who luckily shares your exquisite good taste. *Note:* Smoking is not permitted.

WHERE TO DINE

Galiano has a limited number of fine-dining establishments, though there are many informal places to eat. The convivial **Daystar Market Café** (☎ **250/539-2800**) is just north of Sturdies Bay at the intersection of Georgeson Bay and Porlier Pass roads. This cafe, part of an organic- and health-food store, serves mostly vegetarian meals and baked goods for lunch and dinner daily. **Montague Café,** at the Montague Harbour Marina (☎ **250/539-5733**), offers light dining right on the water.

La Berengerie Restaurant. Montague Rd. ☎ **250/539-5392.** Reservations recommended. 4-course prix-fixe menu C$25 (U.S.$16). MC, V. Daily 5–9pm. FRENCH.

La Berengerie has a truly country-French atmosphere: This old farmhouse overlooking a woodland glade could easily be a Breton cottage by a shaded brook. The menu offers a choice of entree—perhaps duck breast with kumquat sauce, or seafood-stuffed sole—plus soup, salad, and dessert. The dining room is simply decorated (pots of flowers, colorful Provençal linens) yet warm and inviting. The food can be somewhat inconsistent, although on a good day your meal can be very memorable.

✪ **Woodstone Country Inn.** 743 Georgeson Bay Rd. ☎ **250/539-2022.** Reservations required. 4-course dinner C$22–C$27 (U.S.$14–U.S.$18). Minimum charge of C$22 (U.S.$14) per person. AE, DC, MC, V. Sun–Thurs 5–9pm, Fri–Sat 5–10pm. INTERNATIONAL.

The dining room at Woodstone is one of the best restaurants in all of the Gulf Islands. The menu is a compelling blend of classic French cuisine enlivened with vivid international flavors. Roast halibut with a macadamia-nut crust is prepared with a lemon-coconut sauce, while seared duck breast is served atop wild-rice pancakes. Each day's menu includes a choice of three entrees—meat, fish, or vegetarian—which comes with homemade bread, soup, and a delightful salad. Desserts like warm bread pudding and fresh berry sorbets end the meal. The wine list is an interesting mix of Okanagan, California, and French vintages. The light, intimate dining room has lovely views of a wildflower meadow. The absolute professionalism combined with a convivial atmosphere make dining here an enchanting experience.

MAYNE ISLAND

Bucolic Mayne Island is a beautiful medley of rock-lined bays, forested hills, farm fields, and pastureland. Seemingly distant from the pressures of modern life, Mayne was once a center of early Gulf Island agriculture, noted for its apple and tomato production. Many of the island's early farm homes remain, and a rural, lived-in quality is one of Mayne's most endearing features: This feels like a real island community.

GETTING THERE   BC Ferries serves Mayne Island with regularly scheduled runs from both Tsawwassen and Swartz Bay. Three commuter airlines offer floatplane service to and from Vancouver. For more information, see "Essentials," above.

VISITOR INFORMATION   For information, contact the **Mayne Island Community Chamber of Commerce,** Box 2, Mayne Island, BC, V0N 2J0 (no phone; www.gulfislands.com/mayne_chamber).

GETTING AROUND   Call **Midas Taxi** (☎ 250/539-3132) for a ride.

EXPLORING THE ISLAND

Miner's Bay is by default the commercial center of the island, though in most locales this somewhat aimless collection of shops, homes, and businesses along the Active Pass bay front wouldn't really qualify as a village. However, it's this understated approach to life that provides Mayne Island with its substantial charm. Don't let the rural patina fool you: Some of the lodging and dining are world-class, and even though organized activities are few, it's hard to be bored on such a lovely island.

Mayne doesn't boast the provincial parks and public lands that the other Gulf Islands do, though there are several beach access sites that provide opportunities for swimming in warm weather, and beachcombing during other times of the year. **Bennett Bay,** on the northeast coast, is the best swimming beach. **Campbell Bay,** just northwest, is another favorite pebble beach. **Dinner Bay Park** is lovely for a picnic.

On a sunny day, the grounds of the **Georgina Point Lighthouse** provide dramatic viewpoints. Located on the island's northern tip, this lighthouse juts into Active Pass, busy with ferries and pleasure boats, and overlooks the southern shores of Galiano Island, less than a mile distant. The grounds of the lighthouse are now preserved as a national heritage park, with picnic tables and access to the rocky headland.

Mayne Island is home to a number of artists; the widely available map of the island lists more than 20 studios that are open for visitors. The pottery of **John Charowsky,** 490 Fernhill Rd. (☎ 250/539-3488), is especially attractive and versatile.

BIKING   Mayne is one of the best islands for cyclists. The rolling hills provide plenty of uphill challenges, yet the terrain is considerably less mountainous than that of the other islands. Also, the blocky shape of Mayne means roads ring and intersect the island, making a variety of loop trails possible. Bring your bike on the ferry, or rent one from **Bayview B&B,** 764 Steward Dr. (☎ 250/539-2924).

HIKING   The roads on Mayne are usually quiet enough that they can also serve as paths for hikers. Hikers looking for more solitude should consider Mounte Parke Regional Park, off Fernhill Road in the center of the island. The park's best views reward those who take the hour-long hike to Halliday Viewpoint, on the island's crest.

KAYAKING & BOATING   Mayne Island Kayak & Canoe Rentals (☎ 250/539-2667), at Seal Beach in Miner's Bay, rents kayaks and canoes for C$20 (U.S.$13) for 2 hours, or C$42 (U.S.$27) for a full day. The company will drop off kayaks at any of six launching points on the island, and if you get stranded, will even pick up kayaks (and too-weary kayakers) from other destinations. If you'd rather let the wind do the work, call **Island Charters** (☎ 250/539-5040). A half-day excursion (C$135/U.S.$88 for two) lets you explore the coasts of Maynes, Saturna, and the Pender islands, or you can arrange for the sailboat to deliver you to other island destinations (this is the really classy way to get to your country inn).

WHERE TO STAY

Blue Vista Resort. 563 Arbutus Dr., Mayne Island, BC, V0N 2J0. ☎ **250/539-2463.** 8 cottages. C$50–C$75 (U.S.$33–U.S.$49) 1-bedroom cottage, C$80–C$110 (U.S.$52–U.S.$72) 2-bedroom cottage. Extra person C$10 (U.S.$7). Off-season and weekly rates available. MC, V. Closed mid-Jan to mid-Feb. Pets accepted with prior approval only.

This venerable resort is a good example of that rare Gulf Island lodging: a place where families with kids and pets are welcome. Located on the warm eastern side of Mayne Island—close to beaches, kayaking, and hiking—Blue Vista's comfortable cabins are a great value and come with everything you might need: kitchen, private bathroom, fireplace, deck, barbecue, and complimentary bicycles. The parklike setting with beach access makes this an ideal place for a safe, laid-back vacation.

Coach-House On Oyster Bay B&B Inn. 511 Bayview Dr., Mayne Island, BC, V0N 2J0. ☎ **888/629-6322** or 250/539-3368. Fax 250/539-2236. www.monday.com/mlynebb. 3 units. C$115–C$130 (U.S.$75–U.S.$85) double. 2-night minimum stay. Off-season rates available. MC, V. Closed mid-Jan to mid-Feb.

This modern home on a private, wooded bay was designed to look like one of Mayne Island's old heritage farm homes, but with up-to-date comforts. Each room has a private bath, fireplace, patio or balcony, and private entrance. Luxury touches include soft robes, hair dryers, and complimentary in-room sherry. The Landau unit has a private deck with a hot tub and splendid ocean views. A path from the inn leads toward another hot tub, perched just 10 feet from the tide line on a rock ledge. From here, the views toward Tsawwassen across the Strait of Georgia are magnificent. Otters frequently come into the bay, and orcas gather just offshore. Deer feel so at home on this secluded property that they sometimes sleep right in the garden. The Couch-House is convenient to the Active Pass Lighthouse; the inn provides free bikes and tennis rackets for guests' use. In summer, the water along the small private beach is warm enough for swimming. *Note:* Smoking is not permitted.

Fernhill Lodge B&B. 610 Fernhill Rd., Mayne Island, BC, V0N 2J0. ☎ **250/539-5244.** Fax 250/539-2544. 3 units. C$99–C$199 (U.S.$64–U.S.$129). Extra person C$20 (U.S.$13). Rates include breakfast. MC, V.

Drive up a winding road through dense forest to find this secluded inn. Each comfortable room is fancifully designed around a theme: The oak-beamed Jacobean Room is dominated by a huge antique bed from England, while the India Room is swathed with colorful Indian fabric. All units look out onto a dense canopy of forest, making this rural hideaway seem even more private. Each has a private entrance and private bathroom, and two have hot tubs. The innkeepers are serious cooks and gardeners: Expect a delicious breakfast made from homegrown produce. The noted restaurant offers some of the most unusual cuisine in British Columbia (see "Where to Dine," below). Guests are welcome to stroll through the gardens, poke through the library, and relax in the hot tub and sauna. *Note:* Smoking is not permitted.

✪ **Oceanwood Country Inn.** 630 Dinner Bay Rd., Mayne Island, BC, V0N 2J0. ☎ **250/539-5074.** Fax 250/539-3002. www.oceanwood.com. E-mail: oceanwood@gulfislands.com.

12 units. C$149–C$299 (U.S.$97–U.S.$194). Extra person C$25 (U.S.$16). Rates include breakfast and afternoon tea. MC, V. Closed Dec–Feb.

Of all the great places to stay in the Gulf Islands, perhaps the best is the Oceanwood Country Inn, a luxury lodging with an excellent restaurant, attentive staff, and spacious rooms with sumptuous furnishings. Each unit is decorated according to an understated floral and wildlife theme, and all but one have magnificent views of boat-flecked Navy Channel and Saturna Island. The original inn's charming rooms are less expensive, yet still good-sized and beautifully fitted with fine furniture and large bathrooms; two have balconies. The rooms in the new wing are truly large and well appointed, with private decks, large sitting areas, and two-person jetted or soaker tubs facing wood-burning fireplaces. The most deluxe is the Wisteria Suite, a three-tiered unit with two baths, multiple decks, and an outdoor soaker tub.

The inn's public rooms are equally impressive. Facing the gardens are a comfortable living room and library, separated by a double-sided fireplace. The dining room is one of the most sophisticated places to eat in British Columbia (see "Where to Dine," below). Highly recommended, the Oceanwood is a gem of understated elegance, with just the right blend of comfortable formality and relaxed hospitality.

WHERE TO DINE

Manna Bakery Café, on Fernhill Road in Miner's Bay's tiny strip mall (☎ **250/ 539-2323**), is the place to go for a cappuccino and fresh-baked cinnamon roll. Just above the marina in Miner's Bay, the **Springwater Lodge** (☎ **250/539-5521**) is a comfortably ramshackle pub/restaurant with great views; try the fish-and-chips here.

Fernhill Lodge. 610 Fernhill Rd. ☎ **250/539-2544.** Reservations required before 1pm on the same day. 4-course prix-fixe dinner C$28 (U.S.$18). MC, V. Daily 6–9pm. INTERNATIONAL/ HISTORICAL.

The dark-paneled, almost Gothic atmosphere of the Fernhill Lodge dining room is the perfect backdrop to the delightful and unusual food created by chef/owner Brian Crumblehulme, who has researched the role of food in society throughout history, and along the way has become an expert in historical menus and food preparation. The four-course Roman meal begins with appetizers like dates fried in olive oil and honey, followed by squab with mustard and nut sauce. The Renaissance dinner commences with slivers of smoked eel in fruit sauce, followed by game hen with apples, onions, and beer. Crumblehulme also excels at "normal" cooking, though his flair for unusual flavors makes his style of cuisine anything but pedestrian. The daily changing menu features quality meats and the freshest of local produce and fish. Even the choice of menus is unusual: Because the chef enjoys incorporating guests' personal tastes into his cooking, the first couple reserving for the meal gets to help select the menu.

✪ **Oceanwood Country Inn.** 630 Dinner Bay Rd. ☎ **250/539-5074.** Reservations required. 4-course prix-fixe menu C$39 (U.S.$25). AE, DC, MC, V. Sun–Thurs 5:30–9pm, Fri–Sat 5:30–10pm. PACIFIC NORTHWEST.

Refined yet robust, the cuisine at Oceanwood is one of the best expressions of up-to-date, full-flavored cooking in the Gulf Islands. Chef Paul McKinnon brings together the rich bounty of northwest fish, meat, game, and produce in a daily changing tableau of vivid tastes and textures. Dinners include a soup, appetizer, and choice of entrees. The fish selection might be local paupiettes of sole with herb gnocchi and blackberry vinaigrette, while the meat entree could be grilled duck breast with cranberry demiglace served on foie-gras–stuffed ravioli. Service is highly professional, and the decor handsome but unfussy: Why compete with the view? The dining room overlooks a lily pond and garden, with trees framing the vista of Navy Pass.

THE PENDER ISLANDS

The Penders consists of North and South Pender islands, separated by a very narrow channel that's spanned by a one-lane bridge. North Pender is much more developed, though that's all relative out in the Gulf Islands. It has a rather startling housing development on its southwest side, a 1970s suburb plopped down on an otherwise rural island. Neither of the Penders seem to share the long-standing farming economy background of the other Gulf Islands, so forests are thick and all-encompassing. The Penders do have some lovely beaches and public parks with good hiking trails. Toss in a handful of local artists, and you have the recipe for a tranquil island retreat.

GETTING THERE   BC Ferries serves Pender Island with regularly scheduled runs from both Tsawwassen and Swartz Bay. Three commuter airlines offer floatplane service to and from Vancouver. For more information, see "Essentials," above.

VISITOR INFORMATION   Contact the **Pender Island Visitor Info Centre,** 2332 Otter Bay Rd., Pender Island, BC, V0N 2M1 (☎ **250/629-6541;** fax 250/ 629-6541). It's open May 15 to September 2.

EXPLORING THE ISLANDS

Mount Norman Regional Park, which encompasses the northwest corner of South Pender Island, features hiking trails through old-growth forest to wilderness beaches and ridge-top vistas. Access to trails is just across the Pender Island bridge.

The extensive and somewhat confusing network of roads on the Penders makes these islands good destinations for cyclists. Bike rentals are available at **Otter Bay Marina** (☎ **250/629-3579**), where you'll also find **Mouat Point Kayaks** (☎ **250/ 629-6767**). If beachcombing or sunning on the sand is more your style, try Hamilton Beach on the east side of North Pender, or Medicine Beach and the beaches along Beaumont Marine Park, both of which flank Bedwell Harbour.

WHERE TO STAY

Beauty Rest by the Sea. 1301 Mackinnon Rd., N. Pender Island, BC, V0N 2M1. ☎ **250/ 629-3855.** Fax 250/629-3856. www.penderisle.com. E-mail: beauty@gulfislands.com. 2 units. TV. C$120–C$125 (U.S.$78–U.S.$81) double. Extra person C$25 (U.S.$16). Rates include breakfast. MC, V.

An uncommonly dramatic setting—acres of rocky headland overlooking the channel between North Pender and Prevost islands—provides the Beauty Rest with physical charms that other B&Bs can only dream of. The grounds—basically all of a small cliff-sided peninsula—have been in the family for generations. The attractive ranch-style home has two well-appointed guest rooms, each with private entrance, bath, fridge, and coffeemaker. Guests are free to roam the property, watch boats and whales in the channel, sun on the small pebble beach, or read on the deck.

Bedwell Harbour Island Resort. 9801 Spalding Rd., S. Pender Island, BC, V0N 2M3. ☎ **800/663-2899** or 250/629-3212. Fax 250/629-6777. www.islandnet.com/~bedwell. E-mail: bedwell@islandnet.com. 24 units. A/C TV TEL. C$89–C$379 (U.S.$58–U.S.$246) double. Extra person C$12 (U.S.$8). Off-season rates available. AE, MC, V. Closed Oct–Mar.

Bedwell Harbour is the most active place in all South Pender Island. This sprawling complex, with cabins, motel rooms, condo town houses, and a marina, is also the Canadian Customs House for vessels coming in from Washington's San Juan Islands. In summer, this is a very busy spot; you can easily spend an afternoon sitting at a wharf-side table with your favorite drink, watching a parade of boats pass by. The resort is very attractive, particularly the newer condo units with balconies and decks. Families will like the cabins with kitchens, while the motel rooms (many with kitchenettes) represent good value for the Gulf Islands. If your room doesn't have a kitchen, then your rate includes breakfast in the dining room. Bedwell Harbour is currently undergoing a major redevelopment and expansion; the old pub and dining room will be torn down and replaced, and additional units will be added. There's no reason to think the new development will be anything but first-class.

Eatenton House B&B Inn. 4705 Scarff Rd., Pender Island, BC, V0N 2M1. ☎ **888/780-9994** or 250/629-8355. Fax 250/629-8375. www.penderislands.com. E-mail: eatenton@gulfislands.com. 3 units. C$95–C$135 (U.S.$62–U.S.$88) double. Extra person C$20 (U.S.$13). Escape, honeymoon, and anniversary packages available. MC, V. Children must be 15 or older.

This pleasant, contemporary B&B offers wonderful gardens and views of forest and the sparkling waters of Browning Harbour. The spacious guest rooms are great for groups traveling together; the largest is essentially a suite with two bedrooms. A fireplace commands the dining area and antique-filled sitting room. However, on nice afternoons, the deck is where you'll be spending most of your time. If the evening grows chilly, slip into the outdoor garden hot tub. *Note:* Smoking is not permitted.

Inn on Pender Island. 4709 Canal Rd., N. Pender Island, BC, V0N 2M0. ☎ **800/550-0172** or 250/629-3353. Fax 250/629-3167. www.travel.bc.ca/i/innonpender. 12 units. TV. Motel rms C$79 (U.S.$51) double, cabins C$110–C$130 (U.S.$72–U.S.$85) double. Extra person C$10 (U.S.$7). Motel rates include breakfast. MC, V. Small pets C$2 (U.S.$1.30).

The Inn on Pender Island is the name given to an enterprising lodging/dining complex at the center of North Pender. Nine units are in a modern, two-story motel building. These large, unfussy rooms come with TVs and small fridges. Pets and kids are welcome, and breakfast is delivered to your door. These basic motel rooms are a real deal on the otherwise expensive Gulf Islands. Also part of the complex are three brand-new log cabins, set in the forest above the motel. Each has a kitchenette, full bathroom, and deck; two cabins also have private hot tubs. These, too, are a great value when you consider the sky's-the-limit prices of comparable lodgings. Likewise, the restaurant is a just-fine place to eat, with good pizza and Northwest cuisine.

Oceanside Inn. 4230 Armadale Rd., N. Pender Island, BC, V0N 2M3. ☎ **250/629-6691.** www.penderisland.com. E-mail: oceanside@penderisland.com. 4 suites. C$129–C$229 (U.S.$84–U.S.$149) double. Off-season rates and 2-day escape and honeymoon packages available. V. Children must be 15 or older.

Under new ownership, the Oceanside Inn takes its place as one of the nicest and most private getaways on the Penders. The inn is cantilevered above a rocky cliff directly overlooking Navy Channel and Mayne Island. The arbutus trees that line the shore are home to bald eagles and turkey buzzards. The dramatic setting alone strongly recommends the Oceanside Inn; the fact that it has been totally redecorated and renovated, and is now operated by a charming and thoughtful host, makes it even more of a find. Three suites face Navy Channel, and have private decks, hot tubs, and patios; two rooms have fireplaces. All units have private entrances and bathrooms, small fridges, hair dryers, and robes. The glass-fronted dining room is open to guests only; weekend packages include one dinner for two (from C$299/U.S.$194).

WHERE TO DINE

One of the Penders' drawbacks is its lack of many dining options. Your best bet is the **Bedwell Harbour Island Resort** (see "Where to Stay," above), with both a pub and dining room. The dining room has an excellent reputation, but at press time was undergoing a major makeover as part of the resort's redevelopment. Check it out—and feel free to let us know what you think. **Memories,** at the Inn on Pender Island

(☎ **250/629-3353**), is the only other real dining choice. Don't let the rather plain exterior of this family restaurant put you off. The food—ranging from pizza to ribs to fresh fish—is quite tasty. It's open for dinner only.

SATURNA ISLAND

The most remote of the southern Gulf Islands, Saturna Island is both pristine and, compared with its neighbors, mostly vacant. Whereas other islands are best described as rural, mountainous Saturna is wild. It is truly not on the way to anywhere else: Served only by direct ferries from Swartz Bay, Saturna is hard to get to. If you're hoping to add Saturna to your island hopping, you'll find it easiest to ferry to Vancouver Island and then ferry back out: Interisland ferries mostly neglect this beautiful island. Note that ferries from Tsawwassen no longer sail to Saturna.

Its remoteness makes Saturna a favorite destination of outdoors-oriented visitors. The island boasts nice beaches, including Russell Reef, Veruna Bay, and Shell Beach at East Point Park. This park, with its still-active lighthouse, is a good spot to watch for orcas. Hikers can drive to Mount Warburton Pike and follow the Brown Ridge Nature Trail, with great views of the Penders and San Juans. The main kayaking destinations are the rocky islets surrounding Tumbo Island, just offshore Saturna's eastern peninsula. Facilities are few and far between, though in several cases, exemplary. For more information, check out **www.saturnatourism.bc.ca**.

WHERE TO STAY & DINE

Breezy Bay B&B. 131 Payne Rd., Saturna Island, BC, V0N 2Y0. ☎ and fax **250/539-5957**, or 250/539-3339. www.gulfislands.com/saturna/breezybay. E-mail: breezybay@gulfislands. com. 4 units. C$75 (U.S.$49) double. Extra person C$25 (U.S.$16). No credit cards. Closed Oct–Mar.

Fifty acres of farmland surround this beautifully preserved 1890s heritage farmhouse, which overlooks sheep and llama pastures and cliff-lined Breezy Bay. The interior of the house is lined with wainscot and period moldings, while a stone fireplace dominates the lounge and library. The cozy rooms share two bathrooms. Paths lead to the beach, with access for swimming and kayaking. Children are welcome.

Saturna Lodge & Restaurant. 130 Payne Rd., Saturna Island, BC, V0N 2Y0. ☎ **888/ 539-8800** or 250/539-2254. Fax 250/539-3091. www.saturna-island.bc.ca. E-mail: rpage@ pro.net. 7 units. C$120–C$160 (U.S.$78–U.S.$104) double. Rates include buffet breakfast. Special packages available. AE, MC, V.

The best-loved place to stay on Saturna is the Saturna Lodge, a well-established resort that has in recent years been revamped into an upscale country inn. In 1997, Saturna Lodge announced the planting of 87 acres of wine grapes (the region's first major vineyard), marking a new direction for the landmark inn and for the Gulf Islands. Each guest room is named for one of the varietals. All rooms have soaker tubs and views.

Dining: For most guests, the highlight of a weekend at Saturna Lodge is a meal at the restaurant. The daily-changing prix-fixe menu features Saturna Island lamb, local fish and seafood, and organic produce prepared with cutting-edge French élan. In good weather, the menu offers barbecued meats and fish from the outdoor grill, and diners can choose to eat on the several levels of decks that overlook the bay.

4 West of Victoria: Sooke Harbour & Port Renfrew

Port Renfrew: 63 miles (102km) W of Victoria

Following Highway 14 west from Victoria, the suburbs eventually thin; by the time you reach Sooke, the vistas open up to the south, where Washington's Olympic

Mountains prop up the horizon. There are several reasons to explore this part of the island, though the motivations basically boil down to the wild and the civilized.

Highway 14 gives access to a number of beaches and provincial parks with good swimming and recreation, finally leading to Port Renfrew, the southern trailhead for the infamous West Coast Trail. This trail follows the often treacherous wilderness coastline of Pacific Rim National Park for 48 miles (77km), and is considered one of the world's great hikes. (See chapter 6 for complete coverage of the West Coast Trail and Pacific Rim National Park.)

Ambitious backcountry drivers can also make a loop journey from Highway 14. From Port Renfrew, a good logging road leads up the San Juan River valley, connecting to the southern shores of Lake Cowichan just west of Duncan. You can make this drive in one very long day, or divide the trip up by planning to spend the night camping at Lake Cowichan or at one of Duncan's moderately priced hotels.

The civilized reason to make the journey west from Victoria is the superlative Sooke Harbour House, one of the most renowned small inns in all of Canada.

IN & AROUND SOOKE

The little town of Sooke doesn't offer a lot to divert the visitor, but there are a number of recreation areas nearby that warrant a stop. **Sooke Potholes Provincial Park** preserves a curious geologic formation. The Sooke River flows down a series of rock ledges, pooling in waist-deep swimming holes before dropping in waterfalls to another series of pools and waterfalls. In July and August, the normally chilly river water warms up. If the weather's not up to swimming, the trails that link the pools are nice for a casual hike; the park also has picnic facilities. There are more trails in adjacent Sooke Mount Provincial Park. To reach these parks, drive west on Route 14 almost to the town of Sooke; turn right on Sooke River Road. Nine miles (15km) west of Sooke is **French Beach Park,** a sand-and-gravel beach that's one of the best places to watch for passing gray whales. The rock ledges that run into the ocean also make this an excellent place to explore tide pools. The park has 69 campsites right on the beach.

WHERE TO STAY

Point-No-Point Resort. 1505 West Coast Hwy. (Hwy. 14), Sooke, BC, V0S 1N0. ☎ **250/ 646-2020.** Fax 250/646-2294. 22 units. C$70–C$160 (U.S.$46–U.S.$104) cabin. MC, V. Free parking.

Get away from it all, in your own little cabin on the ocean, with 40 acres of wilderness around you, a wide, rugged beach in front of you, and nothing to do but laze the day away in your hot tub. Since 1950, this oceanfront resort has been welcoming guests. Cabins vary depending upon when they were built. All have fireplaces, full kitchens, and bathrooms; newer ones have hot tubs and private decks. Food is not included in the rates, so come prepared. Lunch and supper can be purchased at the small but sunny central dining room. Tables in the dining room are conveniently equipped with binoculars, so you won't miss a bald eagle as you eat your lunch.

✪ **Sooke Harbour House.** 1528 Whiffen Spit Rd., Sooke, BC, V0S 1N0. ☎ **250/ 642-3421.** Fax 250/628-6988. www.sookeharbourhouse.com. E-mail: shh@islandnet. com. 28 units. TEL. C$260–C$465 (U.S.$169–U.S.$302) double. Rates include breakfast and lunch. Dinner C$56 (U.S.$36) extra. Off-season discounts available. AE, ER, JCB, MC, V. Free parking. Take the Island Hwy. (Hwy. 1) to the Sooke/Colwood turnoff (Junction Hwy. 14). Follow Hwy. 14 to Sooke. About 1 mile (1.6km) past the town's only traffic light, turn left onto Whiffen Spit Rd.

This little inn on the end of a sand spit, about 18½ miles (30km) west of Victoria, has earned an international reputation. Each suite is unique, decorated according to a particular northwest theme. The Thunderbird room, for example, reflects the bold colors and striking design of this famous west-coast symbol. Each unit boasts a wood-burning fireplace, fresh flowers, and wonderful views of the water. All but one have sundecks, and many have Jacuzzis. Amenities include in-room breakfast, optional in-room dinner, baby-sitting referrals, and massage by appointment. Sooke Harbour House has one of the best restaurants in the area (see "Where to Dine," below).

WHERE TO DINE

✪ **Sooke Harbour House.** 1528 Whiffen Spit Rd., Sooke. ☎ **250/642-3421.** Reservations required. Main courses C$29–C$36 (U.S.$19–U.S.$23). AE, ER, MC, V. Daily 5–9pm. Take the Island Hwy. to the Sooke/Colwood turnoff (Junction Hwy. 14). Continue on Hwy. 14 to Sooke. About a mile (1.6km) past the town's only traffic light, turn left onto Whiffen Spit Rd. WEST COAST.

In a rambling white house on a bluff overlooking Sooke's Whiffen Spit, this restaurant/hotel offers spectacular waterfront views and a quiet, relaxed atmosphere. Hosts Frederica and Sinclair Philip will immediately make you feel at home as you dine on imaginatively prepared West Coast cuisine, featuring local seafood and organically grown produce. Halibut baked in a crust of herbs, sunflower seeds, and Parmesan is accompanied by a roasted carrot, coriander, and parsley purée, while roasted veal is served with a wild-mushroom, port-wine, and lovage sauce.

JUAN DE FUCA MARINE TRAIL

This new long-distance hiking trail links China Beach Park, just past the town of Jordan River, to Botanical Beach Provincial Park, near Port Renfrew, along a stretch of near-wilderness coastline. Similar to the famed West Coast Trail, but less extreme in the demands it exacts from hikers, the rugged 29-mile (47km) trail offers scenic beauty, spectacular hiking, wildlife viewing, and roaring surf in its course along the Pacific coastline of the Strait of Juan de Fuca. Most of the trail is designed for strenuous day or multiday hiking. Unlike the West Coast Trail, this trail can be easily broken down into daylong segments between trailheads accessed along Highway 14: China Beach, Sombrio Beach, Parkinson Creek, and Botanical Beach. Plan on 3 days to hike the entire thing; campsites are regularly spaced along the trail.

The Juan de Fuca Marine Trail is designed as a wilderness hiking trail. Conditions are always changing, so before proceeding, hikers should obtain up-to-date information by checking the trailhead information shelters. There will be ongoing construction and upgrading on the trail for a number of years. Wear proper footwear and appropriate clothing, and leave a plan of your trip (including which trail you're hiking) with arrival and departure times with a friend or relative.

For information on Juan de Fuca Marine Park, contact **BC Parks,** South Vancouver Island District, 2930 Trans-Canada Hwy., Victoria, BC, V9E 1K3 (☎ **250/391-2300;** fax 250/478-9211; www.bcparks.bc.ca). Another good Web site about the park is at **www.sookenet.com/sooke/activity/trails/jdftrail.html**.

IN & AROUND PORT RENFREW

Port Renfrew is a small seaside village whose main claim to fame is as one of the termini of the West Coast Trail. Day-trippers from Vancouver also make the trip out to visit ✪ **Botanical Beach Provincial Park,** an area with spectacular tide-pool formations, unique geology, and one of the richest intertidal zones on the entire North American west coast. About 2¹/₂ miles (4km) south of Port Renfrew, Botanical Beach is a ledge of sandstone that juts out into the churning waters of the Strait of Juan de Fuca. Over the millennia, tidal action has carved and gouged out pits and pools in the intertidal sandstone, which is where you'll find incredibly rich tide pools filled with sea urchins, clams, coralline algae, periwinkles, giant anemones, chitons and sea stars, and other marine flora and fauna. In spring and fall, watch for passing gray whales. It's a good idea to check local tide tables to maximize opportunities for wildlife and tide-pool viewing. A low tide of 4 feet (1.2m) or less is best for viewing. Various trails lead through the park; picnic facilities and toilets are available.

WHERE TO STAY & DINE

There aren't many choices for spending the night in Port Renfrew, and the lodgings are mostly geared to the long-distance backpacking set coming to or from the West Coast Trail. The **West Coast Motel,** Parkinson Road (☎ **877/299-2288** or 250/ 647-5565), has clean, simple double rooms with kitchenettes for C$89 (U.S.$58).

5 North of Victoria: Goldstream Provincial Park

North of Victoria, the Island Highway climbs up over the high mountain ridge called the Malahat, shedding the suburbs as it climbs. ✪ **Goldstream Provincial Park** is a tranquil arboreal setting that overflowed with prospectors during the 1860s gold-rush days, hence its name. Today, its natural beauty attracts hikers, campers, and birders who stop to spend a few hours or days in the beautiful temperate rain forest.

Hiking trails take you past abandoned mine shafts and tunnels as well as 600-year-old stands of towering Douglas fir, lodgepole pine, red cedar, indigenous yew, and arbutus trees. The **Gold Mine Trail** leads to Niagara Creek and the abandoned mine that was operated by Lt. Peter Leech, a royal engineer who discovered gold in the creek in 1858. The **Goldstream Trail** goes to the salmon-spawning areas (you might also catch sight of mink and river otters racing along this path).

Three species of salmon (chum, chinook, and steelhead) make **annual salmon runs** up the Goldstream River during the months of October, November, December, and February. Visitors can easily observe this natural wonder along the riverbanks.

Goldstream is also a major attraction for bird watchers, as numerous bald eagles winter here each year. January is the best month for spotting these majestic creatures.

For information on Goldstream Provincial Park and all other provincial parks on the South Island, contact **BC Parks** (☎ **250/391-2300**). Goldstream Park's **Freeman King Visitor Centre** (☎ **250/478-9414**) offers guided walks, talks, and programs geared towards kids (but interesting for adults, too) throughout the year. It's open daily from 9:30am to 6pm. Take Highway 1 about 20 minutes north of Victoria.

WHERE TO STAY

✪ **The Aerie.** 600 Ebedora Lane, P.O. Box 108, Malahat, BC, V0R 2L0. ☎ **250/743-7115.** Fax 250/743-4766. www.aerie.bc.ca. 24 units. A/C TV TEL. Apr 25–June 30 and Sept 5– Oct 14 C$180–C$240 (U.S.$117–U.S.$156) double, C$275–C$375 (U.S.$179–U.S.$244) suite; July 1–Sept 4 C$195–C$260 (U.S.$127–U.S.$169) double, C$295–C$425 (U.S.$192– U.S.$276) suite; Oct 15–Apr 24 C$150–C$200 (U.S.$98–U.S.$130) double, C$250–C$300 (U.S.$163–U.S.$195) suite. Rates include full breakfast. Accommodation and dinner packages available. AE, MC, V. Free parking. Take Hwy. 1 to the Spectacle Lake turnoff; take the first right and follow the winding driveway up.

Safe to say, there's nothing else on Vancouver Island like the Aerie. This Mediterranean-inspired villa was designed and decorated by Marie Schuster, an Austrian hotelier with gobs of money and unlimited self-confidence. For some, it's the very picture of paradise. For others, the result is a tad over the top. The setting—on the forested slopes of the Malahat—is certainly spectacular, and the view out over Finlayson Inlet is unsurpassed. Inside, no expense has been spared. Dior duvets sit atop gargantuan four-poster beds, and Persian carpets further soften the rooms. Extras include wet bars, fridges, and coffeemakers. The pricier suites have private decks and fireplaces. Rates include a 7am breakfast hamper at the door and full breakfast later on. Other extras include a helipad, indoor pool, outdoor hot tub, tennis courts, spa treatments, and outdoor wedding chapel. Most guests also stay here to sample the excellent cuisine in the dining room (see below), open to the public only for dinner.

WHERE TO DINE

The Aerie. 600 Ebedora Lane, Malahat. ☎ **250/743-7115.** Reservations required. Main courses C$28–C$32 (U.S.$18–U.S.$21); 7-course set menu C$60 (U.S.$39). AE, MC, V. Daily 5–10pm. Free parking. Take Hwy. 1 to the Spectacle Lake turnoff; take the first right and follow the winding driveway. FRENCH.

Ornate. Overwhelming. Over the top? Depends on your tastes. The dining room of this villa boasts panoramic windows with views of the ocean and mountain, a gold-leaf ceiling, chandeliers, gilt chairs, and faux-marble columns. When it comes to the cooking, over-the-top might be a good thing. Consider, for example, an appetizer of venison-and-pistachio pâté with dried-fruit compote, juniper-and-port glaze, and herbed sunflower croutons. Entrees include beef tenderloin with a caramelized shallot crust in a red-wine-and-rosemary reduction, and roasted lamb chop with a currant-and-cracked-pepper glaze. Topping off the evening is a Belgian-chocolate–and-hazelnut-nougat pyramid with Frangelico ganache. An excellent selection of brandies and coffee will take you over the peak and down the far side.

Six Mile Pub. 494 Island Hwy., View Royal. ☎ **250/478-3121.** Main courses C$4.50–C$8 (U.S.$2.95–U.S.$5). ER, MC, V. Daily 11:30am–2pm and 6–9pm. Pub, Mon–Sat 11am–1am, Sun 11am–midnight. PUB.

Housed in a building dating from 1855, this pub has a rich history. Originally named the Parson's Bridge Hotel (after the man who built Parson's Bridge, which opened the Sooke area to vehicle traffic), it was filled with sailors when the Esquimalt Naval Base opened nearby in 1864. When Victoria elected to continue prohibition until 1952, the Six Mile Pub became the hub for provincial bootleggers. With a lively bar, a huge banquet room, and a few intimate dining rooms, it has broad appeal. Loyal locals come for both the atmosphere and the dinner specials. The food is seasoned with fresh herbs from the pub's own garden. You can enjoy the warm ambiance of the fireside room, which has an oak bar with stained glass, or the beautiful scenery from the outdoor patio. Start with one of the 10 house brews on tap, then enjoy a steak-and-mushroom pie, juicy prime rib, or tasty veggie burger.

6 Duncan & the Cowichan Valley

Duncan: 36 miles (57km) N of Victoria

The Cowichan Valley is one of the richest agricultural areas on Vancouver Island. The Cowichan Indians have lived in the valley for millennia, and today the band's reservation spreads immediately to the south of the town of Duncan. European settlers, drawn by the valley's deep soil and warm temperatures, established farms here in the 1870s. Although the orchards and sheep pastures of yore remain, the valley's providential location also makes it one of the few sites in western British Columbia for vineyards, a new and booming crop.

For visitors, the town of Duncan, at the center of the Cowichan Valley, may seem a pretty low-key place, but its centrality to excellent recreation and cultural sights make it a comfortable, inexpensive hub for exploring this part of Vancouver Island. Lake Cowichan is a popular summertime getaway, with swimming beaches and boating. Maple Bay and Cowichan Bay are marina-dominated harbor towns with good pubs and restaurants, plus enchanting views. And don't forget those wineries: Cowichan Valley is home to several good ones, most with tasting rooms open to the public.

ESSENTIALS

GETTING THERE   Duncan is 36 miles (57km) north of Victoria on Highway 1. It's also a stop on the **E&N Railiner.** For information, contact **VIA Rail** (☎ 800/561-8630; www.viarail.ca). **Laidlaw Coach Lines** (☎ 250/385-4411) passes through Duncan on its Victoria/Nanaimo service.

VISITOR INFORMATION   Contact the **Duncan Visitor Information Centre,** 381A Trans-Canada Hwy., Duncan, BC, V9L 3R5 (☎ 250/746-4636), which is open from April 15 to October 15. For year-round information on Duncan and the entire Cowichan Valley area, contact the **Cowichan Tourism Association,** 135 Third St., Duncan, BC, V9L 1R9 (☎ 250/715-0709; www.cowichan.bc.ca).

EXPLORING THE AREA
DUNCAN: THE CITY OF TOTEM POLES

Duncan is a bustling little city of 5,330, a welcoming place with a population mix of First Nation people and descendants of European settlers. Congested Highway 1 runs to the east of the old town center, and you'll miss Duncan's pleasingly old-fashioned charm if you don't get off the main drag (follow signs for Old Town Duncan).

Downtown Duncan still bustles with stationers, dress shops, bakeries, haberdasheries, cafes, candy shops—it's the quintessential small and friendly Canadian town. **Judy Hill Gallery,** 22 Station St. (☎ 250/746-6663), is an excellent place to shop for Cowichan wood carvings, gifts, and Cowichan sweaters.

The main reason to make a detour downtown is to see the city's impressive collection of modern **totem poles.** This part of Native America is famed for its carving skills. However, most historic totem poles are now in museums or are rotting in front of abandoned villages, and few First Nation Canadians had any reason to keep the old skills and traditions alive. In the 1980s, the mayor of Duncan began an ambitious project of commissioning local native artists to carve new totem poles, which were then erected around the city. Today, with more than 80 totem poles rising above the downtown area, Duncan's public art is one of the world's largest collections of modern totem carving, a wonderful assemblage that represents the continuation of an ancient art form unique to the Northwest coast.

The totem poles are scattered around the city, mostly in the pedestrian-friendly downtown area. Touring the totems can be an ad hoc affair: Simply follow the yellow shoeprints on the pavement, and you'll be led to most of the carvings. You can also take a free walking tour; starting at the Cowichan Valley Museum, in the E&N Railway station at Station Street and Canada Avenue, guides lead hour-long tours, explaining the significance of the figures and symbols. The tours are given May to mid-September from 10am to 1pm. Reserve by calling ☎ 250/715-1700.

The B.C. Forest Discovery Centre. 2892 Drinkwater Rd., 1.2 miles (2km) north of Duncan on Hwy. 1. ☎ 250/715-1113. www.bcforestmuseum.com. May 1 to Labour Day daily 10am–6pm.

British Columbia is one of the world's largest producers of forest products, and the B.C. Forest Discovery Centre explores the history of the logging industry. In recent years, the focus of the exhibits at this extensive 100-acre site has shifted from an unreflective paean to tree cutting to a more thoughtful examination of sustainable forestry practices, woodland ecosystems, and the role (sometimes surprising) of wood products in our lives. No matter what you may think of logging as a practice, the history of forestry in British Columbia is fascinating, and this museum and interpretive center does a good job of presenting both the high and low points. Kids will love the vintage steam train, which circles the grounds on narrow-gauge rails.

✪ **Cowichan Native Village.** 200 Cowichan Way. ☎ **250/746-8119.** www. cowichannativevillage.com. Admission C$6 (U.S.$3.90) adults, C$5 (U.S.$3.25) seniors and students 13–17, C$3 (U.S.$1.95) children 5–12; C$15 (U.S.$10) families. Summer daily 9:30am–5pm, winter daily 10am–4:30pm.

The Cowichan tribe were the original inhabitants of this valley, and the tribe's cultural history and traditional way of life are the focus of Cowichan Native Village, on the southern edge of downtown Duncan. The large, parklike enclosure along the Cowichan River contains several modern longhouse structures flanked by totem poles. Join a guided walking tour of the village, or take a seat in the multimedia theater to watch the excellent presentation *The Great Deeds,* a retelling of Cowichan myth and history. At the building devoted to traditional carving, you can talk to carvers as they work, and even take up a chisel to whittle on a cedar log.

The Cowichan native tribes are famous for their bulky, durable sweaters, knit with bold motifs from hand-spun raw wool. The art gallery is the best place in the valley to buy these hand-knit sweaters (expect to pay around C$250/U.S.$163), as well as carvings, prints, jewelry, and books. In summer, the cafe serves traditional native foods and more-standard fare. It's a good idea to call ahead to time your visit to coincide with special events, such as salmon bakes and powwows.

Cowichan Bay

This small but busy working port town edges along the mouth of the Cowichan River. Once the primary transportation hub of the region and a major fishing port, Cowichan Bay is still an important lumber shipment point and a bustling leisure-boat harbor. Just 4.3 miles (7km) southeast of Duncan, many travelers make the journey to Cowichan Bay to walk the boardwalks and wharves, to enjoy a meal above the marina, and to admire the boats amid the sounds, smells, and sights of a working harborside village.

The **Cowichan Bay Maritime Centre** (☎ **250/746-4955**), which stretches the length of an abandoned pier in the harbor, tells the story of the clash of native and European cultures in the Cowichan Valley. It also serves as a workshop for the building of wooden boats. Admission is C$1 (U.S.65¢).

If the unique ecosystems of Vancouver Island and the Georgia Strait interest you, stop by the **Marine Ecology Station,** on Pier 66. The exhibits in the small, floating-aquarium building are mostly geared for curious students—touch tanks filled with marine life, as well as microscopes for peering at smaller ocean life and minicourses focusing on environmental education. The entire family will enjoy the station's special summer programs, which range from daylong field trips on tide-pool exploration to weeklong ecotours of the Gulf Islands. The programs change yearly, and advance registration is required. Request a schedule from the **Marine Ecology Station,** RR 1, Cowichan Bay, BC, V0R 1N0 (☎ **250/748-4522;** http://mareco.org).

Maple Bay & Genoa Bay

Maple Bay is a lovely little harbor town 4.3 miles (7km) northeast of Duncan. Although there's nothing special to do once here, it's worth the short drive just to take in the view—a placid bay of water beneath steep-sloped, mesalike mountains—which inevitably leads to dreams of buying real estate. There's no better place to ponder the vista than at the ✪ **Brigantine Inn** (☎ **250/746-5422**), a friendly pub with local brews on draft, bar meals, and a bayside deck.

Genoa Bay is directly south of Maple Bay. This tiny harbor is actually on Cowichan Bay, though the mountainous terrain mandates that overland transport make a circuitous route around Mount Tzouhalem and past Birds Eye Cove. Again, the point of the journey is the charm and beauty of the location—mountain slopes dropping off into calm seawaters. Enjoy a meal or drink at the **Grapevine Cafe** (see "Where to Dine," below). The Grapevine also operates **Genoa Bay Charters** (☎ **250/746-0797;** www.cowichan.com/business/grapevine) out of the marina adjacent to the restaurant. The MV *Rendezvous* was built in the 1940s as an Anglican-church mission ship, but now functions as a small cruise ship for sightseeing and adventure charters. If you're traveling with a group or large family, consider a day of Gulf Island exploration, complete with catered meals from the Grapevine.

Cowichan Valley Vineyards

The warm summers and mild winters of the Cowichan Valley make this one of the few areas in western British Columbia where wine grapes flourish. Pinot noir, pinot gris, Marechale Foch, and gewürztraminer are popular varietals. The following wineries welcome guests, and most will arrange tours with sufficient notice.

Blue Grouse Vineyards and Winery, 4365 Blue Grouse Rd., south of Duncan off Kiksilah Road (☎ **250/743-3834**), is open for tastings Wednesday through Sunday from 11am to 5pm. **Alderlea Vineyards,** 1751 Stamps Rd., near Maple Bay (☎ **250/746-7122**), is open Saturday and Sunday from 1 to 5pm.

Cherry Point Vineyards, 840 Cherry Point Rd., in Cobble Hill east of Cowichan Bay (☎ **250/743-1272**), is one of the most prominent Cowichan Valley wineries, with national awards to prove it; the tasting room is open daily from 11am to 6pm.

Vigneti Zanatta Winery and Vineyards, 5039 Marshall Rd., south of Duncan near the little community of Glenora (☎ **250/748-2338**), is open Tuesday through Sunday from noon to 5pm. Its restaurant, Vinoteca, is one of the best places to eat in the Duncan area (see "Where to Dine," below).

Venturi-Schulze Vineyards, 4235 Trans-Canada Hwy., Cowichan Station (☎ **250/743-5630**), is a must for oenophiles, with some of the most outstanding wines in Canada. However, it is only open for tours by appointment. Venturi-Schulze does offer frequent intimate winemaker dinners served in the vineyard's 100-year-old farmhouse, so give them a call in advance and ask about the schedule.

Another twist on the local scene is **Merridale Cider,** 1230 Merridale Rd., Cobble Creek (☎ **800/998-9908**), which produces both apple and pear cider.

Lake Cowichan, Cowichan River & the Backcountry

Lake Cowichan, 19 miles (31km) west of Duncan on Highway 18, is a long, narrow lake nestled between mountain slopes. With a population of 3,116, it's one of the primary summer playgrounds for valley residents. A number of provincial parks provide access to swimming beaches, boat landings, and campsites; Gordon Park Provincial Park, on the lake's south shore, is the most convenient for Duncan-based travelers.

Backcountry explorers can follow the roads along both sides of 18.6-mile-long (30km) Lake Cowichan to access remote areas of Vancouver Island's wilderness west coast. Well-maintained forestry roads from Cayuse and Honeyman Bay, on the south side of the lake, lead to **Port Renfrew,** one of the beginning points of the Pacific Rim National Park's famed West Coast Trail (see section 4, "West of Victoria: Sooke Harbour & Port Renfrew"). From here, paved roads connect to Sooke and Victoria. From the west end of Cowichan Lake, gravel roads lead to **Nitinat Lake,** a tidal lake renowned for its challenging windsurfing. **Carmanah/Walbran Provincial Park,** a vast preserve of misty old-growth forests, is also accessed from these networks of roads.

The Cowichan River flows east out of Lake Cowichan. The **Cowichan River Trail,** a hiking trail that parallels the deep, fast-flowing river through fern glades and forests of cedar and mossy-trunked aspen, provides excellent access to the beautiful, jade-green waters. The 12.4-mile (20km) trail begins just east of Lake Cowichan, below Skutz Falls (follow signs from Hwy. 18 for Skutz Falls Trailhead), and follows the river to Glenora, southeast of Duncan. The river is also popular for steelhead and trout fishing, as well as kayaking. Inquire locally before rafting or kayaking the river: Some canyon rapids are considered too dangerous for passage.

WHERE TO STAY
IN & AROUND DUNCAN

Best Western Cowichan Valley Inn. 6474 Trans-Canada Hwy., RR 4, Duncan, BC, V9L 6C6. ☎ **800/927-6199** or 250/748-2722. Fax 250/748-2207. E-mail: bwcvi@island.net. 42 units. A/C TV TEL. C$95–C$105 (U.S.$62–U.S.$68) double. Extra person C$6 (U.S.$3.90). AE, ER, MC, V. Located 1.2 miles (2km) north of Duncan.

Duncan's most comfortable full-service lodging, and conveniently located for visiting the B.C. Forestry Centre, this Best Western makes it easy to enjoy your stay in the Cowichan Valley. The handsomely furnished guest rooms come with coffeemakers, fridges, and data ports. Facilities include Choices, one of the best family restaurants in Duncan; a fitness center; and a small outdoor pool. The hotel's beer-and-wine shop is one of the best places in town to shop for local wines.

Fairburn Farm Country Manor. 3310 Jackson Rd., Duncan, BC, V9L 6N7. ☎ and fax **250/746-4637.** www.gec.net/fairburn. E-mail: fairburn@gec.net. 7 units. C$110–C$140 (U.S.$72–U.S.$91). Extra person C$20 (U.S.$13). MC, V. Closed Oct 15–Mar 31.

If you dream of an idealized farm vacation, this is your B&B. You'll feel instantly at home, even if the closest you've ever come to rural living is mowing your lawn. Fairburn Farm and its marvelously rambling farmhouse have been in existence since the 1880s. The beautifully preserved farmhouse boasts high ceilings, antique moldings, tiled fireplaces, and a broad columned porch that overlooks gardens, meadows, and mountain slopes. This is one of the few B&Bs that welcome families.

Guests are welcome—but not obliged—to join in farm activities: This is a real working farm, with chickens, cattle, orchards, and a new enterprise—a water-buffalo dairy for the production of authentic mozzarella. You can commune with the hens, turkeys, and friendly sheepdogs, or, if your idea of a vacation is relaxing with a glass of wine in the gazebo, you're invited to watch the cycles of rural life from a distance. The friendly proprietors serve breakfasts of homemade baked goods, fresh Fairburn Farm eggs, and orchard fruit. *Note:* Smoking is not permitted.

Silver Bridge Inn. 140 Trans-Canada Hwy., Duncan, BC, V9L 3P7. ☎ **888/858-2200** or 250/748-4311. Fax 250/748-1774. E-mail: silver@seaside.net. 33 units. A/C TV TEL. C$59–C$74 (U.S.$38–U.S.$48) double. Extra person C$10 (U.S.$7). Kitchen C$5–C$10 (U.S.$3.25–U.S.$7) extra. Weekly, monthly, group, corporate, and sports-team rates and packages available. AE, MC, V.

Moderately priced and well-maintained rooms make the Silver Bridge a good choice. Located next to the Cowichan River, the motel is within walking distance of the Cowichan Native Village. The Silver Bridge Restaurant offers Cantonese and Canadian buffets. The Bridge Pub, with an attractive shaded deck, is a converted century-old house.

Village Green Inn. 141 Trans-Canada Hwy., Duncan, BC, V9L 3P8. ☎ **800/665-3989** in Canada, or 250/746-5126. Fax 250/746-5126. www.bctravel.com/si/villagegreen.html. E-mail: villagegreen@seaside.net. 80 units. TEL. C$64 (U.S.$42) double, C$79 (U.S.$51) suite. Kitchen C$10 (U.S.$7) extra. Senior discounts available. AE, MC, V.

Situated on the Island Highway (Trans-Canada Hwy.) near the Cowichan Native Village, this inn contains accommodations that are tastefully decorated in muted tones. All rooms offer ample amounts of peace and quiet. Some units are equipped with kitchenettes and air-conditioning. Amenities include free local calls, in-room coffee, an indoor pool, a sauna, tennis courts, a beer-and-wine store, and a family-style restaurant and bar and grill.

IN COWICHAN BAY

Inn at the Water Resort (Howard Johnson). P.O. Box 39, 1681 Cowichan Bay Rd., Cowichan Bay, BC, V0R 1N0. ☎ **800/663-7898** or 250/748-6222. Fax 250/748-7122. www.bctravel.com/si/inn-at-the-water.html. E-mail: iatw@bctravel.com. 56 suites. TEL. C$105 (U.S.$68) double. Extra person C$10 (U.S.$7). Children 16 and under stay free in parents' room. Senior discounts, weekend getaway specials, and midweek specials available. AE, DC, ER, MC, V. Small pets accepted.

Located just above the busy boat and seaplane harbor of Cowichan Bay, this all-suite hotel—now operated by the Howard Johnson chain—offers incredible views and high-quality accommodations. The spacious rooms have been recently renovated and refurbished, each containing a balcony and kitchenette. Salt Water Moon is a water-front restaurant serving West Coast cuisine. Other facilities include a lounge with patio, indoor pool, saunas, Jacuzzis, exercise room, and beer-and-wine store.

Old Farm B&B. 2075 Cowichan Bay Rd., Cowichan Bay, BC, V0R 1N0. ☎ **888/240-1482** or 250/748-6410. Fax 250/748-6410. www.cvnet.net/cowb&b/oldfarm. E-mail: oldfarm@ seaside.net. 3 units. C$75–C$120 (U.S.$49–U.S.$78) double. Extra person C$20 (U.S.$13). Rates include breakfast. MC, V. Children must be 12 or over.

This friendly bed-and-breakfast's history begins in 1908, when an English sea captain built his country dream home on the Cowichan River estuary. The handsome main house has three large second-floor guest rooms, all with private bathrooms, brass beds, ceiling fans, and small refrigerators; one unit has a private deck. There are two addi-tional bedrooms on the third floor, each with two twin beds, which can be rented in combination with one of the other guest rooms. (This option is popular with families and with groups traveling together.) The Robert Service Suite—named for the poet laureate of the Klondike, who hailed from near here—is popular with honeymooners. This second-floor cottage suite has a private entrance, small kitchen, deck, and bath-room with two-person Jacuzzi. The hosts pride themselves on the quality of amenities: luxury sheets and towels, along with imported shampoos and lotions. Guests can enjoy the library, sitting room with fireplace, dining room, badminton court, gazebo, and hot tub. *Note:* Smoking is not permitted.

WHERE TO DINE
IN & AROUND DUNCAN

Asta Pasta. 20 Station St. ☎ **250/748-0706.** Reservations recommended. Main courses C$15–C$18 (U.S.$10–U.S.$12). AE, MC, V. Mon–Thurs 10am–9pm, Fri–Sat 10am–10pm. ITALIAN/INTERNATIONAL.

Duncan locals swear by this cheerful Italian deli and cafe, and for good reason: The menu is a balance of fresh, well-seasoned pasta dishes plus a good selection of inter-national choices incorporating local fish, beef, lamb, and poultry. Entrees range from grilled Caribbean lamb T-bone with jerk sauce to grilled swordfish crusted with sesame seeds and served with wasabi and ginger. If you're looking for picnic fare, the deli case is loaded with air-dried sausage, cheeses, salads, and marinated vegetables.

Just Jakes. 45 Craig St. ☎ **250/746-5622.** Reservations not accepted. Main courses C$7–C$16 (U.S.$4.55–U.S.$10). AE, MC, V. Mon–Thurs 11am–9pm, Fri–Sat 11am–10pm. BURGERS/LIGHT DINING.

This laid-back, funky restaurant is a friendly place for a casual meal. The atmosphere is a cross between a fern bar and an old-fashioned soda fountain, and the staff is young and engaging—a mix that's guaranteed to put you at ease. The menu offers a wide selection of boutique burgers, plus entree salads, steaks, and pasta: pleasantly passé food that perfectly mirrors Duncan's attractively slow-paced downtown.

Vinoteca. At Vigneti Zanatta Winery, 5039 Marshall Rd., near Glenora south of Duncan (call for directions). ☎ **250/748-2338.** Reservations recommended. Main courses C$4.50–C$11 (U.S.$2.95–U.S.$7). MC, V. Tues–Wed and Sun noon–5pm; Thurs–Sat noon to dusk. Closed Nov–Apr. LIGHT DINING.

A combination wine-tasting room and tapas bar, Vinoteca is located in a historic farmhouse at the scenic Vigneti Zanatta vineyards (see "Cowichan Valley Vineyards," above). The menu is styled to reflect the family's Italian background and to play counterpoint to the wines produced on the farm. The dishes are based on hearty country fare: salads, marinated vegetables, bruschetta, and a daily fresh-pasta selection. Each menu item is paired with a wine suggestion. As much as possible, the ingredients used at Vinoteca are grown on the farm or nearby. In summer, when days are long and the restaurant is open until dusk, this is a great place for a light meal.

In Cowichan Bay

✪ **Masthead Restaurant.** 1705 Cowichan Bay Rd., Cowichan Bay. ☎ **250/748-3714.** Reservations recommended. Main courses C$15–C$21 (U.S.$10–U.S.$14). AE, MC, V. Tues–Sun 5:30–10pm. WEST COAST.

In the glory days of Cowichan Bay, the building that now houses the Masthead Restaurant was the town's original hotel. The historic hotel's dining room and bar—and a modern deck overlooking the busy marina and harbor—now serves the Duncan area's finest Northwest cuisine. Fish and seafood is the specialty, naturally enough. Appetizers include succulent crab cakes, sauced with a jalapeño lime aioli. Salmon is served two ways: grilled with fresh pesto sauce, or baked in parchment with leek and fennel root. A real showstopper is the halibut, pan-fried with a hazelnut crust and served with an orange ginger butter sauce. Meat-eaters need not fret: The rack of lamb, served with a minted blueberry sauce, is another standout. The light and airy dining room manages to seem nicely traditional without being cloying or overdecorated. In good weather, request a table on the back deck.

Rock Cod Café. 4-1759 Cowichan Bay Rd., Cowichan Bay. ☎ **250/746-1550.** Reservations not accepted. Main courses C$6–C$11 (U.S.$3.90–U.S.$7). MC, V. Daily 9am–11pm. SEAFOOD.

It's no secret that the Rock Cod Café has the best fish-and-chips in the area. The local cod and fries are a full meal and then some, and the fish can't get much fresher than this: From the cafe's back deck, you can watch the fish coming in off the boats. The seafood chowder is also quite good, and the chalkboard menu is crammed with whatever else is fresh; in season, the oysters are superlative. The dining room is strictly utilitarian, but the deck overlooking the harbor is pleasant. Since the cafe has a liquor license—something most British fish-and-chip shops can't boast—you can turn a humble meal of halibut and fries into an afternoon's worth of pleasure.

IN GENOA BAY

✪ **The Grapevine Cafe.** Genoa Bay Marina, in Genoa Bay. ☎ **250/746-0797.** Reservations recommended. Main courses C$17–C$20 (U.S.$11–U.S.$13). MC, V. Mon–Fri 11:30am–2:30pm and 5:30–8pm (last reservation); Sat–Sun 7:30am–2:30pm and 5:30–8pm (last reservation). PACIFIC NORTHWEST.

One of the most delightful dining experiences in the Duncan area is found at the Grapevine, a relaxed yet stylish restaurant adjacent to the Genoa Bay Marina. From the dining room or the umbrella-festooned deck, you can follow the to-ing and fro-ing of pleasure boats and see towering forested bluffs reflected in the waters of the bay, all while sampling innovative, excellently prepared seafood, steaks, ribs, and seasonal specialties. Appetizer favorites include Cajun-spiced fried oysters with the house-secret spicy cream sauce. The prime rib is legendary, as are the baby-back ribs. Each day's menu also includes four fresh-fish or seafood specials, perhaps an arctic char with champagne caviar cream. What makes a meal here so satisfying—besides the dramatic scenery and peaceful atmosphere—is the food's perfect blend of restaurant sophistication and hearty home cooking.

7 En Route to Nanaimo

CHEMAINUS: THE CITY OF MURALS

Settled in the 1850s by European farmers, Chemainus (pop. 562) quickly became a major timber-milling and -shipment point, due to the town's Horseshoe Bay, the oldest deepwater port on the Canadian west coast. Prosperity saw the building of handsome homes and a solid commercial district. By the mid–20th century, the sawmills here were among the largest in the world, fed by the seemingly unending supply of wood from Vancouver Island's vast old-growth forests.

When the mills closed in 1983, the town slid into decline. Economic prospects for Chemainus seemed dim until someone had the bright idea of hiring an artist to paint a mural depicting the town's history. People—notably tourists—took notice, and soon mural painting became the raison d'être of the town. Chemainus claims to be Canada's largest permanent outdoor art gallery. Much of downtown is now covered with murals, most dealing with area history and local events.

Stop by the **Chemainus Visitor Info Centre,** 9758 Chemainus Rd. (☎ 250/246-3944), open from May 1 to September 1, for a walking-tour map of the murals. Across the street in Heritage Park is an informational kiosk where you can join a horse-drawn wagon tour of the murals (C$4/U.S.$2.60 for adults, C$2/U.S.$1.30 for kids). Or simply follow the yellow shoeprints painted on the sidewalks.

There are other reasons to explore the heart of Chemainus. Much of the town is quiet and pedestrian-oriented, making it a pleasant place for a stroll and a good spot for lunch. **Old Town Chemainus,** along Willow and Maple streets, is filled with Victorian cottages converted into shops and cafes.

The **Chemainus Theatre,** 9737 Chemainus Rd. (☎ 250/246-9800; www.ctheatre.bc.ca; e-mail: ctheatre@gec.net), is the town's most eye-catching building, a late-19th-century opera house that now serves as a very popular dinner theater. The season runs from mid-March through December; recent shows have included *The Importance of Being Earnest* and *Marvin's Room.* Ticket prices, which include a buffet lunch or dinner, range from C$38 (U.S.$25) to C$45 (U.S.$29) for adults; theater tickets without the buffet range from C$22 (U.S.$14) to C$26 (U.S.$17). The theater is usually dark on Sunday and Monday. Be sure to call ahead for reservations and to confirm show times.

WHERE TO STAY

Birdsong Cottage Bed & Breakfast. 9909 Maple St., Chemainus, BC, V0R 1K0. ☎ **250/ 246-9910.** Fax 250/246-2909. www.island.net/~birdsong. E-mail: birdsong@island.net. 4 units. C$105 (U.S.$68) rm double, C$325 (U.S.$211) cottage. Extra person C$20 (U.S.$13). Rates include breakfast and afternoon tea. MC, V.

Birdsong is not the kind of place that tries for anonymous decor. Filled with Victorian bric-a-brac and unusual objets d'art, this is an enchanting, English-style garden cottage offering quality accommodations. The owners, both professional musicians, admit to being "a bit theatrical." Rather an understatement: Whimsy pervades the place, from the extensive collection of Victorian hats (which guests are encouraged to try on) to the grand piano and Celtic harp (again, guests are encouraged to make themselves at home) to the recorded sound of birds trilling. The exterior carries on the theme, with a wraparound porch and turreted veranda, burbling fountains, and loads of architectural gingerbread. Everything here is over the top, but lovingly so.

The guest rooms are beautifully outfitted according to an avian theme, with quality furniture, linens, and fresh flowers. The Nightingale Room has access to a private garden and pond. New in 2000 is a cottage-cum-castle located in gardens behind the B&B. Fancifully designed to look like a fairy-tale tower, the luxury cottage has a kitchen, bathroom, dining room, sitting area, and hot tub, plus two balconies (copies of *Romeo and Juliet* are provided). Breakfasts are elaborate affairs. Your hosts will often provide musical divertissement while you eat.

WHERE TO DINE

Chemainus has a number of pleasant, informal places to grab a bite to eat. **Willow Street Café,** 9749 Willow St. (☎ **250/246-2434**), is a hip kind of eatery located in the main floor of an old hotel. The chalkboard menu features sandwiches, wraps, and salads; the umbrella-shaded deck is the best people-watching perch in town.

The Waterford Restaurant. 9875 Maple St. ☎ **250/246-1046.** Reservations recommended. Main courses C$13–C$20 (U.S.$8–U.S.$13). MC, V. Tues–Sun 11:30am–2:30pm and 5–9pm. NORTHWEST.

Located in the heart of historic Old Town, the Waterford is Chemainus's best choice for intimate fine dining. The antique-filled dining room is in a Victorian-era storefront that has been extended to include a lovely garden-side deck—an especially charming spot for lunch. The menu is a combination of seasonal improvisations and signature specialties. Chicken breast Brandon comes stuffed with a mixture of salmon and scallops; the rack of lamb melds the flavors of Dijon mustard, mint, and rosemary. Classics like sole almondine and filet mignon, served with béarnaise and sautéed mushrooms, are local favorites. The husband-and-wife team provide excellent service and accomplished, innovative cuisine.

LADYSMITH

The little community of Ladysmith makes much of the fact that its town is located on the 45th Parallel, which on the mainland separates much of Canada from the United States. A more intriguing reason to visit Ladysmith is to walk through the well-preserved Edwardian town center, and then adjourn to **Transfer Beach Park.** The protected waters here are said to provide the warmest saltwater swimming north of San Francisco, and are easily accessed along a long, pebbly beach. The park also has a large playground, picnicking area, and campsites.

CEDAR & YELLOW POINT

North of Ladysmith and south of Nanaimo, a broad forested peninsula juts out into the waters of the Georgia Strait. The land is rural and mostly undeveloped. The little community of Cedar is as close as the area comes to a town, and although there are a number of pleasant seafront parks here, this wouldn't qualify as much of a destination if it weren't for the fact that one of Vancouver Island's most popular lodges, one of the island's best restaurants, and the island's favorite pub are all located here. The area around Cedar and Yellow Point is a short drive from Nanaimo or Ladysmith, and a detour through the forests and farmland makes for a pleasant break from Highway 1.

WHERE TO STAY

✪ **Yellow Point Lodge.** 3700 Yellow Point Rd., Ladysmith, BC, V0R 2E0. ☎ **250/ 245-7422.** Fax 250/245-7411. 53 units. C$110–C$185 (U.S.$72–U.S.$120) double. Rates include all meals. AE, MC, V. Children must be 16 or older.

Beloved Yellow Point Lodge is located on 180 acres of forested waterfront, with over 1¹/₂ miles (2.4km) of rocky beach and secluded coves. This family-operated resort was established in the 1930s. The three-story log-and-stone building, which sits on a thrust of rock stretching out into the sea, has an enormous lobby, a huge fireplace, and a dining room with communal tables, all with wondrous views of Vancouver Island and the southern Gulf Islands. Inside the lodge are a number of comfortable hotel-like rooms, all with ocean views; scattered around the woods nearby are cabins and cottages in a wide range of styles. Most basic are the beach cabins and the Beach Barracks, rustic camp-style accommodations with communal washhouses. Some of the more luxurious one-, two-, and three-bedroom cottages have fireplaces.

Rates include everything you'll need to have a great vacation. Guests have free use of bikes, kayaks, and canoes, and trails for walking and hiking are on the property and in nearby provincial parks. Other facilities include a saltwater swimming pool, sauna, hot tub, and tennis, volleyball, and badminton courts. Meals are served in the dining room (or you can order a packed lunch), and a real sense of camaraderie develops among the guests. The good, home-style cooking features standards like roast beef and grilled salmon. If this unique blend of summer camp and luxury resort appeals to you, be sure to reserve well ahead. The lodge is a summer tradition for many people, and not just for the wealthy. Part of the charm of Yellow Point is that there are affordable lodging options here for almost everyone, and everyone gets the same friendly service.

WHERE TO DINE

✪ **The Crow & Gate.** 2313 Yellow Point Rd. ☎ **250/722-3731.** Reservations recommended. Main courses C$8–C$13 (U.S.$5–U.S.$8). AE, MC, V. Mon–Thurs 11am–11pm, Fri–Sat 11am–midnight. Take the Island Hwy. (Hwy. 19) north past Cassidy. Turn right on Cedar Rd., which leads onto Yellow Point Rd. Continue for 1 mile (1.6km). PUB.

This classic Tudor-style pub was built in 1972 on a 10-acre working farm. It's a friendly haven of English style and hospitality, flanked by ponds, rose arbors, and lawns. The large stone and half-timbered pub looks right out of the Cotswolds, with low ceilings, handcrafted beams, and gleaming brass accents complemented by a brick fireplace and leaded-glass windows. The menu offers the best of British-pub cooking, including roast beef and Yorkshire pudding, shepherd's pie, pasties, and roasted Cornish game hen. In summer, sit out on the beautiful flower-decked patio.

The Mahle House. At the corner of Cedar and Hemer rds., in Cedar. ☎ **250/722-3621.** Reservations required. Main courses C$14–C$23 (U.S.$9–U.S.$15). MC, V. Wed–Sun 5–10pm. PACIFIC NORTHWEST.

The Mahle (pronounced "Molly") House is located in a tiny country town, in a salmon-pink heritage home overlooking a park. From this unlikely address, it has developed a huge reputation for excellent regional cuisine emphasizing locally grown, mostly organic produce and meats, prepared with contemporary flourishes and traditional finesse. The weekly changing menu features such appetizers as calamari dijonaise or shiitake-and-brown-mushroom soup. For entrees, you might choose duck breast with ginger and mango sauce, chicken and prawns with three-citrus pistachio sauce, or free-range grilled chicken stuffed with goat cheese and chorizo sausage. Whatever you decide on, you can bet that the chef/owner has made use of the freshest possible products from the local area. The award-wining wine list is very extensive.

Central Vancouver Island 6

Central Vancouver Island's major population center is the formerly industrial city of Nanaimo, the arrival point for visitors taking ferries from the mainland and the site of a major 19th-century coal-mining operation. The city has recently begun to move away from its dependence upon resource extraction and is now sparkling with redevelopment, taking advantage of its scenic location—overlooking a bay full of islands, the choppy waters of Georgia Strait, and the not-so-distant glaciated peaks of the British Columbia mainland.

In sharp contrast to the serenity of the east-coast islands, the wild, raging beauty of the Pacific Ocean on Vancouver Island's west coast entices photographers, hikers, kayakers, naturalists, and divers to explore Pacific Rim National Park, Long Beach, and the neighboring towns of Ucluelet, Tofino, and Bamfield. Thousands of visitors arrive between March and May to see as many as 20,000 Pacific gray whales pass close to shore as they migrate north to their summer feeding grounds in the Arctic Circle. More than 200 shipwrecks have occurred off the shores in the past 2 centuries, luring even more travelers to this eerily beautiful underwater world. And the park's world-famous West Coast Trail beckons an international collection of intrepid backpackers and "extreme" hikers to brave the 10-day hike over the rugged rescue trail—established after the survivors of a shipwreck in the early 1900s died from exposure on the beach because there was no land-access route for the rescuers.

On east-central Vancouver Island, the towns of Parksville, Qualicum Beach, Courtenay, and Comox are famous for their warm, sandy beaches and for their numerous championship golf courses, while Denman and Hornby islands, off the east coast, offer visitors their own brand of unique bohemian charm.

Note: See the "Vancouver Island" map (pp. 104–105) to locate areas covered in this chapter.

1 Essentials

GETTING THERE
BY PLANE   See chapter 4 for details on flights to **Victoria,** the main air hub for all of Vancouver Island.

Nanaimo and Comox/Courtenay have regular air service from Vancouver International Airport. Other towns can be reached by scheduled harbor-to-harbor floatplane service, either from Vancouver International's seaplane terminal or from downtown Vancouver's Coal Harbour terminal. Since floatplanes don't require airport facilities, even the most remote fishing camp can be as accessible as a major city.

Air BC (☎ **800/776-3000** in the U.S., 800/663-3721 in B.C., or 250/360-9074), a division of Air Canada, and **Canadian Regional Airlines** (☎ **800/665-1177**), a division of Canadian Air, offer service to Comox/Courtenay, Nanaimo, and Victoria.

Commuter seaplane companies that serve Vancouver Island include **Harbour Seaplanes** (☎ 800/665-9308), **Pacific Spirit Air** (800/665-2359), **Air Rainbow** (604/681-0311), and **Baxter Aviation** (☎ 800/661-5599 or 250/754-1066).

BY FERRY **BC Ferries** (☎ **888/724-5223** in B.C., or 604/444-2890; www.bcferries.bc.ca) operates an extensive year-round network of car and passenger ferries that link Vancouver Island and the Gulf Islands to one another and to the mainland. Major routes include the crossing from Tsawwassen to Swartz Bay and to Nanaimo, and from Horseshoe Bay (west of Vancouver) to Nanaimo. In summer, reserve in advance. Sample fares are included in the regional sections that follow.

BY BUS One of the easiest ways to get to and from Vancouver and Vancouver Island destinations is by bus. Conveniently, the bus will start its journey from a city center (like Vancouver), take you directly to the ferry dock and onto the ferry, and then deposit you in another city center (Victoria or Nanaimo). A lot of the hassle of ferry travel is minimized, and the costs are usually lower than other alternatives. (If you're traveling to Vancouver on the VIA rail system, you'll find bus connections simple, as the buses and trains share the same terminal.)

Pacific Coach Lines (☎ **800/661-1725** or 604/662-8074; www.pacificcoach.com) offers bus service between downtown Vancouver via BC Ferries to downtown Victoria. The one-way fare is C$27 (U.S.$18) for adults, C$13 (U.S.$8) for children; in summer, there are more than a dozen departures daily.

Maverick Coach Tours provides service between Nanaimo and Vancouver; one-way transport is C$19 (U.S.$12). Reserve through Greyhound's network by calling ☎ **800/661-8747** or 604/482-8747. Information on these and other Canadian motor-coach services is available at Greyhound Canada's Web site (**www.greyhound.ca**).

VISITOR INFORMATION

For general information on Vancouver Island, contact the **Tourism Association of Vancouver Island,** Suite 302, 45 Bastion Sq., Victoria, BC, V8W 1J1 (☎ **250/382-3551;** fax 250/382-3523; www.islands.bc.ca; e-mail: tavi@islands.bc.ca).

GETTING AROUND

BY PUBLIC TRANSPORTATION While Vancouver Island has an admirable system of public transport, getting to remote sights and destinations is difficult without your own vehicle.

BC Ferries (☎ **888/724-5223** in B.C., or 604/444-2890; www.bcferries.bc.ca) links Vancouver Island ports to many offshore islands, including Gabriola and Denman and Hornby islands. None of these islands has public transport, so once there you'll need to hoof it, hitch it, hire a taxi, or arrange for bicycle rentals. Most innkeepers will pick you up from the ferry if you've reserved in advance.

Another charming way to get around Vancouver Island is on the **E&N Railway** (☎ **800/561-8630** or 250/383-4324), a division of VIA Rail that makes a daily round-trip run from Victoria to Courtenay in period passenger cars. The *Malahat* passes through beautiful landscapes on the east coast of Vancouver Island, taking about 4¹/₂ hours. Your ticket allows you to get on and off as many times as you'd like: You can stop at Chemainus, Nanaimo, Parksville, or Qualicum Beach and catch the return train back, or take the next day's train north. Ticket prices are very reasonable, especially with 7-day advance purchase. A round-trip between Victoria and Courtenay can cost as little as C$46 (U.S.$30). *Note:* The *Malahat* has no baggage car, and checked baggage service is not available.

Laidlaw Coach Lines (☎ **800/318-0818** or 250/385-4411; www.victoriatours. com) operates Vancouver Island's intercity bus service, which runs along the main highway from Victoria to Port Hardy, and from Nanaimo to Tofino. The one-way fare from Victoria to Nanaimo is C$18 (U.S.$12), from Nanaimo to Tofino C$30 (U.S.$20).

BY CAR   The southern half of Vancouver Island is well served by paved highways. The trunk road between Victoria and Nanaimo is **Highway 1,** the Trans-Canada Highway. This busy route alternates between four-lane expressway and congested two-lane highway, and requires patience and vigilance, especially during the busy summer months. North of Nanaimo, the major road north is **Highway 19,** which is largely a well-maintained two-lane highway, with expressway sections near Parksville and Qualicum Beach, and near Campbell River. The only other major paved road system on the island connects Parksville with Tofino, on the rugged west coast. Access to gasoline and car services is no problem, even in more remote north Vancouver Island.

Rental cars are readily available. Agencies include **Budget Car & Truck Rental** (☎ **800/268-8900** or 250/953-5300), **National Tilden Interrent** (☎ **800/ 387-4747** or 250/386-1213), and **Thrifty Car Rental** (☎ **800/367-2277** or 250/ 383-3659).

2 Nanaimo & Gabriola Island

Nanaimo: 70 miles (113km) N of Victoria

Vancouver Island's second-largest city (pop. 73,000), Nanaimo has come a long way in recent years. For over a century, the city was the center of vast coal-mining operations, developing as a rather drab, socially bifurcated community without much in the way of cultural niceties. In the last 20 years, however, the city has undergone quite a change. With its newly redeveloped waterfront, scenic surroundings, good restaurants, intriguing shops, and a location central to many other Vancouver Island destinations, there's plenty here for several days of exploration.

Just a 20-minute ferry ride from Nanaimo Harbour is Gabriola Island, though it feels a world away from the bustle of Vancouver Island. Gabriola makes a marvelous day trip from Nanaimo: The island provides a little of everything—sandy beaches, fine restaurants, artisans and galleries, petroglyph sites, and tide pools—without surrendering its sense of wooded serenity and isolation.

ESSENTIALS
GETTING THERE   By Plane   Regularly scheduled service between Vancouver International Airport and Nanaimo Airport, 15 miles (24km) south of the city near Cassidy, is offered by **Air BC** (☎ **800/776-3000** in the U.S., 800/663-3721 in B.C., or 250/360-9074) and **Canadian Regional Airlines** (☎ **800/665-1777**).

From Vancouver Harbour, you can fly to Nanaimo Harbour by floatplane. Both **Harbour Air Seaplanes** (☎ **800/665-0212** or 250/714-0900) and **Baxter Aviation** (☎ **800/661-5599** or 250/754-1066) offer scheduled and chartered flights.

By Car   Nanaimo is 70 miles (113km) from Victoria via Highway 1, the Trans-Canada Highway. At Nanaimo, the Trans-Canada crosses Georgia Strait via the Horse-shoe Bay ferry. North of Nanaimo, the main trunk road becomes Highway 19. It's 99 miles (161km) from Nanaimo to Campbell River, 128 miles (206km) to Tofino.

By Ferry   BC Ferries (☎ 888/724-5223 in B.C.) operates two major runs to Nanaimo. The crossing from Horseshoe Bay in West Vancouver to Nanaimo's Depar-ture Bay terminal is one of the busiest in the system, and you can expect delays most mornings. New PacifiCat Ferries began operation on this route in 1999; these catamarans cut the normal 1¹/₂-hour crossing down to just over an hour. The Tsawwassen ferry arrives and departs at Nanaimo's Duke Point terminal, just south of town off Highway 1. Ticket prices for both ferries are C$9 (U.S.$6) per driver or passenger, plus C$30 (U.S.$20) for a vehicle, with slightly higher prices on weekends.

By Train   The **E&N Railiner** operates daily service between Victoria and Courte-nay. The northbound train arrives just before 11am, the southbound at 5pm. For information, contact **VIA Rail** (☎ 800/561-8630; www.viarail.ca).

By Bus   Connections between Nanaimo and Vancouver are operated by Maverick Coach Lines, while buses to and from Victoria, Tofino, and Port Hardy are operated by Laidlaw Coach Lines. Schedules and reservations for both carriers are handled by **Greyhound Canada** (☎ 800/661-8747 or 604/482-8747; www.greyhound.ca).

VISITOR INFORMATION   For information on Nanaimo and vicinity, contact **Tourism Nanaimo,** Began House, 2290 Bowen Rd., Nanaimo, BC, V9T 3K7 (☎ 250/756-0106; fax 250/756-0075; www.tourism.nanaimo.bc.ca; e-mail: info@ tourism.nanaimo.bc.ca). In summer, a **Tourist Info Centre** operates out of the Bastion, the historic fort at Nanaimo's Pioneer Waterfront Plaza.

GETTING AROUND   Nanaimo Regional Transit System provides public trans-port in the Nanaimo urban area. For information, call ☎ 250/390-4531 or contact Tourism Nanaimo (see above). For a cab, call **AC Taxi** (☎ 800/753-1231 or 250/ 753-1231).

The BC Ferries run to and from Gabriola Island leaves from behind the Harbour Park Shopping Centre on Front Street (note that this is not the same ferry dock as either the Tsawwassen- or Horseshoe Bay–bound ferries) roughly every hour; a car passage is C$13 (U.S.$8) round-trip, while a driver, passenger, or pedestrian pays C$5 (U.S.$3.25). Bicycles are carried free of charge on the ferry; Gabriola, though not without challenging ascents, is a great island to explore on two wheels.

EXPLORING NANAIMO

Nanaimo's steep-faced waterfront has been recently restructured with tiers of walk-ways, banks of flowers, cubbyhole storefronts, marina boardwalks, and floating restau-rants. Called **Pioneer Waterfront Plaza,** the area fills on Fridays with the local farmers market. **The Bastion,** a white fortified tower, rises above the harbor as a relic of the 1850s, when the Hudson's Bay Company trading post at Nanaimo needed protection from the local natives (it now holds a summer tourist information center).

Part of the fun of hanging out on the harbor front is watching all of the activity. Nanaimo's busy natural port has ferry links to Vancouver's Horseshoe Bay and to Tsawwassen to the south, as well as to lovely **Gabriola Island** and to **Newcastle Island,** a car-free provincial park on the harbor's northern flank. Throughout the day, floatplanes buzz in and out of the boat basin, shuttling commuters back and forth to Vancouver. If you're up for a stroll or a run, the **Harbourside Walkway** stretches 2.4 miles (4km) from Departure Bay all the way to the waterfront in the heart of the city.

✪ Only in Nanaimo: The World Championship Bathtub Race

From its beginnings in 1967, Nanaimo's signature summer draw has grown into a weeklong series of events that shows off the city's good-natured spirit. Fewer than half of the original racing vessels—old clawfoot tubs fitted with engines—completed the crossing of 36-mile (58km) Georgia Strait from Nanaimo Harbour to Vancouver's Fisherman's Cove. Most capsized at Nanaimo—in fact, the first tub to sink now receives the coveted Silver Plunger Award. These days, most contestants race in specially designed tubs that look like single-person speedboats, but the addition of high technology doesn't dampen the high spirits of the event. The race is the climax of Marine Festival, which includes a street fair, parade, and traditional "Sacrifice to the Bathtub Gods": the ritual burning of a boat in Swy-A-Lana lagoon, followed by fireworks and music. For more information, contact Tourism Nanaimo (see "Visitor Information," above).

The old downtown, centered on Commercial, Front, and Bastion streets, is compressed into a series of winding narrow streets behind the harbor. A mix of old businesses and new boutiques makes this area quite pleasant to explore. The long-established **Scotch Bakery,** 87 Commercial St. (☎ 250/753-2711), is *the* place to sample the city's namesake baked confection. The delicious Nanaimo Bar is a chocolate, caramel cream, coconut, and almond bar cookie that was created as a treat for 19th-century coal miners.

Artisan's Studio, 70 Bastion St. (☎ 250/753-6151), is a co-op gallery that displays the work of Nanaimo-area artists and craftspeople. The **Artery Gallery and Art Centre,** 402-22 Commercial St. (☎ 250/716-2789), is a combination art-supply store/coffeehouse/gallery/performance space.

Another good strolling destination—particularly if you're hungry—is the **Old City Quarter,** an uptown section of the old city center that was severed from the harborfront commercial area when the Island Highway cut through downtown. Now reached from the harbor by walking up the Bastion Street overpass, the 3-block area has been redeveloped into upscale housing, boutiques, and eateries. You'll find some of the city's best restaurants in the courtyards and mews here.

Nanaimo District Museum. 100 Cameron Rd. ☎ **250/753-1821.** Admission C$1.75 (U.S.$1.15) adults, C75¢ (U.S.50¢) children. Daily 9am–5pm.

Nanaimo's regional museum is a worthwhile introduction to the area's long past, first as a home for the Snun-ymuxm and then as an industrial boomtown from the 1850s to the 1950s. An intriguing exhibit links painted dioramas of traditional Snun-ymuxm life with a simulation of an archaeological dig near Discovery Bay in 1992. In drawers beneath the dioramas are the actual artifacts found at the site and pictured in the paintings. Any museum in Nanaimo would need to retell the story of the region's long coal-mining history: The other half of the lower gallery is devoted to a replica of a working coal mine and the tools of early underground mining. The upper galleries present a maze of old storefront facades that re-create the feel of the frontier. There's also a gift shop with wooden carvings from the local Snun-ymuxm.

FERRYING TO NEWCASTLE ISLAND

Just off the Nanaimo coastline, **Newcastle Island Provincial Park** (☎ 250/387-4363) is an ideal destination for hikers, cyclists, and campers. Trails around the island lead through quiet woodlands onto beaches, around caves, and up to high overlooks.

Nanaimo

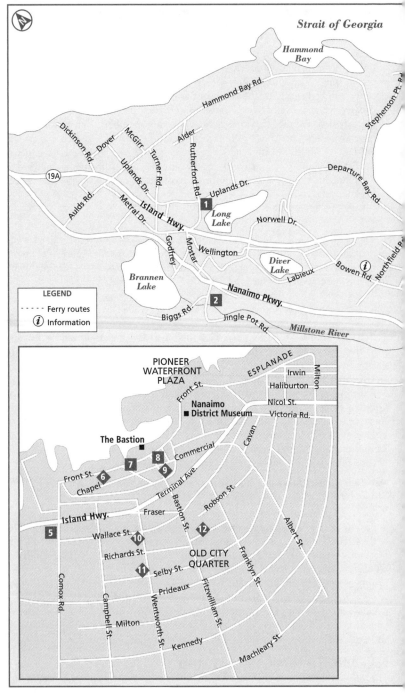

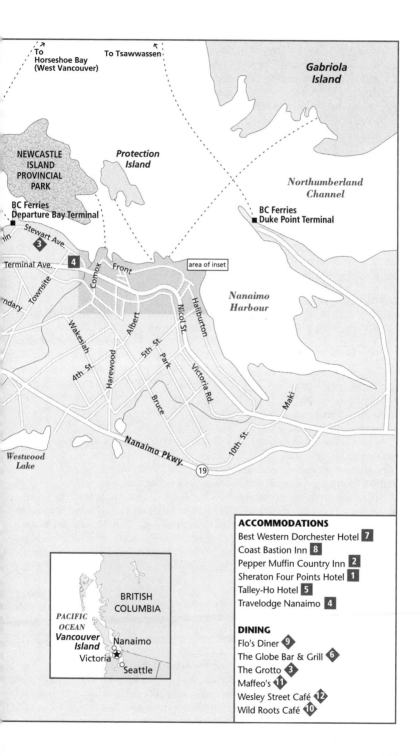

To Horseshoe Bay (West Vancouver)

To Tsawwassen

Gabriola Island

NEWCASTLE ISLAND PROVINCIAL PARK

Protection Island

Northumberland Channel

BC Ferries
■ Departure Bay Terminal

Stewart Ave.

3

Terminal Ave. **4**

BC Ferries
■ Duke Point Terminal

Townsite

Comox

Front

area of inset

Nanaimo Harbour

Wakesiah

Albert

Harewood

5th St.

Park

Nicol St.

Hallburton

4th St.

Bruce

Victoria Rd.

10th St.

Maki

Westwood Lake

Nanaimo Pkwy.

19

ACCOMMODATIONS

Best Western Dorchester Hotel **7**
Coast Bastion Inn **8**
Pepper Muffin Country Inn **2**
Sheraton Four Points Hotel **1**
Talley-Ho Hotel **5**
Travelodge Nanaimo **4**

DINING

Flo's Diner **9**
The Globe Bar & Grill **6**
The Grotto **3**
Maffeo's **11**
Wesley Street Café **12**
Wild Roots Café **10**

PACIFIC OCEAN

BRITISH COLUMBIA

Vancouver Island

Nanaimo

Victoria

Seattle

To get here, take the **ferry** (☎ 250/753-5141, or 250/387-4363 off-season). It leaves daily from the wharf behind Mafeo–Sutton Park's Civic Arena (just north of downtown) from May through October; departures occur almost hourly from 10am to 7:30pm. The 15-minute crossing costs C$4.75 (U.S.$3.10) for adults and C$3.75 (U.S.$2.45) for seniors and kids, round-trip; bikes are an extra C$1.75 (U.S.$1.15).

Newcastle Island was at one time a bustling island community. Two Salish native Indian villages were established here before British settlers discovered coal on the island in 1849. The Canadian-Pacific Steamship Company purchased the island in 1931, creating a resort with a dance pavilion, teahouse, picnic areas, changing houses, soccer field, wading pool, and floating hotel. The island became a provincial marine park in 1961, and now attracts outdoorsy types to its many trails. The popular **Mallard Lake Trail** leads through the wooded interior toward a freshwater lake, while the **Shoreline Trail** runs across steep sandstone cliffs, onto sand and gravel beaches suitable for sunbathing and swimming, past caves and caverns, and up to a great eagle-spotting perch, Giovando Lookout. The park maintains 18 **campsites** on the island's southern tip. Toilets, wood, fire pits, and water are strategically placed at three points on the campgrounds. Rates are C$12 (U.S.$8) per site.

GABRIOLA ISLAND

Much of Gabriola (pop. 3,412) is reached along North Road and South Road, two country lanes that provide a loop route around the island. A third road, Taylor Bay Road, departs from the ferry dock to access Gabriola's rocky northern reaches. It takes about half an hour to drive from one end of the island to the other.

The main commercial center is just up the hill from the ferry terminal and is often referred to as **Folklife Village.** The moniker seems a little precious until you learn that the log structure was originally constructed as the Folklife Pavilion for Vancouver's Expo '86 before being recycled as the island's shopping center. Be sure to stop by **Gabriola Artworks** (☎ 250/247-7412), an excellent gallery of local arts and crafts.

Sandwell Provincial Park, on Lock Bay, is one of Gabriola's nicest beaches and picnic areas, with paths leading through old-growth forests and to views of the Entrance Island lighthouse with the glaciated mainland peaks in the distance. To reach the park, turn off North Road onto Barrett Road and follow the signs.

At the southern end of Gabriola is Silva Bay, a marina resort with the popular **Bitter End Pub** (☎ 250/247-8662) and the outstanding **Latitudes Restaurant** (see "Where to Dine," below). Also near Silva Bay is ✪ **FOGO Folk Art Studio,** 3065 Commodore Way (☎ 250/247-8082; www.fogoart.com). The Lauders are wood-carvers with a sense of humor: Their intricately carved characters perfectly capture the quirks of human nature. Wandering around the studio grounds is a true delight.

Just south of Silva Bay, off South Road on Coast Road, is **Drumbeg Provincial Park,** which has a good swimming beach and picnic areas with views of the boat traffic on Gabriola Pass. A short trail from the parking lot leads to a stand of endangered Garry oaks and to another rocky beach.

Gabriola Island and the area around Nanaimo are rich in prehistoric **petroglyph rock carvings.** On the South Road, near the United Church (about 6.2 miles/10km from the ferry terminal), a short path leads to a group of these carvings. Scratched in sandstone, the carved figures are a mix of fantastical creatures, human forms, and abstract shapes. Park in the church lot and follow the signs.

South Road rejoins North Road near Folklife Village, after passing the nine-hole **Gabriola Golf and Country Club** (☎ 250/247-8822) and the small **Gabriola Historical Museum,** 505 South Rd. (☎ 250/247-9987).

Taylor Bay Road is the island's other road, which leads to more provincial parks and beaches on the north end of the island, as well as one of the finest B&Bs in the area. **Gabriola Sands Provincial Park** protects two of the island's best beaches, at Taylor Bay and Pilot Bay. At **Malaspina Galleries,** waves have differentially eroded a sandstone headland into thin fingers of stone separated by surging coves of water. In some areas, the waves have eaten away at the base of the rock, leaving prominent overhangs; the sheltered areas below are known as galleries.

Toward the end of the road (now called Berry Point Road) is the **Surf Lodge** (☎ 250/247-9231), with a pub and restaurant overlooking the Georgia Strait, and the superlative, seaside **Sunset B&B** (see "Where to Stay," below).

OUTDOOR PURSUITS

BUNGEE JUMPING   Looking for something out of the ordinary? Take the plunge off a 140-foot (43m) trestle at the **Bungy Zone** (☎ 888/668-7874 or 250/753-5867; www.bungyzone.com), off the Island Highway about 15 minutes south of Nanaimo. North America's only legal bridge jump sends you over the Nanaimo River from a specially constructed steel trestle bridge. The first jump costs C$95 (U.S.$62), the second C$75 (U.S.$49). Other adrenaline-pumping activities include the Ultimate Swing, which reaches speeds of 87 miles per hour (140kmph), and a zip line that speeds through a narrow canyon at 62 miles per hour (100kmph). The Bungy Zone is open year-round, daily from 10am to 4:30pm. Reservations are recommended from June through August. You can watch the jumpers for a C$2 to C$4 (U.S.$1.30 to U.S.$2.60) fee. There's free shuttle service from the ferry docks in Nanaimo.

✪ **DIVING**   All of the waters off Vancouver Island—often referred to as the Emerald Sea—are known for their superior scuba-diving opportunities. Nanaimo is an excellent gateway for exploring the undersea world populated by giant Pacific octopii, wolf eels, colorful sea anemones, and herds of marine mammals.

One of the single best dives in the Northwest is at **Dodds Narrows,** between Vancouver Island and Mudge Island. It boasts outstanding visibility, a high concentration of wildlife, dramatic rock formations, and colorful sea gardens of starfish and sponges. Other Nanaimo-area dives include **Snake Island Wall,** with a drop-off that seems to extend into the abyss, and **Gabriola Passage,** at that island's southern tip, across from Valdes Island. The latter dive offers a chance to explore an area rich in wildlife and extreme geological formations, with many cliffs and pinnacles over 100 vertical feet (30m). Probably the most popular dive is the wreck of the **HMCS *Saskatchewan.*** This 366-foot-long Canadian Naval Destroyer was sunk in 1997 as part of Canada's artificial reef project. Only 1¹/₂ miles (3km) from Nanaimo, and 60 feet (18m) below the surface, this sunken ship provides a fascinating showcase of marine-life colonization.

Diving is big business in Nanaimo, and a request to the visitor information center will result in a small mountain of mail. **Ocean Explorers Diving** (☎ 800/233-4145 or 250/753-2055; www.oceanexplorersdiving.com; e-mail: oceanex@islandnet.com) offers packages that include 2 nights' accommodations and 5 boat dives, plus cylinders, air, and weights, with prices starting at C$275 (U.S.$179). It also offers charter dives (from C$80/U.S.$52) and Discover Snorkeling trips (C$45/U.S.$29).

Exta Sea Charters Marine Group (☎ 888/398-2733 or 250/755-9144; www.extasea.com; e-mail: info@extasea.com) is a Nanaimo-based live-aboard dive outfitter that offers charters around the coast of Vancouver Island. Exta Sea's cruisers can accommodate 6 to 10 passengers on trips of 2 to 9 days. Popular excursions include Port Hardy, famed for its dense marine-mammal population, and Barkley Sound and the Broken Group Islands, with a collection of shipwrecks and reefs.

WHERE TO STAY

✪ **Best Western Dorchester Hotel.** 70 Church St., Nanaimo, BC, V9R 5H4. ☎ **800/661-2449** or 250/754-6835. Fax 250/754-2638. 65 units. TV TEL. C$80 (U.S.$52) double. Extra person C$10 (U.S.$7). Senior discounts and corporate and off-season rates available. AE, DISC, ER, MC, V.

The Dorchester stands on the most venerable spot in Nanaimo. This rise of land above the harbor was originally the site of the Hudson's Bay Company trading post in the 1850s, and then became the site of the city's old opera house. Reminders of the opera-house days remain: The handsome chandeliers throughout the lobby and restaurant are all original, as are the ornate columns flanking the dining room. The library (a cozy space to meet friends), marble-lined lobby, and quality Persian-style carpets give the Dorchester a sense of style and history unmatched in Nanaimo. For a historic hotel, the guest rooms are quite large and nicely furnished. Be sure to ask for a bay-side unit, with incredible views of the harbor, islands, and glaciated peaks of the mainland. Nearly all rooms have air-conditioning; smoking is not permitted in two-thirds of the hotel. Best of all, the staff is friendly and professional, and the renovations highlight the historic details while providing fully modern facilities. Café Casablanca offers international fine dining in a harbor-view room; the Oasis Lounge is adjacent.

Coast Bastion Inn. 11 Bastion St., Nanaimo, BC, V9R 2Z9. ☎ **800/663-1144** or 250/753-6601. Fax 250/753-4155. www.coasthotels.com. E-mail: cbastion@nanaimo.ark.com. 179 units. A/C TV TEL. C$145–C$179 (U.S.$94–U.S.$116) double. Extra person C$10 (U.S.$7). Senior discounts, family plans, and off-season rates available. AE, MC, V.

At this modern high-rise hotel, every room boasts a view of Nanaimo's spectacular waterfront, and the Harbourside Walkway scene is just seconds away. While even the standard units are large and pleasant, it's worth the splurge for the Superior Rooms: corner units with more space, upgraded amenities, and views from two sides of the hotel. In-room extras include ironing boards and hair dryers. Cutter's Bistro serves contemporary West Coast cuisine, and the Offshore Lounge has a nice view of the waterfront. Other facilities include an exercise room with sauna, whirlpool, and universal gym. The Coast Bastion connects to the new Park Theatre complex.

Pepper Muffin Country Inn. 3718 Jingle Pot Rd., Nanaimo, BC, V9R 6X4. ☎ **250/756-0473.** Fax 250/756-0421. www.island.net/~pog. E-mail: pog@island.net. 4 units. TV. C$85–C$125 (U.S.$55–U.S.$81) double. Rates include breakfast. AE, MC, V.

This country B&B offers a rural getaway just minutes from downtown. The setting is splendid: a 7-acre farm with grazing cattle in the pasture and yellow Labs bounding around the lawns (the owners raise and train field trial dogs). Running through the property is a stream that plays host to beaver, otter, and trout; across the meadow rise forested mountains. The guest house was built as an inn, and all rooms are totally private and soundproofed. Although newly constructed, the building was designed with quirky angles and rooflines, and is furnished with a mix of antique and modern pieces. Each large room has a private bathroom, balcony, and TV/VCR; one unit has a private deck, another a fireplace. Guests share a sitting room; lounge with refrigerator; and outdoor hot tub. At breakfast, you'll learn what Pepper Muffin refers to: delicious corn muffins flecked with red bell pepper and served with jalapeño jelly.

Sheraton Four Points Hotel. 4900 Rutherford Rd., Nanaimo, BC, V9T 5P1. ☎ **800/325-3535** or 250/758-3000. Fax 250/729-2808. www.fourpoints.com. E-mail: fourpts@island.net. 75 units. TEL. C$125 (U.S.$81) double, C$175–C$250 (U.S.$114–U.S.$163) suite. Extra person C$10 (U.S.$7). AE, DC, DISC, MC, V.

Completed in 1998, the Sheraton is the Nanaimo area's newest and most luxurious lodging. The hotel is part of a golf-and-retirement complex, with an adjacent 18-hole course (another 18-hole course is less than a mile away). The majority of the accommodations are suites. The largest are the 600-square-foot Arbutus suites, with two TVs, a kitchenette, a king bed, and a large desk. The Maple Suites are smaller but equally pleasing, with huge bathrooms, king beds, and a superior floor plan. The standard rooms are a good value for the money. All units are beautifully outfitted with quality furniture and fabrics. The public rooms are handsome, particularly the lobby with its 25-foot ceiling and enormous chandelier. The restaurant and lounge look out onto the walls of a quarry, flanked by manicured lawns. Other facilities include a well-equipped exercise room and an indoor pool.

Tally-Ho Hotel. 1 Terminal Ave., Nanaimo, BC, V9R 5R4. ☎ **800/663-7322** or 250/753-2241. Fax 250/753-6522. 101 units. A/C. C$100–C$112 (U.S.$65–U.S.$73) double. Extra person C$10 (U.S.$7). Off-season rates and senior discounts available. AE, MC, V.

This large motel complex has a convenient location within easy walking distance of downtown, with direct access to the Harbourside Walkway and to lovely Bowen Park via trails that flank the Millstone River. A cut above the average motel, the rooms here are clean, good-sized, and nicely furnished. Facilities include a heated outdoor pool, beer-and-wine store, and Hemingway's Cigar and Martini Bar.

Travelodge Nanaimo. 96 Terminal Ave. N., Nanaimo, BC, V9S 4J2. ☎ **800/667-0598** or 250/724-6355. Fax 250/754-1301. www.vquest.com/traveloddgena. E-mail: travelna@ vquest.com. 78 units. A/C TV TEL. C$79 (U.S.$51) double. Extra person C$6 (U.S.$3.90). Kitchen C$10 (U.S.$7) extra. Rates include continental breakfast. Senior discounts and off-season rates available. AE, DISC, MC, V.

A midprice motel with a great location and generous amenities, this well-maintained Travelodge is just 2 blocks from the Vancouver ferry, and a short walk to the sights and shops of downtown. The rooms are clean and comfortably furnished. All units have balconies or patios, and some come with kitchenettes and ocean views. Extras include free local calls, complimentary continental breakfast and in-room coffee, a sauna, an exercise room, and a meeting room.

ON GABRIOLA ISLAND

✪ **Sunset B&B.** 969 Berry Point Rd., Gabriola Island, BC, V0R 1X0. ☎ **250/247-2032.** www.islandnet.com/~sunsetcl. E-mail: sunsetcl@island.net. 3 units. C$75–C$130 (U.S.$49–U.S.$85) double. Rates include ferry pickup and breakfast. MC, V. Children must be 14 or older.

This wonderful B&B on the rugged eastern shores of Gabriola Island is a marvelous destination for anyone who loves music, books, or the serenity of the sea. The modern home overlooks rocky Orlobar Point and the busy waters of Georgia Strait; paths lead to protected coves, tidal basins, and hidden viewpoints. Set amid rose gardens and tiered flower beds, the home is designed around a spacious open plan with high vaulted ceilings, picture windows, and rich wood floors. The palatial Wild Rose Suite is an amazing series of rooms that extends the entire length of the B&B; it alone is reason enough to make the journey to Gabriola. The suite comprises a sitting room (with fireplace) overlooking the gardens and the water, bedroom, and enormous bathroom filled with luxury toiletries. Two other rooms overlook the side gardens.

As lovely as the accommodations are, the real treasures here are the knowledgeable hosts, Trudy and Gottfried. Once a Vienna Boys Choir singer, Gottfried brings a passion for music to the B&B, while Trudy contributes her love for reading and discussion. Guests are encouraged to browse the selection of classical CDs, linger in the library, and pass the day listening to music, reading a book, or talking to the hosts. Breakfast is an extravagant affair, featuring seasonal fruits, fresh breads and muffins, and—if you're lucky—Gottfried's Viennese scrambled eggs.

WHERE TO DINE

Flo's Diner. 187 Commercial St. ☎ **250/753-2148.** Reservations not accepted. Main courses C$4.50–C$10 (U.S.$2.95–U.S.$7). MC, V. Mon–Fri 8am–7pm, Sat 9am–3pm. DINER.

If you lived in Nanaimo, Flo's is the lunch counter you'd frequent for an old-fashioned sandwich or for Saturday breakfast, all served up with attitude. This campy, kitschy diner is probably the most colorful (in both senses of the word) place in the city, with mannequins and movie-star memorabilia for decor. The clientele ranges from businessmen in mid-deal to arty young things downing espresso. The food is standard diner fare, though prepared with more zest than usual.

✪ **The Globe Bar & Grill.** 25 Front St. ☎ **250/754-4910.** Reservations not accepted. Main courses C$7–C$18 (U.S.$4.55–U.S.$12). MC, V. Daily 11am–1am. PUB.

The pick of Nanaimo's many good pubs, the Globe is housed in a beautifully renovated 1889 hotel with exposed brick, towering ceilings, and massive leaded windows. The menu is extensive, and the quality of preparation better than at most pubs. Dining choices range from burgers, ribs, salads, pasta, and pizza to steaks and fish entrees. The selection of local beers and ales is daunting though wonderful to contemplate— or opt for one of the specialty cocktails. Add pool tables, a large summer patio, and a cigar room, and you've got something for everyone.

The Grotto. 1511 Stewart Ave. ☎ **250/753-3303.** Reservations recommended. Main courses C$12–C$20 (U.S.$8–U.S.$13). MC, V. Tues–Sun 5–10pm. SUSHI/STEAK HOUSE.

If you're looking for Nanaimo's most inventive sushi and fresh fish, head down Stewart Avenue toward the Vancouver ferry docks to the Grotto. While there's plenty of straightforward sashimi on the menu, it's the large selection of "West Coast Sushi Rolls" that truly exhibit the personality of the restaurant. The Martha Stewart Rolls combine asparagus, avocado, shiitake mushrooms, and wasabi in an egg crepe, while the Nanuk Roll brings together egg, crab, avocado, and smoked salmon. As far as entrees are concerned, the Grotto is half steak house, half Pacific Rim fish restaurant. In addition to a full selection of traditional steaks, ribs, and chops, there are seafood dishes like Napa Salmon, a pan-seared fillet with lemon teriyaki dressing, and the house specialty of stuffed almond shrimp.

✪ **Maffeo's.** 538 Wentworth St. ☎ **250/753-0377.** Reservations recommended. Main courses C$11–C$19 (U.S.$7–U.S.$12). AE, MC, V. Mon–Fri 11am–1:30pm; Mon–Sat 5:30–10pm. ITALIAN.

Two Popular Pubs

If you're in the mood for a pint of local ale and a burger, take the 10-minute Protection Connection ferry ride to the **Dinghy Dock Floating Marine Pub,** on Protection Island in Nanaimo Harbour (☎ 250/753-2373). It's exactly what its name says—a floating pub—and is very popular on summer evenings, when the sunset views of Nanaimo and the Vancouver Island mountains are spectacular. The ferry leaves on the hour from the Commercial Inlet boat basin, below Pioneer Waterfront Plaza. You get a wonderful view of the Dinghy Dock Pub—and the rest of the harbor—from the **Lighthouse Bistro,** just off the Harbourside Walkway at 50 Anchor Way (☎ 250/754-3212). This floating pub and drinks-oriented restaurant also serves as the city's floatplane base; it's fun to watch these flying boats take off and arrive from just beside your table.

This converted home in the Old Town Quarter offers an extensive menu of classic pastas and traditional Mediterranean fish and meat dishes. As prepared by the Italian-born and -trained chef/owner, the food at Maffeo's is richly authentic; you won't need to worry about wasabi or Thai peppers creeping into your pasta al pesto. Starting with the appetizers, Maffeo's wins points for serving carpaccio, sadly a rarity in this age of food scares, as well as a fantastic *vitèllo tonnato* (marinated veal with a traditional tuna, anchovy, and caper sauce). The pasta-and-risotto sheet numbers nearly 30 choices. The meat and fish entrees are likewise classics, with rabbit cacciatore, osso bucco, veal piccata, and other well-loved favorites from the grill and sauté pan. The wine list has an excellent selection of Italian rarities. The atmosphere is warm and homey; in summer, you can dine alfresco in the front garden.

✪ **Wesley Street Café.** 321 Wesley St. ☎ **250/753-4004.** Reservations required. Main courses C$14–C$25 (U.S.$9–U.S.$16). AE, MC, V. Daily 11:30am–2:30pm and 5–10pm. WEST COAST CONTEMPORARY.

Nanaimo's premier fine-dining restaurant, the Wesley Street Café serves the most up-to-date food in the city, and quite possibly on Vancouver Island. Served in a comfort-ably formal Old Town Quarter room, the cuisine pairs European tradition with flavors from the Far East, utilizing the stellar produce, seafood, and meats of western Canada. To start, the sweet-potato and house-smoked salmon pancake, served with wasabi mayonnaise, is a standout. Entrees are even more international: Steamed salmon is wrapped in nori and served with wasabi butter and lox, while grilled chicken breast is stuffed with Stilton cheese, walnuts, and apple relish. Evening specials include the freshest of the day's catch from the Nanaimo fishing fleet. The service is friendly, and the wine list extensive and well chosen.

Wild Roots Café. 299 Wallace St. ☎ **250/753-0200.** Reservations not accepted. Main dishes C$7–C$8 (U.S.$4.55–U.S.$5). AE, MC, V. Daily 11am–2pm and 5–8pm. VEGETARIAN.

This friendly cafe, in an old brick storefront on the edge of the Old Town Quarter, serves up "vegetarian cuisine of the world." At lunch, there's an all-you-can-eat buffet starting at C$5 (U.S.$3.25). The evening menu is a mélange of dishes from many dif-ferent cultures: ratatouille, Punjabi curry, vegetable lasagna, and lots of salads and wraps. Friday nights bring live music and a buffet supper for C$8 (U.S.$5). For the money, this is excellent food. Beer and wine are served.

ON GABRIOLA ISLAND

✪ **Latitudes Restaurant.** 3383 South Rd., in the Silva Bay Resort and Marina. ☎ **250/247-8662.** Reservations recommended. Main courses C$14–C$25 (U.S.$9–U.S.$16). AE, MC, V. Thurs–Sun 5:30–10pm. INTERNATIONAL.

Take the 20-minute Gabriola Island ferry and drive to the island's southern tip to find this excellent restaurant. The dining room looks east across the Silva Bay Marina toward the mountains of the mainland, a fitting backdrop to the dramatic cuisine. Starters are outstanding, and you could do far worse than graze your way through a series of shared plates. Skillet-charred yellowfin tuna is served with scallion aioli and traditional Japanese garnishes. Add the grilled local quail, sauced with thyme and fire-weed honey, and a Belgian endive salad with roasted pears, walnuts, figs, and Stilton, and you've got a magical assortment of dishes to nibble at while watching the sunset. Entrees are equally compelling. Local salmon fillets come with a horseradish crust and white truffle cream, and Cioppino Gabriola features scallops, prawns, crab, mussels, and a changing assortment of whitefish in a fennel-and-saffron broth. The wine list offers an intriguing selection of British Columbia bottles. In summer, tables extend along the dock above the marina.

3 Parksville & Qualicum Beach

23 miles (37km) N of Nanaimo

These two resort towns are near the most popular beaches on Vancouver Island: Spending a week on the beach here is a family tradition for many longtime residents of British Columbia. With miles of sand for the kids and six golf courses for the parents, these twin towns are the perfect base for a relaxing vacation. Parksville (pop. 10,000) and Qualicum Beach (pop. 7,000) are also a perfect stopping-off point for travelers making the trip to or from Victoria and Tofino.

ESSENTIALS

GETTING THERE **Laidlaw Coach Lines** (☎ 250/385-4411) offers bus transport to and from the Parksville and Qualicum area along the Highway 1/Highway 19 corridor, as well as to and from Tofino along Highway 4. The **E&N Railiner** (☎ 800/561-8630 or 250/383-4324) has stops in both towns on its daily trip from Victoria to Courtenay. The closest air service is at Nanaimo; for details, see section 2, above.

VISITOR INFORMATION For information on Qualicum Beach, contact **Qualicum Beach Travel Info Centre,** 2711 W. Island Hwy., Qualicum Beach, BC, V9K 2C4 (☎ 250/752-9532; fax 250/752-2923; www.qualicum.bc.ca; e-mail: info@qualicum.bc.ca). The **Parksville Visitor Info Centre** is at 1275 E. Island Hwy. (P.O. Box 99), Parksville, BC, V9P 2G3 (☎ 250/248-3613; fax 250/248-5210; www.chamber.parksville.bc.ca; e-mail: info@chamber.parksville.bc.ca).

For information on this part of Vancouver Island, contact the **Parksville–Qualicum Beach Tourism Association,** 174 Railway St., Box 374, Qualicum Beach, BC, V9K 1S9 (☎ 888/799-3222 or 250/752-2388; fax 250/752-2392; www.oceanside-bc.com; e-mail: info@oceanside-bc.com).

EXPLORING THE AREA

While these towns share similar beaches and are all but connected by country-club developments and marinas, there are differences between the two. Parksville has several large resorts and beachfront hotels, and is more of a long developed strip without much of a town center. In contrast, accommodations in Qualicum Beach are largely in B&Bs, and there is a more traditional town center with shopping and cafes—but this part of town is a couple miles inland, away from the beach.

In Qualicum Beach, you can access the beach from many points along Highway 19A, also called the Island Highway. Likewise, in Parksville, the beach is accessible downtown from the Island Highway, near the junction of Highway 4A, and at the adjacent Parksville Community Beach and Playground. However, the best beaches are preserved in **Rathtrevor Beach Provincial Park,** just east of Parksville's town center. In addition, the 860-acre park offers trails, bird-watching sites, and a campground.

A word about the beaches at both Parksville and Qualicum Beach: If you're looking for miles of dunes or broad, white-sand strands lapped by azure water, then you may be surprised. The sea is quite shallow at Parksville and Qualicum Beach, with a very gentle slope. When the tide goes out, it exposes hundreds of acres of gray-sand flats. When the tide is in—which it is half the time—the beach disappears beneath the shallow waters. There are benefits to this: The summer sun bakes the sand beaches while the tide is out, so when the tides come back in, the shallow water is warmed by the sand, thus making the water agreeable for swimming and wading. Parksville claims to have the warmest ocean-water beaches in all of Canada.

When you're not on the beach, one particularly good place to stop in Qualicum Beach is the **Old School House,** 122 Fern Rd. W. (☎ **250/752-6133**), the town's original school, which now houses several galleries, studios, and a gift shop.

HORNE LAKE CAVES PROVINCIAL PARK

In the mountains west of Qualicum Beach, **Horne Lake Caves Provincial Park** (☎ **250/757-8687**) offers access to a lakeside park area, with camping and canoeing, and a system of caves on the slopes of the Beaufort Range. Two of the caves are open year-round for self-exploration, though you must bring at least two sources of light, and helmets are recommended (in summer, these are available for rent from the park office). From mid-June to Labour Day, the park offers a variety of guided tours, starting with the family-oriented 1^1/$_2$-hour Riverbend Cave Interpretive Program (C$15/U.S.$10 for adults, C$12/U.S.$8 for children). These tours, which focus on conservation of the cave environment, depart daily from 10am to 5pm, and are offered on a first-come, first-served basis.

If you're serious about caving, or just seek more adventure, consider the 5-hour Riverbend Expedition (C$79/U.S.$51), which involves instruction in basic roping and other caving skills, and culminates in roping up a seven-story waterfall known as the Rainbarrel. No prior climbing experience is necessary. If you really want to get the adrenaline pumping, there's the 6-hour Underground Extreme, which pretty much says it all: This time, you get to rappel down the Rainbarrel (C$110/U.S.$72). You must have previous roping experience. For both the latter tours, you must be 15 or older and willing to sign a liability waver. Reservations are required for the two more-difficult expeditions. Contact **Island Pacific Adventures** (☎ **250/248-7829;** fax 250/339-9150; www.hornelake.com; e-mail: adventure@hornelake.com). From the company's teepee camp on the shores of Horne Lake, Island Pacific also offers a series of family adventures and summer camps, which feature caving, rock climbing, kayaking, and wilderness survival courses.

GREAT GOLF

There are six golf courses in the Parksville–Qualicum Beach area, and over a dozen within an hour's drive. **Eagle Crest Golf Club,** 2035 Island Hwy. (☎ **250/752-6311**), is an 18-hole, par-71 course with an emphasis on shot making and accuracy. **Fairwinds,** 3730 Fairwinds Dr., just east of Parksville at Nanoose Bay (☎ **250/468-7666**), is a challenging 18-hole, par-71 course with ocean views and lots of trees to work your way around. **Glengarry Golf Links,** 1025 Qualicum Rd. (☎ **250/752-8786**), has nine links-style holes, plus a forested and scenic back nine. The long-established **Qualicum Beach Memorial,** 115 W. Crescent (☎ **250/752-6312**), has nine holes, stunning ocean views, a pro shop, and a restaurant.

✪ **Morningstar Golf Club,** 525 Lowry's Rd. (☎ **250/248-8161**), is an 18-hole, 7,018-yard-long course with a par-72 rating. Designed by Les Furber, it has seaside links and fairways. **Arrowsmith Golf and Country Club,** north of Qualicum Beach at 2250 Fowler Rd. (☎ **250/752-9727**), is a family-oriented course with 18 holes and a par-61 rating. Each of the above has a driving range, clubhouse, and pro shop.

WHERE TO STAY

If you want to camp, **Rathtrevor Provincial Park,** a former farmstead 1.2 miles (2km) south of Parksville, features a wide sandy beach ideal for water sports and swimming. Rathtrevor also offers hiking, swimming, camping, and evening programs. The campground, with sites going for C$12 to C$19 (U.S.$8 to U.S.$12), is open during the months of July and August. Call ☎ **800/689-9025** for reservations.

✪ **Bahari B&B.** 5101 Island Hwy., Qualicum Beach, BC, V9K 1Z1. ☎ **877/752-9278** or 250/752-9278. Fax 250/752-9038. www.baharibandb.com. E-mail: lhooper@macn.bc.ca. 5 units. TV TEL. C$125–C$175 (U.S.$81–U.S.$114) double, C$250 (U.S.$163) 2-bedroom apt. 2-night minimum stay in apt. Single person deducts C$20 (U.S.$13) per day. Weekly rates and packages available. AE, MC, V. Children accepted in apt; B&B guests must be 16 or older.

Bed-and-breakfasts come in all shapes and styles, but Bahari is unique for its attention to detail and its artistically exquisite sure-handedness. Decorated with a delicate Asian influence that's more Pacific Rim elegant than the usual clutter that typifies many B&Bs, this property could easily take pride of place in *Architectural Digest.* Each unit is uniquely outfitted; even the bathrooms contain one-of-a-kind fixtures, like room no. 2's incredible custom-made counter and sink made of slumped glass. All rooms have original artwork, balconies, robes, and complimentary sherry; the quality of the linens and down comforters alone justifies a visit. Guests are welcome in the sitting room, with its open staircase and incredible wood carvings, and in the more intimate TV room and library, with leather couches and fireplace. Follow the paths to the beach, frequented by seals and eagles, or soak in the hot tub perched above the beach, where you can watch ships ply the waters of the Georgia Strait.

   In addition to the B&B rooms is a 1,200-square-foot, two-bedroom apartment, with one queen and two twin beds, fireplace, balcony, and self-catering kitchen. Kids are allowed in the apartment, which is separated from the main house by a breezeway. Laundry facilities in this section of the house are open to all guests at Bahari.

Best Western Bayside Inn. 240 Dogwood St., Parksville, BC, V9P 2H5. ☎ **800/663-4232** or 250/248-8333. Fax 250/248-4689. www.bwbayside.com. E-mail: reservations@bwbayside.com. 59 units. A/C TV TEL. C$119–C$159 (U.S.$77–U.S.$103) double. Extra person C$10 (U.S.$7). AE, DC, DISC, MC, V.

It doesn't get much more beachfront than this. Perched right above the sands in central Parksville, this full-service resort offers high-quality facilities at relatively moderate prices. Half of the rooms face the beach, while the other half look back onto the mountains of Vancouver Island, and almost all have balconies. Smoking is not permitted in most of the rooms. The grounds are landscaped, with a gazebo and putting green, and best of all, you can step right off the deck onto the beach.

   Heron's Restaurant offers Mediterranean seafood cuisine in a glass-fronted dining room with views of the ocean. In summer, the dining room spills out onto an ocean-front deck; there's a second heated patio as well. Other hotel amenities include an espresso bar, lounge, sports pub, spa treatments, massage, salon, room service, health club, squash courts, pool, whirlpool, steam room, beach volleyball court, basketball court, scuba shop, gift shop, boutiques, and meeting rooms.

✪ **Hollyford Guest Cottage.** 106 Hoylake Rd., Qualicum Beach, BC, V9K 1L7. ☎ **877/224-6559** or 250/752-8101. Fax 250/752-8102. www.hollyford.ca/mail@hollyford.ca. E-mail: hford@island.net. 3 units. TV. C$135 (U.S.$88) double. Rates include full breakfast and refreshment sideboard. MC, V. Children must be 12 or older.

Hollyford Guest Cottage is a marvelous choice if you value the chance to admire fascinating objects and antiques. The bedrooms are large and stylish, and the hosts charming and thoughtful, but what really makes the Hollyford stand out is its fascinating collection of antiques and Canadiana. The lounge's carved black-walnut sideboard—rumored to have been designed for the Banff Springs Hotel—is simply amazing. You'll also see collections of early western Canadian landscape paintings, Native American jewelry, Inuit art, and an homage to the Mounties, complete with a full regalia uniform of red serge. Lest this sound like a museum, let us assure you that the owners of Hollyford have that rare knack for presenting objects as art, not clutter.

The guest rooms are off a long, antique-filled sitting area. Each newly constructed, fully soundproofed room has heated floors, quality new and antique furniture, fine linens, a small garden patio, a fireplace, a beautifully tiled bathroom with deep soaker tub, Aveda toiletries, and handmade local soaps. For the full breakfast served in the original dining room, your hosts will bring out the antique china, Waterford crystal, and silver from the glory days of the Canadian Pacific Railway.

Maclure House B&B Inn. 1015 E. Island Hwy., Parksville, BC, V9P 2E4. ☎ **250/248-3470.** Fax 250/248-6145. www.vancouverisland-bc.com/MaclureHouse. 4 units. C$95–C$130 (U.S.$62–U.S.$85) double. Extra person C$12–C$24 (U.S.$8–U.S.$16). Rates include 3-course breakfast and afternoon treats. Off-season rates available. AE, MC, V.

The Maclure House, an ivy-covered, half-timbered 1921 mansion, was modeled after a Scottish hunting lodge. No expense was spared: You'll see expanses of leaded glass, 30-foot ceilings, ornately carved moldings, and a beautifully landscaped series of gardens. Other aspects of the structure retain the spirit of the local landscape: The ceiling beams and the wood paneling that line the dining room were cut from yellow cedar felled on the property. All guest rooms are decorated according to British Empire themes, but with restraint applied. Two units face the ocean, sharing an ivy-twined balcony and wonderful views. We love the Ocean Suite, which boasts a large bedroom, sitting room with tiled fireplace, and incredible bathroom with original fixtures. See "Where to Dine," below, for a review of the restaurant.

Pacific Shores Nature Resort. 1655 Strougler Rd., Nanoose Bay, BC, V0R 2R0. ☎ **800/500-7212** or 250/468-7121. Fax 250/468-2001. www.pacific-shores.com. E-mail: pacshore@nanaimo.ark.com. 76 units. A/C TV TEL. C$80–C$180 (U.S.$52–U.S.$117) 1-bedroom condo. Off-season rates available. AE, DC, DISC, MC, V.

Pacific Shores is a large time-share development with an environmental twist. The developers have worked hard to integrate this complex of condos, with its extensive health, sports, and spa facilities, into the landscape. It sits above a half mile of pristine waterfront, with a mix of rocky headlands and sandy beach, tucked into a grove of established arbutus and fir trees. Trails lead across the property (guided walks are offered), and the resort even has its own fish hatchery, meant to help replenish the coho salmon in adjacent Beaver Creek. Most impressive are the extensive gardens featuring plants from around the world and separated into areas with species native to South Africa, China, the Pacific Northwest, and so on. Join one of the daily garden tours; if you find a plant you like, chances are good that you'll be able to purchase a cutting from the resort's nursery.

The array of accommodations is not easily summarized. The standard units range in size from 1,300 to 1,400 square feet and have two bedrooms, a full kitchen, fireplaces, a dining area, a stereo, a balcony, and two large bathrooms, one with a jetted tub. The units are filled with natural light and handsomely decorated. It's a good idea to call and discuss the various floor-plan options with the reservations staff. Families are welcome; minimum stays of a week are preferred in summer, although there are often hotel-style rooms available for shorter stays. New for 2000 are a restaurant and lounge. Other facilities include a convenience store and deli, a large pool with "ozonated" water, hot tubs, exercise machines, a weight room, and a wellness spa with massage therapy and aestheticians, plus a licensed naturopathic practitioner.

Peppercorn Cottage B&B. 395 Burnham Rd., Qualicum Beach, BC, V9K 1G5. ☎ **250/752-5851.** Fax 250/752-0086. E-mail: peprcorn@islandnet.com. 3 units. C$125–C$175 (U.S.$81–U.S.$114) double. Rates include breakfast. No credit cards. Closed Nov 1–Feb 14. Children must be 15 or older.

The full scale of this 1929 English-style cottage doesn't become clear until you step inside the high-ceilinged foyer. This very large estate-style home offers spacious, handsomely furnished rooms, with private bathrooms and notably big closets. The entire home has recently been refurbished with new rugs, fresh paint, and new tile. The common rooms are quite splendid: Full cooked breakfasts are served in the formal dining room, and the living room features a massive granite fireplace. With lots of decks to relax on, beautiful gardens to wander about, and the pool and tennis court for amusement, it's easy to while away several days of holiday. A private path leads from the property down to the beach.

✪ **Tigh-Na-Mara Resort Hotel.** 1095 E. Island Hwy., Parksville, BC, V9P 2E5. ☎ **800/ 663-7373** or 250/248-2072. Fax 250/248-4140. www.tigh-na-mara.com. E-mail: info@ tigh-na-mara.com. 142 units. C$104–C$189 (U.S.$68–U.S.$123) double. Extra person C$5–C$10 (U.S.$3.25–U.S.$7). Weekly rates available. AE, DC, MC, V.

This time-honored log-cabin resort just keeps getting better. Established in the 1940s on a forested waterfront beach (near Rathtrevor Beach Provincial Park), Tigh-Na-Mara has expanded over the years: more cottages, lodge-style rooms, and beautifully furnished condo-style suites with stunning ocean views, all log-built. Families will especially appreciate the lengthy list of supervised child-friendly activities (many of them free). With such a long history, you won't be surprised to learn that there are practically as many cottage and condo styles as there are cottages and condos. Accommodation types include studio and one-bedroom lodge rooms, plus one- and two-bedroom cottages. If you're traveling with a group, the duplex cottages can be converted into a series of rooms large enough to sleep eight. The new ocean-side condo units all have views as well as balconies or patios. All rooms and cottages at Tigh-Na-Mara have fireplaces, full bathrooms, and some form of kitchen. The cottages are comfortably lived-in and homey, while the condos are new and lavish.

The restaurant in the log-and-stone lodge serves an eclectic version of Northwest cuisine. There's a full children's menu, adjacent lounge, and Friday barbecues and dances in summer. Other amenities include tennis courts, pool, sauna, hot tubs, exercise rooms, watercraft rentals, video rentals, conference center, children's swimming lessons and activities, and baby-sitting (for a fee).

WHERE TO DINE

Beach House Café. 2775 W. Island Hwy., Qualicum Beach. ☎ **250/752-9626.** Reservations suggested. Main courses C$15–C$18 (U.S.$10–U.S.$12). MC, V. Daily 11am–2:30pm and 5–10pm. INTERNATIONAL.

At this popular beachside restaurant in Qualicum Beach, the flavors of the Orient and Austria blend together, reflecting the birthplaces of the two chef/owners. For a lighter entree, try the Szechuan chicken stir-fry on linguini. An outstanding vegetarian dish is the Madras fruit curry with coconut. On the European side of the menu, the Jagerschnitzel (veal scallops with wild-mushroom sauce) is a standout, as is the traditional paprika goulash. For a real taste explosion, consider the roast duck with a sauce made of local blackberries. For the quality and finesse of the food, the prices are very moderate, and the dining room comfortable and informal, filled with sun and great views. A great choice if you want a good meal without a stuffy atmosphere.

Cola Diner. 6060 W. Island Hwy., Qualicum Bay. ☎ **250/757-2029.** Reservations not accepted. Main courses C$4.95–C$18 (U.S.$3.20–U.S.$12). MC, V. Wed–Mon 8am–10pm. BURGERS.

We've all been to retro 1950s-style restaurants; this is the real thing. Built back when Coca-Cola had its own restaurant/gas station chain, the Cola Diner is a roadhouse north of Qualicum Beach that's been lovingly restored to its former glory, with a soda fountain, jukebox, and lots of Coke memorabilia. The menu is filled with burgers, gravity-defying Dagwood sandwiches, and excellent though heart-stopping side dishes like onion rings and honest-to-Pete french fries. The doting owners are native Germans, so dishes from the homeland also work their way onto the menu.

Kalvas Restaurant. 180 Molliet St., Parksville. ☎ **250/248-6933.** Reservations recommended. Main courses C$11–C$38 (U.S.$7–U.S.$25). AE, MC, V. Daily 5–10pm. FISH/SEAFOOD.

Kalvas is the locals' special-occasion restaurant, a rustic-looking lodge with a bustling dining room. The specialties are steaks, fish, and seafood prepared in traditional supper-club style: sole amandine, grilled halibut, and whole steamed Dungeness crab served with drawn butter. Kalvas makes the most of the excellent oysters from nearby Fanny Bay, with nine preparations available from the oyster bar. Atlantic lobsters, steamed and served with local shrimp and scallops, is another specialty. Meat dishes range from New York steak to pheasant breast with orange brandy sauce.

Lefty's Fresh Foods. 710 Memorial St., Qualicum Beach. ☎ **250/752-7530.** Reservations not accepted. Main courses C$4.95–C$10 (U.S.$3.20–U.S.$7). MC, V. Daily 8am–8pm. HEALTHY/INTERNATIONAL.

Lefty's began as a mostly vegetarian eatery, but over the years has added more chicken and meat dishes to its menu. However, the emphasis remains on fresh flavors and healthy cooking, with a menu that borrows from ethnic cuisines and up-to-date comfort food. At Lefty's (named for the two left-handed owners), this youthful style of cooking is called Left Coast Cuisine, and even the menu reads from left to right. Salads, sandwiches, and focaccia pizza make up the offerings, and all the baking is done on site. Service is bright and cheerful, as is the airy, casual dining room.

Maclure House Restaurant. 1015 E. Island Hwy. ☎ **250/248-3470.** Reservations recommended. Main courses C$11–C$27 (U.S.$7–U.S.$18). AE, MC, V. Daily 8–10:30am, 11:30am–2pm, and 5–10pm. INTERNATIONAL.

One of the loveliest dining rooms in the Parksville–Qualicum Beach area is the Maclure House, a striking 1921 Tudor-style mansion built to resemble a Scottish hunting lodge. It's perfect for a romantic meal or a special occasion. Guests are seated in the formal wood-paneled dining room, the library, or the music room, each with a fireplace and views of the gardens. The snug little lounge, also with fireplace, is a wonderful place for a drink. In summer, tables spill out onto the flagstone veranda.

The menu is comprehensive, with a good selection of appetizers, salads (the hot prawn salad with pesto vinaigrette is a standout), and light pasta dishes. Pan-seared and oven-baked chicken breast comes with a choice of three sauces (we recommend the red-pepper aioli), while the grilled fresh local halibut or salmon come with a choice of four sauces (try the sweet fresh rosemary-cream sauce). The house specialty is rack of lamb, crusted with Dijon mustard and pecans, and served with minted au jus. An inexpensive three-course dinner (C$15/U.S.$10) is also available, with entree choices such as fish-and-chips, shepherd's pie, and seafood lasagna.

Red Pepper Grill. 193 Memorial Ave., Parksville. ☎ **250/248-2364.** Reservations recommended. Main courses C$10–C$18 (U.S.$7–U.S.$12). MC, V. Mon–Thurs 11:30am–9pm, Fri 11am–10pm, Sat 5–10pm, Sun 5–9pm. PACIFIC NORTHWEST.

Located on a quiet block off the busy Island Highway strip in Parksville, the Red Pepper Grill features up-to-date pasta and seafood preparations, plus standards such as steak and ribs. There's a separate children's menu for the younger set. The garden patio is one of downtown Parksville's nicest places to relax on a sunny summer day.

Saigon Garden. 118 Craig St. ☎ **250/248-5667.** Reservations not needed. Main courses C$6–C$10 (U.S.$3.90–U.S.$7). MC, V. Mon–Sat 11am–10pm. VIETNAMESE.

Vietnamese food isn't as common in Canada as in the United States, making this excellent outpost of Southeast Asian cuisine even more of a treat. All of your favorites are here—salad rolls, *pho* (noodle soup), and grilled lemongrass chicken—as well as house specialties like prawn- and pork-filled crepes and *com tay cam do bien,* a seafood hot pot with prawns, scallops, squid, royal mushrooms, and lily flowers all cooked in a delicate fish broth. Saigon Garden also offers free delivery after 3pm in the Parksville area.

Shady Rest Waterfront Pub & Restaurant. 3109 W. Island Hwy., Qualicum Beach. ☎ **250/752-9111.** Reservations not needed. Main courses C$10–C$16 (U.S.$7–U.S.$10). MC, V. Restaurant daily 7am–10pm; pub food service daily 11am–10pm. CANADIAN.

A favorite of locals and tourists alike, the Shady Rest sits right above the sandy shore-line. You can eat in either the restaurant or the pub; both have outdoor seating in good weather, and both serve the same Qualicum Beach–style comfort food. The appetizer menu is extensive, making this a convenient choice if you're not hungry enough for a full-on meal. We like the spicy chicken wings and the oyster Rockefeller. There's also a good selection of salads and stir-fries, including an especially worthy hot scallop salad. Entrees range from seafood thermidor to steaks, burgers, and other stalwarts of pub cooking. The house specialty is the Shady-Style Chicken, a grilled chicken breast topped with scallops, tiger prawns, and cream sauce.

4 En Route to Vancouver Island's Wild West Coast

From Parksville, Highway 4 cuts due west, climbing up over the mountainous spine of Vancouver Island before dropping into Port Alberni, at the head of the Pacific's Alberni Inlet. From here, you can join the mail boats ✪ **MV *Lady Rose*** and **MV *Frances Barkley*** as they ply the inlet's narrow waters, delivering mail, supplies, and passengers to isolated water-side fishing communities. Bamfield, the southern termi-nus of the mail-boat run, is one of the two departure points for the West Coast Trail. Mail boats from Port Alberni also negotiate the waters of Barkley Sound and the Broken Group Islands—a wilderness archipelago that's part of Pacific Rim National Park—before arriving at Ucluelet, once a fishing and logging port, and now a gentri-fying resort town.

North of Ucluelet, Highway 4 parallels Long Beach, another section of Pacific Rim National Park. Miles of wide, sandy wilderness beach contrast with the comforts that await at Tofino, at the northern end of Long Beach. Some of Vancouver Island's finest inns and restaurants are found in Tofino, a fast-growing resort and recreation com-munity on a wave-pounded, spectacularly scenic peninsula.

THE DRIVE TO PORT ALBERNI

Just west of Parksville on Highway 4 is the **North Island Wildlife Recovery Centre,** 1240 Leffler Rd., in Errington (☎ **250/248-8534**). Founded in 1984, the center takes in ill, injured, and orphaned wildlife, with the goal of releasing them back into the wild. Animals that can't fend for themselves remain at the center, where many live in the public viewing areas. Wolves, cougars, bears, and birds can often be seen; the eagle flight cage is the largest in Canada. Hours are from 10am to 4pm daily.

Just 1¹/₂ miles (3km) west of the junction with Highway 19, turn south and follow the signs to **Englishman's Falls Provincial Park.** The icy waters of the Englishman River plunge over a succession of rocky ledges, forming a series of majestic waterfalls. Easy trails lead to both the Upper and Lower Englishman's falls; fishing is very good in the waters below the falls. Picnic tables are available; there's a basic campground near the river.

The community of **Coombs** is an unlikely little tourist town, noted most for the goats that graze on the grassy sod roof of the Old Country Market, one of several old stores clustered around the village center. Crafts, souvenirs, and handmade soaps are offered for sale; you can also find a quick bite to eat here. Kids will enjoy **Butterfly World** (☎ **250/248-7026**), an enclosed zoo with 1,000 free-flying butterflies, and **Emerald Forest Bird Garden** (☎ **250/248-7282**), a small aviary.

West of Coombs, turn north to **Little Qualicum Falls Provincial Park.** Hiking trails follow the Little Qualicum River past good trout-fishing holes to the falls, a series of chutes in a mist-filled glade. The park also offers basic camping facilities.

Just below the cliffs of 5,963-foot (1,818m) Mount Arrowsmith, Highway 4 passes along the shores of **Cameron Lake.** The western end of the lake is preserved as **MacMillan Provincial Park,** a magnificent stand of old-growth forest. Easy trails lead through the park's 340 acres, but the most popular destination is Cathedral Grove, with 200- to 600-year-old Douglas fir trees towering up to heights of 220 feet (67m). These monarchs of the forest are truly awe-inspiring—imagine all of Vancouver Island once covered in these brooding forests.

PORT ALBERNI

Located at the head of Barkley Inlet, the longest inlet in Vancouver Island, Port Alberni is a hard-working little town of nearly 20,000 inhabitants. Logs are milled into lumber, pulp, and paper along the waterfront. The busy port is also home to a number of specialty fishing charters and boat-tour companies, as well as mail boats that offer daylong trips to Bamfield and Ucluelet.

The beauty of the natural location tempers the town's industrial makeup. Hope for good weather when you visit Port Alberni: The clouds and gloom of the Pacific often travel up Alberni Inlet and become trapped at the mountain-ringed port city. In good weather, you'll be treated to stunning views of the deep-blue inlet flanked by near-perpendicular rock walls.

When you arrive in Port Alberni, start your exploring with a stroll around the waterfront. **Harbour Quay,** at the base of Argyle Street, has been redeveloped in recent years to provide visitor access to the docks. A few gift shops and cafes make their home here amid the cry of seagulls and the full-throated honk of ship's horns, and the water-side **Clockworks Restaurant** (see "Where to Stay & Dine," below) is one of the town's best places to eat. On summer Saturdays, Harbour Quay is the site of the local **farmers market.** Just north of Harbour Quay is **Fisherman's Harbour,** where the fishing fleet is docked. If you like your fish really fresh, you can often purchase the Pacific's catch directly from the boats.

If you visit Port Alberni on a summer weekend, you can tour the waterfront on a **historic steam train** built in 1929. Originally used to transport logs and lumber between the mills and the harbor, this 2-8-2T Baldwin steam-powered locomotive leaves from the restored 1912 Port Alberni railway station, traveling along the city's industrial waterfront. On weekends in July and August, the trains run hourly from 11am to 4pm; the fare is C$3 for adults (U.S.$1.95) and C$2 (U.S.$1.30) for children.

Port Alberni also boasts several good museums. Due to open later in 2000 is the **McLean Mill National Historic Site,** which preserves a family-run sawmill built in 1926. More than just a place to cut up lumber, the mill property included bunkhouse accommodations for the 20-odd mill workers, a schoolhouse for the workers' children, and a teacherage, making this essentially a small community. The mill's steam-driven saws are still operational, and the old log skids and chain-driven conveyors provide a fascinating glimpse into the early industrial age of the province's timber industry. It's located on Smith Road, off Beaver Creek Road, west of Port Alberni. Call ☎ **250/ 723-8284** for current information.

The **Alberni Valley Museum,** 4255 Wallace St. (☎ **250/723-2181**), has an excellent display of artifacts—especially grass and cedar-bark basketry—from the native Nuu-chah-nulth. The history of European settlement is also retold, with a focus on the early Port Alberni industrial mainstays, logging and fishing. Hours are Tuesday through Saturday from 10am to 5pm, until 8pm on Thursday.

✪ MV *LADY ROSE* & MV *FRANCES BARKLEY*

Lady Rose Marine Services operates two packet freighters that deliver mail and supplies as well as provide public transport to small communities along the Alberni Inlet and Barkley Sound. In addition, the boats take sightseers on an easy and inexpensive trip to the wild outback of Vancouver Island, offering a fascinating glimpse into the daily life of remote fishing and logging communities. These trips provide lots of wildlife-watching opportunities: You're guaranteed to see bald eagles and probably bears; if you're fortunate, you'll catch a glimpse of orcas or porpoises, too. The freighters also convey kayakers and kayaks bound for the Broken Group Islands; the company now operates a lodge and restaurant at Sechart.

Year-round, the freighters depart from the north side of Harbour Quay at 8am on Tuesday, Thursday, and Saturday. They head to Bamfield via Kildonan, with an hour-long layover before returning to Port Alberni at roughly 5:30pm. From the first Friday in July to the first Friday in September, there's an additional 8am Friday sailing from Port Alberni to Bamfield.

From June through September, freighters also depart at 8am on Monday, Wednesday, and Friday for Ucluelet via Sechart near the Broken Group Islands, arriving back in Port Alberni at 7pm (the freighters are no longer allowed to land in the Broken Group, part of Pacific Rim National Park). From the first Sunday in July to the first Sunday in September, there is an additional 8am Sunday sailing.

One-way fare to Bamfield costs C$20 (U.S.$13); the return is C$40 (U.S.$26). One-way fare to Ucluelet is C$23 (U.S.$15); the return is C$45 (U.S.$29). On all journeys, children ages 8 to 17 pay half; those 7 and younger ride free. Basic food service is available on the freighters; bring windproof jackets and hats, as the weather can change dramatically during the course of the trip. Reservations are required; in summer, the boats reach maximum occupancy quickly.

For freighter ticket information and lodge reservations, contact **Lady Rose Marine Services,** P.O. Box 188, Port Alberni, BC, V9Y 7M7 (☎ **800/663-7192** during business hours from Apr through Sept, or 250/723-8313; fax 250/723-8314).

WHERE TO STAY & DINE

Port Alberni is not the cuisine capital of Vancouver Island. Most restaurants here are designed to fuel the hardworking appetites of loggers and fishermen, and while there's nothing wrong with good old meat and potatoes, you won't be seeing a *Zagat* guide to Port Alberni anytime soon. That said, there are a couple of places worth seeking out. The **Sourdough Bakery Cafe,** 3054 Third Ave. (☎ **250/723-1081**), has fresh-baked goods, espresso, and a lunch menu of light soups, salads, and sandwiches. The **Clockworks Restaurant,** 5440 Argyle St. (☎ **250/723-8862**), has a wonderful location right on Harbour Quay, with views down Alberni Inlet. Open daily for lunch and dinner, the restaurant features fresh seafood, steaks, and pasta.

Best Western Barclay Hotel. 4277 Stamp Ave., Port Alberni, BC, V9Y 7X8. ☎ **800/ 563-6590** or 250/724-7171. Fax 250/724-9691. 86 units. A/C TV TEL. C$75–C$89 (U.S.$49–U.S.$58) double. Extra person C$10 (U.S.$7). AE, DC, DISC, MC, V.

This vintage, totally remodeled hotel offers pleasant guest rooms, some with fridges, microwaves, and coffeemakers. Amenities include a family restaurant, pub, sports bar, seasonal outdoor pool, whirlpool, sauna, and beer-and-wine store. Fishing charters are available as well.

Coast Hospitality Inn. 3835 Redford St., Port Alberni, BC, V9Y 3S2. ☎ **800/663-1144** or 250/723-8111. Fax 250/723-0088. www.coasthotels.com. 50 units. TV TEL. C$130 (U.S.$85) double. Extra person C$10 (U.S.$7). Fishing charters and fishing packages offered. Family plan, senior discounts, and off-season rates available. AE, DC, MC, V.

Considered the finest hotel in Port Alberni, the Coast is well located and has large, nicely furnished guest rooms and landscaped grounds. The Harvest Dining Room specializes in home-style cooking, while Polly's Pub serves a light menu. Also on site is a beer-and-wine store.

Edelweiss B&B. 2610 12th Ave., Port Alberni, BC, V9Y 2T7. ☎ **250/723-5940.** Fax 250/ 723-5925. 3 units. A/C TV. C$70 (U.S.$46) double. Extra person C$15 (U.S.$10). Rates include breakfast. MC, V.

This newly constructed B&B is very convenient to Harbour Quay and the *Lady Rose* freighter docks. The spacious, pleasant guest rooms all have air-conditioning and private bathrooms. The Honeymoon Suite boasts a Jacuzzi tub and French doors that open onto a private sundeck. The Edelweiss offers complimentary pickups from the *Lady Rose* or bus depot. Smoking is permitted outside only.

BAMFIELD

Although it's possible to drive from Port Alberni to Bamfield via long, unpaved roads, the majority of travelers will arrive at this small, isolated maritime community by boat, most likely the packet freighters operated by Lady Rose Marine Services in Port Alberni (see above). Although there's not much to do here—the hour-long layover on the freighter's day trip to Bamfield will be plenty of time for most—consider spending a night if you really want to capture the feel of a remote West Coast fishing community. Bamfield makes a good departure point for kayakers, fishers, and especially divers. Bamfield is also one of the termini of the West Coast Trail (see section 5, below).

There are two sides to Bamfield, separated by about 200 yards of the Bamfield Inlet. The west side of Bamfield is linked by a waterfront boardwalk, which makes for a pleasant stroll past old weather-beaten houses, native plant gardens, cats drowsing in the sun, a shop or two, and even an espresso stand. The east side of Bamfield contains most of the businesses, including the **Hook and Web Pub** (☎ 250/728-3422) and the **Tides and Trails Market and Café** (☎ 250/728-3464). To get back and forth between the two sides of town, you'll need to hitch a ride with a local boat owner or call a water taxi (☎ 250/728-3001).

OUTDOOR PURSUITS

DIVING   Broken Island Adventures (☎ 888/728-6200 or 250/728-3500) offers customized diving on the reefs and wrecks in Barkley Sound. **Bamfield Diving Company** (☎ 250/728-3232) offers diving trips into the sound, as well as scuba and diving instruction. Both outfitters can also arrange kayak and wildlife-viewing tours.

KAYAKING   When you make accommodations reservations, inquire about kayak rentals. Many of the lodges either offer rentals or are affiliated with a local company that can put together tours or excursions for you. If you're coming in on the *Lady Rose* Marine Services freighter, ask about renting kayaks directly from them. **Broken Island Adventures** (☎ 888/728-6200 or 250/728-3500) offers kayak tours and rentals and acts as a clearinghouse for wildlife, fishing, and adventure tours.

WHERE TO STAY & DINE

Bamfield Lodge and Cottages. 275 Boardwalk (Box 23), Bamfield, BC, V0R 1B0. ☎ **250/ 728-3419.** Fax 250/728-3417. www.anglingbc.com/bamfieldlodge. E-mail: bamlodge@ cedar.alberni.net. 2 cottages, 1 two-bedroom house. C$100 (U.S.$65) cottage double, C$250 (U.S.$163) house (sleeps up to 6 persons). Off-season discounts available. 30-day cancellation policy Sept–June; no refunds July–Aug. V. From Port Alberni, it's a 1 1/2-hr. drive (56 miles/ 90km) on a maintained gravel road.

Sip an espresso in this resort's cappuccino bar while watching the birds, whales, and boats pass by. A pair of cottages, a lodge, and a two-bedroom house make up the waterfront accommodations at this marine education center and retreat. The rustic, wood-paneled rooms are simply decorated in earth-tone fabrics. The twin-bed and double-bed cabins and the guest house have fully equipped kitchens. Moorage is available if you boat to the lodge. The staff can arrange hiking, kayaking, fishing, diving, whale-watching, and intertidal field trips. Meal plans are available.

Imperial Eagle Lodge. P.O. Box 59, Bamfield, BC, V0R 1B0. ☎ **250/728-3430.** www. imperialeaglelodge.com. E-mail: impeagl@cedar.alberni.net. 5 units. C$119 (U.S.$77) double. Rates include breakfast. MC, V.

The Imperial Eagle consists of a guest house with a dining room and two guest rooms, plus a cottage and a duplex cabin; all units have private bathrooms. Meal plans are available for guests. The lodge dining room, which serves three meals a day, is open to nonguests as well. The Imperial Eagle also offers fishing charters and kayak tours.

Woods End Landing Cottages. 168 Wild Duck Rd., Bamfield, BC, V0R 1B0. ☎ **250/ 728-3383.** Fax 250/728-3383. www.futuresite.com/woodsend. E-mail: woodsend@island. net. 6 cottages. C$95–C$205 (U.S.$62–U.S.$133) per cottage for up to 4 people. Off-season discounts available. MC, V. Take Hwy. 4 to Port Alberni. There are no access roads; the owners will pick up guests by boat and transport them to the cottages.

The picturesque timbered cottages on this secluded waterfront wilderness property offer full kitchens, propane barbecues, and private porches that look out onto the 2-acre gardens. The decor consists of Canadiana antiques and collectibles, as well as hand-hewn log beds, duvets, farmhouse tables, exposed timber beams, and skylights. Opportunities for hiking, fishing, whale watching, diving, and eagle and sea-lion watching are within walking distance, as are Keeha Beach, part of the West Coast Trail, and the Cape Beale Lighthouse. A private dock, moorage, freezer space, canoe, and fishing tackle are available for guests' use. Smoking is not permitted.

5 The West Coast Trail & Pacific Rim National Park

The west coast of Vancouver Island is a magnificent area of old-growth forests, stunning fjords (called "sounds" in local parlance), rocky coasts, and long, sandy beaches. And although Pacific Rim National Park was established in 1971 as Canada's first marine park, it wasn't until 1993 that the area really exploded into the consciousness of people outside the immediate area. That was when thousands of environmentalists from across the province and around the world gathered to protest the clear-cutting of old-growth forests in Clayoquot Sound. Wherever you stand in that debate, one result

About 20,000 Pacific gray whales migrate here annually. During the second week of March, the ✪ **Pacific Rim Whale Festival** (☎ **250/726-4641**) is held in Tofino and Ucluelet. Crab races, the Gumboot Golf Tournament, guided whale-watching hikes, and a native Indian festival are just a few of the events that celebrate the annual whale migration.

of the protest was incontrovertible. When footage of the protests ran on the evening news, people at home who saw the landscape for the first time were moved to come experience it first-hand. Tourism in the area has never looked back.

There are three units to ✪ **Pacific Rim National Park.** Along the southwest coast is a strip of land that contains the ✪ **West Coast Trail,** which runs between Port Renfrew (covered in chapter 5) and Bamfield (see above). This 48-mile (77km) trail along the wilderness coastline is considered one of the world's great hikes. However, it's not for the inexperienced hiker: It's a grueling 5- to 7-day journey with frequent dangerous river crossings and rocky cliff-side scrambles. The **Broken Group Islands** unit is a wilderness archipelago in the mouth of Barkley Sound, and a popular destination for divers and sea kayakers. The **Long Beach** unit fronts onto the Pacific between the towns of Ucluelet and Tofino. Long Beach is more than 19 miles (30km) long, broken here and there by rocky headlands and bordered by tremendous groves of cedar and Sitka spruce. The beach is popular with birds and marine life, and lately, with wet-suited surfers as well.

The town of **Ucluelet** (pronounced You-*clue*-let, meaning "safe harbor" in the local Nuu-chah-nulth dialect), sits on the southern end of the Long Beach peninsula, on the edge of Barkley Sound. Though it has a winter population of only 1,900, thousands of visitors arrive between March and May to see as many as 20,000 Pacific gray whales. The whales pass close to the shore as they migrate north to their summer feeding grounds in the Arctic Circle.

At the far northern tip of the peninsula, **Tofino** (pop. 1,300) borders beautiful Clayoquot Sound. It's the center of the west-coast ecotourism business, though it's still small. Hikers and beachcombers come to Tofino simply for the scenery, while others use it as a base from which to explore Clayoquot Sound.

ESSENTIALS

GETTING THERE   By Plane   From May through September, **North Vancouver Air** (☎ **800/228-6608**) operates twin-engine, turbo-prop planes that run daily to Tofino from either Vancouver or Victoria; from October through April, it runs four times a week. The one-way fare, including all taxes and airport fees, is C$165 (U.S.$107). Flying time is 45 minutes. **Northwest Seaplanes** (☎ **800/690-0086**) and **Sound Flight** (☎ **800/825-0722**) offer floatplane service between Seattle and Tofino from mid-June to late September.

By Car   From Nanaimo, take the Island Highway (Hwy. 19) north for 31 miles (51.6km). Just before Parksville, there's a turnoff for Highway 4, which leads first to the mid-island town of Port Alberni (about 23 miles/38.3km west) and then the coastal towns of Ucluelet (62 miles/103.3km west) and Tofino (81 miles/135km west of Port Alberni). The road is well paved, but gets windy after Port Alberni.

By Ferry   A 4¹/₂-hour ride aboard the **Alberni Marine Transportation** (☎ 250/ 723-8313) passenger ferry MV *Lady Rose* takes you from Port Alberni through Alberni Inlet to Ucluelet. It makes brief stops to deliver mail and packages to solitary cabin dwellers along the coast, and to let off or pick up kayakers bound for the Broken Group Islands. The *Lady Rose* departs three times a week from Alberni Harbour Quay's Angle Street. The fare to Ucluelet is C$23 (U.S.$15) one-way, C$45 (U.S.$29) round-trip. The service is available in summer only.

By Bus   **Island Coach Lines** (☎ 250/724-1266) operates regular daily bus service between Victoria and Tofino/Ucluelet. The one-way fare for the 7-hour trip, departing from Victoria at 7:30am and arriving in Tofino at 2:45pm, is C$45 (U.S.$29) to Ucluelet and C$48 (U.S.$31) to Tofino. The bus also stops in Nanaimo and picks up passengers arriving from Vancouver on the ferry.

VISITOR INFORMATION   The **Ucluelet Visitor Info Centre,** Junction Highway 4 (P.O. Box 428), Ucluelet, BC, V0R 3A0 (☎ 250/726-4641), is open from July through September, Monday through Friday from 11am to 5pm. The **Long Beach Visitor Information Centre** (☎ 250/726-4212), about a mile (1.6km) from the Highway 4 junction to Tofino, is open from mid-March through September, daily from 10am to 6pm. The **Tofino Visitor Info Centre,** 380 Campbell St. (P.O. Box 476), Tofino, BC, V0R 2Z0 (☎ 250/725-3414), is open March through September, Monday through Friday from 11am to 5pm.

THE HIKE OF A LIFETIME: THE WEST COAST TRAIL

After the SS *Valencia* ran aground in 1906 and most of the survivors died of exposure on the beach, the government built a rescue trail between Bamfield and Port Renfrew. This trail largely retraced an old telegraph route first established in 1890; it follows a rugged shoreline where approximately 66 ships have met their demise along this stretch of "the graveyard of the Pacific." For years, the lifesaving trail was maintained by solitary watchmen who groomed the trail and checked the telephone line.

Upgraded by Parks Canada in the 1970s as part of the new Pacific Rim National Park, the ✪ **West Coast Trail** has gained a reputation as one of the world's greatest extreme hiking and camping adventures. Each year, about 9,000 people hike the entire challenging 43¹/₂-mile (70km) route, and thousands more hike the very accessible **7-mile oceanfront stretch** at the northern trailhead near Bamfield.

The West Coast Trail land is temperate coastal rain forest dominated by old-growth spruce, hemlock, and cedar. Some of the tallest and largest trees in Canada are known to be on or in the vicinity of the West Coast Trail. The topography ranges from sandy beaches to rocky headlands and wide sandstone ledges. Caves, arches, tidal pools, and waterfalls add variety to the shoreline.

Imperative for the full hike are: planning ahead (get a topographic map and tidal table), stamina (besides hiking, you should train for rock climbing), and experience (advanced wilderness-survival and minimum-impact camping knowledge). Veterans recommend going with at least two companion hikers, packing lightweight weatherproof gear, and bringing about 50 feet (15m) of climbing rope per person. To reduce impact on the environment, only 52 people per day are allowed to enter the main trail (26 from Port Renfrew, 26 from Bamfield), and registration with the park office is mandatory. Most people make the hike in 5 to 7 days.

Call **Discover BC** (☎ 800/663-6000) after March 1 to schedule your entry reservation for the coming May-to-September season. In summer, you can also contact the **parks service** (☎ 250/728-3234 or 250/647-5434) for information. Good Web sites to check out include **www.harbour.com/parkscan/pacrim** and **www. boreasbackcountry.com/polaris/hiking/wct.htm**.

Pacific Rim National Park

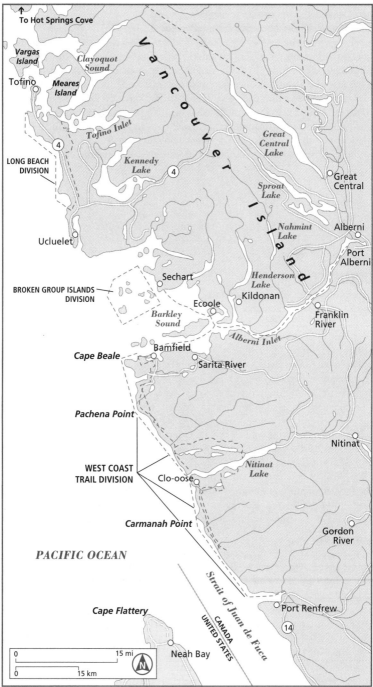

To Hot Springs Cove

Vargas Island

Clayoquot Sound

Tofino

Meares Island

Tofino Inlet

4

LONG BEACH DIVISION

Kennedy Lake

4

Ucluelet

Vancouver Island

Great Central Lake

Sproat Lake

Great Central

Nahmint Lake

Alberni

Port Alberni

BROKEN GROUP ISLANDS DIVISION

Sechart

Ecoole

Barkley Sound

Henderson Lake

Kildonan

Franklin River

Cape Beale

Bamfield

Sarita River

Alberni Inlet

Pachena Point

Nitinat

WEST COAST TRAIL DIVISION

Clo-oose

Nitinat Lake

Carmanah Point

Gordon River

PACIFIC OCEAN

Cape Flattery

Strait of Juan de Fuca

CANADA
UNITED STATES

Port Renfrew

14

0   15 mi
0   15 km

N

Neah Bay

Diving the Graveyard of the Pacific —————————————

The waters off the park's West Coast Trail are known throughout the world as "the graveyard of the Pacific." Hundreds of 19th- and 20th-century shipwrecks silently attest to the hazards of sailing without an experienced guide in these unforgiving waters. The Cousteau Society rates this area one of the world's best. There are even underwater interpretive trails that narrate the area's unique history. Contact the **Victoria Dive Tourism Association,** 2853 Graham St., Victoria (☎ **250/ 725-3318**), for information on island dive outfitters. Prices usually include onboard food and accommodations. For information on diving all around Vancouver Island, check out **www.3routes.com/scuba/na/can/bc/08/index.html**.

Make your reservations as early as possible and be prepared for busy signals and long waiting times. Limited access and increased popularity among international outdoor enthusiasts mean that you might not gain admission if you call too late in the season. The C$25 (U.S.$16) advance booking fee includes the price of a waterproof trail map. There's an additional C$70 (U.S.$46) trail-use fee.

UCLUELET

When fishing was the major industry on the coast, Ucluelet was the big town. Thanks to its harbor, it was here that most of the ships docked, and here that the processing and packing plants were located. With the recent boom in ecotourism, however, roles have been reversed, and Ucluelet is scrambling to catch up. At the moment, it has a beautiful location and a couple of fine B&Bs, but has yet to develop the same range of restaurants and activities as Tofino. Things are changing fast, however, and Ucluelet is still cheaper, just as close to Long Beach, and more likely to have vacancies in the high season, when Tofino is packed.

Fishing, kayaking, and whale watching are the big attractions in Ucluelet. Of the three, fishing still dominates. Charter companies that can take you out after salmon, halibut, and other fish include **Quest Charters,** in the boat basin (☎ **250/ 726-7532**), and the much larger **Canadian Princess Resort** (☎ **800/663-7090**).

Sea Fin Charters (☎ **250/726-2104**) and **Subtidal Adventures** (☎ **250/ 726-7336**) offer charters and whale-watching trips; they'll ferry kayakers out to the Broken Group Islands, too. **Majestic Ocean Kayaking** (☎ **250/726-2868**) runs single- and multiday guided kayak trips. See "Outdoor Pursuits" under "Tofino," below, for information on the **Long Beach Nature Tour Company**'s guided walks.

WHERE TO STAY

Ocean's Edge B&B. 855 Barkley Place, Box 557, Ucluelet, BC, V0R 3A0. ☎ **250/726-7099.** www.oceansedge.bc.ca. 3 units. May–Sept C$120 (U.S.$78) double; Oct–Apr C$95 (U.S.$62) double. Rates include full breakfast. 2-night minimum on long weekends and holidays. MC, V. Children not accepted.

A remarkable place, this little B&B sits on its own tiny peninsula jutting out into the Pacific, with only a thicket of interwoven hemlocks sheltering it from the wind and the surf of the ocean. The rooms are pleasant and spotless without being opulent; the real attraction here is the scenery and abundant wildlife. Last year, owners Bill and Susan McIntyre installed a skylight in the kitchen so that breakfasting guests could keep an eye on a pair of bald eagles and their chicks, which nest in a 200-year-old Sitka spruce in the driveway. The former chief naturalist of Pacific Rim National Park, Bill is a fount of information. See "Outdoor Pursuits" under "Tofino," below, for information on his guided nature tours.

A Snug Harbour Inn. 460 Marine Dr., Box 357, Ucluelet, BC, V0R 3A0. ☎ **888/936-5222** or 250/726-2686. Fax 250/726-2685. www.ucluelet.com/asnugharbourinn. E-mail: asnughbr@island.net. 4 units. June–Sept C$180–C$280 (U.S.$117–U.S.$182) double; Oct–May C$150–C$200 (U.S.$98–U.S.$130) double. Off-season rates and honeymoon and romantic-evening packages available. AE, MC, V. Children must be 14 or older.

A beautiful cliff-top B&B overlooking its own little bay, A Snug Harbour Inn makes the most of its location. There are several large viewing decks at the back of the inn, one with its own hot tub. In addition, guests can make use of a monster-size telescope to watch the sea lions on the reef offshore. Inside, the spacious guest rooms contain opulent bathrooms and jetted tubs. The heart-shaped tub with waterfall may be a bit over the top, but who's complaining? Owner Skip Rowland had the inn built by a shipwright, and the craftsmanship shows. Smoking is permitted outside only.

WHERE TO DINE

Fine dining is only just beginning to have a presence in this sea-coast town, as urban refugees with a flair for cooking arrive and try to make a go of it. Two that have succeeded are the **Kingfisher Restaurant,** 1952 Peninsula Rd. (☎ **250/726-3463**), and the **Matterson Teahouse and Garden,** 1682 Peninsula Rd. (☎ **250/726-2200**). Seafood is the chief focus at the Kingfisher. As for the Matterson, just let Soren, the Danish chef, know what you're interested in, and chances are he can make it.

BROKEN GROUP ISLANDS

Lying off the coast of Ucluelet are the Broken Group Islands, an archipelago of about 300 islands and islets in Barkley Sound that are part of Pacific Rim National Park. Due to the relatively calm waters, abundant wildlife, and dramatic seascapes, these islands are very popular destinations for experienced sea kayakers and ocean canoeists.

Divers can explore historic shipwrecks as well as reefs teeming with beautiful marine life (dive outfitters operate out of Bamfield, described above). The islands are home to branching bryozoans (microscopic sea creatures) that create coral-like reefs where brittle stars, juvenile crabs, and ring-top snails live in protected clusters. The underwater drop-offs shelter large populations of feather stars, rockfish, and wolf eels that grow as long as 7 feet and occasionally poke their heads out of their caves.

Access to the Broken Group Islands is limited. In both Bamfield and Ucluelet, you'll find a number of operators who can help put together a trip to the islands, or you can take a packet freighter from Port Alberni. Lady Rose Marine Services drops off kayakers bound for the Broken Group at Sechart, on a spur of Vancouver Island across from the islands themselves; kayakers then make the crossing on their own.

Sechart is also the site of the **Sechart Whaling Station Lodge,** another operation of the enterprising folks at Lady Rose Marine Services. The lodge building was freighted down the Alberni Inlet from Port Alberni (it was formerly an office building at a paper mill), and positioned on a peaceful cove across from the Broken Group at the site of an early-20th-century whaling station. The lodge primarily serves the needs of kayakers, though it's open to anyone who wants a unique wilderness experience. Rates are C$100 (U.S.$65) double occupancy, including three family-style meals a day, or C$60 (U.S.$39) without meals. The only way to get to the lodge is via one of the company freighters or on your own vessel. Kayak rentals are available at the lodge. For reservations, contact **Lady Rose Marine Services** (☎ **800/663-7192** from Apr to Sept, or 250/723-8313; fax 250/723-8314).

TOFINO

The center of the environmental protests against industrial logging—and the center of the ecotourism business ever since—Tofino remains a rather schizophrenic kind of town. Half of the town is composed of ecotourism outfitters, nature lovers, activists, and serious granolas, while the other half is comprised of loggers and fishermen. Conflict was common in the early years, but recently, the two sides seem to have learned to get along. For a hilarious take on the culture clash between incoming eco-freaks and long-term rednecks during the summer of discontent, pick up *The Green Shadow,* by local eco-freak (and closet redneck) Andrew Struthers.

Outdoor Pursuits

FISHING   Sportfishing for salmon, steelhead, rainbow trout, Dolly Varden char, halibut, cod, and snapper is excellent off the west coast. The nearby provincial hatchery releases more than 10 million fish into these waters annually. Long Beach is also great for bottom fishing. To fish here, you need a nonresident saltwater or freshwater license. Tackle shops sell licenses, offer information on current restrictions, and often carry copies of the publications *BC Tidal Waters Sport Fishing Guide* and *BC Sport Fishing Regulations Synopsis for Non-tidal Waters.* Independent anglers should also pick up a copy of the *BC Fishing Directory and Atlas.*

Chinook Charters (☎ **800/665-3646** or 250/725-3431) organizes fishing charters throughout the Clayoquot Sound area. Fishing, which starts in March or April and lasts until December, can include various species of salmon, halibut, and trout. The company supplies all gear, a guide, and a boat. Prices start from C$85 (U.S.$55) per hour, with a minimum of 4 hours.

GUIDED NATURE HIKES   Owned and operated by Bill McIntyre, former chief naturalist of Pacific Rim National Park, the **Long Beach Nature Tour Company** (☎ **250/726-7099;** fax 250726-4282) offers guided beach walks, storm watching, land-based whale watching, and rain-forest tours, customized to suit your group's needs. We highly recommended Bill's excursions.

Also excellent are the tours offered by wildlife author Adrienne Mason of **Raincoast Communications** (☎ **250/725-2878;** e-mail: amason@port.island.net). A local naturalist and science writer, she can accommodate various group sizes, and will greatly enhance your knowledge of the local flora and fauna and ecology.

HIKING   The 7-mile (11.7km) stretch of rocky headlands, sand, and surf along **Long Beach Headlands Trail** is the most accessible section of the park system, which incorporates Long Beach, the West Coast Trail, and the Broken Group Islands. No matter where you go in this area, you're bound to meet whale watchers in spring, surfers and anglers in summer, hearty hikers, and kayakers year-round.

In and around **Long Beach,** numerous marked trails from a half mile to 2 miles (0.8km to 3.3km) long take you through the thick temperate rain forest that edges the shore. The **Gold Mine Trail** (about 2 miles/3.3km) near Florencia Bay still has a few artifacts from the days when a gold-mining operation flourished amid the trees. And the partially boardwalked **South Beach Trail** (less than a mile/1.6km long) leads through the moss-draped rain forest onto small, quiet coves such as Lismer Beach and South Beach, where you can see abundant life in the rocky tidal pools.

The **Big Cedar Trail** (☎ **250/725-3233**), on Meares Island, is a 2-mile (3.3km) boardwalked path that was built to protect the old-growth forest. Maintained by the Tla-o-qui-aht native Indian band, the trail has a long staircase leading up to the Hanging Garden Tree, the province's fourth-largest western red cedar.

Hot Springs Cove

Hot Springs Cove is a natural hot spring located about 40 miles (66.6km) north of Tofino; it's accessible only by water. Take a water taxi, canoe, or kayak up to Clayoquot Sound to enjoy a swim in the steaming pools and bracing waterfalls. A number of kayak outfitters and boat charters offer trips here (see "Whale Watching & Birding," below).

In town, **Tofino Botanical Garden,** 1084 Pacific Rim Hwy. (☎ **250/725-1220**), is still very much a work in progress, but when it's completed later in 2000, it will feature a landscaped walking garden with native and exotic plants and small architect-designed pavilions, where you can sit and contemplate your surroundings.

✪ **KAYAKING**   Perhaps the quintessential Clayoquot experience, and certainly one of the most fun, is slipping into a kayak and paddling out into the waters of the sound. For beginners, half-day tours to Meares Island (usually with the opportunity to do a little hiking) are an especially good bet. For rentals, lessons, and tours, try **Pacific Kayak** (☎ **250/725-3232;** www.tofino-bc.com/pacifickayak). The **Tofino Sea-Kayaking Company** (☎ **800/863-4664** or 250/725-4222; www.island.net/ ~paddlers) offers packages ranging from 4-hour paddles (from C$52/U.S.$34 per person) to weeklong paddling/camping expeditions.

WHALE WATCHING & BIRDING   A number of outfitters conduct tours throughout this region, which is inhabited by gray whales, bald eagles, porpoises, orcas, seals, and sea lions. **Chinook Charters** (☎ **800/665-3646** or 250/725-3431) offers Clayoquot Sound whale-watching trips on 25-foot Zodiac boats. The company also conducts trips to Hot Springs Cove on its 32-foot Chinook Key. **Jamie's Whaling Station** (☎ **800/667-9913** or 250/725-3919) uses a glass-bottomed 65-foot power cruiser as well as a fleet of Zodiacs for whale-watching tours from March through October. A combined Hot Springs Cove and whale-watching trip aboard a 32-foot cruiser can be booked year-round. Fares for both companies' expeditions generally start at C$75 (U.S.$49) per person for a 3-hour tour; customized trips can run as high as C$200 (U.S.$130) per person for a full day. For an interesting combination, try the 5-hour Sea-to-Sky tour, which starts out with a boat ride, then a hike through the rain forest, and finally a return to Tofino by floatplane; it costs C$109 (U.S.$71) for adults.

From March through November, **Remote Passages** (☎ **800/666-9833** or 250/ 725-3330) runs 2^1/$_2$-hour whale-watching tours on Zodiacs in Clayoquot Sound. Fares are C$50 (U.S.$33) for adults, C$35 (U.S.$23) for kids. A 7-hour combination whale-watching and Hot Springs trip costs C$75 (U.S.$49) for adults, C$50 (U.S.$33) for kids. Reservations are recommended.

For land-based bird watching, contact local naturalist and science-writer Adrienne Mason of **Raincoast Communications** (see "Guided Nature Hikes," above).

RAINY-DAY ACTIVITIES: SHOPPING, STORM WATCHING & MORE

With Tofino becoming more of a tourist destination, art studios and galleries are springing up everywhere. Some focus on native arts and crafts, while others specialize in work from local and Vancouver Island artists. Most are located around Campbell and Main streets. Check for opening hours during the off-season.

If you make only one stop, take a peek at the **Eagle Aerie Gallery,** 350 Campbell St. (☎ **604/725-3235**), which is constructed in the style of a native Indian longhouse. The gallery features the artwork of Roy Henry Vickers, a hereditary chief and son of a Tsimshian native Indian fisherman, including serigraphs, sculptures in glass and wood, carved panels, and totem poles. The **House of Himwitsa,** 300 Main St. (☎ 250/725-2017), is also owned and operated by native Indians. The quality of the shop's artwork, masks, totems, jewelry, and apparel is excellent.

Island Folk Artisans Gallery, 120 Fourth St. (☎ 250/725-3130), mainly represents Vancouver Island artists. The themes are often trees, wildlife, and crafts made out of wood or seashells, a lasting memory of your trip. The more flaky, New Age side of Tofino can be found in the **Reflecting Spirit Gallery,** 441 Campbell St. (☎ 250/725-4229). You'll see medicine wheels and crystals, but also a great selection of native art, carvings, wood crafts, and pottery.

When you're done gallery-hopping, browse the books and grab a steaming latte at the **Wildside Booksellers and Espresso Bar** (☎ 250/745-4222), on Main Street. If you're in the mood for some pampering, treat yourself to a massage or salt glow at the **Ancient Cedars Spa** at the Wickaninnish (☎ 250/725-3100).

Watching the winter storms behind big glass windows has become very popular in Tofino over the past year or so. For a slight twist on this, try the outdoor storm-watching tours offered by the **Long Beach Nature Tour Company** (☎ 250/726-7099; fax 250/726-4282). Owner Bill McIntyre, former chief naturalist of Pacific Rim National Park, will explain how storms work—as well as where to stand so you can get close without getting swept away.

WHERE TO STAY

The Clayoquot Wilderness Resort. P.O. Box 728, Tofino, BC, V0R 2Z0. ☎ **888/333-5405** in North America, or 250/725-2688. Fax 250/725-2689. www.wildretreat.com. 16 units. May–Oct C$249 (U.S.$162) per person, per night; Nov–Apr C$189 (U.S.$123) per person, per night. Rates include 3 meals daily, plus transfer to and from Tofino. AE, MC, V. Parking provided in Tofino.

The latest in absolute luxury in the area, the Clayoquot Wilderness Resort (CWS) floats alone in splendid isolation on Quait Bay, about a half-hour boat ride from Tofino. Guests are encouraged to use the lodge as a base camp for exploring the natural beauty of the sound. The CWS has set up a number of forest trails nearby, and also offers trips to Hot Springs Cove as well as horseback-riding and mountain-biking excursions. The spacious guest rooms offer down duvets, private decks, magnificent views, morning coffee service, aromatherapeutic toiletries, and robes. Meals are prepared by noted West Coast chef Timothy May. The CWS also has four campsites.

House of Himwitsa. P.O. Box 176, 300 Main St., Tofino, BC, V0R 2Z0. ☎ **800/725-2017** or 250/725-2017. Fax 250/725-2361. 4 units. TV TEL. Oct–May C$125–C$185 (U.S.$81–U.S.$120) double; June–Sept C$160–C$225 (U.S.$104–U.S.$146) double. Extra person C$20 (U.S.$13). AE, MC, V.

Overlooking the government dock in the center of town, the House of Himwitsa is a gallery/restaurant on the ground floor, with a small guest house above. Each spacious guest room contains a kitchenette, dining area, and sitting area with pull-out couch. All units have water views, and three have hot tubs outside on a private deck. The ground-floor Sea Shanty restaurant is good though not memorable.

The Inn at Tough City. 350 Main St., P.O. Box 8, Tofino, BC, V0R 2Z0. ☎ **250/725-2021.** Fax 250/725-2088. www.alberni.net/toughcity. E-mail: cityinn@cedar.alberni.net. 6 units. Mar 1–May 15 C$90–C$120 (U.S.$59–U.S.$78) double; May 16–Oct 15 C$140–C$165 (U.S.$91–U.S.$107) double; Oct 16–Feb 28 C$75–C$100 (U.S.$49–U.S.$65) double. MC, V.

This is possibly the nicest small inn in Tofino, and certainly the quirkiest. Built in 1996 from salvaged and recycled material, the inn is chock-full of antiques and bric-a-brac. The guest rooms are spacious, and several feature soaker tubs or fireplaces. Crazy Ron and Johana are your hosts.

Middle Beach Lodge. P.O. Box 100, Tofino, BC, V0R 2Z0. ☎ **250/725-2900.** Fax 250/725-2901. www.middlebeach.com. E-mail: lodge@middlebeach.com. 58 units. C$110–C$165 (U.S.$72–U.S.$107) rm double, C$165–C$275 (U.S.$107–U.S.$179) suite double, C$175–C$370 (U.S.$114–U.S.$241) single cabin, C$160–C$295 (U.S.$104–U.S.$192) duplex cabin, C$110–C$210 (U.S.$72–U.S.$137) triplex cabin, C$125–C$195 (U.S.$81–U.S.$127) sixplex suite. AE, MC, V.

This beautiful complex is located on a headland overlooking the ocean. The rustic look was accomplished by using largely recycled beams, with very pleasing results. Accommodations range from simple lodge rooms to cabins with waterside decks, soaker tubs, fireplaces, and kitchenettes. All guests enjoy access to a lofty common room overlooking the ocean—a good place to sip coffee or something stronger while looking out over the waves crashing in. *Note:* Smoking is not permitted.

Red Crow Guest House. 1084 Pacific Rim Hwy. (Box 37), Tofino, BC, V0R 2Z0. ☎ and fax **250/725-2275.** E-mail: tofinoredcrow@hotmail.com. 3 units, 1 cottage. C$100–C$135 (U.S.$65–U.S.$88) rm, C$160 (U.S.$104) cottage. Extra person C$20 (U.S.$13). V.

Whereas the Wickaninnish and other coastal lodges show you the wild, stormy side of the coast, the Red Crow displays a gentler beauty. Located by the sheltered waters of Clayoquot Sound, this pleasant Cape Cod house looks like it could be set on a lake—that is, until you paddle 50 feet out in a canoe or rowboat (free for guests' use) and see the glaciers. Host Cathy Whitcomb runs an extremely friendly, laid-back establishment. Guests are welcomed with tea and cookies, then given the run of the extensive grounds, often with an affable dog for company. The large, pleasant rooms, outfitted with 1920s-style furnishings, are located on the lower level of the house and have their own porch. Also available is a garden cottage, a cozy, eclectic spot with a full kitchen and woodstove. Substantial hot breakfasts are served downstairs in the sunshine—weather permitting—or under the cover of the veranda.

The Tides Inn on Duffin Cove. 160 Arnet Rd. (Box 325), Tofino, BC, V0R 2Z0. ☎ **250/725-3765.** 3 units. Summer C$90–C$110 (U.S.$59–U.S.$72) double; fall/winter C$80–C$100 (U.S.$52–U.S.$65) double. Small condo in town C$125 (U.S.$81) double. 2-night minimum. No credit cards. Young children not accepted.

The Tides Inn offers three rooms, all with private entrance and spectacular views of Clayoquot Sound. Guests are free to enjoy the hot tub on the grounds; a wooden stairway leads down to a semiprivate beach. *Note:* Smoking is not permitted.

✪ The Wickaninnish Inn. Osprey Lane at Chesterman Beach (P.O. Box 250), Tofino, BC, V0R 2Z0. ☎ **800/333-4604** in North America, or 250/725-3300. Fax 250/725-3110. E-mail: wick@island.net. 46 units. Mar 1–June 25 C$170–C$210 (U.S.$111–U.S.$137) double; June 26–Sept 30 C$240–C$280 (U.S.$156–U.S.$182) double; Oct 1–Nov 1 C$180–C$220 (U.S.$117–U.S.$143) double; Nov 2–Feb 28 C$140–C$180 (U.S.$91–U.S.$117) double. Special packages available year-round. AE, MC, V. Drive 3 miles (5km) south of Tofino toward Chesterman Beach to Osprey Lane.

No matter which room you book in this beautiful new cedar, stone, and glass lodge, you'll wake to a magnificent view of the untamed Pacific. The inn is on a rocky promontory, surrounded by an old-growth forest and the sprawling sands of Chesterman Beach. The spacious guest rooms contain fireplaces, down duvets, soaker tubs (some with views), and private balconies. Rustic driftwood, richly printed textiles, and local artwork highlight the decor. Winter storm-watching packages have become so popular that the inn is as busy in winter as it is in summer. The Pointe Restaurant (see "Where to Dine," below) serves three meals daily. The staff can arrange whale-watching, golfing, fishing, and diving packages. No-Stress Express packages include air transport and accommodations.

CAMPING

The 94 campsites on the bluff at **Green Point** are maintained by **Pacific Rim National al Park** (☎ 250/726-7721). The grounds are full every day in July and August, and the average wait for a site is 1 to 2 days. When you arrive in the area, leave your name at the ranger station to be placed on the list. Sites cost C$14 to C$20 (U.S.$9 to U.S.$13) in July and August, C$12 to C$18 (U.S.$8 to U.S.$12) in the shoulder season. You'll be rewarded for your patience with a magnificent ocean view, pit toilets, fire pits, pumped well water, and free firewood. There are no showers or hookups. The campground is closed from October through March.

Bella Pacifica Resort & Campground, 2 miles (3.3km) south of Tofino on the Pacific Rim Highway (☎ 250/725-3400), is privately owned. It has 165 campsites, from which you can walk to Mackenzie Beach or take the resort's private trails to Templar Beach. Flush toilets, hot showers, water, laundry, ice, fire pits, firewood, and full and partial hookups are available. Rates are C$16 to C$33 (U.S.$10 to U.S.$21) per two-person site. Reserve at least a month in advance for a summer weekend.

Overlooking Grappler Inlet near Bamfield, **Seabeam Fishing Resort & Campground** (☎ 250/728-3286) has 80 campsites and eight rustic lodge rooms. Rates are C$15 to C$20 (U.S.$10 to U.S.$13) per vehicle, C$30 to C$40 (U.S.$20 to U.S.$26) per lodge room. Facilities include hot showers, pay phones, and boat rentals.

WHERE TO DINE

The Common Loaf Bakeshop. 181 First St., Tofino. ☎ **250/725-3915.** Reservations not accepted. Main courses C$3–C$8 (U.S.$1.95–U.S.$5). MC, V. Daily 8am–9pm. BAKERY/CAFE.

Locally famous as the gathering place for granolas, hippies, and other reprobates back when such things mattered in Tofino, the Loaf has recently expanded, which just goes to show you can make money selling idealism along with your muffins. Located at the "far" end of town, on First Street, the Common Loaf does baked goods really well: muffins, cookies, whole-grain breads, and sticky cinnamon buns. It also serves lunch items such as soups, curry, and pizza. You can quench your thirst with herbal tea, coffee, juice, wine, or beer. If it looks crowded downstairs, head up to the loft, where you can have a bird's-eye view of one of the main streets. And to find out about the latest cause célèbre, just have a look at the Loaf's bulletin board.

The Pointe Restaurant. The Wickaninnish Inn, Osprey Lane at Chesterman Beach, Tofino. ☎ **250/725-3110.** Reservations recommended. Main courses C$18–C$30 (U.S.$12–U.S.$20). MC, V. Daily 8am–2:30pm, 2–5pm (for snacks), and 5–9:30pm. PACIFIC NORTHWEST.

Perched on the water's edge at Chesterman Beach is the Pointe, where views of the roaring Pacific serve as the backdrop to an experience that can only be described as pure Pacific Northwest. Chef Rodney Butters applies his talents to an array of local ingredients, including Dungeness crab, spotted prawns, halibut, salmon, and lamb. His signature version of bouillabaisse is a fragrant blend of fish, shellfish, and vegetables simmered in a thick seafood broth. Follow the delectable goat-cheese tarts with grilled lamb chops served with new potatoes, artichokes, and sea asparagus. End with a double-chocolate, mashed-potato brioche, accompanied by a glass of raspberry wine.

The Rain Coast Cafe. Located off Campbell at Fourth St., Tofino. ☎ **250/725-2215.** Main courses C$11–C$20 (U.S.$7–U.S.$13). AE, MC, V. Daily 11:30am–3pm and 5–10pm. WEST COAST/VEGETARIAN.

This cozy restaurant, just off the main street, has developed a deserved reputation for some of the best—and best value—seafood and vegetarian dishes in town. To start off, try one of the most popular appetizers, the Rain Coast salad—smoked salmon, sautéed mushrooms, and chèvre cheese on a bed of greens, served with maple-balsamic vinaigrette. Fresh fish is a big part of the cuisine, and menu items are supplemented with a catch-of-the-day special. Mainstays include seafood and pasta entrees such as linguini with prawns and fresh herbs.

6 Denman & Hornby Islands & Fanny Bay

32 miles (51km) N of Qualicum Beach

Follow Highway 19A, the "old highway" north and west of Qualicum Beach, through forests and past views of Denman and Hornby islands in the Georgia Strait. On the way, you'll drive through several small communities and the small towns of **Qualicum Bay** and **Bowser** before the road joins up again with the Highway 19 expressway. The community of **Fanny Bay** is followed by **Buckley Bay,** the ferry terminus for Denman and Hornby islands.

While none of these little towns are tourist destinations in themselves, they are all pleasant places to while away an hour or two, and some of the B&Bs here are top-notch. The area around Fanny Bay is also Vancouver Island's most renowned oyster-farming area; ask for Fanny Bay oysters by name at local restaurants.

Flower children were attracted to rural **Hornby** (pop. 1,300) and **Denman** (pop. 1,200) during the 1960s and 1970s, when they started organic farms and thriving art communities on the tiny islands off the coast of Vancouver Island. Both islands have maintained their bohemian charm, as well as their mostly deserved reputation as colonies of "alternative" lifestyles. Hornby Island's beaches and provincial parks are another excellent reason to make the journey: Helliwell Provincial Park features a hiking path along the edge of spectacular ocean-fronting cliffs.

During the first 2 weeks in August, the **Hornby Festival** is held at the Community Hall on Hornby Island. Events include live music and theatrical and dance performances. Call ☎ **250/335-2734** for more information.

ESSENTIALS

GETTING THERE   The islands are accessible only by water. Visitors regularly cross by ferry, canoe, or kayak. To reach Hornby, you'll need first to cross to Denman; the Hornby ferry leaves from the southern shore of Denman Island.

By Ferry   BC Ferries (☎ 250/386-3431) operates year-round between these islands and Vancouver Island. The dozen daily trips to each island take 10 minutes one-way and cost C$4.25 to C$4.50 (U.S.$2.75 to U.S.$2.95) per person; vehicles are extra. The ferry from Buckley Bay to Denman Island operates from 7am to 11pm, while the ferry from Denman to Hornby Island operates from 8am to 6:35pm.

VISITOR INFORMATION   On Denman Island, the **Denman General Store,** 1069 Northwest Rd., Denman Island, BC, V0R 1T0 (☎ **250/335-2293**), acts as **Denman/Hornby Visitor Services.** It offers a free island guide as well as a brochure listing the small arts and crafts galleries. You can also get information on the Web at **www.denman.bc.ca** and **www.hornbyisland.com**.

GETTING AROUND   Public transportation on Hornby Island directly reflects this gentle culture: The **Hornby Blue Bus (☎ 250/335-0715)** is a funky 1960s International Harvester. Passengers negotiate with the driver to determine the fare from the ferry. The islands are also great for two-wheel exploration. Visitors can bring bikes on the ferry or go to the **Hornby Island Off-Road Bike Shop,** next to the Co-Op market (☎ **250/335-0444**), or to **Scooter & Bike Rentals,** a 5-minute walk from the ferry in Denman Village (☎ **250/335-2293**).

EXPLORING THE ISLANDS

Hornby and Denman islands are pleasant destinations for strolling or cycling along the sandy beaches. On Hornby, **Tribune Bay Provincial Park** is one of the finest white-sand beaches on the coast. Hornby is also a great destination for birding. The bluffs in **Helliwell Bay Provincial Park** are home to thousands of nesting birds; walking trails edge along the cliffs, making this a dramatically scenic hike.

Denman Island also has its share of sandy beaches, including **Bayle Point,** which has a spectacular view of the Chrome Island Lighthouse. The majestic stands of old-growth Douglas fir in **Fillongley Provincial Park** are an inspiration to many of the local artisans. There's also plenty to see at the many **open studios.** In summer, potters, jewelers, painters, and sculptors open their doors so visitors can view their work.

Sandy Island, off the northern tip of Denman Island, is a favorite destination of sea kayakers. Called "Tree Island" by locals, the island is accessible only by boat or, at low tide, on foot. With only 81 acres, it's essentially a broad sand spit peppered with trees; in summer, the shallow water gets wonderfully warm for swimming. **Denman Island Sea Kayaks,** 1536 Northwest Rd., just north of Denman Village (☎ **250/ 335-2505**), offers rentals and guided excursions; the same folks operate **Sea Canary B&B** and offer lodging/kayaking packages starting at C$65 (U.S.$42). On Hornby, you can rent kayaks from **Hornby Ocean Kayaks** (☎ **250/335-2726**), near the Central Road school building.

Divers will want to look for the rare species of primitive six-gill shark that resides in the deep reefs around Denman and Hornby. Don't worry—the 12-foot-long creatures are very slow-moving because of the unusually warm water temperature. In fact, they seem to enjoy the company of divers who come to mingle with them near the Flora Islet in summer. But more than marine life attracts divers to these waters: Built in 1900, the iron steamer *Alpha* ran aground off **Chrome Island** just south of Denman Island in the 1920s; it's just one of the many wrecks divers will encounter.

WHERE TO STAY & DINE
Near Fanny Bay

The local pub, the **Fanny Bay Inn,** serves a full menu of pub grub and some entree specials. For a memorable meal, order the excellent fiery chicken wings and a pint. The **Harbour View Bistro,** 5575 W. Island Hwy., in Union Bay (☎ **250/355-3277**), has a big local reputation for its French-influenced cuisine. Don't be put off by its unassuming exterior (the bistro is in a trailer house). Reservations are suggested.

✪ **Longhouse Inn at Ships Point.** 7584 Ships Point Rd., Fanny Bay, BC, V0R 1W0. ☎ **800/925-1595** or 250/335-2200. Fax 250/335-2214. www.shipspoint.com. E-mail: innkeeper@shipspoint.com. 2 units. C$174–C$275 (U.S.$113–U.S.$179) double. AE, MC, V.

Longhouse Inn is the perfect place for a romantic weekend or quiet getaway. One of the most beautifully furnished B&Bs on the island, the inn combines the features of your favorite first-class hotel—top-quality amenities, exquisite furnishings, discrete service—with a setting at the edge of a tranquil bay-front beach. The apartment-size suites are off in their own building, which stands above a series of woodland and formal English gardens, which then gives way to the private beach. The Bird's Nest Suite contains a wrought-iron bed, fireplace, sitting area, CD player, fridge with complimentary wine and sodas, and tea/coffeemaker. The bathroom is especially luxurious, with a glass-walled shower and heated slate floors, Aveda toiletries, and terry-lined silk robes. A two-person soaker tub occupies a corner of the suite. Enjoy a view of the bay through the picture windows, or step onto the private deck and watch for seals. The smaller Hummingbird Suite is wheelchair accessible, and otherwise shares the amenities and style of the larger suite. Your hosts are charming and unobtrusive, offering all the service you need and all the privacy you desire. The multicourse breakfast is beautifully presented. The inn offers kayaks for guests' use.

ON DENMAN ISLAND

There aren't many places to eat on Denman. **Café on the Rock,** in Denman Village (☎ 250/335-2999), is open for three meals daily, serving light entrees, vegetarian meals, and homemade desserts. The **Kaleidoscope Market,** in Denman Village (☎ 250/335-0451), has a deli.

Denman Island Guest House. 3806 Denman Rd., Denman Island, BC, V0R 1T0. ☎ 250/335-2688. 5 units (none with private bathroom). C$65 (U.S.$42) double. Rates include breakfast. No credit cards; personal checks (from U.S. and Canadian banks) accepted.

This century-old farmhouse has a laid-back island atmosphere and rustic guest rooms with a shared bathroom. For visitors exploring the island, this is a good location to rest up and fortify yourself with a huge, country-style breakfast before heading out on the overland and marine trails. With garden views, the hotel restaurant is more than passable. The menu changes with the availability of local seafood and produce. Dinner is served Wednesday through Sunday from 4:30 to 9:30pm.

Hawthorn House Bed & Breakfast. 3375 Kirk Rd., Denman Island, BC, V0R 1T0. ☎ 250/335-0905. Fax 250/335-0905. www.nobelmed.com/hawthorn. 3 units. TV. C$70–C$85 (U.S.$46–U.S.$55) double. Extra person C$15 (U.S.$10). Rates include full breakfast. No credit cards; personal checks (from U.S. and Canadian banks) accepted. From the ferry, take Denman Rd. to Northwest Rd., turn left, continue to Kirk Rd., and then turn left.

Children are welcome at this restored 1904 heritage house, which is tastefully decorated with Canadiana. The one single and two double rooms all have private bathrooms. The property's ocean and mountain views are complemented by a secluded garden. Dinner can be prepared for guests on request; fruit and vegetables come from the organic garden, and the fresh-every-morning eggs come from a farm just down the road. Also on the premises are a hot tub, bikes for rent, and a friendly dog. *Note:* Smoking is permitted outside only.

ON HORNBY ISLAND

Hornby Island Resort & Thatch Pub. 4305 Shingle Spit Rd., Hornby Island, BC, V0R 1Z0. ☎ 250/335-0136. Fax 250/335-9136. E-mail: hornbyr@mars.ark.com. 2 rms, 2 cottages, 10 campsites. C$70 (U.S.$46) double (extra person C$5/U.S.$3.25), C$12–C$18 (U.S.$8–U.S.$12) campsite, C$1 (U.S.65¢) electric hookup. Cottages are weekly-only in summer, C$695 (U.S.$452). Vehicles C$12 (U.S.$8). Off-season and weekly rates available. MC, V.

Book your reservations months in advance for the cottages and campsites of this popular waterfront resort located next to the ferry terminal. The rustic cottage rooms are basically furnished; the campsites are well maintained and adequately spaced. Campground facilities include hot showers and laundry. Extras include a playground on the beach, boat rental and moorage service, and a tennis court on the grounds. The resort has a licensed restaurant and pub with a waterfront view, offering casual indoor and outdoor dining year-round as well as barbecues on the deck in summer. The Thatch Pub is a popular local nightspot with live music Thursday through Saturday.

Sea Breeze Lodge. Big Tree 3-2, Hornby Island, BC, V0R 1Z0. ☎ **250/335-2321.**
www.seabreezelodge.com. E-mail: seabreeze@mars.ark.com. 12 cottages. June 15–Sept 15,
full American Plan only, C$230 (U.S.$150) adult double, C$40 (U.S.$26) children 2–6, C$51
(U.S.$33) children 7–12, C$68 (U.S.$44) youths 13–17. Off-season, self-catering only,
C$65–C$95 (U.S.$42–U.S.$62) double. Extra person C$10 (U.S.$7). Weekly rates available.
MC, V.

This well-loved resort offers comfortable beach-side cottages, some with kitchens, all
with fireplaces and private bathrooms. These cottages have been around a while, and
thus have a friendly, lived-in quality that more than makes up for the slightly faded
gentility of the furnishings. In summer, cottage rates include all meals; the dining
room is open at lunch and dinner to nonguests with reservations. Facilities include a
dock, grass tennis court, and hot tub.

7 Courtenay & Comox

37 miles (62km) N of Qualicum Beach

Facing each other across the Courtenay Estuary, Comox (pop. 11,847) and Courtenay (pop. 19,592) are twin towns that provide a bit of urban polish to a region rich
in outdoor recreation and dramatic land- and seascapes. Because Courtenay and
Comox are north of the Victoria-to-Tofino circuit that defines much of the tourism
on Vancouver Island, these towns are refreshingly untouristy and "real" when compared to some of the theme-park burgs to the south. Comox has a working harbor
with a fishing fleet, while Courtenay, a lumber-milling center, has an old downtown
core where the shops haven't yet completely transformed into boutiques. Which isn't
to say that these towns lack sophistication: You'll find excellent lodges, B&Bs, and
restaurants, and the new and opulent Crown Isle Golf Resort is not exactly the kind
of place you'd expect to find in a mill town. In fact, depend on the pace of change to
quicken: The Comox Valley is the fastest growing region of Vancouver Island.

Courtenay and Comox are also stepping-off points for adventures in the Beaufort
Mountains, which reach their highest peaks just to the west. From Mount Washington Alpine Resort and Forbidden Plateau Ski Area, hiking trails lead into the southeast corner of Strathcona Provincial Park. Here, sparkling alpine lakes, massive glacial
basins, and craggy peaks reward hikers. There are also adventures to be had at sea level.
The shallow Courtenay Estuary is home to abundant wildlife, particularly seabirds
and sea mammals. Sea kayaks allow you to explore this rich marine ecosystem with
minimum disturbance to the wildlife.

ESSENTIALS

GETTING THERE   Comox Valley Regional Airport, north of Comox off Ryan
Road, has daily scheduled flights to and from Vancouver on **Canadian Regional
Airlines** (☎ 800/426-7000 in the U.S., 800/665-1177 in Canada) and **Air BC**
(☎ 800/766-3000 in the U.S., 800/663-3721 in Canada).

BC Ferries (☎ 250/386-3431) cross from Little River, just north of Comox off
Anderson Road, to Powell River on the British Columbia mainland. Nanaimo is the
closest ferry terminal with connections to the Vancouver area.

Courtenay, which is 90 minutes north of Nanaimo on Highway 19, is also the terminus for the **E&N Railiner** (☎ 800/561-8630 or 250/383-4324), which offers
daily service from Victoria. **Laidlaw Coach Lines** (☎ 250/385-4411) provides daily
service to Comox/Courtenay from Nanaimo and points south.

VISITOR INFORMATION   For more information on the Comox/Courtenay area,
contact the **Comox Valley Visitor Info Centre,** 2040 Cliffe Ave., Courtenay, BC,

Special Events

The **Filberg Festival** is one of British Columbia's top arts-and-crafts events, attracting over 140 artists and craftspeople from across the province. It all takes place at Filberg Park, with some events in the lodge and others in tents and booths scattered across 9 acres of grounds. The festival has grown quickly in recent years, and now includes musical entertainment, theater, and food booths. It's held the first weekend of August; admission is C$6 (U.S.$3.90) for adults, C$2 (U.S.$1.30) for children 6 to 12. For information, contact the park (see below) or the festival coordinator (☎ 250/334-9242).

V9N 2L3 (☎ 888/357-4471 or 250/334-3234; www.vquest.com/cv.chamber or www.tourism-comox-valley.bc.ca; e-mail: chamber@mars.ark.com).

EXPLORING THE AREA

Highway 19 becomes Cliffe Avenue as it enters Courtenay. It then crosses the Courtenay River and continues north toward Campbell River, bypassing the old town centers of both Courtenay and Comox. This is a comparative blessing, as it allows these commercial districts to quietly gentrify without four lanes of traffic shooting past.

COURTENAY

Courtenay's town center revolves around Fourth, Fifth, and Sixth streets just west of the Courtenay River. It's a pleasant place for a stroll, with a number of coffee shops, galleries, and home-decor shops to browse. An excellent choice for gifts and crafts is the **Artisans Courtyard,** 180A Fifth St. (☎ 250/338-6564), a co-op with more than 60 members. Its retail store is located in a pleasant garden setting. Next door is the **Potter's Place,** 180A 15th St. (☎ 250/334-4613), which offers the works of 29 potters, ranging from earthenware and porcelain to raku and stoneware. The **Comox Valley Art Gallery,** 367 Fourth St. (☎ 250/338-6211), is the regional public gallery, which displays traveling shows and exhibits the work of contemporary and emerging artists from the area. The gift shop offers original handmade art and crafts.

The **Courtenay Museum & Paleontology Centre,** 360 Cliffe Ave. (☎ 250/334-3611; www.courtenaymuseum.bc.ca), is one of those small regional museums that pack a lot of artifacts and information into a modest space. Located in Courtenay's old post office, the museum tells the story of the native First Nation peoples with a good collection of masks, basketry, and other carvings. Other exhibits detail Courtenay's early frontier logging days; there's a massive slide of Douglas fir log that's 1,160 years old. The highlight of the museum is a 40-foot (12m) cast skeleton of an elasmosaur, a Cretaceous-era marine reptile that resembles a modern crocodile.

The Comox Valley was once covered by a tropical sea, and the area now yields a wealth of marine fossils. The Courtenay Museum leads summer **fossil tours** of the exhibits and paleontology lab, culminating in a trip to a local fossil dig. This 3-hour tour is offered on Tuesday, Thursday, and Sunday in July and August. Tickets are C$10 (U.S.$7) for adults, C$8 (U.S.$5) for seniors and students, C$5 (U.S.$3.25) for children, or C$30 (U.S.$20) per family. Call ahead for reservations. Admission to the museum alone is C$2 (U.S.$1.30). Summer hours are daily from 10am to 4:30pm. Winter hours are Tuesday through Saturday from 10am to 4:40pm.

From Courtenay, follow Comox Road east along the Courtenay Estuary. If you're shopping for Native Canadian art and jewelry, stop by the **Native Gallery & Gift Shop** (also called Queneesh Developments), 3310 Comox Rd. (☎ **250/339-7702**). Operated by the Comox band, this shop specializes in works by local native artists.

COMOX

The old center of Comox is small, with just a few shops and cafes to tempt travelers. However, what's definitely worth a stroll is the **marina area** in Comox Harbour. Walkways run along the jetties, offering tremendous views of fishing and pleasure boats and the sparkling waters of the bay. Rising above it all are the jagged peaks of Strathcona Park.

Another excellent place for a stroll—or for unleashing children weary from driving—is **Filberg Lodge and Park,** 61 Filberg Rd. (☎ **250/334-9242;** www. island.net/~filberg). Nine acres of lawn and forest, plus a petting zoo, surround a handsome Arts and Crafts–style home, Filberg Lodge. Once a private residence, the lodge and the grounds are now operated as a public park. The house itself is open for tours, and often serves as the venue for art shows and other events. The lodge is open from 11am to 5pm on Easter weekend plus weekends from May through September.

PARKS, GARDENS & BEACHES

If you're looking for a beach in Comox, continue past the marina on Comox Road to **Gooseneck Park,** a sandy peninsula that hooks to the south of the harbor. It's locals' favorite place to catch a few rays. **Saratoga Beach** (C$18/U.S.$12 per site) and **Miracle Beach,** both provincial parks, are about a half-hour drive north of Courtenay on Highway 19. **Seal Bay Regional Nature Park and Forest,** 15 miles (24km) north of Courtenay off Highway 19, is a 1,764-acre preserve of forest and wetlands laced with hiking and mountain-biking trails. The Coupland Trail leads to Seal Bay, where you may indeed see these marine mammals. Hours are from 6:30am to 11pm.

If the native plants of the northwest coast interest you, visit **Kitty Coleman Woodland Gardens,** RR 2, off Whittaker Road just north of Seal Bay Park (☎ **250/ 338-6901;** www3.bc.sympatico.ca/woodlandgardens). Trails lead through acres of forest and flowers, making this a pleasant stop for the gardener or bird watcher. Hours are 8am to 6pm daily. Guided tours and after-hours visits can be arranged.

CUMBERLAND

Cumberland, 10 miles (16km) south of Courtenay in the foothills of the Beaufort Mountains, is a historic coal-mining town founded in 1888; its population now numbers 2,548. A total of 25 million tons of coal was mined here before the last mine shut down in 1966. Despite a history of devastating fires, many heritage homes and storefronts remain from the 1890s, when the town was home to a diverse population of emigrants from Europe and Asia. Wander the streets and note the vast disparity in the size and style of period homes: This is as much a lesson in sociology as architecture.

A Bird's-Eye View

Parallel Aviation (☎ **250/338-0230**) specializes in sightseeing flights from Courtenay Airport. Popular trips include Comox Glacier tours (C$299/U.S.$194), half-day excursions to the west coast of Vancouver Island, and island-hopper flights from Nanaimo (C$129/U.S.$84). Charter flights are also available. Flights range from C$69 to C$299 (U.S.$45 to U.S.$194) per person with a minimum of two people per flight.

Stop by the **Cumberland Museum & Archives,** 2680 Dunsmuir Ave. (☎ **250/ 336-2445**), which tells the story of the local coal-mining industry; there's even a replica of a coal mine. From mid-May through September, hours are daily from 9am to 5pm. Winter hours are Monday through Saturday from 9am to 5pm. The staff can arrange guided tours of the town.

OUTDOOR PURSUITS

GOLF   One of the finest courses on Vancouver Island is ✪ **Crown Isle Resort & Golf Community,** 339 Clubhouse Dr., Courtenay (☎ **888/338-8439** or 250/ 703-5050; www.crownisle.com). This brand-new, 18-hole links-style championship course has already hosted the Canadian Tour and Canadian Junior Men's Tournament. Facilities are lavish and absolutely top-notch, including an eye-popping clubhouse with a pro shop, formal and casual dining rooms, fitness facilities, steam rooms, and a whirlpool, plus a hotel and villas (see "Where to Stay," below).

KAYAKING   With the Courtenay Estuary and Hornby, Tree, and Denman islands an easy paddle away, sea kayaking is very popular in this area. **Comox Valley Kayaks** (☎ **888/545-5595** or 250/334-2628; www.island.net/~seakayak; e-mail: seakayak@island.net) offers rentals, lessons, and tours. A 3-hour introductory lesson is C$40 (U.S.$26). A day trip to Tree Island goes for C$60 (U.S.$39). **Tree Island Kayaking** (☎ **250/339-0580**) offers lessons, natural-history tours, and rentals.

SKIING   **Mount Washington Ski Resort,** P.O. Box 3069, Courtenay (☎ **888/ 837-4663** or 604/619-0550, or 250/338-1515 for snow report), in the Comox Valley, is British Columbia's third-largest ski area, a 5-hour drive from Victoria and open year-round (for hiking or skiing, depending on the season). A 1,600-foot (488m) vertical drop and 42 groomed runs are serviced by four lifts and a beginners' tow. Nineteen miles (30.4km) of track-set Nordic trails connect to Strathcona Provincial Park. Full-day rates are C$42 (U.S.$27) for adults, C$32 (U.S.$21) for seniors and students, and C$22 (U.S.$14) for kids 7 to 12. Equipment rentals are available at the resort. Take the Strathcona Parkway 23 miles (37km) to Mount Washington.

The condos and lodges at Mount Washington remain open year-round, and offer good value in the summer season. For information, contact **Mount Washington Village** (☎ **888/686-4663**) or **Paradise Ridge Rentals** (☎ **877/287-9491**). Summer rates for a two-bedroom condo with fully equipped kitchen are usually around C$75 (U.S.$49); winter rates are C$115 (U.S.$75).

The family-oriented **Forbidden Plateau Ski Area,** 2050 Cliffe Ave., Courtenay (☎ **250/334-4744,** or 250/338-1919 for snow report), is the island's oldest ski resort, dating back to 1950. The 1,150-foot (351m) vertical and 12 groomed runs, geared to novices, are served by one lift, three T-bars, and a rope-tow. Adult rates are C$29 (U.S.$19); equipment rentals are available. Open Friday, Saturday, and Sunday, this is a casual place where you can avoid the crowds during the January-to-March season. From Courtenay, take the Strathcona Parkway 15½ miles (25km).

WHERE TO STAY

Coast Westerly Hotel. 1590 Cliffe Ave., Courtenay, BC, V9N 2K4. ☎ **800/668-7797** or 250/338-7741. Fax 250/338-5442. www.coasthotels.com. E-mail: coastwes@islandnet.com. 108 units. TV TEL. C$108–C$126 (U.S.$70–U.S.$82) double. Extra person C$10 (U.S.$7). Off-season and senior rates available. AE, MC, V. Ski and golf packages available. Pets accepted.

The Coast Westerly, with a location convenient to downtown Courtenay, presents a rather off-putting visage: The three-story slant-fronted wall of glass that encases the lobby probably seemed like a stylish idea when the hotel was first built. However, once you get past the lobby, you'll discover that the guest rooms are quite spacious and nicely furnished. Of the two wings, the one in back offers rooms with balconies, some overlooking the Courtenay River. Guests can dine in the GreenHouse Restaurant, under the aforementioned wall of glass, and Snooker's Lounge and Gulliver's Pub. Other facilities include an indoor pool, sauna, whirlpool, exercise room, and meeting rooms.

Greystone Manor B&B. 4014 Haas Rd., Courtenay, BC, V9N 8H9. ☎ **250/338-1422.** www.bbcanada.com/1334.html. 3 units. C$80 (U.S.$52) double. Extra person C$20 (U.S.$13). Rates include full home-cooked breakfast. MC, V. Children must be 13 or older.

This much-loved B&B would deserve its vaunted reputation, even without its gardens. But for many guests, the high point of a stay here is a chance to wander the paths among the lush 1½ acres. The charming innkeepers claim that gardening wasn't even a particular passion in their lives until they bought this property, the 1918 summer home of a lumber baron. But a passion it has now become: Every year, they put in more than 3,500 bedding plants, and that's in addition to the perennial beds and well-groomed vegetable garden. The house itself is a handsome Tudor-style Craftsman, with three guest rooms with private bathrooms and stylishly low-key furnishings. Guests share a magnificent wood-paneled sitting room that features loads of unpainted moldings, a grand piano, and comfy couches. Breakfasts incorporate herbs and vegetables from the gardens. *Note:* Smoking is not permitted.

✪ **Kingfisher Oceanside Resort and Spa.** 4330 S. Island Hwy., Courtenay, BC, V9N 8H9. ☎ **800/663-7929** or 250/338-1323. Fax 250/338-0058. www.kingfisher-resort-spa.com. E-mail: stay@kingfisher-resort-spa.com. 45 units. TV TEL. C$99 (U.S.$64) double, C$170 (U.S.$111) suite. Extra person C$10 (U.S.$7). Golf, ski, fishing, spa, and women's wellness packages available. Senior discounts available. AE, DC, MC, V.

Located 4½ miles (7km) south of Courtenay, this long-established resort has recently added a bank of beachfront suites and a classy spa. The older motel units are large, nicely furnished rooms with balconies or patios, most with views of the pool and the Strait of Georgia. The new one-bedroom suites are splendid, each with a full kitchen, two TVs, fireplace, and balcony that juts out over the beach; most suites have a two-person whirlpool tub in addition to a full bathroom with heated tile floors. Our favorite is no. 401, on the end of the building, with banks of windows on two sides.

The Kingfisher restaurant is one of the best places to eat in Courtenay (see "Where to Dine," below). Other amenities include an outdoor pool, hot tub, steam cave, sauna, and canoe and kayak rentals. The spa offers a wide selection of treatments and body work, plus a full exercise room. Trained technicians offer thalassotherapy baths and wraps, massage, reiki, and facials. *Note:* Smoking is not permitted.

Travelodge Courtenay. 2605 Island Hwy., Courtenay, BC, V9N 2L8. ☎ **800/795-9486** or 250/334-4491. Fax 250/334-4694. 91 units. TV TEL. C$66–C$71 (U.S.$43–U.S.$46) double. Extra person C$6 (U.S.$3.90). Kitchens C$10 (U.S.$7) extra. Golf and ski packages available. AAA and senior discounts available. AE, MC, V.

If you don't want to splurge on Courtenay's more upscale accommodations, the Travelodge might be just what you're looking for, as it offers extras at a relatively modest cost. The guest rooms aren't fancy, but if you're mainly interested in a clean, unfussy place to spend a night, this is it. Extras include free local calls, an outdoor pool, a coin-op laundry, and complimentary in-room coffee.

The Villas at Crown Isle Resort. 366 Clubhouse Rd., Courtenay, BC, V9N 9G3. ☎ **888/338-8439** or 250/338-7777. Fax 250/338-7922. www.crownisle.com. 23 villas. MINIBAR TV TEL. C$139–C$199 (U.S.$90–U.S.$129) double. Extra person C$30 (U.S.$20). Golf packages available. AE, MC, V.

For the money, these suites are an incredible deal. Located at Crown Isle Golf Resort, the beautifully furnished one- and two-bedroom villas overlook the first fairway and are just yards away from the spectacular clubhouse. The suites are truly large, and filled with luxury touches: full gourmet kitchens, art, Jacuzzis, fireplaces, multiple TVs and VCRs, top-quality linens, and balconies. Like everything else at Crown Isle, no expense was spared, and the developers certainly didn't stint on architect's fees. Another building with hotel-style rooms is slated to open later in 2000. Guests can dine on contemporary Pacific fare at the Conservatory, or more casual meals at the Timber Room Lounge. Villa guests have full access to the fitness equipment and steam rooms in the resort clubhouse. And of course, there's that golf course.

WHERE TO DINE

Atlas Café. 250 Sixth St., Courtenay. ☎ **250/338-9838.** Reservations recommended. Main courses C$4.95–C$12 (U.S.$3.20–U.S.$8). MC, V. Daily 9am–10pm. INTERNATIONAL.

This pleasant coffee shop and casual cafe is the perfect place to eat if you don't want to run up your credit-card bill but still want good, flavorful food. The menu focuses on multiethnic cooking from the Mediterranean, Mexico, and Asia; many of the dishes are vegetarian. There are regular "theme" evenings, when foods from a particular region are featured. Weekend brunch is served until 2pm.

Bar None Café. 224 Fourth St., Courtenay. ☎ **250/334-3112.** Reservations not accepted. Main courses C$4.95–C$10 (U.S.$3.20–U.S.$10). AE, MC, V. Mon–Sat 7:30am–8pm, Sun 10:30am–5:30pm. VEGETARIAN.

This friendly, youthful vegetarian restaurant specializes in tasty international dishes. The cooks make an effort to use organic, locally raised ingredients and produce from farmers who support responsible agricultural practices. The result? Food that's good for you *and* the planet. The buffet features a range of salads, soups, and hot entrees. Dishes from the buffet cost C$2 (U.S.$1.30) per 100 grams (3.5 oz.). You can also order off the chalkboard menu, which offers a changing selection of pasta dishes, pizza, curries, and wraps and sandwiches. Tuesday is pasta night, with all-you-can-eat pasta for C$8 (U.S.$5), while Friday brings a pay-by-weight East Indian feast. Bar None also has a juice bar and in-house bakery. On a sunny afternoon, grab a smoothie and take a seat on the vine-shaded patio. Bar None's bulletin board is a good source to find out what's going on with the alternative community in Courtenay.

Black Fin Pub. 132 Port Augusta St., Comox. ☎ **250/339-5030.** Reservations not accepted. Main courses C$8–C$15 (U.S.$5–U.S.$10). MC, V. Food service daily 11:30am–1pm and 6:30–9:30pm. PUB/CANADIAN.

On the short walk from downtown Comox to the marina area, you'll pass this hospitable pub, sitting on a shelf of land overlooking the harbor. The menu is large and, for a pub, quite interesting, with a good selection of appetizers and small plates that feature Thai and Chinese flavors. Entrees range from schnitzel and stir-fry to Bengal curry chicken. The usual burgers and sandwiches are also available. Best of all for nonsmokers, the entire pub is smoke-free during dining hours.

Kingfisher Oceanside Restaurant. 4330 S. Island Hwy., $4^1/_2$ miles (7km) south of Courtenay. ☎ **250/338-1323.** Reservations advised. Main courses C$14–C$19 (U.S.$9–U.S.$12). AE, DC, MC, V. Daily 7–10:30am, 11:30am–2pm, and 5–10pm. SEAFOOD.

The dining room at the Kingfisher resort brings together waterfront views of beach, island, and mountains with high-quality seafood and continental cuisine. If you're staying at the Kingfisher to partake of the new spa services, you'll be pleased with the spa menu, which features low-fat, low-calorie entrees such as poached halibut jardiniere. The regular menu offers an extensive selection of seafood appetizers, several featuring Fanny Bay oysters. Local salmon is a favorite on the entree list; one popular preparation is cedar-plank–baked salmon served with a chutney of sage and blackberries. The menu also includes steaks, schnitzels, and lamb dishes. The service is both professional and attentive.

Old House Restaurant. 1760 Riverside Lane, Courtenay. ☎ **250/338-5406.** Reservations recommended. Main courses C$11–C$22 (U.S.$7–U.S.$14). AE, MC, V. Daily 11am–10pm. STEAK HOUSE.

As you might suspect, the Old House Restaurant is located in a heritage home along the banks of the Courtenay River. The parklike setting is lovely, and the home, with four fireplaces and rough-hewn timbers, feels like a venerable country lodge. This is where locals come for special occasions, and if you're looking for steaks, prime rib, or relatively straightforward preparations of fish and seafood, then the Old House is a good if bustling choice. The flower-bedecked patio is a wonderful place for a drink.

✪ **Otters Bistro.** 1805 Beaufort Ave., Comox. ☎ **250/339-6150.** Reservations recommended. Main courses C$14–C$25 (U.S.$9–U.S.$16). Early-bird (5–6pm) 3-course menu C$14 (U.S.$9). AE, MC, V. Daily 11:30am–2:30pm and 5–9:30pm. PACIFIC NORTHWEST.

Easily the best restaurant in the Comox Valley, Otters Bistro also boasts one of the best views in the area. Put the two together, and you have an absolutely first-rate combination. This restaurant and lounge is located just above the marina in Comox, with a spectacular vista across the boat basin and the waters of Courtenay Bay to the sawtooth peaks of Strathcona Park. The dining room is relatively simple and spacious—as it should be when there's such a beautiful view. Request a table on the umbrella-shaded deck if the weather's nice.

Hard to believe, but the food—a successful version of the often disappointing fusion trend—actually measures up to that view. The cuisine is endlessly inventive, from the pizza with Madras duck breast and sweet-pepper confit to the trilogy of seafood cakes—sautéed patties of salmon, crab, and clam. Even the lunchtime burgers are out of the ordinary: There's a halibut version served with roast caper sauce and shoestring potatoes. If you want just a drink and simple bite, stop by the lounge and oyster bar for some fresh Fanny Bar oysters. On the entree list, a real standout is the porcini-mushroom ravioli with scallion-cashew pesto. Using a timeless native cooking method, cedar-plank–roasted salmon is updated with a drizzle of balsamico and Dijon mustard. Service is prompt and friendly, and the wine list formidable. If you eat just one meal in the area, it should be here.

Toscanos. 140 Port Augusta, Comox. ☎ **250/890-7575.** Reservations recommended. Main courses C$9–C$19 (U.S.$6–U.S.$12). MC, V. Mon–Fri 11:30am–2pm; daily 5:30–9:30pm. ITALIAN.

Toscanos is a cheerful Italian restaurant located between downtown Comox and Comox Harbor, with a million-dollar view of the bay and distant Beaufort Mountains. The dining room is rather minimalist, lacking the rustic Mediterranean clutter that usually passes for decor in Italian restaurants. The menu is evenly divided between pasta dishes, such as cheese-stuffed agnoletti with sage butter, and chicken, veal, fish, and seafood entrees. Local fresh salmon is pan-seared and served with a lemon piccata sauce. A favorite is the Italian/Pacific fish soup, a traditional brodetto enhanced with seafood from the waters off Vancouver Island.

Northern Vancouver Island

In this chapter, we cover the portion of Vancouver Island from the town of Campbell River northward. A quick ferry ride away from the "Salmon-Fishing Capital of the World" brings you to the ancient native Indian culture of Quadra Island. West of Campbell River lies Strathcona Provincial Park, the oldest provincial park in British Columbia and the largest on Vancouver Island.

The waters along the island's northeast coast near Port McNeill are home to two species of orca whales: residents, which feed on salmon and live in the area consistently, and transients, which feed on seals and other marine mammals and move annually from Johnstone Strait to the open Pacific. In this vicinity are also two tiny unique communities: the native Indian town of Alert Bay, on Cormorant Island, and Telegraph Cove, a boardwalk community on pilings above the rocky shore.

The Island Highway's final port of call, Port Hardy is the starting point for the Inside Passage ferry cruise up the northern coast. The ferry carries passengers bound for Prince Rupert, where it meets the ferries to the Queen Charlotte Islands (see chapter 9 for complete coverage of these destinations in northern British Columbia).

Note: See the "Vancouver Island" map (pp. 104–105) to locate areas covered in this chapter.

1 Essentials

GETTING THERE

BY PLANE See chapter 4 for information on Vancouver Island's major air hub of **Victoria,** with jet, commuter-plane, and floatplane service from Vancouver and Seattle.

Campbell River and Port Hardy are both served by regular flights from Vancouver International Airport. Other towns can be reached by scheduled harbor-to-harbor floatplane service, either from Vancouver International's seaplane terminal or from downtown Vancouver's Coal Harbour terminal.

Air BC (☎ **800/776-3000** in the U.S., 800/663-3721 in B.C., or 250/360-9074) offers service to Campbell River, while **Canadian Regional Airlines** (☎ **800/665-1177**) flies to Campbell River and Port Hardy.

Commuter seaplanes that serve Vancouver Island include **Harbour Seaplanes** (☎ **800/665-9308**), **Pacific Spirit Air** (☎ **800/665-2359**), **Air Rainbow** (☎ **604/681-0311**), and **Baxter Aviation** (☎ **800/661-5599** or 250/754-1066).

BY FERRY   BC Ferries (☎ 888/724-5223 in B.C., or 604/444-2890; www. bcferries.bc.ca) operates an extensive year-round network of automobile and passenger ferries that link Vancouver Island and the Gulf Islands to one another and to the British Columbia mainland. Major routes include the 15-hour journey through the Inland Passage from Port Hardy to Prince Rupert. In summer, reserve weeks ahead to guarantee space. Sample fares are included in the regional chapters that follow.

If you're traveling with a car, you'll find that ticket prices add up quickly. You may want to consider leaving the car on the mainland and traveling by bus, taxi, or air.

Washington State Ferries (☎ 800/843-3779 in Wash., 206/464-6400 in the rest of the U.S., or 250/381-1551 in Canada; www.wsdot.wa.gov/ferries) has daily ferry service from Anacortes, in northwest Washington, to Sidney, on Vancouver Island. One-way fares for a car and driver cost around U.S.$41 in high season.

BY BUS   Maverick Coach Tours provides service between Nanaimo and Vancouver; a one-way trip is C$19 (U.S.$12). Reserve through Greyhound's network by calling ☎ 800/661-8747 or 604/482-8747. Information on these and other motorcoach services is available at **Greyhound Canada's** Web site (**www.greyhoud.ca**).

Laidlaw Coach Lines (☎ 800/318-0818 or 250/385-4411; www.victoriatours. com) operates Vancouver Island's intercity bus service, which runs along the main highway from Victoria to Port Hardy, and from Nanaimo to Tofino. The one-way fare from Victoria to Nanaimo is C$18 (U.S.$12), from Nanaimo to Tofino C$30 (U.S.$20).

VISITOR INFORMATION

For general information on Vancouver Island, contact the **Tourism Association of Vancouver Island,** Suite 302, 45 Bastion Sq., Victoria, BC, V8W 1J1 (☎ 250/ 382-3551; fax 250/382-3523; www.islands.bc.ca; e-mail: tavi@islands.bc.ca).

GETTING AROUND

BY PUBLIC TRANSPORTATION   While Vancouver Island has an admirable system of public transport, getting to remote sights and destinations is difficult without your own vehicle.

BC Ferries (☎ 888/724-5223 in B.C., or 604/444-2890; www.bcferries.bc.ca) links Vancouver Island ports to many offshore islands, including Quadra Island, Alert Bay, and Cortes Island. None of these islands has public transport, so once there you'll need to hoof it, hitch it, hire a taxi, or arrange for bicycle rentals. Most innkeepers will pick you up from the ferry if you've reserved in advance.

See "Getting There," above, for information on **Laidlaw Coach Lines** (☎ 800/ 318-0818 or 250/385-4411; www.victoriatours.com).

BY CAR   The southern half of Vancouver Island is well served by paved highways. The trunk road between Victoria and Nanaimo is **Highway 1,** the Trans-Canada. This busy route alternates between four-lane expressway and congested two-lane highway, and requires patience and vigilance, especially during the busy summer months. North of Nanaimo, the major road north is **Highway 19,** which is largely a well-maintained two-lane highway, with expressway sections near Parksville and Qualicum Beach, and near Campbell River. The only other major paved road system on the island connects Parksville with Tofino, on the rugged west coast. Access to gasoline and car services is no problem, even in more remote north Vancouver Island.

Rental cars are readily available. Agencies include **Budget Car & Truck Rental** (☎ 800/268-8900 or 250/953-5300), **National Tilden Interrent** (☎ 800/ 387-4747 or 250/386-1213), and **Thrifty Car Rental** (☎ 800/367-2277 or 250/ 383-3659).

2 Campbell River, Quadra Island & Desolation Sound

Campbell River: 31 miles (51.6km) N of Courtenay, 165 miles (266km) N of Victoria

Busy and utilitarian, Campbell River (pop. 29,000) gives the impression of a town that works for a living. For years, it has been known as the "Salmon-Fishing Capital of the World." Between Quadra Island and Campbell River, the broad Strait of Georgia squeezes down to a narrow mile-wide passage called Discovery Channel. All of the salmon that enter the Strait of Juan de Fuca near Victoria to spawn in northerly rivers funnel down into this tight constriction, a churning waterway with 13-foot tides. Historically, vast hauls of incredibly large fish have been pulled from these waters; fishing lodges have lined these shores for decades. However, salmon numbers at Campbell River have fallen drastically in recent years, and the days of pulling 60-pound chinooks from the churning waters are largely over. Today, you're as likely to take a wildlife-viewing trip on the sound as go fishing for salmon.

Salmon or no salmon, there are plenty of other attractions in and around Campbell River. Two excellent museums with world-class collections of native masks and artifacts head the list, while hiking and exploring on Quadra Island and in Strathcona Provincial Park provide recreation for outdoorsy types.

ESSENTIALS

GETTING THERE   By Plane   The **Campbell River and District Regional Airport,** located south of Campbell River off Jubilee Parkway, has regularly scheduled flights on commuter planes to and from Vancouver and Seattle. Contact **Canadian Regional Airlines** (☎ 800/426-7000 in the U.S., 800/665-1177 in Canada) or **Air BC** (☎ 800/766-3000 in the U.S., 800/663-3721 in Canada). Harbor-to-harbor service between Vancouver and Campbell River is available from late June to Labour Day via **Air Rainbow** (☎ 250/287-8371). You can also fly from Seattle's Lake Union to Campbell River harbor on **Kenmore Air** (☎ 800/543-9595).

By Car   On the Island Highway (Hwy. 19), Campbell River is 31 miles (51.6km) north of Courtenay and 165 miles (266km) north of Victoria.

By Bus   **Laidlaw Coach Lines** (☎ 250/385-4411) operates daily bus service from Victoria to Port Hardy, making stops in Campbell River.

VISITOR INFORMATION   The **Campbell River Visitor Info Centre** is at 1235 Shopper's Row, Box 44, Campbell River, BC, V9W 5B6 (☎ 250/287-4636).

CAMPBELL RIVER

Downtown Campbell River won't win any awards for quaintness. Busy Island Highway whizzes through town, and the commercial district is dominated by strip malls and shopping centers. One stop of interest is **Wei Wai Kum,** in the Discovery Harbour Shopping Centre, 1370 Island Hwy. (☎ 250/286-1440), a gallery and gift shop that sells carvings, totem poles, and clothing from the local First Nations people.

The excellent **Willow Point Books,** 2116 S. Island Hwy. (☎ 250/923-5121), has a good section on local travel, recreation, and native lore. The **Public Art Gallery,** 1235 Island Hwy. (☎ 250/287-2261), exhibits shows of art from across the province.

✪ **The Museum at Campbell River.** 470 Island Hwy. ☎ 250/287-3103. www. island.net/~crm_chin. Admission C$2.50 (U.S.$1.65) adults, C$2 (U.S.$1.30) seniors and students, C$8 (U.S.$5) family, free for children under 6. Mid-May to Sept 30 Mon–Sat 10am–5pm, Sun noon–5pm; Oct 1 to mid-May Tues–Sun noon–5pm.

Campbell River

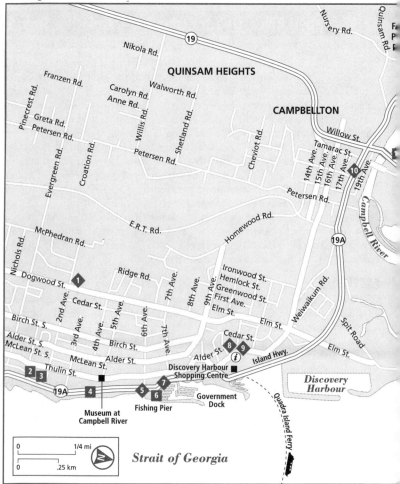

Campbell River's large and captivating museum is located south of the downtown Discovery Harbour area, but it's worth seeking out. The main exhibit hall is devoted to carvings and artifacts from the local First Nations tribes; especially fine is the display of contemporary carved wooden masks. Also compelling is the sound-and-light presentation *The Treasure of Siwidi,* which uses masks to retell an ancient native Indian myth. Another gallery houses a replica of a pioneer-era cabin and a collection of photos and tools from the early days of Vancouver Island logging. The 30-seat theater offers a couple of short films; one, *War of the Land Canoes,* is a 1914 documentary shot in local native villages. The gift shop is one of the best places in Campbell River to buy authentic native art and jewelry.

OUTDOOR PURSUITS

DIVING   Off the shores of Campbell River, dive sites with enticing names like Row and Be Damned, Whisky Point, Copper Cliffs, and Steep Island attract more than

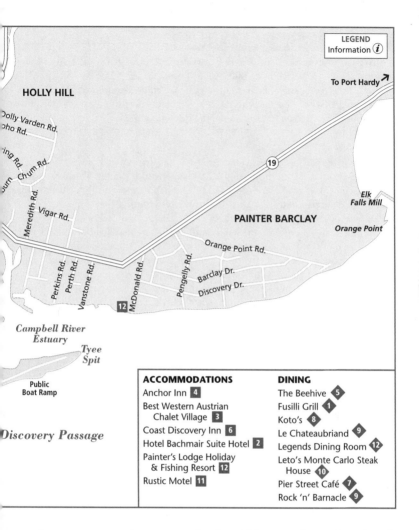

HOLLY HILL

To Port Hardy ↗

LEGEND
Information ⓘ

Dolly Varden Rd.
oho Rd.

ing Rd.   Chum Rd.

Meredith Rd.   Vigar Rd.

Perkins Rd.   Perth Rd.   Vanstone Rd.   McDonald Rd.   Pengelly Rd.

Orange Point Rd.

PAINTER BARCLAY

Elk
Falls Mill

Orange Point

Barclay Dr.

Discovery Dr.

19

12

*Campbell River
Estuary*

*Tyee
Spit*

Public
Boat Ramp

Discovery Passage

ACCOMMODATIONS
Anchor Inn **4**
Best Western Austrian
   Chalet Village **3**
Coast Discovery Inn **6**
Hotel Bachmair Suite Hotel **2**
Painter's Lodge Holiday
   & Fishing Resort **12**
Rustic Motel **11**

DINING
The Beehive ◆**5**
Fusilli Grill ◆**1**
Koto's ◆**8**
Le Chateaubriand ◆**9**
Legends Dining Room ◆**12**
Leto's Monte Carlo Steak
   House ◆**10**
Pier Street Café ◆**7**
Rock 'n' Barnacle ◆**9**

strawberry anemones and sponges to the clear tidal waters. **Beaver Aquatic,** 760 Island Hwy. (☎ **250/287-7652**), rents scuba equipment for about C$55 (U.S.$36) per day and can provide site information and diving advice.

✪ **FISHING** Fishing isn't what it once was in Campbell River. Some salmon runs are now catch-and-release only, while others are open for limited catches; many fishing trips are now billed more as wildlife adventures than hunting-and-gathering expeditions.

The coho salmon in these waters weigh up to 20 pounds, and even these are dwarfed by the tyee salmon. Some tyee have tipped the scales at more than 75 pounds, but now the average is around 30 pounds. Between mid-July and mid-September, fishermen vie for membership in the **Tyee Club.** The requirements include fishing from an unpowered, guided rowboat in a small, designated area called a tyee pool. Only certain types of poles and line weights can be used to catch a record-weight tyee salmon.

To fish here, you need nonresident saltwater and freshwater licenses, available at outdoor-recreation stores throughout Campbell River, including **Painter's Lodge,** 1625 MacDonald Rd. (☎ 250/286-1102). The staff here can also provide information on guided boats and fishing rules. This resort's beautiful waterfront deck makes the perfect spot to view all of the action (see "Where to Stay," below).

If you'd like to get out onto the waters and fish, be sure to call ahead and talk to an outfitter or the Visitor Info Centre to learn what fish are running during your visit, and if the seasons have been opened. Because of plummeting numbers of salmon, as well as recently concluded treaties with the United States, the next few years will see even more restrictions on fishing seasons in the waters off Vancouver Island. Don't be disappointed if there's no salmon fishing when you visit, or if the salmon you do hook is catch-and-release only. For one thing, there are other fish in the sea: Not all types of salmon are as threatened as the coho and tyee, and fishing is also good for halibut and other bottom fish. And if all you really want is to get out on the water for a little adventure, consider a wildlife-viewing boat tour.

There are dozens of fishing guides in the Campbell River area, with a range of services that extend from basic to pure extravagance. Expect to pay around C$45 to C$50 (U.S.$29 to U.S.$33) per hour for 4 to 5 hours of fishing with a no-frills outfitter. A flashier trip on a luxury cruiser can cost more than C$120 (U.S.$78) per hour. The most famous guides are associated with the Painter's Lodge and its sister property, April Point Lodge (see "Where to Stay," below). Other smaller fishing-guide operations include **Destiny Sportfishing** (☎ 250/286-9610), **CR Fishing Village** (☎ 250/287-3630), **Larry Craig Salmon Charters** (☎ 250/287-2592), and **King Salmon Adventures** (☎ 604/664-4999). You can also check out the Info Centre's directory to fishing guides at **www.vquest.com/crtourism/member/fishi.html**.

Most hotels in Campbell River also offer fishing/lodging packages; ask when you reserve. For C$1 (U.S.65¢), you can fish off **Discovery Pier,** in Campbell River right at Campbell Harbour. Cutthroat and rainbow trout inhabit the nearby rivers.

GOLF   Golfers find this part of Vancouver Island a little bit of paradise. The Les Furber–designed **Morningstar,** 525 Lowry Rd., Parksville (☎ 250/248-8161), integrates large lakes in open areas with several seaside links and rolling fairways that run in and out of the woods. The 18-hole championship par-72 course has a 74 rating.

Because it was carved out of a dense forest, you may see wildlife grazing on the fairway and roughs at **Storey Creek Golf Club,** Campbell River (☎ 250/923-3673). Gentle creeks and ponds also wind through this course.

HIKING   For day hikes, drive to Strathcona Provincial Park (see below) or explore the trails at Quadra Island's Mount Seymour or Morte Lake parks. For a pleasant hike closer to Campbell River, drive west 3.7 miles (6km) on Highway 28 toward Gold River to **Elk Falls Provincial Park.** Easy 1- to 2-hour hikes within the park lead to a fish hatchery and let you explore a stream with beaver ponds. From the park, you can also join the **Canyon View Trail,** a great loop hike that follows the banks of the Campbell River. You can frequently see migrating salmon in the river; the bridge that crosses the gorge affords spectacular views of the rushing water below.

WILDLIFE TOURS   For a full listing of adventure- and wildlife-tour operators in the Campbell River area, check out **www.vquest.com/crtourism/member/ adven.html#adventuretours**.

  Eagle Eye Adventures (☎ **250/286-0809;** www.havannah.bc.ca/eagle-eye), offers a range of excursions via Zodiac and floatplane. A $3^1/_2$-hour bear- and wildlife-watching trip to Bute Inlet costs C$89 (U.S.$58) for adults, C$69 (U.S.$45) for kids under 13. A 6-hour whale- and bear-watching excursion begins by boating to Johnstone Strait to view orcas and black bears. At Port Neville, a floatplane whisks you away for an eagle's-eye view of the Inside Passage (see chapter 9) and returns you to Campbell River. The cost, which includes snacks, is C$149 (U.S.$97) for adults, C$119 (U.S.$77) for kids. Call or check the Web site for other seasonal tours.

  Tide Rip Tours (☎ **888/643-9319** or 250/339-5320; www.tiderip.com; e-mail: tiderip@bc.sympatico.ca) also offers a variety of wildlife-viewing trips, depending on the season and conditions. Single-day options range from trips to Mitlenotch Island, with the largest seabird population in the Georgia Strait, and Desolation Sound (C$89/U.S.$59) to excursions to watch grizzly bears fish for salmon in the waters of Knight Inlet (C$245/U.S.$159). Tours are conducted in inflatable Zodiac boats.

  Painter's Lodge (see "Fishing," above) also offers a full range of wildlife-watching and ecotours.

WHERE TO STAY

Anchor Inn. 261 Island Hwy., Campbell River, BC, V9W 2B3. ☎ **800/663/7227** or 250/ 286-1131. Fax 250/287-4055. 77 units. TV TEL. C$94–C$139 (U.S.$61–U.S.$90) double. Extra person C$15 (U.S.$10). AE, MC, V.

If you're looking for an ocean view during your Campbell River stay, the Anchor Inn is a good choice. Although the guest rooms contain standard motel-type fixtures and amenities, each is spacious and has a balcony and ocean view. Best of all, the Anchor Inn is on the ocean side of busy Island Highway, so you won't have to look over the traffic to see the view. On site, Season's Bistro and Lounge offers fine dining, Sushi By the Sea serves up Japanese cuisine, and Wily Coyote's Bar and Grill features informal dining. Amenities include a pool, whirlpool, free local calls, and meeting facilities. Whale-watching and sightseeing tours are offered.

Best Western Austrian Chalet Village. 462 S. Island Hwy., Campbell River, BC, V9W 1A5. ☎ **800/667-7207** or 250/923-4231. Fax 250/923-2840. www.vquest.com/austrian. E-mail: austrian@vquest.com. 55 units. TV TEL. C$89–C$149 (U.S.$58–U.S.$97) double. Extra person C$10 (U.S.$7). Kitchen units C$10 (U.S.$7) extra. Off-season discounts available. AE, MC, V.

Overlooking Discovery Passage, this newly renovated oceanfront hotel is conveniently located right on the Island Highway. You'll have a choice of regular or housekeeping units (with fully equipped kitchenettes and fridges); some rooms are in loft chalets. On the premises are a restaurant, which serves three meals daily, and a casual pub. Other facilities include a pool, sauna, whirlpool, table tennis, and mini–putting green. The staff can arrange whale-watching, fishing, or golfing trips.

Coast Discovery Inn. 975 Shoppers Row, Campbell River, BC, V9W 2C4. ☎ **800/ 663-1144** or 250/287-7155. www.coasthotels.com. E-mail: coastdi@vquest.com. 90 units. A/C TV TEL. C$99–C$144 (U.S.$64–U.S.$94) double. Extra person C$10 (U.S.$7). Family plan, senior discounts, and corporate and off-season rates available. AE, DC, DISC, MC, V.

Part of the sprawling Discovery Harbour Marina and Shopping Centre development, the Coast is right downtown and convenient to both fishing and wildlife-viewing trips. The views from the upper stories, with Quadra Island and Discovery Passage right below, are dramatic. The guest rooms are spacious and nicely furnished. Facilities include the Brasserie Restaurant for fine dining, the Sgt. O'Flaherty Deli Pub for casual meals and drinks, and a health club with exercise room and whirlpool.

✪ **Hotel Bachmair Suite Hotel.** 492 S. Island Hwy., Campbell River, BC, V9W 1A5. ☎ **888/923-2849** or 250/923-2848. Fax 250/923-2849. www.bctravel.com/ni/hotelbachmair.html. 23 units. TV TEL. C$79–C$130 (U.S.$51–U.S.$85) double. Extra person C$10 (U.S.$7). Fishing charters arranged. AE, MC, V.

This hotel on the southern edge of town offers very large and beautifully furnished rooms at moderate prices. Accommodations range from standard hotel rooms to two-bedroom suites; one of the penthouse suites can sleep eight. The suites all come with large bedrooms, kitchens, sitting rooms, and dining areas. Furnishings are exquisite: leather couches, fine carpeting, and hand-painted armoires. Kitchens are fully equipped with china, utensils, and appliances. Most units have balconies and views of Discovery Passage. The hotel itself—wrapped in carved-wooden-rail balconies lined by flower boxes—is handsome in the Bavarian style so favored in Canada.

✪ **Painter's Lodge Holiday & Fishing Resort.** 1625 MacDonald Rd., Box 460, Campbell River, BC, V9W 4S5. ☎ **800/663-7090** or 250/286-1102. Fax 250/598-1361. www.obmg.com. E-mail: obmg@pinc.com. 94 units. TV TEL. C$110–C$145 (U.S.$72–U.S.$94) double, C$150–C$360 (U.S.$98–U.S.$234) cottage. Extra person C$15 (U.S.$10). Off-season discounts available. AE, MC, V. Closed Nov–Mar.

This resort has been a favorite fishing hideaway for film stars such as John Wayne, Bob Hope, and Goldie Hawn and Kurt Russell. Once you see the awe-inspiring wooded coastal location, you'll understand why. Built in 1924 on a point overlooking the Discovery Passage, the lodge retains a rustic grandeur, with spacious rooms and suites decorated in natural wood and pastels. Four secluded, self-contained cottages nestled near the lodge are also available for rent. Guests can enjoy all three meals and cocktails in the Legends Dining Room (see "Where to Dine," below), Tyee Pub (offering burgers and pub food), and Fireside Lounge. Amenities include guided fishing trips, tennis courts, fitness center, and airport shuttle.

Rustic Motel. 2140 N. Island Hwy., Campbell River, BC, V9W 2G7. ☎ **800/567-2007** or 250/286-6295. Fax 250/286-9692. www.bctravel.com/ni/rusticmotel.html. E-mail: rusticmo@mail.island.net. 41 units, 1 cabin. C$70 (U.S.$46) double. Extra person C$10 (U.S.$7). Kitchen C$10 (U.S.$7) extra. Rates include continental breakfast. AE, DC, MC, V.

The Rustic is the place to stay if you want a moderately priced room in Campbell River. Located on 2 acres of parkland beside the river, the motel has clean rooms with everything you'll need for a comfortable stay: fridge, coffeemaker, microwave, and, in the older wing, a full kitchen. There are also three two-bedroom kitchen suites that can each sleep five, plus a three-bedroom cabin with full kitchen. The Rustic is well maintained and decked out in summer with baskets of flowers. Amenities include sauna, Jacuzzi, barbecues, laundry, modem phones, and voice mail.

CAMPING

If you're looking for a campground, you'll find 122 sites in a wooded, riverside setting at **Elk Falls Provincial Park** (☎ 250/954-4600), 3.7 miles (6km) west of Campbell River on Highway 28. The park has an extensive trail system, linking waterfalls, river gorges, and wildlife-viewing areas. Sites are C$12 (U.S.$8).

WHERE TO DINE

In addition to the full-service restaurants below, try **Koto's,** 80 10th Ave. (☎ 250/286-1422), an excellent sushi bar (closed Sun and Mon).

The Beehive. 921 Island Hwy. ☎ **250/286-6812.** Reservations recommended. Main courses C$9–C$14 (U.S.$6–U.S.$9). AE, MC, V. July 1 to Labour Day daily 7am–10pm; Labour Day to June 30 Mon–Fri 7am–3pm, Sat–Sun 7am–5pm. CANADIAN.

A family dining place and sister restaurant to the Rock 'n' Barnacle (and just below it), the Beehive offers good eggy breakfasts, moving on to a menu of burgers, fish-and-chips, and sandwiches during the day. The dinner offerings expand to include steak and seafood dishes, such as grilled halibut with sun-dried cranberry butter.

Fusilli Grill. 220 Dogwood St., #4. ☎ **250/830-0090.** Reservations recommended. Main courses C$8–C$16 (U.S.$5–U.S.$10). AE, MC, V. Mon–Thurs 11am–9:30pm, Fri–Sat 11am–10pm, Sun 5–9pm. ITALIAN.

A very good, casual Italian restaurant located in the suburbs southwest of downtown, Fusilli Grill makes almost all of its own pasta on the premises, and prepares all of its own sauces as well, utilizing local produce, meats, fish, and seafood as much as possible. At lunch, freshly baked focaccia forms the basis of a variety of sandwiches. At dinner, diners have a choice of steak, fish, and chicken dishes. A few Mexican and Asian selections make their way onto the menu for variety. There's a separate kids' menu. Evening three-course take-out specials are just C$8 (U.S.$5).

Le Chateaubriand. 1170 Island Hwy. ☎ **250/287-4143.** Reservations recommended. Main courses C$16–C$24 (U.S.$10–U.S.$16). AE, MC, V. Tues–Sun 6–10pm. CONTINENTAL.

This long-established restaurant, surveying downtown Campbell River from its third-floor vantage point, is a relic of mid-20th-century fine dining. Yes, you can actually order a real Chateaubriand here, an arm-sized roast of beef tenderloin drizzled with béarnaise and topped with asparagus (C$52/U.S.$34 for two). Other well-prepared classics of Kennedy-era cuisine, like duck with orange sauce, veal Oscar (local veal scallops topped with crab and hollandaise), and even frogs' legs, are additional menu stalwarts. Daily fresh seafood specials receive more contemporary preparations. The dimly lit dining room has changed little since Sputnik. Chateaubriand isn't exactly a food museum—it's more like time travel, and great fun at that.

✪ Legends Dining Room. At Painter's Lodge, 1625 MacDonald Rd. ☎ **250/286-1102.** Reservations recommended. Main courses C$12–C$25 (U.S.$8–U.S.$16). AE, MC, V. Daily 7am–10pm. Closed Nov 1–Mar 31. INTERNATIONAL.

The beautiful tiered dining room at Painter's Lodge is entirely flanked by windows, affording every table a view of busy Discovery Passage and the free speedboat taxi that runs between the hotel and April Point Lodge, on mist-shrouded Quadra Island. If you're having dinner here, consider hopping that water taxi to April Point for a cocktail or predinner appetizer at its sushi bar. Return with salt spray in your hair, ready for a great meal at Legends. Appetizers feature local seafood; especially good is the smoked-salmon–stuffed mushroom caps, which come to the table with a drizzle of hot-pepper cream. The entrees range from jambalaya to Cuban-style pork chops, marinated in rum and tandoori spices and served with apple and sun-dried cranberry chutney. As you'd expect at a fishing resort, fish and seafood are menu favorites; the specials feature the day's fresh catch. Service is friendly and professional.

Leto's Monte Carlo Steak House. 1850 Island Hwy. ☎ **250/287-9969.** Reservations recommended. Main courses C$10–C$22 (U.S.$7–U.S.$14). MC, V. Mon–Fri 11am–10pm, Sat 5–10pm, Sun 5–9pm. GREEK/STEAK HOUSE.

It's not clear why Greek immigrants run the best steak houses in Canada, but they do. It's easier to comprehend why native Greeks run the best Greek restaurants. Put the two together, and you get Leto's, a restaurant that brings the best of eastern Mediterranean cuisine—souvlaki, dolmades, kebabs, moussaka—together with perfectly grilled certified Angus beef. The fried calamari, served with zesty tzatziki, is excellent, making a great appetizer course for a 10-ounce New York steak. The menu also features roast and grilled lamb, Italian-style veal, and some pasta dishes. Not much here for a vegetarian except the fine Greek salad.

Pier Street Café. 871 Island Hwy., 2nd floor. ☎ **250/287-2772.** Reservations suggested. Main courses C$10–C$19 (U.S.$7–U.S.$12). MC, V. Daily 11am–10pm. SEAFOOD.

Ask a local where to eat seafood, and chances are you'll be steered to Pier Street Café. A long list of daily fresh fish specials augments the extensive menu, which includes steaks, pasta, stir-fries, and burgers. The fish preparations tend to be rather undramatic, but when the fish is this fresh, you don't need fancy sauces. The dining room is on the plain side, but the deck overlooking the docks can be quite pleasant.

Rock 'n' Barnacle. 921 Island Hwy. ☎ **250/286-6812.** Reservations recommended. Main courses C$13–C$19 (U.S.$8–U.S.$12). AE, MC, V. July 1 to Labor Day daily 11:30am–2pm and 5:30–10pm; Labor Day to Jan 1 and Mar 1–June 30 daily 5:30–9pm. Closed Jan–Feb. CANADIAN/SEAFOOD.

A casual, almost spare dining room with views over the pier, the Rock 'n' Barnacle serves a menu of standard pasta, steak, and chicken dishes, along with a selection of fresh local fish. The specialty is salmon, offered in three different preparations. Boiled shrimp, served with drawn butter, are available by the pound. We like the tasty West Coast bouillabaisse. In summer, there's deck seating above the harbor.

QUADRA ISLAND

A visit to Quadra Island, which sits right across Discovery Channel from Campbell River, should definitely be on the itinerary of anyone exploring the area. A 10-minute ferry runs between Campbell River and Quathiaski Cove, on Quadra. There are two trips per hour; the fare is C$4.50 (U.S.$2.95) per person, C$12 (U.S.$8) per vehicle.

The main reason to make the ferry crossing is to see the excellent ✪ **Kwagiulth Museum and Cultural Centre,** WeiWai Road, in Cape Mudge Village (☎ 250/285-3733). It boasts one of the world's best collections of artifacts, ceremonial masks, and tribal costumes, once used by the Cape Mudge Band in elaborate potlatch ceremonies conducted to celebrate births, deaths, tribal unity, the installment of a new chief, marriages, and other important occasions. Potlatches became more and more ostentatious as the centuries went by: Bands and villages spent months, even years, planning feasts and performances, carving totem poles, and amassing literally tons of gifts for their guests. The Canadian government outlawed the practice in 1922 as part of the short-lived enforced-assimilation policy, and lifted the ban in 1951. During the time potlatches were outlawed, the artifacts in the Kwagiulth Museum were removed to museums and private collections in eastern Canada and England, where they were preserved and cataloged. The collection was repatriated to the Cape Mudge Band in the early 1990s, when the tribe built the present spectacular museum.

Behind the museum is K'Ik'Ik G'Illas, or "The House of Eagles," a new longhouselike structure used to teach carving, dancing, and other traditional ways of life. Ask at the museum to tour the building, which contains an especially impressive totem pole, colorful carvings, wall murals, and two house posts (the main external support posts for longhouses, carved into fanciful forms). In the lobby, you can make petroglyph rubbings from fiberglass castings of ancient stone carvings. Across from the museum is a park where a series of petroglyphs document a few of the island's ancient legends.

The museum is open Monday through Saturday from 10am to 4:30pm. In summer, it's also open Sunday from noon to 4:30pm. Admission is C$3 (U.S.$1.95) for adults and C$2 (U.S.$1.30) for seniors and students. The road to the museum is not well marked. From the ferry, take Cape Mudge Road south about 3 miles (5km); watch for signs for WeiWai Road and a hand-painted sign saying MUSEUM.

In addition to the Kwagiulth Museum, other Quadra destinations include the scenic **Cape Mudge Lighthouse** and **Rebecca Spit,** a sandy swimming beach. **Heriot Bay,** Quadra's other village, is home to the century-old Heriot Bay Inn, with a pub and restaurant (see "Where to Stay," below). A number of artists and craftspeople live on Quadra and keep informal hours at their studios; watch for signs.

OUTDOOR PURSUITS

BIKING   If you'd like to explore Quadra by bike, call ahead and reserve one from **Island Cycle** (☎ 250/285-3627), located in the little village of Quathiaski Cove at the terminal for the ferry to and from Campbell River. There are mountain-biking trails at Morte Lake and Mount Seymour park.

DIVING   The decommissioned HMCS *Columbia* was sunk in 1996 near the sealife–rich waters of Seymour Narrows off Quadra Island's west coast. For information on diving to this artificial reef and to other sites in the Campbell River area, contact **Beaver Aquatics** (☎ 250/287-7652).

KAYAKING   The protected waters of Sutil Channel, between Cortes and Quadra islands, are very popular with sea kayakers. **Spirit of the West Adventures** (☎ 800/307-3982 or 250/285-2121; www.kayak-adventures.com) offers rentals and a variety of excursions. Day trips include an exploration of Rebecca Spit, which goes for C$49 (U.S.$32) for a half day, C$69 (U.S.$45) for a full day. Spirit of the West also offers multiday trips to the Discovery Islands, Desolation Sound, Nootka Sound, and the orca sanctuary at Johnstone Strait. Kayak rentals range from C$16 to C$20 (U.S.$10 to U.S.$13) for a single, C$25 to C$30 (U.S.$16 to U.S.$20) for a double.

WHERE TO STAY

April Point Lodge & Fishing Resort. April Point Rd., Quadra Island. c/o Box 1, Campbell River, BC, V9W 4Z9. ☎ **800/663-7090** or 250/285-2222. www.obmg.com. E-mail: obmg@ pinc.com. 30 units, 6 guest houses. A/C TV TEL. C$139–C$199 (U.S.$90–U.S.$129) double; C$189–C$249 (U.S.$123–U.S.$162) guest house. Extra person C$15 (U.S.$10). AE, MC, V.

The secluded April Point Lodge, world-famous for its saltwater fishing charters, has magnificent views of the Discovery Passage in a tranquil, private setting. This luxury fishing resort and Painter's Lodge, just across the channel, are under the same ownership; there's free boat-taxi service between the two properties, which makes going for drinks or dinner here both easy and adventuresome if you're in Campbell River. The one- to six-bedroom guest houses at the water's edge are comfortable and tastefully furnished, containing hot tubs, fireplaces, and kitchens. The lodge suites are also spacious and nicely appointed. The restaurant features Northwest cuisine; there's also a sushi bar and a cocktail lounge with deck seating (see "Where to Dine," below). Amenities include helicopter access and seaplane service to Vancouver, British Columbia, and Seattle, Washington; a full array of fishing and adventure tours; kayak, bicycle, and scooter rentals; and a full-service marina.

Heriot Bay Inn & Marina. Heriot Bay Rd. (Box 100), Heriot Bay, Quadra Island, BC, V0P 1H0. ☎ **250/285-3322.** Fax 250/285-2708. www.oberon.ark.com/~heriot/index.html. E-mail: heriot@oberon.ark.com. 10 units, 4 cottages. C$60 (U.S.$39) rm double, C$145 (U.S.$94) cottage double. Extra person C$6 (U.S.$3.90). Inn room rates include breakfast. AE, MC, V.

For an inexpensive, fun place to stay, try the century-old Heriot Bay Inn, with a waterfront location in Heriot Bay, Quadra Island's largest village. There's nothing fancy about the rooms or the cottages, but everything is clean and shipshape. Tent and RV sites are also available for C$10 to C$18 (U.S.$7 to U.S.$12). On site are a family restaurant and pub. Boat rentals, canoe and kayak rentals, fishing charters, and hiking packages are available.

✪ **Tsa-Kwa-Luten Lodge.** Lighthouse Rd., Box 460, Quathiaski Cove, Quadra Island, BC, V0P 1N0. ☎ **800/665-7745** or 250/285-2042. Fax 250/285-2532. www.capemudgeresort.bc.ca. E-mail: tkllodge@connected.bc.ca. 30 suites, 4 cabins. TEL. C$60–C$125 (U.S.$39–U.S.$81) suite; C$100–C$350 (U.S.$65–U.S.$228) cabin (sleeps up to 8). Meal plan available. AE, DC, MC, V. Free parking.

Owned and operated by the Laichwiltach, or the Cape Mudge Band, this is a modern luxury resort designed to resemble a native Big House and to harmonize with the landscape and with native traditions. Overlooking the Discovery Passage, Tsa-Kwa-Luten offers both lodge suites and waterfront cabins. Some suites have lofts, Jacuzzis, or fireplaces; all have balconies. The two- and four-bedroom waterfront cabins contain fully equipped kitchens; some have fireplaces and hot tubs. All accommodations are beautifully decorated with native Canadian–inspired furnishings and accessories, as well as contemporary native art. The lodge restaurant features fresh fish, seafood, and steaks prepared with continental finesse and an eye toward native traditions (see "Where to Dine," below). Native dancing and entertainment are offered. Other amenities include a cocktail lounge, fitness center, sauna, whirlpool, and boat, bike, and moped rentals. The staff can arrange fishing trips and heli-fishing charters.

WHERE TO DINE

April Point Lodge. April Point Rd. ☎ **250/285-2222.** Reservations recommended. Main courses C$14–C$25 (U.S.$9–U.S.$16). AE, MC, V. Daily 7–10:30am, 11am–2pm, and 5–10pm. PACIFIC NORTHWEST.

The waterfront restaurant at this well-loved fishing resort boasts a stellar view across Discovery Passage, accompanied by well-prepared Pacific Northwest cuisine. For an appetizer, try pan-seared Fanny Bay oysters with chili and lime crème fraîche, or choose from the menu of the adjoining sushi bar. Daily changing seafood specials, the highlight of the restaurant, join the regular menu's selection of salmon, shrimp, and halibut dishes. If you're not in the mood for fish, perhaps the filet mignon, with crisp latkes and caramelized red-onion glaze, will tempt you. You can get here from Campbell River by taking the free water taxi from Painter's Lodge.

Big House Restaurant. At Tsa-Kwa-Luten Lodge, Lighthouse Rd. ☎ **250/285-2042.** Reservations recommended. Main courses C$14–C$19 (U.S.$9–U.S.$12). AE, MC, V. Daily 7–10:30am, 11am–2pm, and 5–10pm. CONTINENTAL.

Set on the bluffs above the entrance to Discovery Passage, the dining room of Tsa-Kwa-Luten Lodge offers a stunning land- and seascape as a backdrop for its high-quality cuisine. The chowder, studded with fish and seafood from nearby waters, is excellent. Among the entrees, standouts include the venison Bourguignon, with wild mushrooms and traditional bannock bread, and salmon Wellington, a fillet of wild sockeye stuffed with seafood and wrapped in puff pastry. The excellent seafood cakes come with a Thai-style dipping sauce.

CORTES ISLAND & DESOLATION SOUND

This remote island (pop. 900) is the stepping-off point for exploration of Desolation Sound, one of the Canadian west coast's most famed sailing and kayaking destinations. The island is reached by ferry from Heriot Bay, on Quadra, to Whaletown Bay, on the west coast of Cortes.

Adventurers can combine camping with sailing or kayaking lessons at **T'ai Li Lodge,** Box 16, Cortes Bay, BC, V0P 1Z0 (☎ **800/939-6644** or 250/935-6749; www.island.net.~taili). The staff will pick you up from Quadra or Cortes islands and transport you to the beautiful wilderness hideaway (see "Where to Stay," below). Most visitors join one of the various tours or New Age-y workshops held here.

T'ai Li Lodge also offers a number of **sailing** and **kayaking** tours on Desolation Sound. Mothership Tours combine sailing, kayaking, and camping; a weeklong trip in Desolation Sound ranges from C$1,425 to C$1,675 (U.S.$926 to U.S.$1,089). Weeklong kayak-only camping explorations of Desolation Sound cost from C$750 to C$1,150 (U.S.$488 to U.S.$748). Other tours include naturalist-led kayak and sailboat expeditions and women-only kayak trips. Call the lodge for more information.

WHERE TO STAY

T'ai Li Lodge. Box 16, Cortes Bay, BC, V0P 1Z0. ☎ **800/939-6644** or 250/935-6749. www.island.net/~taili. 2 units (neither with private bathroom). C$84 (U.S.$55) double. MC, V.

This remote but beautifully located lodge is popular with sea kayakers and the back-to-the-wilderness New Age set. There are only two rooms in the rather rustic lodge, but many people opt to stay in the platform tent rooms, which are essentially wooden frame tents with foam mattresses (C$65/U.S.$42). Lodge and tent guests share shower, sink, and toilet facilities. American Plan meals (three meals) are available for C$34 (U.S.$22) daily. T'ai Li Lodge also offers regular tent campsites at C$10 (U.S.$7) per night. There's a solar-heated shower and pit toilet for campers' use.

3 Strathcona Provincial Park

24 miles (38km) W of Campbell River

British Columbia's oldest provincial park, and the largest on Vancouver Island at 250,000 hectares (617,500 acres), ✪ **Strathcona Park** is located west of Campbell River and Courtenay. Mountain peaks, many glaciated or mantled with snow, dominate the park, while lakes and alpine meadows dot a landscape laced with rivers, creeks, and streams.

Western red cedar, Douglas fir, grand fir, and western hemlock of the coast forest cover much of the valleys and lower mountain slopes, giving way to subalpine fir, mountain hemlock, and creeping juniper in the subalpine areas. Throughout the summer, the park offers a spectacular floral display in various areas from sea level to above 5,904 feet (1,800m). Roosevelt elk, Vancouver Island marmot and wolf, and black-tailed deer have evolved into distinct species, due to Vancouver Island's separation from the mainland. Birds include the chestnut-backed chickadee, red-breasted nuthatch, winter wren, and kinglet, as well as blue grouse, ruffed grouse, and a limited number of unique Vancouver Island white-tailed ptarmigan.

Buttle Lake, named for Commander John Buttle, who explored the area in the 1860s, is the major body of water in the park. Buttle and many of the other lakes and waterways provide good fishing for cutthroat and rainbow trout and Dolly Varden. Lake swimming is also popular near the Buttle Lake and Ralph River campgrounds.

ESSENTIALS

GETTING THERE   The cities of Campbell River (pop. 30,672) and Courtenay (pop. 18,420) are the primary access points for Strathcona Provincial Park.

Highway 28 passes through the northern section of the park and provides access to Buttle Lake, 30 miles (48km) west of Campbell River.

There are two access routes to the Forbidden Plateau area from Courtenay. To reach Paradise Meadows from Courtenay and Highway 19, follow signs to Mount Washington Resort via the Strathcona Parkway. Fifteen miles (25km) up the parkway, you'll come to the resort's Nordic Lodge road on the left. Go another mile (1.6km) to the Paradise Meadows parking lot. To reach Forbidden Plateau, follow the signs on the Forbidden Plateau road from Highway 19 and Courtenay. It's 12 miles (19km) to the Forbidden Plateau Ski Area and the trailhead.

VISITOR INFORMATION   For advance information, contact **BC Parks District Manager,** Box 1479, Parksville, BC, V9P 2H4 (☎ **250/248-3931**).

SEASONS   Summers in Strathcona are usually pleasantly warm; evenings can be cool. Winters are fairly mild except at higher elevations, where heavy snowfall is quite common. Snow remains year-round on the mountain peaks and may linger into July at higher elevations. Rain can be expected at any time of year.

SEEING THE HIGHLIGHTS

The Buttle Lake area (off Hwy. 28) and the Forbidden Plateau area (accessed through Courtenay) both have some visitor-oriented developments. Just outside the park boundaries, **Strathcona Park Lodge** (see "Accommodations," below) offers lodging, dining, and a wide variety of adventure-oriented activities. The rest of the park is largely undeveloped and appeals primarily to visitors seeking wilderness surroundings. To see and enjoy much of the park's scenic splendor requires hiking or backpacking into the alpine wilderness.

A paved road joins **Highway 28** (the Gold River Hwy.) near the outlet of Buttle Lake and winds its way southward, hugging the shoreline. Along this scenic road are numerous cataracts and creeks that rush and tumble into the lake. **Myra Falls,** on the west side of Buttle Lake near the south end, is the largest.

Some of the more prominent peaks include Mount McBride, Marble Peak, Mount Phillips, and Mount Myra. **Elkhorn Mountain,** at 7,190 feet (2,192m), is the second-highest mountain in the park. Elkhorn, along with Mount Flannigan and Kings Peak, can be seen from Highway 28. The highest point on Vancouver Island at 7,216 feet (2,200m), the **Golden Hinde** stands almost in the center of the park to the west of Buttle Lake.

A second area of the park, **Forbidden Plateau,** is accessed by gravel road from Courtenay. The plateau was believed, according to Indian legend, to be inhabited by evil spirits that consumed women and children who dared to venture into the area. Today, those who hike into the plateau are rewarded with an area of subalpine beauty. Small lakes dot the plateau, while views extend from the surrounding glaciers and mountains to the farmlands and forest that stretch eastward to the Strait of Georgia.

The 1,443-foot (440m) **Della Falls,** the highest nonseasonal waterfall in North America, is located in the southern section of the park, and is reached by a rugged 2-day, 20-mile hike. The trail departs from Great Central Lake, accessible from Highway 4 between Port Alberni and Tofino.

HIKING

FROM THE BUTTLE LAKE AREA The 1.9-mile (3km) **Upper Myra Falls Trail** starts just past the Westmin mine operation and follows a gravel road for 2,296 feet (700m) before turning into a forested trail. This 2-hour hike leads through old-growth forests and past waterfalls. The 4.1-mile (6.6km) **Marble Meadows Trail** starts at Phillips Creek Marine Campsite on Buttle Lake. Marble Meadows features viewpoints, alpine meadows, and limestone formations. Allow 6 hours round-trip for this hike.

The 2,952-foot (900m) **Lady Falls Trail,** which begins at the Highway 28 viewing platform, takes about 20 minutes to hike and leads to a picturesque waterfall. The short, circular 20-minute walk on the 2,624-foot (800m) **Lupin Falls Trail** features cool forest and, in season, Indian Pipe and Candystick flowers. **Karst Creek Trail** covers 1.2 miles (2km) as it passes through a limestone wonderland including sinkholes, disappearing streams, and waterfalls. The hike takes about 45 minutes.

FROM THE PARADISE MEADOWS TRAILHEAD (MT. WASHINGTON) The 1.4-mile (2.2km) **Paradise Meadows Loop Trail** is an easy walk through subalpine meadows, taking about 45 minutes. The **Helen McKenzie–Kwai Lake–Croteau Lake Loop Trail,** 8.6 miles (14km) long, offers access to beautiful subalpine lakes and mountain vistas. There's designated camping at Kwai Lake. Suggested hiking time is 6 hours. From Lake Helen McKenzie, the trail follows forested slopes over rougher terrain before rising to a rolling subalpine area to Circlet Lake. The Hairtrigger Lake area provides spectacular views. Circlet Lake offers designated camping as well. Allow 4 hours for this hike.

FROM FORBIDDEN PLATEAU The 3.1-mile (5km), 2-hour **Mount Becher Summit Trail** starts at the ski lodge and goes up one of the runs to the trailhead near the T-bar. The trail and summit provide excellent views of the Comox valley and northern Strait of Georgia.

OTHER TRAILS IN STRATHCONA PARK The **Della Falls Trail** is 20 miles (32km) round-trip. It starts at the west end of Great Central Lake (between Port Alberni and Tofino on Hwy. 4) and follows the old railway grade up the Drinkwater Valley to near the base of the falls. Della Falls, at 1,443 feet (440m), is one of the 10 highest waterfalls in the world. The trail passes by historic sites from the early days of railroad logging and accesses Love Lake and Della Lake. Some unbridged river crossings can be hazardous. Handrails on the bridge over the Drinkwater River are removed for the winter season.

CAMPING

Buttle Lake, with 85 sites, and **Ralph River,** with 76 sites, are both located on Buttle Lake, accessible via Highway 28 (the Gold River Hwy.) west of Campbell River. Sites go for C$15 (U.S.$10). The campgrounds have water, toilets, and firewood.

WHERE TO STAY

✪ **Strathcona Park Lodge.** 25 miles (40km) west of Campbell River on Hwy. 28. Mailing address: Hwy. 28, Box 2160, Campbell River, BC, V9W 5C9. ☎ **250/286-3122.** www. strathcona.bc.ca. E-mail: info@strathcona.bc.ca. 20 chalet rms, 8 two-bedroom suites, 10 cabins, 1 eight-bedroom chalet. From C$70–C$120 (U.S.$46–U.S.$78) double. 2- or 3-night minimum stays in cabins. AE, MC, V. American Plan (3 meals) available from C$150–C$215 (U.S.$98–U.S.$140) double.

This rustic lodge, just north of Strathcona Park along upper Campbell Lake, is far more than just a place to stay in the woods. With a wide variety of educational and adventure programs appealing to everyone from families to Elderhostel Golden Agers to those seeking accreditation in mountaineering, the lodge has something to offer anyone who loves the outdoors. One guest called it "a cross between Outward Bound and Club Med." Activities include training in climbing, rappelling, and wilderness survival, along with gentler pursuits such as canoeing, fishing, swimming, and hiking. Because the options for activities/lodging packages are numerous, it's a good idea to call the lodge to discuss what fits your interests. One popular program is the 4-day Adventure Sampler, which includes lodging, meals, and activities (climbing, kayaking, orienteering, hiking, and more) for C$680 (U.S.$442) per person. Guides and instructors can also be hired by the hour. Even if you choose not to participate in any of the adventure programs, the lodge is a lovely place to hang out and use as a base for exploring the park. All accommodations are sparely yet comfortably furnished. Some chalet units have shared bathrooms; all other rooms and cabins have private baths. The lakefront cabins, with full kitchens, are the most charming, though you must call well in advance to reserve. In summer, the Whale Room serves three meals daily; off-season, it offers a buffet. Guests sit at communal long tables.

4 West to Gold River & Nootka Sound

Highway 28 continues past Strathcona Park another 6 miles (9km) to **Gold River** (pop. 2,049), a logging port and mill town on the Muchalet Inlet, and the only community on Vancouver Island's west coast reachable by paved road besides Tofino and Ucluelet. This extremely wild coastline was the site of the first European settlement in the northwest. In 1774, Spanish soldiers established a short-lived post on **Nootka Sound.** They were followed by Capt. James Cook, who traded with natives for otter furs in 1792. The tiny coastal communities here are almost completely isolated from roads, and rely on the **MV** *Uchuck III,* a converted World War II minesweeper, for public transport and movement of goods. Passengers are welcome to join the MV *Uchuck III* as it goes between Gold River, Nootka Sound, and Kyuquot Sound.

The year-round Tahsis Day Trip leaves on Tuesday at 9am, traveling into Nootka Sound and up the Tahsis Inlet between Vancouver and Nootka islands to the village of Tahsis. The 9-hour trip costs C$45 (U.S.$29) for adults, C$41 (U.S.$27) for seniors, and C$23 (U.S.$15) for children 7 to 12.

On Thursdays year-round, the boat departs for Kyuquot Sound, to the north. This 2-day trip goes through Nootka Sound and up the Tahsis and Esperanza inlets to the open sea and eventually the village of Kyuquot, where passengers stay overnight at a B&B before returning the following day. Costs, which include accommodation, are C$170 (U.S.$111) single, C$285 (U.S.$185) double. The departure time is 7am from April 1 to October 31, 6am the rest of the year. Children traveling with an adult pay C$70 (U.S.$46). Rates do not include the evening meal.

From July to the week after Labour Day, the boat makes day trips to Friendly Cove on Nootka Island, the spot where the Spanish settled and the English traded. These 7- to 8-hour trips leave Gold River at 10am on Wednesday and Saturday; tickets are C$40 (U.S.$26) for adults, C$37 (U.S.$24) for seniors, and C$20 (U.S.$13) for kids.

For more information or to make reservations, contact **Nootka Sound Services,** P.O. Box 57, Gold River, BC, V0P 1G0 (☎ 250/283-2325; fax 250/283-7582; www.island.net/~mvuchuck; e-mail: mvuchuck@island.net). To reach the departure dock, go 8¹/₂ miles (14km) past Gold River on Highway 28.

If you need accommodations in Gold River, contact the **Tourist Info Centre** (☎ 250/283-2202) or try the **Ridgeview Motel,** 395 Donner Court

(☎ **800/989-3393** or 250/283-2277), where doubles range from C$89 to C$125 (U.S.$58 to U.S.$81).

5 Telegraph Cove, Port McNeill, Alert Bay & Port Hardy

Telegraph Cove: 123 miles (198km) N of Campbell River

It's a winding 123-mile (198km) drive through thickly forested mountains along the Island Highway (Hwy. 19) from Campbell River to **Port McNeill** on northern Vancouver Island. But the majestic scenery, the crystal-clear lakes, and the unique wilderness along the way make it worthwhile.

The highway rejoins the coast along **Johnstone Strait,** an area that's home to a number of orca pods, which migrate annually from the Queen Charlotte Strait south to these salmon-rich waters. (Orcas, or killer whales, live in groups from a few to 50 individuals, known as pods.) Whale-watching trips out of Port McNeill and Telegraph Cove are the principal recreational activities; this is one of the most noted whale-watching areas in British Columbia.

Also worth a visit is the island community of **Alert Bay,** a traditional First Nations town site festooned with totem poles and carvings. The cultural museum houses a famous collection of ceremonial masks and other historic artifacts.

The Island Highway's terminus, **Port Hardy,** is 32 miles (51.6km) north of Port McNeill. Although it's a remote community of only 5,470, Port Hardy is the starting point for three unique experiences: the Inside Passage ferry cruise (see chapter 9) to Prince Rupert, the Discovery Coast ferry cruise (see chapter 9), and the untamed rain forest and coastline of Cape Scott Provincial Park (see section 6, below).

ESSENTIALS

GETTING THERE   There are three principal ways to get to Vancouver Island's northernmost towns and islands: by car, bus, and plane. You can also reach Port Hardy from the north via the Inside Passage ferry from Prince Rupert (see chapter 9).

By Plane   Pacific Coastal Airlines (☎ **800/663-2872**), a partner of Canadian Airlines, flies three times daily into Port Hardy Airport from Vancouver.

By Car   Telegraph Cove is 123 miles (198.3km) north of Campbell River along the Island Highway (Hwy. 19). Port McNeill is another 5 miles (8.8km) north. Port Hardy is 148 miles (238km) north of Campbell River.

By Bus   Laidlaw Coach Lines (☎ **250/385-4411**) operates daily service between Nanaimo and Port McNeill and Port Hardy. The one-way fare to Port Hardy is C$75 (U.S.$49).

VISITOR INFORMATION   Although there's no official visitor center in Telegraph Cove, you can contact **Information for Tourists,** Telegraph Cove, BC, V0N 3J0 (☎ **250/928-3185**).

The **Port McNeill Visitor Info Centre,** 1626 Beach Dr., Box 129, Port McNeill, BC, V0N 2R0 (☎ **250/956-3131;** e-mail: pmccc@island.net), is open from May 15 to September 15, daily from 10am to 6pm.

The **Alert Bay Visitor Info Centre,** 116 Fir St., Box 28, Alert Bay, BC, V0N 1A0 (☎ **250/974-5213;** e-mail: info@alertbay.com), is near the ferry terminal. It's open in summer, daily from 9am to 6pm, and the rest of the year, Monday through Friday from 9am to 5pm.

The **Port Hardy Visitor Info Centre,** 7250 Market St., Box 249, Port Hardy, BC, V0N 2P0 (☎ **250/949-7622;** e-mail: chamber@trinet.bc.ca), is open from June 1 to Labour Day, Monday through Friday from 8am to 9pm, Saturday and Sunday from 9am to 9pm; Labour Day to October 20, Monday through Friday from 9am to 5pm, Saturday and Sunday from 9am to 9pm; October 21 to May 31, Monday through Friday from 8:30am to 4:30pm (plus May 1 to 31, Sat and Sun from 9am to 5pm).

TELEGRAPH COVE

Telegraph Cove, 5 miles (8km) south of Port McNeill, offers an unusual story. The town's 12 residents live in one of the few remaining elevated-boardwalk villages on Vancouver Island, overlooking Johnstone Strait. This postcard-perfect fishing village's buildings are perched on stilts over the water, making it an entertaining destination for a stroll, especially since whales have been spotted close to shore many times.

First a sawmill and fishing port, then an army camp, now a resort, Telegraph Cove's once isolated charm is quickly changing. For years, the town has largely been dominated by comfortably dilapidated **Telegraph Cove Resort,** which offers many of the town's historic boardwalk homes and structures as rental units. With a good restaurant, busy boat basin, and wonderful bay and island views, the resort village is a longtime family favorite. However, the beauty of the area hasn't been lost on one present-day resort developer, who is in the process of building a massive full-scale resort on Telegraph Cove, complete with golf courses, luxury condos, and a hotel.

From May to mid-October, a passenger-only **ferry** (☎ **250/974-5225**) travels between Telegraph Cove and the fascinating native village of **Alert Bay** (see below). One-way tickets for the half-hour trip are C$20 (U.S.$13) for adults, C$10 (U.S.$7) for children. In high season, the ferry departs every 2 hours from 9am to 9pm.

WHALE WATCHING

Telegraph Cove is the closest settlement to Johnstone Strait, a narrow passage that serves as the summer home to hundreds of orcas as well as dolphins, porpoises, and seals. Bald eagles also patrol the waterway, and more unusual birds pass through the area, an important stop on the Pacific Flyway.

Ten miles (16.5km) south of Telegraph Cove and accessible by boat charter, the ✪ **Robson Bight Ecological Reserve** provides some of the most fascinating whale watching in the province. Orcas, some the size of small school buses, regularly beach themselves in the shallow waters of the Bight's world-famous pebbly "rubbing beaches" to remove the barnacles from their tummies. Occasionally, grey and minke whales are also seen in this area. Boaters, including kayakers and tour operators, are not allowed to enter the reserve, but you can visit nearby areas.

Stubbs Island Whale Watching (☎ **800/665-3066** or 250/928-3185; www.stubbs-island.com; e-mail: stubbs.island.net), located near the end of the Telegraph Cove boardwalk, offers whale-watching trips to Johnstone Strait, passing near the Robson Bight Reserve. The boats are 60-foot vessels equipped with hydrophones, so you can hear the whales' underwater communication. The 4-hour tours are offered June through September; call ahead for reservations. The cost is C$65 (U.S.$42) for adults. Seniors, children 12 and under, and individuals in groups of four or more (with reservations) pay C$59 (U.S.$38).

WHERE TO STAY & DINE

Although both of the following establishments have mailing addresses in Port McNeill, they are located in or near Telegraph Cove.

Hidden Cove Lodge. Lewis Point, Box 258, Port McNeill, BC, V0N 2R0. ☎ **250/ 956-3916.** 8 units, 3 cabins. C$125–C$150 (U.S.$81–U.S.$98) double, C$250 (U.S.$163) cabin. Extra person C$25 (U.S.$16). Rates include continental breakfast. MC, V. Closed Dec–Apr. Take the Island Hwy. (Hwy. 19) to Telegraph Cove/Beaver Cove; turn right and follow the signs. The lodge is 4 miles (6.6km) from Telegraph Cove.

Built years before a road reached this isolated little harbor, Hidden Cove Lodge was meant to be approached by boat, and it still saves its best face for those who arrive this way. The handsome two-story lodge is nestled beside a secluded cove overlooking the Johnstone Strait. The split-level, cathedral-ceilinged great room and dining room are comfortably furnished, and the lodge's clean and simply decorated guest rooms all have private bathrooms. Facing onto the strait are three new two-bedroom, one-bathroom cabins, each with an efficiency kitchen and large deck. Hidden Cove's easy-going, unaffected atmosphere belies the fact that it attracts the rich and famous: Folks like the United Nations Secretary General and entertainment stars have been guests here. The resort's restaurant serves high-quality international dishes and a daily selection of seasonal choices based on locally caught seafood. The dining room is open to nonguests by reservation only. The hosts can arrange whale-watching, bird- and wildlife-watching, guided fishing, heli-fishing, and hiking tours.

Telegraph Cove Resorts. Box 1, Telegraph Cove, BC, V0N 3J0. ☎ **800/200-HOOK** or 250/928-3131. www.telegraphcoveresort.com. E-mail: tcrltd@island.net. 19 units. C$115–C$155 (U.S.$75–U.S.$101) double. Extra person C$5 (U.S.$3.25). MC, V. Located 5 miles (8km) south of Port McNeill.

Most of the lodgings offered by Telegraph Cove Resorts are refurbished older homes from the early 20th century, scattered along the bayside boardwalk. Each accommodation is different, ranging from small double rooms in a former fishermen's boardinghouse to three-bedroom homes that sleep up to nine. All units have private bathrooms and kitchens, but no phones or TVs. There are also hotel-style rooms (no cooking facilities) available at the Wastell Manor, a large home built in 1912. Although none of the resort's properties are exactly fancy, these historic buildings are clean, simply furnished, and charming, and make for a unique lodging experience. In addition, 121 wooded campsites are a short walk from the cove and the boardwalk. Open May through October, the campground provides hot showers, laundry, toilets, fire pits, and drinking water. Sites are C$23 (U.S.$15).

The Killer Whale Café offers a seafood-rich Canadian menu, while the Old Saltery Pub serves up burgers and lighter fare. Both have outdoor seating. On Sunday, the resort encourages all guests to join the afternoon potluck. Amenities include moorage, fishing charters, and kayak rentals.

PORT MCNEILL & ALERT BAY

Port McNeill (pop. 3,014) is a hard-bitten little logging and mill town that, aside from access to whale-watching tours and the ferry to Alert Bay, has little to offer travelers. Alert Bay (pop. 612), on the other hand, is a fascinating destination for anyone interested in First Nations culture, both historic and present-day. One of the best-preserved and easily accessible native villages in British Columbia, Alert Bay has a wonderful collection of totem carvings and wall murals, as well as historic buildings.

If you're here the second week of June, the Nimpkish Reserve hosts **June Sports & Indian Celebrations** (☎ 250/974-5556) on the soccer field in Alert Bay. Traditional tests of strength and agility are demonstrated by the island's tribal members.

BC Ferries (☎ **888/724-5223** in B.C.) operates runs between Port McNeill and Alert Bay 10 times daily from 8:40am to 9:50pm. The crossing takes about 45 minutes; fares are C$6 (U.S.$3.90) per passenger, C$14 (U.S.$9) per vehicle.

Additionally, a private passenger-only ferry operates between Telegraph Cove and Alert Bay in summer (see "Telegraph Cove," above).

EXPLORING ALERT BAY

Alert Bay on Cormorant Island has a rich native Indian heritage that can be seen in the architecture and artifacts that are proudly preserved on the tiny island. It has been a Kwagiulth tribal village for thousands of years. The integration of Scottish immigrants into the area during the 19th and 20th centuries is clearly depicted in the design of the **Anglican Church,** on Front Street (☎ 250/974-5213). The cedar building was erected in 1881; its stained-glass window designs reflect a fusion of native Kwagiulth and Scottish design motifs. It's open in summer, Monday through Saturday from 8am to 5pm.

Walk a mile (1.6km) from the ferry terminal along Front Street to the island's two most interesting attractions. A 173-foot (53m) **totem pole**—the world's highest—stands next to the Big House (the tribal community center), which is not open to the public. Visitors are welcome, however, to enter the outside grounds to get a closer look at this building covered with traditional painted figures. Erected in 1973, the cedar totem pole features 22 hand-carved figures of bears, orcas, and ravens, plus a sun at the top.

A few yards down the road from the Big House and totem pole is the ✪ **U'Mista Cultural Centre,** Front Street (☎ 250/974-5403), which displays a collection of carved-wood ceremonial masks, cedar baskets, copper jewelry, and other potlatch artifacts that were confiscated by the Canadian government when the potlatch was banned in 1922. The items were only recently returned to the island's native Indian community. Revolving exhibits explain the Kwagiulth tribe's culture and history. Admission is C$5 (U.S.$3.25) for adults, C$4 (U.S.$2.60) for seniors, and C$1 (U.S.65¢) for children under 12. In summer, the museum is open daily from 9am to 6pm. In winter, hours are Monday through Friday from 9am to 5pm.

WHALE WATCHING & OTHER OUTDOOR PURSUITS

Orcas, dolphins, and eagles all gather along Johnstone Strait to snack on salmon and other fish that converge at this narrows between Vancouver Island and a series of tightly clustered islands.

From Port McNeill, **Mackay Whale Watching Ltd.** (☎ 877/663-6722 or 250/956-9865; e-mail: mackaybd@island.net) offers daily tours to Johnstone Strait on the *Naiad Explorer,* a 55-foot passenger cruiser with bathroom facilities and a hydrophone. The cost for a 4- to 5-hour trip is C$60 (U.S.$39) per person, with group and family discounts available. Call for schedules and reservations.

From Alert Bay, families or small groups can join **Headwind Charters** (☎ 800/947-2032 or 250/974-2032; www.alertbay.com/headwind; e-mail: headwind@island.net) for Johnstone Strait whale-watching trips on the 35-foot, hydrophone-equipped MV *Kvitsoy.* Rates are C$60 (U.S.$39) per hour per group, with a 3-hour minimum and 6-person maximum.

You can also get up close and personal with the orcas on a guided sea-kayak tour. **Robson Bight Adventures** (☎ 877/956-2582 or 250/956-2581) offers year-round excursions along the Johnstone Bight. **Seasmoke Tours** (☎ 800/668-6722 or 250/974-5225) offers sailing trips from June through October. Excursions through the Johnstone Strait aboard a 44-foot, hydrophone-equipped yacht include a seafood lunch and Devonshire tea. Half-day tours with both Robson Bight and Seasmoke cost between C$75 and C$115 (U.S.$49 and U.S.$75) per person.

WHERE TO STAY & DINE

Groceries are available at supermarkets such as **IGA Plus,** 1705 Campbell Way (☎ 250/956-4404). You'll find a number of restaurants along Beach Drive in Port McNeill. **Sportsman's Steak & Pizza,** on Beach Drive (☎ 250/956-4113), offers a hearty menu of basics such as roast chicken, steaks, burgers, and pizzas.

Port McNeill has a number of modest homestay B&Bs and older motels. If you can't get into the recommended Telegraph Cove–area resorts and don't want to continue on to Port Hardy or Campbell River, try the **Dalewood Inn,** 1703 Broughton Blvd. (☎ 250/956-3304), a motor inn with rooms starting at C$66 (U.S.$43).

Oceanview Cabins. 390 Poplar St., Alert Bay, BC, V0N 1A0. ☎ **250/974-5457.** Fax 250/974-2275. 12 cottages (2 with shower only). TV. C$50–C$65 (U.S.$33–U.S.$42) double. Extra person C$5 (U.S.$3.25). MC, V.

Overlooking Mitchell Bay and only a mile from the ferry terminal, this quiet, waterfront resort is the island's best value. The property offers simply furnished, comfortable cabins with queen-size beds, kitchens, and full bathrooms (in all but two cabins). Be sure to reserve a few months in advance.

CAMPING

Oceanview Camping & Trailer Park, Alder Road, Box 28, Alert Bay, BC, V0N 1A0 (☎ 250/974-5213; fax 250/974-5470), has a great view of the Johnstone Strait and a number of nature trails that fan out from the 23 campsites. Rates are C$10 to C$15 (U.S.$7 to U.S.$10) per vehicle. Full hookups, flush toilets, free hot showers, a free boat launch, boat charters, and boat tours make this a great deal.

PORT HARDY

Port Hardy is the final stop on the Island Highway. This down-on-its-luck community is slowly moving away from a resource-based economy: Fishing, forestry, and the mining of copper, gold, and molybdenum have waned, and the town is gradually making the transition to an economy based on tourism.

The principal reason to venture here is the ferry to **Prince Rupert**—in fact, the ferry is the mainstay of the local tourism industry. The night before the 15-hour Inside Passage ferry runs, the town is booked up and reservations are needed at most restaurants—not exactly what you'd expect in such a remote town. Port Hardy is also the point of departure for the Discovery Coast ferry cruise (see chapter 9).

People also visit for the outdoor recreation: diving, hiking, and excellent halibut and salmon fishing. Sportfishing is very good here, as the runs of salmon in local rivers continue to be strong and are therefore open to more fishing than at threatened runs elsewhere. Port Hardy is also the launching point for a land-based journey to **Cape Scott,** a wilderness park at the northern tip of Vancouver Island.

In the small downtown, the **Port Hardy Museum,** 7110 Market St. (☎ 250/949-8143), holds relics from early Danish settlers, plus a collection of stone tools from about 8000 B.C. found in archaeological digs just east of town. That ancient village is one of the earliest known human settlements in British Columbia.

Special Events

Even at Vancouver Island's northernmost point, you'll find daring swimmers diving into the icy waters on New Year's Day at the annual **Polar Bear Swim** (☎ 250/949-7622). It takes place on Seagate Dock in Port Hardy.

Admission is C$1 ((U.S.65¢). The gift shop is one of the few places in town where you can find local carving and artwork.

Outdoor Pursuits

✪ **DIVING**   Diving is excellent in the Port Hardy area. The strong tides and ocean currents keep the water very clear, and within a small area, you'll find many kinds of dive environments with abundant sea life. For more information on north Vancouver Island diving, go to **www.3routes.com/scuba/na/can/bc/08/index.html**.

In Port Hardy, **North Island Diving and Water Sports,** at the corner of Market and Hastings (☎ **250/949-2664**), is a full-service dive supply store; equipment rentals and instruction are available. For an entire vacation's worth of diving, contact **God's Pocket Resort,** Box 130, Port Hardy, BC, V0N 2P0 (☎ **888/5-DIVEBC** or 250/949-9221; www.3routes.com/scuba/godspocket). Located on Hurst Island 7.4 miles (12km) north of Port Hardy in Queen Charlotte Strait, the resort offers complete diving (and fishing) packages, including meals and accommodations. A 3-day package goes for C$499 (U.S.$324) and includes all boat transport between the resort and Port Hardy, all meals and accommodations, two boat dives per day, plus air and weight belts. Divers must provide their own personal diving gear and show a "C" level diving card.

FISHING   If you want to base yourself in Port Hardy, you can arrange day charter trips with local outfitters. **Catala Charters and Lodge** (☎ **800/515-5511** or 250/ 949-7560; www.capescott.net/labrador; e-mail: catala@capescott.net) offers guided fishing trips for salmon, halibut, and other bottom fish. It also operates the **C-View B&B,** so you can arrange lodging and fishing with one phone call. Another established outfitter is **Codfather Charters** (☎ **250/949-6696**), with year-round fishing for salmon, ling cod, halibut, and red snapper. Accommodations are in the company's waterfront lodge. Both outfitters offer many different kinds of charters, but most cost roughly C$350 (U.S.$228) per day, including lodging, meals, and gear.

If you simply want to rent a boat and get started on your own, contact **Hardy Bay Boat Rental** (☎ **250/949-7048**). In addition to a variety of boat rentals ranging from C$13 to C$22 (U.S.$8 to U.S.$14) an hour, Hardy Bay also rents fishing gear.

Port Hardy is the stepping-off point for trips to remote **fishing camps,** many with long pedigrees and well-to-do clientele. One of the most famous is **Nimmo Bay Resort,** Nimmo Bay, Box 696, Port McNeill, BC, V0N 2R0 (☎ **800/887-HELI** or 250/949-2549; fax 250/956-2000), an all-inclusive, full-service resort where a week's fishing will cost around C$3,295 (U.S.$2,142). Another resort with similar prices and facilities is **Eagle Manor Retreat,** Quatsino Sound, c/o Box 72, Coal Harbour, BC, V0N 1K0 (☎ **604/949-7895**). Both camps require reservations in advance, and offer lodging and fishing to registered guests only. Access is by floatplane or boat.

One of the only camps directly accessed from Port Hardy is **Duval Point Lodge,** Goletas Channel, Box 818, Port Hardy, BC, V0N 2P0 (☎ **250/949-6667;** www.island.net/~duval; e-mail: duval@island.net), which offers 3- and 4-day packages from its base camp about 5 miles (8km) north of town. Guests receive a short training session; groups are then given their own boat and pointed to the channel, which is alive with halibut, cod, and, in season, salmon. From here on, you keep your own schedule and run expeditions as you see fit. Lodging is in two two-story floating lodges, each with four bedrooms, a mix of private and shared bathrooms, and full kitchen. The outfitter provides rod and reel, bait, boat, cleaning area, and freezers for storage, plus bedding and kitchen equipment. Guests do their own cooking. Guides are available, though part of the fun here is the satisfaction of running your own boat and interacting with other guests. Brand-new at the lodge are two land-based log cabins, each with three bedrooms, two baths, and full kitchen. Rates are C$185 (U.S.$120) a night, with a 4-night minimum. The lodge is closed from October through May. Duval Point Lodge is not for those looking for five-star comforts and pampering. However, if you want access to excellent fishing and adventure with congenial hospitality, it's a great value.

HIKING   For serious hikers, the best destination on North Vancouver Island is **Cape Scott Provincial Park,** at the island's northwest point (see below).

KAYAKING   Duval Point Lodge (see "Fishing," above) now offers kayaking adventures. The dozens of uninhabited islands in the Goletas Channel directly offshore from the lodge are excellent for exploration by kayak, as is the coastline west of Duval Point, which is dotted with rocky headlands and tiny sandy coves. Experienced kayakers can choose to base themselves at the lodge and explore on their own with a 5-day package (C$720/U.S.$468), or join a 5-day guided and supported kayak/camping trip that takes in several islands and remote beach campsites (C$780/U.S.$507). Tents, kayaks, and meals are included in the price.

   North Island Kayak (☎ **877/949-7707** or 250/949-7707; www.island.net/ ~nikayak; e-mail: nikayak@island.net), offers kayak rentals, instruction, and a wide range of tours. It has locations both in Port Hardy and on the Johnstone Strait, and offers a number of tours to view orcas. A day trip onto Johnstone Strait costs C$99 (U.S.$64); a daylong instruction course on calmer waters is C$69 (U.S.$45). Longer expeditions are also available. Half-day rentals start at C$20 (U.S.$13) for a single kayak, C$35 (U.S.$23) for a double kayak.

WHERE TO STAY

Port Hardy has several well-worn hotel complexes. Reserve well in advance— especially on days when the ferries run, as lodgings usually fill up completely.

Airport Inn. 4030 Byng Rd., Box 2039, Port Hardy, BC, V0N 2P0. ☎ **250/949-9434.** Fax 250/949-6533. www.capescott.net/~airportinn. E-mail: airportinn@capescott.net. 45 units. TV TEL. C$85–C$95 (U.S.$55–U.S.$62). Extra person C$5 (U.S.$3.25). Kitchen C$7 (U.S.$4.55) extra. AE, MC, V.

Although the Airport Inn is 8 miles (12.8km) from downtown, this newly remodeled motel deserves mention because it's the best maintained of Port Hardy's many older motor inns. Rooms are large and furnished with all of the basics, plus in-room coffeemakers; some have kitchenettes as well. On site are a coffee shop, dining room, and pub. The hotel is within walking distance of the airport.

Kay's Bed & Breakfast. 7605 Carnarvon Rd., Box 257, Port Hardy, BC, V0N 2P0. ☎ **250/ 949-6776.** 4 units (2 with shared bathroom). TV. C$58 (U.S.$38) double. Extra person C$15 (U.S.$10). Rates include continental breakfast, complimentary tea and coffee all day, and kitchen use. Off-season rates available. No credit cards.

This conveniently located B&B has a lovely ocean view and offers free pickup service from the Port Hardy ferry terminal. Each self-contained guest room is furnished with a comfortable queen bed and a fully equipped kitchen. The complimentary breakfast features fresh baked goods, jams, and coffee.

Oceanview B&B. 7735 Cedar Place, Box 1837, Port Hardy, BC, V0N 2P0. ☎ and fax **250/ 949-8302.** www.island.net/~oceanvue. E-mail: oceanvue@island.net. 3 units (2 with shared bathroom). TV. C$85 (U.S.$55) double. Rates include buffet breakfast. No credit cards; cash and traveler's checks accepted. Children must be 12 or older.

Perched on a bluff overlooking Port Hardy Bay, Oceanview is a large and comfortably furnished modern home. A large room with two queen beds and a private bathroom overlooks the cul-de-sac and front gardens, while another large room with one queen bed offers views of the bay. The entire house is absolutely spotless. The hostess, a long-time Port Hardy resident, offers a friendly welcome and advice on local travel.

Pioneer Inn (Port Hardy). 4965 Byng Rd., Box 669, Port Hardy, BC, V0N 2P0. ☎ **800/663-8744** or 250/949-7271. Fax 250/949-7334. 36 units. TV TEL. C$85–C$99 (U.S.$55–U.S.$64). Extra person C$8 (U.S.$5). 25 RV sites. C$21 (U.S.$14) per vehicle. Electricity, sewer, and water included; cable TV and telephone hookup extra. AE, MC, V.

Pioneer Inn is located in a parklike setting on the banks of the Quatse River, 5 miles (8km) south of Port Hardy on the road to Coal Harbour. The rooms are well maintained and basic; some larger family units contain kitchens. Inn guests get free local calls. There are often vacancies here on the nights before the ferry departs, when the downtown motels fill up. Facilities include a campground, restaurant, coffee shop, laundry, and playground and picnic area.

Quarterdeck Inn. 6555 Hardy Bay Rd., P.O. Box 910, Port Hardy, BC, V0N 2P0. ☎ **250/902-0455.** Fax 250/902-0454. www.capescott.net/~quarterdk. E-mail: quarterdk@capescott.net. 40 units. C$102 (U.S.$66) double. Rates include continental breakfast. AE, MC, V.

Opened in 1999, the Quarterdeck has more going for it than just its comparative youth. Perched directly above the busy Quarterdeck Marina, all units have great views onto a large fishing and pleasure-boat port. Rooms are spacious (some are practically suites) and outfitted with quality beds, furniture, and amenities; some contain kitchenettes. The Quarterdeck also has an RV park (C$20/U.S.$13 full hookup). IV's Quarterdeck Pub is adjacent to the inn. Guests will enjoy the on-site hot tub.

CAMPING

The shaded **Wild Woods Campsite,** Forestry Road, Box 801, Port Hardy, BC, V0N 2P0 (☎ **250/949-6753**), is on the road to the Port Hardy ferry terminal. The 60 campsites are a great value, offering fire pits, hot showers, toilets, picnic tables, beach access, and moorage for C$7 to C$20 (U.S.$4.55 to U.S.$13) per vehicle. There's a store on the premises.

WHERE TO DINE

For a simple meal or snack, or to get provisions for a picnic, stop by the **Stink Creek Bakery Cafe,** 7030 Market St. (☎ **250/949-8117**), a somewhat unfortunately named small bakery right downtown that also offers lunchtime soups and sandwiches.

IV's Quarterdeck Pub. Hardy Bay Rd. ☎ **250/949-6922.** Reservations not accepted. Main courses C$7–C$16 (U.S.$4.55–U.S.$10). AE, MC, V. Daily 11am–midnight. PUB/CANADIAN.

This friendly pub and dining room, right above the marina, offers a large menu of appetizers, salads, burgers, and a selection of entrees—North American standards like steaks, ribs, and chicken. Locals will be quick to tell you that this is the best casual dining in Port Hardy; the clientele is a friendly mix of local fishermen, tradesmen, and travelers.

Sam's Place. North Island College. ☎ **250/949-9733.** Reservations recommended. Main courses C$5–C$18 (U.S.$3.25–U.S.$12). AE, MC, V. Daily 11am–10pm. Located a half mile (1km) south of Port Hardy on Hwy. 19. GREEK/CANADIAN.

It doesn't look like much from the outside, but this cozy restaurant in a mostly abandoned shopping center offers Port Hardy's best dining. The broad menu encompasses excellent Greek cooking (such as seafood souvlaki), pizza, steak and seafood combinations, and continental-style chicken and veal entrees. The house specialty is

Yani's Veal, with peppercorn sauce and tiger shrimp. Light dinners, burgers, and pasta dishes are available for smaller appetites.

6 Cape Scott Provincial Park

42 miles (68km) W of Port Hardy

Cape Scott Provincial Park is a 54,000-acre rugged coastal wilderness at the northwest tip of Vancouver Island. The park is characterized by 40 miles (64km) of spectacular ocean frontage, including about 14 miles (23km) of wide, sandy beaches, running from Nissen Bight in the north to San Josef Bay in the south and interspersed with rocky promontories and headlands. **Nels Bight,** about midway between the eastern boundary of the park near Nissen Bight and the Cape Scott Lighthouse, is a 1 1/2-mile-long, 700-foot-wide (213m) beach with fine white sand; it's considered the most impressive of the nine beaches in the park. Inland areas of Cape Scott are covered with forests of red and yellow cedar, lodgepole pine, hemlock, and fir.

Hansen Lagoon is a stopping place for Canada geese and a variety of waterfowl traveling the Pacific Flyway. The ubiquitous gull and other seabirds frequent the shoreline. Deer, elk, black bear, otter, cougars, and wolves are in evidence in the forested and open uplands, while seals and sea lions inhabit offshore islands.

The heavy rainfalls and violent windstorms of the Cape Scott area have shaped its history. Annual precipitation, almost totally in the form of rain, is nearly 200 inches. Even in summer, prolonged sunny periods are a rarity. High winds, rain, and generally stormy conditions can be expected at any time of the year.

A combination of factors—weather conditions, distance from markets, and lack of suitable access routes—spelled the death knell of two settlement attempts. In 1897 and again in 1910, hardy Danish pioneers arrived at Hansen Lagoon to settle, raise crops, and fish. After several years of hardship, they were forced by the elements of nature and conditions beyond their control to give up their struggles and leave.

Cape Scott Provincial Park is true wilderness, preserving magnificent areas of coastal British Columbia. Visitors can expect to find little development other than trails. Anyone contemplating a visit should be prepared for adverse weather conditions, which are the rule year-round rather than the exception. There is no best time to visit the park, although midsummer is generally preferred.

ESSENTIALS

GETTING THERE   Hiking trails, frequently muddy, provide the only access to the park. The trailhead for all park trails, in the extreme southeast corner of the park, is reached by a 42-mile (67km) part-paved, part-gravel road. From Port Hardy, follow signs for Winter Harbour or Holberg.

VISITOR INFORMATION   For information, contact **BC Parks District Manager,** Box 1479, Parksville, BC, V9P 2H4 (☎ **250/248-3931**).

HIKING

The easiest and most popular hike in the park is the 1 1/2-mile (2.5km) one-way trail from the trailhead to **San Josef Bay.** The trail leads through forest along the San Josef River, reaching the beach in about 45 minutes. Once at the beach, you can explore the ruins of the Henry Ohlsen home and post office, a relic of the Danish settlements of the early 1900s. The first section of beach is wide and white, punctuated by occasional sea stacks and flanked by rocky cliffs, and makes a great destination for a picnic. At the north end of this beach, the cliffs reach out into the surf. At low tide, hikers can skirt this rocky point (stop to look at the sea cave), which is the easiest way to reach a second, equally beautiful section of beach on the north shore of San Josef Bay. At high tide, hikers must scale the rocky promontory on a steep, rough trail. San Josef Bay is a good place to explore by kayak; surfers ride the high waves here as well.

The highlight of the park is the 14.6-mile (23.6km) one-way trail out to **Cape Scott.** This trip takes a minimum of 2 days and involves hiking along trails that are frequently very muddy. Most hikers manage this trail in 3 days, with 2 nights spent at Nels Bight—which means you won't be carrying your gear on the final leg to Cape Scott. Along the way, the trail passes some massive old-growth groves and remnants from early settlement. Nels Bight is a spectacular coastline of sand and rocky beaches, and is a popular place to camp; freshwater is available. After one inland portion just past Nels Bight, the rest of the trail to Cape Scott and its lighthouse basically follows the beach. Note that access to the cape itself is restricted due to liability issues. You can easily see the cape from the lighthouse, however.

Facilities in the park are minimal. There are a few wilderness campgrounds with dry toilets, notably at San Josef Bay's second beach, Nels Bight, and at Eric Lake. Be sure to wear waterproof boots, and if you're spending the night, be prepared for sudden and extreme changes of weather.

The Sunshine Coast & Whistler

One of British Columbia's most scenic drives and the province's most celebrated year-round recreation center are both just north of Vancouver, making great destinations for a weekend away or a short road trip. The Sunshine Coast Highway is the name given to Highway 101 as it skirts the islands, fjords, and peninsulas of the British Columbia mainland's Strait of Georgia coast. The scenery is spectacular, and the little fishing and logging communities along the route offer friendly hospitality. No small part of the charm of this drive are the ferry rides: To reach road's end at Lund, you'll need to take two ferries, both offering jaw-dropping vistas of glaciered peaks floating above deep blue waters. To make this route into a full loop trip, catch a third ferry from Powell River across the Strait of Georgia to Comox, and begin your exploration of Vancouver Island (covered in chapters 5 through 7).

The road to Whistler is equally spectacular, as it follows fjordlike Howe Sound, flanked by cliffs and towering glaciered peaks. But there's more to do here than gawk at the landscape. Whistler is Canada's premier skiing destination in winter, and a hiking and white-water rafting mecca in summer (as well as a major convention center). Lodging, dining, and recreational facilities are absolutely first-class, and the well-planned residential and lodging developments have yet to overwhelm the natural beauty of the valley.

1 The Sunshine Coast

Powell River: 88 miles (142km) N of Vancouver

It's a travel writer's truism that the "getting there" part of a trip is half the fun. In the case of the Sunshine Coast—that strip of wildly scenic waterfront real estate north of Vancouver, along the mainland Strait of Georgia coast—the "getting there" is practically the entire reason for making the journey. But what a journey!

Backed up against the high peaks of the glaciated Coastal Mountain range, overlooking the tempestuous waters of the Strait of Georgia and onto the rolling mountains of Vancouver Island, this maritime-intensive trip involves two ferry rides and a lovely canoodling drive between slumbering fishing villages, eventually terminating at Lund, the end of the road for the Pacific Coast's Highway 101.

Powell River is the only town of any size along this route. Long a major lumber-milling center, Powell River is beginning to focus on tourism as a supplement to its resource-based economy. Diving in the sealife-rich waters of the Georgia Strait is a particularly popular activity along the Sunshine Coast.

ESSENTIALS

GETTING THERE   By Car & Ferry   Getting to Powell River and the Sunshine Coast requires taking a couple of ferry rides. From West Vancouver's **Horseshoe Bay BC Ferries** (☎ 888/223-3779) terminal, ferries embark for Langdale, a 40-minute crossing. Driving north along Highway 101, the road hugs the coast along the Sechelt Peninsula, terminating 50 miles (81km) later at Earls Cove, where another ferry departs for a 50-minute crossing to Saltery Bay. The fare for each of these ferries is C$8 (U.S.$5) per passenger, C$28 (U.S.$18) per vehicle. From Saltery Bay, Powell River is another 19 miles (31km). Lund, the terminus of Highway 101, is another 17 miles (28km).

You can also cross to **Comox/Courtenay,** on central Vancouver Island, from Powell River. This popular 75-minute crossing makes for a highly scenic loop tour of British Columbia's rugged coast and islands. There are four ferries daily; the passenger fare is C$8 (U.S.$5), C$25 (U.S.$16) for a vehicle. (See chapter 6 for coverage of Comox and Courtenay.)

By Bus   Malaspina Coach Lines (☎ 604/485-5030 in Powell River, **604/ 682-6511** in Vancouver), offers service from Vancouver to Powell River via Highway 101 and the Sechelt Peninsula. Buses leave from the Pacific Central Station bus terminal (at Terminal and Main in Vancouver).

By Plane   Pacific Coastal Airlines (☎ 800/663-2872 or 604/273-8666) flies between Vancouver International Airport and Powell River roughly every 2 hours.

VISITOR INFORMATION   The **Powell River Visitors Bureau** is at 4690 Marine Ave., Powell River, BC, V8A 2L1 (☎ **604/485-4701;** e-mail: prvb@prcn.org).

EXPLORING THE AREA

Although Powell River is only 88 miles (142km) north of Vancouver, it feels light years removed from the mad scramble of urban sprawl. It's probably because of the ferries: Commuting from the Sunshine Coast—the name given to the rocky, mountain-edged coastline that lies in the rain shadow of Vancouver Island—wouldn't make sense if you worked in Vancouver's financial district.

Highway 101 is a very scenic route, with soaring 10,000-foot (3,048m) peaks to the east and the swelling blue waters of the Strait of Georgia to the west. The first town north of the Horseshoe Bay–Langdale Ferry is **Gibsons** (pop. 3732), a bucolic seaside community with an attractive waterfront district. Gibsons served as the setting for the popular 1980s television series *The Beachcombers.* Much of the action took place in **Molly's Reach Café,** 647 School Rd. (☎ 604/886-9710), which has evolved from a film set of a restaurant into a real eatery with fine home-style cooking. Wander along the Gibsons Seawalk, which leads from the Government Wharf to Gibsons Marina, and watch fishing boats unload their catch. **Roberts Creek Provincial Park,** 5¹/₂ miles (9km) north of town, has a great tide-pool area that's perfect for picnicking; campsites are C$12 (U.S.$8).

Seventeen miles (28km) north of Gibsons is **Sechelt** (pop. 7,343), an arty little town on a sandy finger of land. This narrow stretch of sand is all that connects the Sechelt Peninsula to mainland British Columbia. The town is a delightful clutter of galleries and cafes, well worth a stop. The **Sechelt Indian Nation** is headquartered here; the imposing House of Hewhiwus contains a cultural center, museum, and gift shop. A couple miles north of Sechelt is **Porpoise Bay Provincial Park,** with a nice sandy beach, campground, and riverside hiking trail.

Southwestern British Columbia

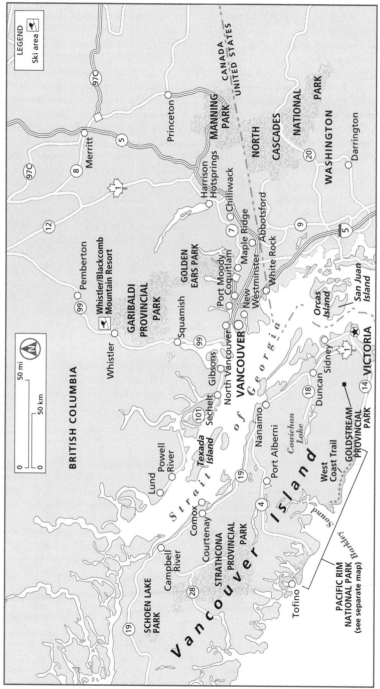

LEGEND
Ski area

BRITISH COLUMBIA

97C

Princeton
5
Merritt
8
97C
12

MANNING PARK

CANADA
UNITED STATES

NORTH
CASCADES NATIONAL PARK
WASHINGTON

Darrington

20

Harrison Hotsprings
Chilliwack
7
Maple Ridge
Abbotsford
9
White Rock
5

Pemberton
Whistler/Blackcomb Mountain Resort
99
GARIBALDI PROVINCIAL PARK
GOLDEN EARS PARK
Squamish
99

Port Moody
Coquitlam
New Westminster
VANCOUVER
North Vancouver

Orcas Island
San Juan Island

Strait of Georgia

Whistler

50 mi
50 km
0
0

Gibsons
Sechelt
101

Sidney
VICTORIA
1
14

Nanaimo
19

Duncan
18

Lund
Powell River
Texada Island

Cowichan Lake

GOLDSTREAM PROVINCIAL PARK

Comox
Courtenay
4

Port Alberni

West Coast Trail

Barkley Sound

STRATHCONA PROVINCIAL PARK

Campbell River
28

Vancouver Island

SCHOEN LAKE PARK
19

Tofino

PACIFIC RIM NATIONAL PARK
(see separate map)

213

Continue north along Highway 101, admiring views of Vancouver Island. Drive past the Earls Cove ferry terminal to **Skookumchuck Narrows Provincial Park.** All of the seawater that lies behind 25-mile-long (40km) Sechelt Peninsula—which includes three major ocean inlets—churns back and forth through this passage in an amazing display of tidal fury. It's about an hour's walk to the park's viewing area, which overlooks this rocky cleft between the mountains. Tides are so fierce, they actually roar, causing boiling whirlpools and eddies. With tidal speeds of 12 to 14 knots, you'll want to keep well away from the water when the tides are in action.

Take the ferry from Earls Cove to **Saltery Bay Provincial Park,** one of the most popular dive sites on the coast. Divers can actually count on seeing a mermaid here: A 10-foot bronze of one was sunk in the waters to lend a somewhat fabled atmosphere to an area already highly populated with sea life. (See "Outdoor Pursuits," below.)

Powell River (pop. 14,143) is dominated by one of the world's largest pulp and paper mills. That said, the town sits on a lovely location, and if you're feeling adventurous, Powell River is a major center for scuba diving and kayaking.

The old portion of town is called the **Homesite,** a company town that grew up alongside the original lumber mill near the harbor. The only designated National Historic Region in British Columbia, the Homesite contains more than 30 commercial buildings and about 400 residential buildings, all built in late-Victorian style. Ask at the visitor center for the heritage walking-tour brochure and have a wander through the old town core. The **Powell River Historic Museum,** 4800 Marine Dr. (☎ **604/ 485-2222**), has one of the largest archives of historic photos in the province, along with artifacts from the native Sechelt. It's open from mid-May to Labour Day, daily from 10am to 5pm; the rest of the year, Monday through Friday from 10am to 5pm. Admission is C$2 (U.S.$1.30).

From Powell River, many travelers take the ferry over to Comox/Courtenay on Vancouver Island and continue the loop back south. However, Powell River isn't the end of the road. That honor goes to tiny **Lund,** 17 miles (28km) north of Powell River on Highway 101. The main reason to make the trip is to say you did it, and to pop into the century-old Lund Hotel for a drink or a meal.

OUTDOOR PURSUITS

CANOEING & KAYAKING   The entire Sunshine Coast, with its fjord-notch coastline, myriad islands, and protected waters, makes for excellent kayaking. The **Desolation Sound** area, north of Lund, is especially popular. However, the granddaddy of the region's paddling routes is the **Powell Forest Canoe Route,** a 4- to 8-day backcountry paddle that links four lakes in a 50-mile circuit.

For more information on canoeing and kayaking in the area, contact **Powell River Sea Kayaks,** 6812E Alberni St. (☎ **604/485-2144;** www.prcn.org/kayak), which offers kayak and canoe rentals as well as tours of Desolation Sound.

DIVING   Powell River is the center for diving along the Sunshine Coast. Water clarity is excellent, with visibility of 100-plus feet in winter, lots of sea life, and varied terrain. The many area dive spots include five large shipwrecks and several boats sunk as artificial reefs. **Don's Dive Shop,** 6789 Wharf St. (☎ **604/485-6969;** http:// donsdiveshop.powellriver.net), is one of the area's leading outfitters, with a variety of tours starting at C$50 (U.S.$33) an hour.

WHERE TO STAY & DINE
IN SECHELT

✪ **Four Winds B&B.** 5488 Hill Rd., Sechelt, BC, V0N 3A0. ☎ **800/543-2989** or 604/ 885-3144. Fax 604/885-3182. 2 units. C$120–C$140 double (U.S.$78–U.S.$91). Rates include breakfast and afternoon tea. MC, V.

It's hard to imagine a more compelling site: a thrust of bare rock stretching out into the Strait of Georgia, backed up against a grove of fir and spruce. This modern home is lined with picture windows, all the better to capture the astonishing view of islands and sea, frequently visited by whales, herons, and seals. Guest rooms are beautifully decorated. Amenities include a hot tub; one of the owners is a licensed massage therapist, and will schedule sessions utilizing craniosacral therapy and neuromuscular techniques. Plan to arrive at 4:30pm to sample the fresh scones and afternoon tea.

IN POWELL RIVER

Beach Gardens Resort Hotel. 7074 Westminster Ave., Powell River, BC, V8A 1C5. ☎ **800/663-7070** or 604/485-6267. Fax 604/485-2343. 66 units. A/C TV TEL. C$88 (U.S.$57) double. AE, MC, V.

Popular with divers and kayakers, the Beach Gardens has large, comfortable guest rooms and a handsome location overlooking Malaspina Strait; most units have views. Some kitchen units are available. Amenities include a restaurant, pub, pool, sauna, fitness center, marina, tennis courts, and beer-and-wine store.

Coast Town Centre Hotel. 4660 Joyce Ave., Powell River, BC, V8A 3B6. ☎ **800/663-1144** or 604/485-3000. Fax 604/485-3031. www.coasthotels.com. 71 units. A/C TV TEL. C$105–C$149 (U.S.$68–U.S.$97) double. AE, MC, V.

Right downtown, the Coast Town Centre is Powell River's newest hotel, offering large, well-appointed rooms. There's casual dining in the Garden Court, and a light bar menu in TC's Pub. Extras include full health-club facilities (an exercise room and whirlpool) and in-room coffeemakers.

Desolation Resort. 2694 Dawson Rd, Okeover Inlet, Powell River, BC, V8A 4Z3. ☎ **604/483-3592.** Fax 604/483-7942. www.prcn.org/desolation. E-mail: desolres@prcn.org. 7 units. C$120–C$240 double (U.S.$78–U.S.$156). AE, MC, V.

If you're looking for luxury and a wilderness experience rolled into one, this is the place for you. Desolation Resort is a recreation-oriented getaway 20 minutes north of Powell River on the way to Lund. Guests stay in either apartmentlike suites (one- or two-bedroom) in two duplex cabins or in three stand-alone chalets, each with two bedrooms. All of these attractive log structures, built by local craftspeople, contain full kitchens. The resort sits above Okeover Inlet, just a matter of feet from your balcony. Rental kayaks and canoes are available; the staff will help arrange diving trips as well.

2 Whistler: North America's Premier Ski Resort

74 miles (120km) N of Vancouver

The premier ski resort in North America, according to *Ski* and *Snow Country* magazines, the Whistler/Blackcomb complex boasts more vertical, more lifts, and more ski terrain (and more varied at that) than any other resort in North America. If you're not into downhill skiing, there's backcountry, cross-country, snowboarding, snowmobiling, heli-skiing, and sleigh riding. In summer, the outdoor options include rafting, hiking, golfing, and horseback riding.

And then there's Whistler Village. Back in the 1970s, the city fathers made a conscious decision to build a resort town. The results are impressive—40,000 beds, arranged around a central village street in a sufficiently compact style, enabling you to park your car and remain a pedestrian for the duration of your stay.

What was sacrificed in this drive to become the perfectly planned community was space for the odd, the funky, the quaint, and the nonconformist. Whistler has none of the strip malls, cheap motels, or gas stations that mar some resort towns, but neither will you find that quaint and wonderful little restaurant run by an old Tyrolean couple, tucked away on an out-of-the-way hillside. So it goes.

The towns north of Whistler, **Pemberton** and **Mount Currie,** are refreshment stops for touring cyclists and hikers, and the gateway to the icy alpine waters of **Birkenhead Lake Provincial Park** (see "Fishing," below) and the majestic **Cayoosh Valley,** which winds through the glacier-topped mountains to the Cariboo town of Lillooet.

ESSENTIALS

GETTING THERE   By Car   Whistler is about 2 hours from Vancouver along Highway 99, also called the Sea to Sky Highway. The drive is spectacular, winding first along the edge of Howe Sound before climbing up through the mountains. Parking at the mountain is free for day skiers. For overnight visitors, most hotels charge about C$7 (U.S.$4.55).

By Bus   Whistler Express (☎ 604/266-5386 in Vancouver, or 604/905-0041 in Whistler) operates buses from Vancouver International Airport to the Whistler Bus Loop, plus drop-off service at many hotels. In summer, there are five departures daily between 8:30am and 7:30pm. In winter, there are eight departures daily between 9:30am and 11:30pm, with extra service on weekends. The trip takes about 3^1/$_2$ hours; the round-trip adult fare is C$86 (U.S.$56) in summer and C$98 (U.S.$64) in winter, while children pay C$50 (U.S.$33) in summer and C$58 (U.S.$38) in winter. Children under 5 ride free. Reservations are required year-round.

Greyhound, Pacific Central Station, 1150 Station St., Vancouver (☎ 604/662-8051 in Vancouver, 604/482-8747 in Whistler), offers six daily trips from Vancouver to the Whistler Bus Loop. The trip takes about 2^1/$_2$ hours; one-way fares are C$18 (U.S.$12) for adults, C$9 (U.S.$6) for children 5 to 12.

By Train   BC Rail (☎ 604/984-5246) operates the *Cariboo Prospector* year-round. It leaves the North Vancouver train terminal daily at 7am, chugs up the Howe Sound coastline through the Cheakamus River valley and Garibaldi Provincial Park, and arrives at 10:35am at the Whistler train station. The same train leaves Whistler at 6:10pm and returns to North Vancouver at 8:45pm. A one-way ticket is C$31 (U.S.$20) for adults, C$28 (U.S.$18) for seniors, C$19 (U.S.$12) for children 2 to 12, and C$6 (U.S.$3.90) for kids under 2. The 2^1/$_2$-hour trip includes a meal.

VISITOR INFORMATION   The **Whistler Visitor Info Centre,** 2097 Lake Placid Rd., Whistler, BC, V0N 1B0 (☎ 604/932-5528), is open year-round daily from 9am to 5pm. An **information kiosk** on Village Gate Boulevard at the entry to Whistler Village is open mid-May to early September, daily from 9am to 5pm. The **Whistler Resort Association,** 4010 Whistler Way, Whistler, BC, V0N 1B0 (☎ 604/932-3928), provides general information and can assist with event tickets and last-minute hotel bookings.

GETTING AROUND   On Foot   Compact and pedestrian-oriented, Whistler Village has signed trails and paths linking all shops and restaurants. If you're staying in the village, you can park your car and leave it for the duration of your stay. The walk between the Whistler Mountain (Whistler Village) and Blackcomb Mountain (Upper Village) resorts takes about 5 minutes.

By Bus   A year-round **public transit service** (☎ 604/932-4020) operates frequent daily buses from the Tamarisk district and the BC Rail Station to the neighboring districts of Nester's Village, Alpine Meadows, and Emerald Estates. Bus service from the Village to Village North and Upper Village accommodations is free. For other routes,

Special Events at Whistler

Dozens of **downhill ski competitions** are held between December and May. These include the Whistler Snowboard World Cup (Dec), Owens-Corning World Freestyle Competition (Jan), Power Bar Peak to Valley Race (Feb), Kokanee Fantastic Downhill Race (Mar), and World Ski and Snowboard Festival (Apr).

Mountain bikers compete in the **Power Bar Garibaldi Gruel** (Sept) and the **Cheakamus Challenge Fall Classic Mountain Bike Race** (Sept).

During the third week in July, **Whistler's Roots Weekend** (☎ 604/ 932-2394) brings the sounds of Celtic, zydeco, bluegrass, Delta blues, Latin, folk, and world-beat music down to the villages and up to the mountains. The **Whistler Summit Concert Series** (☎ 604/932-3434) is held on August weekends. The mountains provide a stunning backdrop for performers such as the Barenaked Ladies, Blue Rodeo, and others.

The **Alpine Wine Festival** (☎ 604/932-3434), which takes place on the mountaintop on the first weekend in September, features tastings, a winemakers' dinner, and other events highlighting North America's finest vintages.

The second weekend in September ushers in the **Whistler Jazz & Blues Festival** (☎ 604/932-2394), with live performances in the village squares and surrounding clubs—a great opportunity to hear jazz, gospel, R&B, and blues.

November's **Cornucopia** (☎ 604/932-3434) is Whistler's premier wine-and-food festival. The opening gala showcases 50 top wineries from the Pacific region. Other events include a celebrity chef competition, food and wine seminars, and wine tastings.

---

one-way fares are C$1.50 (U.S.$1) for adults, C$1.25 (U.S.80¢) for seniors and students, and free for children under 5.

By Taxi The village's taxis operate around the clock. Taxi tours and airport transport are also offered. Call **Airport Limousine Service** (☎ 604/273-1331), **Whistler Taxi** (☎ 604/938-3333), or **Sea to Sky Taxi** (☎ 604/932-3333).

By Car Rental cars are available from **Budget,** at the Holiday Inn Sunspree, 4295 Blackcomb Way (☎ 604/932-1236), and **Thrifty,** in the Listel Whistler Hotel, 4121 Village Green (☎ 604/938-0302).

HITTING THE SLOPES

Now that both areas are jointly operated by Intrawest as ✪ **Whistler/Blackcomb Mountain Resorts,** 4545 Blackcomb Way, Whistler, BC, V0N 1B4 (☎ 604/ 932-3434; snow report 604/687-1032; www.whistler-blackcomb.com), your pass gives you access to both ski areas.

Whistler Mountain has 5,006 feet (1,526m) of vertical and 100 marked runs, served by a high-speed gondola and eight high-speed chairs, plus four other lifts and tows. Helicopter service from the top of the mountain makes another 100-plus runs on nearby glaciers accessible. Facilities include cafeterias, gift shops, and a restaurant on the peak. **Blackcomb Mountain** has 5,280 feet (1 mile) of vertical and 100 marked runs that are served by nine high-speed lifts, plus three other lifts and tows. The cafeteria and gift shop aren't far from the peak; the restaurant is worth the ride even if you're not skiing. The view is spectacular, the food decent. Both mountains also have bowls and glade skiing, with Blackcomb offering glacier skiing well into August.

In the winter 2000 season, lift tickets are C$59 to C$61 (U.S.$38 to U.S.$40) for adults, C$50 to C$52 (U.S.$33 to U.S.$34) for youths and seniors, and C$30 (U.S.$19.50) for children. A variety of multiday passes are also available.

LESSONS & PROGRAMS   Whistler/Blackcomb offers ski lessons and guides for all levels and interests. (For skiers looking to try snowboarding, the rental/half-day lesson package is a particularly attractive option.) Call **Guest Relations** (☎ **604/ 932-3434**) for details.

Ski and snowboard gear can be rented at the base of both Whistler and Blackcomb Village, just prior to purchasing your lift ticket, on a first-come, first-served basis. Arrive by 8am, and you'll be on the gondola by 8:15am. Arrive at 8:30am, however, and you won't be up until 9:15am. **Summit Ski** (☎ **604/938-6225** or 604/ 932-6225), at various locations including the Delta Whistler Resort and Market Pavilion, rents high-performance and regular skis, snowboards, cross-country skis, and snowshoes.

BACKCOUNTRY SKIING   The **Spearhead Traverse,** which starts at Whistler and finishes at Blackcomb, is a well-marked backcountry route that has become extremely popular in the past few years. **Garibaldi Provincial Park** (☎ **604/898-3678**) maintains marked backcountry trails at **Diamond Head, Singing Pass,** and **Cheakamus Lake.** All trails in the rugged backcountry are ungroomed and unpatrolled and you must be self-reliant: This means you should be at least an intermediate skier and bring appropriate clothing and avalanche gear.

HELI-SKIING   For those intermediate and advanced skiers who can't get enough fresh powder or vertical on the regular slopes, there's always heli-skiing. **Whistler Heli-Skiing** (☎ **888/HELISKI** or 604/932-4105; www.heliskiwhistler.com), one of the more established operators, will whisk you and fellow skiers and boarders up to the pristine powder. A three-run day, with 8,000 to 10,000 feet (3,048m) of vertical helicopter lift, goes for C$430 (U.S.$280) per person.

CROSS-COUNTRY SKIING   Well-marked, fully groomed cross-country trails run throughout the area. The 18 miles (29km) of easy-to-very-difficult marked trails at **Lost Lake** start a block from the Blackcomb Mountain parking lot. They're groomed for track skiing and for ski-skating. They're also patrolled. Passes are C$8 (U.S.$5); a 1-hour cross-country lesson runs about C$35 (U.S.$23) and can be booked at the same station where you purchase your trail pass. The **Valley Trail System** in the village becomes a well-marked cross-country ski trail during the winter.

OTHER WINTER PURSUITS

SNOWMOBILING & ATVing   The year-round combination ATV and snowmobile tours offered by **Canadian Snowmobile Adventures Ltd.,** Carleton Lodge, 4290 Mountain Sq., Whistler Village (☎ **604/938-1616;** www.cdn-snowmobile.com), are a unique way to take to the Whistler Mountain trails. All tours are weather and snow conditions permitting. In 1999, there was so much snow on top of Whistler Mountain that the company was still offering full snowmobile tours in early August. A gondola ride takes you up the mountain, where a 1-hour tour costs C$59 (U.S.$38) for a driver and C$39 (U.S.$25) for a passenger. Drivers on both snowmobiles and ATVs must have valid driver's licenses.

On Blackcomb Mountain, **Snowmobile Adventures** (☎ **604/938-1616**) offers a popular ATV trip, the 2-hour Mountain Explorer. It costs C$109 (U.S.$71) for a driver and C$54 (U.S.$35) for a passenger. Conditions permitting, inquire about the combined ATV/snowmobile trip, in which you ride up to the snowline on the ATV and then switch to a snowmobile for a summertime snow ride. In winter, snowmobile rides start at C$69 (U.S.$45) for a single rider and C$44 (U.S.$29) for a shared rider.

Blackcomb Snowmobile (☎ **604/905-7002;** www.snowmobiling.bc.ca) offers 4- to 8-hour guided snowmobile tours on Blackcomb Mountain. The cost is C$159 double (U.S.$103) for a 4-hour tour, C$229 (U.S.$149) for an all-day tour.

SNOWSHOEING   Snowshoeing is the world's easiest form of snow locomotion: It requires none of the training and motor skills of skiing or boarding. You can wear your own warm, waterproof shoes or boots, strap on your snowshoes, and off you go!

Outdoor Adventures@Whistler (☎ **604/932-0647;** www.adventureswhistler. com; e-mail: outdoors@whistler.net) offers guided tours for novices at C$39 (U.S.$25) for $1^{1}/_{2}$ hours. A 4-hour tour to a ghost town costs C$69 (U.S.$45), including lunch. If you want to rent just the snowshoes and find your own way around, rentals are C$15 (U.S.$10) per day. **Whistler Backcountry Adventures,** 36-4314 Main St., Whistler (☎ **888/297-2222** or 604/932-4086; www.whistlerbackcountry. com), has guided tours to the Cougar Mountain area. The 2-hour tour costs C$49 (U.S.$32).

SLEIGH RIDING & DOGSLEDDING   Dogsled rides are offered by **Whistler Backcountry Adventures** (see "Snowshoeing," above). A musher and his team of Inuit sled dogs will take you into the backcountry for C$249 (U.S.$162) per sled, with a maximum of two riders or 400 pounds.

For a different kind of sleigh ride, contact **Blackcomb Horsedrawn Sleigh Rides,** 103-4338 Main St., Whistler (☎ **604/932-7631;** www.whistlerweb.net/resort/ sleighrides). In winter, tours are offered for C$45 (U.S.$29) per adult and C$25 (U.S.$16) per child. The tour takes you up past the ski trails and onto a wooded trail with a magnificent view of the lights at Whistler Village. A stop at a cabin for hot chocolate will warm you up for the ride home.

WARM-WEATHER PURSUITS

BIKING   You'll find some of the best mountain-bike trails on Whistler and Blackcomb mountains. Some of the backcountry trails at Lost Lake are marked for biking as well. Lift tickets at both mountains range from C$19 to C$30 (U.S.$12 to U.S.$20) per day; discounted mountain-bike passes are available.

Bike rentals are available at **Blackcomb Ski & Sports,** Blackcomb Mountain Day Lodge, Upper Village (☎ **604/938-7788**); **Trax & Trails,** Chateau Whistler Hotel, 4599 Chateau Blvd., Upper Village (☎ **604/938-2017**); and the **Whistler Bike Company,** Delta Whistler Resort, 4050 Whistler Way, Whistler Village (☎ **604/ 938-9511**). Prices range from C$10 (U.S.$7) an hour to C$30 (U.S.$20) per day.

M.X. Mountain Bike Vacations (☎ **604/905-4914;** www.mx.whistler.bc.ca) offers affordable 6- and 8-day camps for ages 15 and over. Packages include lodging, meals, mountain-bike coaching, and activities such as white-water rafting.

CANOEING & KAYAKING   The 3-hour River of Golden Dreams Tour offered by **Whistler Sailing & Water Sports Center Ltd.** (☎ **604/932-7245**) is a great way for novices, intermediates, and experts to get acquainted with an exhilarating stretch of water that runs between Green Lake and Alta Lake behind the village of Whistler. Packages start at C$29 (U.S.$19), including gear and return transportation to the village. Also available are lessons, clinics, and sailboat and windsurfing rentals.

FISHING   Spring runs of steelhead, rainbow trout, and Dolly Varden char, summer runs of cutthroat and salmon, and fall runs of coho salmon attract anglers from around the world to the many glacier-fed lakes and rivers in the area and to

Birkenhead Lake Provincial Park, 40 miles (65km) north of Pemberton. Bring your favorite fly rod and don't forget to buy a fishing license, available at **Whistler Backcountry Adventures,** 36-4314 Main St., Whistler (☎ 604/932-3474).

Whistler River Adventures (see "Jet Boating," below), **Sea to Sky Reel Adventures** (☎ 604/894-6928), and **Off the Beaten Track Wilderness Expeditions** (☎ 604/938-9282; www.otbt.bc.ca) all offer half- and full-day catch-and-release fishing trips in the surrounding rivers. Rates are C$99 to C$250 (U.S.$64 to U.S.$163) per person, including gear, round-trip transport, and a snack or lunch.

GOLF **A-1 Last Minute Golf Hotline** (☎ 800/684-6344 or 604/878-1833) can arrange next-day tee times at Whistler golf courses with savings of as much as 40%. Call between 3 and 9pm for the next day or before noon for the same day.

Robert Trent Jones's **Chateau Whistler Golf Club,** at the base of Blackcomb Mountain (☎ 604/938-2092; pro shop 604/938-2095), is an 18-hole, par-72 course. With an elevation gain of more than 400 feet (122m), this course traverses mountain ledges and crosses cascading creeks. Midcourse, there's a panoramic view of the Coast Mountains. Greens fees range from C$110 to C$175 (U.S.$72 to U.S.$114).

The award-winning course **Nicklaus North at Whistler** (☎ 604/938-9898) is a 5-minute drive north of the village on the shores of Green Lake. The par-71 course's mountain views are spectacular. This is just the second Canadian course designed by Nicklaus, and the only one in the world to bear his name. Greens fees range from C$100 to C$125 (U.S.$65 to U.S.$81).

Whistler Golf Club (☎ 800/376-1777 or 604/932-4544), designed by Arnold Palmer, features nine lakes, two creeks, and magnificent vistas. In addition to the 18-hole, par-72 course, the club offers a driving range, putting green, sand bunker, and pitching area. Greens fees are C$125 (U.S.$81).

HIKING You'll discover numerous easy hiking trails in and around Whistler. In summer, you can take a lift up to the high mountain trails of Whistler and Blackcomb. There are a number of other choices as well; we describe our favorites below.

Lost Lake Trail starts at the north end of the day-skier parking lot at Blackcomb. The lake is less than a mile from the trailhead. The 18 miles (30km) of marked trails, which wind around creeks, beaver dams, blueberry patches, and lush cedar groves, are ideal for biking, cross-country skiing, or just strolling and picnicking.

The **Valley Trail System** is a well-marked, paved trail that connects different parts of Whistler. The trail starts on the west side of Highway 99, adjacent to the Whistler Golf Course, and winds through residential areas as well as golf courses and parks.

Garibaldi Provincial Park's **Singing Pass Trail** is a 4-hour hike of moderate difficulty. We recommend taking the Whistler Mountain gondola to the top, then walking down the well-marked path that ends in the village on an access road. Winding down from above the tree line, the trail takes you through stunted alpine forest into Fitzsimmons Valley.

Nairn Falls Provincial Park, about 20 miles (33km) north of Whistler on Highway 99, features a mile-long trail that leads to a stupendous view of the icy-cold Green River as it plunges 196 feet (60m) over a rocky cliff into a narrow gorge. There's also an incredible view of Mount Currie peeking over the treetops.

On Highway 99 north of Mount Currie, **Joffre Lakes Provincial Park** offers an intermediate-level hike that leads past several brilliant-blue glacial lakes up to the very foot of a glacier.

The **Ancient Cedars** area of Cougar Mountain is an awe-inspiring grove of towering cedar and Douglas fir. (Some of the trees are more than 1,000 years old.) This

$2^1/_2$-mile (4km) hike can be made even more exciting by taking a 4x4 up the back-country route. **Off the Beaten Track Wilderness Expeditions** (see "Fishing," above) offers this unique off-road experience and provides a knowledgeable guide. Three- and 6-hour tours depart from the Whistler Village Bus Loop. Prices range from C$59 to C$89 (U.S.$38 to U.S.$58) per person, including snacks.

HORSEBACK RIDING **Whistler River Adventures** (see "Jet Boating," below) offers 2-hour (C$49/U.S.$32) and 5-hour (C$109/U.S.$71) trail rides along the Green River, through the forest, and across the Pemberton Valley from its 10-acre riverside facility in nearby Pemberton. You'll need your own transportation to get to Pemberton, a 35-minute drive north of Whistler.

JET BOATING **Whistler River Adventures,** Whistler Mountain Village Gondola Base (☎ **888/932-3532** or 604/932-3532; fax 604/932-3559; www.whistler-river-adv.com), will take you up the Green River just below Nairn Falls, where moose, deer, and bear sightings in the sheer-granite canyon are common. The Lillooet River tour goes past ancient petroglyphs, fishing sites, and the tiny native Indian village of Skookumchuck. In summer, **Whistler Jet Boating Company Ltd.** (☎ **604/ 894-5200**) can run you down the Green River or take you speed-cruising through the Lillooet River valley, water levels permitting. Tours by both companies range from 1-hour (C$69/U.S.$45) to 4-hour cruises (C$135/U.S.$88).

RAFTING **Whistler River Adventures** (see "Jet Boating," above) offers 2-hour and full-day round-trip rafting runs down the Green, Elaho, or Squamish rivers. Tours, which include equipment and ground transport, cost C$57 to C$125 (U.S.$37 to U.S.$81). Children who weigh at least 90 pounds are welcome, as long as they are able to hold on by themselves. Novices are taken to the Green River, where small rapids and snowcapped-mountain views are the highlights of a half-day trip. Experts head to the Elaho or Squamish rivers for full-day, Class IV excitement. Trips depart daily from May through August. The full-day trip includes a barbecued-salmon lunch. The company also conducts 3-hour round-trip jet-boat tours of the river for C$69 (U.S.$45) per person, which include ground transport and wet suit.

For first-timers, **Wedge Rafting,** Carleton Lodge, Whistler Village (☎ **604/ 932-7171;** www.whistler.net/wedgerafting; e-mail: wedge@whistlernet.com), offers tours of the Green or Birkenhead rivers. The $2^1/_2$-hour Green River trip picks you up in Whistler, takes you to the wilderness launch area for briefing and equipping, and then treats you to an exciting hour or more on icy rapids. After the run, rafters relax with a snack at the outfitter's log lodge before being shuttled back into town. The cost is C$57 (U.S.$37). The Birkenhead River tour takes about 4 hours and costs C$75 (U.S.$49). Discounts are available for youths 10 to 16 who weigh at least 90 pounds.

TENNIS **Whistler Racquet & Golf Resort,** 4500 Northland Blvd. (☎ **604/ 932-1991;** e-mail: whisracq@whistler.net), features three covered courts, seven out-door courts, and a practice cage, all open to drop-in visitors. Indoor courts are C$24 (U.S.$16) per hour, outdoor courts C$12 (U.S.$8) per hour. Adult and junior tennis camps are offered in summer. Prices for a 3-day camp range from C$250 to C$350 (U.S.$163 to U.S.$228). Kids' camps cost C$36 (U.S.$23) per day for drop-ins, or C$150 (U.S.$98) for a 5-day camp. Book early, as these camps fill up very quickly.

Mountain Spa & Tennis Club, Delta Whistler Resort, Whistler Village (☎ **604/ 938-2044**), and the **Chateau Whistler Resort,** Chateau Whistler Hotel, Upper Village (☎ **604/938-8000**), offer courts to drop-in players. Prices run about C$10 (U.S.$7) per hour; racquet rentals are available at C$5 (U.S.$3.25) an hour.

There are **free public courts** (☎ 604/938-PARK) at Myrtle Public School, Alpha Lake Park, Meadow Park, Millar's Pond, Brio, Blackcomb Benchlands, White Gold, and Emerald Park.

MORE TO SEE & DO
A WORTHWHILE MUSEUM

To learn more about Whistler's heritage, flora, and fauna, visit the **Whistler Museum & Archives Society,** 4329 Main St., off Northlands Boulevard (☎ 604/932-2019), established in 1986. The exhibits reveal the life and culture of the native Indian tribes who have lived in the lush Whistler and Pemberton valleys for thousands of years. There are also re-creations of the village's early settlement by British immigrants during the late 1800s and early 1900s. Hours are daily from 10am to 4pm in summer; call ahead in winter. Admission is C$1 (U.S.65¢) for adults, free for those under 18.

SHOPPING

The **Whistler Marketplace,** in the center of Whistler Village, and the area surrounding the **Blackcomb Mountain lift** brim with clothing, jewelry, craft, gift, and equipment stores that are open daily from 10am to 6pm. **Horstman Trading Company** (☎ 604/938-7725), beside the Chateau Whistler at the base of Blackcomb, carries men's and women's casual wear, from swimwear and footwear to fleece vests and nylon shells. **Escape Route** (☎ 604/938-3228), at Whistler Marketplace and Crystal Lodge, has a great line of outdoor clothing and equipment. **Whistler Backcountry Adventures,** 4314 Main St. (☎ 604/932-3474), sells fishing licenses and carries a nice selection of rods, tackle, sports gear, and outdoor clothing.

GALLERIES

Whistler Inuit Gallery, Chateau Whistler Resort, 4599 Chateau Blvd. (☎ 604/938-3366), specializes in Inuit, West Coast, and contemporary artists. **Keir Fine Jewelry,** Village Gate House (☎ 604/932-2944), sells handmade jewelry in addition to Italian gold and Swiss watches. **Gallery Row,** in the Delta Whistler Resort, consists of three galleries: the **Whistler Village Art Gallery** (☎ 604/938-3001), **Northern Lights Gallery** (☎ 604/932-2890), and the **Adele Campbell Gallery** (☎ 604/938-0887). Their collections include fine art, sculpture and glass.

SPAS

That resort lifestyle can be hard on the body, so why not try some relaxation at one of Whistler's outstanding spas? The **Spa at Chateau Whistler Resort** (☎ 604/938-2086) is considered the best in the area. It offers massage, aromatherapy, skin care, wraps, steam baths, and more. **Whistler Body Wrap,** 210 St. Andrews House, next to the Keg in the Village (☎ 604/932-4710), can nurture you with an array of services, such as shiatsu massage, facials, pedicures and manicures, waxing, and aromatherapy.

If something didn't go quite right on the slopes or on the trails, call **Whistler Physiotherapy,** 339-4370 Lorimer Rd. or 202-2011 Innsbruck Dr. (☎ 604/932-4001 or 604/938-9001). The therapists treat many professional athletes and have extensive experience with the typical ski, board, and hiking injuries.

ESPECIALLY FOR KIDS

Whistler Village and the Upper Village sponsor daily activities that are tailor-made for active kids of all ages. Offerings include mountain-bike races, an in-line-skating park, a trapeze, a trampoline, wall-climbing lessons, summer skiing, snowboarding, and snowshoeing. There's even a first-run multiplex movie theater.

The *Whistler Explorer:* All Aboard for a Backcountry Ramble

For centuries, the arid canyons, alpine meadows, and crystal-clear lakes of the area between Whistler and Kelly Lake were inaccessible to all but the most experienced hikers. Now, **BC Rail's** (☎ **604/984-5246**) *Whistler Explorer* offers visitors a leisurely way to see the remote landscape.

Departing from the Whistler train station on Lake Placid Road at 8am, the *Explorer* takes an 8¹/₂-hour round-trip ramble through Pemberton Valley and past Setoff and Anderson lakes before arriving at Kelly Lake, which is adjacent to the historic Cariboo Gold Rush Trail.

After a 1-hour stretching-and-strolling break, passengers reboard the train, returning to Whistler at 5:30pm. It's the ideal way to discover the backcountry without braving an overnight camping and hiking expedition into this stretch of pristine wilderness. The round-trip fare is C$114 (U.S.$74) for adults and C$78 (U.S.$51) for children ages 2 to 12.

Based at Blackcomb Mountain, the **Dave Murray Summer Ski Camp** (☎ **604/932-5765**) is North America's longest-running summer ski camp. Junior programs cost about C$1,200 (U.S.$780) per week from mid-June to mid-July. Packages include food, lodging, and lift passes as well as tennis, trapeze, and mountain-biking options. Mornings and early afternoons are spent skiing, boarding, or free-riding on the excellent terrain parks. The rest of the day is occupied by a wide range of other activities. This ski and board camp is not for beginners; it caters to youths 10 to 18. The comprehensive instruction and adult supervision are excellent.

WHERE TO STAY

The Whistler valley contains 40,000 guest beds, but first you'll have to decide whether to stay in or outside of Whistler Village. If you opt for a place in the village, you can forget your car for the duration of your visit and walk along cobblestone paths from hotel to ski lift to restaurants and pubs. Tourists from around the world stroll from shop to shop, stopping for breaks at outdoor cafes—expect to hear French, Japanese, German, and Chinese being spoken. The village is thus a lively place, but it's never completely quiet. And because all of the village hotels were built around the same time, and according to pretty much the same pattern, all of the condo units and hotel suites are similar in terms of room quality. Higher-end options typically offer extra amenities, such as heated pools and Jacuzzis.

If you stay outside the village, you'll have a short drive to the lifts and restaurants (though many places offer shuttle service), but you'll also have a touch more of that mountain tranquillity. You'll also find a bit more variety among lodging options.

Wherever you decide to stay, determine your budget first, and then call one of these booking agencies. Studios, town houses, chalets, and one- to five-bedroom, furnished condo units are available year-round. Prices range from C$90 to C$1,400 (U.S.$59 to U.S.$910) per night. **Whistler Central Reservations** (☎ **800/944-7853** or 604/664-5625; fax 604/938-5758; www.whistler-resort.com) has more than 2,000 units to choose from. Its staff can arrange packages that include lift tickets and air or ground transportation to and from Vancouver. **Whistler Chalets and Accommodations Ltd.** (☎ 800/663-7711 in Canada, or 604/932-6699; www.whistlerchalets.com) and **Rainbow Retreats Accommodations Ltd.** (☎ 604/932-2343; www.whistler.net/rainbow) also have many properties to suit every budget and group size.

Reservations for peak winter periods should be made by September at the latest.

IN THE VILLAGE

Canadian Pacific Chateau Whistler Resort. 4599 Chateau Blvd., Whistler, BC, V0N 1B4. ☎ **800/441-1414** in the U.S., 800/606-8244 in Canada, or 604/938-8000. Fax 604/938-2055. 563 units. MINIBAR TV TEL. Summer C$299–C$335 (U.S.$194–U.S.$218) double, C$425–C$1,000 (U.S.$276–U.S.$650) suite; winter C$385–C$435 (U.S.$250–U.S.$283) double, C$570–C$1,200 (U.S.$371–U.S.$780) suite. AE, ER, MC, V. Underground valet parking C$15 (U.S.$10).

The one exception to the everything's-the-same-in-Whistler rule, the Chateau Whistler is simply outstanding. The Canadian Pacific hotel chain spared little expense re-creating the look and feel of an old-time country retreat at the foot of Blackcomb Mountain. In the lobby, massive wooden beams support an airy peaked roof, while in the hillside Mallard Bar, double-sided stone fireplaces cast a cozy glow on the leather armchairs. Rooms and suites feature duvets, robes, and soaking tubs; one wheelchair-accessible unit is available. Gold-service guests can enjoy breakfast or relax après-ski in a private lounge that has the warm and slightly musty feel of a Victorian library.

The Wildflower Restaurant offers perhaps the best buffet-style brunch in the village, daily from 7 to 11am (C$16.95/U.S.$11 per person). It's also an excellent spot for West Coast cuisine. The Mallard Bar, with a great view of the Blackcomb lifts, offers cocktails, coffee, light meals, and good beer. Amenities include room service, concierge, spa, massage, indoor/outdoor pool, sauna, steam room, weight room, tennis courts, golf course, terrace barbecue, and ski and bike storage.

The Pan Pacific Lodge Whistler. 4320 Sundial Crescent, Whistler, BC, V0N 1B4. ☎ **888/905-9955** or 604/905-2999. Fax 604/905-2995. www.panpac.com. 121 suites. A/C MINIBAR TV TEL. Summer C$109–C$199 (U.S.$71–U.S.$129) double; winter C$155–C$375 (U.S.$101–U.S.$244) double. AE, ER, MC, V. Underground valet parking C$15 (U.S.$10).

The guest rooms are similar to those in all of the other hotels in the village, but the Pan's location is killer: right at the foot of the Whistler Mountain gondola. While you take a swim in the heated outdoor pool or, better yet, a soak in one of two outdoor Jacuzzis, you can look up at the snow-covered runs and wonder at the ameliorative effects of warm water on aching muscles. Also on the property, Arthur's offers fine dining, but you'll get more fun and better value at the Dubh Linn Gate Irish Lounge/Pub, a convincing re-creation of a Dublin pub, complete with fireplaces, wood paneling, quality grub and beer, and, more often than not, a balladeer singing a song or two. Amenities include room service, concierge, fitness center, steam room, laundry, and storage for skis, bikes, and golf bags.

OUTSIDE THE VILLAGE

Cedar Springs Bed & Breakfast Lodge. 8106 Cedar Springs Rd., Whistler, BC, V0N 1B8. ☎ **800/727-7547** or 604/938-8007. Fax 604/938-8023. www.whistlerinns.com/cedarsprings. 9 units (7 with bathroom). C$80–C$199 (U.S.$52–U.S.$129) double, C$129–C$199 (U.S.$84–U.S.$129) suite. Rates include full breakfast. MC, V. Take Hwy. 99 north toward Pemberton, 2.4 miles (4km) past Whistler Village. Turn left onto Alpine Way. Drive 1 block to Rainbow Dr. and turn left. Drive 1 block to Camino St. and turn left. The lodge is 1 block down at the corner of Camino and Cedar Springs Rd.

This charming lodge is comfortably modern yet understated. The honeymoon suite boasts a fireplace and balcony. A sauna and hot tub on the deck overlooking the gardens add to the pampering after a day of play. The sitting room contains a TV, VCR, video library, and phone. A gourmet breakfast is served in the dining room, and guests are welcome to enjoy an afternoon tea. Owners Joann and Jackie Rhode can provide box lunches and special-occasion dinners at their warm, cozy hideaway. The complimentary Alpine Meadows bus provides transportation to and from the village.

✪ **Durlacher Hof Pension Inn.** 7055 Nesters Rd. (P.O. Box 1125), Whistler, BC, V0N 1B0. ☎ **604/932-1924.** Fax 604/938-1980. www.durlacherhof.com. 8 units. TV TEL. Summer (June 19–Sept 30) C$120–C$199 (U.S.$78–U.S.$129) double; winter (Dec 18–Mar 31) C$179–C$259 (U.S.$116–U.S.$168) double. Extra person C$30 (U.S.$20). Discounted rates in spring and fall. Rates include full breakfast and afternoon tea. MC, V. Free parking. Take Hwy. 99 north about half a mile (0.8km) north of Whistler Village to Nesters Rd. Turn left; the inn is immediately on the right.

Peter and Erika Durlacher run a lovely Austrian-style mountain chalet that fits perfectly with its surroundings. Guests will feel completely spoiled by the fine European service, decor, and cuisine. Each room contains a down duvet, fluffy robes, a private bathroom (some with jetted tubs), deluxe toiletries, and an incredible mountain view from a private balcony. The library room has been adapted for wheelchair access, complete with roll-in shower. The cocktail lounge has a welcoming fireplace and offers complimentary après-ski appetizers. On selected nights, dinners are offered for an additional charge; they're often prepared by a celebrated guest chef. Extras include an on-site sauna and whirlpool.

Hostelling International Whistler. 5678 Alta Lake Rd., Whistler, BC, V0N 1B0. ☎ **888/ 203-4303** or 604/932-5492. Fax 604/932-4687. www.hihostels.bc.ca. 33 beds in 4- to 6-bed dorms. C$19 (U.S.$12) IYHA members, C$23 (U.S.$15) nonmembers. Annual adult membership C$27 (U.S.$18). Family and group memberships available. MC, V. Free parking.

One of the few inexpensive spots in Whistler, the hostel also happens to have one of the nicest locations: on the south edge of Alta Lake, with a dining room, deck, and lawn overlooking the lake toward Whistler Mountain. Inside, the hostel is extremely pleasant, with a lounge with wood-burning stove, a common kitchen, a piano, Ping-Pong tables, a sauna, a drying room for ski gear, and storage for bikes, boards, and skis. In summer, guests have use of a barbecue, canoe, and rowboat. As with all hostels, most rooms and facilities are shared. Beds book up very early; reserve by September at the latest for the winter ski season.

Camping

South of Whistler on the Sea to Sky corridor is the very popular **Alice Lake Provincial Park.** Spots can be reserved by calling **Discover Camping** (☎ 800/689-9025). About 16 miles (27km) north of Whistler, the well-maintained, more adult-oriented campground at **Nairn Falls,** on Highway 99 (☎ 604/898-3678), offers 88 sites, pit toilets, pumped well water, fire pits, and firewood, but no showers. Its proximity to the roaring Green River and the town of Pemberton makes it appealing to many hikers, and the sound of the river is sweeter than any lullaby. Prices are C$15 (U.S.$10) per night, on a first-come, first-served basis.

The 85 campsites at **Birkenhead Lake Provincial Park,** off Portage Road, Birken (☎ 604/898-3678), fill up very quickly during the summer high season. Call **Discover Camping** (☎ 800/689-9025) to reserve a spot. Boat launches, great fishing, and well-maintained tent and RV sites make this an angler's paradise and one of the province's top 10 camping destinations. Facilities include fire pits, firewood, pumped well water, and pit toilets. Campsites are C$12 (U.S.$8) per night.

WHERE TO DINE

Whistler literally overflows with dining options. On-the-go gourmets can find a quick meal at **Chef Bernard's,** 4573 Chateau Blvd., Whistler Village (☎ **604/932-7051**), which serves breakfasts, soups, salads, sandwiches, and hot entrees. Locals are drawn to restaurant/nightspot **Citta Bistro,** in Whistler Village Square (☎ **604/932-4177**). It serves thin-crust pizzas, gourmet burgers, and finger foods ranging from bruschetta to nachos. The terrace tables offer the best people-watching corner in town. Equally fun indoor dining can be had at the **Dubn Linn Irish Lounge/Bar** in the Pan Pacific Lodge (see "Where to Stay," above).

At the other end of the epicurean spectrum, those who prefer linen napkins, the clink of silver, and truly fine dining have seen their options multiply in recent years. Brand-new to Whistler but long known in Vancouver for its quality beef is **Hy's Steakhouse,** 4308 Main St. (☎ **604/905-5555**). Over Blackcomb way, the **Wildflower,** in the Chateau Whistler (see "Where to Stay," above), does innovative West Coast cuisine in a quiet and civilized room.

✪ **Araxi Restaurant & Bar.** 4222 Village Sq. ☎ **604/932-4540.** Reservations recommended. Main courses C$11–C$27 (U.S.$7–U.S.$18). AE, MC, V. Daily 11am–10:30pm. ITALIAN/WEST COAST.

A consistent award winner for its wine list, and voted "Best Restaurant in Whistler" by readers of *Vancouver* magazine, this is one of the top places to dine. And thanks to renovations in 1999, Araxi's now has storage enough for its 12,000-bottle inventory of fine British Columbia and foreign wines. Outside, the heated patio seats 80 amid barrels of flowers, while inside, the artwork, antiques, and terra-cotta tiles give Araxi's a subtle Italian ambiance. The menu, however, is less Italian and more West Coast, with an emphasis on fresh regional products, including B.C. ostrich, salmon, and scallops. Various soups and salads are made from scratch with fresh ingredients, including Pemberton sheep cheese and Okanagan tomatoes. Main courses include seafood such as ahi tuna, salmon, and scallops. The locally caught trout is smoked in the Araxi kitchen. Meat lovers can choose rack of lamb, tenderloin, or pork loin. And considering the near-encyclopedic length of Araxi's famous wine list, don't hesitate to ask sommelier Chris Van Nus for suggestions to make the most out of your meal.

Caramba! Restaurant. 12-4314 Main St., Town Plaza. ☎ **604/938-1856.** Reservations recommended. Main courses C$11–C$17 (U.S.$7–U.S.$11). Daily noon–10:30pm. AE, MC, V. MEDITERRANEAN.

The dining room here is bright and filled with the pleasant buzz of nattering diners. The kitchen is open, with tantalizing hints of fennel and artichoke wafting out. These are all good signs. Worrisomely, however, the waitresses bear the 300-watt smiles of Amway reps, welcoming every guest with an overly enthusiastic greeting. That, and the menu notes indicating Caramba! is part of a chain, might have you wondering whether you've wandered into a glorified burger bar, a kind of Denny's in disguise. Blissfully, your first instincts will prove to be correct. Caramba! may be casual dining, but its Mediterranean-influenced menu offers fresh ingredients, consistently prepared with a great deal of pizzazz. Try the pasta, free-range chicken, or roasted pork loin. Better still, if you're feeling especially good about your dining companions, order a pizza or two, a plate of grilled calamari, and let the games begin.

Uli's Flipside. 4433 Sundial Place (upstairs). ☎ **604/935-1107.** Reservations recommended. Main courses C$11–C$17 (U.S.$7–U.S.$11). Mon–Sat 3pm–1am, Sun 3pm–midnight. AE, DC, MC, V. PASTA/ITALIAN.

At least one longtime Whistler resident threatened dire if unspecified consequences if a travel writer wrote about this little local favorite. It's not that Uli's is the best restaurant in town, or even the best pasta place (although it's certainly in the running). It's just that few other spots offer the same combination of excellent pasta, a good wine list, and a warm and pleasant room with vaulted ceilings and intimate booths, all at moderate prices. Given that Whistler shares the West Coast affliction of early dining (few kitchens are open as late as 10pm), Uli's is also your best bet for late-night bites. Try for yourself and see—just don't say you heard it from me.

WHISTLER AFTER DARK

Après-ski refers to that delicious hour after a hard day on the slopes, when you sit back with a cold drink, nurse the sore spots, and savor the glow that comes from a day well skied. On the Blackcomb side, **Merlin's Bar** (☎ 604/938-3775), at the base, is the most obvious spot, but hidden away inside the Chateau Whistler is something better: the **Mallard Bar** (☎ 604/938-8000), one of the most civilized après-ski bars on earth.

For a town of just 8,000, Whistler has a more than respectable nightlife scene. Bands touring through Vancouver regularly make the trip up the Sea to Sky; some even make Whistler their Canadian debut. Show listings can be found in the *Pique,* a free local paper available at cafes and food stores.

Tommy Africa's, underneath the Pharmasave at the entrance to the Main Village (☎ 604/932-6090), and the dark and cavernous **Maxx Fish,** in the Village Square below the Amsterdam Cafe (☎ 604/932-1904), cater to the 18- to 22-year-old crowd: lots of beat and not much light. The clientele at **Garfinkel's,** at the entrance to Village North (☎ 604/932-2323), is similar, although the cut-off age can reach as high as 26 or 27 if your tan's good and your glutes are in shape.

The **Boot Pub,** on Nancy Green Drive just off Highway 99 (☎ 604/932-3338), advertises itself as Whistler's living room, and more than lives up to its billing: Throngs of young Australian ski-lift operators cram into the room, bouncing to the band or DJ, and spilling draught beer onto the floor and their mostly unwashed clothes. **Buffalo Bills,** across from the Whistler Gondola (☎ 604/932-6613), and the **Savage Beagle,** in the village (☎ 604/938-3337), cater to the 30-something crowd. Bills is bigger, with a pool table and video ski machine, smallish dance floor, and music straight from the 1980s. The Beagle has a fabulous selection of beer and bar drinks, with a pleasant little pub upstairs and a house-oriented dance floor below.

9 Northern British Columbia

When you begin talking about the "north" in Canada, you have to be careful. Although the following destinations are certainly northerly—reached by at least one day's very long drive from Vancouver, or by a 15-hour ferry trip from Vancouver Island—most of this chapter's towns and sights are geographically in British Columbia's midsection. However, by the time you reach Prince George or Prince Rupert, you'll feel the palpable sense of being in the north: The days are long in summer and short in winter, and the spruce forestlands have a primordial character, as if they had just recently been released from the grip of the ice ages. First Nation native Indians make up a greater percentage of the population here than in more southerly areas, and native communities and heritage sites are common.

One of the most dramatic ways to reach northern British Columbia is by ferry. The BC Ferries Inside Passage route operates between Port Hardy, on Vancouver Island, and Prince Rupert, on the mainland; this full-day ferry run passes through mystical land- and seascapes, with excellent wildlife-viewing opportunities. From Prince Rupert—a fishing town with an excellent native-arts museum—you can catch another ferry to the Queen Charlotte Islands, which lie truly on the backside of beyond. A part of these islands is preserved as Gwaii Haanas National Park Reserve, a refuge of rare flora and fauna, and the ancient homeland of the Haida people.

Inland from Prince Rupert, the Yellowhead Highway (Hwy. 16) follows the mighty Skeena and Bulkley rivers past native villages, isolated ranches, and massive lake basins, finally reaching Prince George, the largest city in northern British Columbia. Prince George is also a transportation gateway. Whether you're coming west from Edmonton, east from Prince Rupert, north from Vancouver, or south from Alaska, you'll pass through this city at the junction of the Fraser and Nechako rivers.

From Highway 16, there are two options for travelers who wish to explore realms even farther north. The famed 1,413-mile (2,280km) Alaska Highway—the only overland route to the 49th state—begins at Dawson Creek. More than 600 miles (960km) of the route wind across northern British Columbia, through black-spruce forest, over the Continental Divide, and across plateaus rutted with the trails of not-so-ancient land glaciers. The Alaska Highway exercises an irresistible attraction to die-hard road-trippers, many of them retirees with RVs. Another route north, the Stewart-Cassiar Highway, also labeled Highway 37, leaves the Yellowhead Highway west of the Hazeltons, cutting behind the towering Coast Mountains to eventually join the Alaska Highway in the Yukon.

While all the major highways in northern British Columbia remain open year-round, frigid weather and short daylight make winter travel difficult; it's far better to see this beautiful wilderness landscape under the glow of the summer's midnight sun.

1 The Inside Passage & Discovery Coast

The ferry cruise along British Columbia's Inside Passage combines the best scenic elements of Norway's rocky fjords, New Zealand's majestic South Island, Chile's Patagonian range, and Nova Scotia's wild coastline. Less than half a century ago, there was only one way to explore this rugged coastline: by booking the 4-day passage on an Alaska-bound cruise ship or freighter.

Since 1966, BC Ferries has operated the **Inside Passage ferry** between Port Hardy (on northern Vancouver Island, discussed in chapter 7) and Prince Rupert (on the mainland, discussed below), with stops at the small Discovery Coast communities of Bella Coola, Ocean Falls, Shearwater, McLoughlin Bay, and Klemtu. These stopovers became so popular that in 1994, the company added the **Discovery Coast ferry** to its schedule.

The ferry system also connects Prince Rupert to the remote **Queen Charlotte Islands,** the ancestral home of the Haida tribe (see below).

For information on the region, contact the **Northern BC Tourism Association,** 11-3167 Tatlow Rd. (Box 1030), Smithers, BC, V0J 2N0 (☎ **250/847-5227**).

✪ THE INSIDE PASSAGE

Fifteen hours may seem like a long time to be on a ferry. But you'll never get bored as the ✪ *Queen of the North* noses its way through an incredibly scenic series of channels and calm inlets, flanked by green forested islands. Humpback whales, orcas, Dall porpoises, salmon, bald eagles, and sea lions line the route past the mostly uninhabited coastline. The 304-mile (491km) BC Ferries run between Port Hardy and Prince Rupert follows the same route as expensive Alaska-bound cruise ships, but at a fraction of the cost. And in midsummer, with the north's long days, the trip is made almost entirely in daylight.

The ferry from Port Hardy initially crosses a couple hours worth of open sea—where waters can be rough—before ducking behind Calvert Island. Except for a brief patch of open sea in the Milbanke Sound north of Bella Bella, the rest of the trip follows a narrow, protected channel between the mainland and a series of islands.

The actual Inside Passage begins north of Bella Bella, as the ferry ducks behind Princess Royal Island and then Pitt Island, both as large as New England states, but far more mountainous. The high-walled passage between these islands and the mainland is very narrow—often less than a mile (1.6km) wide. The scenery is extraordinarily dramatic: Black cliffs drop thousands of feet directly into the channel, notched with hanging glacial valleys and fringed with forests. Powerful waterfalls drop from dizzying heights directly into the sea. Eagles float along thermal drafts, while porpoises cavort in the ferry's wake.

Even in poor conditions (the weather is very changeable along the north Pacific coast), this is an amazing trip. Wisps of clouds drifting along the cliffs only enhance the brooding primordial beauty of this land- and seascape.

The 410-foot *Queen of the North* carries up to 750 passengers and 157 vehicles. You can wander around the ferry, lounge on seating either inside or on the deck, or rest in a private dayroom or overnight cabin. Onboard, you'll find a cafeteria, snack bar, buffet-style dining, playroom, business center, and gift shop. Reservations are mandatory, especially in the busy summer season. You'll also want to have lodging reservations in Prince Rupert or Port Hardy, as the ferry arrives late in the evening; by the time the ship docks and you wait to drive your car off, it can be close to midnight.

The **BC Ferries** (☎ **888/223-3779**) Inside Passage line operates the *Queen of the North* between Port Hardy on Vancouver Island and Prince Rupert on the mainland, normally a 15-hour trip. From June through September, the ferry makes the journey north one day, returning south the next; in June, July, and September, it goes southbound on even-numbered days, and in August, heads south on odd-numbered days. The northbound ferry follows the same schedule on opposite days. In May, the ferry makes the journey every second day. The rest of the year, service through the Inside Passage gradually drops to one ferry per week each way in midwinter; contact BC Ferries for schedules.

Summer one-way fares between Prince Rupert and Port Hardy are C$104 (U.S.$68) per car passenger or walk-on, C$214 (U.S.$139) for a normal-size vehicle. A car with two passengers adds up to C$346 (U.S.$225). Reservations are mandatory. The ship's cabins rent for between C$43 and C$52 (U.S.$28 and U.S.$34).

In summer, the ferry leaves both Prince Rupert and Port Hardy at 7:30am, so under normal circumstances, you'll arrive at your destination at 10:30pm later that same day; you probably won't need a sleeping berth.

At Prince Rupert, you can also catch an **Alaska Marine Highway ferry,** which stops here on its run between Bellingham, Washington, and Skagway, Alaska. Passenger fare from Prince Rupert to Skagway is U.S.$130; a vehicle under 15 feet long costs U.S.$299. It's about 52 hours from Prince Rupert to Skagway. For information on the Alaska Marine Highway system, call ☎ **800/642-0066.**

THE DISCOVERY COAST PASSAGE

Also departing from Port Hardy, the Discovery Coast's *Queen of Prince Rupert* connects small, mostly First Nations communities along the fjords and islands of the northern coast, including Namu, Bella Bella, Shearwater, Ocean Falls, and Klemtu. The most popular part of this run is the summer-only service to Bella Coola, which links to Highway 20, a paved and gravel road that's a day's drive from Williams Lake, in central British Columbia's Fraser Valley (see "Williams Lake," in chapter 10).

In summer, there are two direct ferry runs on Tuesday and Thursday to Bella Coola, plus a Saturday circular run that goes north to Klemtu before returning to Port Hardy via Bella Coola. These trips depart from Port Hardy at 9:30am; the Tuesday and Saturday departures require a night on the boat. In high season, fares between Port Hardy and Bella Coola are C$110 (U.S.$72) per passenger, C$214 (U.S.$139) for a car. Berths rent for between C$43 and C$52 (U.S.$28 and U.S.$34).

2 Prince Rupert

304 miles (491km) N of Port Hardy, 470 miles (756km) W of Prince George

British Columbia's most northerly city, Prince Rupert (pop. 17,681) is a city in transition. For years a major fishing and timber port, it has recently felt the decline in these industries, and is now turning to tourism to bolster its economy. Although scarcely a fancy place, Prince Rupert has much to offer travelers. Ecotourism has taken off, with outfitters offering wildlife-viewing excursions both on the ocean and in the wilderness.

Prince Rupert

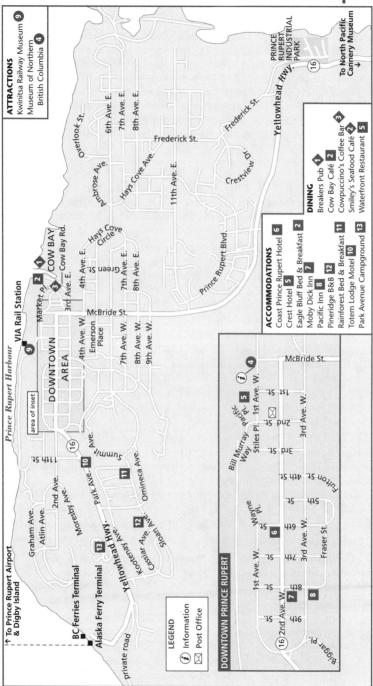

ATTRACTIONS

Kwinitsa Railway Museum ⑨
Museum of Northern
British Columbia ④

DINING

Breakers Pub ①
Cow Bay Café ②
Cowpuccino's Coffee Bar ③
Smiley's Seafood Café ②
Waterfront Restaurant ⑤

ACCOMMODATIONS

Coast Prince Rupert Hotel ⑥
Crest Hotel ⑤
Eagle Bluff Bed & Breakfast ②
Moby Dick Inn ⑦
Pacific Inn ⑧
Pineridge B&B ⑫
Rainforest Bed & Breakfast ⑪
Totem Lodge Motel ⑩
Park Avenue Campground ⑬

LEGEND

ⓘ Information
⊠ Post Office

DOWNTOWN PRINCE RUPERT

Prince Rupert Harbour

COW BAY

DOWNTOWN AREA

VIA Rail Station

To Prince Rupert Airport & Digby Island

BC Ferries Terminal
Alaska Ferry Terminal

Yellowhead Hwy.

To North Pacific Cannery Museum →

PRINCE RUPERT INDUSTRIAL PARK

231

Sportfishing is excellent in local rivers and in the protected waters of Chatham Sound; the city's claim to be the fishing capital of British Columbia is well justified. And Prince Rupert is a convenient hub for exploring the sights of the Pacific Northwest. From here, ferries go north to Alaska, west to the remote Queen Charlotte Islands, and south to Vancouver Island and Bellingham, Washington.

Prince Rupert exudes a hard-working, good-natured vigor, and the population is a well-integrated mix of First Nations and European-heritage Canadians. You'll experience the palpable sense of being on the northern edge of the world, which gives the city—situated on a series of rock ledges above the broad expanse of the Pacific—a sense of purpose and vitality.

ESSENTIALS

GETTING THERE　By Ferry　For information on BC Ferries service from Port Hardy and Alaska Marine Highway service between southeast Alaska and Washington State see "The Inside Passage," above. For information on BC Ferries service to the Queen Charlottes, see below.

By Train　The **VIA Rail** (☎ 888/842-7245) train departs from Prince Rupert on Monday, Thursday, and Saturday at 8am and arrives in Prince George at 8:10pm. One-way fares start at C$67 (U.S.$44); the station is off Second Street, near the waterfront. The train follows the same route as the Yellowhead Highway along the scenic Skeena River valley. At Prince George, travelers can continue east on VIA's cross-Canada rail service, or travel south to Vancouver on the *Cariboo Prospector.*

By Plane　Air BC (☎ 800/766-3000 in the U.S., 800/663-3721 in Canada) and **Canadian Regional Airlines** (☎ 800/426-7000 in the U.S., 800/665-1177 in Canada) provide service between Vancouver and the Prince Rupert Airport, located east of the city off Highway 16. **Harbour Air** (☎ 800/665-0212 or 250/627-1341) departs from the seaplane base at Seal Cove with scheduled service to the Queen Charlotte Islands and many other smaller communities along the coast and islands. Harbour Air also offers flightseeing tours of the region.

By Car　Prince Rupert is the terminus of the Yellowhead Highway, Canada's most northerly transcontinental roadway. Between Prince Rupert and Prince George, the route is 450 miles (724km) of extraordinary scenery, particularly the portion along the Skeena Valley. The road is open year-round.

Car-rental agencies in Prince Rupert include **Budget** (☎ 800/268-8900) and **Tilden** (☎ 800/387-4747).

By Bus　Greyhound buses (☎ 800/661-8747) serve Prince Rupert and Prince George with two buses daily each way. The one-way fare is C$88 (U.S.$57).

VISITOR INFORMATION　The **Prince Rupert Visitor Info Centre,** 100 First Ave. E., at the corner of McBride Street (Box 669), Prince Rupert, BC, V8J 3S1 (☎ 800/667-1994 in Canada, or 250/624-5637; fax 250/627-8009; e-mail: prtravl@ citytel.net), is open year-round, daily from 9am to 5pm.

Special Events

During the second week in June, Prince Rupert hosts **Seafest** (☎ 250/624-9118), which features a fishing derby, parades, games, food booths, bathtub races, and the annual blessing of the fleet.

EXPLORING THE AREA

Prince Rupert gets more than 18 hours of sunlight a day in summer. And despite its far-north location, this coastal city enjoys a mild climate most of the year. Mountain biking, cross-country skiing, fishing, kayaking, hiking, and camping are just a few of the region's popular activities.

Northern British Columbia's rich native Indian heritage has been preserved in Prince Rupert's museums and archaeological sites. But you don't need to visit a museum to get a sense of the community's history. Relics of the city's early days are apparent in its old storefronts, miners' shacks, and churches. Built on a series of rocky escarpments, the city rises ledge by ledge, starting at the harbor with a well-established train station and the **Kwinitsa Railway Museum** (☎ 250/627-1915). This area is overlooked by the old commercial center, which itself is overlooked by the historic residential area, dominated by massive stone churches. The historic **Cow Bay** district on the north waterfront, with galleries, gift shops, and good cafes and restaurants, plus a couple of B&Bs, is Prince Rupert's major center for tourist activity.

Museum of Northern British Columbia. 100 First Ave. ☎ **250/624-3207.** Admission C$5 (U.S.$3.25) adults, C$2 (U.S.$1.30) students, C$1 (U.S.65¢) children 6–11, C$10 (U.S.$7) per family. Summer Mon–Sat 9am–8pm, Sun 9am–5pm; winter Mon–Sat 10am–5pm.

This recently renovated museum displays artifacts created by the Tsimshian (Nisga'a) and Haida tribes, who have inhabited this area for more than 10,000 years. There are also artifacts and photographs from Prince Rupert's 19th-century European settlement. In summer, the museum sponsors a number of special programs, ranging from 2-hour archaeological boat tours of the harbor (which allow you to see the area's many active dig sites at ancestral villages that date back more than 5,000 years) to walking tours of the city. As the museum shares space with the visitor center, this is a good place to find out about tours of all kinds. The excellent gift shop is one of the best places in town to buy native art. Also sponsored by the museum is the **Carving Shed,** a working studio located a block away on Market Place. Native carvers use the space to work on their art; visitors are welcome, but are encouraged to be discreet while the carvers concentrate. Save your ticket to the museum, as it will get you in free to *The Prince Rupert Story,* a 1-hour dramatization and slide show in the auditorium.

✪ **North Pacific Cannery Museum.** 12 miles (20km) south of Prince Rupert in Port Edward. Mailing address: Box 1104, Prince Edward, BC, V0V 1G0. ☎ **250/628-3538.** Admission C$6 (U.S.$3.90) adults, C$3 (U.S.$1.95) students, free for children under 6. May 1–Sept 30 daily 9am–6pm. Call for off-season hours.

Salmon canning was one of the region's original industries, back when the salmon run up the Skeena River was one of the greatest in North America. The province's oldest working salmon-cannery village, built on the waterfront of Inverness Passage in 1889, was home to hundreds of First Nation, Japanese, Chinese, and European workers and their families. Every summer, fishing fleets dropped off their catches at the cannery, where the salmon was packed and shipped out to world markets. This company-owned community reached its apex from 1910 to 1950, when the work force numbered 400 and the community grew to about 1,200; the cannery has been closed since 1968.

Now a National Historic Site, the North Pacific Cannery Village Museum complex includes the cannery building, various administration buildings and residences, the company store, a hotel, and a dining hall—a total of over 80 structures linked by a long boardwalk (the land is so steep here that most of the houses were built on wharves). Workers were segregated by race: the Chinese, Japanese, and native

Canadian workers had their own micro-neighborhoods along the boardwalk, all over-seen by the European bosses. Guided tours of the cannery complex, offered on the hour, provide a very interesting glimpse into a forgotten way of life.

The **boardinghouse** is now open for B&B accommodations, with doubles going for C$65 (U.S.$42); the dining hall is open during museum hours.

ARCHAEOLOGICAL, WILDLIFE & ADVENTURE TOURS

Prince Rupert is at the center of an amazingly wild and scenic area, but unless you have your own boat, you'll find it hard to get around. A good option is to sign on with a local tour operator. One of the most unique excursions is the **Pike Island Archaeo-logical Tour,** operated by the Metlakata First Nation band. Tiny Pike Island is 5^1/$_2$ miles (9km) from Prince Rupert in Venn Passage, and is at the center of a rich archaeological area that was once one of the most densely populated regions in pre-Contact Native America. The island has three village sites, which were abandoned 18 to 20 centuries ago. Although none have been excavated, guides point out the house depressions in the forest floor and discuss the midden deposits, the shellfish and bone piles that were essentially the garbage pits of these prehistoric people. Tours are offered daily from late June to Labour Day, starting at 11:30am and returning to Prince Rupert at 4pm. The crossing is made on a small ferry; the trails on the island are not difficult, but are not wheelchair accessible. Tickets are C$42 (U.S.$27), including lunch, and can be purchased at the museum or reserved by calling ☎ 250/628-3201. For more information, see **www.citytel.net/library/pike**.

If you're into adventure and want to see wildlife in pristine landscapes, consider a 4-day sailing expedition into the **Khutzeymateen Grizzly Bear Preserve.** Offered by **Sunchaser Charters** (☎ 250/624-5472; www.citytel.net/sunchaser), the trip involves sailing up the Khutzeymateen Inlet, northwest of Prince Rupert. There's no other access to the preserve—the first bear sanctuary in the world—except by boat or floatplane, and humans are forbidden to actually land. Most transport is on the 40-foot sailing ketch *Sunchaser,* which has eating and sleeping facilities; some trips also include a floatplane link. The all-inclusive cost is C$1,100 (U.S.$715).

A handy place to sign up for a variety of tours is **Seashore Charters** (☎ 250/624-5645), which has a trailer office at the corner of First Avenue East and McBride Street. Among the options available are harbor tours by boat and city tours by bus, each costing C$20 (U.S.$13), and whale-watching tours for C$65 (U.S.$42). Seashore also arranges fishing charters, flightseeing, and Northern Pacific Cannery tours.

West Coast Launch Ltd. (☎ 250/624-3151; www.citytel.net/westwhales; e-mail: ddavis@citytel.net) offers whale-watching tours from June through September (C$75/U.S.$49), kayak drop-off and pickup, and circle tours of Kaien Island.

For a historical walking tour of the city, contact the **Heritage Walking Tour** (☎ 250/624-3207). This guided 2-hour tour leaves daily in summer at 2pm from the museum; it costs C$4 (U.S.$2.60) for adults and C$2 (U.S.$1.30) for youths.

OTHER OUTDOOR PURSUITS

FISHING　Prince Rupert is famed for its excellent sportfishing. Area waters boast strong salmon runs and great bottom fishing. There are dozens of charter operators based in town. If you'd like to fish but don't feel comfortable dealing with the outfit-ters, the **Visitor Info Centre** (☎ 250/624-5637) or **Seashore Charters** (☎ 250/624-5645) can steer you to the one that best serves your needs.

Nass-Skeena Marine Charters (☎ 250/624-8243) operates the floating Palmer-ville Lodge east of Prince Rupert and offers day or overnight charters. Fishing charters are C$375 (U.S.$244) for a half day, C$600 (U.S.$390) for a full day. Packages that include all three meals plus lodging go for C$100 (U.S.$65) per night. The lodge is also open to B&B guests at a rate of C$50 (U.S.$33) per person.

Squadaree Lodge and Chartering Service (☎ 250/624-3328) is 20 nautical miles west of Prince Rupert on Stephen's Island. The lodge offers fishing charters, sailboat charters, and kayak trips. Fishing charters are C$375 (U.S.$244) for 8 hours, daylong sailboat trips are C$475 (U.S.$309), and C$275 (U.S.$179) buys you unlimited kayaking or skiffing. Prices include meals, lodging, and boat transport.

Fishing charters can range in length from a half-day to weeklong trip, and range in facilities from rough-and-ready boats to luxury cruisers. Expect a guided trip to cost from C$350 (U.S.$228) for a half day. Long-established companies include **Frohlich's Fish Guiding** (☎ 250/627-8443), offering both river and bottom fishing, and **Predator Fishing Charters** (☎ 250/627-1993), which provides charters for salmon, halibut, ling cod, snapper, and crab fishing, as well as diving. **New Pacifica Charters/Expeditions** (☎ 250/624-3272) offers charters for salmon, halibut, cod, and crab; wildlife-viewing and photography trips; and diving charters.

HIKING   **Kalen Sports,** 344 Second Ave. W. (☎ 250/624-3633), and **Far West Sports,** 221 Third Ave. W. (☎ 250/624-2568), are the two best sources for information about hiking and mountain-biking trails and directions. The area experiences annual as well as seasonal changes in trail conditions, and some hiking and back-country ski areas are too challenging for beginners. Both of these outfitters can supply clothing and equipment for camping, climbing, and skiing.

There are a number of good hiking options right in Prince Rupert. Trails from the Park Avenue Campground lead through the woods to the BC Ferries terminal. Another in-town trail follows Hays Creek from McBride Street down to the harbor. Just 4 miles (6.4km) east on Highway 16 is a trailhead for three more wilderness hikes. The 2¹/₂-mile (4km) loop Butze Rapids Trail winds through wetlands to Grassy Bay and to Butze Rapids, a series of tidal cataracts. The trails to the Tall Trees—a sometimes-steep trail that explores a grove of old-growth cedars—and to the viewpoint on Mount Old-field require more stamina.

KAYAKING & CANOEING   The waters surrounding Prince Rupert are tricky, and rough tidal swells and strong currents are common. **Eco Trek Adventures** (☎ 250/624-8311; www.citytel.net/ecotreks; e-mail: ecotrks@citytel.net) offers guided half-day trips (C$45/U.S.$29) and expeditions to the grizzly sanctuary (C$175/U.S.$114). Kayak rentals start at C$25 (U.S.$16) for a half day.

WHERE TO STAY

Coast Prince Rupert Hotel. 118 Sixth St., Prince Rupert, BC, V8J 3L7. ☎ **800/663-1144** or 250/624-6711. Fax 250/624-3288. www.coasthotels.com. E-mail: coastprh@citytel.net. 92 units. A/C TV TEL. C$105–C$110 (U.S.$68–U.S.$72) double. Extra person C$10 (U.S.$7). Family plan, corporate and off-season rates, and senior discounts available. AE, MC, V.

Right downtown, the Coast Prince Rupert offers views of the harbor and mountains from every room. Accommodations are large and comfortable, with extras such as in-room coffeemakers. Friendly service and good dining options make this a fine lodging choice. Amenities include Charlie Hays Restaurant, which serves fresh local seafood; horse-race betting in the Turf Lounge; Bogey's Cabaret; a beer-and-wine store; and guided charter fishing boats in summer.

✪ **Crest Hotel.** 222 First Ave. W., Prince Rupert, BC, V8J 3P6. ☎ **800/663-8150** or 250/624-6771. Fax 250/627-7666. www.cresthotel.bc.ca. E-mail: info@cresthotel.com. 102 units. TV TEL. C$109–C$119 (U.S.$71–U.S.$77) double. AE, ER, MC, V.

If you're looking for one package that offers the best views, good dining, and beautifully furnished rooms, then you're looking for the Crest. Situated on the bluff's edge overlooking Tuck Inlet, Metlakata Pass, and the busy Prince Rupert harbor, the Crest is one of the finest hotels in northern British Columbia. The views are fabulous and the rooms nicely furnished, though in a style more beholden to the 1980s than the 21st century. The wood-paneled lobby and common rooms are gracious and opulent.

The coffee shop is open for three meals daily. The Waterfront Restaurant, with incredible views and patio dining, is one of the best places to eat (see "Where to Dine," below). With a heated deck, Charley's Lounge has the city's best year-round view from a bar stool. Amenities include a hot tub, fitness center, steam room, meeting rooms, modem phones, fishing charters, and sealife-viewing trips.

Eagle Bluff Bed & Breakfast. 201 Cow Bay Rd., Prince Rupert, BC, V8J 1A2. ☎ **800/ 833-1550** in Canada, or 250/627-4955. Fax 250/627-7945. E-mail: eaglebed@citytel.net. 5 units. TV. C$55–C$65 (U.S.$36–U.S.$42) double. MC, V.

One of the best-located B&Bs in the city—at least if you like Prince Rupert's maritime ambiance—the Eagle Bluff sits right on the wharf at Cow Bay. Step outside your door and directly into a tour boat or kayak; the cafes and coffee shops are just steps away. All rooms have great views of the bustling harbor. Accommodations include single, double, and family units, with a mix of private and shared bathrooms.

Moby Dick Inn. 935 Second Ave. W., Prince Rupert, BC, V8J 1H8. ☎ **800/663-0822** or 250/624-6961. Fax 250/624-3760. TV TEL. C$79–C$89 (U.S.$51–U.S.$58) double. Children under 12 stay free in parents' room. AE, MC, V.

Well established and serviceable, the Moby Dick is a good choice if you're looking for a clean, unfussy place to stay. It has a central location between downtown and the ferry docks. Rooms are spacious and nicely outfitted. Wheelchair-accessible units are available. The owner's collection of native carving is on display in the lobby. Facilities include a dining room, popular pub, sauna, whirlpool, and laundry.

Pacific Inn. 909 Third Ave. W., Prince Rupert, BC, V8J 1M9. ☎ **888/663-1999** or 250/ 627-1711. 77 units. TV TEL. C$75–C$85 (U.S.$49–U.S.$55) double. Rates include continental breakfast. AE, MC, V.

Newly renovated, this motor lodge is a good value if you're in search of large, clean rooms in a convenient location, midway between downtown proper and the ferry docks. The owners take pride in the motel, and it shows. Boulet's Seafood House serves up local fish and seafood.

Pineridge B&B. 1714 Sloan Ave., Prince Rupert, BC, V8J 3Z9. ☎ **888/733-6733** or 250/627-4419. www.citytel.net/pineridge. E-mail: pineridge@citytel.net. 3 units. C$80 (U.S.$52) double. MC, V.

Pine Ridge is a comfortable B&B located near downtown and the ferry terminals. The spacious, newly renovated home offers three units, each with private bathroom. Guests have access to two large sitting rooms, one with a fireplace. The entire house is nicely decorated with local art and crafts, and your hosts are friendly and gracious.

Rainforest Bed & Breakfast. 706 Ritchie St., Prince Rupert, BC, V8J 3N5. ☎ **888/ 923-9993** or 250/624-9742. Fax 250/627-5551. www.pixsell.bc.ca//bb/6399htm. E-mail: Rain4est@citytel-net. 3 units. C$60–C$70 (U.S.$39–U.S.$46) double. Rates include full breakfast. Children 8–13 can share parent's room for C$5 (U.S.$3.25) per night. Personal checks, traveler's checks, and cash only. Free parking and short-term vehicle storage. From the ferry terminal, drive 3 min. (0.8km/0.5 mile) on Hwy. 16, which is also called Park Ave. on the coastal side of town. Turn right on Ritchie St.

Located in a quiet, residential section of Prince Rupert, this cozy, homey B&B offers guests a shared kitchenette for making lunch or dinner, plus a TV room. Breakfast, served in the dining room, includes fresh-squeezed juices and delicious homemade cinnamon rolls. Your hosts offer free ferry and airport pickup and drop-off.

Totem Lodge Motel. 1335 Park Ave., Prince Rupert, BC, V8J 1K3. ☎ **800/550-0178** in North America, or 250/624-6761. Fax 250/624-3831. 31 units. TV TEL. C$65–C$79 (U.S.$42–U.S.$51) double. Kitchen units C$7 (U.S.$4.55) extra. AE, ER, MC, V. Hwy. 16 becomes McBride St. when it first enters town. It then becomes Third Ave. and finally Park Ave. From the ferry terminals, drive 1 mile (1.6km) into town on Park Ave.

This motel offers tidy, quiet, simply furnished rooms with kitchens and satellite TV. It's the closest lodging to the Alaska and BC Ferries terminal. Facilities include car storage and a coin-op laundry.

CAMPING

A mile (1.6km) from the ferry terminal, **Park Avenue Campground,** 1750 Park Ave., Box 612, Prince Rupert, BC, V8J 4J5 (☎ **250/624-5861;** fax 250/627-8009), has 97 full-hookup and tent sites. Facilities include laundry, showers, toilets, playground, mail drop, and phones. Reserve in advance in summer, as this campground is the best in the area. It's also an ideal location if you're catching the morning ferry to Port Hardy or to Skagway, Alaska. Rates are C$14 to C$19 (U.S.$9 to U.S.$12) per site.

WHERE TO DINE

One excellent reason to visit the Cow Bay area is **Cowpuccino's Coffee Bar,** 25 Cow Bay Rd. (☎ **250/627-1395**), a friendly and slightly funky coffee shop with comfortable chairs and good homemade muffins and sweet breads.

✪ **Breakers Pub.** 117 George Hills Way (on the Cow Bay Wharf). ☎ **250/624-5990.** Reservations not needed. Main courses C$6–C$21 (U.S.$3.90–U.S.$14). AE, DC, MC, V. Daily 11am–midnight. PUB.

Breakers is a popular local pub with a harbor view and a huge menu of well-prepared international food. The offerings ranges from salads, wraps, and sandwiches to pasta and pizza, and on to grilled local fish and seafood. Breakers is also a hopping social spot; the young and prosperous of Prince Rupert gather here to admire the views and get happy with a microbrew or two.

Cow Bay Café. 205 Cow Bay Rd. ☎ **250/627-1212.** Reservations recommended. Main courses C$8–C$13 (U.S.$5–U.S.$8). MC, V. Tues–Sat noon–9pm. PACIFIC NORTHWEST.

This homey place is like a little Vancouver street cafe plunked down on the edge of a dock. The casual, slightly hippie atmosphere feels refreshing so far north, and is nicely matched by the menu, which features lots of vegetarian and light-dining options. Most dishes change daily, which ensures that the cooks focus on what's freshest. Choices include salads, pastas, soups, and sandwiches; at night, there's always a selection of fresh fish prepared with up-to-date zest. Desserts are all homemade. The cafe is perched right on the edge of the harbor, and the views are magnificent.

Smiley's Seafood Café. 113 Cow Bay Rd. ☎ **250/624-3072.** Reservations not accepted. Main courses C$7–C$23 (U.S.$4.55–U.S.$15). MC, V. Daily 11am–10pm. SEAFOOD.

Open since 1922, Smiley's serves seafood in every shape and form, from oyster burgers and seafood salads to heaping platters of fried fish. Located on the waterfront in the historic Cow Bay district, Smiley's is essentially an old-fashioned, vinyl-seated diner whose base clientele are the town's fishermen and -women. Take a seat and listen to the locals talk about the day's catch. In summer, this small establishment is always busy, but it's worth the wait. Fish-and-chips is a specialty.

Waterfront Restaurant. In the Crest Hotel, 222 First Ave. W. ☎ **250/624-6771.** Reservations suggested. Main courses C$8–C$32 (U.S.$5–U.S.$21). AE, DC, MC, V. Daily 11:30am–2:30pm and 5–10pm. PACIFIC NORTHWEST.

Easily Prince Rupert's most sophisticated restaurant, the Waterfront is flanked by banks of windows that overlook the city's busy harbor and offshore islands. The white-linen-and-crystal elegance of the dining room is matched by the inventiveness of the cuisine. Understandably, much of the menu is devoted to local fish and seafood; Skeena River salmon, for example, is baked with sun-dried cranberries and served with honey lemon butter. Steaks and rack of lamb will win the favor of meat eaters. The Waterfront also has a full page of "casual plates," dinners that feature smaller portions, salads, and tempting appetizers such as a seafood club sandwich.

3 Queen Charlotte Islands

The misty and mysterious Queen Charlotte Islands provided inspiration for 19th-century painter Emily Carr, who documented her impressions of the towering carved-cedar totem poles and longhouses at the abandoned village of Ninstints, on Anthony Island. The islands still lure artists, writers, and photographers wishing to experience their haunting beauty.

The Queen Charlottes—also called by their native name, Haida Gwaii—are the homeland of the Haida people, the most warlike of the First Nation tribes of the northwest. Sometimes referred to as the Vikings of the Pacific, the Haida were mighty seafarers, and during raiding forays, ranged as far south along the Pacific Coast as Oregon. The Haida were also excellent artists, carvers of both totems and argillite, a slate-like rock that they transformed into tiny totemic sculptures and pendants. The Haida today make up about half of the islands' population of 5,500.

The Queen Charlottes have a reputation as the "Canadian Galapagos," as these islands—ranging between 32 and 85 miles (51 and 136km) from the mainland—have evolved their own endemic species and subspecies of flora and fauna. In recognition of the islands' unique natural and human history, the Canadian government preserved the southern portion of Moresby Island as ✪ **Gwaii Haanas National Park Reserve and Haida Heritage Site.** UNESCO followed suit by naming the islands a World Heritage Site.

The Queen Charlottes are primordial and beautiful, but visiting them requires some planning. In fact, if you're reading this in Prince Rupert and are thinking about a spur-of-the-moment trip to the Charlottes, you may want to reconsider. Lodging on the islands is limited, and reservations are necessary year-round. The most interesting parts of the islands—the abandoned Haida villages—are accessible only by boat, and the Gwaii Haanas Park limits the number of people who can daily access the archaeological sites. There are only 78 miles (125km) of paved roads, and none of them even come close to the park or the islands' wild western coastline. If you haven't already signed up with an outfitter, you'll end up driving these roads through deep forest and visiting isolated maritime villages—pleasant enough, but perhaps not quite the adventure you were anticipating. In short, simply showing up on the Queen Charlottes is not a good idea. The best way to visit is by arranging, in advance, to join a tour guide or outfitter on a kayak, flightseeing, sailboat, or powerboat excursion that will provide adventure while transporting you to a primitive and fabled wilderness.

ESSENTIALS
GETTING THERE   By Ferry   BC Ferries (☎ **888/223-3779**) operates a car-and-passenger ferry that crosses between Prince Rupert and Skidegate, on northerly

Graham Island. The 8-hour crossing can be quite rough, as storms and currents in Hecate Strait are intense and unpredictable. If you're prone to seasickness, it's a good idea to take precautions. Ferries run daily in summer, though the schedule is confusing; call ahead to find out times and to reserve (recommended in summer). Tickets are C$24 (U.S.$16) for a passenger, C$90 (U.S.$59) for a vehicle.

By Plane   Canadian Regional Airlines (☎ 800/665-1177) and **Harbour Air** (☎ 800/689-4234) provide two scheduled daily flights between Vancouver and the Sandspit Airport on northern Moresby Island. Harbour Air also has one seaplane flight daily from Prince Rupert to Sandspit and to Masset, on Graham Island. Charter seaplanes offer transport around the islands as well as flightseeing trips (see below).

VISITOR INFORMATION   The **Queen Charlotte Islands Visitor Info Centre,** 3220 Wharf St. (Box 819), Queen Charlotte, BC, V0T 1S0 (☎ 250/559-8316), is open May to Labour Day, daily from 8am to 8pm. On Graham Island, the **Masset Visitor Info Centre,** 1455 Old Beach Rd. (Box 68), Masset, BC, V0T 1M0 (☎ 250/626-3982), is open in July and August, daily from 11am to 5pm. You can also check out **www.qcinfo.com** or e-mail: qcvic@island.net.

GETTING   AROUND   In the Queen Charlotte Islands, the Graham Island–to–Moresby Island **Skidegate–Alliford Bay ferry** operates 12 daily sailings. Fares are C$4.50 (U.S.$2.95) per passenger, C$12 (U.S.$8) for a car. There is no other public transport available.

With so few roads on the islands, it's fair to ask if it even makes sense to take a car on a short trip. Car rentals are available from **Budget** (☎ 800/577-3228), **Rustic Car Rentals** (☎ 250/559-4641), **Tilden** (☎ 250/626-3318), and **Thrifty** (☎ 250/559-8050).

Bike rentals are available from **Northern Exposure ATV Rentals,** in Masset (☎ 250/626-3793), and **Premier Creek Lodging,** in the town of Queen Charlotte (☎ 888/322-3388).

EXPLORING THE ISLANDS

Most visitors come to the Charlottes to view its abundant and unusual wildlife, and to visit the ancient Haida villages renowned from painting and photographs. In both cases, you'll need to either have your own boat or arrange for a guide to get you from the islands' small settlements to the even more remote areas. The islands provide superlative wilderness adventures—camping, hiking, diving, sailing, kayaking, and fishing—although due to their isolation and sometimes extreme weather, you'll need to plan ahead and know what you're getting into before setting out.

Graham Island is the more populous of the two major islands. **Queen Charlotte City** is a fishing and logging town with a population of about 1,200, sitting above the scenic waters of Beaverskin Bay. QCC, as the village is sometimes dubbed, has the majority of lodgings and facilities for travelers, as well as the administrative headquarters for **Gwaii Haanas National Park Reserve** (☎ 250/559-8818).

Skidegate Village, just east of the Skidegate ferry terminal, is home to the **Haida Qwaii Museum** (☎ 250/559-4643), which houses the world's largest collection of argillite carvings, made from the slatelike stone found only in the Queen Charlottes. Next to the museum is the longhouse-style office of the **Haida Gwaii Watchmen,** the native guardians of the island's Haida villages. Ask here for information on visiting the archaeological sites; also note the modern carved canoe on the lawn next door.

Heading north from Skidegate on Highway 16, **Tlell** is an old agricultural community and now somewhat of an artists' colony; watch for signs pointing to studios. Past the logging town of Port Clements, the highway ends at **Masset.** The island's largest town with a population pushing 1,300, Masset was until the early 1990s a major military and sea-rescue base. **Old Massett,** just north of Masset, is one of the largest Haida settlements on the island, and is a good place to shop for carvings and jewelry. Just north of the Masset town center, trails lead through the **Delkatla Wildlife Sanctuary.** A birder's paradise, it's one of the first southerly landfalls for the migrating species of bird life that use the Pacific Flyway.

East of Masset, **Naikoon Provincial Park** is an 180,000-acre wildlife reserve on the northeast tip of Graham Island, where whales can be spotted from the beaches. Peregrine falcons fly overhead, and Sitka deer silently observe as you walk along trails through the dense temperate rain forest. The **Agate Beach Campground (☎ 250/847-7320)** is a popular place to camp (C$12/U.S.$8). To reach the park from Masset, continue north and then east on Tow Hill Road.

On **Moresby Island,** the principal—and just about only—center of population is **Sandspit** (pop. 750). In summer, Parks Canada operates an information center for visitors headed to the wilderness ✪ **Gwaii Haanas National Park Reserve and Haida Heritage Site.** There are no roads or shore facilities in the park, and access is by boat or chartered floatplane only. While there are many amazing sights in this part of the Queen Charlottes, you'll need to be committed to the journey to get here: The distances are great and the costs high. If you're a dedicated wildlife watcher, it may be worth it to see the array of rare fauna and flora. Perhaps the most famous site in the park is **Ninstints,** on Anthony Island, an ancient native village revered as sacred ground by the modern-day Haida tribe. Centuries-old totem poles and longhouses proudly stand in testimony to the culture's 10,000-year heritage.

You will need permission to visit Gwaii Haanas Park and must attend mandatory orientation sessions before entering. The **Haida Gwaii Watchmen,** Box 609, Skidegate, Haida Gwaii, BC, V0T 1S0 (☎ **250/559-8225**), control access to Ninstints and to other ancient villages in the park. For more information, contact **Gwaii Haanas,** Box 37, Queen Charlotte City, BC, V0T 1S0 (☎ **250/559-8818;** www.harbour.com/parkscan/gwaii; e-mail: gwaiicom@qcislands.net).

TOURS & EXCURSIONS TO GWAII HAANAS NATIONAL PARK RESERVE

Outfitters must be registered with park officials; the list of authorized tour operators is the best place to start shopping for expeditions into the park. The park entry fees are C$60 (U.S.$39), and are not usually included in the tour packages.

Many outfitters, such as **Butterfly Tours Great Expeditions (☎ 800/663-3364** or 604/264-1668), offer all-inclusive kayaking packages that suit all ages and experience levels. Longtime sea-kayak outfitter **Ecosummer Expeditions (☎ 800/465-8884** or 604/669-7741; www.ecosummer.com) offers 1- and 2-week trips to Gwaii Haanas, with prices starting at C$1,445 (U.S.$939). **Pacific Rim Paddling Company (☎ 250/384-6103;** www.islandnet.com/~prp; e-mail: prp@islandnet.com) has both 7- and 14-day kayak trips to Gwaii Haanas, with prices from C$1,355 (U.S.$881).

Sailing into Gwaii Haanas is another popular option, and most sailboat operators also have kayaks aboard for guests' use. **Queen Charlotte Adventures (☎ 250/559-8990;** www.island.net/infobus/qca; e-mail: qciadven@island.net) offers tours to Ninstints on a 53-foot schooner. Prices include lodging, meals, and a skipper and crew. Tours range from 2 days (C$1,100/U.S.$715) to 5 days (C$2,750/U.S.$1,788). Queen Charlotte Adventures also offers daylong powerboat tours of the park.

South Moresby Air Charters (☎ 888/551-4222 or 250/559-4222; www.island.net/smoresby; e-mail: smoresby@qcislands.net) offers sightseeing seaplane flights to a number of sites in Gwaii Haanas, including Ninstints. The tour includes a landing at

Rose Bay and a 40-minute boat ride to the ancient village, plus a guided tour. For three people, the charge is C$933 (U.S.$606).

Scuba-diving charters can be arranged through **Gwaii Haanas Tours and Diving Adventure** (☎ **250/637-5666**).

FISHING

One of the most beautiful lodges in western Canada, **Langara Lodge, Ltd.,** 436 W. Second Ave., Vancouver, BC, V5Y 1E2 (☎ **604/873-4228;** fax 604/873-5500), also offers the most complete all-inclusive fishing packages to the islands. Geared toward anglers and ecotourists who want to be pampered, the lodge picks up guests at Vancouver Airport and delivers them to Sandspit. From here, it's a quick hop by float-plane to Langara Island, just north of Graham Island. The rooms at this log-lodge complex are large and luxurious. The dining room serves expertly prepared Pacific Northwest dishes complemented by an impressive wine list. Fishing packages include round-trip air transport from Vancouver, lodging, meals, boats, tackle, weather gear, survival suits, and freezing, canning, and taxidermy services. Guided fishing costs extra, as do whale-watching, ecotouring, and heli-touring charters. Rates start at C$3,125 (U.S.$2,031) per person for a 4-day trip.

For something a little more low-key, **Naden Lodge,** 1496 Kelkatla St., Box 648, Masset, BC, V0T 1M0 (☎ **800/771-8933** or 250/626-3322), offers B&B accommodations and guided fishing trips from a lovely location right above Masset's boat basin. **R&J Charters,** Box 587, Queen Charlotte, BC, B0T 1S0 (☎ **250/559-8940** May–Sept, or 250/772-3217 in winter), runs by-the-hour fishing trips.

WHERE TO STAY & DINE

There's not a lot to be said about dining on the Charlottes. Food on these remote islands is pretty perfunctory. After a long day of exploration, stop in at **Daddy Cool's Neighbourhood Pub,** Collison Avenue at Main Street, Masset (☎ **250/626-3210**), for a pint and a fish tale or two. The **Cafe Gallery,** Collison Avenue at Orr Street, Masset (☎ **250/626-3672**), serves hearty portions of seafood, steaks, pasta dishes, sandwiches, and salads. **Harry Martin's Eatery,** 3207 Wharf St., Queen Charlotte City (☎ **250/559-4773**), is a bakery, cafe, and crafts gallery rolled into one.

Dorothy & Mike's Guest House. 3127 Second Ave. (Box 595), Queen Charlotte City, BC, V0T 1S0. ☎ **250/559-8439.** Fax 250/559-8439. 8 units. C$40 (U.S.$26) rm with shared bathroom, C$75 (U.S.$49) suite with private bathroom. Rates include breakfast. MC, V. Drive 2 miles (3.3km) away from the Skidegate ferry terminal on Second Ave.

The atmosphere here has an island flavor: A large deck overlooks the Skidegate Inlet, while a serene garden surrounds the house. The warm, cozy guest rooms are filled with local art and antiques; the suites come with full kitchens and private bathrooms. The inn is within walking distance of the ocean, restaurants, and shopping.

Premier Creek Lodging. 3101 Third Ave. (Box 268), Queen Charlotte City, BC, V0T 1S0. ☎ **888/322-3388** or 250/559-8415. www.qcislands.net/premier. E-mail: premier@ qcislands.net. 12 units. TV TEL. C$55–C$70 (U.S.$36–U.S.$46) double. AE, MC, V.

This heritage lodge dates back to 1910, though it has been recently remodeled and modernized. Many of the rooms have great views over gardens to Bearskin Bay. There's a range of accommodations, from small hostel-style units with shared bathrooms to suites with full kitchens and large, private bathrooms.

Sea Raven Motel. 3301 Third Ave. (Box 519), Queen Charlotte, BC, V0T 1S0. ☎ **800/ 665-9606** or 250/559-4423. www.searaven.com. E-mail: searaven@qcislands.net. 29 units. TV TEL. C$70 (U.S.$46). MC, V.

The largest lodging in the Queen Charlottes, the Sea Raven is a comfortable motel with many room types, ranging from simple single units to those with kitchenettes to deluxe accommodations with decks. Some units are smoke-free, and many have ocean views. The accommodations are simply furnished, but very clean. The cafe is open for three meals daily. The Sea Raven also arranges fishing charters.

Spruce Point Lodging. 609 Sixth Ave., Queen Charlotte City, Graham Island, BC, V0T 1S0. ☎ **250/559-8234.** 7 units. TV TEL. C$65 (U.S.$42) double. Kitchen unit C$10 (U.S.$7) extra. Rates include breakfast. MC, V. Drive a half mile (0.8km) away from the Skidegate ferry terminal on Sixth Ave.

This rustic inn, overlooking the Hecate Strait, features rooms with private entrances as well as excellent views. Each unit has a fridge and a choice of either private shower or tub. Some rooms even have full kitchen facilities, and all have complimentary tea and coffee service. The shared balcony is used as a guest lounge. Your friendly hosts can arrange kayaking packages to the surrounding islands.

4 The Yellowhead Highway: From Prince Rupert to Prince George

It's a long 447 miles (715km) from Prince Rupert to Prince George. Even though it's possible to make the journey in one long day's drive, it's far more pleasant to take it slowly, enjoy the extravagant mountain scenery, and stop at some of the cultural sites along the way.

The route initially follows the glacier-carved, dramatically beautiful Skeena River valley inland, through the industrial city of **Terrace** and to the **Hazeltons,** twin towns with a lovely river setting and an excellent First Nations cultural center. **Smithers,** cradled in a rich agricultural valley beneath craggy peaks, is another scenic spot, and the most pleasant place along the route to spend a night. Between Burns Lake and Fort Fraser is a series of long, thin lakes, famed for trout angling and rustic fishing resorts.

ESSENTIALS

GETTING THERE   By Car   Terrace is 91 miles (151.6km) east of Prince Rupert on the Yellowhead Highway (Hwy. 16). From Terrace to Prince George, it's another 357 miles (571km).

By Train   VIA Rail (☎ 888/842-7245 or 800/561-3949) operates three-times-weekly passenger-train service between Prince George and Prince Rupert, with stops including Smithers, New Hazelton, and Terrace. The east-bound train operates on Wednesday, Friday, and Sunday; the west-bound runs on Monday, Thursday, and Saturday. The train follows the same route as the Yellowhead Highway.

By Bus   Greyhound buses (☎ **800/661-8747**) travel twice daily between Prince Rupert and Prince George, with stops at almost all of the communities along the way. One-way fare from Prince Rupert to Terrace is C$21 (U.S.$14).

VISITOR INFORMATION   The **Northern BC Tourism Association,** 11-3167 Tatlow Rd. (Box 1030), Smithers, BC, V0J 2N0 (☎ **250/847-5227**), can provide extensive and detailed information on the area.

TERRACE & NISGA'A MEMORIAL LAVA BEDS PROVINCIAL PARK

The Yellowhead Highway (Hwy. 16) follows the lush Skeena River valley from Prince Rupert, on the coast of the Inside Passage, to the province's interior. It's the gateway to the land-based return route from the Inside Passage ferry cruise. The long, winding valley is home to a diverse community of fishers, loggers, and aluminum and paper mill workers in Terrace, and is the ancestral home of the Gitksan, Haisla, and Tshimshian (Nisga'a) tribes, who have lived in the area for over 8,000 years.

If you've had trouble understanding glacial geology, driving up the Skeena River valley will provide instant illumination. It's easy to picture the steep-sided valley choked with a bulldozer of ice, grinding the walls into sheer cliffs. In many places, the rock walls are still so barren and precipitous that they barely support vegetation. Streams running into the Skeena drop thousands of feet in a series of waterfalls to reach the valley floor, making for eye-popping scenery. There are many small picnic areas along this route; plan on stopping beside the Skeena to admire the view.

Terrace is a grimly industrial town of 13,372, with little to offer tourists. However, there are two shops here you shouldn't miss: The **Northern Light Studio, 4820 Halliwell Ave.** (☎ **250/638-1403**), has a Japanese garden and a walkway built completely out of British Columbia jade. The studio features jewelry, fine arts, native crafts, and totem poles. Owned by the Kitsumkalum tribal band, the **House of Sim-oi-ghets,** off Highway 16 (☎ **250/635-6177**), is a cedar longhouse decorated with traditional Nisga'a motifs. The store offers jewelry, carvings, moccasins, bead and leather work, and books. The complex also includes a riverside campground.

Many Indian legends focus on the Skeena River valley surrounding Terrace and the incredibly rare wildlife in this region. Twenty-five miles (40km) northwest of town, the **Khutzeymateen** ("confined space of salmon and bears") is the province's first official grizzly-bear sanctuary. The 240-square-mile (622km^2) reserve protects the 50 **grizzlies** that live in a fragile estuary habitat. You need permission to enter the park, and you must be part of an authorized group or accompanied by a ranger to observe these amazing creatures (see "Archaeological, Wildlife & Adventure Tours," above).

North America's rarest subspecies of black bear, the **kermodei,** also makes its home in the valley and on Princess Royal Island in the Douglas Channel. The kermodei is unique, a nonalbino black bear born with white fur, ranging from dark chestnut blond to blue-gray glacier white. One of every 10 black bears born here is a kermodei. Its teddy-bear face, small eyes, and round ears are endearing, but the kermodei is even larger than the impressive Queen Charlotte Islands black bear. This amazing animal was on the verge of extinction until a decade ago, when naturalists managed to prevent the logging industry from decimating its remaining territory.

At the **Nisga'a Memorial Lava Beds Provincial Park,** vegetation has only recently begun to reappear on the lava plain created by a volcanic eruption and subsequent lava flow in 1750, which consumed this area and nearly all of its inhabitants.

The route to the park's near-lunar landscape begins in Terrace at the intersection of the Yellowhead Highway (Hwy. 16) and Kalum Lake Road (Nisga'a Hwy.). Follow the narrow gravel highway north along the Kalum River past Kalum Lake. Along the way, there's a **pioneer graveyard** and the **Deep Creek Fish Hatchery** (☎ **250/635-3471**), which releases chinook salmon from August through September and coho salmon from October through November. Just past the tiny settlement of Rosswood is **Lava Lake,** then the town of **New Aiyansh** (the valley's largest Nisga'a village), and finally the park. The entire trip is 48 miles (80km); allow at least 2 hours.

For information on the Terrace area, stop by or contact the **Terrace Visitor Info Centre,** 4511 Keith Ave., Terrace, BC, V8G 1K1 (☎ **250/635-2063;** e-mail: terrace.tourism@osg.net), open from June 1 to September 30, daily from 10am to 6pm; and October 1 to May 31, Monday through Friday from 10am to 6pm.

WHERE TO STAY & DINE

Best Western Terrace Inn. 4553 Greig Ave., Terrace, BC, V8G 1M7. ☎ **250/635-0083.** Fax 250/635-0092. www.bestwestern.com/ca/terraceinn. E-mail: res@terraceinn.com. 68 units. A/C TV TEL. C$99–C$109 (U.S.$64–U.S.$71) double. Group, corporate, senior, and weekend discounts available. AE, CB, DC, DISC, MC, V. Free parking. Small pets accepted for C$10 (U.S.$7) fee.

Overlooking the surrounding mountains, these comfortable, well-appointed rooms feature a number of little touches not normally found this far into the backcountry: complimentary coffee, clock radios, and hair dryers. Facilities include a restaurant, piano bar and lounge, and casual pub with live entertainment. Lava-bed and hiking tours are available upon request.

Coast Inn of the West. 4620 Lakelse Ave., Terrace, BC, V8G 1R1. ☎ **800/663-1144** or 250/638-8141. Fax 250/638-8999. www.coasthotels.com. 58 units. A/C TV TEL. C$115–C$135 (U.S.$75–U.S.$88) double. AE, DISC, ER, MC, V.

This high-rise hotel dominates downtown Terrace, and is within easy walking distance of the two shopping malls that constitute the city center. The guest rooms are attractively furnished and quite large. On site are the White Spot family restaurant and Fanny's Lounge. The hotel is close to a fitness and swimming center as well.

Miles Inn on the T'seax. Nass Valley (Box 230), New Aiyansh, BC, V0J 1A0. ☎ and fax **250/633-2636.** www.kermode.net/milesinn. E-mail: milesinn@kermode.net. 4 units, 2 with private bathroom. C$75 (U.S.$49) double. Rates include breakfast. No credit cards.

Overlooking the Nisga'a Memorial Lava Beds Provincial Park, this beautiful lodge is nestled in the Nass River valley. A hot tub is available for relaxing tired muscles after a day of hiking the lava beds and crater, rock climbing, canoeing or kayaking the Nass River, fishing the T'seax River, or simply lounging around the lodge. Home-cooked dinners are available for an extra charge. *Note:* Smoking is not permitted.

THE STEWART-CASSIAR HIGHWAY: NORTH TO ALASKA

Forty-seven miles (75km) east of Terrace (30 miles/48km west of the Hazeltons) is the junction of Highway 16 and the Stewart-Cassiar Highway (also labeled as Hwy. 37), one of two roads leading to the far north of British Columbia, eventually to join the famed Alaska Highway in the Yukon. This route is not as popular as the Alaska Highway, which begins farther east in Dawson Creek, though the scenery is more spectacular and the road conditions about the same. The route is now mostly paved, with a few gravel sections; you can depend on delays due to road construction. It's a total of 446 miles (714km) between the Yellowhead Highway and the junction of the Alaska Highway near Watson Lake, the Yukon.

Even if you don't want to drive all the way to the Yukon or Alaska, consider a side trip to the twin communities of Stewart, British Columbia, and Hyder, Alaska. These two boundary-straddling villages lie at the head of the Portland Canal, a very long and narrow fjord—in fact, the world's fourth longest. The setting alone—the two ports huddle below high-flying peaks and massive glaciers—is worth the drive.

After turning north at the Highway 16 junction, stop in the native village of **Gitwangak** to view the historic totem poles. Some of the poles are more than 100 years old. Similar totem poles can also be seen 15 miles (24km) farther up the Stewart-Cassiar Highway at **Kitwancool.** One totem pole here, the "Hole in the Ice" pole, is reckoned to be the oldest in the world, carved around 1850.

Ninety-six miles (154km) north on the Stewart-Cassiar Highway is Meziadin Junction, where Highway 37A heads west to **Stewart** and **Hyder.** It's just 40 miles (64km) to Stewart from the junction, but what a 40 miles! The road arches up immediately to cross the mighty glacier-choked Coast Mountains before plunging precipitously down to sea level at Stewart. You'll want to stop at the Bear Glacier Rest Area, where massive **Bear Glacier**—glowing an eerie aqua blue—descends into Strohn Lake, frequently bobbing with icebergs. Watch for mountain goats and bears.

Stewart (pop. 858) is Canada's most northerly ice-free port, and is now a major copper-mining center. The tidy little town contrasts vividly with Hyder (pop. 70), Stewart's grubby Alaskan cousin: One feels like an outpost of an empire, while the other feels like the end of the road. Facilities are basic but serviceable; the best place to stay is the **King Edward Hotel and Motel,** on Fifth Avenue in Stewart (☎ **800/ 663-2126** in B.C., or 250/636-2244), with doubles going for C$80 (U.S.$52).

From Hyder, continue along graveled Fish Creek Road for 5 miles (8km) to **Fish Creek,** where in July, black and grizzly bears gather to fish for spawning chum salmon. Follow the road another 20 miles (32km) to an astonishing vista of Salmon Glacier gouging its steep-sided valley.

Continuing north from Meziadin Junction, the route follows rushing rivers in narrow, mountain-flanked valleys, framed by forests of spruce. Facilities are very limited; there's camping at **Kinaskan Lake Provincial Park,** 130 miles (208km) north of Meziadin Junction, and 17 miles (27km) farther north at the **Tatogga Lake Resort** (no phone), with rustic cabins (C$55/U.S.$36 double), a woodsy restaurant, and campsites.

The town of **Dease Lake** (pop. 700) will seem like a metropolis by the time you reach it. Since it's about midway on the Stewart-Cassiar Highway, it's the natural place to spend the night. The **Northway Motor Inn,** on Boulder Street (☎ **250/ 771-5341**), is a standard motel/restaurant complex with double rooms for C$72 (U.S.$47). There are a number of campgrounds along Dease Lake itself.

If you think Dease Lake is isolated, consider a side trip to **Telegraph Creek,** 70 miles (112km) west on a gravel road. The road parallels the powerful Stikine River as it trenches a precipitous canyon on its way to the Pacific. Don't even think of driving this road if you have vertigo! There are frequent narrow, steep, and cliff-edged portions—the grade is 20% in some sections—and you'll live in dread of meeting oncoming traffic. However, the scenery is absolutely compelling, and the little community of **Telegraph Cove** (pop. 300), with both a native village and frontier-era town, is friendly and welcoming. Just about the only place to stay is the **RiverSong Lodge** (☎ **250/235-3196**), formerly the Hudson's Bay Company trading post. Inquire at the RiverSong about boat and flightseeing tours in the Stikine Valley.

Back on the Stewart-Cassiar Highway, from Dease Lake it's a straightforward 145 miles (232km) of mountains and forests to the junction with the Alaska Highway, 13 miles (21km) east of Watson Lake.

THE HAZELTONS

The Skeena and Bulkley rivers join at the Hazeltons (pop. 1,165), a friendly community with a long history and a beautiful location. Straddling two river canyons and set below the rugged Rocher de Boule mountains, the Hazeltons are actually three separate towns: **Hazelton** itself, **South Hazelton,** and **New Hazelton,** all in a 5-mile (8km) stretch. The junction of these two mighty rivers was home to the Gitksan and Wet'suwet'en peoples, for whom the rivers provided both transport and a wealth of salmon. This was an important trade center in native Canada. Beginning in the 1860s, it was the upriver terminus for riverboat traffic on the Skeena, and Hazelton became a commercial hub for miners, ranchers, and other frontier settlers farther inland.

Both the First Nations and the frontier history are still on view. The old town center of Hazelton, though small, has the feel of a pioneer settlement. The first thing you'll notice as you drive into historic Hazelton from New Hazelton is the one-lane **suspension bridge** across the Bulkley River Canyon. Controlled by traffic lights, this bridge sways 250 feet above the river. The Gitksan and Wet'suwet'en used to cross this gorge on a footbridge constructed of poles lashed together with cedar-bark rope.

The homeland of the Gitksan people, the area around the Hazeltons has been inhabited for at least 7,000 years. You can get a sense of the culture of the Gitksan by visiting ✪ **'Ksan Historical Village,** off Highway 62 (☎ 250/842-5544; www.ksan. org; e-mail: ksan@ksan.org), a re-creation of a traditional village, complete with a carving school and a museum of historic artifacts and ceremonial items. 'Ksan is located in a large grassy meadow near the confluence of the Skeena and Bulkley rivers, and is filled with vividly painted longhouses and towering totem poles. Some of the longhouses serve as studios, where you can watch native artists carve masks, totem poles, and wall panels as well as design and hammer silver jewelry.

'Ksan is also the home of the Kitanmax School of Northwest Coast Indian Art, a formal 4-year program dedicated to the renewal of Northwest coast design. If possible, plan your visit to coincide with a performance by the **'Ksan Performing Arts Group,** a troupe of singers and dancers who entertain visitors with music, masks, costumes, and pageantry. The shop here is a great source for native art and gifts, and the Wilp Tokx, or the House of Eating, is a good place to try native cooking.

There's a C$2 (U.S.$1.30) admission for the grounds themselves, which gets you access to the gift shop, museum, restaurant, carving shed, and totem poles. However, to see the interior of the clan longhouses, you'll need to join a tour. Each of these three houses demonstrates a different aspect of Gitksan culture. The **Frog House** (Wilp Lax See'l)—the house of the distant past—represents Gitksan culture before European contact. The **Wolf House** (Wilp Lax Gibuu), the feast house, presents the Gitksan governance and inheritance system commonly referred to as the potlatch. The **Fireweed House** (Wilp Gisk'aast), or the treasure house, displays the ceremonial clothing and artifacts used at feast times and by the 'Ksan Performing Arts Group.

The guided tour costs C$8 (U.S.$5) for adults, C$7 (U.S.$4.55) for seniors and youths 5 to 17. If you take the tour, you don't have to pay the grounds fee. 'Ksan is open April 15 to October 15, daily from 9am to 6pm. The rest of the year, only the museum and shop are open, Monday through Friday from 10am to 5pm.

Continue your tour of Gitksan ceremonial art and carving by driving 8 miles (13km) north to the native village of **Kispoix.** Fifteen historic totem poles stand guard over the village, many carved a century or more ago. Wander the streets of Kispoix and watch for small signs advertising native carvers and box makers. Respectful visitors are welcome at the village.

To get advance information on the area, contact the **Hazeltons Travel InfoCentre,** P.O. Box 340, New Hazelton, BC, V0J 2J0 (☎ 250/842-6071 in summer, 250/842-6571 Oct–May). The summer-only **visitor center** is located at the junction of Highways 16 and 62 (Main St.).

WHERE TO STAY & DINE

Your best bet for a good meal is the **Hummingbird Restaurant,** on Highway 62 heading into Hazelton (☎ 250/842-5628). It serves good Austrian and Canadian cooking at all three meals. For a more relaxed atmosphere, stop by the **Garage Pub and Grill,** just off Highway 16 in South Hazelton (☎ 250/842-5488). The pub, in a renovated auto-repair garage from the 1950s, features lots of period memorabilia.

28 Inn. 4545 Yellowhead Hwy. 16, Box 358, New Hazelton, BC, V0J 2J0. ☎ **877/842-2828** or 250/842-6006. Fax 250/842-6340. E-mail: 28inn@osg.net. 32 units. A/C TV TEL. C$51–C$54 (U.S.$33–U.S.$35) double. Extra person C$6 (U.S.$3.90). Kitchen C$6 (U.S.$3.90) extra. MC, V.

There aren't many lodging choices in the Hazeltons, but the 28 Inn is clearly the best. The motel is newly constructed, with large standard rooms and good-quality furnishings. Some units have kitchens; all have fridges. On site are a beer-and-wine store and restaurant and pub.

CAMPING

Seeley Lake Provincial Park, 6 miles (9.6km) west of New Hazelton on Highway 16 (☎ **250/847-7320**), has 20 sites (C$12/U.S.$8) and good fishing, but dry toilets. The **'Ksan Historical Village** (see above) operates a campground near the confluence of the Bulkley and Skeena rivers at Hazelton.

SMITHERS & THE BULKLEY VALLEY

Smithers is located in a stunningly beautiful valley, flanked on three sides by vast ranges of glaciated peaks and cut through by the fast-flowing Bulkley River. While many communities in North America boast of being Bavarian look-alikes, the countryside around here truly does look like the northern Alps, except for the cattle and horse ranches that sprawl across the valley. Approximately midway between Prince Rupert and Prince George, Smithers makes a good place to take a break, as you'll find good hotels and restaurants, plus ample recreational opportunities nearby.

The heart of Smithers is the old commercial strip on **Main Street,** which is perpendicular to the current fast-food–and-motel-laden Highway 16. This bustling and attractive area is lined with Bavarian-theme storefronts that offer outdoor clothing and gear, gifts, and local crafts.

Directly across Highway 16 from Main Street is **Centre Park** and the **Bulkley Valley Museum** (☎ **250/847-5322**), a shake-sided heritage building that formerly served as the courthouse. The museum tells the story of the community's railroad and agricultural history, and boasts a replica blacksmith shop as well as displays of fossils from the Driftwood Canyon fossil beds (see below). In the same building is the **Smithers Art Gallery** (☎ **250/847-3898**), which exhibits the work of local and regional artists. Both the museum and gallery are open mid-May to Labour Day, daily from 10am to 5pm; admission is C$2 (U.S.$1.30) for adults.

What Smithers really has to offer is its gorgeous and dramatic mountain backdrop. With 8,600-foot-high (2,621m) **Hudson Bay Mountain** rising directly behind the town, snowcapped mountain ranges ringing the valley, and the area's fast-flowing rivers and streams, you'll feel the urge to get outdoors and explore.

Driftwood Canyon Provincial Park, 7 miles (11km) northeast of Smithers, preserves fossil-bearing formations laid down 50 million years ago, when this area was a subtropical wetland. Considered one of the world's richest fossil beds, the park has interpretive trails leading through a section of exposed creek bed, which was carved by an ice-age glacier. Fossil collecting is not permitted. To reach the park, drive 2 miles (3km) east of Smithers and turn east on Babine Lake Road.

Additional information on this region can be obtained from the **Smithers Visitor Info Centre,** 1411 Court St. (P.O. Box 2379), Smithers, BC, V0J 2N0 (☎ **250/847-3337;** www.bulkley.net/~smicham; e-mail: smicham@bulkley.net).

OUTDOOR PURSUITS

HIKING   You don't have to go far to find hiking trails in Smithers. The popular **Perimeter Trail** rings the town, linking parks, golf courses, and residential areas. The 5¹/₂-mile (9km) trail is a good place to stroll or jog; one especially lovely stretch is along the Bulkley River in Riverside Park. You can access the trail at many areas throughout town.

Two excellent hikes are on **Hudson Bay Mountain.** Two miles (3km) west of Smithers, take Kathlyn Lake Road and follow it 6¹/₂ miles (10.4km) to the clearly marked trailhead. It's an easy half-mile (0.8km) stroll to view the impressive **Twin Falls,** which plunge 500 feet (152m) down a thundering 1¹/₂-mile-wide (2.4km) gulch carved in the side of the mountain. Also from the same trailhead, sturdy hikers can climb up to Glacier Gulch and visit the toe of **Kathlyn Glacier.** This strenuous hike is just less than 4 miles (6.4km) one-way, but allow at least 3 hours to make the climb. Views across the valley and onto the face of the glacier are fantastic.

On the southern slopes of Hudson Bay Mountain is another good hiking destination. Follow Hudson Bay Mountain Road west out of Smithers for 6¹/₂ miles (10.4km) to **Smithers Community Forest,** with an extensive trail system that passes through ecosystems ranging from alpine to wetlands. The easy 2¹/₂-mile (4km) Interpretive Nature Trail makes a loop through the forest.

For longer and more rugged hiking, **Babine Mountains Recreation Area** protects 80,000 acres of subalpine meadows, glacier-fed lakes, and craggy peaks. This roadless area is accessible only on foot, but many exquisite sights are within the range of day hikers. One of the best hikes is **Silver King Basin Trail,** which passes through subalpine forest before reaching an alpine meadow that explodes with wildflowers in July. To reach the Babine Mountains, go 2 miles (3km) east of Smithers and take Babine Lake Road. The recreation-area boundary is 9 miles (14km) from the highway.

FISHING   With so many lakes and rivers around, you'll find it hard not to think about trophy-worthy trout and cohos as you drive across the Bulkley Valley. The Bulkley River has excellent fishing for steelhead, chinook, and coho salmon, though restrictions apply. The best fishing areas on the Bulkley are from the confluence of the Morice River south of Smithers to the town of Telkwa.

WHERE TO STAY

Aspen Motor Inn. 4268 Hwy. 16 (Box 756), Smithers, BC, V0J 2N0. ☎ **800/663-7676** or 250/847-4551. Fax 250/847-4492. 60 units. A/C TV TEL. C$75–C$79 (U.S.$49–U.S.$51) double. AE, MC, V.

This well-maintained motel complex has everything you'll need: an indoor pool, restaurant, and large, comfortable rooms. Some units have kitchens. Other perks include a sauna and whirlpool.

Hudson Bay Lodge. 3251 Hwy. 16 E. (Box 3636), Smithers, BC, V0J 2N0. ☎ **800/663-5040** or 250/847-4581. Fax 250/847-4878. E-mail: hblodge@mail.netship.net. 99 units. A/C TV TEL. C$87 (U.S.$57) double. AE, ER, MC, V.

The largest and most comfortable hotel in Smithers, the Hudson Bay Lodge is a popular stop for the tour-bus crowds making their way to and from the Prince Rupert ferries. The crowds notwithstanding, the facilities here are high quality. Facilities include the Twin Falls Dining Room (see "Where to Dine," below), a coffee shop, a pub, and a sauna.

Stork Nest Inn. 1485 Main St. (Box 2049), Smithers, BC, V0J 2N0. ☎ **250/847-3831.** Fax 250/847-3852. www.bulkley.net/~stork. E-mail: stork@mail.bulkley.net. 23 units. A/C TV TEL. C$65 (U.S.$42) double. Rates include full breakfast. MC, V.

Billing itself as a European-style hotel, the Stork Nest does more than most Smithers lodgings to look Bavarian, with gables, lots of flowers, and a corbelled roofline. However, what really makes the Stork Nest such a prize is the value it offers. These clean, nicely furnished rooms aren't the largest in the province, but if all you need is a pleasant space with all of the standard facilities, this is it.

CAMPING

Riverside Park Municipal Campsite, 1600 Main St. N. (☎ **250/847-1600**), has 40 riverside sites next to the town golf course, with dry toilets, fire pits, fishing, water, and a playground. No hookups are available.

WHERE TO DINE

Alpenhorn Pub and Bistro. 1261 Main St. ☎ **250/847-5366.** Reservations not accepted. Main courses C$7–C$17 (U.S.$4.55–U.S.$11). MC, V. Daily 11am–11pm. PUB.

The Alpenhorn is a pleasant, sports-bar type of pub with a large selection of gourmet burgers—like the chicken cordon bleu burger—as well as a selection of pastas, sandwiches, and salads. If you're feeling like something more substantial, go for the steak or ribs.

✪ **Rainbow Alley Restaurant and Gallery.** 1089 Main St. ☎ **250/847-6121.** Reservations suggested. Main courses C$12–C$24 (U.S.$8–U.S.$16). MC, V. Mon–Fri 11am–2:30pm; daily 5–10pm. INTERNATIONAL.

Easily the best restaurant in the valley, the Rainbow Alley serves up a vivid and well-prepared selection of dishes that borrows ably from world cuisines. The starters include an interesting salad of grilled romaine hearts with roasted garlic vinaigrette, as well as barbecued salmon sushi. Moving on to the entrees, you have the chance to travel the world, from rack of lamb with Oriental barbecue sauce to Jamaican jerk prawns with lime crème fraîche. In lesser hands, these kinds of dishes can end up a muddle of flavors, but here the preparations are refined and exciting. The lively dining room provides the perfect backdrop for this outstanding food.

Twin Falls Dining Room. In the Hudson Bay Lodge, 3251 Hwy. 16 E. ☎ **250/847-4581.** Reservations suggested. Main courses C$13–C$33 (U.S.$8–U.S.$21). Daily 5:30–10pm. AE, MC, V. PACIFIC NORTHWEST.

Twin Falls Dining Room is a comfortably old-fashioned, steak-house-style restaurant in the popular Hudson Bay Lodge. The menu offers a number of German and continental dishes, like schnitzels and sauerbraten, as well as more up-to-date selections such as chicken linguini with red pesto. But the stock-in-trade here is the beef, with prime rib and steaks receiving expert attention. The Twin Falls even has a number of table-side presentations: Try the pepper steak flambé and meld performance art with fine dining.

THE LAKES DISTRICT

Between Smithers and Prince George lies a vast basin filled with glacier-gouged lakes, dense spruce forests, and rolling mountains—but not many people. There are over 300 lakes in this region, ranging from small ponds to bodies of water dozens of miles long. The combined lake shorelines here add up to a length of more than 3,000 miles (4,800km), which is more than the number of people in the region's largest town, Burns Lake. Not surprisingly, sportfishing is the main draw here, and rustic fishing lodges are scattered along the lake shores.

However, this isn't an easy place to plan a casual visit. Many of the lodges are fly-in or boat-in, and offer only weeklong fishing packages. Most are very rustic indeed. If this is what you're looking for, contact the Burns Lake Chamber of Commerce (see below), which can connect you with the lodge or outfitter that suits your needs. Ask for the free *Burns Lake 3,000 Miles of Fishing* map and information sheet, and you'll get a sense of the complex and isolated network of lodges in the area.

If you have a day to spare and want to explore the region, there's a paved loop starting in Burns Lake that explores the shores of four of the lakes. Take Highway 35 south from Burns Lake, past Tchhesinkut Lake to Northbank on François Lake. From here, take the free half-hour ferry across François Lake and continue south through woodlands to Ootsa Lake. Here, the road turns west to follow Ootsa Lake, eventually returning to François Lake and Burns Lake.

Burns Lake is nominally the center of the Lakes District, and if you end up here needing a place to stay, the **Burns Lake Motor Inn,** on Highway 16 West (☎ **800/663-2968** or 250/692-7545), offers double rooms for C$70 (U.S.$46). For information on the region, contact the **Burns Lake Chamber of Commerce,** P.O. Box 339, Burns Lake, BC, V0J 1E0 (☎ **250/692-3493**).

At Vanderhoof, 83 miles (133km) east of Burns Lake, take Highway 27 north 37 miles (59km) to ✪ **Fort St. James,** one of the most interesting historic sites in northern British Columbia. Fort St. James was the earliest non-native settlement in the province, a fur-trading fort established in 1806. Now preserved as the Fort St. James National Historic Site, the fort and grounds are an open-air museum of frontier life. The wooden fortress stretches across a wide swath of Stuart Lake, which in the days of canoe travel was the center of a network of lakes and rivers in New Caledonia, as the region was then known. In summer, the fort is a hive of activity, with costumed docents acting out the roles of traders, craftsmen, and explorers. There's a museum with artifacts from the original fort, as well as a short audiovisual presentation on the fort's history. The park is open mid-May through September, daily from 9am to 5pm; the museum is open year-round during the same hours. Admission is free.

Stuart Lodge, on Stones Bay Road (☎ **250/996-7917;** www.wdcomputers.com; e-mail: roesslet@mail.wdcomputers.com), is the best place to stay in the area, with double rooms going for C$60 (U.S.$39).

5 Prince George

246 miles (396km) W of Jasper, Alberta; 470 miles (756km) E of Prince Rupert

The largest city in northern British Columbia, Prince George (pop. 77,996) makes a natural base for exploring the sites and recreational opportunities of the province's north-central region, which is filled with forested mountains, lakes, and mighty rivers.

There has been settlement at the junction of the Fraser and Nechako rivers for millennia; the two river systems were as much a transportation corridor for the early First Nation people as for the European settlers who came later. The first whites to pass through here in 1793 were scouting the region for furs; a trading post was established in the early 1800s. The Grand Trunk Railroad, which passed through here in 1914, put Prince George on the map.

What makes the city's economic heart beat is lumber—and lots of it. Prince George is at the center of vast softwood forests, and three major mills here turn trees into pulp, and pulp into paper. The economic boom that these mills introduced has brought a degree of sophistication to the lumber town—there's a civic art gallery, good restaurants, and the University of Northern British Columbia—but not so much that you're likely to forget that you're in the north. The downtown area is a little ragged on the edges, though full of character, and the recently built malls that sprawl on the edges of the city bring the products of globalization to this northern outpost.

ESSENTIALS

GETTING THERE   By Plane   Air BC (☎ 800/663-3721) and **Canadian Regional Airlines** (☎ 800/665-1177) both offer air service between Prince George and Vancouver.

Special Events

The **Ol' Sawmill Bluegrass Jamboree,** held 16 miles (26km) up North Nechako Road in mid-August, is a musical event for the whole family, with weekend camping, music workshops, arts and crafts, play areas for the kids, and many talented bluegrass performers. For more information, call ☎ **250/564-8573.**

By Train   Prince George is served by **BC Rail's** *Cariboo Prospector* (☎ **604/ 984-5246**) from North Vancouver. It departs three times a week from North Vancouver at 7am with stops at Whistler, Lillooet, 100 Mile House, Williams Lake, and Quesnel; it arrives here at 8:30pm. The one-way fare is C$170 (U.S.$111).

By Bus   **Greyhound** serves Prince George with four buses to and from Vancouver daily. One-way fare is C$91 (U.S.$59). Greyhound also has two buses daily between Prince George, Jasper, and Edmonton. One-way fare to Jasper is C$47 (U.S.$31).

By Car   Prince George is about a third of the way across the province on the east-west Yellowhead Highway (Hwy. 16). South from Prince George, Highway 97 drops down through the Cariboo District on its way to Kelowna (445 miles/712km) and Vancouver (via Hwy. 1, 505 miles/808km). From Prince George, you can also follow Highway 97 north to join the Alaska Highway at Dawson Creek (263 miles/421km).

VISITOR INFORMATION   Contact the **Prince George Visitor Info Centre** at 1198 Victoria St., Prince George, BC, V2L 2L2 (☎ **800/668-7646** or 250/ 562-3700; fax 250/563-3584; www.tourismpg.bc.ca).

GETTING AROUND   The local bus system is operated by **Prince George Transit** (☎ **250/563-0011**). For a cab, call **Emerald Taxi** (☎ **250/563-3333**).

Car-rental agencies include **Avis** (☎ **250/562-2847**), **Tilden** (☎ **250/564-4847**), and **Hertz** (☎ **250/963-7454**).

EXPLORING THE AREA

Downtown Prince George is located on a spur of land at the confluence of the Fraser and Nechako rivers. The old commercial district at first seems a bit forlorn and gritty, but a stroll around the city center—concentrated around Third Avenue and George Street—reveals a down-and-dirty charm that's reminiscent of towns in the Yukon or Northwest Territories. And the prevalence of tattoo parlors, pawn shops, sporting-goods stores, and old-fashioned coffee shops enhances the impression that this is at heart a rough-and-ready frontier community.

In 1999, the **Prince George Art Gallery** (☎ **888/221-1155** or 250/563-6447) moved into its stylish space in the Civic Centre Plaza, at Patricia Boulevard and Dominion Street. This architecturally innovative, C$5-million structure houses a collection of works by mostly local artists. There's also a sculpture garden, gift shop, and cafe. Hours are Tuesday through Saturday from 10am to 5pm, Sunday from 1 to 5pm. Between May and September, it's also open Monday between 10am and 5pm. After viewing the gallery, cross Patricia Street and wander the trails in **Connaught Hill Park.** From the top of the hill are good views of the Fraser River and downtown.

The **Prince George Native Art Gallery,** 1600 Third Ave. (☎ **888/221-1155** or 250/614-7762), features the works of native artists in the Prince George region. You can see birch-bark biting art, cedar-wood carvings, beadwork, and limited-edition prints. The gallery is open Tuesday through Saturday from 10am to 4:30pm.

Railway buffs should stop by the **Prince George Railway & Forestry Industry Museum,** 850 River Rd. (☎ **250/563 7351**). Open May through September daily from 10am to 5pm, the museum features a 1914 Grand Trunk Station moved from Penny, British Columbia; a 1903 Russell snowplow; and early logging equipment. Admission is C$3 (U.S.$1.95) for adults and C$1.50 (U.S.$1) for kids.

Prince George is rightly proud of its parks. There are more than 120 parks within the city limits, many of them linked by the Heritage Rivers trail system. The best is 89-acre **Fort George Park,** on the site of the original fur-trading post. On the grounds are a First Nations burial ground, a working miniature railway, the original Fort George rail station, an old one-room schoolhouse, and the outstanding **Fraser Fort George Regional Museum** (☎ 250/562-1612), which details the region's history, starting with exhibits on the customs of the native Carrier people, moving on through the fur-trading and logging past. Admission is C$7 (U.S.$4.55) for adults, C$5.50 (U.S.$3.60) for seniors, C$4.50 (U.S.$2.95) for children, or C$10 (U.S.$7) per family. Fort George Park is located on the Fraser River end of 20th Avenue. From downtown, take Queensway Street south, then turn east on 20th Avenue.

The **Heritage River Trails** take you on a 7-mile (11km) circuit covering the historic sights of town. The loop starts at Fort George Park, goes along the Fraser River, passes through Cottonwood Island Park and along the Nechako River to the Cameron Street bridge, and leads through town and back to Fort George Park.

WHERE TO STAY

If you're looking for a bed-and-breakfast, try the **Prince George B&B Hotline** (☎ **877/562-2626** or 250/562-222; www.pgonline.com/bnb/hotline.html).

Coast Inn of the North. 770 Brunswick St., Prince George, BC, V2L 2C2. ☎ **800/ 663-1144** or 250/563-0121. Fax 250/563-1948. www.coasthotels.com. 150 units. A/C MINIBAR TV TEL. C$155 (U.S.$101) double. Extra person C$10 (U.S.$7). Family plan, corporate and off-season rates, and senior discounts available. AE, MC, V.

One of the best of British Columbia's Coast chain of hotels is right in the thick of things in downtown Prince George. The guest rooms here are very nicely furnished; ask for a corner room and you'll get a balcony. Facilities include a pub, three restaurants, saunas, whirlpools, indoor pool, dance club, gift shop, travel agency, fitness center, tanning salon, hair salon, florist, and boutique.

Connaught Motor Inn. 1550 Victoria St., Prince George, BC, V2L 2L3. ☎ **800/663-6620** or 250/562-4441. Fax 250/562-4441. 98 units. A/C TV TEL. C$65–C$75 (U.S.$42–U.S.$49) double. Extra person C$5–C$10 (U.S.$3.25–U.S.$7). Kitchen C$10 (U.S.$7) extra. Senior discounts and off-season and weekly rates offered. AE, MC, V. Pets accepted.

A rambling motor-court lodging just south of downtown, the Connaught is an easy-in, easy-out kind of place with clean, large rooms, and lots of extras. On-site facilities include a restaurant, indoor pool, hot tub, and sauna.

Econo Lodge. 1915 Third Ave., Prince George, BC, V2M 1G6. ☎ **888/566-6333** or 250/563-7106. Fax 250/561-7216. 30 units. A/C TV TEL. C$55–C$75 (U.S.$36–U.S.$49) double. Extra person C$10 (U.S.$7). Rates include continental breakfast. MC, V.

If you're looking for value, it's hard to beat the Econo Lodge. Right downtown, it's fairly new and offers clean, unfussy guest rooms. Extras include in-room coffee, free local calls, data ports, an exercise room, and a whirlpool.

Ramada Hotel (Downtown Prince George). 444 George St., Prince George, BC, V2M 3C2. ☎ **800/830-8833** or 250/563-0055. Fax 250/563-6042. 200 units. A/C TV TEL.

C$73–C$160 (U.S.$48–U.S.$104) double. Extra person C$20 (U.S.$13). Senior discounts available. AE, MC, V. Free covered parking.

The grandest of hotels in Prince George, the Ramada offers a variety of room styles—from standard to presidential—right in the center of the city. The Ramada also has the only casino in Prince George, so this is a very busy and popular place, in many ways the focal point of downtown. Besides that huge casino, amenities include a restaurant, sports bar, whirlpool, pool, sauna, meeting rooms, and airport service.

Sandman Inn. 1650 Central St., Prince George, BC, V2M 3C2. ☎ **800/SANDMAN** or 250/563-8131. Fax 250/563-8613. www.sandman.ca. E-mail: sandho@mail.fronet.com. 118 units. A/C TV TEL. C$81–C$133 (U.S.$53–U.S.$86) double. Senior discounts and 13th-night-free program available. AE, MC, V. Small pets C$5 (U.S.$3.25) per day.

The brand-new Sandman, along the Highway 97 strip west of downtown, offers large, comfortable guest rooms. It also leases a number of furnished and unfurnished apartments. Amenities include 24-hour room service from the on-site Denny's, indoor pool, sauna, and complimentary in-room coffee and tea.

A Tangled Garden B&B. 2957 Sullivan Crescent, Prince George, BC, V2N 5H6. ☎ **250/964-3265.** Fax 250/964-3248. E-mail: dpcc@mag-net.com. 2 units. TV TEL. C$60 (U.S.$39) double. Extra person C$15 (U.S.$10). No credit cards.

This comfortable, centrally located home has two guest rooms, both with private bathrooms and TV/VCRs. One unit has a kitchenette, private entrance, and queen bed, while the other offers a panoramic view and both a queen and a twin bed. Guests will enjoy using the hot tub.

WHERE TO DINE

For a quick breakfast or light meal, head to **Java Mugga Mocha,** 304 George St. (☎ **250/562-3338**), a fun hangout for espresso drinks, sandwiches, and baked goods.

Buffalo Brewing Co. Restaurant & Pub. 611 Brunswick. ☎ **250/564-7100.** Reservations not accepted. Main courses C$8–C$17 (U.S.$5–U.S.$11). AE, MC, V. Mon–Fri 11:30am–midnight. PUB.

Housed in a former church vestry, the Buffalo brewpub is a large and airy space with a broad menu of pasta, pizza, burgers, and regular entrees. The pub's signature salad is an excellent calamari dish with a spicy lime dressing. The wood-burning oven is used for specialty pizzas and rotisserie meats; the fire-roasted chicken is simultaneously succulent and crisp. Cowboy-style prime rib—slow-roasted, sliced, tossed on the grill for a moment, and served with seasoned butter—is a standout.

Cosmos. 1205 Third Ave. ☎ **250/564-9792.** Reservations recommended. Main courses C$14–C$18 (U.S.$9–U.S.$12). AE, MC, V. Daily 11:30am–2:30pm and 5–10pm. GREEK.

The locals regard this Greek restaurant highly, and with good reason: The classic eastern-Mediterranean food at Cosmos is very good. The dining room is thankfully free of the more obnoxious of Greek kitsch, though it maintains a certain masculine formality. All of your favorite Greek dishes are here; the roast lamb is especially tasty. Vegetarians should try *briam,* a casserole of zucchini, egg, and potatoes.

✪ **Da Moreno.** 1493 Third Ave. ☎ **250/564-7922.** Reservations recommended. Main courses C$13–C$24 (U.S.$8–U.S.$16); 5-course tasting menu C$40 (U.S.$26). AE, DC, MC, V. Mon–Fri 11:30am–2pm; daily 4:30–10pm. ITALIAN.

A coolly elegant space with excellent Italian cuisine, Da Moreno is easily the best place to eat in Prince George. This restaurant would pass muster in Chicago or New York, which makes its presence in Prince George's ramshackle downtown seem an anomaly— and makes it all the more special. The regular menu offers a selection of antipasti, pasta, meat, and fish dishes, but the real soul of the restaurant is the list of daily chang- ing specials based on what's fresh and in season—perhaps rack of lamb crusted with mustard and goat cheese, or halibut with braised fennel root. Service is very profes- sional, and the wine list well selected.

Kelly O'Bryans. 1375 Second Ave. ☎ **250/563-8999.** Reservations not accepted. Main courses C$7–C$33 (U.S.$4.55–U.S.$21). MC, V. Daily 11am–midnight. PUB.

It's hard to imagine a more ambitious pub menu than Kelly O'Bryans. Weighing in at 16 pages, it's more like a novel than a menu, and it comes complete with puzzles and answers to pertinent questions like what men wear under their kilts (or just ask your be-kilted waiter). This lively pub covers almost every food group, from "pachos"—an appetizer of lattice fried potatoes topped with melted cheese and green onions—to lobster. Grilled chicken, stir-fries, and pasta round out the menu.

6 The Alaska Highway

Constructed as a military freight road during World War II to link Alaska to the Lower 48, the Alaska Highway (also known as the Alcan Hwy., and Hwy. 97 in B.C.) is now a popular tourist route to the Last Frontier. Now as much a phenomenon as a road, the Alaska Highway has become something of a pilgrimage route. The vast majority of people who make the trip are recent retirees, who take their newly purchased RVs and head up north; it's a rite of passage.

Strictly speaking, the Alaska Highway starts at the Mile 1 marker in **Dawson Creek,** on the eastern edge of British Columbia, and travels north and west for 1,520 miles (2,452km) to **Fairbanks, Alaska,** passing through the Yukon along the way. As recently as 15 years ago, much of the talk of the Alaska Highway had to do with con- ditions of the road itself: where the really torn-up sections were, the freak rain and snowstorms, and the far-flung gas pumps. However, for the road's 50th anniversary in 1992, the final stretches of the road were paved.

While the days of tire-eating gravel roads and extra gas cans are largely past, there are several things to consider before casually setting out to make this journey. First, this is a very *long* road. Popular wisdom states that if you drive straight out, it takes 3 days between Fairbanks and Dawson Creek. But if you're in that much of a hurry to get to Fairbanks, then consider flying: Much of the road is very winding, slow- moving RV traffic is heavy, and considerable portions are under reconstruction every summer. If you try to keep yourself to a 3-day schedule, you're going to have a miserable time.

WHAT TO EXPECT

Summer is the only window of opportunity to repair the road, so construction crews really go to it; count on lengthy delays and some very rugged detours. Total delays of 2 to 4 hours are common in each daylong segment of the trip. Visitor centers along the way receive faxes of construction schedules and conditions. Stop and ask if you don't want to be surprised, or call ☎ **867/667-5893** for **24-hour highway information.**

While availability of gasoline isn't the problem that it once was, there are a couple of things to remember. Gas prices are high—about a third higher than in Edmonton or Vancouver. While there's gas at most of the little communities that appear on the provincial road map, most close up early in the evening, and some outfits are less than friendly. You'll find 24-hour gas stations and plenty of motel rooms in the towns of Dawson City, Fort St. John, Fort Nelson, Watson Lake, and Whitehorse.

Try to be patient when driving the Alaska Highway. In the high season, the entire route, from Edmonton to Fairbanks, is one long caravan of RVs. Many people have their car in tow, a boat on the roof, and several bicycles chained to the spare tire. Thus encumbered, they lumber up the highway at top speeds of 45 miles per hour (70kmph); loath (or unable) to pass one another, convoys of RVs stretch on forever, the slowest of the party setting the pace for all. If you're not part of the RV crowd, driving the Alaska Highway will demand a lot of patience.

DRIVING THE ALASKA HIGHWAY

The route begins (or ends) at Dawson Creek in British Columbia. Depending on where you start from, Dawson Creek is a long 365-mile (590km) drive from Edmonton or a comparatively short 252 miles (406km) from Prince George on Highway 97. Dawson Creek is a natural place to break up the journey, and there are ample tourist facilities throughout this stretch of the highway.

If you want to call ahead to ensure a room, try the **Lodge Motor Inn & Café,** 1317 Alaska Ave. (☎ **800/935-3336** or 250/782-4837), with doubles from C$56 (U.S.$36), or call the **Trail Inn,** 1748 Alaska Ave. (☎ **800/663-2749** or 250/782-8595), with doubles starting at C$69 (U.S.$45).

From Dawson Creek, the Alaska Highway soon crosses the Peace River and passes through **Fort St. John,** in the heart of British Columbia's far-north ranch country. The highway continues north, parallel to the Rockies. First the ranches thin, and then the forests thin, with pointy spruce trees replacing pine and fir. Wildlife-viewing opportunities are good: Moose are often seen from the road.

From Fort St. John to **Fort Nelson,** you'll find gas stations and cafes every 40 to 50 miles (65 to 81km), though lodging options are dubious. At Fort Nelson, the Alaska Highway turns west and heads into the Rockies; from here, too, graveled Highway 7 continues north to Fort Liard and Fort Simpson, the gateway to **Nahanni National Park.** Fort Nelson is thick with motels and gas stations; since it's hours from any other major service center, this is a good place to spend the night. Try the **New Caledonia Motel,** 167 Douglas Ave. (☎ **250/996-8051**), with doubles going for C$45 to C$64 (U.S.$29 to U.S.$42).

The road through the Rockies is mostly narrow and winding; you can depend on finding a construction crew working along this stretch. The Rockies are relatively modest mountains in this area, not as rugged or scenic as they are farther south in Jasper National Park. Once over the Continental Divide, the Alaska Highway follows tributaries of the Liard River through Stone Mountain and Muncho Lake provincial parks. Rustic lodges and cabin resorts are scattered along the road; this is also a good place to find a campsite. The lovely log ✪ **Northern Rockies Lodge,** at Muncho Lake (☎ **250/776-3481**), offers rooms in the lodge and in standalone chalets at C$69 to C$89 (U.S.$45 to U.S.$58), plus campsites for C$17 to C$27 (U.S.$11 to U.S.$18).

At the town of **Liard River,** be sure to stop and stretch your legs or go for a soak at Liard Hot Springs. The provincial parks department maintains two nice soaking pools in the deep forest; the boardwalk out into the mineral-water marsh is pleasant even if you don't have time for a dip.

As you get closer to **Watson Lake** in the Yukon, you'll notice that mom-and-pop gas stations along the road will advertise that they have cheaper gas than at Watson Lake. Believe them, and fill up: Watson Lake is an unappealing town whose extortionately priced gas is probably its only memorable feature. We don't recommend the town, but if you have to spend the night, the **Gateway Motor Inn,** on the Alaska Highway (☎ 867/536-7744), is a just-fine place.

The long road between Watson Lake and **Whitehorse** travels through rolling hills and forest to Teslin and Atlin lakes, where the landscape becomes more mountainous and the gray clouds of the Gulf of Alaska's weather systems hang menacingly on the horizon. Whitehorse is the largest town along the route of the Alaska Highway, and unless you're in a great hurry, plan to spend at least a day here. You'll want to wash the dust off the car and eat a decent meal before another day of driving.

Whitehorse is a relatively large commercial center, where you should have no trouble finding decent accommodations. If you want to call ahead, the **Westmark Whitehorse,** 201 Wood St. (☎ **800/544-0970** or 867/668-4700), is one of the city's best lodgings, with double rooms at C$125 (U.S.$81).

Hope for good weather as you leave Whitehorse, since the trip past **Kluane National Park** is one the most beautiful parts of the entire Alaska Highway route. The two highest peaks of Canada straddle the horizon, while glaciers push down mountain valleys. The road edges by lovely Kluane Lake before passing Beaver Creek and crossing over into Alaska. From the border crossing to Fairbanks, it's another 298 miles (481km).

A number of guidebooks deal exhaustively with the Alaska Highway drive; particularly good is the mile-by-mile classic, the annual *Alaska Milepost.*

The Cariboo Country & the Thompson River Valley

10

South of Prince George along Highway 97 and beyond into British Columbia's interior, the Canadian Wild West hasn't changed much in the past century. This is Cariboo Country, a vast landscape that changes from alpine meadows and thick forests to rolling prairies and arid, granite-walled canyons before it encounters the gigantic glacial peaks of the Coast Mountains. The Cariboo's history is synonymous with the word *gold.*

From Vancouver, the Sea to Sky Highway (Hwy. 99) passes through Whistler and the Cayoosh Valley, eventually descending into the town of Lillooet, which was Mile 0 of the Old Cariboo Highway during the gold-rush days of the 1860s. Prospectors and settlers made their way north up what's now called the Cariboo Gold Rush Trail (Hwys. 99 and 97).

Highway 97 follows the gold-rush trail through 70 Mile House, 100 Mile House, 108 Mile House, and 150 Mile House. The towns were named after the mile-marking roadhouses patronized by prospectors and settlers headed north to the goldfields.

The gold-rich town of Barkerville sprang up in the 1860s after a British prospector named Billy Barker struck it rich on Williams Creek. Completely restored by the parks service, the town brings the rough gold-rush days to life. The streets are only 18 feet (5.5m) wide, thanks to a drunken surveyor. And the town burned to the ground in 1868, when a miner knocked over an oil lamp while in hot pursuit of a dance-hall girl. It was rebuilt almost overnight, but abandoned after World War II. Nowadays, you can try your hand at panning for the shiny gold flakes and nuggets that still lie deep within Williams Creek.

Gold isn't the only thing that attracts thousands of visitors to this area year-round. Cross-country skiers and snowmobilers take to the creek-side paths in winter, while canoeists head a few miles north of Barkerville to a 72-mile (120km) circular route called Bowron Lakes.

From Williams Lake, back-roads enthusiasts can also drive Highway 20 west to the Pacific coastal community of Bella Coola, which in the early days of European exploration was one of the most important First Nations communities on the Pacific Northwest coast. From Bella Coola, you can catch the Discovery Coast ferry to Port Hardy on the northern tip of Vancouver Island (see chapter 7).

Due east, on the opposite side of Cariboo Country, the Thompson River valley's arid and hilly lowlands attract fishers and boaters to the shores of the lower Thompson River and the Shuswap Lakes. Heading

The Cariboo Country & the Thompson River Valley

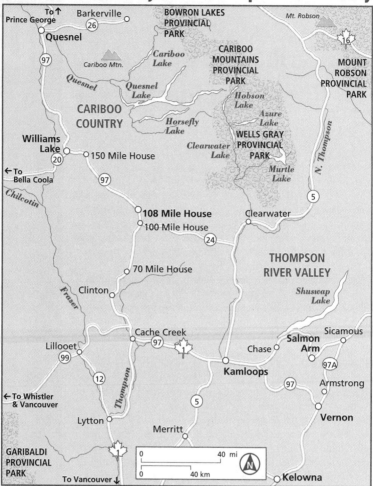

north from this dry terrain, you'll reach a majestic 3,211,000-acre forested mountain wilderness formed by glaciers and volcanoes—Wells Gray Provincial Park.

1 Cariboo Country Essentials

GETTING THERE

Whether you travel by train or by car, the trip from Whistler to Cariboo Country is a visually exhilarating experience.

BY CAR The shortest and most scenic route to the Cariboo from Vancouver is along Highway 99 past Whistler to Lillooet, continuing to Highway 97 and turning north to 100 Mile House and points north. From Vancouver to Quesnel, it's 360 miles (600km). If you want to bypass the dramatic but slow Highway 99 and head straight up to the central Cariboo district, you can also take the Highway 1 expressway east from Vancouver, then jump onto Highway 97 at Merritt.

BY TRAIN   BC Rail's (☎ **604/984-5246**) *Cariboo Prospector* departs North Vancouver three times a week. The first part of the route, from Vancouver to Lillooet, is extraordinarily scenic. The train continues north to 100 Mile House, Williams Lake, and Quesnel, and terminates in Prince George. Reserve at least 48 hours in advance.

BY BUS   Greyhound buses (☎ **800/661-8747**) travel from Vancouver through the Cariboo to Prince George via Highway 1 and Highway 97, passing through 100 Mile House, Williams Lake, and Quesnel. Note that this route does not pass through Lillooet, which has no bus service.

BY PLANE   Air BC (☎ **800/776-3000** in the U.S., 800/663-3721 in B.C., or 250/360-9074) offers three-times-daily service between Quesnel and Vancouver. It also offers three daily flights between Williams Lake and Vancouver.

VISITOR INFORMATION

Contact the **Cariboo Chilcotin Coast Tourist Association,** 266 Oliver St., Williams Lake, BC, V2G 1M1 (☎ **800/663-5885** or 250/392-2226; www.cariboocountry. org; e-mail: cta@cariboocountry.org).

2 Lillooet

84 miles (135km) NE of Whistler

There's nothing subtle about the physical setting of Lillooet (pop. 2,058). To the west, the soaring glaciated peaks of the Coast Mountains are *right there,* filling up half the sky. To the east rise the steep desert walls of the Fountain Range, stained a rusty red and ochre. And cleaving the two mountain ranges is the massive and roaring **Fraser River.** From the Coast Range peaks immediately behind Lillooet to the surging river, it's a drop of nearly 9,000 feet (2,743m), making an incredibly dramatic backdrop.

The entire 1½-hour drive up Highway 99 from Whistler is extravagantly scenic, and it's fair to say that getting to Lillooet is at least as exciting as actually being there. From Whistler, drive north on Highway 99 through Pemberton and Mount Currie. About 4 miles (6.6km) later, you begin your ascent up a number of switchbacks into the spectacular Cayoosh Valley. For 60 miles (100km), this portion of Highway 99 winds through rolling alpine meadows, with the icy waters of the valley's creeks racing alongside. The scenery then shifts to stark granite walls and cavernous canyons that plunge hundreds of feet below the roadway. Suddenly, you'll find yourself in a mountainous antelope-brush desert in the rain shadow of the looming Coast Mountains. Lillooet is nestled in this valley, where the muddy Fraser River is fed by the crystal-clear waters of the Cayoosh Valley creeks.

In town, the **Lillooet Pioneer Museum,** 790 Main St. (☎ **250/256-4308**), is housed in a former Anglican church. Built in the 1960s, it's a replica of the original structure, which was carried in pieces by miners headed up the gold-rush trail in 1860. The museum houses an eclectic collection, including Indian artifacts, farming tools, and mining implements. Hours are daily from 9am to 5pm; admission is by donation.

Lillooet was Mile 0 of the 1860s **Cariboo Gold Rush Trail.** In 1858, a trail was established from the Fraser Valley goldfields in the south to the town of Lillooet. At the big bend on Main Street, a cairn marks "Mile 0" of the original Cariboo Wagon Road, cut in 1861 as an access route to the gold-rich creeks of Barkerville. The towns along this road (now Hwy. 97) are named after the roadhouses along the way: 70 Mile House, 100 Mile House, 108 Mile House, and 150 Mile House. There are still signs of **gold fever** in and around Lillooet. Visitors try their luck, panning a few shovelfuls along the river's edge. The **Chinese Rock Piles** just outside town were formed by early Chinese prospectors, who patiently gathered minute grains of gold from the remains of spent claims abandoned by miners looking for fist-sized nuggets.

The nearby **ghost towns** of Bradian and Brexton, in the Bridge River valley, are accessible by car. The tiny settlements of **Bralorne** and **Gold Bridge** were established when the Pioneer-Bralorne mine was built in the 1930s. The mine produced over C$145 million in gold and employed 5,000 miners before it closed in 1970. You can reach these inhabited towns on the unpaved Hurley River Road above Lillooet.

For information on the region, contact the **Lillooet Visitor Info Centre,** 790 Main St. (Box 441), Lillooet, BC, V0K 1V0 (☎ **250/256-4308**). Situated inside the Lillooet Pioneer Museum, it's open May 24 to October 31, daily from 10am to 6pm.

If you happen to be visiting during the second week in June, catch the parade, exhibits, live performances, and food at **Only in Lillooet Days** (☎ **250/256-7972**).

OUTDOOR PURSUITS

FISHING   Anglers hit the surrounding lakes, rivers, and creeks for rainbow and lake trout at places like Tyaughton Lake, Hat Creek, and Turquoise Lake.

GOLF   The **Sheep Pasture Golf Course,** just outside Lillooet (☎ **250/256-4484**), is a nine-hole course with a pro shop, clubhouse, driving range, and sheep. That's right, loads of sheep. The course is located on a working sheep ranch that was established in 1858. The views and the warm desert climate make this course a welcome diversion. Tee times are not required.

SKIING   Miles of cross-country ski trails weave around near Gold Bridge and Bralorne above Lillooet; try the trail that encircles Tyaughton Lake.

WHERE TO STAY & DINE

Don't expect anything fancy in Lillooet. You can catch some local color at the **Hotel Victoria Dining Room,** 667 Main St. (☎ **250/256-4112**), or dine on Greek fare at **Dina's Place Restaurant,** 690 Main St. (☎ **250/256-4264**).

If you want to camp, the 26 sites at **Marble Canyon Provincial Park,** Highway 99, between Lillooet and Highway 97 (☎ **250/851-3000**), are open from April through November, offering excellent canoeing, fishing, kayaking, and swimming, but minimum facilities (pit toilets, fire pits, and pumped well water). Campsites are $12 (U.S.$8) per night. See also the campsites at Tyax Mountain Lake Resort, below.

Tyax Mountain Lake Resort. Tyaughton Lake Rd., Gold Bridge, BC, V0K 1P0. ☎ **250/238-2221.** Fax 250/238-2528. www.tyax.bc.ca. E-mail: fun@tyax.bc.ca. 29 lodge rms, 5 chalets, 12 campsites. TEL. C$98–C$129 (U.S.$64–U.S.$84) double lodge rm; C$220–C$398 (U.S.$143–U.S.$259) chalet; C$24 (U.S.$16) per 2-person campsite. AE, MC, V. Drive 2 hr. (57 miles/92km) from Lillooet up the unpaved Tyaughton Lake Rd. Follow signs to the resort.

Set high above the town of Lillooet, Tyaughton Lake is the perfect alpine setting for a romantic vacation. On its shores stands this huge log lodge, which offers guests luxurious accommodations and a host of activities, ranging from heli-fishing and heli-skiing trips to barbecues on the lake. Guest rooms are comfortably furnished with queen-size beds. The resort restaurant serves Pacific Northwest cuisine. Also on the premises are a lounge, sauna, fitness center, whirlpool, and tennis court. Fly-out fishing charters, floatplane sightseeing, canoe rentals, horseback riding, cross-country ski trails, heli-skiing, heli-fishing, and mountain-bike rentals are available.

Rafting the Fraser & Thompson Rivers: A Side Trip to the Fraser River Canyon

South from Lillooet, Highway 12 edges along the Fraser River valley's precipitous canyon walls. The vistas are astonishing as the raging river trenches its way beneath the horizon-filling peaks of the Coast Range. While the road is perfectly safe, there are frequent cliff-edge areas that are prone to landslides. In spring, ask in Lillooet about road conditions.

Forty-two miles (67km) from Lillooet, Highway 12 joins Highway 1 at **Lytton,** a small community at the confluence of the Thompson and Fraser rivers. In pre-Contact times, this was one of the most densely populated areas in Native America, as these two mighty rivers each supported vast runs of wild salmon.

Nowadays, Lytton is known as a white-water rafting capital. **Hyak Wilderness Adventures** (☎ 800/663-7238) offers trips on the Thompson River. A day trip drops through 19 named rapids (C$99/U.S.$64); a weekend trip travels 52 miles (83km) on the Thompson and includes a night of camping on an island, meals, gear, and ground transport (C$229/U.S.$149).

Kumsheen Raft Adventures (☎ 800/663-6667; www.kumsheen.com) offers a number of different trips, ranging from the 3-hour "Whitewater Quickie" (C$82/U.S.$53) to full days on the Thompson (C$108/U.S.$70) to 2-day rafting adventures on both the Fraser and Thompson rivers. The 2-day packages typically include a night of camping, meals, and ground transport, with costs ranging from C$160 to C$268 (U.S.$104 to U.S.$174) for adults.

3 En Route to 100 Mile House

From Lillooet, Highway 99 heads north along the Fraser River Canyon, affording many more dramatic vistas before turning east to its junction with Highway 97. Immediately before the junction is **Hat Creek Ranch** (☎ 800/782-0922 or 250/457-9722), a provincial heritage site. Hat Creek House was built in 1861 and served as a stagecoach inn for miners during the gold rush. The inn and ranch buildings have all been restored, now serving as an open-air museum of frontier life. The grounds have more than 20 period buildings, including a blacksmith shop, 1894 barn, and stable. There's also a good exhibit on the culture of the region's First Nations Shuswap tribe. In summer, concessionaires operate horse-drawn wagon and horseback rides. You can stroll the grounds year-round; however, regular visitor services and guided tours are offered only from mid-May to Labour Day, daily from 10am to 6pm.

Nineteen miles (30km) north on Highway 97 is **Clinton,** the self-avowed "guest-ranch capital of British Columbia." This is certainly handsome ranch country, with broad cattle- and horse-filled valleys rolling between dry mountain walls.

The **Big Bar Guest Ranch** (☎ and fax **250/459-2333;** www.bigbarranch.com) is just north of Clinton off Highway 97. The centerpiece of the property is the **Harrison House,** a hand-hewn log home built by pioneers in the 1800s. Besides taking horseback-riding and pack trips year-round, you can canoe, fish, hike, pan for gold, and cross-country ski on the beautiful grounds. Lodge rooms go for C$250 (U.S.$163), including meals; self-contained log cabins have kitchens, bathrooms, and fireplaces (C$144/U.S.$94). There are six campsites for C$30 (U.S.$20), as well as a number of teepees that sleep up to four (C$79/U.S.$51 per person).

Echo Valley Ranch Resort (☎ 800/253-8831 or 250/459-2386; www.evranch.
com; e-mail: evranch@uniserve.com) is a more upscale ranch, complete with spa.
Guests stay in lodge rooms or cabins. Facilities include a pool, sauna, hot tub, and spa
with beauty treatments and massage. The ranch raises its own beef, chicken, and
turkey, and has an organic garden that provides much of the produce used by
the excellent restaurant. Activities include riding, fishing, hiking, and rafting, plus
unusual options like watching falcons being trained. The base rate of C$205
(U.S.$133) includes meals and access to all facilities; horseback riding and guided
activities cost extra. In high season, there's a 3-night minimum stay.

4 100 Mile House & the South Cariboo District

100 Mile House: 109 miles (174km) N of Lillooet, 200 miles (320km) S of Prince George

Named for the roadhouse inn that marked the hundredth mile north of Lillooet in the
days of the Cariboo gold rush, 100 Mile House (pop. 1,978) is an attractive ranching
community at the heart of a vast recreational paradise. There are thousands of lakes in
the valleys that ring the town, making canoeing, fishing, and boating very popular
activities. In winter, the gently rolling landscape, combined with heavy snowfalls,
make 100 Mile House a major cross-country ski destination.

The old commercial center of 100 Mile House is along **Birch Avenue,** 1 block east
of Highway 97. Just east of downtown is pleasant **Centennial Park,** which flanks
Bridge Creek as it passes through the town. Eight miles (13km) north of 100 Mile
House is **108 Mile House,** another frontier-era community now famed for its golf
course and **108 Mile House Heritage Site** (☎ 250/791-5288). This collection of
ranch buildings includes an enormous log barn built to stable 200 Clydesdales, the
horsepower that drove the stagecoaches.

For information on this region, contact the **South Cariboo Visitor Info Centre,**
422 Hwy. 97 S., Box 2312, 100 Mile House, BC, V0K 2E0 (☎ **250/395-5353;** fax
250/395-4085; www2.bcinternet.net/~100mile/sccofc).

FISHING & WATER SPORTS

100 Mile House is a pleasant enough little town, but it's the outdoor recreation in the
surrounding South Cariboo Lakes District that brings most people here. There are
dozens of lakes, nearly all with rustic fishing resorts as well as provincial parks offering campgrounds and public boat launches. Be sure to pick up the *Cariboo-Chilcotin
Fishing Guide* at the visitor center. For tackle, licenses, and advice, head to **Donex
Pharmacy,** 145 Birch St., 100 Mile House (☎ **250/395-4004**).

One lake-filled area lies southeast of 100 Mile House along Highway 24, which
connects Highway 97 with Highway 5 at Little Fort, on the Thompson River. This
very scenic drive climbs up along a high plateau between the watersheds of the Fraser
and Thompson rivers. The road leads to so many excellent fishing lakes that it's often
referred to as the "Fishing Highway."

On Sheridan Lake, the **Loon Bay Resort,** 25 miles (40km) southeast of 100 Mile
House (☎ **250/593-4431**), rents tackle, canoes, and motorboats; sells licenses; and
maintains small log cabins (from C$65/U.S.$42) and campsites.

At Bridge Lake, 40 miles (64km) east of 100 Mile House, the **Bridge Lake Provincial Park** offers campsites as well as fishing access to the lake. Also on the lake, the
Nature Hills Resort (☎ **250/593-4659**) has guided fishing trips plus boat and tackle
rentals. Cabins are C$60 to C$70 (U.S.$39 to U.S.$46).

Perhaps the most beautiful of all these lakes is **Lac des Roches,** 55 miles (88km)
east of 100 Mile House; the place to go here is the handsome **Lac Des Roches Resort**

(☎ 250/593-4141). Boat rentals, campsites (C$16/U.S.$10), and lakeside cabins (from C$69/U.S.$45) are among the offerings at this full-service resort.

Northeast of 100 Mile House is another lake-filled valley. **Canim Lake** is the most developed and largest of these lakes, with good swimming beaches. The venerable **Ponderosa Resort** (☎ 250/397-2243) offers boat rentals, guided fishing trips, and horseback riding. Cabins are C$85 to C$130 (U.S.$55 to U.S.$85), while campsites go for C$18 to C$22 (U.S.$12 to U.S.$14). At **Canim Beach Provincial Park,** 28 miles (45km) from 100 Mile House, lakeside campsites are C$12 (U.S.$8).

If you're looking for a wilderness canoeing experience, **Moose Valley Provincial Park** preserves a series of small glacial lakes that are linked by short portage trails. The most popular route begins at Marks Lake and links with 11 other lakes, making for a leisurely 2-day loop paddle. For more information on the park, contact **BC Parks,** Cariboo District (☎ 250/398-4414).

OTHER OUTDOOR PURSUITS

CROSS-COUNTRY SKIING   When the snow's on the ground, things heat up in 100 Mile House. Every February, the town hosts the **Cariboo Marathon,** a 32-mile (50km) race that draws more than 1,000 contestants. There's an extensive public trail system with 125 miles (200km) of groomed trails in the area, with some parts lit at night. Many resorts and guest ranches also have groomed trails. For ski rentals and advice, contact **100 Mile Sport Shop,** 409 Hwy. 97 (☎ 250/395-9812).

GOLF   The region's finest course is undoubtedly at **108 Ranch Resort,** in 108 Mile House (☎ 800/667-5233 or 250/791-5211). The 18-hole championship course has 6,800 yards of undulating, tree-lined fairways and fast putting greens. The resort also offers practice greens, a driving range, a pro shop, and lessons.

WHERE TO STAY & DINE

Best Western 108 Resort. 4618 Telqua Dr., Box 2, 108 Mile Ranch, BC, V0K 2Z0. ☎ **800/ 667-5233** or 250/791-5211. Fax 250/791-6537. www.108resort.com. E-mail: 108rst@ bcinternet.net. 62 units and 11 campsites. A/C TV TEL. C$125–C$155 (U.S.$81–U.S.$101) double. Extra person C$10 (U.S.$7). Campsites C$15 (U.S.$10) per vehicle with a C$5 (U.S.$3.25) charge for electricity. Off-season rates and packages available. AE, MC, V.

This upscale hotel and resort 8 miles (13km) north of 100 Mile House centers on its fantastic golf course, although even if you're not a duffer, there's a lot to like here. Guest rooms are large and beautifully furnished, all with balconies that overlook either the golf course or a small lake. Facilities include a restaurant serving Northwest cuisine, lounge, ski and bike rentals, stables, pool, and gift shop. Golf, cross-country skiing, and horseback-riding packages are available.

Hills Health & Guest Ranch. Hwy. 97, 108 Mile Ranch, P.O. Box 26, BC, V0K 2Z0 ☎ **250/ 791-5225.** Fax 250/791-6384. www.grt-net.com/thehills. E-mail: thehills@bcinternet.net. 46 units. Lodge C$100–C$120 (U.S.$65–U.S.$78) double, chalet C$129–C$149 (U.S.$84– U.S.$97) double. All-inclusive packages available. AE, DISC, MC, V.

This full-service spa offers guests a full complement of beauty and health treatments as well as outdoor activities such as horseback riding, hayrides, guided hiking trips, and cross-country skiing on more than 100 miles (167km) of private trails. The large guest rooms feature ranch-style natural pine decor. Also available are self-contained chalet accommodations with kitchens and full bathrooms; each sleeps up to six people. There are 10 campsites on this amazing property as well, going for C$15 (U.S.$10).

The restaurant serves guests and the public a unique blend of cowboy favorites and spa cuisine, such as Italian fish stew, made with fresh cod fillets. Reservations are recommended. The spa offers exercise classes, wellness workshops, hydrotherapy pools, massage, wraps, facials, reflexology, and body packs. There's also a sauna, indoor pool, hot tub, and fully equipped fitness facility.

100 Mile Lodge B&B. 150 Hwy. 97, 100 Mile House, BC, V0K 2E0. ☎ **888/667-7451** or 250/395-9099. www.bbcanada.com/2732.html. E-mail: lodgebnb@bcinternet.net. 4 units, none with private bathroom. C$70 (U.S.$46) double. MC, V.

Spend your visit in a monument to the history of 100 Mile House. The 100 Mile Lodge is a historic inn built in 1930 to replace the original inn that gave the town its name. The large, plank-sided inn is in a quiet, shady location on Little Bridge Creek, but within easy walking distance of both downtown and the Highway 97 strip. The guest rooms contain comfortable period furnishings; they share two bathrooms. Guests enjoy a cozy fireside sitting area and, in the morning, a full country-style breakfast.

Red Coach Inn. 170 Hwy. 97 N., Box 760, 100 Mile House, BC, V0K 2E0. ☎ **800/663-8422** or 250/395-2266. Fax 250/395-2446. 49 units. A/C TV TEL. C$79–C$92 (U.S.$51–U.S.$60) double. Extra person C$6 (U.S.$3.90). Senior and corporate discounts available. AE, MC, V.

This large and handsome motel is all you need for a good night's stay in 100 Mile House. The rooms are clean and nicely furnished, and all the facilities are shipshape. Facilities include a restaurant, lounge, pool, whirlpool, hot tub, and sauna.

5 Williams Lake

56 miles (90km) N of 100 Mile House, 337 miles (539km) N of Vancouver

Unabashedly a ranch town, Williams Lake (pop. 11,398) is known across the West for its large, hell's-a-poppin' rodeo, the **Williams Lake Stampede,** held the first weekend of July. At the center of a vast cattle-ranching area, Williams Lake is also the gateway to the Chilcotin, the coastal mountainous area to the west.

As the trade center for a large agricultural area, the little lakeside town in a steep-sided canyon bustles with activity. The downtown area is west of the Highway 97 strip, centered on Oliver Street. Amid the boot shops and western-clothing stores are a couple of interesting stops. The **Cariboo Friendship Society Native Arts and Crafts Shop,** 99 S. Third Ave. (☎ 250/398-6831), sells the work of local native artists; the building that houses the shop was built to resemble a pit-house dwelling used by the Shuswap Indians. The town's old train depot has been in part converted into the **Station House Gallery,** at the foot of Oliver Street right above the lake (☎ 250/392-6113). The Station House is both an exhibition space for the work of regional artists as well as a sales gallery with local arts and crafts.

The **Museum of the Cariboo Chilcotin,** 113 N. Fourth Ave. (☎ 250/392-7404), contains artifacts from the area's ranching history, an exhibit on the ranching women of the Cariboo Chilcotin, native arrowheads, and a replica blacksmith shop. The museum is open June 1 to August 31, Monday through Saturday from 10am to 4pm; the rest of the year, Tuesday through Saturday during the same hours.

For information, contact the **Williams Lake Visitor Centre,** 1148 Broadway S., Williams Lake, BC, V2G 1A2 (☎ 250/392-5025; e-mail: wldc@stardate.bc.ca).

OUTDOOR PURSUITS

Red Shreds Bike and Board Shop, 95 S. First Ave. (☎ 250/398-7873), offers a bounty of information on local hiking, mountain biking, and kayaking; bicycle and kayak rentals; and a number of specialty trail maps for the area.

The Williams Lake Stampede

The Williams Lake Stampede is one of Canada's top rodeos, and is the only rodeo on the Canadian Professional Rodeo Association circuit held in British Columbia. Begun in the 1920s as an amusement for area cowboys, the Stampede has grown into a 4-day festival of events. Rodeo cowboys from across Canada and the western United States gather here to compete for prizes in excess of C$80,000 (U.S.$52,000).

What makes the Stampede such a popular event is that in addition to the usual rodeo events—barrel racing, bareback and saddle bronco riding, calf roping, bull riding, and so on—there are also a number of unusual races and competitions that provide lots of laughs and action. The Ranch Challenge Competition pits real working cowboys from area ranches in a pouch-passing pony express race, a hilarious wild cow–milking contest, and a cattle-penning contest. There's also chariot races with two-horse teams and a chuck-wagon race with four-horse teams. In a variation on British sheepdog trails, the Top Dog Competition pits a cowboy and his ranch dog against three unruly cows. The dog puts the cows through a course of barrels, then into a pen; the fastest dog wins.

Other Old West events, like barn dances, a parade, midway rides, and grandstand entertainment, add to the festival spirit. Because the Stampede is very popular, accommodations go fast in July—make plans well ahead. For more information, contact the **Williams Lake Stampede,** P.O. Box 4076, Williams Lake, BC, V2G 2V2 (☎ **250/392-6585;** www.imagehouse.com/rodeo). Reserved seats are C$10 (U.S.$7) for adults, C$7 (U.S.$4.55) for children and seniors. For tickets, call ☎ **800/717-6336.**

FISHING   There are more than 8,000 lakes in the area, and as many streams and rivers. Stop by **Harry's Sporting Supply,** 615 Oliver St. (☎ **250/398-5959**), to find out where the fish are biting.

✪ **WHITE-WATER RAFTING**   The Chilko-Chilcotin-Fraser river system that runs from the Coast Mountains east is a major white-water rafting destination, though not for the faint of heart. The Fraser is an enormous river that runs with the fury of a steep mountain stream. These are not rivers for the unguided novice. Inquire at **Red Shreds** (see above) for information on area rivers and kayak rentals. If the thrills and spills sound like good fun, contact **Chilko River Expeditions** (☎ **800/967-7238** or 250/398-6711; fax 250/398-8269; www.chilkoriverexpeditions.com; e-mail: rapids@chilkoriverexpeditions.com), which offers a variety of trips on the three rivers, including a 1-day trip on the Chilcotin for C$99 (U.S.$64), a 2-day screamer down the Chilko River's Lava Canyon for C$299 (U.S.$194), and a 6-day trip that runs all the way from Lava Canyon down to the Fraser for C$1,595 (U.S.$1,037).

WHERE TO STAY & DINE

Caesar Inn. 55 Sixth Ave. S., Williams Lake, BC, V2J 1K8. ☎ **800/663-6893** or 250/392-7747. Fax 250/392-4852. 100 units. A/C TV TEL. C$75 (U.S.$49) double. Kitchen C$10 (U.S.$7) extra. Extra person C$5 (U.S.$3.25). Monthly rates available. AE, MC, V. Small pets accepted.

If you want a clean, no-fuss place to stay, the Caesar Inn is a good choice. It's right downtown, service is friendly, and the restaurant is one of the best in town. The guest rooms are large and moderately priced; some kitchens units are available. Facilities include a sauna and laundry.

✪ **Georgio's** is a very good Greek/Canadian restaurant, far better than the dingy cafes usually found in motels. As much as possible, meats and produce are sourced locally from area ranchers and farmers, and everything is made from scratch. The main focus is on steaks; the house-specialty garlic tenderloin goes for C$16 (U.S.$10). Other choices include Bella Coola salmon with honey lime glaze.

Fraser Inn. 285 Donald Rd., Williams Lake, BC, V2G 4K4. ☎ **888/452-6789** or 250/ 398-7055. Fax 250/398-8269. www.Fraserinn.com. E-mail: book@Fraserinn.com. 75 units. A/C MINIBAR TV TEL. C$69–C$92 (U.S.$45–U.S.$60) double. Kitchen C$10 (U.S.$7) extra. Extra person C$7–C$10 (U.S.$4.55–U.S.$7). AE, MC, V. Pets accepted.

The Fraser Inn overlooks Williams Lake from its hillside perch north of town along Highway 97. Large and modern, the Fraser offers a level of facilities not usually found in small ranch towns, plus a good steak-house restaurant. Amenities include room service, a universal gym, a whirlpool, and a sauna.

The **Great Cariboo Steak Company** is the town's leading place for steaks and prime rib (C$16/U.S.$10), also offering grilled chicken, soups, a salad bar, and a selection of pasta dishes. It's open for three meals daily.

Sandman Inn. 664 Oliver St., Williams Lake, BC, V2G 1M6. ☎ **800/SANDMAN** or 250/ 392-6557. Fax 250/392-6242. www.sandman.ca. E-mail: sandho@mail.fronet.com. 59 units. A/C TV TEL. C$81–C$133 (U.S.$53–U.S.$86) double. Senior discounts offered. AE, MC, V. Small pets C$5 (U.S.$3.25) per day.

Conveniently located 2 blocks from downtown, the Sandman has a newly constructed wing of large suite-style rooms with kitchenettes, plus an older wing with regular motel units. You'll find the place clean, friendly, and shipshape. Amenities include a 24-hour Denny's restaurant, indoor pool, sauna, in-room coffee, and laundry.

6 West on Highway 20 to Bella Coola

285 miles (456km) W of Williams Lake

Highway 20 cuts through a rugged land of lakes and towering mountains on its way to Bella Coola, a native village on a Pacific inlet. This scenic journey takes the adventurous driver from Williams Lake and the desert canyons of the Fraser River to glaciated peaks and finally to the shores of a narrow fjord. It's an amazingly scenic trip, but be ready for lots of gravel roadbeds and very steep grades. "The Hill" is the somewhat understated name given to a 20-mile (32km) section of the route as it drops from Heckman Pass to sea level. There aren't a lot of facilities along the route, so start out with a full tank of gas and some food to snack on, and give the tires a quick kick.

After climbing up out of the Fraser Canyon, Highway 20 winds along the **Chilcotin Plateau,** miles and miles of spacious grasslands that are home to some of the largest ranches in North America. Blink-and-you'll-miss-it hamlets like Riske Creek, Hanceville (with its fascinating general store), and Alexis Creek are about the only signs of human habitation you'll see in the first couple hours of the drive.

At **Hanceville,** the route drops onto the Chilcotin River, famed worldwide for its white-water rafting and kayaking. The **Chilcotin Hotel,** in Alexis Creek (☎ **250/ 394-4214**), is a popular place to stop for a home-style meal or perhaps a drink in the pub; a double here is C$51 (U.S.$33). A popular place to camp right on the river is **Bull Canyon Provincial Parks,** with 20 sites at C$12 (U.S.$8). The park is 6 miles (10km) west of Alexis Creek, 79 miles (126km) west of Williams Lake.

Just past Redstone, Highway 20 leaves the Chilcotin River and climbs up the Chilanko River valley as the Coast Mountains begin to fill the western horizon. **Puntzi Lake,** noted for its kokanee salmon, is also home to a number of old-time fishing resorts. The **Poplar Grove Resort** (☎ 800/578-6804 or 250/481-1186) has boat and tackle rentals, as well as lakefront campsites for C$12 to C$15 (U.S.$8–U.S.$10) and cabins from C$35 to C$80 (U.S.$23–U.S.$52).

As Highway 20 presses closer to the Coast Mountains, the landscape is increasingly dotted with lakes and marshes. At the wee community of **Tatla Lake,** the pavement ends and the gravel begins. **Anahim Lake**, 205 miles (328km) west of Williams Lake and the largest settlement on the Chilcotin Plateau (pop. 522), is noted for its fishing and outdoor recreation. The long-established **Escott Resort** (☎ 888/380-8802 or 250/742-3233) has cabins starting at C$60 (U.S.$39). The general store in Anahim Lake is over a century old, and its coffeepot is always on. The enormous glaciated peak that dominates the southern skyline is **Mount Waddington,** which at 13,175 feet (4,016m) is the highest point in the Coast Mountains.

As you begin the final ascent up to 4,900-foot-high (1,494m) **Heckman Pass,** note the mountains that crowd the western horizon. Called the **Rainbow Range,** these 8,000-foot-plus (2,400m+) peaks are brilliantly colored by purple, red, and yellow mineralization. Nineteen miles (30km) from Anahim Lake, Highway 20 crests Heckman Pass, and then begins **"The Hill."**

Bella Coola residents had long dreamed of a road connection to the rest of the province, and a succession of provincial governments promised to build a road from the Chilcotin Plateau down to the Pacific. However, when years went by and nothing happened—civil engineers doubted that a safe road could be made down the steep western face of the Coast Mountains—the locals took matters in their own hands. In summer 1953, two men in bulldozers set out, one from Heckman Pass, the other from the end of the road at the base of the Coast Mountains. In just 3 months, the two bulldozers kissed blades at the middle of the mountain, and Highway 20 was born. The route is often referred to as the "The Freedom Road," since Bella Coolans were now free to reach the outside world by vehicle.

It may be "The Freedom Road," but that doesn't mean that it's a superhighway. You'll feel your heart in your mouth on a number of occasions as you corkscrew your way down the road. The most notorious portion of the route is 6 miles (10km) of switchbacks, with gradients up to 18%, that drop 4,600 feet (1,402m). In summer, the dust—for this portion of the road is gravel—will only add to your discomfort.

This portion of Highway 20 passes through **Tweedsmuir Provincial Park,** British Columbia's second-largest park at 2.45 million acres. This vast wilderness park of soaring mountains, interlocking lakes, and abundant wildlife is accessible by long-distance hiking trails, floatplane, and canoe. In fact, the Eutsuk Lake–Whitesail Lake circuit in the northern section of the park provides more than 200 miles (320km) of canoeing waters with just one portage. For information, contact **BC Parks,** 281 First Ave. N., Williams Lake, BC, V2G 1Y7 (☎ 250/398-4414).

The town at the end of the road, **Bella Coola** (pop. 992) is a disorganized little burg in a green glacier-carved valley. Ancestral home to the Bella Coola tribe, Bella Coola once held a Hudson's Bay Company trading fort, then became a fishing center for Norwegian settlers. There's not a lot to do here now. The waterfront is a busy place in summer, with fishing and pleasure boats coming and going.

Besides the lure of the end of the road, the main reason to drive to Bella Coola is to catch the **BC Ferries Discovery Coast** service. This summer-only car-and-passenger ferry connects Bella Coola with other even more isolated coastal communities along the rugged Pacific coastline, like Ocean Falls, Bella Bella, Shearwater, Klemtu, and Rivers Inlet. The ferry terminates at Port Hardy on the northern end of Vancouver Island, making this an increasingly popular loop trip. From late May to mid-September, there are runs to Port Hardy on Monday, Wednesday, and Friday. The journey lasts 12 to 13¹/₂ hours. In high season, fares between Bella Coola and Port Hardy are C$110 (U.S.$72) per adult, C$214 (U.S.$139) for a car.

WHERE TO STAY & DINE

There are basic camping sites (pump your own water, pit toilets) at **Bailey Bridge Campsite** (☎ 250/982-2342). See also the Bella Coola Motel, below.

Bella Coola Motel. Clayton St., Box 188, Bella Coola, BC, V0T 1C0. ☎ **250/799-5323.** Fax 250/799-5323. 10 units. TV TEL. C$65–C$75 (U.S.$42–U.S.$49) double. Extra person C$10 (U.S.$7). AE, MC, V.

Located right downtown, this motel occupies the site of the old Hudson's Bay Company trading post on the waterfront. All of the guest rooms are large and have full kitchens. There are also tent camping sites here. Shuttle service and scooter, bicycle, and canoe rentals are available.

Cedar Inn. MacKenzie St., Box 183, Bella Coola, BC, V0T 1C0. ☎ **888/799-5316** or 250/799-5316. Fax 250/799-5610. 20 units. TV TEL. C$66–C$95 (U.S.$43–U.S.$62) double. Extra person C$10–C$15 (U.S.$7–U.S.$10). AE, MC, V.

Newly renovated, the Cedar Inn (also called the Bella Coola Valley Inn) is close to the ferry terminal. The rooms are standard motel-style units with queen beds, in-room coffee, and fridges. Amenities include courtesy airport and ferry shuttle service, a BC Ferries ticket agency, the Smuggler's Cove Restaurant, and the Salty Dog Pub.

7 Quesnel

75 miles (120km) N of Williams Lake, 409 miles (654km) N of Vancouver, 63 miles (101km) S of Prince George

Like most other towns in the Cariboo District, Quesnel (pop. 8,588) was founded during the gold-rush years in the 1860s. Now mostly a logging center, Quesnel serves as gateway to the ghost town of Barkerville and other historic mining sites, as well as to the canoe paddler's paradise, the Bowron Lakes.

Quesnel is located on a jut of land at the confluence of the Fraser and Quesnel rivers. The small downtown area is almost completely surrounded by these rivers. **Ceal Tingley Park,** on the Fraser side, is a pleasant place for a stroll, and it's one of the few spots where you can get right down to the huge and powerful Fraser. Directly across the street from the park is a Hudson's Bay Company trading post built in 1882; it currently houses a restaurant (see Heritage House under "Where to Dine," below).

The main commercial strip is **Reid Street,** a block east of Highway 97. A walk along Reid Street reveals the kinds of old-fashioned shops and services that have been gobbled up by behemoths like Walmart in the United States.

Over on the Quesnel River side of downtown is **LeBourdais Park,** which contains the visitor center and the **Quesnel and District Museum and Archives,** 405 Barlow Ave. (☎ **250/992-9580**), which tells the story of the gold rush and has good exhibits on the Chinese who worked in the camps. It's open mid-June to Labour Day, daily from 8am to 6pm; May to mid-June and Labour Day through October, daily from 8:30am to 4:30pm; and the rest of the year, Monday through Friday from 1 to 4pm.

The Quesnel Rodeo, a horseshoe tournament, river-raft races, and more than 100 other events attract thousands to Quesnel during the second week of July for **Bill Barker Days** (☎ 800/992-4922 in Canada, or 250/992-8716).

The **Quesnel Visitor Info Centre** is in Le Bourdais Park, 705 Carson Ave., Quesnel, BC, V2J 4C3 (☎ **800/992-4922** or 250/992-8716; fax 250/992-2181; e-mail: visitorinfo@cityquesnel.bc.ca). It's open from March through October.

WHERE TO STAY

Ten Mile Lake Provincial Park (☎ **250/398-4414**) is 7 miles (11km) north of Quesnel off Highway 97. This attractive, forested campground has 141 campsites for C$12 to C$15 (U.S.$8 to U.S.$10). Open May through October, the park has dry and flush toilets, a sani-station, a playground, lake swimming, and showers.

Talisman Inn. 753 Front St., Quesnel, BC, V2J 2L2. ☎ **800/663-8090** or 250/992-7247. Fax 250/992-3126. 87 units. A/C TV TEL. C$63–C$75 (U.S.$41–U.S.$49) double. Kitchen C$10 (U.S.$7) extra. Extra person C$5 (U.S.$3.25). Corporate and senior rates available. AE, MC, V.

A well-maintained older motel close to downtown, the Talisman has large, light-filled rooms that overlook a grassy courtyard. A standard unit comes with microwave, minifridge, and toaster; full kitchen units are also available. Some rooms have Jacuzzis. There's also a coin laundry on the premises.

Tower Inn. 500 Reid St., Quesnel, BC, V2J 2M9. ☎ **800/663-2009** or 250/992-2201. Fax 250/992-5201. 63 units. A/C TV TEL. C$75 (U.S.$49) double. Extra person C$5 (U.S.$3.25). AE, MC, V.

Right downtown, the Tower Inn offers clean, crisply new rooms that come with hair dryers, complimentary coffee, and VCRs. The on-site Begbie's Bar and Bistro is a popular Quesnel eatery and hangout.

Wheel Inn Motel & Restaurant. 146 Carson Ave., Quesnel, BC, V2J 2A8. ☎ **250/992-8975.** 24 units. A/C TV TEL. C$45 (U.S.$29) double. AE, MC, V.

This compact, older motor-court motel has recently been given a rejuvenating face-lift and now offers B&B-style lodgings. The complimentary breakfast is served in the small, dinerlike restaurant, which is also open for three meals daily. The Wheel Inn is a cheerful place, festooned with flowerpots.

WHERE TO DINE

Heritage House. 102 Carson Ave. ☎ **250/992-2700.** Reservations not needed. Main courses C$7–C$15 (U.S.$4.55–U.S.$10). MC, V. Daily 7am–9pm. CANADIAN.

The Heritage House is just that—a historic structure built in 1882 that once housed a Hudson's Bay Company trading post. Although there's plenty of standard Canadian fare on the menu, the restaurant also offers a number of dishes, such as Veal Voyageur and Hudson Bay Stew, that hearken back to Quesnel's frontier past. Heritage House is also the place to come for a big, old-fashioned breakfast.

Mr. Mike's Grill. 450 Reid St. ☎ **250/992-7742.** Reservations recommended. Main courses C$7–C$16 (U.S.$4.55–U.S.$10). AE, MC, V. Daily 10am–midnight. CANADIAN.

Mr. Mike's is probably the hippest place to hang out in Quesnel, with a menu of cocktails that would make a Yaletown club in Vancouver proud. The dining room serves up eclectic fare that remains mostly focused on steaks, grilled local salmon, and boutique burgers. A few Mexican- and Thai-influenced dishes also make their way onto the menu. Service is friendly.

8 East to Barkerville & Bowron Lakes

Barkerville: 52 miles (83km) E of Quesnel

Barkerville is one of the premier tourist destinations in interior British Columbia, as well as one of the most intact ghost towns in Canada. However, what lures paddlers and campers to the Cariboo Mountains today isn't a flash of gold, but the splash of water at the Bowron Lakes. These are a chain of six major and a number of smaller interconnecting lakes that attract canoeists and kayakers who paddle and portage around the entire 72-mile (115km) circuit.

Follow the signs in Quesnel to Highway 26 east. The 52-mile (86.6km) drive to Barkerville takes you deep into the forests of the Cariboo Mountains, where moose and deer are often spotted from the road. The paved highway ends at Barkerville. Bowron Lakes is another 18 miles (30km) northeast on a gravel road.

EXPLORING BARKERVILLE: AN OLD WEST GHOST TOWN

The 1860 Cariboo gold rush was the reason thousands of miners made their way north from the played-out Fraser River gold deposits to Williams Creek, east of Quesnel. The town of ✪ **Barkerville** was founded on its shore after Billy Barker discovered one of the region's richest gold deposits, 50 feet below the water line in 1862. The town sprang up practically overnight; that year, it was reputedly the largest city west of Chicago and north of San Francisco. Many of the claims continued to produce well into the 1930s, but Barkerville's population moved on, leaving behind an intact ghost town that was designated a historic park in the 1950s.

The original 1869 **Anglican church** and 125 other buildings have been lovingly reconstructed or restored. The church holds daily services. Aside from the **visitor center** at the park's entrance (☎ **250/994-3302**), little has changed. The **Richland courthouse** stages trials from the town's past. From May to Labour Day, the "townspeople" dress in period costumes and bring Barkerville back to life. Visitors can pan for gold outside the general store, learn about the big strikes, enjoy a meal in the Chinatown section, or take a stagecoach ride.

In winter, the town becomes a haven for **cross-country skiers,** who take to the trail from Barkerville and Richfield down to Likely and Quesnel Forks. During the holidays, Barkerville hosts a special **Victorian Christmas** celebration.

Two-day admission to the town is C$7 (U.S.$4.55) for adults, C$4.25 (U.S.$2.75) for seniors and students, and C$1 (U.S.65¢) for children. Barkerville is open year-round, daily from dawn to dusk. For information, contact **Barkerville Historic Town,** Box 19, Barkerville, BC, V0K 1B0 (☎ **250/994-3302;** www.heritage.gov. bc.ca).

WHERE TO STAY & DINE

There are three campgrounds in **Barkerville Provincial Park,** Highway 26, Barkerville (☎ **250/398-1414**), open year-round. Sites go for C$12 to C$15 (U.S.$8–U.S.$10). **Lowhee Campground** is the best and closest to the park entrance. The well-spaced sites accommodate both tents and RVs. Hot showers, flush toilets, pumped well water, and a sani-station are available.

On the way up to Barkerville, be sure to stop at the **Cottonwood House** (☎ **250/ 992-3997**), about half an hour's drive from Quesnel. Formerly a stage stop on the way to the goldfields, Cottonwood House has been serving meals to travelers since 1865. It's open for breakfast and lunch only, from mid-May to Labour Day.

The Wells Hotel. Pooley St. (Box 39), Wells, BC, V0K 2R0. ☎ **800/860-2299** in Canada, or 250/994-3427. Fax 250/994-3494. www.wellshotel.com. E-mail: goldcity.net. 40 units, 24 with private bathroom. C$70–C$120 (U.S.$46–U.S.$78) double. Rates include breakfast. AE, MC, V.

Established in 1933, this restored hotel is filled with lovely antique furnishings and offers amenities that you'll truly appreciate after a day of hiking, canoeing, skiing, or gold panning: fine dining, a frothy cappuccino, and a soothing hot tub. All guest rooms are tastefully decorated in earth-tone textiles and locally created artwork. Some units have private bathrooms and/or fireplaces. The hotel added another 23 rooms in a new wing in 1999. Dining options range from the Pooley Street Café and an espresso shop to the Wells Hotel Pub and Fireplace Lounge. Amenities include bike rentals, conference rooms, hot tub, and massage.

EXPLORING BOWRON LAKES: A CANOEIST'S PARADISE

Eighteen miles (30km) northeast of Barkerville over an unpaved road, there's access to a circle of lakes that attracts canoeists and kayakers from around the world. The 304,000-acre ✪ **Bowron Lakes Provincial Park** is a majestic paddler's paradise set against a backdrop of glacial peaks.

The 7-day circular route is 72 miles (120km) of unbroken wilderness. It begins at Kibbee Creek and Kibbee Lake, flows into Indianpoint Lake, Isaac Lake, and the Isaac River, and continues to McCleary, Lanezi, Sandy, and Una lakes before entering the final stretch: Babcock Lake, Skoi Lake, the Spectacle Lakes, Swan Lake, and finally Bowron Lake. The long, narrow lakes afford visitors a close look at both shores. More than occasionally, you'll catch sight of moose, mountain goats, beavers, black bears, and grizzly bears. Be prepared to portage for a total of 5 miles (8.3km) between some of the creeks that connect the lakes. The longest single portage is 1³/₄ miles (2.9km). You must pack everything in and out of the wilderness camps.

To protect the wilderness experience, the number of canoes and people allowed to enter the park per day is restricted in summer. Permit bookings are handled by the provincial tourist information service **Super Natural British Columbia** (☎ **800/663-6000** or 250/387-1642). Fees for a full circuit of the park are C$50 (U.S.$33) per person per one-person canoe/kayak, or C$100 (U.S.$65) per two-person canoe/kayak. There's a reservation fee of C$18 (U.S.$12) plus tax for each canoe booked. Payment must be made at the time of reservation, by Visa or MasterCard only. After September 15, permits can purchased at the **Bowron Lakes Park office,** at the start of the circuit (☎ **250/398-4414**). The park does not close in winter, but there are no rangers or other staff in the park after mid-October, so extreme caution must be used. For information on Bowron Lakes Provincial Park, contact the **District Manager,** Suite 301, 640 Borland St., Williams Lake, BC, V2G 4T1 (☎ **250/398-4414;** www.elp.gov.bc.ca/bcparks/explore/parkpgs/bowron.htm).

You don't have to make the entire journey to enjoy this incredible setting. Open from May through October, the **campground** at the park's entrance is a relaxing spot to camp, fish, boat, or simply relax and observe the abundant flora and fauna.

WHERE TO STAY

✪ **Bowron Lake Lodge & Resorts.** Bowron Lake, 672 Walken St., Quesnel, BC, V2J 2J7. ☎ **250/992-2733.** 24 units, 50 campsites. C$55–C$150 (U.S.$36–U.S.$98) double; C$16–C$20 (U.S.$10–U.S.$13) campsite. MC, V. Closed Nov–Apr.

This rustic, lakeside lodge resort provides all the creature comforts you could ask for in a wilderness setting. Guests can choose from comfortable lodge rooms (with double beds, private bathrooms, and optional fully equipped kitchens), self-contained cabins, or tree-shaded campsites by the lake. Mountain-bike, canoe, and motorboat rentals are available. The lodge has 3 miles (5km) of private hiking trails, 2,000 feet (610m) of private sandy beach, a private airstrip, and a restaurant and cocktail lounge.

9 The Thompson River Valley

Kamloops: 220 miles (356km) NE of Vancouver, 135 miles (218km) W of Revelstoke

From its juncture with the Fraser River at Lytton, the Thompson River cuts north, then east through an arid landscape. The countryside is grazed by cattle; in the vibrantly green valleys, farmers grow a variety of crops. **Kamloops,** a major trade center for this agricultural region, is increasingly a retirement center for refugees from the gloom of the Pacific coast. In the South Thompson River valley, the **Shuswap Lakes** are popular with houseboaters. It's easy to navigate the 620 miles (1,000km) of waterways, landing at campsites and beaches along the way. Rent a houseboat in **Salmon Arm,** then spend a relaxing vacation at one of the area's marine parks.

Rising up from the dry terrain of Kamloops, heading north along Highway 5, the road enters the cool forests of the High Country. High above the town of **Clearwater** is the pristine wilderness of **Wells Gray Provincial Park.** Drive up the winding dirt road to the **Green Point Observatory** for a perfect overview of the park from the three-story wooden observation tower.

KAMLOOPS

At the confluence of the north and south forks of the Thompson River, Kamloops (pop. 79,566) is the province's fifth-largest city. The forest-products industry— logging and milling—is the city's primary economic force, although Kamloops is also a major service center for ranchers and farmers.

ESSENTIALS

GETTING THERE **By Plane & Car** You can fly into Kamloops, a 50-minute flight from Vancouver, and rent a car at the airport. **Air BC** (☎ **604/688-5515**) and **Canadian Regional Airlines** (☎ **800/426-7000** in the U.S. or 800/363-7530 in Canada) operate daily flights. Car-rental firms have desks at the airport.

By Car Kamloops is a junction point of many provincial roadways, including the Trans-Canada and the Coquihalla highways. The fastest route from Vancouver is by far the Coquihalla, or Highway 5. Note that this is a toll highway; passenger vehicles pay C$10 (U.S.$7) on the 220-mile (356km) Vancouver/Kamloops route.

By Bus There are seven **Greyhound** (☎ **800/661-8747**) buses daily between Kamloops and Vancouver; the one-way adult fare is C$47 (U.S.$31). Four of these buses continue on to Calgary; the one-way fare is C$77 (U.S.$50).

By Train **VIA Rail** passenger trains (☎ **800/561-8630**) pass through Kamloops on the main transnational route. Kamloops is also the overnight stop for the luxury **Rocky Mountaineer Railtour** train (☎ **800/665-7245**).

VISITOR INFORMATION Contact the **Kamloops Visitor Info Centre,** 1290 W. Trans-Canada Hwy. (exit 368), Kamloops, BC, V2C 6R3 (☎ **800/662-1994** or 250/828-9500; www.city.kamloops.bc.ca).

EXPLORING THE AREA

Kamloops is a sprawling city in a wide river valley flanked by high desert mountains. A major service center for local timber products and agricultural industries, Kamloops

Special Events

Departing from a different ranch each year, the annual ✪ **Kamloops Cattle Drive,** Box 1332, Kamloops, BC, V2C 6L7 (☎ **250/372-7075;** www.cattledrive.bc.ca; e-mail: cattledr@mail.netshop.net), has grown immensely popular over the past 7 years. More than 1,000 people participate in the 6-day ride during the second week in July. Cattle, cowboys, and visitors from around the world ride through the High Country's rolling prairies for 5 days, finishing with a grand arrival and a big party in Kamloops. Horses, gear, and even seats on the chuck wagons are available for rent.

isn't exactly a tourist town. However, the downtown core centered around **Victoria Street** is a pleasant, tree-lined area. North of downtown along the Thompson is **Riverfront Park,** a lovely expanse of green in an otherwise arid landscape. The 85-foot sternwheeler *Wanda-Sue* (☎ 250/374-7447 or 250/374-1505) plies the waters of the river, providing narrated sightseeing tours.

The **Kamloops Art Gallery,** 101-465 Victoria St. (☎ **250/828-3543**), is the only public art museum in the Thompson region and the largest in the province's interior, with a collection of more than 1,200 works by Canadian artists. The worthwhile **Kamloops Museum & Archives,** 207 Seymour St. (☎ **250/828-3576**), tells the story of human history in the Thompson Valley. There's a fur trader's cabin, livery stable, and blacksmith shop, plus cultural artifacts from the native Shuswap.

The kids will enjoy the 120-acre **Kamloops Wildlife Park,** on the Trans-Canada Highway, 15 minutes east of Kamloops (☎ **250/573-3242;** www.kamloopswildlife. com), with more than 70 species of endangered wildlife. Most popular is the grizzly exhibit; you'll also see Siberian tigers, cougars, and wolves.

Secwepemc Museum & Heritage Park. 355 Yellowhead Hwy. ☎ **250/828-9801.** www. secwepemc.org. Admission C$6 (U.S.$3.90) adults, C$4 (U.S.$2.60) children 7–12 and seniors 60 and over, free for children under 6. June 1 to Labour Day Mon–Fri 8:30am–8pm, Sat–Sun and holidays 10am–6pm. Labour Day to May 31 Mon–Fri 8:30am–4:30pm. Summer admission includes performances.

The Secwepemc (pronounced *She*-whep-m, anglicized as Shuswap) people have lived along the Thompson River for thousands of years. At their reserve just north of the river on Highway 5, this heritage park presents a very interesting series of exhibits. The park contains an actual archaeological site—a winter village inhabited by the Secwepemc people 1,200 to 2,400 years ago—plus reconstructions of traditional villages from five different eras, from 5,000 years ago to the 19th century. Also featured are performances of traditional song and dance; displays of native plants and their traditional uses; a replica of a salmon-netting station; and a collection of historic Secwepemc artifacts. The gift shop sells native arts and crafts.

OUTDOOR PURSUITS

FISHING   There are more than 200 lakes within a 2-hour drive of Kamloops, and "Gone Fishing" describes the general attitude in summer. For licenses, equipment, and advice, try **Wilderness Outfitters,** 1304 Battle St. (☎ **604/327-2127**). An authorized Orvis shop, it stocks a great selection of rods, reels, flies, and supplies.

GOLF   The one thing Kamloops has in abundance is golf courses; in fact, the city is practically surrounded by full-sized courses. **Aberdeen Hills Golf Links,** 1185 Links Way (☎ **205/828-1149** or 250/828-1143; www.come.to/aberdeenhills), is an 18-hole course with full facilities and panoramic views from almost every hole. The

Dunes, 652 Dunes Dr. (☎ **888/881-4653** or 250/579-3300), is a Graham Cooke–designed 18-hole championship course. **Kamloops Golf & Country Club,** 3125 Tranquille Rd. (☎ **250/376-8020** or 250/376-3231), is an 18-hole semiprivate championship course with full facilities. **Pineridge Golf Course,** 4725 E. Trans-Canada Hwy. (☎ **250/573-4333**), is an 18-hole course designed to be "the best short course ever built."

○ **Rivershore Estates and Golf Links** (☎ **250/573-4622**) is an award-winning Robert Trent Jones signature design and has been host to the Canadian National Championships. **Sun Peaks Resort and Golf Course,** 280 Alpine Rd. (☎ **877/828-9989** or 250/578-7222), is a Graham Cooke–designed course adjacent to the ski-resort village at Sun Peaks, north of Kamloops. Horseback riding, shopping, and six resort hotels are close to the first tee. For family-friendly golf, the **McArthur Island Golf Centre** (☎ **250/554-3211**) is a good choice. Located on McArthur Island, this nine-hole course includes a driving range, mini golf course, pro shop, and restaurant.

SKIING ○ **Sun Peaks Resort,** Tod Mountain Road, Heffley Creek (☎ **250/578-7232,** or 250/578-7232 for snow report), is a great powder-skiing and open-run area with a vertical rise of 2,854 feet (870m). The 63 runs are serviced by a high-speed quad chair with bubble cover, a fixed-grip quad chair, a triple chair, a double chair, a T-bar, and a beginner platter. Snowboarders have a choice of two half pipes, one with a superlarge boarder-cross. At the bottom of this 3,000-foot (914m) run are handrails, cars, a fun box, hips, quarter pipes, burly tabletops, transfers, and fat gaps that were designed by Ecosign Mountain Planners and some of Canada's top amateur riders. Cross-country and snowmobile trails are also available. Lift tickets are C$41 (U.S.$27) for adults, C$36 (U.S.$23) for children over 12, and C$23 (U.S.$15) for children 12 and under.

WHERE TO STAY

In addition to the following lodgings, most of which are downtown, you'll find a phalanx of easy-in, easy-out motels at Highway 1, exit 368, south and west of the city center.

Best Western Kamloops Towne Lodge. 1250 Rogers Way, Kamloops, BC, V1S 1J3. ☎ **800/665-6674** or 250/828-6660. Fax 250/828-6698. 122 units. A/C TV TEL. C$122–C$157 (U.S.$79–U.S.$102) double. Extra person C$10–C$15 (U.S.$7–U.S.$10). AE, MC, V. Take Hwy. 1, exit 368.

New and attractive, this large complex offers plenty of facilities and spacious, nicely furnished guest rooms. In-room perks include complimentary coffee, hair dryers, and fridges. The three-story courtyard with indoor pool is filled with tropical plants. Additional facilities include Forsters Restaurant and Lounge (see "Where to Dine," below), whirlpool, hot tubs, exercise room, and beer-and-wine store.

Coast Canadian Inn. 339 St. Paul St., Kamloops, BC, V2C 2J5. ☎ **800/663-1144** or 250/372-5201. Fax 250/372-9363. www.coasthotels.com. 94 units. A/C TV TEL. C$105 (U.S.$68) double. Extra person C$10 (U.S.$7). Family plan, corporate and off-season rates, and senior discounts available. AE, DC, MC, V.

Located right downtown, the Coast Canadian is one of the top hotels in Kamloops, with spacious guest rooms, professional service, and lots of extra features, like complimentary passes to a full health club and gym. The Pronto Restaurant is one of the best in the city (see "Where to Dine" below), while Sgt. O'Flaherty's Deli Pub serves a light menu. Other amenities include room service, two pools, exercise equipment, a hot tub, a sauna, and a beer-and-wine store.

Hostelling International-Kamloops. 7 W. Seymour St., Kamloops, BC, V2C 1E4. ☎ **250/828-7991.** Fax 250/828-2442. www.hihostels.bc.ca. E-mail: kamloops@hihostels. bc.ca. 70 beds. C$15 (U.S.$10) dorm rm; C$35–C$44 (U.S.$23–U.S.$29) private rm double. Group and off-season rates available. MC, V.

One of the best and grandest hostels in all of Canada, the Kamloops hostel is located in the old district courthouse, built in 1909. The stone-and-brick structure has been modernized with up-to-date comforts, but still retains many historical and architectural features of interest, such as stained-glass windows and Gothic arches. The old courtroom is now a sitting room, while the old jail cells now serve as bathrooms.

Scott's Inn—Downtown. 551 11th Ave., Kamloops, BC, V2C 3Y1. ☎ **800/665-3343** or 250/372-8221. Fax 250/372-9444. www.scottsinn.kamloops.com. E-mail: scottsinn@ kamloops.com. 51 units. A/C TV TEL. C$54–C$68 (U.S.$35–U.S.$44) double. Kitchen C$10 (U.S.$7) extra. Extra person C$6–C$10 (U.S.$3.90–U.S.$7). Group, senior, corporate, and CAA-member discounts and off-season rates available. AE, MC, V.

If what you're looking for is a clean and comfortable room in a convenient location at a moderate price, Scott's Inn is a good option. A standard motel with many extra features, Scott's is located in a quiet residential neighborhood within easy walking distance of downtown. Facilities include an on-site restaurant, laundry, indoor pool, hot tub, and rooftop sundeck.

Stockman's Hotel & Casino. 540 Victoria St., Kamloops, BC, V2C 2B2. ☎ **800/663-2837** or 250/372-2281. Fax 250/372-1125. www.stockmentshotel.com. E-mail: frontdesk@ stockmentshotel.com. 150 units. A/C TV TEL. C$99–C$149 (U.S.$64–U.S.$97) double. Extra person C$15 (U.S.$10). Family plan and off-season rates available. AE, MC, V.

Smack-dab in the center of downtown, the Stockman is practically synonymous with central Kamloops. This block-square hotel is the one lodging everyone knows about in Kamloops, and with good reason: Service is commendable, rooms are good-sized and comfortable, and you can walk everywhere you need to go. On the property are the Nuggets Grill and Restaurant, the Black Jack Lounge, and a casino.

WHERE TO DINE

Chapters Viewpoint Restaurant. 610 Columbia St. ☎ **250/374-3224.** Reservations recommended. Main courses C$11–C$24 (U.S.$7–U.S.$16). AE, MC, V. Daily 11:30am–2:30pm and 5–10pm. MEXICAN.

Perched on a hill above Kamloops, Chapters offers a great view over the city; the terrace is the place to be for a summer drink. The menu, which features a large selection of salads and appetizers, has a Mexican flavor, although there's also pasta and steaks. A local favorite is the Steak Ranchero, a red-pepper-marinated New York strip that's grilled and served with a topping of cheese.

Forsters Restaurant. In the Best Western Kamloops Towne Lodge, 1250 Rogers Way. ☎ **250/372-5312.** Reservations recommended. Main courses C$14–C$24 (U.S.$9–U.S.$16). AE, MC, V. Daily 7–10:30am, 11:30am–2:30pm, and 5–10pm. Take Hwy. 1, exit 368. CANADIAN.

This bright and lively restaurant is a good choice if you want good food but don't want to negotiate downtown Kamloops. The house specialty is prime rib in a variety of sizes, including a mammoth 2-pound portion that will more than satisfy your meat cravings. There's also a selection of pasta, chicken, and seafood dishes.

Pronto Restaurant. In the Coast Canadian Inn, 339 St. Paul St. ☎ **250/372-5201.** Reservations suggested. Main courses C$14–C$33 (U.S.$9–U.S.$21). AE, MC, V. Daily 5–10pm. CONTINENTAL/SEAFOOD.

Kamloops's finest restaurant, Pronto is an elegant and sophisticated choice that's a favorite for special occasions. About half of the menu is devoted to seafood: Grilled steelhead trout is dusted with lemon pepper and served with tomato sherry sauce. The meat dishes have a European flavor, ranging from pork schnitzel to veal medaillons with Gorgonzola sauce to rack of lamb with mint and merlot.

THE SHUSWAP LAKES

From Kamloops, the South Thompson River valley extends east to the Shuswap Lakes, a series of waterways that is an extremely popular summer destination for family houseboating parties. With more than 620 miles (1,000km) of shoreline, these long, interconnected lakes provide good fishing, waterskiing, and other boating fun.

The main commercial center for the Shuswap Lakes is **Salmon Arm** (pop. 15,034), 67 miles (108km) east of Kamloops on Highway 1, although small lakeside resorts are scattered throughout the area. While Salmon Arm has plenty of facilities for the traveler, there's not much in the way of sights. Have a stroll through the commercial district and walk out to the **Salmon Arm Wharf,** a long boardwalk that thrusts out into the lake. The wharf is the longest marina structure in inland British Columbia.

The **Salmon Arm Visitor Info Centre,** 751 Marine Park Dr. NE (Box 999), Salmon Arm, BC, V1E 4P2 (☎ **250/832-2230;** e-mail: sacofc@shuswap.net), is open from September 2 to May 30, Monday through Friday from 9am to 5pm, and June 1 to September 1, daily from 9am to 5pm. The staff can help with travel plans throughout the Shuswap Lakes region.

The other sizable commercial center on the lakes is **Sicamous** (pop. 3,088), which has the largest numbers of houseboat-rental agencies.

OUTDOOR PURSUITS

Fishing and houseboating are the area's biggest lures. With a shoreline filled with sandy beaches, coves, and narrow channels, visitors come to while away summer days aboard houseboats or fishing charters, enjoying the tranquil beauty of the lakes.

BOAT RENTALS   Sicamous Creek Marina (☎ **250/836-4611**) rents ski boats, fishing boats, and other power watercraft, as well as kayaks and canoes.

FISHING   To fish here, you need a nonresident freshwater license. Pick up copies of *BC Tidal Waters Sport Fishing Guide* and *BC Sport Fishing Regulations Synopsis for*

The Salmon Run & Other Special Events

During the second week in January, the **Reino Keski-Salmi Loppet** (☎ **250/832-7740**) attracts cross-country skiers from across North America to the Larch Hills Cross-Country Ski Hill in Salmon Arm.

One of nature's most amazing phenomena, the ✪ **Adams River Salmon Run,** takes place annually in late October. Every 4 years, an estimated 1.5 to 2 million sockeye salmon struggle upstream to spawn in the Adams River near Squilax. Trails provide riverside viewing, a "Salute to Salmon" program offers displays, and trained staff are ready to interpret this spectacle. Take the Trans-Canada Highway (Hwy. 1) to Squilax (about 6 miles/10km east of Chase). Follow the signs north to Roderick Haig-Brown Provincial Park.

The annual **Salmon Arm Bluegrass Festival** (☎ **250/832-3258**), held in Salmon Arm's R. J. Haney Heritage Park on the first weekend in July, features performers from Canada, the United States, and Europe.

Non-Tidal Waters. Independent anglers should also get a copy of the *BC Fishing Directory and Atlas.*

GOLF   There are 15 golf courses in the Shuswap Lakes area, making this heaven for golfers. One of the best is the **Salmon Arm Golf Club,** 3641 Hwy. 97B SE, Salmon Arm (☎ **250/832-4727;** e-mail: sagolf@jetstream.net), an 18-hole, par-72, 6,738-yard course that's rated among the province's top 20. Equipment rentals and lessons are offered. Greens fees start at C$45 (U.S.$29). Also tops is the **Shuswap Lakes Estate Golf & Country Club,** 2404 Centennial Rd., Sorrento (☎ **800/661-3955** in Canada, or 250/675-2315), offering an 18-hole, par-71, 6,438-yard course with generous fairways and four scenic lakes. Greens fees start at C$42 (U.S.$27). Facilities include a driving range, two practice greens, and a pro shop offering equipment rentals and lessons.

HIKING   On the northern shore of Shuswap Lake near the town of Squilax, **Shuswap Lake Provincial Park** (☎ **250/851-3000**) offers wonderful strolling, with abundant old-growth ponderosa pines. About a mile (1.6km) offshore, the park's **Copper Island** has a pleasant trail that leads to a high point, where boaters looking for a dry-land hiking experience can survey the lake and surrounding countryside.

WHERE TO STAY & DINE

Many visitors come here to hire a houseboat and cruise the lakes in a leisurely fashion (see "Houseboating on the Shuswap Lakes," below). However, you'll also find good land-based accommodations in all price ranges, though some of the lower-priced motels see pretty hard use in summer—and it shows.

Because most people use the kitchen facilities on their boats, notable restaurants haven't really taken hold here. One exception is the **Orchard House,** 720 22nd St. NE (☎ **250/832-3434**), with up-to-date New Canadian cooking.

Best Western Villager West Motor Inn. 61 10th St. SW, Salmon Arm, BC, V1E 1E4. ☎ **800/528-1234** or 250/832-9793. Fax 250/832-5595. 78 units. A/C TV TEL. C$50–C$90 (U.S.$33–U.S.$59) double. Kitchen C$7 (U.S.$4.55) extra. Extra person C$7 (U.S.$4.55). Commercial and off-season discounts available. AE, MC, V.

This Best Western isn't lakefront, but it offers good value and is within easy walking distance of central Salmon Arm and the wharf. Amenities include a pool and whirlpool; it's adjacent to two restaurants. Lake tours can be arranged.

Coast Shuswap Lodge. 200 Trans-Canada Hwy., Box 1540, Salmon Arm, BC, V1E 4N3. ☎ **800/663-1144** or 250/832-7081. Fax 250/832-6753. www.coasthotels.com. 40 units. A/C. C$79–C$150 (U.S.$51–U.S.$98) double. Extra person C$10 (U.S.$7). Family plan, corporate and off-season discounts, and senior rates available. AE, MC, V.

At the very center of Salmon Arm, this brand-new hotel offers the most comfortable rooms in town, with spacious and beautifully furnished accommodations accompanied by excellent, friendly service. Facilities include the ABC family restaurant, lounge, heated outdoor pool, whirlpool, patio, and beer-and-wine store.

✪ **Quaaout Lodge.** Little Shuswap Lake Rd. (Box 1215), Chase, BC, V0E 1M0. ☎ **800/663-4303** or 250/679-3090. Fax 250/679-3039. E-mail: quaaout@quaaout.com. 72 units. A/C TV TEL. C$119–C$175 (U.S.$77–U.S.$114) double. AE, MC, V. Free parking. Take the Trans-Canada Hwy. (Hwy. 1) through the town of Chase. About 10 miles (16km) east, turn left at the Squilax Bridge underpass. Take the overpass; the lodge is on the first road on the left.

This gorgeous resort draws heavily on Native Indian tradition in its design and decor. Set on the sandy shores of Little Shuswap Lake, it's owned and operated by the Shuswap band of the Secwepemc tribe, who built it in 1992. Six well-appointed rooms

Houseboating on the Shuswap Lakes

The best way to see the lakes is to rent a houseboat for a few days. After all, Shuswap is the "Houseboating Capital of Canada." Houseboats come equipped with staterooms, full bathrooms, and fully equipped kitchens. All you need to bring is your bedding and food. Reserve well in advance; by late spring, all boats are usually rented for the high season, from mid-June to Labour Day. Low-season rates are up to half off the prices below. Of the numerous houseboat-rental operations along the Shuswap Lakes, the following are three of the largest.

Admiral House Boats, Sicamous Creek Marina (RR 1, Site 6, Comp 30), Sicamous, BC, V0E 2V0 (☎ 250/836-4611; fax 250/836-4614), rents houseboats from April through October. There are two sizes: The Admiral boats, which sleep up to 8, have 2 private staterooms and 1½ bathrooms, while the larger Super Admirals have 3 private bedrooms and 1½ bathrooms, and can sleep up to 10. Rentals are available in 3-, 5-, and 7-day increments. In high season, a week on an Admiral houseboat goes for C$1,755 (U.S.$1,141), while a week on a Super Admiral costs C$2,065 (U.S.$1,342). Pricier hot-tub models are available as well.

Blue Water Houseboats, 110 Weddup (Box 248), Sicamous, BC, V0E 2V0 (☎ 800/663-4024 or 250/836-2255; fax 250/836-4955; www.shuswap.bc.ca/sunny/bluewtr.htm; e-mail: bluwater@sicamous.com), rents boats from April through October. There are a variety of boat types, including luxury liners that can sleep up to 16. High-season weekly prices range from C$895 (U.S.$582) for a small one-bedroom boat that sleeps 4 to C$1,595 (U.S.$1,037) for a Suncruiser that sleeps 10. The 16-passenger cruiser rents for C$4,695 (U.S.$3,052) per week. Rentals of 3-, 5-, and 7-day increments are available.

Twin Anchors Houseboat Vacations (e-mail: houseboat@mail.netshop.net) has two locations, one in Salmon Arm at 750 Marine Park Dr. (Box 1480), Salmon Arm, BC, V1E 4P6 (☎ 800/665-7782 or 250/832-2745; fax 250/836-4824), and the other in Sicamous at 101 Martin St. (Box 381), Sicamous, BC, V0E 2V0 (☎ 800/663-4026 or 250/836-2450; fax 250/836-4824). It offers four types of houseboats, from a Commander that sleeps 8 and costs C$1,595 (U.S.$1,037) per week to a Cruisecraft that sleeps 15 and costs C$3,995 (U.S.$2,597). Rentals are available in 3-, 4-, 5-, and 7-day increments.

---

contain fireplaces and Jacuzzis. The excellent restaurant offers a menu featuring many traditional dishes, including alder-smoked salmon, venison, and a fried bread called bannock. Amenities include a pool, saunas, gym, hiking and biking trails, fishing, cross-country skiing, canoeing, and playground. Adventurous kids can opt to spend a night in a large teepee provided by the lodge.

CAMPING

The 280 campsites at **Shuswap Lake Provincial Park** (☎ 250/851-3000), 19 miles (31.6km) northeast of Highway 1 at Squilax, cost C$19 (U.S.$12) per night. Facilities include free hot showers, flush toilets, a playground, and a nature house. The 35 sites at **Silver Beach Provincial Park** (☎ 250/851-3000) are accessible by an unpaved road from the town of Anglemount, by ferry from Sicamous, or by boating to the north end of Seymour Arm. Facilities include pit toilets and fire pits; sites are

C$8 (U.S.$5) per night. There are 51 campsites at **Herald Provincial Park** (☎ **250/ 851-3000**), 9 miles (15km) northeast of Highway 1 at Tappen. Facilities include free hot showers, pit toilets, a sani-station, and a boat launch. Sites are C$19 (U.S.$12) per night.

THE UPPER THOMPSON RIVER VALLEY

From Kamloops, the North Thompson River flows north into increasingly rugged terrain. The little town of **Clearwater** is the gateway to **Wells Gray Provincial Park,** known for its waterfalls and wilderness lakes. Wells Gray Provincial Park, which contains the high glaciers of the Cariboo Mountains, is increasingly the mountain wilderness park of choice for purist hikers and outdoor adventurers, as the nearby Canadian Rockies become increasingly crowded and commercialized.

Although **Greyhound** offers bus service daily between Vancouver and Clearwater, you'll need a car to explore the best areas of the High Country, especially Wells Gray Provincial Park. Clearwater is 62 miles (103km) north of Kamloops on Highway 5.

For visitor information, stop by the **Clearwater–Wells Gray Info Centre,** 425 E. Yellowhead Hwy. 5 (Box 1988, RR 1), Clearwater, BC, V0E 1N0 (☎ **250/ 674-3693;** www.profiles.net/chamber; e-mail: clwcofc@mail.wellsgray.net), at the intersection of Highway 5 and Wells Gray Park Road. From October 16 to April 14, it's open Monday through Saturday from 9am to 5pm; April 15 to June 30 and September 1 to October 15, daily from 9am to 6pm; July 1 to August 31, daily from 8am to 8pm.

EXPLORING WELLS GRAY PROVINCIAL PARK

Established in 1939, **Wells Gray Provincial Park** (☎ **604/371-6400**) is British Columbia's second-largest park, encompassing more than 1.3 million acres of virgin wilderness: mountains, rivers, volcanic formations, lakes, glaciers, forests, and alpine meadows. Wildlife abounds, including mule deer, moose, grizzly and black bears, beaver, coyote, hummingbirds, timber wolves, mink, and golden eagles.

Wells Gray has something to offer every outdoor interest: excellent birding and wildlife-viewing opportunities, hiking for every ability, boating, canoeing, and kayaking. Guide operations offer horseback riding, canoeing, river rafting, fishing, and hiking. The history enthusiast can learn about the early homesteaders, trappers, and prospectors, or about the natural forces that produced Wells Gray's many volcanoes, waterfalls, mineral springs, and glaciers.

Most of Wells Gray is remote wilderness that can only be viewed after a vigorous hike or canoe excursion. However, in the southern quarter of the park, a road runs 21 miles (34km) from the park entrance to Clearwater Lake. Called simply the **Corridor,** from this road system you can explore many of the park's geological, cultural, and natural features. The road also connects to three campgrounds and to many trailheads. Stop by the Wells Gray Info Centre in Clearwater to inquire about trail conditions.

Twice as tall as Niagara Falls, the park's **Helmcken Falls** is an awesome sight easily reached by paved road. Also easily accessible is the broad cascade known as **Dawson Falls.** Boating, canoeing, kayaking, and fishing are popular pastimes on **Clearwater, Azure, Mahood,** and **Murtle lakes.** The wilderness campgrounds along these lakes make perfect destinations for overnight canoe or fishing trips.

Multiday hiking destinations include the area around Ray Farm Homestead, Rays Mineral Spring, and the thickly forested **Murtle River Trail** that leads to **Majerus Falls, Horseshoe Falls,** and **Pyramid Mountain,** a volcanic upgrowth that was shaped when it erupted beneath miles of glacial ice that covered the park millions of years ago.

GUIDED TOURS & EXCURSIONS

Besides excellent accommodations, **Trophy Mountain Buffalo Ranch** and **Wells Gray Backcountry Chalets** (see "Where to Stay," below) offer half-day to weeklong horseback-riding, cross-country skiing, and hiking trips. Rates start at C$45 (U.S.$29) per person at both companies.

Wells Gray Guest Ranch, Wells Gray Road (RR 1, Box 1766), Clearwater (☎ 250/674-2792 or 250/674-2774), offers guided packages that include hiking, canoeing, rafting, fishing, biking, and motorboating (on Clearwater and Azure lakes) in summer; and dogsledding, cross-country and downhill skiing, snowshoeing, snow-mobiling, and ice fishing in winter. Excursions range from half-day to weeklong trips.

Crazy Moon Enterprises, Helmcken Falls Lodge, Wells Gray Road, Clearwater (☎ 250/674-3657), offers half- and full-day hikes and canoeing trips through the park and environs. **Interior Whitewater Expeditions** (☎ 250/674-3727) conducts a variety of rafting and kayaking packages, ranging from half- to 5-day trips, on some of the wildest, most beautiful stretches of the Adams and North Thompson rivers.

WHERE TO STAY

Most campers head to Wells Gray Provincial Park's ✪ **Spahats, Clearwater,** and **Dawson Falls campgrounds** (☎ 250/851-3000). The park has 88 available sites; check the sign outside the Clearwater Visitor Info Centre to make sure the grounds aren't full before driving all the way up to the park. Sites are C$12 (U.S.$8) per night. Facilities include fire pits, firewood, pumped well water, pit toilets, and boat launches.

Dutch Lake Motel and Campground. 333 Roy Rd. (RR 2, Box 5116), Clearwater, BC, V0E 1N0. ☎ **877/674-3325** or 250/674-3325. Fax 250/674-2916. www.mypage.direct.ca/ d/dutch_lk. E-mail: dutch_lk@direct.ca. 27 units. A/C TV TEL. C$80 (U.S.$52) double; camp-sites C$20 (U.S.$13). AE, MC, V.

The nicest lodging in the town of Clearwater itself, the Dutch Lake Motel overlooks its namesake lake in a quiet setting away from the highway. All guest rooms have balconies, while some rooms have kitchenettes as well. The Dutch Lake Village Restaurant offers family dining. Canoe rentals can be arranged.

Nakiska Ranch. Trout Creek Rd. (off Wells Gray Park Rd.), Clearwater, BC, V0E 1N0. ☎ **250/674-3655.** Fax 250/674-3387. www.nakiskaranch.bc.ca. 3 units, 4 cabins. Summer C$105 (U.S.$68) double, C$115–C$135 (U.S.$75–U.S.$88) cabin. Winter C$80 (U.S.$52) double, C$89–C$95 (U.S.$58–U.S.$62) cabin. MC, V. Drive up Wells Gray Park Rd. for 25 miles (41.6km); it will take about 40 min. Turn right at the ranch sign onto Trout Creek Rd. The ranch is a 10-min. drive from the park entrance. Small pets accepted.

Gorgeous log cabins, acres of mowed meadows, and Wells Gray's majestic forests and mountains surround the main log house on this working ranch. The immaculate interiors of both the lodge and the individual cabins are straight out of the pages of *House Beautiful,* featuring open kitchens, hardwood floors, lots of windows, and Scandinavian-style wood furnishings. The two-story cabins are pristine hideaways that can sleep up to six comfortably. Breakfast is served in the lodge house, but you must bring your own groceries for other meals. The lodge guests can request access to the main kitchen. (It's a 30-min. drive to the nearest restaurant or store.)

✪ **Trophy Mountain Buffalo Ranch Bed & Breakfast and Campground.** RR 1 (P.O. Box 1768), Clearwater, BC, V0E 1N0. ☎ **250/674-3095.** Fax 250/674-3131. E-mail: buffranch@hotmail.com. 4 units, 15 campsites, 4 camping cabins. C$45–C$60 (U.S.$29–U.S.$39) double; C$14–C$17 (U.S.$9–$11) campsite; C$11 (U.S.$7) cabin. Rm rates include full breakfast. MC, V. Drive up Wells Gray Park Rd. for 20 miles (33.3km); it will take about 30 min. Turn left at the ranch sign.

You can't miss the small buffalo herd casually grazing in a fenced pasture as you drive up the Wells Gray Park Road. Beyond this pastoral setting stand a log lodge, campsites, and four cabins nestled in the woodlands. The four lodge rooms are cozy and clean, with warm comforters and soft pillows. Guests in the lodge enjoy a hearty breakfast in the dining room.

The camping cabins, tent sites, and RV sites are extremely well kept. Dishwashing sinks are set up on the deck of the shower house, where hot water flows liberally. There's plenty of free firewood; fire-pit grills are available for a nominal fee. Hiking and horseback-riding trails surround the ranch. Guided rides run through the forest to the cliffs overlooking the Clearwater River valley and to the base of a secluded waterfall. Prices start at C$48 (U.S.$31) for a 2^1/$_2$-hour trip. If you get a sudden urge to venture deep into the woods near Trophy Mountain, your hosts can give you directions and outfit you with rental gear, from canoes to cookware.

Wells Gray Backcountry Chalets. Box 188B, Clearwater, BC, V0E 1N0. ☎ **888/ SKI-TREK** or 250/587-6444. Fax 604/587-6446. 3 chalets. Summer C$35 (U.S.$23) per person; winter C$40 (U.S.$26) per person. MC, V. Drive up Wells Gray Park Rd. for 22 miles (36.6km). The road takes about 35 min. to drive. Turn left at the ranch sign.

Ian Eakins and Tay Briggs run a family-owned outdoor guiding company that maintains three year-round chalets nestled deep in the park. Each chalet sleeps up to 12 and is fully equipped with a kitchen, bedding, books, sauna, and propane-generated lighting and heat. It's the best of both worlds: You can experience untrammeled wilderness *and* great rural hospitality. Two of the nicest people you could hope to have as guides and hosts, Ian and Tay are extremely knowledgeable about the wildlife and history of the park. They offer guided or self-catered hiking and cross-country ski packages that include stays in these backcountry hideaways, as well as guided 3- and 6-day canoe trips on Clearwater and Azure lakes that are custom-designed for families. Summer hikes are C$125 (U.S.$81) per person per day; winter cross-country ski trips are C$135 (U.S.$88) per person per day.

WHERE TO DINE

There aren't many restaurants to choose from in Clearwater. The **Clearwater Country Inn,** 449 Yellowhead Hwy. E. (☎ **250/674-3455**), has good home-style cooking like fried chicken and breaded veal cutlets; it's open from 4am to 9pm. The **Helmcken Falls Lodge,** Wells Gray Park Road, Clearwater (☎ **250/674-3657**), and the **Wells Gray Guest Ranch,** Wells Gray Park Road, Clearwater (☎ **250/674-2774**), offer buffet-style dinners daily at 7pm sharp, for C$25 (U.S.$16) per person.

If you're just looking for a light meal, the **River Café,** 73 Old N. Thompson Hwy. (☎ **250/674-0088**), is a friendly and informal place offering salads, espresso drinks, and fresh-baked snacks. River Café shares space with Interior Whitewater Expeditions. Campers usually stock up on provisions at the **Safety Mart,** Brookfield Mall, Old North Thompson Highway. It's open daily from 9am to 6pm.

11

The Okanagan Valley

Just south of the high country on Highway 97, the arid Okanagan Valley with its long chain of crystal-blue lakes is the ideal destination for freshwater-sports enthusiasts, golfers, skiers, and wine lovers. Ranches and small towns have flourished here for more than a century; the region's fruit orchards and vineyards will make you feel as if you've been transported to the Spanish countryside. Summer visitors get the pick of the crop—at insider prices—from the many fruit stands that line Highway 97. Be sure to stop for a pint of cherries, homemade jams, and other goodies.

An Okanagan-region chardonnay won gold medals in 1994 at international competitions held in London and Paris. And more than three dozen other wineries produce vintages that are following right on its heels. Despite this coveted honor, the valley has received little international publicity. Most visitors are Canadian, and the valley is not yet a major tour-bus destination. Get here before they do.

Many Canadian retirees have chosen the Okanagan Valley as their home for its relatively mild winters and dry, desertlike summers. It's also a favorite destination for younger visitors, drawn by boating, waterskiing, sportfishing, and windsurfing on 80-mile-long (128km) Lake Okanagan. In the summer high season, the valley's population increases five-fold from its winter average of about 35,000.

The town of Kelowna in the central valley is the hub of the province's wine-making industry and the valley's largest city. The town of Vernon is a favorite destination for cross-country and powder skiers, who flock to the northern valley's top resort—Silver Star Mountain.

1 Essentials

GETTING THERE

BY CAR The 242-mile (387km) drive from Vancouver to the Okanagan via the Trans-Canada Highway (Hwy. 1) and Highway 3 rambles through rich delta farmlands and the forested mountains of Manning Provincial Park and the Similkameen River region before descending into the Okanagan Valley's antelope-brush and sagebrush desert. For a more direct route to the towns of Kelowna and Vernon, take the Trans-Canada Highway to the Coquihalla Toll Highway, which eliminates more than an hour's driving time. The 126-mile (203km) route runs from Hope through Merritt over the Coquihalla Pass into Kamloops. The highway toll is C$10 (U.S.$7) per car.

BY BUS   Greyhound (☎ 800/661-8747) operates bus runs between Vancouver and Penticton, Kelowna, and Vernon, with service continuing on to Banff and Calgary. There are seven buses daily between Vancouver and Kelowna.

BY PLANE   Canadian Airlines (☎ **800/426-7000** in the U.S., 800/363-7530 in Canada) and **Air BC** (☎ **800/667-3721**) have frequent daily commuter flights from Calgary and Vancouver to Penticton and Kelowna.

VISITOR INFORMATION

Call the **Okanagan Similkameen Tourism Association,** 1332 Water St., Kelowna, BC, V1Y 9P4 (☎ **250/860-5999**); it's open daily year-round from 9am to 6pm.

2 Touring the Wineries

British Columbia has a long history of producing wines, ranging from mediocre to truly bad. In 1859, missionary Father Pandosy planted apple trees and vineyards and produced sacramental wines for the valley's mission. Other monastery wineries cropped up, but none of them worried about the quality of their bottlings. After all, the Canadian government had a reputation for subsidizing domestic industries, such as book publishing and cleric wineries, to promote entrepreneurial growth.

In the 1980s, the government threatened to pull its support of the industry unless it could produce an internationally competitive product. The vintners listened. Root stock was imported from France and Germany, and European-trained master vintners were hired to oversee the development of the vines and the wine-making process. The climate and soil conditions turned out to be some of the best in the world for wine making, and today, British Columbian wines are winning international gold medals. Competitively priced, in the C$7 to C$50 (U.S.$4.55 to U.S.$33) range, they represent some great bargains in well-balanced chardonnays, pinot blancs, and gewürztraminers; full-bodied merlots, pinot noirs, and cabernets; and dessert ice wines that surpass the best muscat d'or.

Because U.S. visitors are allowed to bring 33.8 ounces (1 liter) of wine back home without paying additional duty, Americans can bring a bottle (about 750ml) of their favorite selection back home if they've visited Canada for more than 24 hours. (The duty on additional bottles can be as high as U.S.25¢ per ounce!) Travelers from the United Kingdom can take back up to 2 liters of still wine without paying duty.

The valley's more than three dozen vineyards and wineries conduct free tours and wine tastings throughout the year. The **Okanagan Wine Festival** (☎ **250/861-6654**) is a celebration of wine and food at area vineyards and restaurants. Contact local visitor centers for specific information. See specific winery recommendations in the following sections on Oliver, Penticton, and Kelowna.

3 Oliver

32 miles (52km) S of Penticton

The absolute center of the Okanagan fruit-growing orchards is Oliver (pop. 4,285). What makes the area interesting to travelers, however, is its many wineries. Scarcely a tourist town, Oliver exists to serve the needs of local farmers, orchardists, and winemakers. It makes a reasonable stop if you're not obsessed with the resort and watersports lifestyle prevalent in the rest of the Okanagan Valley.

Many of the long-established wineries that put the region's name on the wine-producing map are within a short drive from Oliver. Especially proud of their location are the wineries along the "Golden Mile," situated on the slopes of the mountains west of Oliver along Road 8. The **Festival of the Grape** (☎ 250/498-6321) occurs on the first weekend of October, and is part of the larger Okanagan Wine Festival.

Notable wineries that welcome visitors include **Domaine Combret Estate Winery,** on Road 13 (☎ **250/498-8878;** fax 250/498-8879; e-mail: domaine_combret@bc.sympatic.ca), which has won medals at the annual Chardonnay du Monde competition in Burgundy. **Gehringer Brothers Estate Winery,** Road 8 (☎ **250/498-3537),** offers German-style wines, including Riesling, pinot gris, pinot noir, and pinot blanc. Try the crisp Ehrenfelser white wine, which carries intense flavors of apricot and almond. The tasting room is open June through October daily.

Hester Creek Estate Winery, Road 8 (☎ **250/498-4435;** e-mail: info@hestercreek.com), has a boutique that's open daily, plus tours by appointment. Especially nice is the patio, an inviting spot for picnickers. Superior growing conditions found at Hester Creek produce intense fruit flavors. **Inniskillin Okanagan,** Road 11 (☎ **250/498-6663**), offers daily tours and tastings. This winery produces a distinct selection of red wines such as cabernet sauvignon, merlot, and pinot noir.

Tinhorn Creek Vineyards, Road 7 (☎ **250/498-3734;** fax 250/498-3228; e-mail: winery@tinhorn.com), is one of the top Okanagan wineries. Self-guided tours allow you to linger; guided tours can be arranged by appointment. Specialties include gewürztraminer, pinot gris, chardonnay, pinot noir, cabernet franc, merlot, and ice wine. Adjacent to a wilderness area and bird sanctuary overlooking Vaseaux Lake, **Blue Mountain Vineyards & Cellars,** Allendale Road (☎ 250/497-8244), offers tours by appointment and operates a wine shop and tasting room.

For more information on the region, contact the **Oliver Visitor Info Centre,** 36205 93rd St. (Box 460), Oliver, BC, V0H 1T0 (☎ **250/498-6321**).

The **Southwind Inn,** 34017 Hwy. 97 S. (☎ **800/661-9922** or 250/498-3442), is the nicest place to stay in Oliver, with a restaurant and double rooms for C$75 to C$85 (U.S.$49–U.S.$55).

4 Penticton

50 miles (80km) N of Oliver, 37 miles (60km) S of Kelowna, 245 miles (396km) W of Vancouver via the Coquihalla Hwy.

One of the belles of the Okanagan, Penticton (pop. 32,219) is a lovely midsize city with two entirely different lakefronts. Above the town is the toe-end of vast Okanagan Lake, while to the south is Lake Skaha. It's a lovely setting, and a peach of a place for a recreation-dominated holiday. "Peach" has additional significance here, as Penticton is also the center for apple, peach, cherry, and grape production. But there's a lot more to Penticton than agriculture. Facilities range from hostels to world-class resorts, while the restaurants are among the best in this part of British Columbia.

ESSENTIALS

GETTING THERE **By Car** Penticton is 50 miles (80km) north of Oliver on Highway 97, and 37 miles (60km) south of Kelowna. Via the Coquihalla Highway, the town is 245 miles (396km) west of Vancouver.

By Bus Four **Greyhound** (☎ 800/661-8747) buses connect Penticton and Vancouver daily. The one-way fare is C$50 (U.S.$33).

By Plane Both **Air BC** (☎ 800/667-3721) and **Canadian Regional Airlines** (☎ 800/665-1177) offer flights between Penticton and Vancouver.

VISITOR INFORMATION The **Penticton Visitor Info Centre** is at 888 Westminster Ave. W., Penticton, BC, V2A 8R2 (☎ **800/663-5052** or 250/493-4055).

Special Events

The town's big summer celebration is the **Penticton Peach Festival,** held the first week of August. It includes parades, water-sports competitions, live entertainment, street dances, midway rides, and a general and pervasive air of fun. Be the first to taste the valley's best chardonnay, pinot noir, merlot, and ice wine at the **Okanagan Wine Festival** (☎ 250/861-6654), during the first and second weeks in October at wineries and restaurants throughout Penticton.

The visitor center also houses the British Columbia Wine Information Centre and a good wine shop with all sorts of local vintages.

EXPLORING THE TOWN

It's hard to beat Penticton's location. With Lake Okanagan lapping at the northern edge of town, Lake Skaha's beaches forming the town's southern boundary, and the Okanagan River cutting between the two, Penticton has the feel of a real oasis. Hemmed in by lakes and desert valley walls, Penticton has a pleasantly compact feel and in summer fairly hums with activity. As elsewhere in the Okanagan Valley, water sports are the main preoccupation, but Penticton also has an air of gentility that suggests there's a little more going on than just jet skiing.

The old commercial center is along **Main Street** toward the north end of town; there's also a lot of activity along **Lakeshore Drive,** the boulevard that parallels the beachfront of Lake Okanagan. Lined with hotels and restaurants on one side, clogged with sun worshippers on the other, Lakeshore Drive is a very busy place in summer.

Right on the lakefront is the **SS *Sicamous,*** a sternwheeler that plied the waters of Lake Okanagan from 1914 to 1935. There are plans to restore it as an operating tour boat, but meanwhile, it's beached in the sand, and currently houses a scale model of the Kettle Valley Railway. It's open in summer daily from 9am to 5pm; the rest of the year, Monday through Friday from 9am to 5pm.

Even if you're not into sunbathing, a saunter along the **beachfront promenade** is called for (dodge the madly peddled surrey carts). Beach volleyball, sand castles, and a drinks kiosk in the shape of a giant peach are just the beginning of what you'll encounter along this long, broad strand: It's prime people-watching territory.

At the eastern end of the beachfront is the **Art Gallery of the South Okanagan,** 199 Front St. (☎ 250/493-2928), a showcase for local artists. The gift shop is a good spot to pick up a souvenir. Just beyond the gallery is the **Marina on Lake Okanagan** (☎ 250/770-2000), where you can rent all manner of watercraft.

The beach along Skaha Lake is usually more laid-back than the Okanagan Lake front. The relatively more secluded nature of this beach, plus a large water park for the kids, makes it a good destination for families. The **Skaha Lake Marina** (☎ 250/ 492-7368), at the east edge of the beach, will get you out onto the water.

TOURING THE WINERIES

The two main wine-producing areas near Penticton are north along the east slopes of Okanagan Lake near the community of Naramata, and north along the west lake slopes near Summerland. From Penticton, follow Upper Bench Road, which turns into Naramata Road and leads to **Naramata,** 9 miles (14km) north and one of the first British Columbian wine-growing regions. One of the first small wineries in the province was **Lang Vineyard,** 2493 Gammon Rd. (☎ 250/496-5987). The tasting-and-sales room is open May through September daily.

Hillside Estate, 1350 Naramata Rd. (☎ 250/493-4424; www.hillsideestate.com), is open daily (call ahead in midwinter). From Easter weekend until the Okanagan Wine Festival, Hillside Estates operates a patio restaurant at the winery. The tasting room at **Lake Breeze Vineyards,** 930 Sammet Rd. (☎ 250/496-5659), is open May 1 to October 15 daily. Its restaurant is open for lunch from May 1 to September 30.

North of Penticton along Highway 97 is another wine-producing area. **Sumac Ridge Estate Winery,** 17403 Hwy. 97 (☎ 250/494-0451; www.sumacridge.com), conducts tours daily from May to mid-October. Besides operating a shop and tasting room, the winery runs the fine Cellar Door Bistro (see "Where to Dine," below).

Located 26 miles (43.3km) north of Penticton, **Hainle Vineyards Estate Winery,** 5355 Trepanier Bench Rd. (☎ 250/767-2525; www.hainle.com), was the first Okanagan winery to produce ice wine. The wine shop is open May through October, Tuesday through Sunday. From November through April, the shop is open for tastings Thursday through Sunday. The bistro Amphora is open Tuesday through Sunday.

THE KETTLE VALLEY STEAM RAILWAY

The Kettle Valley Railway was completed in 1914 to link the British Columbian coastal communities to the burgeoning mining camps in Kettle River valley, one valley east of the Okanagan Valley. Laying rails through this extreme landscape was considered quite an engineering feat, as the grade climbed from sea level to 4,000 feet (1,219m) and crossed 18 trestle bridges. Many portions of this highly scenic railway have been converted into rails-to-trails pathways for hikers and mountain bikers, but one section remains in use by original steam trains.

The **Kettle Valley Railway Society,** 18404 Bathville Rd., Summerland (☎ 877/ 494-8424 in B.C., or 250/494-8422; e-mail: big_ideas@bc.sympatico.ca), operates a 2-hour journey on a 6-mile (10km) section of the original track west of Summerland, 10 miles (16km) north of Penticton. From July 1 to Labour Day, the train runs Thursday through Monday at 10:30am and 1:30pm, departing from the Prairie Valley Station off Bathville Road; from late May through June and from Labour Day to mid-October, the train runs at the same times but from Saturday through Monday only. Fares are C$11 (U.S.$6.95) for adults, C$10 (U.S.$6.50) for seniors and youths, C$8 (U.S.$5) for children 4 to 12, and C$39 (U.S.$25) for families.

OUTDOOR PURSUITS

BIKING   The best Okanagan Valley off-road bike trail is the old ✪ **Kettle Valley Railway** route. The most scenic and challenging section of the route is from Naramata, north of Penticton along the east side of Okanagan Lake. The rails-to-trails route climbs up steep switchbacks to Chute Lake and then across 17 trestles as it traverses Myra Canyon. The entire mountain-bike route from Naramata to Westbridge in the Kettle River valley is 108 miles (175km) and can take from 3 to 5 days. For more information, contact the visitor center or **Sun Country Cycle,** 533 Main St. (☎ 250/ 493-0686), which also offers rentals and lots of friendly advice.

BOATING & WATER SPORTS   Penticton's local marinas offer full-service boat rentals. **Okanagan Boat Charters,** 291 Front St. (☎ 250/492-5099), rents houseboats with fully equipped kitchens that can accommodate up to 10; a week starts at C$1,295 (U.S.$842). The **Marina on Okanagan Lake,** 291 Front St. (☎ 250/ 492-2628), rents ski boats, fishing boats, and tackle.

Wonderful Waterworld, 225 Yorkton Ave. (☎ 250/493-8121), is the place for water slides, slot-car racing, and nine-hole mini golf. If you have a hankering to parasail, contact **Okanagan Parasailing,** on Lake Okanagan just west of the art museum

(☎ 250/492-2242). A popular activity is renting a rubber raft from **Coyote Cruises** (☎ 205/492-2115), in the blue building along the river at Riverside Drive, then floating from Okanagan Lake down to Skaha Lake. On a hot summer day, you'll be joined by hundreds of other people in rafts, inner tubes, and rubber dinghies; the water fight of your life is almost guaranteed. After you reach Skaha Lake—it takes about 2 hours—Coyote Cruises will transport you back to headquarters.

GOLF   Penticton Golf & Country Club (☎ 250/492-8727) is an 18-hole, par-70 course just west of downtown on the Okanagan River. Greens fees are C$35 (U.S.$23) Monday through Friday, C$45 (U.S.$29) Saturday and Sunday. The club offers equipment rentals, a driving range, and a clubhouse. **Twin Lakes Golf Resort,** 11 miles (18km) south of Penticton off Highway 97 (☎ 250/497-5359), is another 18-hole course, located in a steep-walled canyon; greens fees start at C$35 (U.S.$23).

SKIING   Cross-country and powder skiing are the Okanagan Valley's main winter attractions. Intermediate and expert downhill skiers frequent the **Apex Resort,** Green Mountain Road (☎ 800/387-2739, 250/492-2880, 250/292-8111, or 250/ 492-2929 for snow report), where 56 runs are serviced by a quad chair, a triple chair, a T-bar, and a beginner tow/platter. The 31 miles (51.6km) of cross-country ski trails are well marked and well groomed, offering both flat stretches and hilly ascents. Facilities include an ice rink, snow golf, sleigh rides, casino nights, and racing competitions.

WHERE TO STAY

There are three major lodging areas: the northern lakefront on Okanagan Lake, the southern lakefront on Lake Skaha, and the Main Street strip that connects the two. Penticton has a lot of older motels, many of which have seen years of hard use.

Bear's Den B&B. 189 Linden Ave., P.O. Box 172, Kaleden, BC, V0H 1K0. ☎ **250/ 497-6721.** Fax 250/497-6453. E-mail: bearsden@vip.net. 3 units. C$85–C$100 (U.S.$55– U.S.$65) double. V.

This friendly B&B is 10 minutes south of Penticton in the small village of Kaleden. Perched high above Skaha Lake, views from the patio and balconies are expansive, from the neighboring orchards to the glittering lake and mountain slopes beyond. There are three guest rooms: the Music Room and the Rabbit Warren, each with whimsical decor, plus the Bear's Den, a master suite with canopy bed, enormous bathroom with 6-foot soaker tub, and that million-dollar view. The teddy-bear theme might not be to everyone's taste, but there's no denying the first-rate quality of the accommodations, the gracious welcome, and the wonderful multicourse breakfast.

Bel Air Motel. 2670 Skaha Lake Rd., Penticton, BC, V2A 6G1. ☎ **800/766-5770** or 250/492-6111. Fax 250/492-8035. E-mail: bel-air@uniserve.som. 42 units. A/C TV TEL. High season C$68 (U.S.$44) double. Kitchen C$16 (U.S.$10) extra. AE, MC, V.

This well-maintained older motor-court motel is just the ticket if you don't want to spend a fortune on a room in Penticton. Guest rooms are large and stylish, and the balconies and parking areas decked with flowers. You'll need to drive to get to the beaches, but otherwise this is a good, inexpensive place to stay. On-site facilities include an outdoor pool, hot tub, sauna, barbecues, laundry, and playground. The motel is near both restaurants and shopping.

Best Western Inn at Penticton. 3180 Skaha Lake Rd., Penticton, BC, V2A 6G4. ☎ **800/ 668-6746** or 250/493-0311. Fax 250/493-5556. www.bestwestern.bc.ca. E-mail: bestwest@bc.ca. 67 units. A/C TV TEL. High season C$109–C$119 (U.S.$71–U.S.$77) double. Kitchen C$20 (U.S.$13) extra. AE, DISC, MC, V.

Roughly midway between the two lake beaches, this new Best Western is a short drive from the beach scene, but it's a handsome hotel with nicely furnished rooms and especially nice facilities, such as the beautifully landscaped courtyard and banks of flowers everywhere. The family-dining restaurant serves three meals daily; other perks are the indoor and outdoor pools, hot tub, and barbecues.

Hostelling International–Penticton. 464 Ellis St., Penticton, BC, V2A 4M2. ☎ **250/ 492-3992.** Fax 250/492-8755. www.hihostels.bc.ca. E-mail: penticton@hihostels.cb.ca. 50 beds. High season C$12–C$19 (U.S.$8–U.S.$12) dorm rm, C$35–C$42 (U.S.$23–U.S.$27) private rm double. AE, MC, V.

Right in the heart of downtown, the Penticton hostel is in a historic home once owned by a pioneer banker. Facilities include a kitchen, laundry, outdoor barbecue area, and bike rentals.

Penticton Lakeside Resort. 21 W. Lakeshore Dr., Penticton, BC, V2A 7M5. ☎ **800/ 663-9400** or 250/493-8221. Fax 250/493-0607. www.rpbhotels.com. E-mail: lakeside@ rpbhotels.com. 204 units. A/C TV TEL. C$155 (U.S.$111) double; C$159–C$205 (U.S.$103–U.S.$133) suite. AE, CB, DC, DISC, MC, V. Free parking. When you arrive in town, follow the signs to Main St. Lakeshore Dr. is at the north end of Main St. Pets accepted with C$10 (U.S.$7) fee.

Set on the water's edge, the Penticton Lakeside Resort has its own stretch of sandy Lake Okanagan beachfront, where guests can sunbathe or stroll along the adjacent pier. This year-round resort is also close to great golf courses and the Apex Mountain ski area. The deluxe suites feature Jacuzzis, and the lakeside rooms are highly recommended for their view. The menus at the Okanagan Surf N' Turf Company Restaurant and the Barking Parrot Bar & Patio feature locally grown ingredients. Other facilities include a pool, sauna, whirlpool, fitness center, tennis courts, salon, gift shop, volleyball, and running trails.

Spanish Villa Resort. 890 Lakeshore Dr., Penticton, BC, V2A 1C1. ☎ **800/552-9199** or 250/492-2922. Fax 250/492-2922. 60 units. A/C TV TEL. High season C$68–C$108 (U.S.$44–U.S.$70) double. Kitchen C$20 (U.S.$13) extra. AE, DISC, MC, V.

Of the many motel complexes that line Lakeshore Drive, the Spanish Villa, directly across the street from the Lake Okanagan beaches, is the most attractive and best maintained. The rooms are large and furnished with a Mediterranean flair. The most expensive units boast great views. Guests have access to a pool and laundry; the Villa is also close to dozens of restaurants and shops, right in the thick of things.

Travelodge Penticton. 950 Westminster Ave., Penticton, BC, V2A 1L2. ☎ **800/578-7878** or 250/492-0225. Fax 250/493-8340. 34 units. A/C TV TEL. C$70–C$90 (U.S.$46–U.S.$59) double. Kitchen C$10 (U.S.$7) extra. AE, MC, V.

For a moderately priced motel within walking distance of Lake Okanagan, the Travelodge offers clean, unfussy rooms with lots of extras. The coffee shop is open for breakfast and lunch. Amenities include an indoor and outdoor pool with water slide, free in-room coffee, sauna, and whirlpool. One of the best values in Penticton.

Waterfront Inn. 3688 Parkview St., Penticton, BC, V2A 6H1. ☎ **800/563-6006** or 250/492-8228. Fax 250/492-8228. E-mail: watfront@bc.sympatico.ca. 21 units. A/C TV TEL. High season C$58–C$80 (U.S.$38–U.S.$52) double. Kitchen C$10 (U.S.$7) extra. AE, MC, V.

The Waterfront Inn is an older, standard-issue motel in a great location: across a quiet street from a park with beach access to Lake Skaha. The rooms are clean and basic, but if you're here for the action on the lakefront, you'll enjoy the relative quiet of this location and the fact that you won't have to cross four lanes of traffic to get to the water. Some units have full kitchens. Guests can use the laundry and gas barbecues.

WHERE TO DINE

Cellar Door Bistro. 17403 Hwy. 97, Summerland, 10 miles (17km) north of Penticton. ☎ **250/494-3316.** Reservations recommended. Main courses C$14–C$24 (U.S.$9–U.S.$16). AE, MC, V. Thurs–Sat noon–3pm; Tues–Sat 5–9pm. CONTINENTAL.

The microbrewery boom got us used to eating in breweries; now we have restaurants in wineries. This excellent, attractive choice is hidden inside the Sumac Ridge Estate Winery in Summerland, just north of Penticton. The menu changes monthly to emphasize what's fresh. The cuisine has a hearty country-French finesse, such as a savory mushroom tart, prime rib with Roquefort herb butter, and pan-seared halibut with local wild mushrooms. The dishes are paired with wines from Sumac Ridge.

Granny Bogners. 302 W. Eckhardt. ☎ **250/493-2711.** Reservations required. Main courses C$11–C$19 (U.S.$7–U.S.$12). AE, DC, MC, V. Tues–Sun 5:30–9:30pm. FRENCH.

Granny Bogners is in a shake-sided heritage home in a quiet residential area in central Penticton. Granny's tops the list when it comes to the locals' favorite special-occasion restaurant. The menu is slightly old-fashioned: The well-prepared dishes here almost qualify as upscale comfort food. Roast duck is served with Grand Marnier sauce, pan-fried fillet of red snapper Cleopatra is prepared with capers and shrimp, and oysters come on a bed of spinach, bacon, and cheese. Sweetbreads, New York steaks, and veal medaillons in port-and-mushroom sauce are other choices. The dining room is filled with white linen and crystal, yet retains a kind of rustic nonchalance.

Historic 1912 Restaurant. Lakehill Rd., Kaleden. ☎ **250/497-6868.** Reservations recommended. Main courses C$19–C$35 (U.S.$12–U.S.$23). MC, V. Tues–Sun 5:30–10pm. Drive 10 min. south of Penticton on Hwy. 97. Take the second left after the Okanagan Game Farm onto Lakehill Rd. CONTINENTAL.

The Historic 1912 Restaurant is the quintessential romantic hideaway. At the end of a long, winding road, the lakeside restaurant is in a stone building that served as a general store when it was built in 1912. The decor is Victorian, featuring dark-wood paneling and white linens. The menu offers seafood specialties like lemon vodka prawns, steak and rack of lamb, pasta dishes, and rich desserts. A specialty are four-course, prix-fixe dinners for two or four that feature table-side cooking and carving. Prices for these dinners range from C$59 to C$109 (U.S.$38 to U.S.$71) for two.

✪ Mambo's Italiano Restaurant. 274 W. Lakeshore Dr. ☎ **250/493-6556.** Reservations suggested. Main courses C$12–C$18 (U.S.$8–U.S.$12). AE, MC, V. Daily 11am–2pm and 5–10pm. ITALIAN.

Mambo's has a great location right on Lakeshore Drive, across from the Lake Okanagan beachfront. Guests dine in either the pleasantly casual main room or the large second-story patio with views across the lake. Mambo's serves the most up-to-date cooking in Penticton, a mix of hearty Italian and zippy Northwest cuisine that combines the best features of both. Appetizers are fresh and appealing: The yam-and-roast-garlic soup is a standout, as are the crispy oysters with apple, pancetta, and smoked chili cream sauce. There's also a selection of entree salads if you want something light, plus many vegetarian pasta and pizza choices. The eclectic entrees range from beef tournedos, with local goat cheese and merlot demiglace, to chicken Parmesan served with blackberry and black-pepper sauce.

Theo's Greek Restaurant. 687 Main St. ☎ **250/492-2923.** Reservations recommended. Main courses C$10–C$18 (U.S.$7–U.S.$12). AE, DC, ER, MC, V. Mon–Sat 11am–11pm, Sun 5–11pm. GREEK.

When you mention that you're going to Penticton, don't be surprised if previous visitors immediately offer testimonials about Theo's, a popular place with excellent, highly flavored cooking. The casual taverna-style dining room has whitewashed walls, a stone floor, and lush greenery. The traditional menu features delectable calamari, succulent marinated lamb, and standard favorites like dolmades and moussaka. Even the requisite local salmon is baked with an oregano-and-garlic crust.

Villa Rossa Ristorante. 795 W. Westminster Ave. ☎ **250/490-9595.** Reservations suggested. Main courses C$12–C$25 (U.S.$8–U.S.$16). AE, MC, V. Mon–Fri 11:30am–2:30pm; daily 5–10pm. ITALIAN.

Villa Rossa is one of the top Penticton restaurants for more traditional Italian cuisine. It has an especially attractive patio shaded by grapevines, just the spot on a warm evening. The menu is varied, with classic dishes like osso bucco, chicken Marsala, and pasta joining Canadian specialties like steaks and salmon. Good wine list, too.

5 Kelowna

245 miles (395km) E of Vancouver

Kelowna (pop. 93,403) is the largest city in the Okanagan, and one of the fastest-growing areas in Canada. You won't have to spend much time here to understand why: Kelowna sits astride 80-mile-long (128km) Okanagan Lake at the center of a vast fruit-, wine-, and vegetable-growing area, with lots of sun and a resort lifestyle. This is about as close to California as it gets in Canada. Kelowna is especially popular with retirees, who stream here to escape the Pacific pall of Vancouver and the winter cold of Alberta. Predictably, water sports and golf are the main leisure activities, and it's hard to imagine a better outdoor-oriented family-vacation spot.

With plenty of marinas and a beautiful beachfront park that flanks downtown, you'll have no problem finding a place to get wet. In fact, Kelowna's only problem is its popularity. The greater area now has a population of 150,000, with a sizable percentage of these people arriving since 1990. Traffic is very heavy, especially on the Okanagan Lake Floating Bridge, which simply can't handle its present traffic load.

ESSENTIALS

GETTING THERE **By Plane** The Kelowna airport is north of the city on Highway 97. **Air BC** (☎ 800/667-3721 in Canada, 800/776-3000 in the U.S.) and **Canadian Air** (☎ 800/665-1177 in Canada, 800/426-7000 in the U.S.) offer regular flights from Calgary, Vancouver, and other cities. **Horizon Air** (☎ 800/547-9308) offers service from Seattle. **WestJet** (☎ 800/538-5696; www.westjet.com) operates flights from Vancouver, Victoria, Calgary, and Edmonton.

By Car With the completion of the Peachland Connector to the Coquihalla Highway (Hwy. 5) in 1990, high-speed freeways linked Kelowna and the Okanagan to the Vancouver area. You can make the 245-mile (395km) drive from Vancouver in about 4 hours. From Kelowna to Calgary, it's 386 miles (623km) over slower roads.

By Bus Seven **Greyhound** buses (☎ 800/661-8747) travel between Vancouver and Kelowna daily. The adult fare is C$51 (U.S.$33). Three buses per day continue on to Calgary; adult fare is C$75 (U.S.$49).

VISITOR INFORMATION The **Kelowna Visitor Info Centre** is at 544 Harvey Ave., Kelowna, BC, V1Y 6C9 (☎ 800/663-4345 or 250/861-1515; www.bcyellowpages.com/advert/k/kcc; e-mail: kelownachamber@awine.com).

GETTING AROUND The local bus service is operated by **Kelowna Transit System** (☎ 250/860-8121). A one-zone fare is C$1.75 (U.S.$1.15). For a taxi, call **Checkmate Cabs** (☎ 250/861-1111).

Kelowna gets its busy summer festival season off to a bang with the **Knox Mountain Hill Climb** (☎ **250/861-1990**), held for nearly half a century on the second-to-last weekend in May. This motor sport race involves both cars and motorcycles, and is the longest hill-climb race in North America. The **Okanagan Wine Festival** (☎ **250/861-6654**) is celebrated in early October in wineries and restaurants throughout the area.

EXPLORING THE CITY

Kelowna is a big, sprawling place that has engulfed both sides of Okanagan Lake, but the sights of most interest to travelers are contained in a relatively small area. And that's good, because traffic in Kelowna can be vexing. Beware of the heavily traveled **Harvey Street** and the **Okanagan Lake Floating Bridge;** on the latter, delays of an hour are not uncommon.

Downtown Kelowna is a pleasant retail area that retains a number of older buildings that now house shops, galleries, and cafes. The main commercial strip is **Bernard Street.** The showpiece of Kelowna is lovely **City Park,** which flanks downtown and the bridge's east side and has over half a mile (1km) of wide sandy beach. At the north edge is a large marina where you can rent boats and recreational equipment, or sign up to learn to water-ski and parasail. Here, too, is where you board **MV *Fintry Queen,*** which offers paddle-wheel boat tours of the lake (see below).

Continue north through the busy marina to **Waterfront Park,** with an island band shell and promenades along the lakefront and lagoons. The **Grand Okanagan Lakefront Resort** towers above the park, and it's worth a stop to step inside the modern opulent lobby, or to enjoy a drink beside the pool. Adjacent to the resort between Water and Ellis streets is a modern complex of structures housing many of Kelowna's top cultural sites and civic buildings, including the city hall, post office, and **Kelowna Visual and Performing Arts Centre,** to be completed later in 2000.

Kelowna Centennial Museum. 470 Queensway. ☎ **250/763-2417.** Admission by donation. July 1 to Labour Day, Mon–Sat 10am–5pm, Sun 2–5pm; rest of the year, Tues–Sat 10am–5pm.

This large and ambitious museum touches on the history of almost every aspect of life in the Okanagan Valley. Starting out with local fossils, moving on through the prehistoric culture and artifacts of the native Okanagans and on to the lives of the farmers and ranchers, it's all here. Eclectic only begins to describe the collection—radios, dolls, books—but everything is well curated, and you're sure to find something of interest. A couple of high points are the re-creation of the original 1861 Kelowna trading post and a winter dwelling of the early native inhabitants.

B.C. Orchard Industry Museum. 1304 Ellis St. ☎ **250/763-0433.** Admission by donation. Tues–Sat 10am–5pm.

This museum, housed in an old apple-packing plant, tells the story of the region's apple-and-soft-fruit industry, with archival photos, old equipment, and a hands-on discovery corner. Sharing space with the Orchard Museum is the **Wine Museum** (☎ **250/868-0441**), with a few exhibits on the relatively brief history of Okanagan wine production. The wine shop sells a good selection of regional vintages.

Kelowna Art Gallery. 1315 Water St. ☎ **250/762-2226.** www.islandnet.com/~bcma/museums/kelowna. E-mail: kagchin@bc.sympatico.ca. Admission by donation. July–Aug Mon–Sat 10am–5pm, Sun 1–5pm; rest of year Tues–Sat 10am–5pm.

Kelowna

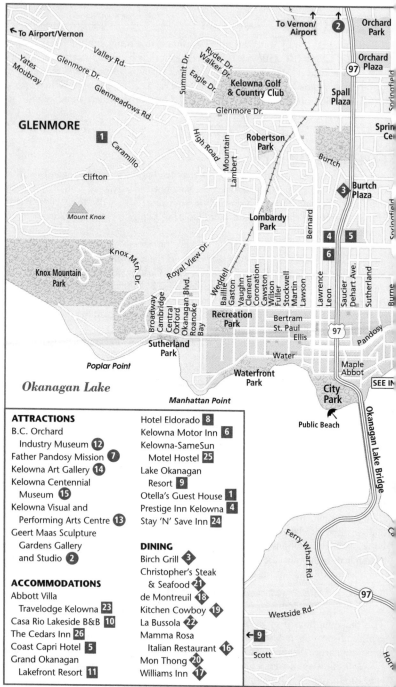

To Vernon/Airport

To Airport/Vernon →

Valley Rd.
Glenmore Dr.
Yates
Moubray
Glenmeadows Rd.
Summit Dr.
Ryder Dr.
Walker Dr.
Eagle Dr.

Orchard Park

Orchard Plaza

97

Spall Plaza

Kelowna Golf & Country Club

Glenmore Dr.

GLENMORE

1

Caramillo

Clifton

Robertson Park

Burtch

Spri
Ce

Mount Knox

High Road
Mountain
Lambert

Lombardy Park

Bernard

3 **Burtch Plaza**

4   5

6

Knox Mtn. Dr.

Knox Mountain Park

Royal View Dr.

Weddell
Baillie
Gaston
Vaughn
Clement
Coronation
Cawston
Wilson
Fuller
Stockwell
Martin
Lawson

Lawrence
Leon

Saucier
Dehart Ave.
Sutherland
Burne

Broadway
Cambridge
Central
Oxford
Okanagan Blvd.
Roanoke
Bay

Recreation Park

Bertram
St. Paul
Ellis

97

Pandosy

Sutherland Park

Water

Poplar Point

Maple
Abbot

SEE IN

Waterfront Park

City Park

Okanagan Lake

Manhattan Point

Public Beach

Okanagan Lake Bridge

Ferry Wharf Rd.

97

Westside Rd.

9 ←

Scott

ATTRACTIONS

B.C. Orchard
  Industry Museum **12**
Father Pandosy Mission **7**
Kelowna Art Gallery **14**
Kelowna Centennial
  Museum **15**
Kelowna Visual and
  Performing Arts Centre **13**
Geert Maas Sculpture
  Gardens Gallery
  and Studio **2**

ACCOMMODATIONS

Abbott Villa
  Travelodge Kelowna **23**
Casa Rio Lakeside B&B **10**
The Cedars Inn **26**
Coast Capri Hotel **5**
Grand Okanagan
  Lakefront Resort **11**

Hotel Eldorado **8**
Kelowna Motor Inn **6**
Kelowna-SameSun
  Motel Hostel **25**
Lake Okanagan
  Resort **9**
Otella's Guest House **1**
Prestige Inn Kelowna **4**
Stay 'N' Save Inn **24**

DINING

Birch Grill **3**
Christopher's Steak
  & Seafood **21**
de Montreuil **18**
Kitchen Cowboy **19**
La Bussola **22**
Mamma Rosa
  Italian Restaurant **16**
Mon Thong **20**
Williams Inn **17**

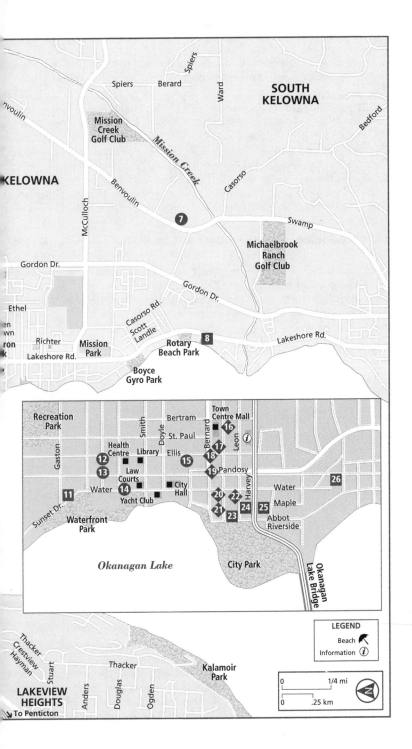

Kelowna's new art gallery hosts 16 shows per year of work by regional, national, and international artists. The permanent collection is a good body of works by primarily British Columbian artists. The shop is a great place for unique handcrafted gifts.

Father Pandosy Mission. South of the city center at the corner of Benvoulin and Casorso rds. ☎ 250/860-8369. Free admission. Easter to mid-Oct daily 9am–dusk. From downtown, take Richter St. south. Take a left on Cedar, then right on Casorso. Follow Casorso to the T-junction with Benvoulin.

The first nonnative person to settle in the Kelowna area was the oblate Father Pandosy, who established a mission here to convert the native Okanagans. On the original site now stands a life-size replica of the log mission buildings, which are filled with period household items. Also on the grounds are a collection of old horse-drawn wagons and carriages and early farm equipment. A free brochure leads you on a self-guided tour of the site.

Geert Maas Sculpture Gardens Gallery and Studio. 250 Reynolds Rd. ☎ 250/860-7012. E-mail: gmsg@silk.net. Free admission. May 1–Oct 1 Mon–Sat 10am–5pm.

Geert Maas is an internationally acclaimed artist and sculptor whose work fills a large parklike meadow in the hills above Kelowna. The mostly bronze pieces are large, voluminous, and amply curved in the manner of Henry Moore. Wander among the sculpture and then go inside to see more intimate pieces by Maas, including paintings and multimedia assemblages.

TOURING THE WINERIES

Calona Wines, 1125 Richter St., Kelowna (☎ 250/762-3332; e-mail: wineboutique@cascadia.ca), conducts daily tours through western Canada's oldest and largest (since 1932) winery. Many antique wine-making machines are on display, alongside the state-of-the-art equipment the winery now uses. At **Summerhill Estate Winery,** 4870 Chute Lake Rd., Kelowna (☎ 800/667-3538 in Canada, or 250/764-8000), the wine shop and tasting room are open year-round daily.

The neighboring town of Westbank is home to **Mission Hill Wines,** 1730 Mission Hill Rd. (☎ 250/768-7611; e-mail: kmoul@markanthony.com). In July and August, tours are conducted daily; the rest of the year, on Saturday and Sunday. An experience worth savoring even if you're not an oenophile is the **Quail's Gate Estate,** 3303 Boucherie Rd., Kelowna (☎ 250/769-4451); be sure to taste the ice wines. Tours are conducted May 30 to Labour Day daily. The tasting room is in the restored log home of the Allison family, pioneers who arrived in the valley during the 1870s.

North of Kelowna is **Gray Monk Estate Winery,** 1055 Camp Rd., Okanagan Centre (☎ 800/663-4205 or 250/766-3168; www.graymonk.com), noted for its pinot noirs. Gray Monk boasts a patio lounge and gives winery tours from May 1 to October 31 daily. The tasting room is open daily year-round.

GUIDED TOURS & EXCURSIONS

Built in 1948, the paddle wheeler **MV *Fintry Queen,*** on the dock off Bernard Avenue (☎ 250/763-2780), was once a working ferry but is now a tour boat and restaurant. Call for details on sailings and special lunch and dinner cruises.

The **Okanagan Valley Wine Train** (☎ 888/674-8725; www.incentre.net/funtrain) travels from Kelowna to Vernon and on to Armstrong. The trip is made in vintage rail cars; the train includes a cafe, gift shop, and, of course, a club car pouring local vintages. The 6- to 7-hour excursion travels along the eastern shores of Okanagan Lake and then Kalamalka Lake before passing through the bucolic dairy country near Armstrong, where there's an optional buffet-style dinner and entertainment. The schedule and rates are rather complex; call for details.

If you want to visit the wineries themselves, contact **Okanagan Wine Country Tours** (☎ 250/868-9463), which offers packages ranging from a 3-hour "Afternoon Delight" (C$30/U.S.$20) to the "Daytripper" for C$85 (U.S.$55).

OUTDOOR PURSUITS

BIKING   The Kettle Valley Railway's ✪ **Myra Canyon** route near Kelowna crosses 18 trestle bridges and passes through two tunnels that were carved out of the mountains. This rails-to-trails route is challenging, but one of the most scenic mountain-biking routes in British Columbia. Knox Mountain Park (see "Hiking," below) also has mountain-biking trails. Guided biking tours are organized by **Monashee Adventure Tours Inc.** (☎ 250/762-9253) and **Silver Star Mountain Resort** (see "Outdoor Pursuits" under section 6, Vernon). To rent bikes, contact **Sports Rent,** 3000 Pandosy St. (☎ 250/861-5699).

GOLF   There are more than a dozen golf courses in the Kelowna area, and golf is second only to water sports as the region's recreational drawing card. The greens fees throughout the Okanagan Valley range from C$30 to C$85 (U.S.$20 to U.S.$55)—a good value not only for the beautiful locations but also for the quality of service you'll find at each club. **A-1 Last Minute Golf Hotline** (☎ 800/684-6344 or 604/878-1833) can arrange next-day tee times at local courses. Savings can be as much as 40%. Call between 3 and 9pm for the next day, or before noon for the same day.

Gallagher's Canyon Golf and Country Club, 4320 McCulloch Rd. (☎ 250/861-4240), has a Les Furber–designed 18-hole course that features one hole overlooking the precipice of a gaping canyon and another that's perched on the brink of a ravine. It also has a nine-hole course, midlength course, and double-ended learning center. **Harvest Golf Club,** 2725 Klo Rd. (☎ 250/862-3103), is one of the finest courses in the Okanagan, a championship course in an orchard setting. The ✪ **Okanagan Golf Club** (☎ 800/898-2449 or 250/765-5955) has two 18-hole courses, the Jack Nicklaus–designed Bear Course and the Les Furber–designed Quail Course. These courses are just off Highway 97 near the airport.

HIKING   The closest hiking trails to Kelowna are in **Knox Mountain Park,** immediately north of the city. From downtown, follow Ellis Street to its terminus, where there's a parking area and trailhead. The most popular trail climbs up the cactus-clad mountainside to Knox Mountain summit, from which you'll enjoy magnificent views of the lake and orchards.

SKIING & SNOWBOARDING   British Columbia's second-largest ski area and one of North America's snowboarding capitals, ✪ **Big White Ski Resort,** Parkinson Way, Kelowna (☎ 250/765-3101, 250/765-SNOW for snow report, or 250/765-8888 for lodge reservations; www.bigwhite.com), is famed for its hip-deep champagne powder snow. The resort spreads over a broad mountain, featuring long, wide runs. Skiers here cruise open bowls and tree-lined glades. There's an annual average of 18 feet of fluffy powder, so it's no wonder the resort's 102 named runs are so popular. There are three high-speed quad chairs, a fixed-grip quad, a triple quad, a double chair, a T-bar, a beginner tow, and a platter lift. The resort also offers more than 15 miles (25km) of groomed cross-country ski trails, a recreational racing program, and night skiing 5 nights a week. An adult day lift ticket is C$45 (U.S.$29). Big White is 34 miles (55km) southeast of Kelowna off Highway 33.

Only a 15-minute drive from Westbank, **Crystal Mountain Resorts Ltd.** (☎ 250/768-5189, or 250/768-3753 for snow report) has a range of programs for all types of skiers, specializing in clinics for children, women, and seniors. This friendly, family-oriented resort has 20 runs, 80% of which are intermediate-to-novice grade. They're serviced by a double chair and two T-bars, and are equipped for day and night skiing. There's also a half pipe for snowboarders. Lift tickets start at C$32 (U.S.$21) for adults and C$20 (U.S.$13) for juniors. Half-day and night discounts are available.

WATER SPORTS   The marina just north of City Park has a great many watercraft outfitters that can rent you a boat, jet ski, windsurfing board, paddleboat, and just about any other form of water-borne fun. If you want to call ahead, contact **Dockside Marine Centre** (☎ 250/765-3995), which has a wide range of boats and watercraft. If you'd like to try parasailing, call **Kelowna Parasail Adventures** (☎ 250/868-4838), which offers flights at C$45 (U.S.$29).

WHERE TO STAY

Abbott Villa Travelodge Kelowna. 1627 Abbott St., Kelowna, BC, V1Y 1A9. ☎ **800/578-7878** or 250/763-7771. Fax 250/762-2402. www.travelodge.com. 53 units. A/C TV TEL. High season C$75–C$99 (U.S.$49–U.S.$64) double. Kitchen C$10 (U.S.$7) extra. AE, MC, V.

For the money, this is the best place to stay in Kelowna, as it has one of the best locations downtown—right across from the City Park beaches. You'll be able to walk to the lakefront and to your favorite restaurants. For a central location like this, the rates are very reasonable. The rooms are fairly standard-issue motels units, but are clean, well maintained, and contain everything you need for a pleasant stay. On the property are a restaurant, outdoor pool, whirlpool, and steam room.

✪ **Casa Rio Lakeside B&B.** 485 Casa Rio Dr., Kelowna, BC, V1Z 3L6. ☎ **800/313-1033** or 250/769-0076. Fax 250/769-4488. E-mail: casario@silk.net. 3 units. A/C. High season C$100–C$125 (U.S.$65–U.S.$81) double. Kitchen C$40 (U.S.$26) extra. MC, V. Call for directions.

This superlative B&B is like your own private resort. It sits right on the waterfront across the bridge from Kelowna, on the west shores of Okanagan Lake. The modern, elegant three-story home rises above tiered formal gardens, ponds, and fountains, stepping down to 150 feet (46m) of private lake beachfront complete with a long dock. Casa Rio has traditional B&B rooms, which are spacious and beautifully furnished, or you can rent the entire ground floor of the home as an enormous 1,200-square-foot suite with private entrance, full kitchen, dining room, huge bathroom, sitting area, and separate bedroom. It's perfect for families or couples who seek space and privacy. Guests have free use of paddleboats and canoes; you'll probably end up spending all of your time out on the decks, in the outdoor hot tub, or on the beach.

✪ **The Cedars Inn.** 278 Beach Ave., Kelowna, BC, V1Y 5R8. ☎ **800/822-7100** or 250/763-1208. Fax 250/763-1109. E-mail: cedars@bc.sympatico.ca. 3 units. C$125 (U.S.$81) double. 2-night minimum on holiday weekends. MC, V.

If you prefer beautifully restored, historic B&Bs, then the Cedars is where you should stay. This gracious English-cottage–style home was built in 1906 with an eye for detail. The wainscoting, box beams, native granite fireplaces, and built-in cabinets with stained-glass panels perfectly capture an early-20th-century Canadian dream of elegance. The owners have beautifully maintained the spirit of the original home while transforming the bedrooms into a gracious contemporary vision of sumptuous fabrics and antiques. The inn sits on a quarter acre of gardens, with a pool, hot tub, and landscaped terrace. Add to that the house's location, a block from Okanagan Lake beaches in a quiet residential neighborhood, and the thoughtfulness and charm (and culinary talents) of your hosts, and you have a memorable experience ahead of you.

Coast Capri Hotel. 1171 Harvey Ave., Kelowna, BC, V1Y 6E8. ☎ **800/663-1144** or 250/860-6060. Fax 250/762-3430. www.coasthotels.com. 185 units. A/C. High season C$109–C$175 (U.S.$71–U.S.$114) double. AE, MC, V.

Somewhat apart from the downtown area, the Coast Capri offers large and graciously furnished rooms, all with balconies, and a good restaurant. You'll need to drive to the beaches from here, and the surrounding blocks are filled with strip malls, but if you can't get into one of the beachfront hotels yet still want high-quality lodgings, then this your next-best choice. The Vintage Dining Room is a great old-fashioned steak house—probably the best place in town for an elegant dinner of prime rib or steak. There's casual fare in the Garden Café, plus drinks in the lounge and pub.

Grand Okanagan Lakefront Resort & Conference Centre. 1310 Water St., Kelowna, BC, V1Y 9P3. ☎ **800/465-4651** or 250/763-4500. Fax 250/763-4565. www.grandokanagan.com. E-mail: sales@grandokanagan.com. 325 units. A/C TV TEL. C$199–C$265 (U.S.$129–U.S.$172) double; C$240–C$420 (U.S.$156–U.S.$273) suite or condo. Extra person C$15 (U.S.$10). Off-season discounts available. AE, DC, MC, V. Free parking. On Hwy. 97, cross the Lake Okanagan Bridge. At the first set of lights, turn left onto Abbott St. At the second set of lights, turn onto Water St.

This elegant lakeshore resort sits on 25 acres of beach and parkland; its atmosphere is reminiscent of Miami Beach in the 1920s. The atrium lobby of the modern hotel has a fountain with a sculpted dolphin as its centerpiece. The guest rooms, suites, and condos (with full kitchens) are decorated in salmon, sea blue, and shell white, exuding a relaxed yet elegant atmosphere. It's an ideal location for visitors who want to feel pampered in sophisticated surroundings during their stay. The restaurant and lounge overlook the resort's private marina, where guests can moor their small boats. Other facilities include a pool, salon, shops, and fitness center. Motorized swans and boats sized for kids offer fun for children in a protected waterway.

✪ **Hotel Eldorado.** 500 Cook Rd. (at Lakeshore Rd.), Kelowna, BC, V1W 3G9. ☎ **250/763-7500.** Fax 250/861-4779. www.sunnyokangan.com/el. 20 units. A/C TV TEL. C$139–C$179 (U.S.$90–U.S.$116) double. AE, DC, MC, V. Free parking. From Hwy. 97, cross the Lake Okanagan Bridge. Turn right at the second set of traffic lights onto Pandosy Rd. Drive 1 mile (1.6km) past the hospital and the shopping center. Turn right on Cook Rd.

One of Kelowna's oldest hotels, the Eldorado was floated down the lake from its original location to its present site on the water's edge south of downtown. It has been fully restored and is now decorated with a unique mix of antiques. The third-floor guest rooms with views of the lake are the largest and quietest. Some rooms also feature lakeside balconies. On the premises are a boardwalk cafe, lounge, and dining room. The staff can arrange boat moorage, boat rentals, and waterskiing lessons.

Kelowna Motor Inn. 1070 Harvey Ave., Kelowna, BC, V1Y 8S4. ☎ **800/667-6133** or 250/762-2533. Fax 250/868-3874. www.kminn.bc.ca. E-mail: kelownainn@wkpowerlink.com. 50 units. A/C TV TEL. High season C$75–C$99 (U.S.$49–U.S.$64) double. AE, MC, V.

Kelowna has a number of exclusive and wonderful lodging options, but sometimes you just need a good, clean motel room that doesn't overtax the credit card. The Kelowna Motor Inn is centrally located to dining and entertainment, offers large and simply furnished rooms, and has all the facilities you'll need to have a pleasant night or two in town. Some one- and two-bedroom accommodations are available, as are units with kitchens. Facilities include a pool, whirlpool, and steam bath.

Kelowna-SameSun Motel Hostel. 245 Harvey Ave., Kelowna, BC, V1Y 6C2. ☎ **250/763-9814.** Fax 250/763-9814. www.samesun.com. E-mail: samesun@silk.net. 68 beds. C$15–C$19 (U.S.$10–U.S.$12) single. MC, V.

If you're traveling on a budget, this very centrally located hostel-in-an-old-motel is just the ticket. Right downtown, you'll be close to the beach as well as downtown eats and nightlife. Facilities include a kitchen, laundry, and common room with TV.

Lake Okanagan Resort. 2751 Westside Rd., Kelowna, BC, V1Z 3T1. ☎ **800/663-3273** or 250/769-3511. Fax 250/769-6665. www.lakeokanagan.com. 140 units. A/C TV TEL. C$160–C$215 (U.S.$104–U.S.$132) 1-bedroom suite, C$325 (U.S.$211) 3-bedroom suite. Off-season discounts and packages available. AE, MC, V. Free parking. Drive 11 miles (18.3km) up Westside Rd., which overlooks the lake.

The long, winding road that leads to this secluded hideaway is a sports-car driver's dream come true. And there are many more activities to keep guests occupied once they arrive at this woodsy resort with its country-club atmosphere. Located on 300 acres of Okanagan Lake's hilly western shore, it offers one-bedroom units with kitchenettes, as well as three-bedroom suites and rooms. Because the resort is built on a hillside, every room has a terrific view. Amenities include a cafe, restaurants, bar, pools, Jacuzzis, fitness center, par-3 golf course, tennis courts, horseback riding, biking and hiking trails, private beach, marina, and summer kids' camp.

✪ **Otella's Guest House.** 42 Altura Rd., Kelowna, BC, V1V 1B6. ☎ **888/858-8596** or 250/763-4922. Fax 250/763-4982. 3 units. A/C TEL. High season C$85–C$95 (U.S.$55–U.S.$62) double. MC, V.

Otella's is located in the hills behind Kelowna, in a quiet, upscale neighborhood. When the owners bought this modern chalet-style home to convert into a bed-and-breakfast, they knew they didn't want a frilly B&B. Instead, they transformed this expansive A-frame into a coolly elegant, sophisticated guest house filled with quality furniture, local art, and restrained good taste. The two nicest rooms, which share a small balcony, are on the third floor (we like the African Room). The intriguing setting is at the end of a steep cul-de-sac against the desert hillside; the backyard incorporates ledges of rock that form a two-tiered lawn. It's favored by the local quail, which stroll down for a peck at the manicured grasses. One of the owners is a professionally trained chef, so expect breakfast to be exemplary.

Prestige Inn Kelowna. 1675 Abbott St., Kelowna, BC, V1Y 8S3. ☎ **87/PRESTIGE** or 250/860-7900. Fax 250/860-7997. 65 units. High season C$110–C$146 (U.S.$72–U.S.$95) double. AE, DISC, MC, V.

One of the closest hotels to the City Park beaches, the Prestige Inn is a cornerstone of downtown Kelowna. The rooms and exterior went through a major renovation in 1999, and emerged more comfortable and handsome than ever. All units have glass-fronted balconies, small fridges, hair dryers, and voice mail. If you ask for a suite, you'll get a canopy bed, robes, VCR, and double Jacuzzi. On site are the Tuscany Grill and Lounge, Blue Gator Bar and Grill (one of Kelowna's premier clubs for live blues and jazz), indoor pool, hot tub, and fitness center.

Stay 'N' Save Inn. 1140 Harvey Ave., Kelowna, BC, V1Y 6E7. ☎ **800/663-0298** or 250/862-8888. Fax 250/862-8884. www.staynsave.com. E-mail: staynsave@staynsave.com. 101 units. A/C TV TEL. High season C$104–C$114 (U.S.$68–U.S.$74) double. Kitchen C$10 (U.S.$7) extra. MC, V.

So you're heading into Kelowna on a summer weekend, and even though you're dreaming of a beachfront hotel, you didn't call 6 months ago to secure a room. Every place is absolutely booked. You're going to have to stay in a decent, basic motel, and you just hope it's clean, new, and functional. This is it. Facilities include a family restaurant, outdoor pool, hot tub, sauna, and exercise room.

CAMPING

The contact number for both of the following parks is ☎ **250/494-6500. Okanagan Lake Provincial Park** (☎ **250/494-6500**), 7 miles (11km) north of Summerland and 27 miles (44km) south of Kelowna on Highway 97, has 168 campsites nestled amid 10,000 imported trees. Sites go for C$19 (U.S.$12). Facilities include free hot showers, flush toilets, a sani-station, and a boat launch. Closer to Kelowna is **Bear Creek Provincial Park** (☎ **250/494-6500**), 6 miles (9km) north of Highway 97 on Westside Road, about 2 miles (3km) west of the Okanagan Lake Floating Bridge. The park has 80 sites for C$19 (U.S.$12) each.

WHERE TO DINE

Birch Grill. 8-1470 Harvey Ave. ☎ **250/860-2223.** Reservations recommended. Main courses C$11–C$13 (U.S.$7–U.S.$8). AE, MC, V. Mon–Thurs 11:30am–10pm, Fri 11:30am–11pm, Sat 5–11pm. CONTINENTAL.

Its location in a strip mall along Kelowna's busiest street belies the fact that the Birch Grill is a sophisticated little bistro with moderately priced meals. The dining room is casual, but filled with rich color and stone tile, and you'll get to watch the cooks in action in the adjoining kitchen. The menu, which changes daily, features lots of appetizers and small plates, plus pasta dishes—like portobello ravioli with tomato cream sauce—and grilled fish and chicken. The staff is friendly, youthful, and professional. The Birch Grill also keeps later hours than most Kelowna eateries.

Christopher's Steak & Seafood. 242 Lawrence Ave. ☎ **250/861-3464.** Reservations recommended. Main courses C$10–C$23 (U.S.$7–U.S.$15). AE, DC, MC, V. Daily 4:30–10pm. STEAK HOUSE.

Christopher's is a local favorite for drinks and steaks in a dark, fern-bar–like dining room. The decor and the menu haven't changed much since the early years of the Reagan administration, but that's a plus if you're looking for Alberta beef served up in simple abundance. The menu features appetizers like sautéed oysters as well as old-fashioned bar favorites like deep-fried zucchini sticks. The house specialty is prime rib. Steaks, pasta, chicken, and seafood are also offered.

☉ de Montreuil. 368 Bernard Ave. ☎ **250/860-5508.** Reservations recommended. Main courses C$18–C$24 (U.S.$12–U.S.$16). AE, MC, V. Mon–Fri 11am–10pm, Sat–Sun 5–11pm. CONTEMPORARY CANADIAN.

This low-key, high-performance restaurant produces the Okanagan's most exciting cooking. The menu is simply divided into four sections: Appetizers, Bowls, Salads, and Main Plates. You can order à la carte or, better yet, follow the simple pricing system in which any two-course meal (main course plus appetizer, salad, or soup) is C$28 (U.S.$18) and a three-course meal is C$34 (U.S.$22). The menu changes weekly, but expect everything to be fresh and filled with hearty earthiness. As an appetizer, try pan-seared goose liver with fiddleheads and morel mushroom risotto. A couscous salad is served with asparagus spears and fresh apricots, then drizzled with orange ginger dressing. For an entree, choose roast free-range chicken with red curry and coconut yogurt sauce. An impressive wine list and friendly, sophisticated staff make de Montreuil even more noteworthy.

Kitchen Cowboy. 353 Bernard Ave. ☎ **250/868-8288.** Reservations not needed. Main courses C$8–C$15 (U.S.$5–U.S.$10). AE, MC, V. Daily 10am–11pm. CANADIAN.

If you're looking for a scene that's casual but on the edge of trendy, with unfussy food at a reasonable price, then try Kitchen Cowboy, in the heart of downtown. The building was once a pioneer drugstore (note the hammered-tin ceiling), but the interior has been done up in a strikingly contemporary design. This is a good place for lunch, as the entire front of the restaurant opens to the street; you can watch the to-ing and fro-ing of tourists as you choose from salads, wraps, and sandwiches. At dinner, the menu is eclectic and international, with lots of fish, chicken, and pasta dishes.

La Bussola. 234 Leon Ave. ☎ **250/763-3110.** Reservations recommended. AE, MC, V. Main courses C$10–C$28 (U.S.$7–U.S.$18). Mon–Sat 5–10pm. ITALIAN.

La Bussola is a traditional Italian restaurant with a big local reputation. All of your favorite Italian pastas and meat dishes are here—pasta al pesto, lasagna, chicken piccata—along with an especially large selection of veal specialties, like veal escallop with wild mushrooms. The house signature dish is grilled chicken breast with a creamy white vermouth sauce. A solid and dependable restaurant.

Mamma Rosa Italian Restaurant. 561 Lawrence Ave. ☎ **250/763-4114.** Reservations not needed. C$8–C$14 (U.S.$5–U.S.$9). AE, MC, V. Mon–Sat 5–10pm, Sun 5:30–9pm. ITALIAN.

Mamma Rosa's is a big, friendly, family-style Italian restaurant with the kind of hearty cooking that fulfills gastronomic stereotypes. You'll find very good pizza here, plus a broad selection of house-made pastas—spicy Sicilian fettuccine, gnocchi in creamy pesto sauce—and well-prepared Italian stalwarts like chicken cacciatore.

Mon Thong. 1530 Water St. ☎ **250/763-8600.** Reservations not needed. Main courses C$9–C$13 (U.S.$6–U.S.$8). MC, V. Daily 11am–2:30pm and 5–11pm. THAI.

Mon Thong has an encyclopedic six-page menu of house specialties, making this the best Thai restaurant in the Okanagan. Almost all dishes can be made vegetarian. Choose from red, green, or yellow curries, or from signature dishes like Goong Pad Num Prick Pao, stir-fried shrimp with fresh vegetables in special fiery Thai sauce.

✪ **Williams Inn.** 526 Lawrence Ave. ☎ **250/763-5136.** Reservations required. Main courses C$12–C$28 (U.S.$8–U.S.$18). AE, DC, MC, V. Mon–Thurs 11am–2pm and 5:30–9pm, Fri 11am–2:30pm and 5:30–10pm, Sat 5:30–10pm, Sun 5:30–9pm. CONTINENTAL.

The chefs at this 1906 heritage home, on the edge of downtown, have extensive experience cooking in some of Europe's finest restaurants, and they bring that savoir faire to the native ingredients of the Canadian west. The simple rustic lines of the historic home contrast nicely with the white-linen-and-crystal formality of the table service; in summer, there's dining on the shaded deck. Among the well-loved hit parade of classic French-style dishes—escargot, lamb rack with mustard-herb crust, and beef chateaubriand with béarnaise—are entrees that reflect the tastes of the region. Venison from neighboring Nicole Valley is served with local blue cheese and wine sauce, and Fraser Valley pheasant with blackberry glaze. The wine list promotes the finest vintages of the Okanagan. Expect friendly, courteous service.

KELOWNA AFTER DARK

The brand-new **Kelowna Visual and Performing Arts Centre,** to be completed later in 2000, will be "a home to all the arts," according to its promoters. The complex includes a 300-seat theater, art gallery, studio space, rehearsal rooms, and two restaurants. It's located on Water Street at Cawston Street, near the Grand Okanagan Resort. The **Kelowna Community Theatre,** at the corner of Water and Doyle streets (☎ 250/763-9018), is home to a number of performing-arts groups, including the Okanagan Symphony Orchestra, Shakespeare Kelowna, and other theater groups.

6 Vernon

29 miles (47km) N of Kelowna, 47 miles (75km) S of Sicamous

North of Kelowna, Highway 97 cuts between Okanagan Lake to the west and a chain of smaller glacial lakes to the east. This is rich agricultural land, settled by ranchers in the mid–19th century, long before the more arid Okanagan Valley was consigned to the irrigation ditch. Vernon (pop. 23,514) is the oldest city in the Okanagan, and while it doesn't have the lakeside location and the fierce recreational spirit of Penticton and Kelowna, it's nonetheless a handsome town in the midst of lakes and farms.

Although it's what's nearby that makes a visit here worthwhile, downtown Vernon is, nevertheless, compact and pleasant. The **Greater Vernon Museum and Archives,** 3009 32nd Ave. (☎ **250/542-3142**), explores the area's history with relics of the early gold-rush prospectors and of the large open-range cattle ranches that moved in to take advantage of belly-deep grasslands. Most notable for travelers is **Silver Star Mountain,** a major ski and summer resort, and the **Historic O'Keefe Ranch,** one of the province's earliest and now preserved as a public heritage park.

In early February, colorful balloons meet to fly the valley's air thermals at Vernon's **Annual Winter Carnival & Hot Air Balloon Festival** (☎ **250/545-2236**). Events include arts and crafts exhibits, food stands, and musical entertainment.

For culture of another sort, plan to attend a performance of the **Sen'klip Native Theater Co.** (☎ **250/549-2921**), held on weekends in July and August. This native dance and acting troupe reenacts Indian legends on an outdoor stage at Newport Beach Resort and RV Park, $3^1/2$ miles (5.5km) down Westside Road from Highway 97 north of Vernon. Call for details; admission is by donation.

Although Vernon doesn't front onto a lake, there are excellent lake beaches just minutes away. One of the most popular is **Kal Beach,** south of town off Kalamalka Road. The beach is at the northern shores of strikingly green Kalamalka Lake. The aquamarine color of the waters is due to underwater springs that circulate millennia-old glacial till. Also convenient is **Kin Beach,** off Tronson Road, west of Vernon on Okanagan Lake. Take 25th Avenue west from downtown and follow the signs.

The first ranch in the Okanagan Valley was established by Cornelius O'Keefe and Thomas Greenhow in 1867, and at one time these early cattle barons controlled over 20,000 acres of prime grassland. Many of the original ranch buildings are preserved as the **Historic O'Keefe Ranch** (☎ **250/542-7868;** www.okeeferanch.bc.ca), 8 miles (13km) north of Vernon off Highway 97. The original log house, as well as the Victorian "mansion" built in 1886 in the ranch's heyday, are open for viewing, as are a general store, Catholic church, and blacksmith. The ranch is open May to mid-October, daily from 9am to 5pm. Admission is C$6 (U.S.$3.90) for adults, C$5 (U.S.$3.25) for seniors, C$4.50 (U.S.$2.95) for students 13 to 17, C$4 (U.S.$2.60) for children 6 to 12, or C$17 (U.S.$11) per family.

To get further information on this area, contact the **Vernon Visitor Info Centre,** 701 Hwy. 97 S. (Box 520), Vernon, BC, V1T 6M4 (☎ **250/542-1415;** www.vernontourism.com). Vernon offers a one-call reservations service for hotels, golf and ski packages, and adventure holidays at ☎ **800/665-0795.**

OUTDOOR PURSUITS

BIKING & HIKING   Kalamalka Lake Provincial Park, on the northeast slopes of Kalamalka Lake, has an extensive network of trails that wind through forests to vistas over the lake. To reach the park, follow Kalamalka Road south past Kal Beach to Kidston Road. See also Silver Star Mountain Resort under "Skiing," below.

GOLF   Resting high on a wooded ridge between two lakes, Les Furber's **Predator Ridge,** 360 Commonage Rd., Vernon (☎ 250/542-3436), has hosted the B.C. Open Championship in recent years. Greens fees start at C$75 (U.S.$49).

SKIING   One of the fastest-growing and most popular ski and summer resorts in British Columbia is the ✪ **Silver Star Mountain Resort,** 12 miles (20km) northeast of Vernon. The resort boasts two ski hills, with a maximum of varied terrain, 84 runs, and a vertical drop of 2,500 feet (762m). The Vance Creek side offers long, rolling cruisers, while the Putnam Creek side is a little wilder with groomed and ungroomed double-blacks, glades, and bumps. For snowboarders, there's a half pipe and a terrain park. Silver Star has nine lifts, including two high-speed detachable quads. Day lift tickets are C$40 (U.S.$26) for adults and C$20 (U.S.$13) for youths. For cross-country skiers, there are 51 miles (85km) of groomed and track-set trails.

The resort remains open in summer, when the lifts transport hikers and mountain bikers to the top of the mountain. A chairlift ride to the top of the mountain and a naturalist-guided hike back down through subalpine meadows costs C$18 (U.S.$12) for adults and C$14 (U.S.$9) for children. Or rent a bike and cycle back down for C$30 (U.S.$20) per adult, C$18 (U.S.$12) per child. For more information, contact **Silver Star Mountain Resort,** P.O. Box 3002, Silver Star Mountain, BC, V1B 3M1 (☎ 800/663-4431 or 250/542-0224; www.silverstarmtn.com; e-mail: reserv@ junction.net). The resort's five hotels are open year-round and can all be reserved through the central reservation number.

WHERE TO STAY

✪ **Best Western Vernon Lodge.** 3914 32nd St., Vernon, BC, V1T 8G4. ☎ 800/ 663-4422 or 250/545-3385. Fax 250/545-7156. E-mail: Vernon_Lodge@bc.sympatico.ca. 131 units. A/C. High season C$109–C$130 (U.S.$71–U.S.$85) double. AE, DC, DISC, MC, V.

Completely renovated in 1999, this large complex has a wide variety of room types, but be sure to ask for one that faces the courtyard, an amazing three-story space with extensive gardens flanking a pool, restaurant, and hot tubs. And that stream isn't an artificial water feature: Swan Lake Creek is a live stream with real fish in it. The guest rooms are large and very nicely furnished with quality cherry-wood furniture. All units facing the atrium have balconies. King suites come with two TVs, work desk, fridge, large seating area, and two-person soaker tub. Facilities include a pub with an outdoor deck, convention facilities, and a wine-and-beer store.

Prestige Inn. 4411 32nd St., Vernon, BC, V1T 9G8. ☎ 87/PRESTIGE or 250/558-5991. Fax 250/558-5996. 104 units. TV. High season C$110–C$126 (U.S.$72–U.S.$82) double. AE, MC, V.

This classy hotel with brand-new rooms and top-notch facilities is located on the strip north of Vernon. The folks who own the Prestige hotels don't assume that just one room type fits all needs, so the Vernon Prestige Inn offers a number of layouts, from standard rooms to one-bedroom suites to two-story loft units—even two-bedroom apartments with kitchens. Amenities include a pool, hot tub, fitness center, laundry, good restaurant, and lounge. All in all, excellent quality and great service.

WHERE TO DINE

Demetri's Steak House. 2705 32nd St. ☎ 250/549-3442. Reservations recommended. Main courses C$8–C$19 (U.S.$5–U.S.$12). AE, MC, V. Mon–Fri 11am–2pm; daily 4–10pm. GREEK.

Half steak house, half taverna, Demetri's has equally good beef and Greek specialties, such as souvlaki, moussaka, and spanikopita. The restaurant has a nicely formal atmosphere that's mostly free of the usual Greek kitsch.

Eclectic Mediterranean Restaurant. 100-3117 32nd St. ☎ **250/558-4646.** Reservations recommended. Main courses C$12–C$20 (U.S.$8–U.S.$13). AE, MC, V. Mon–Fri 11am–2pm and 5–10pm, Sat 5–10pm, Sun 5–9pm. INTERNATIONAL.

It would take a large menu to represent a world's worth of cuisine, and the 30 entrees at the Eclectic Mediterranean do their best to circle the globe a time or two. The menu is a mélange of southern European, Thai, and West Coast cuisines, and while such breadth sometimes means unfocused cooking, here it translates into favorite dishes with bright new flavors. As an appetizer, local goat cheese blistered with honey offers a nice contrast between sweet and earthy. Moroccan lamb is grilled and served with apricots, pine nuts, and bell peppers, while Salmon Stinger is the name for parchment-baked fillet with vodka and lime juice. The atmosphere here is upbeat and casual.

Intermezzo. 3206 34th Ave. ☎ **250/542-3853.** Reservations recommended. Main courses C$12–C$23 (U.S.$8–U.S.$15). AE, DC, MC, V. Sun–Thurs 5–9pm, Fri–Sat 5–10pm. CONTINENTAL.

Vernon's preeminent supper club, the Intermezzo serves up a wide menu of pasta, veal, chicken, steak, and seafood to locals celebrating special events and to travelers looking for an elegant dining experience. The preparations are mostly Italian- and French-inspired, though the produce, meat, and fish are sourced regionally. Good service and an intriguing wine list.

12 Southeastern British Columbia & the Kootenay Valley

With the high-flying Rockies to the east and the rugged Purcell and Selkirk mountain ranges to the west, southeastern British Columbia has as much beauty and recreation to offer as anywhere else in the province. If you're looking to avoid the crowds at Banff and Jasper national parks on the Alberta side of the Rocky Mountains, try one of the smaller parks covered in this chapter.

Trenched by the mighty Kootenay and Columbia rivers, this region has a long history of mining, river transport, and ranching. However, these parts of British Columbia have yet to succumb to the resortification that characterizes much of the rest of the province and neighboring Alberta. And while that means that you may not have the ultimate dining experience while here, it also means that prices are lower across the board—and you won't have to compete with tour-bus hordes while you hike the trails.

In pre-Contact native America and the early years of western exploration, the Kootenay Valley was a major transportation corridor. Due to a curious accident of geology, the headwaters of the vast Columbia River—which flows north from Columbia Lake for 171 miles (275km) before bending south and flowing to the Pacific at Astoria, Oregon—are separated from the south-flowing Kootenay River by a low, 1.2-mile-wide (2km) berm of land called Canal Flats. The Kootenay River then zigzags down into the United States before flowing back north into Canada to join the Columbia at Castlegar, British Columbia.

Because a short portage was all that separated these two powerful rivers, Canal Flats was an important crossroads when canoes and river boats were the primary means of transport. The fact that an easily breached ridge was all that separated two major rivers caught the imagination of an early entrepreneur, William Adolph Baillie-Grohman. In the 1880s, he conceived a plan to breach Canal Flats and divert much of the Kootenay's flow into the Columbia. Unsurprisingly, he ran into opposition from people living and working on the Columbia, and had to settle for building a canal and lock system between the two rivers. Only two ships ever passed through the canal, and today this curiosity is preserved as Canal Flats Provincial Park, 27 miles (44km) north of Cranbrook, with picnic tables and a boat launch on Columbia Lake.

For advance visitor information on southeastern British Columbia, contact **Tourism Rockies,** P.O. Box 10, Kimberley, BC, V1A 2Y5 (☎ 250/427-4838; www.bcrockies.com; e-mail: info@bcrockies.com).

1   Revelstoke

254 miles (410km) W of Calgary, 350 miles (565km) NE of Vancouver

Located on the Columbia River at the foot of Mount Revelstoke National Park, Revelstoke sits in a narrow fir-cloaked valley between the Selkirk and the Monashee mountains. It's a spectacular, big-as-all-outdoors setting, and unsurprisingly, Revelstoke makes the most of the outdoor-recreation opportunities on its doorstep. Winter is high season here, as the city is a major center for heli-skiing and snowmobiling. Summer activities include rafting, hiking, and horseback riding.

The town was established in the 1880s, when the Canadian Pacific Railway pushed through. Much of the handsome downtown core was built then; most restaurants and hotels are housed in century-old buildings. For all its beauty and charm, Revelstoke is surprisingly unheralded. With a setting that rivals Banff and Jasper, Revelstoke's congenial and sleepy isolation can't last. Plan a visit before the throngs arrive.

ESSENTIALS

GETTING THERE   Revelstoke is 119 miles (192km) from Kelowna on Highway 1. It's 350 miles (565km) northwest of Vancouver and 254 miles (410km) west of Calgary.

Greyhound (☎ **800/661-8747** or 403/260-0877; www.greyhound.ca) operates six buses daily from Vancouver, costing C$65 (U.S.$42) one-way. Four buses daily connect Revelstoke to Calgary, which costs C$52 (U.S.$34) one-way.

VISITOR INFORMATION   Contact the **Revelstoke Visitor Information Centre** at 204 Campbell St. (P.O. Box 490), Revelstoke, BC, V0E 2S0 (☎ **800/487-1493** or 250/837-5345; www.revelstokecc.bc.ca; e-mail: cocrev@junction.net).

EXPLORING THE AREA

Downtown Revelstoke (pop. 8,507) sits on a shelf of land above the confluence of the Columbia and Illecillewaet rivers. Founded in the 1880s, the town center retains a number of original storefronts and buildings, and is pleasant to explore. You'll find plenty of coffeehouses, galleries, and cafes, plus some standout architectural jewels like the domed **Revelstoke Courthouse,** 1123 Second St. W. **Grizzly Plaza,** near the corner of Victoria Road and Campbell Avenue, is a courtyard lined with redbrick storefronts. It's the site of the Saturday-morning farmers market, as well as free live music Monday through Saturday from 7 to 10pm, from July 1 to Labour Day.

The **Revelstoke Museum,** 315 W. First St. (☎ 250/837-3067), located in the town's original post office, contains memorabilia from Revelstoke's pioneer mining and railroading days. Upstairs is the community art gallery. Admission is by donation; it's open in summer, Monday through Friday from 1 to 5pm, and the rest of the year on Monday, Wednesday, and Friday from 1 to 4:30pm.

It's the railroad that really put Revelstoke on the map. The **Revelstoke Railway Museum,** across from downtown on Victoria Road (☎ 250/837-6060; www. railwaymuseum.com; e-mail: railway@junction.net), houses a collection of antique rolling stock, including a beautifully restored Canadian Pacific Railway steam engine from the 1940s—one of the largest ever to operate in Canada. Other exhibits focus on the building of the first transcontinental line across Canada and the communications systems that kept the trains running safely. From July 1 to Labour Day, the museum is open daily from 9am to 8pm; from March 1 to June 30 and from Labour Day to November 30, it's open daily from 9am to 5pm; the rest of the year, hours are Monday through Friday from 1 to 5pm. Admission is C$5 (U.S.$3.25) for adults, C$3

Touring the Dams

The Columbia River has the steepest descent of any large river in North America, and in terms of volume, is the continent's third-largest river. This combination of characteristics makes it irresistible to hydroelectric dam builders.

Two of the many electricity-generating dams on the river are near Revelstoke, and both are open for tours. **Revelstoke Dam,** $2^1/_2$ miles (4km) north of Revelstoke on Highway 23, is 1,541 feet (54m) across and 574 feet (175m) high, and contains more than 2 million cubic meters of concrete. Self-guided tours of the visitor center explain how hydroelectricity is produced and how the dams impact the local ecosystem. An elevator shoots to the top of the dam, where you get a feeling for the immensity of this structure. The visitor center is open May to mid-June, daily from 9am to 5pm, and mid-June to mid-September, daily from 8am to 8pm. Admission is free.

If you enjoy the Revelstoke Dam, consider taking the 87-mile (140km) drive up Highway 23 along the shores of Revelstoke Lake to **Mica Dam,** the first large dam on the Columbia. And large it is, much larger than the Revelstoke Dam. Mica Dam is more than 2,600 feet (792m) across and 656 feet (200m) high. The dam forms Kinbasket Lake, which stretches for more than 100 miles (160km) and contains 14.8 trillion cubic meters of water. The visitor center is open mid-June to Labour Day, daily from 10:30am to 4:30pm. Guided tours of the power station are offered at 11am and 1:30pm.

(U.S.$1.95) for seniors, C$2 (U.S.$1.30) for students, and free for children 5 and under. Family admission is C$10 (U.S.$7).

OUTDOOR PURSUITS

Grizzly Tours (☎ 800/667-8865 or 250/837-6500; www.grizzlyvacations.com; e-mail: gcmc@mindlink.bc.ca) offers hiking, canoeing, mountain biking, and ATV excursions in summer. In winter, the focus shifts to snowmobile tours, cross-country skiing, snowshoeing, and dogsledding. The trips are customized to your needs, experience level, and price point. **Revelstoke Alpine Adventure Company** (☎ 250/837-5417; www.raamountainguides.com; e-mail: guides@raamountainguides) offers many of the same options, plus mountaineering, climbing, and helicopter-enhanced hiking and fishing trips. In winter, ski touring and customized cross-country and heli-skiing trips are available.

SKIING   Revelstoke is surrounded by rugged mountains with extremely heavy snowfalls, but there's only one traditional ski resort. **Powder Springs Ski Area,** 4 miles (6km) south of Revelstoke on Camozzi Road (☎ 877/422-8754 or 250/837-5151), has 1,000 feet (305m) of vertical drop, with 3,500 feet (1,067m) of total runs. There are two chairlifts, a T-bar, and a rope tow; lift tickets are C$26 (U.S.$17).

CMH Heli-Skiing (☎ 800/661-0252; www.cmhski.com) offers helicopter skiing to remote slopes and glaciers in the Monashee and Selkirk mountains. Packages include all meals, lodging, and use of specially designed heli-skis. Choose from 3-, 4-, and 7-day packages. Prices for a week of heli-skiing range from C$3,341 to C$5,612 (U.S.$2,172 to U.S.$3,648). Pickup at the Calgary airport can be arranged.

Revelstoke's long-established **Selkirk Tangiers Heli Skiing** (☎ 800/663-7080; www.selkirk-tangiers.com; e-mail: selkirk@rockies.net) offers helicopter-assisted skiing

Southeastern British Columbia

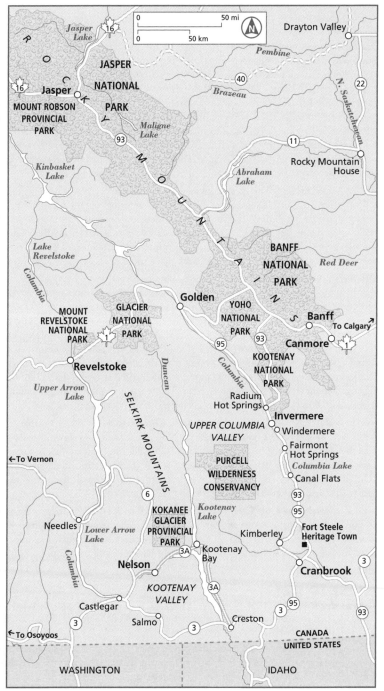

and snowboarding trips to more than 200 approved areas in the Monashee and Selkirk mountains, with some runs up to 7,200 feet (2,195m) in length. In addition, the company's Albert Canyon base, located 22 miles (35km) east of Revelstoke on Highway 1, offers heli-skiing in the Selkirks. Three-, 5-, and 7-day packages are available; a week of midwinter skiing goes for C$4,892 (U.S.$3,180).

Cat Powder Skiing (☎ 800/991-4455; www.catpowder.com; e-mail: catski@ junction.net) uses Snowcats to transport skiers and snowboarders to backcountry slopes. The Snowcat takes skiers to the 7,500-foot (2,286m) elevation of Mount Mackenzie, where they can choose from a number of runs up to 3,500 feet (1,067m) long, including a half pipe and a terrain park; skiers are guaranteed five runs each day. Each of the 2- to 5-day packages includes guide service, unlimited skiing, lodging, and meals. Three days of Cat skiing in midwinter costs C$1,275 (U.S.$829).

SNOWMOBILING The mountains around Revelstoke receive an annual snowfall of almost 60 feet (18m), which make them tempting terrain for a variety of winter activities, including snowmobiling. A detailed brochure of snowmobiling trails is available from the visitor center, or contact **Great Canadian Snowmobile Tours** (☎ 800/667-8865; www.snowmobilerevelstoke.com; e-mail: info@ snowmobilerevelstoke.com) for guided customized trips.

BIKING The mountains around Revelstoke are etched with old logging roads that have been converted into mountain-bike trails. Ask at the visitor center for a map of routes. At **High Country Cycle and Sports,** 118 Mackenzie Ave. (☎ 250/ 814-0090), bike rentals start at C$7 (U.S.$4.55) an hour or C$35 (U.S.$23) a day. If you're looking for a guided cycle trip that includes the magical 17-mile (27km), 5,000-foot (1,524m) descent down Mount Revelstoke, contact **Summit Cycle Tours** (☎ 250/837-3734; www.compusmart.ab.ca/sumcycle; e-mail: sumcycle@ compusmart.ab.ca). Its most popular tour is a 4-hour trip that begins with a short hike through Mount Revelstoke's alpine meadows before screaming down the mountain on a bike; it's C$56 (U.S.$36) for adults, C$46 (U.S.$30) for children.

WHITE-WATER RAFTING **Apex Rafting Company,** Box 1754, Revelstoke, BC, V0E 2S0 (☎ 888/232-6666 or 250/837-6376), offers excursions down Illecillewaet River's Albert Canyon. The trip provides thrills, but nothing too extreme. In summer, three 3-hour trips are offered daily, costing C$42 (U.S.$27) for adults and C$32 (U.S.$21) for youths 10 to 17. Apex also offers trips down the challenging Kicking Horse River east of Golden, starting at C$85 (U.S.$55).

GOLF **Revelstoke Golf Club** (☎ 800/991-4455 or 250/837-4276) is a championship 18-hole, par-72 course established in 1924, with narrow fairways lined with mammoth conifers and small lakes. The club—one of the oldest in British Columbia—has a driving range, clubhouse with lounge and restaurant, and pro shop. Greens fees are C$33 (U.S.$21).

WHERE TO STAY

Cat Powder Ski Lodge. 1601 Third St. W., Revelstoke, BC, V0E 2S0. ☎ **800/991-4455** or 250/837-5151. www.catpowder.com. E-mail: catski@junction.net. 18 units. A/C TV TEL. C$53 (U.S.$34) double. AE, MC, V.

This is a pleasant place to stay, particularly in summer. During the lodge's winter high season, it serves as the base for backcountry Snowcat skiers, but in summer, the comfortable rooms are priced at a discount. All units have queen beds and in-room coffee and tea; some kitchen units are available as well. On the property are a family restaurant and whirlpool.

⭕ **Mulvehill Creek Wilderness Inn and Bed & Breakfast.** 4200 Hwy. 23 S. (P.O. Box 1220), Revelstoke, BC, V0E 2S0. ☎ **877/837-8649** or 250/837-8649. www.mulvehillcreek. com. E-mail: mulvehil@junction.net. 8 units. C$85 (U.S.$55) double, C$115–C$195 (U.S.$75–U.S.$127) suite. Rates include breakfast. MC, V.

One of the most superlative inns in all of British Columbia, the Mulvehill Creek Wilderness Inn is located on Arrow Lake, 12 miles (19km) south of Revelstoke on Highway 23. The inn sits in a clearing in the deep forest, just steps away from the lake and from a magnificent 300-foot waterfall. The long, cedar-shake-sided lodge has three rooms with queen beds, two with twin beds, and one king room, plus a family suite (with a king bed and a queen sofa bed) and a honeymoon suite, which comes with a king bed, two-person Jacuzzi, and private deck. The rooms are all beautifully decorated with rich colors, locally made pine furniture, and original folk art.

The comfortable lounge is lined with bookcases; grab a novel and curl up by the fireplace. From the deck, look onto the heated pool and the organic garden, which produces much of the fruit and vegetables served here; the inn's hens provide the eggs. Guests have free use of the hot tub, gym, and canoes on the lake. Children are welcome at Mulvehill—there's even a playground. Your hosts are happy to arrange cross-country ski or snowshoe excursions, horseback riding, and fishing and motor-boat trips. The breakfast buffet includes fresh breads and baked goods, along with homemade jams and jellies. A couple days at Mulvehill may well be the highlight of your trip to British Columbia. In its first year of operation, the word "paradise" appeared 106 times in guest-book comments.

Regent Inn. 112 First St. E., Revelstoke, BC, V0E 2S0. ☎ **888/245-5523** or 250/837-2107. Fax 250/837-9669. E-mail: regent@regentinn.com. 50 units. A/C TV TEL. C$88–C$129 (U.S.$57–U.S.$84) double. Rates include breakfast. AE, MC, V.

The finest lodging in downtown Revelstoke, the Regent is a refurbished heritage hotel facing historic Grizzly Plaza. The large bedrooms are nicely furnished, the One Twelve Restaurant offers fine dining, and guests can enjoy the outdoor heated pool, hot tub, and sauna. Also on site are Dapper Dan's Pub, which serves drinks and light meals, and the Grizzly Lounge, where you can order a cocktail.

Revelstoke Traveller's Hostel & Guest House. 400 Second St. W., Revelstoke, BC, V0E 2S0. ☎ **250/837-4050.** Fax 250/837-5600. www.hostels.bc.ca. E-mail: info@hostels.bc.ca. 26 beds. Dorm beds C$15 (U.S.$10) HI members, C$19 (U.S.$12) nonmembers. MC, V.

Located on the edge of downtown, the Revelstoke Hostel is in a spacious older home with oak floors and French doors. The hostel offers a full kitchen, TV room, and free use of a computer with Web access. There are also tenting sites in the large backyard.

Three Valley Chateau. 12 miles (19km) west of Revelstoke on Hwy. 1 (P.O. Box 860), Revelstoke, BC, V0E 2S0. ☎ **888/667-2109** or 250/837-2109. Fax 250/837-5220. 200 units. A/C TV TEL. C$85–C$109 (U.S.$55–U.S.$71) double. AE, ER, DC, DISC, MC, V.

This huge new development can't be missed: With its bright red, steeply pitched, six-story tin roof cleaved by dozens of sharply peaked gables, this hotel and entertainment complex stands out, to put it mildly. The hotel sits amid formal gardens at the head of Three Valley Lake, a small body of water with sandy swimming beaches. The guest rooms are quite large, most with balconies; if you're interested, ask about the theme suites (the interior of the Cave Suite is lined completely in native stone). Guests have a choice of two dining rooms plus a cafeteria and lounge. In the hotel's Walter Moberly Theatre is a nightly revue with cowboy songs and skits about the frontier days. Part of the Three Valley Chateau development is its Historic Town, a collection of historic buildings that have been moved to the property to form an ad hoc ghost town. The more-typical hotel facilities include a pool, whirlpool, and guest laundry.

Wintergreen Inn. 312 Kootenay St., Revelstoke, BC, V0E 2S0. ☎ **800/216-2008** or 250/837-3369. E-mail: wintergreen@bctravel.com. 10 units. A/C. C$90 (U.S.$59) double. MC, V.

The Wintergreen Inn is newly built, but designed to fit in architecturally with its long-established historic neighbors close to downtown Revelstoke. Each of the comfortable guest rooms has a private bathroom, hardwood floors, and quality furniture; they're decorated in themes that reflect local history and recreation. Guests share a living room with a large fireplace and a recreation room with darts, games, and a TV.

CAMPING

Martha Creek Provincial Park, just north of Revelstoke on Highway 23 (☎ **250/ 837-3500**), sits on Lake Revelstoke and has 28 sites that go for C$12 (U.S.$8) each.

WHERE TO DINE

One Twelve Restaurant. In the Regent Inn, 112 First St. E. ☎ **250/837-2107.** Reservations suggested. Main courses C$12–C$26 (U.S.$8–U.S.$17). AE, MC, V. Mon–Fri 11:30am–2pm and 5:30–9pm, Sat 5:30–9pm. WESTERN CANADIAN.

This handsome restaurant is Revelstoke's fine-dining option, with a good selection of steaks, seafood (about half the menu is fish or seafood), and continental cuisine. Veal fillet is served with a wild-mushroom sauce, and fresh lobster tails with drawn butter. Good service and an intriguing wine list enhance the experience.

Three Bears Bistro. 122 Mackenzie Ave. ☎ **250/837-9575.** Reservations not accepted. Main courses C$12–C$17 (U.S.$8–U.S.$11). MC, V. Mon–Sat 8am–9pm, Sun 11am–4pm. CASUAL DINING.

The Three Bears is a convivial little spot in Grizzly Plaza with sidewalk patio seating as well as deck seating in the garden. At lunch, the menu includes homemade soup, salads, wraps, fajitas, and sandwiches, while the evening menu shifts to pasta, pot pies, and paella. The bistro also has good desserts, espresso drinks, and specialty teas.

2 Mount Revelstoke National Park

Just west of Glacier National Park (see below) is Mount Revelstoke National Park, a glacier-clad collection of craggy peaks in the **Selkirk Range.** Comprising only 161 square miles (417km²), Mount Revelstoke can't produce the kind of awe that its larger neighbor, Glacier National Park, can in good weather; however, Revelstoke does offer easier access to the high country and alpine meadows.

The park is flanked on the south by Highway 1, the Trans-Canada Highway. The park has no services or campgrounds, but all tourist services are available in the neighboring town of Revelstoke (see above).

ESSENTIALS

For information, contact **Mount Revelstoke National Park,** P.O. Box 350, Revelstoke, BC, V0E 2S0 (☎ **250/837-7500;** e-mail: revglacier_reception@pch.gc.ca).

Entry to the park is C$4 (U.S.$2.60) for adults, C$3 (U.S.$1.95) for seniors, C$2 (U.S.$1.30) for children 6 to 16, and C$10 (U.S.$7) per family.

EXPLORING THE PARK

The most popular activity in the park is the drive up to the top of 6,000-foot (1,829m) **Mount Revelstoke,** with great views of the Columbia River and the peaks of Glacier Park. To reach Mount Revelstoke, take the paved Meadows in the Sky Parkway north from the town of Revelstoke and follow it 14 miles (23km) to Balsam Lake.

Mount Revelstoke & Glacier National Parks

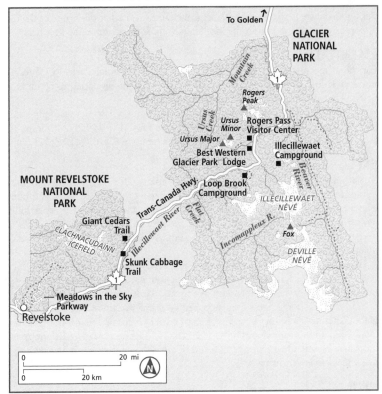

The parkway is closed to trailers and motor coaches, as it is a very narrow mountain road with 16 steep switchbacks.

At **Balsam Lake,** at the Meadows in the Sky area, free shuttle buses operated by the parks department make the final ascent up to the top of Mount Revelstoke, but only after the road is clear of snow, usually from early July to late September. If the shuttle isn't running, you have a choice of several easy hiking trails around Balsam Lake that lead past rushing brooks through wildflower meadows. The **Eagle Knoll Trail** and the **Parapets** are two easy options that take less than an hour to complete. At the summit are longer trails, including the 3.7-mile (6km) **Eva Lake Trail.**

If you don't make the trip up to the Meadows in the Sky area, you can enjoy a short hike in the park from along Highway 1. The **Skunk Cabbage Trail** is a boardwalk which winds through a marsh that explodes with bright yellow and odiferous flowers in early summer. Another popular hike is the **Giant Cedars Trail,** a short boardwalk out into a grove of old-growth cedars that are more than 1,000 years old.

3 Glacier National Park

44 miles (72km) E of Revelstoke, 50 miles (80km) W of Golden

Located amid the highest peaks of the Selkirk Mountains, Canada's Glacier National Park amply lives up to its name. More than 400 glaciers repose here, with 14% of the park's 837 square miles (2,168km²) lying under permanent snowpack. The reason that this high country is so covered with ice is the same reason that this is one of the more unpopulated places to visit in the mountain West: It snows and rains a lot here.

ESSENTIALS

For more information on the park, contact **Glacier National Park,** P.O. Box 350, Revelstoke, BC, V0E 2S0 (☎ **250/837-7500;** e-mail: revglacier_reception@pch. gc.ca). The visitor center is at Rogers Pass.

There's no fee if you pass through the park on Highway 1 without stopping, but if you do stop to hike or picnic, the entry fee is C$4 (U.S.$2.60) for adults, C$3 (U.S.$1.95) for seniors, C$2 (U.S.$1.30) for children, or C$10 (U.S.$7) per family.

EXPLORING THE PARK

The primary attractions in the park are viewpoints onto craggy peaks and hiking trails leading to wildflower meadows and old-growth groves; heavy snow and rainfall lend a near-rain-forest feel to the hikes. Spring hikers and cross-country skiers should beware of avalanche conditions, a serious problem in areas with high snowfall and steep slopes. Call the park information number (☎ **250/837-7500**) for weather updates.

Glacier Park is crossed by the Trans-Canada Highway and the Canadian Pacific Railway tracks. Each has had to build snowsheds to protect its transportation systems from the effects of heavy snows and avalanches. **Park headquarters** are just east of 4,100-foot (1,250m) Rogers Pass; stop here to watch videos and see the displays on natural and human history in the park. New exhibits focus on the role of the railroads in opening up this rugged area of Canada. You can sign up for ranger-led interpretive hikes here as well. On a typically gray and wet day, the information center may be the driest place to enjoy the park.

HIKING

Several easy trails leave from the park's Rogers Pass visitor center. **Abandoned Rails Trail** follows a rails-to-trails section of the old CPR track for an hour-long round-trip with a gentle grade through a wildflower-studded basin. The **Balu Pass Trail** is a more strenuous 3-mile (5km) hike up to the base of the glaciers on 8,950-foot (2,728m) Ursus Major.

The other important trailhead is at **Illecillewaet Campground,** west of Rogers Pass along Highway 1. Seven major trails head up into the peaks from here, including the **Asulkan Valley Trail,** which follows a stream up a narrow valley to a hiker's hut. These trails require more exertion than the trails at Rogers Pass, and will take most of a day to complete.

Further down the Illecillewaet Valley are two other popular routes. **Loop Brook Trail** is an hour-long saunter through a riparian wetland. The quarter-mile (0.4km) **Rockgarden Trail** climbs up a valley wall of moss-and-lichen–covered boulders to a vista point onto 9,446-foot (2,880m) Smart Peak. Stop at the **Hemlock Grove Picnic Area** and follow the boardwalk through the old-growth hemlock forest.

The longest hike in the park is the 26-mile (42km) **Beaver Valley Trail,** which follows the Beaver River on the eastern edge of the park. This trail takes 3 days, one-way, to complete. If you plan on backcountry camping, you'll need to register at the visitor center and purchase a C$6 (U.S.$3.90) wilderness pass.

WHERE TO STAY

Best Western Glacier Park Lodge. Rogers Pass, BC, V0E 2S0. ☎ **800/528-1234** or 250/837-2126. Fax 250/837-2130. 50 units. TV TEL. C$125–C$150 (U.S.$81–U.S.$98) double. AE, DISC, ER, MC, V.

Just below Rogers Pass, where Highway 1 edges over the Selkirk Range in Glacier National Park, is this large complex. The setting is spectacular: The glaciered faces of towering peaks crowd around a broad cirque blanketed with wildflowers and boulders, at the center of which sits this handsome lodge. Eighty-seven miles (139km) of hiking/cross-country ski trails lead from the lodge out into the wilderness. The rooms are very comfortable and nicely furnished with lodgelike rusticity. Facilities include a dining room, 24-hour cafeteria, heated outdoor pool, sauna, and gas station.

CAMPING

Illecillewaet and **Loop Brook** campgrounds are both just west of Rogers Pass off Highway 1 and along the Illecillewaet River. Both operate on a first-come, first-served basis. Facilities include flush toilets, kitchen shelters, firewood, and drinking water. Illecillewaet offers guided hikes and fireside programs as well. Rates at both campgrounds are C$13 (U.S.$8) a night.

4 Golden

83 miles (134km) W of Banff, 442 miles (713km) E of Vancouver

For more than a century, Golden (pop. 4,107) has been known primarily as a transport hub, first as a division point on the transcontinental Canadian Pacific Railway, then as the upstream steamboat terminus on the Columbia River, and then as a junction of two of Canada's busiest highway systems.

Nowadays, Golden is known for its outdoor recreation. The town sits in a breathtaking location in the trenchlike Columbia River valley, between the massive Rocky Mountains and the soaring Purcell Range, within a 90-minute drive from five major national parks. The fact that Golden is near—and not in—the parks is in large part the reason for the area's recent phenomenal growth. Outfitters that offer heli-skiing, heli-hiking, and other recreation that isn't allowed in the national parks (for conservation reasons) choose to make Golden their base. And with park towns like nearby Banff trying to limit further development, businesses and outfitters that want a Rocky Mountain hub find Golden a convenient and congenial center.

Golden won't win any awards for charm, however. It's basically a functional little town with lots of motel rooms in a magnificent location.

Note that Golden and the other communities in this part of the Columbia Valley are in the mountain time zone, an hour earlier than the rest of British Columbia.

ESSENTIALS

GETTING THERE   Golden is at the junction of Highway 1 (the Trans-Canada Hwy.) and Highway 95. The closest airport to Golden is in Calgary.

Greyhound (☎ 800/661-8747 or 403/260-0877; www.greyhound.ca) operates buses that link Golden to Vancouver, Banff, and Calgary, and to Cranbrook to the

Special Events

The **Golden Festival of Birds and Bears** (☎ 800/622-4653) is held during the second week of May. Events include field trips, free kids' programs, musical entertainment, and wildlife and conservation seminars. The **Golden Rodeo** brings a bit of the Wild West to the Canadian Rockies during the first weekend of August, with a pancake breakfast, street dance, barbecues, and, of course, bucking bulls and broncos, roping, and races. The rodeo grounds are a mile (1.6km) south of Golden off Highway 95. For information, contact the visitor center.

south. There are four buses daily between Golden and Vancouver; the one-way adult fare is C$82 (U.S.$53). Four buses daily link Golden to Calgary; the one-way adult fare is C$35 (U.S.$23).

VISITOR INFORMATION   Contact the **Golden Visitor Info Centre** at 500 10th Ave. N. (P.O. Box 1320), Golden, BC, V0A 1H0 (☎ **800/622-4653** or 250/344-6688; e-mail: goldcham@rockies.net).

GETTING AROUND   If you need a rental car while in Golden, contact **Tilden,** 915 11th Ave. (☎ **250/344-9899**).

EXPLORING THE AREA

You could spend several days in the Golden area without realizing that the town has an older downtown core. It's a block west of busy 10th Avenue, on **Main Street.** There's not much here—just a handful of shops and cafes—but it's a pleasant break from the commercial sprawl along Highways 1 and 95. The town itself is mostly charm-free and hasn't yet developed the kind of boutique infrastructure or tourist attractions that you find in other Canadian mountain towns.

The **Golden and District Museum,** 1302 11th Ave. (☎ **250/344-5169**), tells the story of Golden's rail history. It also has an on-site old log schoolhouse and blacksmith's shop. The museum is open Monday through Friday from 10am to 6pm in May, June, and September, and daily in July and August. Admission is by donation.

Rafter J Frontier Village, 1870 Upper Donald Rd., north of Golden (☎ **250/344-6432;** www.rockies.net/~rafterj), is a private open-air museum housed in a re-created frontier village. Guides conduct tours, pointing out native and cowboy artifacts. Texas longhorn cattle roam through the village. A gift shop sells collectibles and antiques. Village tours cost C$5 (U.S.$3.25) and are free for children 10 and under. Rafter J also offers campsites for C$10 to C$15 (U.S.$7 to U.S.$10).

OUTDOOR PURSUITS

HELI-HIKING   Although based in Banff, **CMH Heli-Hiking** (☎ **800/661-0252** or 403/762-7100; fax 403/762-5879; www.cmhhike.com) offers a variety of helicopter-assisted hiking trips and vacation packages in the mountains west of Golden. If you're short on time, daylong trips head into the Cariboo Mountains for C$261 (U.S.$170). Five-, 6-, and 8-day heli-hiking trips involve staying at remote high-country lodges accessible only by long hiking trails or by helicopter. Prices vary quite a bit depending on time of year and individual lodge, but plan on a 5-day trip to cost between C$1,700 and C$1,950 (U.S.$1,105 and U.S.$1,268); rates include all lodging, food, and helicopter transport to the lodge and to hiking areas.

From June 15 to September 30, **Purcell Heli-Hiking** (☎ **877/435-4754** or 250/344-5410) offers daylong heli-hiking in the Purcell Mountains west of Golden. Guided alpine day hikes start at C$200 (U.S.$130) and go to C$400 (U.S.$260), including lunch. Helicopter sightseeing tours start at C$100 (U.S.$65).

✪ **HELI-SKIING**   Golden is at the center of one of the world's best terrains for helicopter-assisted skiing. The Bugaboo, Purcell, Selkirk, and Cariboo mountains all rear up behind Golden, and since they are unencumbered with national-park status (unlike the Canadian Rockies), they're available to licensed heli-skiing operations. Banff-based **CMH Heli-Skiing** (see "Heli-Hiking," above) has eight high-country lodges in the mountain ranges near Golden, which serve as bases for weeklong heli-skiing holidays. Rates include lodging, food, nonalcoholic drinks, helicopter transport, use of specialized powder skis, and ground transport from the nearest large airport (usually Calgary). Prices vary greatly depending on the lodge and

A Bird's-Eye View

Alpenglow Aviation (☎ 888/244-7117 or 250/344-7117; www.rockiesairtours. com) offers a variety of flightseeing trips into the magnificent mountain ranges that ring Golden. Two of the most popular trips are the Glaciers & Granite Tour, a 1-hour flight over the incredible spires of the Bugaboo Mountains south of Golden (C$98/U.S.$64 per person), and the Icefields & Waterfalls Tour, which flies along the Continental Divide between Yoho and Banff national parks. This $1^1/_4$-hour tour also flies over the Columbia Icefield, the largest nonpolar ice cap in the world; the cost is C$125 (U.S.$81) per person.

Air tours require a minimum of two passengers. The Golden Airport is just west of Golden, off Fisher Road. Alpenglow Aviation also offers, for an extra fee, pickup and drop-off van service anywhere in Canmore, Banff, or Lake Louise. If you happen to be in Golden on a clear day, you should definitely take advantage of these awe-inspiring air tours.

---

time of year, but range between C$3,700 and C$6,000 (U.S.$2,405 and U.S.$3,900) for a week.

Great Canadian Heli-Skiing (☎ 250/344-2326; fax 250/344-2316; www. greatcanadianheliski.com; e-mail: heliski@rockies.net) offers weeklong helicopter-assisted trips in the Selkirk and Purcell mountains. Accommodations are in the company's private lodge near Golden. Prices vary, but average between C$6,000 and C$7,000 (U.S.$3,900 and U.S.$4,550) per week, including all lodging, food, skis, helicopter transport, and ground transport from the Calgary airport.

SKIING   In addition to heli-skiing, Golden offers more-conventional alpine and Nordic skiing. **Whitetooth Ski Area,** just west of Golden across the Columbia River (☎ 800/622-GOLD or 250/344-6114; www.rockies.net/~whitetooth), has 22 deep powder runs with 1,740 vertical feet (530m) of drop, plus a ski school, rental shop, and day lodge with cafeteria. The resort also has $10^1/_2$ miles (17km) of cross-country trails. Day lift passes are C$28 (U.S.$18) for adults, C$20 (U.S.$13) for youths 13 to 18 and seniors 60 and over, and C$12 (U.S.$8) for children 6 to 12.

Keep your eye on Whitetooth: The ski area is poised for a major redevelopment as the four-season ✪ **Golden Peaks Resort.** The new resort will feature a 4,000-foot-long (1,219m) gondola lift that will take skiers up above elevations of 8,000 feet (2,348m), making this one of the highest ski areas in North America. It will have six new chairlifts (in addition to the gondola) and over 4,000 acres of skiable terrain and 4,100 feet (1,250m) of vertical drop. With two four-star hotels in the works, plus a variety of ski lodges and country inns all planned for the new development, promoters claim that the Golden Peaks Resort is poised to become the Whistler of the Rockies.

WHITE-WATER RAFTING   The **Kicking Horse River,** which enters the Columbia at Golden, is one of the most exciting white-water rafting trips in Canada, with constant Class III and Class IV rapids as it tumbles down from the Continental Divide through Yoho National Park. Rafting trips are usually offered from mid-May to mid-September. A trip down the Kicking Horse will be a highlight of a vacation in the Canadian Rockies. **Alpine Rafting** (☎ 888/599-5299 or 250/344-6778; www. recnet.ca/alpineraft) offers a daylong trip for C$80 (U.S.$52), including a barbecue steak lunch. A gentler introduction to white water goes for C$45 (U.S.$29) for adults and C$25 (U.S.$16) for children 14 and under, with lunch included.

Canadian Whitewater Adventures (☎ 888/577-8118 or 403/720-8745; www.canadianwhitewater.ca) offers rafting trips and combination rafting-and-hiking or rafting-and-rappelling trips. Rafting packages include Upper Canyon for C$69 (U.S.$45), Lower Canyon for C$49 (U.S.$32), and the Upper & Lower Combo for C$99 (U.S.$64). The hiking package goes for C$39 (U.S.$25), the rafting/hiking package C$99 (U.S.$64), the rappelling package C$99 (U.S.$64), and the rafting/rappelling package C$149 (U.S.$97). All packages include equipment, guides, and lunch. A shuttle from Banff and Lake Louise costs C$10 (U.S.$7).

Glacier Raft Company (☎ 250/344-6521; e-mail: glacierraft@redshift.bc.ca) offers a variety of options. The easygoing scenic float day trip goes to the gentle upper valley of the Kicking Horse; it's for those who want an introduction to rafting or who don't want the thrills of white water. Cost is C$55 (U.S.$36) for adults and C$29 (U.S.$19) for kids 6 to 12. Two separate day trips (one with a portage around Class VI rapids) explore the white-water sections of the Kicking Horse and cost C$85 to C$99 (U.S.$55 to U.S.$64). All day trips include a lunchtime steak barbecue.

Rocky Mountain Rafting Co. (☎ 888/518-7238 or 250/344-6979) offers full-day Kicking Horse trips, including lunch, starting at C$79 (U.S.$51). A calmer, family white-water trip in the upper valley costs C$49 (U.S.$32). If you just want the thrills, you can choose a 1½-hour rafting trip that shoots through the longest section of continuous Class IV rapids in western Canada (C$49/U.S.$32), or a 4-hour trip for the adventurous that focuses on the two most extreme sections of white water (C$99/U.S.$64). Lunch is included in the full-day and family white-water trips. A daily shuttle from Banff, Canmore, and Lake Louise is available for C$10 (U.S.$7).

Wet 'n' Wild Adventures (☎ 800/668-9119 or 250/344-6546; www.canadianrockies.net/wetnwild) offers daily Kicking Horse trips from Banff, Lake Louise, and Golden. The standard day trip is C$76 (U.S.$49), with lunch included. If you just want to shoot the rapids of the lower canyon, a half-day trip is available for C$55 (U.S.$36). For beginners, a morning introduction to white water is C$50 (U.S.$33) for adults and C$35 (U.S.$23) for children 12 and under, including lunch.

Whitewater Voyageurs Ltd. (☎ 800/667-7238 or 250/344-7335; www.raftingcanada.com) has a full-day trip of continuous white-water adventure (lunch included) for C$118 (U.S.$77). The half-day white-water trip is C$64 (U.S.$42). If you're really keen about rafting, consider the 2-day Kicking Horse trip, which starts gently in the upper valley. After a night of camping, be ready to shoot down the lower canyon's Class III and IV rapids. Cost is C$235 (U.S.$153), all meals and tents provided (you bring a sleeping bag). You also have the choice of floating the scenic Blaeberry River for C$55 (U.S.$36); children 12 and under pay half-price.

FISHING   The Columbia River runs through town and offers fair fishing for rainbow trout and kokanee salmon. There's better fishing in the **Kinbasket Lake** section of the river, which begins just north of Golden. For guided fishing trips in more-remote lakes and streams, contact **Kinbasket Adventures** (☎ 250/344-6012; www.rockies.net/~kbasket; e-mail: kbasket@rockies.net).

GOLF   **Golden Golf & Country Club** (☎ 250/344-2700; www.golfcanada.com) is an 18-hole championship course along the banks of the Columbia River. Bill Newis designed the front nine holes, while Les Furber took care of the back nine. The clubhouse includes a pro shop with equipment rentals. Greens fees are C$42 (U.S.$27).

Exploring the Columbia River Wetlands

South (upstream) from Golden are the Columbia River Wetlands, a 90-mile-long (144km) Wildlife Management Area that supports an incredible diversity of wildlife. More than 270 bird species have been seen in this stretch of river, marsh, and lake. The largest wetland west of Manitoba, the Columbia River Wetlands is also a major breeding ground for the bald eagle, osprey, and great blue heron. Mammals, including moose, elk, mink, and beaver, make their home here as well. Two Golden-based outfitters offer wildlife-viewing and bird-watching trips through the wetlands.

Eco Excursions Ltd. (☎ **888/210-2211** or 250/344-5060) has tours from May 1 to September 10. Two-hour family float trips are C$40 (U.S.$26) per seat (with children free). Three-hour adult-only float trips are C$40 (U.S.$26) per seat. Eco Excursions is located 13 miles (20km) south of Golden on Highway 95.

Kinbasket Adventures (☎ **250/334-6012;** www.rockies.net/~kbasket; e-mail: kbasket@rockies.net) has two different wetlands tours. Leisurely 2$^{1}/_{2}$-hour pontoon trips are C$40 (U.S.$26) for adults and C$15 (U.S.$10) for children 12 and under. This trip is suitable for all ages as well as for those with disabilities. You can also opt for longer guided canoe trips with a stronger bird-watching focus. Both half- (C$50/U.S.$33) and full-day (C$80/U.S.$52) trips are available; the full-day trip includes lunch. Canoe rentals are also available.

HORSEBACK RIDING Located in the lovely Blaeberry River valley, **Triple C Backcountry Riding,** Goat Mountain Lodge, 236 Blaeberry Rd. (☎ **877/ 240-RIDE** or 250/344-6579; e-mail: goatmtn@rockies.net), offers a variety of rides. The trails follow the river along the same routes traversed by native Canadians and early frontier explorers. One-, two- and half-day guided rides range from C$30 to C$50 (U.S.$20 to U.S.$33) for adults and C$25 to C$45 (U.S.$16 to U.S.$29) for children 12 and under. Full-day trips are C$75 (U.S.$49) for adults and C$65 (U.S.$42) for kids. A "Sundowner trip" with an evening cookout goes for C$55 (U.S.$36) per adult and C$50 (U.S.$33) per child. A basic backcountry riding lesson is included with all trips.

Canyon Creek Trail Rides, southwest of Golden at 896 Cedar Lake Rd. (☎ **250/ 344-5585**), offers guided horseback rides. Rates are C$25 (U.S.$16) for 1 hour, C$35 (U.S.$23) for 2 hours, C$40 (U.S.$26) for 3 hours, C$50 (U.S.$33) for half a day, and C$70 (U.S.$46) for a full day. Lunch is provided for those on 1-day rides by request. Reservations are required; there's a maximum of eight riders per group.

WHERE TO STAY

✪ **Alpine Meadows Lodge.** 717 Elk Rd., Golden, BC, V0A 1H0. ☎ **888/700-4477** or 250/344-5863. Fax 250/344-5853. www.alpinemeadowslodge.com. E-mail: alpmeadow@ redshift.bc.ca. 9 units. C$89–C$99 (U.S.$58–U.S.$64) double. Rates include breakfast. MC, V.

Located high above Golden, looking across onto the face of the Rockies, this friendly, family-owned lodge enjoys a great location—removed from the bustle of Golden, yet only 10 minutes to skiing, golf, and tourist services in town. The lodge, which was constructed from timber felled on the property, consists of a large building with a central three-story great room, flanked by wraparound balconies and open staircases. A huge, two-sided stone fireplace dominates the living area. The guest rooms are light-filled and airy, with simple, unfussy decor. All units have private bathrooms with Jacuzzis and showers. Outdoor recreation is literally right out the door, with paths from the lodge leading to hiking trails in neighboring federal forestland. The owner, who is very knowledgeable about local lore and activities, will make it easy to get you out into the wilderness or onto the fairways. A number of well-priced packages include lodging, golf, skiing, white-water rafting, and flightseeing.

Columbia Valley Lodge. 14 miles (23km) south of Golden on Hwy. 95 (Box 2669), Golden, BC, V0A 1H0. ☎ **250/348-2508.** Fax 250/348-2505. www.bbcanada.com/ 2081.html. 12 units. TV TEL. C$70 (U.S.$46) double. Extra person C$10 (U.S.$7). Children under 6 stay free in parents' room. Rates include full breakfast. Senior and off-season discounts and weekly rates available. AE, MC, V.

This homey lodge sits on a wetlands lake beside the Columbia River, offering a relaxing place to stay for those who want to be close to nature but who don't want to backpack to get to it. The flower-box–bedecked, Tyrolean-style inn overlooks a broad, grassy meadow with picnic tables and play structures for the kids; a 2-minute walk leads to the lake, where guests have free use of canoes (this is a great place for birders). The rooms are clean and basic, all with private bathrooms; half have balconies. Families are welcome here. The lodge's restaurant is open to the public in the evening; it features Canadian and Austrian cuisine.

Golden Rim Motor Inn. 1416 Golden View Rd., Golden, BC, V0A 1H0. ☎ **250/ 344-2216.** Fax 250/344-6673. 69 units. A/C TV TEL. C$80 (U.S.$52) double. AE, MC, V.

There are dozens of motels in Golden, but this is the pick of the litter. Standing above the precipitous Kicking Horse River valley, just half a mile (1km) east of Golden, the Golden Rim boasts sweeping views of the Rockies and the Columbia Valley. It offers standard queen-bed motel accommodations, with some housekeeping and Jacuzzi units available. Facilities include a dining room, indoor and outdoor pools, water slides, a sauna, a whirlpool, and a recreation center.

Hillside Lodge & Chalets. 1740 Seward Frontage Rd., Golden, BC, V0A 1H0. ☎ **250/ 344-7281.** www.mistaya.com/hillside/. E-mail: hillside@rockies.net. 9 units. C$90 (U.S.$59) lodge double, C$98 (U.S.$64) 1-bedroom chalet. Rates include full German-style breakfast. MC, V.

This stylish European-style lodge with five stand-alone chalets sits on 60 forested acres above the quiet Blaeberry River, about 10 minutes north of Golden. You have a choice of staying in one of the four comfortable lodge rooms, with king beds and private bathrooms, or one of the delightful one-bedroom chalets, each with twin or queen beds, private bathroom, handcrafted furniture, woodstove, and deck. Both the lodge and the chalets are newly built, so you'll find all the facilities completely ship-shape. Rates include a full German-style breakfast, with the option of family-style dining in the lodge. The central lodge also contains a reading area, TV room, and lounge.

✪ **Kapristo Lodge.** 1297 Campbell Rd., Golden, BC, V0A 1H0. ☎ **250/344-6048.** Fax 250/344-6755. www.kapristolodge.com. E-mail: kapristolodge@redshift.bc.ca. 6 units (some with shared bathroom). C$145 (U.S.$94) double. Rates include breakfast. MC, V.

If you're looking for a recreation-oriented vacation with homey, lodge-style accommodations, the Kapristo will prove an excellent choice. It sits high above the Columbia Valley, with sweeping views of the Purcell Mountains from the very large flagstone-and-planking patio. Also quite spacious is the cathedral-ceilinged living room, filled with couches and tables flanked by a stone fireplace. Adjoining are a sun-room and a dining room, where homemade breakfasts are served. The guest rooms are comfortably furnished with down quilts and handsome furniture; one unit has its own kitchen, fireplace, and Jacuzzi. There's a mix of private and shared bathrooms. What sets this apart from other lodges around Golden is its friendly informality and its owner's efforts to ensure that guests have a good time, whether rafting a river, riding horseback, or sunning on the deck.

Prestige Inn Golden. 1049 Trans-Canada Hwy., Golden, BC, V0A 1H0. ☎ **877/737-8443** or 250/344-7990. Fax 250/344-7902. 82 units. A/C TV TEL. From C$110 (U.S.$72) double. AE, ER, DISC, MC, V.

Easily the swankest place to stay in Golden, the Prestige Inn is newly constructed and luxurious, with excellent facilities, a variety of room types, and a good restaurant. Guest rooms are spacious and richly appointed, each with two phones and voice mail, iron and board, coffeemaker, and hair dryer. Some kitchenette units are available as well. On-site amenities include room service, concierge, indoor pool, hot tub, fitness center, and meeting facilities.

WHERE TO DINE

There are a lot of exceptional aspects to Golden, but fine dining isn't one of them. If you're staying at a lodge that offers a meal plan, take advantage of it. **Norberts & Doris Bakery Café,** 505 Ninth Ave. (☎ 250/344-5506), is a continental-style bakery with lunchtime soup, salads, and sandwiches, while **Sisters & Beans,** 1122 10th Ave. S. (☎ 250/344-2443), offers a largely vegetarian light-dining menu.

La Cabina Ristorante. 1105 Ninth St. ☎ **250/344-2330.** Reservations recommended. Main courses C$10–C$23 (U.S.$7–U.S.$15). AE, MC, V. Mon–Fri 11am–2pm; daily 5–10pm. ITALIAN.

Golden's only fine-dining option is housed in a historic log cabin near downtown. The menu features both traditional Italian favorites and house specialties with the zing of *nuova cucina*. The enticing appetizers include *gamberi alla cabina,* tiger prawns sautéed with Pernod and tomatoes. The pasta selection is broad and well prepared, but the kitchen really shines with its beef, veal, chicken, and fish dishes. Pollo Cleopatra is a pan-fried chicken breast topped with shrimp and finished with a sauce of white wine, garlic, and capers, while Bistecca alla Cassinesa is a New York steak grilled and served with red-bell-pepper butter.

Ricco's Family Restaurant. 417 Ninth Ave. N. ☎ **250/344-2665.** Reservations not needed. Main courses C$7–C$13 (U.S.$4.50–U.S.$8). MC, V. Daily 8am–11pm. PIZZA/ CANADIAN.

Ricco's is an unprepossessing little eatery with a big local reputation for its pizza. However, if you're traveling with a group that can't make up its mind about what to eat, Ricco's is still a good choice, as the menu offers a wide selection of pasta, steak, veal, and chicken dishes. Take out and free delivery are available.

The Timber Inn. 3483 Hwy. 95 S. ☎ **250/344-2228.** Reservations recommended. Main courses C$13–C$23 (U.S.$8–U.S.$15). MC, V. Daily 11:30am–2:30pm and 5–9pm. GERMAN/CONTINENTAL.

Located 20 miles (32km) south of Golden in the little community of Parsons, this country inn contains an excellent dining room. The menu offers a number of appe-tizer salads, such as the Turino salad with tuna and onion, plus excellent bruschetta. Moving on to the main courses, choose from three types of schnitzel, steaks, roast lamb, and chicken. The small room overlooks the Columbia Valley and the Purcell Mountains. It's a lovely drive to Parsons on a long summer evening.

5 The Upper Columbia Valley

Invermere: 8 miles (13km) S of Radium Hot Springs, 79 miles (127km) N of Cranbrook

INVERMERE & WINDERMERE

South of Radium Hot Springs, the Columbia Valley is broad and green, flanked by the towering peaks of the Rockies to the east and the Purcell Mountains to the west. Nestled in the valley are two lovely lakes, **Windermere Lake** and **Columbia Lake,** the latter considered the birthplace of the Columbia River. This entire area is undergoing extensive development as a resort area, mostly in the form of golf courses and country clubs. Other outdoor-recreation activities—skiing, mountain biking, hiking, and rafting—are also developing as a major focus.

The main towns in this part of the Columbia Valley are **Invermere** (pop. 2,271) and **Windermere** (pop. 1,273), on opposite sides of Windermere Lake but separated by only 4¹/₂ miles (7km). Of the two, Invermere is by far the more attractive. Situated on the shores of the lake, it offers a pleasant town center and easy beach access at **Kinsman Beach Park,** off the end of Seventh Avenue. Also in the park is **Pynelogs Cultural Centre,** a historic building built in 1915 that now houses art shows, exhibits, and concerts. **James Chabot Provincial Park,** on the north edge of town, is another beach access point with good swimming and a playground.

Wings Over the Rockies Bird Festival (☎ 888/933-3311 or 250/342-3210; www.adventurevalley.com/wings) features interpretive walks, floats on the Columbia River, workshops, art displays, a children's festival, and music to celebrate the return of migratory birds to the Columbia Valley in early May. The Columbia River Wetlands are home to 270 species of birds.

OUTDOOR PURSUITS

✪ **GOLF**   Invermere is at the center of Columbia Valley golfing. The area between Radium and Fairmont—a distance of about 20 miles (32km)—boasts 12 major courses, making this one of the top golf destinations in British Columbia. The popular 18-hole **Windermere Valley Golf Course,** 1¹/₄ miles (2km) east of Highway 93 on the Windermere Loop Road (☎ 250/342-3004), has easy terrain and challenges for every level of player. Facilities include a pro shop, putting green, and driving range. Greens fees are C$22 (U.S.$14) Saturday and Sunday, C$20 (U.S.$13) Monday through Friday. The new-in-1999 **Eagle Pines Ranch Golf,** off Athalmer Highway on the east side of Windermere Lake (☎ 877/877-3889 or 250/342-0820), is a 6,800-yard, 18-hole golf course and country-club resort with challenging holes and scenic vistas over the lake.

WHITE-WATER RAFTING & BOATING   The rivers in the upper Columbia Basin are popular with local rafters. The **Kootenay River Runners** (☎ 800/599-4399 or 250/347-9210) offers a number of tours, including a half-day Kootenay River float for C$49 (U.S.$32) and a full-day trip for C$95 (U.S.$62). The company also has white-water rafting trips down the famed Kicking Horse, with free transport from Windermere, Invermere, or Fairmont Hot Springs. A half-day trip is C$75 (U.S.$49), while a full-day Lower Canyon Kicking Horse River trip is C$95 (U.S.$62).

You can also explore the upper reaches of the wildlife-rich Columbia Wetlands from Invermere or Windermere. **Columbia River Outfitters** (☎ 250/342-7397) offers

Babin Air (☎ **250/342-3565** at the Invermere Airport, or 250/345-0022 at the Fairmont Airport; fax 250/342-0086; www.babinair.com; e-mail: info@BabinAir. com) has a number of flightseeing trips into the Purcell and Rocky mountains. Options include the 1-hour Ultimate Alpine tour, for C$85 (U.S.$55) per person, and the 45-minute Hanging Glacier tour, for C$65 (U.S.$42) per person. Flights may be chartered for custom tours as well.

half-day wetlands tours in a canoe or kayak for C$40 (U.S.$26). Sunset kayak trips on Lake Windermere are C$30 (U.S.$20). Relive the days of the fur trappers and paddle a 22-foot canoe down the Columbia for C$35 (U.S.$23). Lessons and kayak rentals (from C$20/U.S.$13 for 2 hr. to C$40/U.S.$26 for a full day) are available, as is free transportation from Fairmont, Windermere, Invermere, and Radium.

FISHING   For the best lake fishing in the upper Columbia River valley, try the smaller lakes at the base of the Rockies, like Whiteswan, Alces, Premier, and Dunbar lakes. Skookumchuk Creek is noted for its good fly-fishing. **Columbia Valley Guided Fishing Services** (☎ **250/342-9811**) offers custom lake and creek fishing trips; equipment rentals are offered as well.

✪ PANORAMA MOUNTAIN VILLAGE RESORT

Panorama, a major new golf and ski resort 24 miles (40km) west of Invermere on Panorama Road (☎ **800/663-2929** or 250/342-6941; www.panoramaresort.com; e-mail: paninfo@intrawest.com), is a four-seasons resort and upscale residential area. Besides golf and skiing, Panorama offers a host of other activities, including horseback riding, white-water rafting, ATV touring, tennis, hiking, and mountain biking. One of the most unusual facilities is the landscaped outdoor water slide that's pumped with heated water, allowing it to remain open year-round.

Greywolf Golf Course has bent grass greens and fairways, plus spectacular mountain vistas from every hole. Water comes into play on 14 of the 18 holes. The course, which in 1999 was named best new Canadian course by *Golf Digest,* has a signature 16th hole that requires a drive across a steep-sided gorge. The course is 7,140 yards in length. Greens fees are C$85 (U.S.$55) Monday through Friday, C$90 (U.S.$59) Saturday and Sunday.

The **Panorama Ski Resort** boasts the second-highest vertical drop in Canada, at 4,000 feet (1,219m). There are more than 100 named runs in 2,000 acres of skiable terrain, serviced by nine lifts, including one high-speed quad; 55% percent of the runs are rated intermediate or advanced, and 25% are expert. Adult lift tickets are C$49 (U.S.$32). The resort is also home to the Bilodeau School of Skiing and Snowboarding and the Becky Scott Nordic Ski Centre, with 10 miles (16km) of groomed trails; the access fee is C$7 (U.S.$4.55) per day. **Heli-skiing** packages take guests into the Purcell Mountains. A day trip with three helicopter-assisted descents, including breakfast and lunch, is C$517 (U.S.$336) per person.

Panorama offers a range of lodging options, from traditional hotel rooms, condos, and town houses to private-home rentals. Rates begin at C$132 (U.S.$86) double; for information and reservations, call ☎ **800/663-2929.** The resort currently has four restaurants and four bars, pubs, and nightclubs, with more of everything on the way.

FAIRMONT HOT SPRINGS

People have been visiting the hot-water springs at Fairmont for millennia, but the early natives who came here to cure their aches and pains wouldn't recognize it now. The springs are now the center of **Fairmont Hot Springs Resort,** 10 miles (16km) south of Windermere on Highway 93/95 (☎ **800/663-4979** or 250/345-6311; fax 250/345-6616; www.fairmontresort.com). This four-seasons resort has a number of large country-club developments linked with a winter ski area, though for many families, the big draw remains the hot springs. The mineral water here is rich in calcium but contains no sulfur, the odiferous agent that fouls the air at most hot-springs resorts.

The main attraction is the 3,200-square-foot lap pool filled with hot mineral water, plus a diving pool and several soaker pools. Amazingly, all the water in the pools is drained nightly and refilled with fresh water. At Fairmont, more than 1.4 million gallons per day flow out of the mountain and through the pools. Single entry to the pool complex is C$6 (U.S.$3.90) for adults, C$6 (U.S.$3.90) for seniors and youths 13 to 17, and C$4 (U.S.$2.60) for children 4 to 12. Multiple-entry day passes are C$8 (U.S.$5) for adults, C$7.50 (U.S.$4.85) for seniors and youths, and C$6 (U.S.$3.90) for children. Massage, hydrotherapy, and esthetic services are available.

If you're not into the hot springs, Fairmont also boasts two 18-hole golf courses. The oldest course in the region is **Mountainside Golf Course,** just below the hot springs off Fairway Drive (☎ **250/345-6514**). A par-72 course, Mountainside's most famous hole is its 600-yard fourth hole. **Riverside Golf Resort,** off Riverview Road (☎ **800/665-2112** or 250/345-6346; www.golfriverside.com), is a championship 18-hole course, with a driving range, practice area, pro shop, and lessons. Riverside is unique in that it spans the Columbia River, and uses the mighty river as a natural water hazard. The Riverside course is 6,527 yards in length and was named Canada's golf course of the year in 1998. Greens fees for both courses are C$55 (U.S.$36).

Fairmont Hot Springs Ski Resort offers a half pipe and snowboard park, triple chair, and 13 runs. Fairmont is not as large as other resorts in the Columbia Valley—it has a vertical drop of 1,000 feet (305m)—but it's a good place for families or beginners. Adult day lift tickets are C$29 (U.S.$19).

Accommodations at Fairmont Hot Springs Resort are in the rambling 140-room lodge. Double rooms go for between C$139 and C$210 (U.S.$90 and U.S.$137).

6 The Kootenay Valley: Cranbrook, Creston & Nelson

CRANBROOK

50 miles (80km) N of the U.S.–Canadian border

The largest city in southeastern British Columbia, Cranbrook (pop. 18,780) exists mostly as a trade center for loggers and agriculturists. The town itself has few tourist sites, but Cranbrook is central to a number of historic and recreational areas and offers ample numbers of hotel rooms as well as a few good places to eat. The town's setting is spectacularly dramatic: a broad forested valley that looks onto the sky-piercing Canadian Rockies and backside of the U.S. Glacier National Park.

ESSENTIALS

GETTING THERE   Cranbrook is near the junction of two major road systems, the north-south Highway 93/95 corridor and the east-west Highway 3. **Greyhound** (☎ **800/661-8747**) operates buses that travel on both of these road systems. Bus service between Cranbrook and Golden costs C$32 (U.S.$21) one-way; between

Special Events

Sam Steele Days celebrate the Wild West heritage of the Cranbrook area. This annual festival, held the third weekend of June, features an indoor Bull-o-Rama rodeo, a parade, a western-style barbecue, a pancake breakfast, street dances, sports tournaments, and family fun. For more information, call the Sam Steele headquarters at ☎ **250/426-4161.**

Cranbrook and Calgary, C$53 (U.S.$34); and between Cranbrook and Creston, C$16 (U.S.$10). There's also daily service to and from Spokane, Washington.

Both **Air BC** (☎ **800/663-3721**) and **Canadian Regional Airlines** (☎ **800/ 665-1177**) have flights from Vancouver to the Cranbrook Airport, north of town.

VISITOR INFORMATION   The **Cranbrook Visitor Info Centre** is at 2279 Cranbrook St. N., Box 84, Cranbrook, BC, V1C 4H6 (☎ **800/222-6174** or 250/ 426-5914; fax 250/426-3873; www.cyverlink.bc.ca/~cbkchamber).

EXPLORING THE AREA

It's worth getting off the grim Highway 95 strip to visit the pleasant downtown area around Baker Street. As you stroll the broad, tree-lined streets, you'll see a number of heritage brick storefronts and commercial buildings. Especially impressive is the grand, turreted 1909 **Imperial Bank** building at Baker and Eighth streets.

Canadian Museum of Rail Travel. In the train depot at Hwy. 3 and Baker St. ☎ **250/ 489-3918.** Admission C$7 (U.S.$4.55) adults, C$5 (U.S.$3.25) seniors, C$3 (U.S.$1.95) students, C75¢ (U.S.50¢) preschoolers, C$17 (U.S.$11) per family. Each admission is good for a 1-hr. tour and, in summer, complimentary tea or coffee from the dining car. July–Aug daily 8am–8pm; dining car daily 10am–6pm. Sept to mid-Oct and Easter to June daily 10am–6pm; mid-Oct to Easter Tues–Sat noon–5pm. Tours given on the hour.

Cranbrook was established as a rail division point, so it's fitting that the town is home to this fascinating rail museum. Devoting itself to the social history of rail travel, the museum preserves a number of historic rail cars, including those designed for royalty. The highlight is 12 cars built in 1929 by the Canadian Pacific Railway for its Trans-Canada Limited run. Rather like a traveling luxury hotel, the cars are a vivid testament to the craftsmanship and taste of the early 20th century. The beautifully restored cars gleam with brass and inlaid walnut and mahogany. These cars were the last of their type built in Canada, and the museum's collection is the largest intact historic railcar set in North America. In summer, the dining car offers tea service.

✪ **Fort Steele Heritage Town.** 10 miles (16km) northeast of Cranbrook on Hwy. 93/95. ☎ **250/489-3351,** or 250/426-6923 for recorded information. www.fortsteele.bc.ca. Grounds, year-round daily 9:30am–5:30pm. Evening entertainment and restaurant, late June to Labour Day Tues–Sun. Admission to grounds, May to mid-Oct, C$8 (U.S.$5) adults, C$5 (U.S.$3.25) seniors, C$4.50 (U.S.$2.95) youths 13–18, C$2 (U.S.$1.30) children 6–12, C$17 (U.S.$11) per family; free admission to grounds rest of year. Tickets good for 2 consecutive days. Reduced 1-day evening admission also available. Free evening admission for theater and restaurant patrons.

During the 1864 gold rush, a cable ferry stretched across a narrow section of the Kootenay River, enabling prospectors to safely cross the turbulent waters. A small settlement sprang up, and after another mining boom—this time for silver, lead, and zinc—Fort Steele had more than 4,000 inhabitants and was the leading town in the region, as well as the head of steamboat navigation on the Kootenay River. However, when the railroad pushed through, it bypassed Fort Steele in favor of Cranbrook.

Within 5 years, all but 150 of the citizens had left. In the 1960s, the crumbling ghost town was declared a heritage site, and a long period of restoration ensued.

Today, more than 60 restored and reconstructed buildings grace the townsite. In summer, the population spikes with the addition of living-history actors who give demonstrations of period skills and occupations. The buildings include a hotel, storefronts, churches, saloons, a courthouse and jail, and private homes. Additionally, there's a steam train, free horse-drawn wagon rides, and a musical variety show at the Wild Horse Theatre. The International Hotel Restaurant serves Victorian fare.

OUTDOOR PURSUITS

BIRD WATCHING & HIKING If you're a birder or if you're just looking for a short leg-stretcher in a lovely natural setting, drive just west of Cranbrook to the visitor information center. The center is on the shores of Elizabeth Lake, a small lake and marshy area where songbirds and migrating birds stop over. Trails ring the lake.

FISHING Eighteen area rivers, including the Elk River, St. Mary River, and Kootenay, are often rated among the country's top 10 fly-fishing destinations. Trophy fish are taken all season long. For lake fishing, Moyie Lake, 19 miles (30km) south of Cranbrook, has a good stock of kokanee, rainbow, and bull trout. **Rocky Mountain Angler** (☎ 250/489-4053) can help you land that big one with hourly, half-day, and full-day instruction. Women-only trips are available as well.

GOLF The **Cranbrook Golf Club,** 2700 Second St. S. (☎ **888/211-8855** or 250/426-6462), is a long-established 18-hole course with greens fees starting at C$35 (U.S.$23). The newer **Mission Hills Golf Course** (☎ **250/489-3009**) has 18 holes and a par-3 rating, plus a clubhouse and restaurant. Greens fees are C$18 (U.S.$12).

KAYAKING & WHITE-WATER RAFTING Several large rivers just east of Cranbrook make thrilling destinations for rafters and kayakers. **Mountain High River Adventures** (☎ 250/489-2067; www.elkvalley.net/riveradventures) offers daylong raft trips on the Elk River (C$79/U.S.$51) and the Bull River (C$89/U.S.$58). Trips are also offered on the White River near White Swan Lake Provincial Park (C$89/U.S.$58). If you'd rather hit the water in an inflatable kayak, guided day trips are offered on a number of rivers for C$94 (U.S.$61). Overnight white-water and overnight float trips go for C$131 (U.S.$85).

SKIING Fifty-seven miles (93km) east of Cranbrook, on the western face of the Rockies, is one of the best ski and snowboard areas in British Columbia. **Fernie Alpine Resort,** Ski Area Road, Fernie, BC, V0B 1M1 (☎ **250/423-4655;** fax 250/423-6644; www.skifernie.com; e-mail: info@skifernie.com), is a relatively unheralded resort that's popular with in-the-know snowboarders. Average snowfall is about 30 feet, with a vertical drop of 2,811 feet (857m). There are 97 trails in five alpine bowls, with a total of more than 2,500 acres of skiable terrain served by three quads, two triples, two T-bars, a Poma, and a handle tow with the capacity to handle 12,300 skiers per hour (but it's never *that* busy). Adult lift tickets are C$46 (U.S.$30). Amenities include lodging (☎ **800/258-SNOW** for reservations), restaurants, rentals, and instruction. The resort, lodges, and lifts remain open in summer, with hiking, mountain biking, and horseback riding the main activities.

WHERE TO STAY

Best Western Coach House Motor Inn. 1417 Cranbrook St. N., Cranbrook, BC, V1C 3S7. ☎ **800/528-1234** or 250/426-7236. 76 units. A/C TV TEL. C$70 (U.S.$46) double. Extra person C$10 (U.S.$7). Kitchen unit C$6 (U.S.$3.90) extra. Family plan available. AE, DC, DISC, MC, V.

A well-maintained motor-court motel, the Coach House offers especially large rooms. The motel is located on the busy Highway 95 strip north of town. Facilities here include a dining room, lounge, and outdoor pool.

Cedar Heights B&B. 1200 13th St., Cranbrook, BC, V1C 5V8. ☎ **800/497-6014** or 250/426-0505. Fax 250/426-0045. www.pixsell.bc.ca/bb/4309.htm. E-mail: cedarheights@ cyberlink.bc.ca. 3 units. A/C TV TEL. C$85 (U.S.$55) double. Extra person C$10–C$25 (U.S.$7–U.S.$16). Rates include full breakfast. MC, V. Children must be 12 or older.

This modern home is situated in a residential area just minutes from downtown Cranbrook. The rooms are very nicely furnished, with private bathrooms and private entrances. The B&B offers two guest lounges, one with a fireplace and couches, the other with a wet bar, fridge, and games. From the spacious deck or the hot tub, you can take in the view of the magnificent Rocky Mountains.

Mount Baker Hotel. 1017 Baker St., Cranbrook, BC, V1C 1A6. ☎ **888/489-3433** or 250/489-3433. Fax 250/489-3818. www.intek.com/mtbakerhotel. E-mail: mtbakerhotel@ cintek.com. 29 units. A/C TV TEL. C$58 (U.S.$38) double, C$150 (U.S.$98) suite. AE, DISC, MC, V.

The only lodging in downtown Cranbrook, the historic Mount Baker Hotel was restored and remodeled in 1999 and now shines with its former glory. For a historic hotel, the guest rooms are fair-sized and comfortable. The friendly staff will make you feel like you're part of the family. Facilities include the Corralz restaurant (see "Where to Dine," below) and the Colonel Baker Lounge.

Nomad Motel. 910 Cranbrook St. N., Cranbrook, BC, V1C 3S3. ☎ **800/863-6999** or 250/ 426-6266. Fax 250/426-1871. 34 units. A/C TV TEL. C$52–C$65 (U.S.$34–U.S.$42) double. Extra person C$5–C$10 (U.S.$3.25–U.S.$7). Kitchen unit C$6 (U.S.$3.90) extra. Rates include continental breakfast. AE, MC, V.

Of the many moderately priced motels along the Highway 95 strip north of Cranbrook, the well-maintained Nomad offers the most facilities for the money. Although the motel doesn't have its own restaurant, it's next door to a 24-hour Smitty's and the Apollo steak house (see "Where to Dine," below). Other amenities include a pool, in-room minifridges and microwaves, a business center, and a playground.

Prestige Rocky Mountain Resort & Convention Centre. 209 Van Horne St. S., Cranbrook, BC, V1C 6R9. ☎ **887/773-7844** or 250/417-0444. Fax 250/417-0400. www. prestigeinn.com. 108 units. A/C TV TEL. C$105 (U.S.$68) double, C$125 (U.S.$81) suite. Extra person C$15 (U.S.$10). Off-season rates and golf/ski packages available. AE, DISC, MC, V.

By far the poshest place to stay in Cranbrook, the new Prestige resort features very large and stylish rooms, with lots of extras such as voice mail, minifridges, irons and ironing boards, and coffeemakers. There's fine dining in Delmonico's Restaurant, drinks and lighter meals in Chattanooga's Bar and Grill, and an espresso bar for your caffeine fix. Other perks range from a full athletic club (with pool, hot tub, and exercise equipment) to a spa offering aromatherapy and massage.

CAMPING

The **Fort Steele Resort & RV Park** is 10 miles (16km) north of Cranbrook on Highway 95 (☎ **250/489-4268**). With 300 sites costing from C$18 to C$26 (U.S.$12 to U.S.$17), this is one of the largest campgrounds in the area. It offers pull-throughs, a tenting area, hot showers, and a rentable log cabin. Trail rides are also available.

WHERE TO DINE

Apollo Ristorante & Steak House. 1012 Cranbrook St. N. ☎ **250/426-3721.** Main courses C$9–C$18 (U.S.$6–U.S.$12). AE, MC, V. Daily 11am–10pm. GREEK/STEAK HOUSE.

Ask a local to recommend a restaurant, and Apollo is sure to be among the first choices—and for good reason. The extensive menu covers not only traditional Greek dishes, but also a broad selection of pasta, steaks and prime rib, sandwiches, seafood, even pizza. With such a large dining room and ambitious menu, you might suspect that quality would suffer. But someone in the kitchen here knows how to cook, and you'll be pleased with the hearty, slightly old-fashioned tastiness of the results.

Corralz. In the Mount Baker Hotel, 1017 Baker St. ☎ **250/489-3433.** Reservations not needed. Main courses C$13–C$23 (U.S.$8–U.S.$15). AE, ER, MC, V. Daily 7am–9pm. STEAK HOUSE.

The new dining room at the restored Mount Baker Hotel is the best place downtown for steak, prime rib, and barbecued chicken and ribs. The house Sasquatch Sauce is the chef's own barbecue sauce—and it packs a wallop.

Heidi's Restaurant. 821C Baker St. ☎ **250/426-7922.** Reservations recommended. Main courses C$11–C$17 (U.S.$7–U.S.$11). AE, MC, V. Mon–Thurs 11am–2pm and 5–9pm; Fri–Sat 11am–2pm and 5–10pm. CONTINENTAL.

Although the large menu at this pleasantly refined restaurant travels the globe for inspiration, the food is dominated by the cuisines of Germany and Italy. The attention-getting appetizer list ranges from empanadas with cumin beef to classic escargots. Entrees include steaks from local beef, schnitzels, pastas like ricotta-and-spinach cannelloni, fresh fish, and specialties like seared duck breast with black-currant sauce and spaetzle. The decor is dominated by redbrick walls and potted plants.

CRESTON & THE EAST SHORE OF KOOTENAY LAKE

66 miles (107km) SW of Cranbrook on Hwy. 3

After its brief sojourn in Montana and Idaho, the Kootenay River heads north and crosses into Canada again, where it drains into Kootenay Lake, a long, slim lake between the Purcell and Selkirk mountain ranges. Along the way, it passes Creston, an agricultural town surrounded by orchards, berry fields, and dairies. Although not a tourist center, Creston (pop. 4,843) is at the crossroads of a number of popular tourist routes—in particular the East Shore Kootenay Lake route, which explores Kootenay Lake before crossing a lake ferry on its way to the lovely town of Nelson.

Creston is set at the base of 62-mile-long (100km) Kootenay Lake. While you won't plan your vacation around the town, you may well spend a night here, especially if you're driving north from the United States on Highway 95.

Born of the Kootenay gold rush in the 1860s, the Creston region's real destiny was agriculture. By diking the Kootenay River, which annually flooded its broad valley at Creston, farmers have reclaimed 20,000 acres of rich farmland. The mild climate and rich soil make this a major center for fruit and vegetable growing. Roads in the area are lined with farm stands selling fresh produce, jams, and honey.

While friendly and pleasant, Creston has only a couple of activities for tourists. The town is home to the **Columbia Brewery,** 1220 Erickson St. (☎ **250/428-9344**), makers of popular Kokanee beer. Free tours are offered mid-June to mid-September daily at 10am, 12:30pm, and 2:30pm. Closed-toe shoes must be worn on the tour.

The history of Creston's development from native Ktunaxa (anglicized as Kootenay) encampment to gold camp to national fruit-growing capital is retold at the **Stone House Museum,** 219 Devon St. (☎ **250/428-9262**). The most interesting item here

---

Marsh Crawls Through a Wetlands Preserve

While diking the Kootenay River has been good for agribusiness, it hasn't been so good for the migrating birds and wildlife who lived in the marshy valley. A portion of the wetlands have been preserved as the 17,000-acre **Creston Valley Wildlife Management Area,** 6.8 miles (11km) northwest of Creston on Highway 3 (☎ 250/428-3259; www.cwildlife.bc.ca). More than 265 species of birds and 50 species of mammals make their home in this lush, marshy wetland, including a large population of nesting ospreys, moose, and river otters. Tundra swans and snow geese pass through during spring and fall migrations.

The refuge has an excellent visitor center that is dedicated to teaching the importance of wetlands. The center offers a variety of guided activities, including wildlife-viewing canoe trips and "marsh crawls." A number of hiking trails lead through the forest. The preserve is open year-round, but the interpretative center is open April through October only, daily from 9am to 4pm. Admission is C$3 (U.S.$1.95) for adults, C$2 (U.S.$1.30) for students, and C$9 (U.S.$6) per family or C$12 (U.S.$8) for a group of four to six people.

---

is an authentic Ktunaxa canoe. The Ktunaxa built canoes with so-called "sturgeon nosees" that point down into the water at both ends; the only other aboriginal group to build similar-style canoes were the Goldi peoples in Russia's Amur River basin. Guided tours are offered May through October, daily from 10am to 3:30pm. Admission is C$2 (U.S.$1.30) for adults and C$1 (U.S.65¢) for youths 6 to 16.

For more information, contact the **Creston Visitor Info Centre,** 1711 Canyon St., Box 268, Creston, BC, V0B 1G0 (☎ 250/428-4342; fax 250/428-9411; e-mail: crescofc@kootenay.net). You can also check out the Web site **www.crestonbc.com.**

Greyhound buses (☎ 800/661-8747) link Creston to Vancouver (C$94/U.S.$61) and to Calgary (C$65/U.S.$42). Creston is 68 miles (109km) from Sand Point, Idaho. From Nelson, it's 69 miles (112km) via the Highway 219 East Shore Kootenay Lake/Kootenay Lake ferry route. Via Highways 3 and 6, it's 77 miles (124km).

WHERE TO STAY

Hacienda Inn. 306 Northwest Blvd., Creston, BC, V0B 1G4. ☎ 800/567-2215 or 250/428-2224. Fax 250/428-2324. 50 units. A/C TV TEL. C$50–C$70 (U.S.$33–U.S.$46) double. Extra person C$5 (U.S.$3.25). Kitchen unit C$7 (U.S.$4.55) extra. Family plan, golf packages, commercial rates, and senior discounts available. AE, MC, V.

The Hacienda Inn, on the west entrance to Creston overlooking the Kootenay River valley, is a well-maintained older motel. In addition to standard motel rooms, the Hacienda offers one-bedroom kitchen units and two-bedroom suites. All accommodations have fridges. Facilities include a family dining room and lounge, an outdoor pool, a hot tub, a sauna with solarium, and an exercise room.

The Sweetapple Bed & Breakfast. 3939 Hwy. 3 E., Box 93, Erickson, BC, V0B 1K0. ☎ 250/428-7205. Fax 250/428-0310. www.sweetapple.bc.ca. E-mail: doull@cancom.net. 2 units. C$60 (U.S.$39) double. Family rates, golf packages, and senior discounts available. No credit cards.

The Sweetapple B&B, 5 minutes east of Creston in the neighboring village of Erickson, is a lovely little cottage sitting on 10 verdant acres beside the trout-filled Goat River. The two guest rooms and the guest lounge are located on one full floor of the cottage. One room has a queen bed, the other two twins; both rooms have sinks and toilets, although they share a shower. Flanking the guest rooms is a 60-foot-long balcony with fantastic views of the Skimmerhorn Mountains.

DRIVING THE EAST SHORE OF KOOTENAY LAKE TO NELSON

From Creston, you have two choices if you're driving to Nelson. You can follow Highway 3 to Salmo, 77 miles (124km), or you can drive the east shore of Kootenay Lake, cross the lake on a free car ferry from Kootenay Bay to Balfour, and then follow the west arm of Kootenay Lake to Nelson, a distance of 69 miles (112km). We highly recommend the latter route, which connects little lakeside resorts, antiques stores, and artisans' studios—it's one of the most scenic drives in British Columbia.

Kootenay Lake is rather unusual. Trapped between the majestic Selkirk and Purcell ranges, this narrow 62-mile-long (100km) lake is fed by two major rivers from opposite ends of its valley; the lake's outflow is through its West Arm, a cleft in the Selkirks. The lake is famed for its fishing—the world's largest rainbow trout reside here, and freshwater kokanee salmon spawn here in August—and for its wildlife. The greatest concentration of ospreys in North America is along Kootenay Lake.

Driving north from Creston, follow Highway 3A along the estuarial Kootenay River valley. The valley's steep walls and flat base belie its glacial birth. Watch on the west side of the road for a **horse farm** that raises rare Norwegian fjord draft horses, the largest horse breed in the world. **Duck Lake,** a marshy body of water barely separated from Kootenay Lake, is renowned for its bass fishing. The little hamlet of Sirdar sits on the shores of Duck Lake; the **Sirdar Pub,** 8068 Hwy. 3A (☎ **250/ 866-5522**), is a good spot for home-style cooking.

Just past Duck Lake, the road drops onto the southern shores of Kootenay Lake, opening up vistas of the Selkirk Mountains. Drive through the wee burg of Sanca and then watch for the **Glass House,** 25 miles (40km) north of Creston (☎ **250/ 223-8372**). This curious landmark is a castlelike house constructed of 150,000 square glass embalming-fluid containers. The structure was built in the 1950s by a local architect, and served as his home for a number of years. Today, it's a gift shop and saddlery.

Boswell is a small community of 200 citizens with a number of venerable lakefront resorts and marinas. It's just south of **Lockhart Creek Provincial Park** (☎ **250/ 825-3500**), which offers forest hiking trails, access to a swimming beach, and a boat launch. Campsites go for C$12 (U.S.$8). One of the nicer resorts here is the **Destiny Bay Resort,** 11935 Hwy. 3A (☎ **800/818-6633** or 250/223-8234), with a central lodge and eight sod-roofed cottages, all with fireplaces and lakeside verandas. Cottages for two start at C$160 (U.S.$104).

Be sure to stop at **Crawford Bay** (pop. 312), home to a number of unusual artisans' studios. Craftspeople at the **North Woven Broom Co.** (☎ **250/227-9245**) fashion traditional brooms from local wood and unprocessed broomcorn. At the **Kootenay Forge** (☎ **250/227-9466**), artist blacksmiths create functional household items using centuries-old hammer-and-forge techniques. **Weavers' Corner Handweaving Studio & Shop** (☎ **250/227-9655**) uses traditional looming methods to make one-of-a-kind clothing and household items. These three studios are open mid-May to mid-October, daily from 9am to 5pm. In winter, hours are more fluid, but normally the studios are open Saturday and Sunday from 9am to 5pm.

Also at Crawford Bay is the 18-hole championship ✪ **Kokanee Springs Golf Resort** (☎ **800/979-7999** or 250/227-9226). One of British Columbia's top courses, it has glorious views of the lake and the glaciered face of the Selkirks. Long fairways and rolling greens make this course a challenge even for veteran golfers. Greens fees are C$41 to C$46 (U.S.$27 to U.S.$30). Lessons, rentals, RV camping, dining, and lodging are also available at the resort.

On the way to the ferry terminal at Kootenay Bay, you'll pass the **Yasodhara Ashram Retreat** (☎ 250/227-9224), a long-established yoga and retreat center on the shores of the lake. You can visit the Temple of Divine Light, browse the bookstore, or spend the night: The Ashram offers simple rooms for C$45 (U.S.$29).

The 5¹/₂-mile (9km) Kootenay Bay–Balfour **ferry** service is apparently the longest free ferry ride in the world. The 40-minute crossing offers a good chance to take in the magnificent mountain-and-fjord scenery. Ferries operate from 6am to midnight; in high season, there are 18 crossings daily.

At Balfour, turn north on Highway 31 and watch for the power poles wearing neckties. If days on the road have made you stiff and sore, **Ainsworth Hot Springs Resort,** 9 miles (15km) north of Balfour (☎ **800/668-1171** or 250/229-4212; www. hotnaturally.com), is a popular place with an unusual steam-bath cave. The hot springs here were popular with the native Ktunaxa, although the springs ran fuller after early gold miners made a mine shaft out of the cave from whence the waters flowed. The 114°F (42°C) water flows out of the cave into a large lakeside pool. You can also follow the 65-foot-long lighted cave back and soak in a waist-deep pool, with hot mineral water dripping from the cave ceiling. Single entry to the pool system is C$7 (U.S.$4.55) for adults; a day pass is C$10 (U.S.$7). The resort also offers modern lodge rooms from C$86 (U.S.$56). The dining room serves three meals daily.

From Balfour, Highway 3A follows the West Arm of Kootenay Lake past more marinas and fishing resorts. **Kokanee Creek Provincial Park** (☎ **250/825-3500**) is a great campground with long, sandy beaches and lots of recreational opportunities. This is also the best spot for **kokanee salmon fishing and viewing;** in late summer, guides lead tours of man-made spawning channels. To find good hiking trails, turn north from Kokanee Creek Provincial Park and follow a fair gravel road for 10 miles (16km) to **Kokanee Glacier Provincial Park.** This wilderness park contains the high country of the Slocan peaks, including 9,100-foot-high (2,774m) **Kokanee Peak,** draped with glaciers. The park has a large network of trails.

From the park entrances, Highway 3 continues along the West Arm, finally crossing over the lake to enter the lovely resort town of Nelson.

NELSON

15 miles (24km) N of the U.S.–Canadian border

Nelson (pop. 9,585) is quite possibly the most pleasant and attractive town in the British Columbian interior. The late-19th-century commercial district is still intact and still in use with an eclectic mix of old-fashioned businesses, coffeehouses, and fancy boutiques and galleries. Nelson also offers high-quality bed-and-breakfasts, hotels, and restaurants, and the setting—along a shelf of land above the West Arm of Kootenay Lake—is scenically splendid.

Nelson was born as a silver-mining town in the 1880s, and its veins proved productive and profitable. By 1900, Nelson was the third-largest city in the province, with an architecturally impressive core of Victorian and Queen Anne–style homes and civic buildings. Today, the gracious town center, coupled with convenient access to recreation in nearby lakes, mountains, and streams, has added to Nelson's new-found luster as an arts capital. Nelson claims to have more artists and craftspeople per capita than any other city in Canada. It certainly has an appealingly youthful, comfortably countercultural feel, and makes a great place to spend a day or two.

ESSENTIALS

GETTING THERE   Nelson is 15 miles (24km) north of the U.S.–Canada border, 151 miles (242km) north of Spokane, Washington, and 407 miles (657km) east of Vancouver. **Greyhound** (☎ **800/661-8747**) operates two buses per day from Vancouver; the one-way fare is C$87 (U.S.$58). The buses continue on to Cranbrook (C$30/U.S.$20) with connections to Banff and Calgary. **North Vancouver Air** (☎ **800/228-5141**) offers one flight daily between Vancouver and Nelson.

VISITOR INFORMATION   Contact the **Nelson Visitor Info Centre** at 225 Hall St., Nelson, BC, V1L 5X4 (☎ **250/352-3433;** www.city.nelson.bc.ca; e-mail: chamber@netidea.com).

EXPLORING THE AREA

Nelson's main attractions are, in order, the city itself and what's just beyond the city. As an introduction to the town's wonderful Victorian architecture, go to the visitor center and pick up brochures for both the driving and the walking architectural tours of Nelson's significant heritage buildings.

Not to be missed are the château-style **City Hall,** 502 Vernon St., and **Nelson Court House,** designed by F. M. Rattenbury, famed for his designs for the B.C. Parliament Buildings and the Empress hotel, both of which continue to dominate Victoria. Along Baker Street, note the three-story, turreted storefront at the corner of Baker and Ward streets, and the **Mara-Barnard building,** 421–431 Baker St., once the Royal Bank of Canada building, with elaborate brickwork and bay windows.

The story of Nelson's human history is told at the **Nelson Museum,** 402 Anderson St. (☎ **250/352-9813**), which has a number of artifacts from the native Ktunaxa and from the silver-mining days when Nelson was one of the richest towns in Canada. One of the most fascinating exhibits is on the Doukhobor, a Russian Christian sect that settled along Kootenay Lake in the 1890s. The museum is open in summer, daily from 1 to 6pm, and the rest of the year, Monday through Saturday from 1 to 4pm. Admission is C$3 (U.S.$1.95) for adults, C$2 (U.S.$1.30) for seniors and students.

If you're interested in Nelson's mining past, visit the free **Chamber of Mines Eastern B.C. Museum,** just next door to the visitor center at 215 Hall St. (☎ **250/ 352-5242**). The museum contains the largest mineral collection in the province.

Nelson has a number of beautiful parks. **Gyro Park,** at Vernon and Park streets, features formal gardens, an outdoor pool, and panoramic views of Kootenay Lake and the Selkirk Mountains. **Lakeside Park,** which flanks Kootenay Lake near the base of the Nelson Bridge, offers swimming beaches, tennis courts, and a playground.

You can explore Nelson's lakefront on foot on the **Waterfront Pathway,** which winds along the shore from near the Prestige Resort to Lakeside Park. Or, in summer, hop on the restored **Streetcar no. 23,** which runs from Lakeside Park to Hall Street, along the waterfront. At the turn of the 20th century, Nelson had a streetcar system and was the smallest city in Canada to boast such public transport. The system

A Bird's-Eye View

For a flightseeing tour of the area, contact **Nelson Mountain Air Inc.** (☎ **250/ 354-1456**), which offers 1-hour floatplane tours of the Kokanee Glacier and the surrounding Selkirk Mountains for C$75 (U.S.$49), with a minimum of two passengers. The tours begin at the floatplane base at the small Nelson airport, along the waterfront at Hall Street.

fell out of use in the 1940s, but a stretch of the track, which traces the waterfront, remains intact. From mid-May to Labour Day, the streetcar runs daily from noon to 6pm. Tickets are C$2 (U.S.$1.30) for adults and C$1 (U.S.65¢) for seniors and students.

OUTDOOR PURSUITS

FISHING   Fishing is legendary in 656-foot-deep (200m) Kootenay Lake, which has 310 miles (500km) of lakefront. Especially along the West Arm—where the currents quicken as the lake begins to drain into the Kootenay River—the lake offers exemplary fishing for kokanee salmon, Dolly Varden, and rainbow trout. For guided trips and advice, contact **Screamin' Reel Fly and Tackle,** Balfour ferry landing, 21 miles (34km) northeast of town on Highway 3A (☎ **250/229-5262**).

GOLF   **Granite Pointe Golf Club,** 1123 Richards St. W. (☎ **250/352-5913**), is a hilly 18-hole, par-72 course with fantastic views of Kootenay Lake. Greens fees are C$32 (U.S.$21); the club offers rentals, a clubhouse with dining, and a driving range.

HIKING   The closest wilderness hiking is at **Kokanee Glacier Provincial Park** (see "Driving the East Shore of Kootenay Lake to Nelson," above), 13 miles (21km) northeast of Nelson on Highway 3A, then 10 miles (16km) north on a gravel road. Accessible right in Nelson is a 5$\frac{1}{2}$-mile (9km) **rails-to-trails system** on the old Burlington Northern line that follows the southern edge of the town along the flanks of Toad Mountain. You can join the path at a number of points; from downtown, follow Cedar Street south to find one entry point.

MOUNTAIN BIKING   The visitor center has a free map of old logging roads and rail lines that are available for biking. The Burlington Northern rails-to-trails system (see "Hiking," above) is also open to mountain bikers. For information on rentals and trail conditions, contact **Gerick Cycle & Sports,** 702 Baker St. (☎ **800/665-4441**).

SKIING   Ten miles (16km) south of Nelson off Highway 6 is the **Whitewater Ski Resort** (☎ **800/666-9420** or 250/354-4944; www.skiwhitewater.com; e-mail: info@ skiwhitewater.com), with some of British Columbia's best snow conditions. The ski area is in a natural snow-catching bowl below an escarpment of 8,300-foot (2,530m) peaks. The average snowfall is 40 feet, and that snow falls as pure powder. The mountain consists of groomed runs, open bowls, glades, chutes, and tree skiing; 80% of the runs are rated either intermediate or advanced. There are two double chairs and a handle tow; the vertical drop is 1,300 feet (396m). A day lift ticket costs C$36 (U.S.$23). Facilities include a day lodge with rentals, dining, and drinks.

WHERE TO STAY

Best Western Baker Street Inn. 153 Baker St., Nelson, BC, V1L 4H1. ☎ **888/255-3525** or 250/352-3525. Fax 250/352/2995. www.netidea.com/bakerst/. E-mail: bwbaker@ wkpowerlink.com. 70 units. A/C TV TEL. C$89–C$109 (U.S.$58–U.S.$71) double. Extra person C$10 (U.S.$7). AE, DISC, ER, MC, V.

The Baker Street Inn stands at the end of the historic downtown area, and is within easy walking distance of both shopping and dining. The guest rooms are rather basic, but very clean and comfortable. There's a restaurant on the property.

Casa Blanca Bed & Breakfast. 724 Second St., Nelson, BC, V1L 2L9. ☎ **888/354-4431** or 250/354-4431. Fax 250/354-4431. www.bbcanada.com/1941.html. E-mail: casabb@ netidea.com. 2 units (neither with private bathroom). C$60–C$75 (U.S.$39–U.S.$49) double. Extra person C$15 (U.S.$10). MC, V.

This exotic 1938 art-deco mini-mansion offers two spacious queen bedrooms (which share one bathroom) in a great location across from Kootenay Lake. The detailing in the house is amazing: The guest living room boasts tropical wood paneling, beveled glass doors, a quartz fireplace, and inlaid hardwood floors. This common area also contains such modern comforts as a TV, VCR and movies, CD player, and books and magazines. It's an easy walk to downtown Nelson or to Kootenay Lake beaches.

Dancing Bear Inn. 171 Baker St., Nelson, BC, V1L 4H1. ☎ 250/352-7573. Fax 250/ 352-9818. www.dancingbearinn.com. E-mail: dbear@netidea.com. 35 beds. C$17 (U.S.$11) dorm bed, C$39 (U.S.$25) double. Rates include use of kitchen. Family and group rates and seasonal vacation packages available. MC, V.

The Dancing Bear is a first-rate hostel right in the thick of things on downtown Nelson's Baker Street. The atmosphere and furnishings are more like you'd expect to find in a B&B—a grimy backpackers' flophouse this is definitely not. The inn offers both dorm-style and private-room accommodations, with shared and private bathrooms. The furniture is locally made from pine, beds are covered with down duvets, and paintings by area artists grace the walls. Facilities include a guest kitchen, dining area, patio, laundry, computer with Internet access, and common room with library, TV, and VCR. This is not your everyday hostel, and even if you're not into the hostelling scene, you'll find it a great place to meet people.

Heritage Inn. 422 Vernon St., Nelson, BC, V1L 4E5. ☎ **250/352-5331.** Fax 250/ 352-5214. www.heritageinn.org. E-mail: info@heritageinn.org. 41 units. C$69–C$89 (U.S.$45–U.S.$58) double. Extra person C$10–C$15 (U.S.$7–U.S.$10). Kitchen unit C$10 (U.S.$7) extra. Golf and ski packages available. Rates include breakfast. AE, MC, V.

One of Nelson's originals, this beautifully preserved 1898 hotel has been renovated to accommodate modern ideas of comfort while maintaining its vintage charm. For an antique hotel, the rooms are good-sized. Facilities include the General Store Restaurant with Italian cuisine, Taffy Jack's Cabaret, Library Lounge, Mike's Pub, wine-and-beer store, and salon. You'll want to visit the Heritage Inn even if you're not staying here, just to check out the wonderful bars and lobby area.

Inn the Garden Bed & Breakfast. 408 Victoria St., Nelson, BC, V1L 4K5. ☎ **800/ 596-2337** or 250/352-3226. Fax 250/352-3284. www.inthegarden.com. 7 units. A/C. C$70–C$130 (U.S.$46–U.S.$85) double in main house, C$150 (U.S.$98) 3-bedroom cottage. Extra person C$15–C$25 (U.S.$10–U.S.$16). Rates for guests in main house include full breakfast. Golf and ski packages available. AE, MC, V. Children accepted in cottage only.

This spacious B&B is perched on a hill just a block off downtown's Baker Street, with views of the lake and Kootenay Peak. The main house, a handsome painted lady–style Victorian, has six rooms with a mix of private and shared bathrooms, plus a large guest lounge. There's a terraced front garden and a patio and deck. Next door is a separate three-bedroom cottage that rents as one unit—perfect for families or groups. The cottage has a full kitchen, living room with TV and VCR, and its own backyard. Rates for guests staying in the main house include full breakfast; cottage guests get the makings for breakfast plus fresh baked goods delivered to their door.

Prestige Lakeside Resort & Convention Centre. 701 Lakeside Dr., Nelson, BC, V1L 6G3. ☎ **877/737-8443** or 250/352-7222. Fax 250/352-3966. 101 units. A/C TV TEL. C$110 (U.S.$72) double. Extra person C$10–C$20 (U.S.$7–U.S.$13). Off-season rates available. AE, DC, DISC, ER, MC, V.

Down on the lakeshore, the Prestige is Nelson's new full-service resort, offering spacious, beautifully furnished rooms with all the services you'd expect in a luxury hotel. All units have balconies, and you have a choice of accommodation types, including a number of theme rooms that will spice up a special occasion. Dining options include the Kootenay Waterfront Restaurant, Chillano's for sandwiches and soup, the Elephant Mountain Bar and Grill, a sushi bar, and a cappuccino bar. Other amenities include room service, concierge, marina, recreation rentals, pool, spa, fitness center, hot tub, gift shop, florist, salon, and meeting facilities.

WHERE TO DINE

You'll have no problem finding excellent food in Nelson. The restaurants at the **Prestige Resort** and the **Heritage Inn** (see "Where to Stay," above) are very good, and a wander down **Baker Street** will reveal literally dozens of small cafes, coffeehouses, and inexpensive ethnic restaurants, most with street-side tables.

Don't miss the **Dominion Café,** 334 Baker St. (☎ **250/352-1904**), an old diner offering sandwiches, light entrees, and baked goods. For Nelson's most popular hangout, go to **Jigsaws Coffee Co.,** 503 Baker St. (☎ **250/352-5961**). The curiously named **Rice Bowl Sushi Whole Foods,** 301 Baker St. (☎ **250/354-4129**), serves fast-food Thai and Japanese favorites. Get some sushi to go and have a picnic.

✪ **All Seasons Café.** 620 Herridge Lane. ☎ **250/352-0101.** Reservations required. Main courses C$13–C$25 (U.S.$8–U.S.$16). AE, MC, V. Daily 5–10pm; Sun brunch 10am–2:30pm. NORTHWEST.

If you're a fan of fresh, innovative cuisine, then the All Seasons Café is reason enough to visit Nelson. Located on a back alley a block off busy Baker Street, the All Seasons isn't easy to find, but if you want to eat at British Columbia's best restaurant east of Vancouver, then persevere. It's located on the main floor of a handsome old heritage home, decorated with casual flair and lots of fresh flowers.

The cuisine is eclectic, and the menu reads like a novel. For appetizers, try the outstanding Brie and asparagus flan with Italian figs and warm honey, or go for the Dungeness crab and potato latkes with fresh salsa. The main courses include a number of vegetarian and fish options. Red lentil and vegetable curry is served with cucumber raita and a seasonal fruit chutney, while seared salmon and halibut strips come with fennel, leeks, and fettuccine with lavender–pinot blanc wine butter. The wine list is thoughtfully selected, and the service friendly and professional.

Max and Irma's Kitchen. 515A Kootenay St. ☎ **250/352-2332.** Reservations not needed. Main courses C$8–C$12 (U.S.$5–U.S.$8). MC, V. Sun–Thurs 11am–9pm, Fri–Sat 11am–11pm. NEW ITALIAN.

The focus at bright, lively Max and Irma's Kitchen is the wood-fired oven. Located half a block off Baker Street, this restaurant serves very tasty and moderately priced, California-influenced Italian cuisine. The large menu encompasses a selection of individual pizzas, calzones, toasted panini sandwiches, and pastas.

13 Gateways to the Canadian Rockies: Calgary & Edmonton

Stretching from the Northwest Territories to the U.S. border of Montana in the south, flanked by the Rocky Mountains in the west and the province of Saskatchewan in the east, Alberta is a big, beautiful, empty chunk of North America, with 255,285 square miles (661,188km²). The province has 2.5 million inhabitants, over half of whom live in Edmonton, the provincial capital, and Calgary, a former cow town grown large and wealthy with oil money.

Both Calgary and Edmonton serve as gateways to the famed Canadian Rockies that rise on their western horizons. Since both cities function as air hubs for the major national parks—there are no scheduled flights to destinations within the Canadian Rockies—and since both Calgary and Edmonton are on major east-west road systems, chances are good you'll spend some time here. (See chapter 14 for complete coverage of the Rockies.)

Culturally, Calgary and Edmonton are a beguiling mix of rural Canadian sincerity and big-city swagger and affluence. Both cities are models of modern civic pride and hospitality; in fact, an anonymous behavioral survey recently named Edmonton Canada's friendliest city.

Early settlers first came to Alberta for its wealth of furs; the Hudson's Bay Company established Edmonton House on the North Saskatchewan River in 1795. The Blackfoot, one of the West's most formidable Indian nations, maintained control of the prairies until the 1870s, when the Royal Canadian Mounted Police arrived to enforce the white man's version of law and order. The Mounties' Fort Calgary was established on the Bow River in 1875. Open-range cattle ranching prospered on the rich grasslands, and agriculture is still the basis of the rural economy. Vast oil reserves were discovered beneath the prairies in the 1960s, introducing a tremendous 40-year boom across the province.

Plan to take a day or two to explore these lively cities. Calgary has excellent museums and one of the most exciting restaurant scenes in Canada, while Edmonton, dominated by its university and its capital status, has a vital arts scene and—not to be dismissed lightly—one of the largest shopping malls–cum–entertainment palaces in the world.

four-star hotel: two TVs, two phones, and modem hookups. Some units have full kitchens. Recent renovations include new carpets and furniture throughout, and a face-lift to all bathrooms. Amenities include a restaurant, lounge, room service, massage, courtesy car, pool, Jacuzzi, fitness room, and sauna. The downside? The three elevators date from the days when this was an apartment building; in summer, when tour buses hit, it can be exasperating to wait for them to serve guests on all 35 floors.

✪ **Palliser Hotel.** 133 Ninth Ave. SW, Calgary, AB, T2P 2M3. ☎ **800/441-1414** or 403/262-1234. Fax 403/260-1260. www.cphotels.ca. 421 units. A/C MINIBAR TV TEL. C$180–C$289 (U.S.$117–U.S.$188) double, from C$225 (U.S.$146) suite. AE, DC, DISC, ER, MC, V. Valet parking C$16 (U.S.$10) per day; self-parking C$12 (U.S.$8).

Opened in 1914 as one of the Canadian Pacific Railroad hotels, the Palliser is Calgary's landmark historic hotel. The vast marble-floored lobby, surrounded by columns and lit by gleaming chandeliers, is the very picture of Edwardian sumptuousness. Guest rooms are large for a hotel of this vintage—the Pacific Premier rooms would be suites at most other properties—and they preserve the period charm while incorporating modern luxuries. All units feature cordless phones, voice mail, and business desks with modem jacks. Entree Gold–class rooms come with their own concierge and a private lounge with complimentary breakfast, drinks, and hors d'oeuvres. The Palliser's C$30-million renovation continues, with new carpets, upholstery, and furniture throughout.

Guests can dine in the Rimrock Room, with vaulted ceilings, period murals, a massive stone fireplace, and hand-tooled leather panels on teak beams. The lounge bar looks like a gentlemen's West End club. Amenities include concierge, room service, secretarial services, valet parking, lap pool, health club, whirlpool, steam room, sauna, and business center with Internet access.

✪ **Westin Hotel.** 320 Fourth Ave. SW, Calgary, AB, T2P 2S6. ☎ **800/937-8461** or 403/266-1611. 525 units. A/C MINIBAR TV TEL. C$129–C$230 (U.S.$84–U.S.$150) double, C$247–C$380 (U.S.$161–U.S.$247) suite. Extra person C$20 (U.S.$13). Ask about weekend packages, which can bring the rate under C$100 (U.S.$65), with C$37 (U.S.$24) worth of in-hotel coupons. Family and senior rates also available. AE, DC, DISC, ER, MC, V. Parking C$9 (U.S.$6) per day.

The Westin is a massive modern luxury block in the heart of the financial district, and probably the single nicest hotel in Calgary. The entire property has undergone a major renovation over the past 5 years. Gone is the anonymous business-hotel atmosphere, replaced by a subtle western feel that's reflected in the new, very comfortable Mission-style furniture, Navajo-look upholstery, feather duvets, and in-room period photos that commemorate Calgary's bronco-busting and oil-boom past. Beautiful barn-wood breakfronts and lowboys dispel the feeling that you're in one of the city's most modern hotels. Each unit has two phones and a data port, voice mail, and an iron and ironing board. For C$20 (U.S.$13), upgrade to a Westin Guest Office room, with fax, printer, and copier.

Budget Options

The 120 beds at the **Calgary International Hostel,** 520 Seventh Ave. SE, Calgary, AB, T2G 0J6 (☎ **403/269-8239;** fax 403/266-6227; www.hostellingintl.ca/ Alberta/Hostels/Calgary.html), go for C$16 (U.S.$10) for members and C$20 (U.S.$13) for nonmembers. It's near downtown, convenient to bars and restaurants along Stephen Avenue and theaters near the performing-arts center. Facilities include laundry, two family rooms, and a common area.

Guests can choose from seven dining venues, from a buffet to the exquisite Owl's Nest (see "Where to Dine," below). Amenities include room service (radio-dispatched for maximum efficiency), panoramic 17th-floor indoor pool, sauna, and whirlpool. The hotel rolls out the welcome mat for kids, with a full array of children's furniture, baby-sitting, and a children's menu. Special needs are anticipated, from strollers, potty chairs, and playpens to room-service delivery of fresh diapers!

Moderate & Inexpensive

Travelers on a budget have excellent though limited choices in downtown Calgary. Luckily, Calgary's light-rail system makes it easy to stay outside the city center, yet have easy access to the restaurants and sights of downtown.

Best Western Suites Downtown. 1330 Eighth St. SW, Calgary, AB, T2R 1B3. ☎ **800/981-2555** or 403/228-6900. Fax 403/228-5535. 123 units. A/C TV TEL. C$125–C$145 (U.S.$81–U.S.$94) junior suite, C$165 (U.S.$107) 1-bedroom suite, C$185 (U.S.$120) 2-bedroom suite. Extra person C$10 (U.S.$7). Senior, weekly, and monthly rates available. AE, DISC, ER, MC, V. Free parking.

This all-suites hotel is an excellent value. You get a choice of standard, one-, or two-bedroom units; some come with efficiency kitchens (microwave and fridge). The rooms are quite large, almost apartment-size, and fitted with quality furniture and fixtures. This Best Western is a few blocks from downtown, but it's near the trendy street life of 17th Avenue. The motel has its own lounge and restaurant.

Lord Nelson Inn. 1020 Eighth Ave. SW, Calgary, AB, T2P 1J3. ☎ **800/661-6017** or 403/269-8262. Fax 403/269-4868. 57 units. A/C TV TEL. C$95 (U.S.$62) double, C$105 (U.S.$68) suite. Extra person C$10 (U.S.$7). Children under 18 stay free in parents' room. AE, ER, MC, V. Free parking.

One of the best deals in the city, the Lord Nelson is a modern nine-story structure with recently renovated rooms and suites. Although on the edge of downtown, it's just a block from downtown's free C-Train, which will put you in the heart of things in 5 minutes. The inn has a cozy lobby with redbrick pillars and comfortable armchairs. Adjoining are a coffee shop and tavern with outdoor patio. Each bedroom comes with two TVs, a couch, a desk, a fridge, and a balcony; the suites have Jacuzzis.

✪ **Sandman Hotel.** 888 Seventh Ave. SW, Calgary, AB, T2P 3J3. ☎ **800/726-3626** or 403/237-8626. Fax 403/290-1238. 301 units. A/C TV TEL. C$99–C$135 (U.S.$64–U.S.$88) double, C$175 (U.S.$114) suite. Children under 16 stay free in parents' room. Off-season rates available. AE, DC, DISC, MC, V. Parking C$4 (U.S.$2.60).

This 23-story hotel on the west end of downtown is one of Calgary's best deals. The Sandman is conveniently located on the free rapid-transit mall, just west of the main downtown core. The standard rooms are good-sized, but the real winners are the very large corner units, which feature small kitchens and great views. The Sandman is a popular place with corporate clients, due to its central location and good value. It also boasts the most complete fitness facility of any hotel in Calgary. Its private health club, available free to guests, has a pool, three squash courts, aerobics, and weight-training facilities. A massage therapist is available by appointment. Room service is available 24 hours a day, and there are three restaurants and two bars on the premises.

ALONG THE MACLEOD TRAIL

This was once a cattle track, but now it's the main expressway heading south toward the U.S. border. The northern portions of the Macleod Trail are lined with inns and motels—from upper middle range to economy.

En Route to the Rockies: The Old West

The Old West isn't very old in Alberta. If you're interested in the life and culture of cowboys and ranchers, stop at one of the following sights. Both are short and very scenic detours on the way from Calgary to the Rocky Mountains.

The **Western Heritage Centre** (☎ 403/932-3514; www.whcs.com) is 15 minutes west of Calgary in the little ranching town of Cochrane. This museum and interpretive center is located at the Cochrane Ranche Provincial Historic Site, which preserves Alberta's first large-scale cattle ranch, established in 1881. The center commemorates traditional farm and ranch life, contains a rodeo hall of fame, and offers insights into this most western of sporting events. Special events—often rodeo-related—are scheduled throughout the summer; call for a schedule. To reach Cochrane, follow Crowchild Trail (which becomes Hwy. 1A) out of Calgary; or from Highway 1 to Banff, take Highway 22 north to Cochrane. Admission is C$8 (U.S.$5) for adults, C$6 (U.S.$3.90) for students and seniors, C$3.50 (U.S.$2.30) for children, and C$20 (U.S.$13) for a family. The center is open from late May to early September.

An hour southwest of Calgary is another Old West destination. The ✪ **Bar U Ranch National Historic Site** (☎ 403/395-2212) is a well-preserved and still-operating cattle ranch that celebrates both past and present traditions. Tours of the ranch's 35 original buildings (some date from the 1880s) are available; a video of the area's ranching history is shown in the interpretive center. Special events include displays of ranching activities and techniques; since this is a real ranch, you might get to watch a branding or roundup. To get here, follow Highway 22 south from Calgary to the little community of Longview. Admission is C$6 (U.S.$3.90) for adults, C$4.60 (U.S.$3) for seniors, and C$2.90 (U.S.$1.90) for children. It's open from mid-May to mid-October.

If you're just looking for a convivial drink, head to **Bottlescrew Bill's Old English Pub,** First Street and 10th Avenue SW (☎ 403/263-7900), a friendly neighborhood pub with outdoor seating and Alberta's widest selection of beers.

CASINOS   Calgary has several legitimate casinos whose proceeds go wholly to charities. None impose a cover. **Cash Casino Place,** 4040B Blackfoot Trail SE (☎ 403/243-4812), operates Monday through Saturday from noon to midnight. The **Elbow River Inn Casino,** 1919 Macleod Trail S. (☎ 403/266-4355), part of a hotel by the same name (see "Where to Stay," above), offers the usual games plus a variation called Red Dog. The minimum stake is C$2 (U.S.$1.30), the maximum C$500 (U.S.$325). Open Monday through Saturday from 10am to 3am.

2 Edmonton

176 miles (283km) N of Calgary, 224 miles (361km) E of Jasper

Edmonton is Alberta's capital and has the largest metropolitan population in the province, currently around 850,000. Located on the banks of the North Saskatchewan River, Edmonton is a sophisticated city noted for its easygoing friendliness.

Edmonton grew in spurts, following a boom-and-bust pattern as exciting as it was unreliable. During World War II, the boom came in the form of the Alaska Highway, with Edmonton as the material base and temporary home of 50,000 American troops and construction workers.

The ultimate boom, however, gushed from the ground in February 1947, when a drill at Leduc, 25 miles (40km) southwest of the city, sent a fountain of crude oil soaring skyward. Some 10,000 other wells followed, all within a 100-mile (161km) radius of the city. In their wake came the petrochemical industry and the major refining and supply conglomerates. In 20 years, the population of the city quadrupled, its skyline mushroomed with glass-and-concrete office towers, a rapid-transit system was created, and a C$150-million civic center rose. Edmonton had become what it is today—the oil capital of Canada.

ESSENTIALS

GETTING THERE   By Plane   Edmonton is served by most major airlines, including **Air Canada** (☎ 800/776-3000) and **Canadian Airlines** (☎ 800/426-7000), which also operates more than a dozen shuttle flights per day to Calgary. The **Edmonton International Airport** (☎ 800/268-7134) lies 18 miles (29km) south of the city on Highway 2, about 45 minutes away. By cab, the trip costs about C$35 (U.S.$23); by Airporter bus, C$11 (U.S.$7).

By Car   Edmonton straddles the **Yellowhead Highway,** western Canada's new east-west interprovincial highway. Just west of Edmonton, the Yellowhead is linked to the Alaska Highway. The city is 320 miles (515km) north of the U.S. border, 176 miles (283km) north of Calgary.

By Train   The **VIA Rail Station** is at 104th Avenue and 100th Street (☎ 800/561-8630 or 780/422-6032). **Greyhound** buses link Edmonton to points in Canada and the United States from the depot at 10324 103rd St. (☎ 780/413-8747).

VISITOR INFORMATION   Contact **Edmonton Tourism,** 9797 Jasper Ave. NW, Edmonton, AB, T5J 1N9 (☎ 800/463-4667 or 780/496-8400; www.tourism.ede. org). There are also visitor centers located at City Hall and at Gateway Park, both open from 9am to 6pm, and on the Calgary Trail at the southern edge of the city, open from 9am to 9pm.

CITY LAYOUT   The winding **North Saskatchewan River** flows right through the heart of the city, dividing it into roughly equal halves. Most of this valley has been turned into public parklands.

The street numbering system begins at the corner of **100th Street** and **100th Avenue,** which means that downtown addresses have five digits and that suburban homes often have smaller addresses than businesses in the very center of town. Edmonton's main street is **Jasper Avenue** (actually 101st Avenue), running north of the river. The "A" designations you'll notice for certain streets and avenues downtown add to the confusion: They're essentially old service alleys between major streets, many of which now are pedestrian areas with sidewalk cafes.

At 97th Street, on Jasper Avenue, rises the massive pink **Canada Place,** the only completely planned government complex of its kind in Canada. Across the street is the **Edmonton Convention Centre,** which stair-steps down the hillside to the river.

Beneath the downtown core stretches a network of pedestrian walkways—called **Pedways**—connecting hotels, restaurants, and shopping malls with the library, City Hall, and the Citadel Theatre. These Pedways not only avoid the surface traffic, but are also climate-controlled.

At the northern approach to the High Level Bridge, surrounded by parkland, stand the buildings of the Alberta Legislature. Across the bridge, to the west, stretches the vast campus of the **University of Alberta.** Just to the east is **Old Strathcona,** a

Edmonton

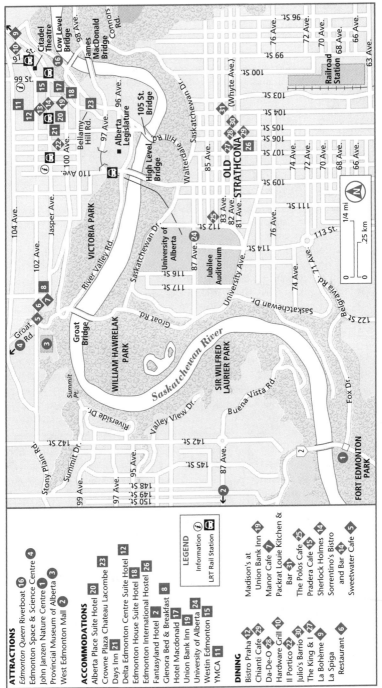

ATTRACTIONS
Edmonton Queen Riverboat 16
Edmonton Space & Science Centre 4
John Janzen Nature Centre 1
Provincial Museum of Alberta 3
West Edmonton Mall 2

ACCOMMODATIONS
Alberta Place Suite Hotel 20
Crowne Plaza Chateau Lacombe 23
Days Inn 21
Delta Edmonton Centre Suite Hotel 12
Edmonton House Suite Hotel 18
Edmonton International Hostel 26
Fantasyland Hotel 2
Glenora Bed & Breakfast 8
Hotel Macdonald 17
Union Bank Inn 19
University of Alberta 24
Westin Edmonton 15
YMCA 11

LEGEND
ⓘ Information
🚆 LRT Rail Station

DINING
Bistro Praha 12
Chianti Cafe 29
Da-De-O 28
Hardware Grill 10
Il Portico 22
Julio's Barrio 30
The King & I 27
La Bohème 9
La Spiga
Restaurant 6
Madison's at
Union Bank Inn 19
Manor Cafe 7
Packrat Louie Kitchen &
Bar 31
The Polos Cafe 25
Pradera Cafe 13
Sherlock Holmes 14
Sorrentino's Bistro
and Bar 14
Sweetwater Cafe 5

353

✪ Klondike Days

The gold rush that sent an army of prospectors heading for the Yukon in 1898 put Edmonton "on the map," as they say. Although the actual goldfields lay 1,500 miles (2,415km) to the north, this little settlement became a giant supply store, resting place, and "recreation" ground for thousands of men who stopped here before tackling the hazards of the Klondike Trail, which led overland to Dawson City in the Yukon. Edmonton's population quickly doubled in size, and its merchants, saloonkeepers, and ladies of easy virtue grew rich in the process.

Since 1962, Edmonton has commemorated the event with one of the greatest and most colorful extravaganzas staged in Canada. The **Klondike Days** are held annually in late July, with street festivities and the great Klondike Days Exposition at Northlands Park lasting 10 days.

Locals and visitors dress up in period costumes, street corners blossom with impromptu stages featuring anything from country bands to cancan girls, stage-coaches rattle through the streets, and parades and floats wind from block to block.

The 16,000-seat Coliseum holds nightly spectacles of rock, pop, variety, or western entertainment. Northlands Park turns into Klondike Village, complete with the Chilkoot Gold Mine, Silver Slipper Saloon, and gambling casino—legal for this occasion only. The Walterdale Playhouse drops serious stage endeavors for a moment and puts on hilarious melodramas with mustachioed villains to hiss and dashing heroes to cheer.

Immense "Klondike breakfasts" are served in the open air, marching bands compete in the streets, and down the North Saskatchewan River float more than 100 of the weirdest-looking home-built rafts ever seen, competing in the "World Championship Sourdough River Raft Race."

For more information on Klondike Days, call ☎ **888/800-PARK** or 780/471-7210.

---

bustling neighborhood of cafes, galleries, and hip shops that's now a haven for Edmonton's more alternative population. The main arterial through Old Strathcona is **Whyte Avenue,** or 82nd Avenue. Running south from here in a straight line is 104th Street, which becomes the **Calgary Trail** and leads to the Edmonton airport.

West of downtown Edmonton, Jasper Avenue shifts and twists to eventually become Stony Plain Road, which passes near **West Edmonton Mall,** the world's largest shopping and entertainment center, before merging with Highway 16 on its way to Jasper National Park.

GETTING AROUND   Edmonton Transit (☎ **780/496-1611**) operates the buses and the LRT (Light Rail Transit). This electric rail service connects downtown Edmonton with Northlands Park to the north and the University of Alberta to the south. The LRT and buses have the same fares: C$1.60 (U.S.$1.05) for adults and C$1 (U.S.65¢) for seniors and children; a day pass goes for C$4.75 (U.S.$3.10) adults, C$3.75 (U.S.$2.45) children. You can transfer from one to the other at any station on the same ticket. On weekdays from 9am to 3pm, downtown LRT travel is free between Churchill, Central, Bay, Corona, and Grandin stations.

In addition to the following downtown locations, **Tilden,** 10131 100A St. (☎ **780/422-6097**); **Budget,** 10016 106th St. (☎ **780/448-2000**); and **Hertz,** 10815 Jasper Ave. (☎ **780/423-3431**), each has a bureau at the airport.

Call **CO-OP Taxi** (☎ **780/425-2525** or 780/425-8310) for a ride in a driver/owner-operated cab.

FAST FACTS   There's an **American Express** office at 10180 101st St., at 102nd Avenue (☎ **780/421-0608**). The **Alberta Motor Association,** 11220 109th St. (☎ **780/471-3550**), affiliated with the Canadian Automobile Association, reciprocates with the AAA, offering members free travel information, advice, and services.

In case of emergency, dial ☎ **911.** The **Royal Alexandra Hospital,** 10240 Kingsway Ave. (☎ **780/477-4111**), offers emergency care.

If you need nonemergency medical care, check the phone book for the closest branch of **Medicentre,** which offers walk-in medical services daily. If you need a pharmacy, **Shoppers Drug Mart** has over a dozen locations in Edmonton, including one branch at 8210 109th St. (☎ **780/433-2424**). Most are open until midnight.

The main **post office** is located at 103A Avenue (at 99th Street).

EXPLORING THE CITY

Moored outside the convention center, the *Edmonton Queen* Riverboat (☎ **780/424-2628**) plies the North Saskatchewan River. Call for details on cruises.

Edmonton Space & Science Centre. 11211 142nd St., Coronation Park. ☎ **780/451-3344.** www.edmontonscience.com. E-mail: essc@planet.eon.net. Admission C$7 (U.S.$4.55) adults, C$6 (U.S.$3.90) seniors and youths, C$5 (U.S.$3.25) children 3–12, C$26 (U.S.$17) families. Summer daily 10am–10pm, winter Tues–Sun and holidays 10am–10pm. Bus: 17 or 22. Free parking.

This is one of the most advanced facilities of its kind in the world. It contains, among other wonders, an IMAX theater (☎ **780/493-4250**), the largest planetarium theater in Canada, high-tech exhibits (including a virtual-reality showcase and a display on robotics), and an observatory open on clear afternoons and evenings. The programs include star shows, laser shows, and IMAX films that have to be seen to be believed.

✪ **Fort Edmonton Park.** On Whitemud Dr. at Fox Dr. ☎ **780/496-8787.** www.gov. edmonton.ab.ca/fort. Admission to Fort Edmonton Park C$7 (U.S.$4.55) adults, C$5 (U.S.$3.25) seniors and youths, C$3.50 (U.S.$2.30) children, C$21 (U.S.$14) families. Admission to John Janzen Nature Centre by donation. Park: mid-May to late June Mon–Fri 10am–4pm, Sat–Sun 10am–6pm; late June to early Sept daily 10am–6pm. Nature Centre: May 18–June 30 Mon–Fri 9am–4pm, Sat–Sun 11am–4pm; July 1–Sept 7 Mon–Fri 9am–6pm, Sat–Sun 11am–6pm. LRT to University Station, then bus no. 32.

Fort Edmonton Park is a complex of townscapes that reconstruct various eras of Edmonton's history. Perhaps most interesting is the complete reconstruction of the old Fort Edmonton fur-trading post from the turn of the 18th century. This vast wooden structure is a warren of rooms and activities: Blacksmiths, bakers, and other docents ply their trades. On 1885 Street, you'll see Frontier Edmonton, complete with blacksmith, saloon, general store, and Jasper House Hotel, which serves hearty pioneer meals. On 1920 Street, sip an old-fashioned ice-cream soda at Bill's confectionery. You can ride streetcar no. 1, a stagecoach, or a steam locomotive between the various streets. As an open-air museum, the park is very impressive; the variety of activities and services here make this a great family destination.

Adjoining Fort Edmonton, the **John Janzen Nature Centre** (☎ **780/496-2939**) offers exhibits and trails. You can go bird watching, see a living beehive, and take courses in everything from building a log cabin to game tracking.

✪ **Old Strathcona.** Around 82nd Ave., between 103rd and 105th sts. Bus: 46 from downtown.

This historic district used to be a separate township, but was amalgamated with Edmonton in 1912 and still contains some of the best-preserved landmarks in the city.

It's best seen on foot, guided by the brochures given out at the **Old Strathcona Foundation,** 10324 82nd Ave., fourth floor (☎ **780/433-5866**). It's easy to spend an afternoon here, just wandering the shops, sitting at street-side cafes, and people watching. This is hipster-central for Edmonton, where students, artists, and the city's alternative community come to hang out. Be sure to stop by the **Old Strathcona Farmers Market** (☎ **780/439-1844**), at 83rd Avenue and 103rd Street, an open-air market with fresh produce, baked goods, and local crafts. It's open Saturday year-round, plus Tuesday and Thursday afternoons in summer.

✪ **Provincial Museum of Alberta.** 12845 102nd Ave. ☎ **780/453-9100.** Fax 780/454-6629. www.pma.edmonton.ab.ca. Admission C$7 (U.S.$4.55) adults, C$6 (U.S.$3.90) seniors, C$3 (U.S.$1.95) children, C$15 (U.S.$10) families; Tues are half-price. Daily 9am–5pm. Bus: 1.

Expertly laid out, this 200,000-square-foot modern museum displays Alberta's natural and human history in three permanent galleries. The Habitat Groups show wildlife in astonishingly lifelike dioramas; these picture windows into Alberta's diverse ecosystems are sure to captivate the kids and have adults marveling at the trompe-l'oeil paint job. The redesigned Aboriginal Peoples Gallery tells the 11,000-year story of Alberta's native inhabitants, incorporating artifacts, film, interactive media, and native interpreters; it's one of Canada's foremost exhibits on native culture. The Natural History Gallery has fossils, minerals, and a live-bug room.

✪ **West Edmonton Mall.** 8882 170th St. ☎ **800/661-8890** or 780/444-5200. www.westedmontonmall.com. Bus: 10.

You won't find many shopping malls mentioned in this book, but the West Edmonton Mall is something else. Although it contains 800 stores and services, including 90 eateries, it looks and sounds more like a large slice of Disneyland that has somehow broken loose and drifted north. The locals modestly call it the "Eighth Wonder of the World." More theme park than mall, it encompasses 5.2 million square feet, and houses the world's largest indoor amusement park, including a titanic roller coaster, bungee-jumping platform, and enclosed wave-lake, complete with beach and enough artificial waves to ride a surfboard on. It has walk-through bird aviaries, a huge ice-skating palace, 19 (count 'em, 19) movie theaters, a lagoon with performing dolphins, and several absolutely fabulous adventure rides (one of them by submarine to the "ocean floor"). In the middle of it all, an immense fountain with 19 computer-controlled jets weaves and dances in a musical performance.

Of course, you can shop here, too, and some of Edmonton's most popular restaurants are located in the mall. On Saturdays at 2pm, you can even tour the rooms at the mall's excellent "theme" hotel, called Fantasyland. Roll your eyes all you want, but do go. You have to see the West Edmonton Mall to believe it.

SHOPPING

See "Exploring the City," above, for the West Edmonton Mall.

DOWNTOWN   Most of downtown's shops are in a few large mall complexes; all are linked by the Pedway system, which gives pedestrians protection from summer heat and winter cold. **Edmonton Centre** has 140 stores and shares the block with the **Hudson's Bay Company. Eaton Centre** contains over 100 stores, including the flagship Eatons. All face 102nd Avenue, between 103rd and 100th streets.

OLD STRATHCONA   If you don't like mall shopping, then wandering the galleries and boutiques along Whyte Avenue might be more your style. About the only part of Edmonton that retains any historic structures, Old Strathcona is trend-central for students and bohemians. Shop for antiques, gifts, books, and crafts. Be sure to stop by the **Farmers Market** at 103rd Street and 102nd Avenue.

HIGH STREET   This small district, which runs from 102nd to 109th avenues along 124th Street, has Edmonton's greatest concentration of art galleries, housewares shops, boutiques, and bookstores. Great restaurants, too.

WHERE TO STAY

For B&Bs, try **Alberta and Pacific Bed and Breakfast** (☎ **604/944-1793;** fax 604/552-1659) or the **Alberta Bed and Breakfast Association (www.bbalberta. com)**. Note that accommodations are scarce during Klondike Days.

EXPENSIVE

Delta Edmonton Centre Suite Hotel. Eaton Centre, 10222 102nd St., Edmonton, AB, T5J 4C5. ☎ **780/429-3900.** Fax 780/428-1566. 169 units. A/C MINIBAR TV TEL. C$132–C$250 (U.S.$86–U.S.$163) standard business suite, C$218 (U.S.$142) deluxe executive suite. Ask about summer family discounts, weekend packages, and special rates for business travelers. AE, DC, ER, MC, V. Parking C$9 (U.S.$6) per day; valet parking C$12 (U.S.$8) per day.

This all-suite establishment forms part of the upscale Eaton Centre in the heart of downtown. Three-quarters of the windows look into the mall, so you can stand behind the tinted one-way glass (in your pajamas, if you like) and watch the shopping action outside. Most units are deluxe executive suites, each with a large sitting area (with TV and wet bar) and separate bedroom (with another TV and a plate-glass wall looking into the mall). If you need lots of room, or have work to do in Edmonton, these very spacious rooms are just the ticket. All units have two phones and jetted tubs.

Facilities and amenities include a restaurant, concierge, dry cleaning/laundry, babysitting, business center, health club, and whirlpool. Without having to stir out of doors, you can access 140 shops in the mall, plus movie theaters and an indoor putting green. Four other malls are connected to the hotel via Pedway.

✪ **Fantasyland Hotel.** 17700 87th Ave., Edmonton, AB, T5T 4V4. ☎ **800/737-3783** or 780/444-3000. Fax 780/444-3294. 354 units. A/C TV TEL. C$138–C$165 (U.S.$90–U.S.$107) standard rm, C$225–C$295 (U.S.$146–U.S.$192) double. Extra person C$10 (U.S.$7). Weekend and off-season packages available. AE, ER, MC, V. Free parking.

From the outside, this solemn tower at the end of the huge West Ed Mall reveals little of the wildly decorated rooms found within. Fantasyland is a cross between a hotel and Las Vegas: It contains a total of 116 themed rooms decorated in nine different styles (as well as 238 large, well-furnished regular rooms). Theme rooms aren't just a matter of subtle touches; these units are exceedingly clever, very comfortable, and way over the top. Take the Truck Room: Your bed is located in the back end of a real pickup, the pickup's bench seats fold down into a child's bed, and the lights on the vanity are real stoplights. In the Igloo Room, a round bed is encased in a shell that looks like ice blocks; statues of sled dogs keep you company, and the walls are painted with amazingly lifelike arctic murals. The dogsleds even become beds for children. And so on, through the Canadian Rail Room (train berths for beds), the African Room, and more. All theme rooms come with immense four-person Jacuzzis and plenty of amenities. The hotel offers tours of the different theme types on Saturdays at 2pm.

It's not all fantasy here, though. The nontheme rooms are divided into superior rooms, with either a king or two queen beds, and executive rooms, with a king bed and Jacuzzi. The hotel's restaurant is quite good; of course, you have all-weather access to the world's largest mall and its many eateries as well. Other amenities include room service, business center, small workout room, and passes to the mall's water park.

✪ **Hotel Macdonald.** 10065 100th St., Edmonton, AB, T5J 0N6. ☎ **800/441-1414** or 780/424-5181. Fax 780/429-6481. www.hotelmacdonald.ca. 198 units. A/C MINIBAR TV TEL. High season C$229–C$249 (U.S.$149–U.S.$162) deluxe standard rm, C$265–C$277 (U.S.$172–U.S.$180) Pacific Premier suite, C$349 (U.S.$227) executive suite, C$429–C$699 (U.S.$279–U.S.$454) specialty suite. Weekend and off-season discounts available. AE, DC, DISC, ER, MC, V. Parking C$15 (U.S.$10) per day. Pets accepted.

The palatial Hotel Macdonald opened in 1915. After a long and colorful career, it was bought by the Canadian Pacific chain in 1988. What ensued was a masterwork of sensitive renovation and restoration. The guest rooms were completely rebuilt to modern luxury standards, while retaining all of their original charm. Signature elements like the deep tubs, brass door plates, and paneled doors were kept intact, while important additions like new plumbing were installed. Rooms are beautifully furnished with amazingly comfortable beds, luxurious upholstery, feather duvets and pillows, and a bin for recyclables—a thoughtful touch.

The Library Bar resembles an Edwardian gentlemen's club, while the Harvest Room offers panoramic views of the valley as well as a garden terrace for summer dining. Amenities include concierge, room service, dry cleaning/laundry, business center, pool (with Roman pillars), and health club (with pro shop, juice bar, weight room, sauna, steam room, squash courts, massage, and personal trainers).

From the outside, with its limestone facade and gargoyles, the Mac looks like a feudal château—right down to the kilted staff. High ceilings and crystal chandeliers grace the lobby. Even pets, which are welcome, get special treatment: a gift bag of treats and a map of pet-friendly parks. Needless to say, there aren't many hotels like this in Edmonton, or in Canada for that matter.

Westin Edmonton. 10135 100th St., Edmonton, AB, T5J 0N7. ☎ **800/937-8461** or 780/426-3636. Fax 780/428-1454. www.westin.ab.ca. E-mail: sales@westin.ab.ca. 413 units. A/C MINIBAR TV TEL. From C$135 (U.S.$88) double. AE, CB, DC, DISC, ER, MC, V. Parking C$14 (U.S.$9) per day, valet parking C$17 (U.S.$11) per day.

Located in the heart of the downtown shopping and entertainment district, this modern hotel offers some of the city's largest rooms. Although the lobby is a bit austere, the guest rooms are very comfortably furnished and come equipped with nice touches like a coffeemaker, two phones, voice mail, and an ironing board and iron. For an extra C$20 (U.S.$13), you can request a Westin Guest Office room, which comes with a printer and fax. Seventy percent of the rooms are no-smoking. Guests frequent one of two restaurants, including Pradera, one of Edmonton's most inventive establishments (see "Where to Dine," below); there are also two lounges. Amenities include concierge, room service, laundry, exercise facilities, pool, sauna, and whirlpool.

MODERATE

Alberta Place Suite Hotel. 10049 103rd St., Edmonton, AB, T5J 2W7. ☎ **800/661-3982** or 780/423-1565. Fax 780/426-6260. 86 units. TV TEL. C$81–C$120 (U.S.$53–U.S.$78) double, C$104 (U.S.$68) double 1-bedroom suite. Extra person C$8 (U.S.$5). Children 16 and under stay free in parents' room. AE, DC, ER, MC, V. Free parking.

This downtown apartment hotel is an excellent choice for travelers who need extra space or for families who want full cooking facilities. The apartments, of various sizes, are very well furnished and comfortable. On site are a pool, hot tub, and sauna. The hotel is located half a block from public transport, and is within easy walking distance of most business and government centers.

Crowne Plaza Chateau Lacombe. 10111 Bellamy Hill, Edmonton, AB, T5J 1N7. ☎ **800/ 661-8801** or 780/428-6611. Fax 780/425-6564. www.crowneplaza.net. E-mail: cpcl@ planet.eon.net. 330 units. A/C MINIBAR TV TEL. C$79–C$129 (U.S.$51–U.S.$84) double, C$185–C$350 (U.S.$120–U.S.$228) suite. Extra person C$15 (U.S.$10). Weekend packages available. AE, DC, ER, JCB, MC, V. Parking C$8 (U.S.$5) per day.

Centrally located downtown, the Crowne Plaza, a round 24-story tower sitting on the edge of a cliff overlooking the North Saskatchewan River, possesses some of the city's best views. The unusual design blends well with the dramatic skyline, yet it's instantly recognizable from afar—a perfect landmark. The nicely furnished rooms and suites aren't huge, though the wedge-shaped design necessitates that they are broadest toward the windows, where you'll spend time looking over the city. Two private executive floors, no-smoking floors, and wheelchair-accessible rooms are available. Extras include a revolving restaurant at the top of the tower, a cocktail lounge, concierge, room service, laundry/dry cleaning, and fitness center.

✪ **Edmonton House Suite Hotel.** 10205 100th Ave., Edmonton, AB, T5J 4B5. ☎ **800/ 661-6562** or 780/420-4000. Fax 780/420-4008. www.edmontonhouse.com. 300 units. TV TEL. C$69–C$140 (U.S.$45–U.S.$91) 1-bedroom suite. Extra person C$5 (U.S.$3.25). Weekend packages and weekly/monthly rates available. AE, DC, ER, MC, V. Free parking.

This is a great alternative to pricier downtown hotels: The rooms are big and well decorated, and you don't have to pay stiff parking fees. With a great location right above the North Saskatchewan River, the all-suite hotel has one of the best views in Edmonton. Each suite comes with a full kitchen and dining area, bedroom, separate sitting area with fold-out couch, balcony, two phones, and a data port. Amenities include room service, restaurant, lounge, pool, sauna, exercise room, and laundry facilities. Edmonton House is within easy walking distance of most downtown office areas and to public transport.

Glenora Bed & Breakfast. 12327 102nd Ave. NW, Edmonton, AB, T5N 0I8. ☎ **780/ 488-6766.** Fax 780/488-5168. 18 units. C$70–C$140 (U.S.$46–U.S.$91) double. Rates include breakfast. AE, MC, V.

Located in the heart of the High Street district, just west of downtown, the Glenora occupies the upper floors of a 1912 heritage boardinghouse. There's an array of room types, from simple units with a mix of shared and private bathrooms to studios, suites, and rooms that are best thought of as apartments. All are pleasantly furnished with period antiques and rich designer fabrics. A deluxe continental breakfast is served.

✪ **Union Bank Inn.** 10053 Jasper Ave., Edmonton, AB, T5J 1S5. ☎ **780/423-3600.** Fax 780/423-4623. www.unionbankinn.com. 29 units. A/C MINIBAR TV TEL. C$125–C$145 (U.S.$81–U.S.$94) double. Rates include full breakfast. AE, DC, ER, MC, V. Free parking.

If you're weary of anonymous corporate hotels, this is a wonderful choice. The stylish Union Bank, built in 1910, now houses an elegant restaurant and intimate boutique hotel. The owner asked Edmonton's top interior designers to each design a room. The results are charming, with each unique guest room displaying its own style, colors, furniture, and fabrics. All units, however, have the same amenities, including fireplaces, voice mail, modem jacks, feather duvets, and nice toiletries. The rooms vary in layout and aren't incredibly big; if you're in town with work to do, ask for one of the larger units. Service is very friendly and professional. The restaurant/bar, Madison's, is a great place to meet friends (see "Where to Dine," below).

INEXPENSIVE

The **YMCA,** 10030 102A Ave. (☎ **780/421-9622;** fax 780/428-9469), accommodates men, women, and couples in 106 rooms (C$42/U.S.$27 double). Extras include
a cafeteria, pool, gym, and racquetball court. The **Edmonton International Hostel**
sleeps 104 in its new location in Old Strathcona at 10647 81st Ave. (☎ **780/
988-6836;** fax 780/988-8698; e-mail: eihostel@hostellingintl.ca).

In summer, 1,200 dorm rooms in Lister Hall at the **University of Alberta,**
87th Avenue and 116th Street (☎ **780/492-4281;** fax 780/492-7032; www.hfs.
ualberta.ca; e-mail: conference@ualberta.ca), are thrown open to visitors. Most are
standard bathroom-down-the-hall rooms for C$33 (U.S.$21). Available year-round
are guest suites, two-bed dorms that share a bathroom with only one other suite,
costing C$40 (U.S.$26). The university is right on the LRT line and not far from
trendy Old Strathcona. Parking is C$3 (U.S.$1.95) per day.

Days Inn. 10041 106th St., Edmonton, AB, T5J 1G3. ☎ **800/267-2191** or 780/423-1925.
Fax 780/424-5302. www.daysinn.com. E-mail: daysinn@compusmart.ab.ca. 76 units. A/C TV
TEL. C$59–C$89 (U.S.$38–U.S.$58) double. Children 11 and under stay free in parents' room.
Senior, AAA, and corporate discounts available. AE, CB, DC, DISC, ER, MC, V. Free parking.

For the price, this is one of downtown Edmonton's best deals. Located just 5 minutes
from the city center, the motor inn has everything you need for a pleasant stay, including guest laundry and king or queen beds in comfortably furnished rooms.

WHERE TO DINE

Edmonton has a vigorous dining scene, with lots of hip new eateries joining traditional steak and seafood restaurants. In general, fine dining is found downtown and
on High Street, close to the centers of politics and business. Over in Old Strathcona,
south of the river, are trendy—and less expensive—cafes and bistros.

DOWNTOWN
Expensive
✪ **Hardware Grill.** 9698 Jasper Ave. ☎ **780/423-0969.** www.hardwaregrill.com.
Reservations suggested. Main courses C$20–C$30 (U.S.$13–U.S.$20). AE, MC, V. Mon–Fri
11:30am–2pm; Mon–Thurs 5–9:30pm, Fri–Sat 5–10pm. Closed first week of July and first
week of Jan. NEW CANADIAN.

Housed in a historic building that was once Edmonton's original hardware store, this
is easily one of the city's most exciting restaurants. The building may be historic, but
there's nothing antique about the dining room. Postmodern without being stark, the
room is edged with glass partitions, with exposed pipes and ducts painted a smoky
rose. The menu here reflects new cooking styles and regional ingredients. There are
as many appetizers as entree selections, making it tempting to graze through a series
of smaller dishes. Sautéed sweetbreads are served with a hearty potato hash, wild-
mushroom ragout spills over grilled polenta, and smoked duck comes in crispy spring
rolls. But it's hard to resist entrees like maple-smoked pork loin with sweet corn sauce,
or lamb sirloin with herb gnocchi and mint aioli. The wine list is extensive.

La Bohème. 6427 112th Ave. ☎ **780/474-5693.** Reservations required. Main courses
C$15–C$29 (U.S.$10–U.S.$19). AE, MC, V. Mon–Sat 11am–3pm, Sun 11am–3:30pm; daily
5–11pm. FRENCH.

La Bohème consists of two small, lace-curtained dining rooms in a historic building
northeast of downtown. The cuisine is French, of course, and so is the wine selection,
with a particular accent on Rhône Valley vintages. There's a wide selection of appetizers and light dishes, including a number of intriguing salads. The entrees are hearty,

classic preparations of lamb, chicken, and seafood. The restaurant also features daily changing vegetarian entrees. Desserts are outstanding.

Madison's at Union Bank Inn. 10053 Jasper Ave. ☎ **780/423-3600.** Reservations suggested. Main courses C$14–C$21 (U.S.$9–U.S.$14); table d'hôte C$25 (U.S.$16). AE, ER, MC, V. Daily 7am–11pm. NEW CANADIAN.

One of the loveliest dining rooms and casual cocktail bars in Edmonton is Madison's. Once an early-20th-century bank, the formal architectural details remain, but they share the light and airy space with modern art, avant-garde furniture, and excellent food. The menu is up-to-date, with grilled and roast fish and meats, pasta dishes, interesting salads (one special featured rose petals, baby lettuce, and shaved white chocolate), and several daily specials. Many entrees boast an international touch, such as prawns with cilantro and tequila lime cream served over pasta.

Pradera Cafe. In the Westin Edmonton, 10135 100th St. ☎ **780/426-3636.** Fax 780/428-1454. Reservations recommended. Main courses C$15–C$25 (U.S.$10–U.S.$16). AE, DC, DISC, MC, V. Mon–Fri 6:30am–2pm, Sat–Sun 7am–2pm; daily 5–11pm. INTERNATIONAL.

One of downtown's most inventive restaurants is Pradera, featuring creative fusion cooking. The menu free-associates across several cuisines, notably Asian, Italian, and Canadian, to arrive at new dishes that succeed at being more than just the sum of their parts. The herb-crusted rack of lamb is served with polenta and Sambuca coffee jus, grilled mahimahi comes with a potato spring roll and papaya relish, and prime rib is served with a horseradish profiterole. Service is excellent.

Sorrentino's Bistro and Bar. 10162 100th St. ☎ **780/424-7500.** Reservations suggested. Main courses C$17–C$25 (U.S.$11–U.S.$16). AE, DC, MC, V. Mon–Fri 7–11am, 11:30am–2:30pm, and 5:30pm–midnight; Sat 5pm–midnight. ITALIAN.

This new and upscale branch of a local chain of Italian restaurants is a good addition to the downtown scene. The coolly sophisticated dining room and bar—flanked by the Havana Room, where Cuban cigars are available with port and single-malt Scotch—is a popular meeting place for the captains of the city's business and social life. The food is excellent: You can't do better than a plate from the daily appetizer table, which features grilled vegetables, salads, and marinated anchovies. Entrees range from risotto to wood-fired pizza to imaginative choices like tournedos of salmon and scallops, veal and chicken dishes, and several rotisserie specials.

Moderate & Inexpensive

Bistro Praha. 10168 100A St. ☎ **780/424-4218.** Reservations recommended on weekends. Main courses C$13–C$18 (U.S.$8–U.S.$12). AE, DC, ER, MC, V. Mon–Fri 11am–2am, Sat noon–2am, Sun 4pm–midnight. CENTRAL EUROPEAN.

Bistro Praha is one of several side-by-side casual restaurants—all with summer street-side seating—that take up the single block of 100A Street. It's also the best of these restaurants, and features a charming, wood-paneled interior, a mural-covered wall, and very good Eastern European cooking. The menu offers a wide selection of light dishes, convenient for a quick meal or mid-afternoon snack. The entrees center on schnitzels, as well as a wonderful roast goose with sauerkraut. Desserts tend toward fancy, imposing confections like Sacher torte. The clientele here is mainly young, stylish, and cosmopolitan. Service is friendly and relaxed.

✪ **Il Portico.** 10012 107th St. ☎ **780/424-0707.** Reservations recommended on weekends. Main courses C$11–C$23 (U.S.$7–U.S.$15). AE, DC, DISC, MC, V. Mon–Fri 11:30am–2pm; Mon–Sat 5:30–11pm, Sun 5–10pm. ITALIAN.

One of the most popular Italian restaurants in town, Il Portico has a wide menu of well-prepared traditional but updated dishes. With excellent selections of grilled meats, pastas, and pizza, it's one of those rare restaurants where you want to try everything. The Caesar salad will remind you how wonderful these salads can be if prepared properly. Service is impeccable, and the wine list one of the best in the city: Remarkably, the staff will open any bottle on the list (except reserve bottles) if you buy a half liter. The dining room is nicely informal but classy.

Sherlock Holmes. 10012 101A Ave. ☎ **780/426-7784.** www.thesherlockhomes.com. Main courses C$7–C$10 (U.S.$4.55–U.S.$7). AE, ER, MC, V. Mon–Sat 11:30am–2am, Sun noon–8pm. ENGLISH.

The Sherlock Holmes is a tremendously popular English-style pub with local and regional beers on tap (as well as Guinness) and a very good bar menu. The pub is housed in a charming building with a picket fence around the outdoor patio. The menu has a few traditional English dishes—fish-and-chips, steak-and-kidney pie—but there's a strong emphasis on new pub grub like chicken-breast sandwiches, beef curry, burgers, and salads. There are two other Sherlock Holmeses in Edmonton, one in the West Edmonton Mall and the other in Old Strathcona at 10341 82nd Ave.

HIGH STREET

La Spiga Restaurant. 10133 125th St. ☎ **780/482-3100.** Fax 780/488-3225. Reservations recommended on weekends. Main courses C$13–C$23 (U.S.$8–U.S.$15). AE, DC, MC, V. Mon–Fri 11:30am–2pm; Mon–Sat 5–11pm. ITALIAN.

La Spiga, located along gallery row, offers nouveau Italian cooking with an emphasis on fresh, stylish ingredients and unusual tastes and textures. The rack of lamb is marinated in fresh herbs and grappa, while the prawns and scallops are paired with a white-wine lemon sauce and served over angel-hair pasta.

Manor Cafe. 10109 125th St. ☎ **780/482-7577.** Fax 780/488-7763. Reservations recommended on weekends. Main courses C$9–C$15 (U.S.$6–U.S.$10). AE, DC, ER, MC, V. Sun–Thurs 11am–11pm, Fri–Sat 11am–midnight. PACIFIC RIM.

Housed in a stately mansion overlooking a park, the Manor Cafe offers one of the most fashionable outdoor dining patios in Edmonton. Recently renamed and redesigned, this longtime favorite now offers Pacific Rim cuisine, which brings the tastes of Asian food together with international ingredients and techniques. Hoisin lamb tenderloin is served on a bed of couscous; smoked duck wontons are among the intriguing appetizers. The food is eclectic, but always delicious.

Sweetwater Cafe. 12427 102nd Ave. ☎ **780/488-1959.** Main courses C$5–C$12 (U.S.$3.25–U.S.$8). AE, MC, V. Mon–Thurs 11am–10pm, Fri 11am–midnight, Sat 9am–midnight, Sun 10am–5pm. INTERNATIONAL/SOUTHWESTERN.

Here's a bright and lively bistro with good, inexpensive food; in summer, you can sit on the charming outdoor deck in the back, thankfully far from the roar of traffic. The food is international but leans towards the southwestern—sandwiches are served in tortillas, and there are several types of quesadillas.

OLD STRATHCONA

Chianti Cafe. 10501 82nd Ave. ☎ **780/439-9829.** Reservations required. Main courses C$7–C$15 (U.S.$4.55–U.S.$10). AE, DC, DISC, MC, V. Sun–Thurs 11am–11pm, Fri–Sat 11am–midnight. ITALIAN.

Chianti is a rarity among Italian restaurants: very good and very inexpensive. Pasta dishes begin at C$6 (U.S.$3.90) and run to C$10 (U.S.$7) for fettuccine with scallops, smoked salmon, curry, and garlic; even veal dishes (more than a dozen are offered!) and seafood specials barely top C$12 (U.S.$8). Chianti is located in a hand-somely remodeled post-office building; the restaurant isn't a secret, so it can be a busy and fairly crowded experience.

Da-De-O. 10548A 82nd Ave. ☎ **780/433-0930.** Main courses C$6–C$18 (U.S.$3.90–U.S.$12). MC, V. Mon–Wed 11:30am–11pm, Thurs–Sat 11am–11:30pm. CAJUN/SOUTHERN.

This New Orleans–style diner is authentic right down to the low-tech, juke-box-at-your-table music system. The food is top-notch, with good and goopy po' boy sand-wiches, fresh oysters, and five kinds of jambalaya. Especially good is the Sorochan Angel, seafood in Pernod cream over angel-hair pasta. Relax in a vinyl booth, listen to Billie Holiday, and graze through some crab fritters.

Julio's Barrio. 10450 82nd Ave. ☎ **780/431-0774.** Main courses C$9–C$19 (U.S.$6–U.S.$12). AE, MC, V. Mon–Wed 11:45am–11pm, Thurs 11:45am–midnight, Fri–Sat noon–1am, Sun noon–11pm. MEXICAN.

This Mexican restaurant and watering hole is a great place to snack on several light dishes while quaffing drinks with friends. The food ranges from enchiladas and nachos to sizzling shrimp fajitas. The atmosphere is youthful, high energy, and minimalist-hip: no kitschy piñatas or scratchy recordings of marimba bands here.

The King & I. 8208 107th St. ☎ **780/433-2222.** Main courses C$11–C$19 (U.S.$7–U.S.$12). AE, MC, V. Mon–Thurs 11:30am–10:30pm, Fri 11:30am–11:30pm, Sat 4:30–11:30pm. THAI.

This is the place for excellent, zesty Thai food, which can be a real treat after the beef-rich cooking of western Canada. Many dishes are vegetarian, almost a novelty in Alberta. Various curries, ranging from mild to sizzling, and rice and noodle dishes are the house specialties. For a real treat, try the lobster in curry sauce with asparagus.

✪ **Packrat Louie Kitchen & Bar.** 10335 83rd Ave. ☎ **780/433-0123.** Reservations rec-ommended on weekends. Main courses C$8–C$17 (U.S.$5–U.S.$11). MC, V. Tues–Sat 11:30am–11:30pm. ITALIAN.

Bright and lively, this very popular bistro has a somewhat unlikely name. Menu choic-es range from specialty pizzas to fine entree salads to grilled meats, chicken, and pasta. Most dishes cast an eye toward light or healthy preparations without sacrificing com-plexity. A grilled chicken breast comes with an arresting mélange of puréed spinach and red bell pepper; grilled lamb chops are garnished simply with plenty of fresh tomatoes, feta cheese, and polenta.

✪ **The Polos Cafe.** 8405 112th St. ☎ **780/432-1371.** Reservations suggested. Main courses C$10–C$24 (U.S.$7–U.S.$16). AE, DC, MC, V. Mon–Fri 11am–2:30pm; Mon–Thurs 5–10pm, Fri–Sat 5pm–midnight. ITALIAN/CHINESE/FUSION.

The Polo in question is Marco Polo, the first European to travel between Italy and China, and the namesake and inspiration for this exciting restaurant. The menu brings together classic Italian and Chinese cooking in a new cuisine loftily hailed as "Orie-ital." And it works: The food here is always delicious. Lamb rack with cilantro-garlic pesto and Marsala wine reduction is a typical hybrid; Italian pasta and Shang-hai noodles are tossed together with a variety of Sino-Italian sauces; tea-smoked duck comes with caramelized apples in merlot. The dining room has art-hung mauve walls, cool pools of light, and eager diners. Definitely worth a visit.

EDMONTON AFTER DARK

Tickets to most events are available through **Ticketmaster** (☎ **780/451-8000**). For listings of current happenings, check the Friday arts section of the *Edmonton Journal* or the alternative weekly *See* (**www.see-edmonton.com/events**).

Summertime Special Events

The **Jazz City International Music Festival** (☎ 780/432-7166) is a citywide celebration of jazz that takes over most music venues in Edmonton during the last week of June and first week of July.

The **Edmonton Folk Fest** (☎ 780/429-1899; www.efmf.ab.ca) is the largest folk-music festival in North America. Held in mid-August, it brings in musicians from around the world, from the Celtic north to Indonesia, plus major rock stars playing "unplugged." All concerts are held outdoors.

For 10 days in mid-August, Old Strathcona is transformed into a series of stages for the **Fringe Theatre Festival** (☎ 780/448-9000). Only Edinburgh's fringe festival is larger than Edmonton's—more than 60 troupes attend from around the world.

A masterpiece of theatrical architecture, the **Citadel Theatre,** 9828 101A Ave. (☎ 780/426-4811), which looks like a gigantic greenhouse, takes up the entire city block adjacent to Sir Winston Churchill Square. It houses five different theaters, workshops and classrooms, a restaurant, and a magnificent indoor garden with a waterfall. The Citadel is one of the largest, busiest theaters in Canada.

The **Northern Alberta Jubilee Auditorium,** 11455 87th Ave. (☎ 780/427-2760; fax 780/422-3750), is home to the Edmonton Opera and the Alberta Ballet.

THE CLUB & BAR SCENE   The flashy, upscale country-and-western scene is the name of the game, with new places opening up all the time. The hottest country dance bar in town is **Cook County Saloon,** 8010 103rd St. (☎ 780/432-2665).

There are plenty of options if you're not into Garth Brooks. For something uniquely Edmonton without the twang, check out the versatile **Sidetrack Cafe,** 10333 112th St. (☎ 780/421-1326), offering everything from Australian rock to progressive jazz. **Blues on Whyte,** 10329 82nd Ave. (☎ 780/439-5058), in the vintage Commercial Hotel in Old Strathcona, is Edmonton's best blues club. The **Rev,** 10032 102nd St. (☎ 780/424-2745), is the premier spot for the alternative-music scene. Edmonton's gay and lesbian bar of choice is the **Roost,** 10345 104th St. (☎ 780/426-3150).

The most romantic place for a drink is the **Library Bar** at the Hotel Macdonald, 10065 100th St. (☎ 780/424-5181).

CASINOS   In Alberta, the money from casinos goes to charities. The casinos are privately owned and provide comfortable surroundings, food and liquor service, and an amiable staff. The games are blackjack, roulette, baccarat, red dog, and sic bo; bets range from C$2 to C$500 (U.S.$1.30 to U.S.$325); and the play goes daily from 10am to 3am. Try your luck at **Casino ABS,** City Centre, 10549 102nd St. (☎ 780/424-9467), or **Casino ABS,** Southside, 7055 Argyll Rd. (☎ 780/466-9467). The **Palace Casino,** 8770 170th St. (☎ 780/444-2112), operates in the West Edmonton Mall.

Jasper Townsite & Jasper National Park

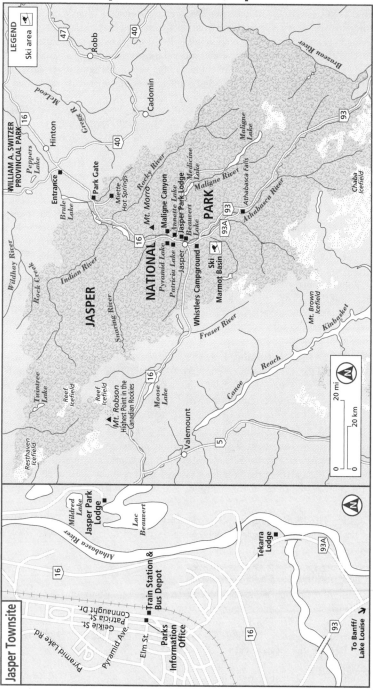

RAFTING Jasper is the jumping-off point for float and white-water trips down several rivers. A raft trip is a good option for that inevitable drizzly day, as you're going to get wet anyway. The mild rapids (Class II to III) of the wide Athabasca River make a good introductory trip, while wilder runs down the Maligne River (Class III) will appeal to those needing something to brag about. **Maligne River Adventures** (☎ 780/852-3370; fax 780/852-3405) offers trips down both rivers, as well as a 3-day wilderness trip on the Kakwa River (Class IV-plus).

Wilder white-water runs (Class III to IV) are available on the Fraser River in Mount Robson Park from **Sekani Mountain Tours** (☎ 780/852-5211). "Salmon-spawning" floats take place on the Fraser's calmer stretches in mid-August and mid-September.

Trips generally include most equipment and transportation. Jasper is loaded with rafting outfitters; a stroll along the main streets of town reveals a half-dozen options. Or just ask your hotel concierge for advice and help booking a trip.

HORSEBACK RIDING One of the most exhilarating experiences the park can offer is trail riding. Guides take your riding prowess (or lack of it) into account and select trails slow enough to keep you mounted. The horses used are steady, reliable animals not given to sudden antics. For a short ride, call **Pyramid Stables** (☎ 780/852-3562), which offers 1- to 3-hour trips around Pyramid and Patricia lakes.

Long-distance trail rides take you into the backcountry. **Skyline Trail Rides** (☎ 888/582-7787 or 780/852-4215; www.discoverjasper.com/trailrides/skyline) offers a number of short day trips costing roughly C$25 (U.S.$16) per hour, as well as 3- to 4-day trips to a remote, albeit modernized, lodge. Sleigh rides are offered in winter.

FISHING **Currie's Guiding Ltd.** (☎ 780/852-5650) conducts fishing trips to beautiful Maligne Lake; the cost is C$149 (U.S.$97) per person (minimum two persons) for an 8-hour day. Tackle, bait, boat, and lunch are included. Ask about special single and group rates. Patricia and Pyramid lakes, north of Jasper, are more convenient to Jasper-based anglers who fancy trying their luck at trout fishing.

CLIMBING **Jasper Climbing School** (☎ 780/852-3964), offers beginner, intermediate, and advanced climbing in daylong private courses. Basics are taught at the foot of Mount Morro, 12 miles (19km) from Jasper. The guided climbing fee is C$250 (U.S.$163) a day. For C$30 (U.S.$20), beginners can sample rappelling in a 3-hour workshop. Food, transport, and accommodations (in private homes) cost extra.

GOLF The 18-hole course at ✪ **Jasper Park Lodge,** east of Jasper Townsite, is one of the most popular and challenging courses in the Rockies, with 73 sand traps and

Organized Tours of the Park

Some of the principle outfitters and guides also offer transportation to outlying park beauty spots. Organized tours of the park's major sites—notably the Athabasca snowfields (C$78/U.S.$51) and a Maligne Lake cruise (C$56/U.S.$36)—are offered by **Brewster** (☎ 780/852-3332) and **Maligne Tours** (☎ 780/852-3370).

Beyond the Beaten Path (☎ 780/852-5650; e-mail: curries@ycs.ab.ca) also offers excursions to these popular destinations, as well as trips to Miette Hot Springs (C$42/U.S.$27) and more intimate sightseeing, photography, wildlife-viewing, and picnic options. In addition, the company offers a shuttle service for hikers and rafting parties.

other, more natural hazards—like visiting wildlife. *Score Magazine* ranked this the best golf course in Alberta. Call ☎ **780/852-6090** for information.

JASPER TOWNSITE

Jasper isn't Banff, and to listen to most residents of Jasper, that's just fine with them. Born as a railroad division point, Jasper Townsite lacks its southern neighbor's glitz and slightly precious air of an internationalized alpine fantasyland. Instead, it gives off a lived-in, community-oriented feel that's largely lacking in Banff. The streets are thronged with avid young hikers and mountain bikers rather than the shopping hordes. Chances are, the people you meet in town will be a little muddy or wet, as if they've just gotten in from the river or the mountain. Chances are they have.

However, development is rapidly approaching: New nightclubs, restaurants, and shops geared toward tourists are springing up along Patricia Street, and that sound you hear in the distance is the thunder of tour buses.

ESSENTIALS

GETTING THERE   Jasper is on the Yellowhead Highway System, linking it with Vancouver, Prince George, and Edmonton—and is therefore an important transportation hub. The town is 178 miles (287km) northwest of Banff.

VIA Rail connects Jasper to Vancouver and Edmonton with three trains weekly; the train station (☎ **780/852-4102**) is at the town center, along Connaught Street. The train tracks run due north before they start the long easterly sweep that leads to Edmonton. Also headquartered at the train station is the **Greyhound** bus station (☎ **780/852-3926**) and **Brewster Transportation** (☎ **780/852-3332**), which offers express service to Banff, as well as a large number of sightseeing excursions.

VISITOR INFORMATION   For information on the townsite, contact **Jasper Tourism and Commerce,** P.O. Box 98, Jasper, AB, T0E 1E0 (☎ **780/852-3858;** fax 780/852-4932).

ORIENTATION   Jasper Townsite is much smaller than Banff. The main street, **Connaught Drive,** runs alongside the Canadian National Railway tracks, and is the address of the majority of Jasper's hotels. **Patricia Street,** a block west, is quickly becoming the boutique street, with new shops and cafes springing up. Right in the center of town, surrounded by delightful shady gardens, is the **Parks Information Offices** (☎ **780/852-6146**). The post office is at the corner of Patricia and Elm streets. At the northern end of Connaught and Geike streets, a quarter mile (0.4km) from downtown, is another complex of hotels.

GETTING AROUND   For a rental car, contact **Tilden,** 638 Connaught Dr. (☎ **780/852-3798**). Call a **taxi** at ☎ **780/852-5558** or 780/852-3600.

EXPLORING THE AREA

The **Jasper Tramway** (☎ **780/852-3093;** www.worldweb.com/JasperTramway) starts at the foot of Whistler's Mountain, 4 miles (6km) south of Jasper off Highway 93. Each car takes 30 passengers (plus baby carriages, wheelchairs, and the family dog) and hoists them 1¼ miles (2km) up to the summit (7,400 ft./2,256m) in a breathtaking sky ride. At the upper terminal, you'll step out into alpine tundra, the region above the tree line where some flowers take 25 years to blossom. A wonderful picnic area carpeted with mountain grass is alive with squirrels. You'll also see the "whistlers"—actually hoary marmots—that the mountain is named for. The ride costs C$16 (U.S.$10) for adults and C$9 (U.S.$6) for children; cars depart every 10 to 15 minutes. Or consider a sunset ride followed by a three-course dinner at the terminal's restaurant for C$30 (U.S.$20); buffet breakfast and lunch are also available.

Just northeast of Jasper, off the Jasper Park Lodge access road, the Maligne River drops from its high mountain valley to cut an astounding canyon into a steep lime-stone face on its way to meet the Athabasca River. The chasm of **Maligne Canyon** is up to 150 feet (46m) deep at points, yet only 10 feet (3m) across; the river tumbles through the canyon in a series of powerful waterfalls. A sometimes-steep trail follows the canyon down the mountainside, bridging the gorge six times. Interpretive signs describe the geology. In summer, a teahouse operates at the top of the can-yon.

An incredibly blue mountain lake buttressed by a ring of high-flying peaks, **Maligne Lake** is 45 minutes east of Jasper, and is one of the park's great beauty spots. Maligne is the largest glacier-fed lake in the Rockies, and the second largest in the world. The native Canadians, who called the lake Chaba Imne, had a superstitious awe of the region. White settlers didn't discover Maligne until 1908.

Today, droves of tour buses go to the "hidden lake," and the area is a popular destination for hikers, anglers, trail riders, and rafters. No matter what else they do, most visitors take a boat cruise to **Spirit Island,** at the head of the lake. The 90-minute cruise leaves from below the **Maligne Lake Lodge,** an attractive summer-only facility with a restaurant, bar, and gift shop (but no lodging). Cruise tickets cost C$32 (U.S.$21) for adults, C$29 (U.S.$19) for seniors, and C$16 (U.S.$10) for kids.

Maligne Lake waters are alive with rainbow and eastern brook trout, and the Maligne Lake Boathouse is stocked with licenses, tackle, bait, and boats. **Guided fishing trips** include equipment, lunch, and hotel transportation, with half-day excur-sions starting at C$120 (U.S.$78). You can rent a boat, canoe, or sea kayak to ply the waters. Morning and afternoon **horseback rides** up the Bald Hills depart from the Chalet at Maligne Lake; the cost is C$55 (U.S.$36).

All facilities at Maligne Lake, including lake cruises, fishing, trail rides, and a white-water raft outfitter that offers trips down three Jasper Park rivers, are operated by **Maligne Tours.** Offices are located at the lake, next to the lodge; in Jasper at 626 Connaught Dr. (☎ **780/852-3370;** www.jaspertravel.com/malignelake; e-mail: maligne@ycs.ab.ca); and at the Jasper Park Lodge (☎ **780/852-4779**). Maligne Tours also operates a shuttle bus between Jasper and the lake.

Downstream from Maligne Lake, the Maligne River flows into **Medicine Lake.** This large body of water appears regularly every spring, grows 5 miles (8km) long and 60 feet (18m) deep, and then vanishes in fall, leaving only a dry gravel bed through the winter. The reason for this annual wonder is a system of underground drainage caves. The local Indians believed that spirits were responsible for the lake's annual dis-appearance, hence the name.

Miette Hot Springs (☎ **780/866-3939**) is 37 miles (60km) northeast of Jasper off Highway 16, one of the best **wildlife-viewing routes** in the park. Watch for elk, deer, coyotes, and moose en route. The springs can be enjoyed in a beautiful swimming pool or two soaker pools, surrounded by forest and an imposing mountain backdrop. Campgrounds and an attractive lodge with refreshments are nearby. In summer, the pool is open daily from 8:30am to 10:30pm. Admission is C$5 (U.S.$3.25) for adults, C$4.50 (U.S.$2.95) for children and seniors, or C$15 (U.S.$10) per family.

SHOPPING

Weather can be unpredictable in Jasper. If it's raining, you can while away an after-noon in the town's shops and boutiques. The arcade at the Jasper Park Lodge, called the **Beauvert Promenade,** has a number of excellent clothing and gift shops. In Jasper itself, Patricia Street contains most of the high-quality choices. A number of galleries feature Inuit and native arts and crafts: Check out **Our Native Land,** 601 Patricia St. (☎ 780/852-5592). Fashionable yet functional outdoor gear is the specialty of **Wild Mountain Willy's,** 610 Patricia St. (☎ 780/852-5304).

WHERE TO STAY

As in Banff, there's a marked difference in rates between high season and the rest of the year, so if you can avoid the June-to-September crush, you may save up to 50%. All prices listed below are for high season. Call for off-season rates. Reserve well in advance if possible. If you can't find a room, or don't want to bother with the details, contact **Reservations Jasper** (☎ 780/852-5488; fax 780/852-5489; e-mail: resjas@ incentre.net), which charges a fee for its services.

If you find the prices too astronomical in Jasper, or just can't find a room, consider staying east of the park near **Hinton** (see below).

Very Expensive

✪ **Chateau Jasper.** 96 Geikie St., Jasper, AB, T0E 1E0. ☎ **800/661-9323** or 780/ 852-5644. Fax 780/852-4860. E-mail: chjasper@agt.net. 119 units. A/C TV TEL. C$290 (U.S.$189) double, C$335–C$390 (U.S.$218–U.S.$254) suite. AE, CB, DC, DISC, MC, V. Free covered, heated parking.

Usually considered Jasper Townsite's best hotel, the Chateau Jasper is a refined three-story lodging with some of the best staff and service in town. The grounds are beautifully landscaped, with colorful floral patches scattered throughout the courtyards. The nicely decorated guest rooms come with all the amenities you'd expect at a four-star lodging. About half of the hotel's floors are smoke-free. The noted Beauvallon Dining Room is just off the lobby. Amenities include room service, dry cleaning/ laundry, baby-sitting, complimentary shuttle to the train and bus station, ski lockers, pool, hot tub, and sundeck. The Chateau Jasper is about the only downtown hotel that offers concierge service.

Jasper Park Lodge. P.O. Box 40, Jasper, AB, T0E 1E0. ☎ **800/465-7547** in Alberta, 800/ 441-1414 elsewhere in North America, or 780/852-3301. Fax 780/852-5107. www. cphotels.ca. 446 units. C$149–C$459 (U.S.$97–U.S.$298) double, C$289–C$689 (U.S.$188–U.S.$448) suite, from C$1,677 (U.S.$1,090) cabin. AE, DC, DISC, ER, JCB, MC, V. Free parking.

Jasper's most exclusive lodging, the Jasper Park Lodge was built by the Canadian Pacific Railroad and has the same air of luxury and gentility as their other properties, but with a more woodsy feel—sort of like an upscale summer camp. The hotel's wooded, elk-inhabited grounds are located along Lac Beauvert, about 5 miles (8km) east of Jasper proper. The amazing, lofty great room offers huge fireplaces to snuggle by. The accommodations are all extremely comfortable, though a bit hard to characterize, as there are a wide variety of cabins, lodge rooms, chalets, and cottages available—all from different eras, all set amid the forest, and all within easy walking distance of the beautiful central lodge. Since the rooms vary so much, it's a good idea to call and find out what suits your budget, needs, and group size. Families or groups can opt for one of the wonderful enormous housekeeping cabins, some of which have up to eight bedrooms.

Guests have a choice of four restaurants, including the famed four-star Edith Cavell Dining Room, with four-course dinners going for C$60 (U.S.$39). The Tent City Lounge is one of Jasper's youthful hangouts. Amenities include room service, dry cleaning/laundry, secretarial service, baby-sitting, the classy Beauvert Promenade shopping arcade, stables, tennis courts, outdoor pool, health club, one of the best golf courses in Canada, and access to all of the mountain sports available in Jasper.

Expensive

Amethyst Lodge. 200 Connaught Dr. (P.O. Box 1200), Jasper, AB, T0E 1E0. ☎ **800/ 661-9935** or 780/852-3394. Fax 780/852-5198. 97 units. A/C TV TEL. C$196–C$206 (U.S.$127–U.S.$134) double. AE, CB, DC, MC, V.

If you're sick of the faux-alpine look prevalent in the Canadian Rockies, then you may be ready for the Amethyst Lodge, a comfortable and unabashed motor inn. All rooms come with two double or two queen beds; half of the rooms have balconies. The Amethyst is more central to downtown Jasper than most lodgings. On site are a large restaurant and lounge, where afternoon tea is served daily. Other amenities include two hot tubs and laundry/dry cleaning service.

✪ **Jasper Inn.** 98 Geikie St. (P.O. Box 879), Jasper, AB, T0E 1E0. ☎ **800/661-1933** or 780/ 852-4461. Fax 780/852-5916. www.jasperinn.com. E-mail: jasperin@telusplanet.net. 157 units. TV TEL. C$175–C$202 (U.S.$114–U.S.$131) double, C$212–C$325 (U.S.$138– U.S.$211) suite. Extra person C$10 (U.S.$7). Children 16 and under stay free in parents' room. AE, DC, ER, MC, V. Free parking.

The Jasper Inn, on the northern end of town but set back off the main road, is one of the nicest lodgings in town. Rooms are available in four different buildings, and in many different size and bed configurations. If you're looking for a good value, ignore the standard and efficiency units (which are perfectly nice rooms, mind you); instead, fork over C$10 (U.S.$7) more and reserve a spacious one-bedroom suite with a fireplace and full kitchen. Even nicer are the extra-spacious guest rooms in the separate Maligne Suites building (all no-smoking), which come with enormous marble- and granite-lined bathrooms, fireplaces, wet bars, Jacuzzis, and balconies. (The top of the line is Elke Sommers's former room; ask for it by name.) Also available are two-bedroom chalet-style rooms, which can sleep up to seven. With the full kitchen, balcony, fireplace, and loads of room, these are perfect for families.

The Inn Restaurant, in a gardenlike atrium, offers tasty Canadian fare, with good prime rib, salmon, and pasta. Other on-site facilities include a sauna, steam room, hot tub, small pool, coin-op laundry, ski wax room, and small meeting facility.

✪ **Lobstick Lodge.** 96 Geikie St. (P.O. Box 1200), Jasper, AB, T0E 1E0. ☎ **888/852-7737** or 780/852-4431. Fax 780/852-4142. www.mtn-park-lodges.com. 139 units. TV TEL. C$196 (U.S.$127) double, C$211 (U.S.$137) kitchenette unit. Children under 15 stay free in parents' room. AE, DC, ER, MC, V. Free parking.

The Lobstick Lodge was totally renovated in 1995, and now features both a lounge and elevators, good additions to one of Jasper's most popular hotels. Standard units here are the largest in Jasper. Even more impressive are the huge kitchen units, which come with a full-size fridge, four-burner stove, and microwave, plus double and twin beds and a fold-out couch. These are perfect for families and go fast—reserve early. The upstairs meeting room has great views; when it's not in use, guests can play cards or lounge here. Also available are a restaurant, cocktail lounge, pool, whirlpool, hot tubs, patio, and dry cleaning/laundry.

Marmot Lodge. 86 Connaught Dr., Jasper, AB, T0E 1E0. ☎ **800/661-6521** or 780/852-4471. Fax 780/852-3280. 107 units. TV TEL. C$190 (U.S.$124) double, C$206 (U.S.$134) kitchen unit. Children under 15 stay free in parents' room. AE, DC, MC, V.

At the northern end of Jasper's main street, the Marmot Lodge offers very pleasant rooms in three buildings, each with different types of accommodations. One building contains kitchen units with fireplaces, popular with families. The building facing the street offers smaller, less expensive rooms with two single or one queen bed, while the third building features very large deluxe rooms. All have been decorated with a Native

American theme; some have tapestrylike weavings on the walls. Amenities include a barbecue patio, newly renovated dining room, fireside lounge, and heated, picture-windowed pool with sauna and whirlpool.

Sawridge Hotel Jasper. 82 Connaught Dr., Jasper, AB, T0E 1E0. ☎ **800/661-6427** or 780/852-5111. Fax 780/852-5942. 154 units. A/C TV TEL. C$207–C$229 (U.S.$135–U.S.$149) double, C$325–C$375 (U.S.$211–U.S.$244) suite. AE, ER, MC, V.

The three-story lobby of this hotel is large and rustic, opening onto a long central atrium lit with skylights, where you'll find the award-winning dining room, pool, and hot tub. The one-bedroom guest rooms face this atrium, while the two-queen-bedded rooms overlook the town and offer balconies as well. The entire hotel has recently been redecorated, and all units are very comfortable. Also on site are an informal garden cafe, Jacuzzis, lounge, and sports bar. The Sawridge, on the northern edge of Jasper, is unique in that it's owned by the Sawridge Cree Indian Band.

Moderate

In high season, it seems that nearly half the dwellings in Jasper let rooms, B&B-style; contact **Jasper Home Accommodation Association,** P.O. Box 758, Jasper, AB, T0E 1E0, for a full list. B&Bs listed with the local visitor association have little signs in front; if you arrive early enough in the day, you can comb the streets looking for a likely suspect. Note that B&Bs here are much less grand than those in Banff, and less expensive as well. Double-occupancy accommodations are in the C$50 to C$75 (U.S.$33 to U.S.$49) range at most homes. You'll need to pay cash for most. There's no central booking agency in Jasper, so contact your host directly.

Athabasca Hotel. 510 Patricia St., Jasper, AB, T0E 1E0. ☎ **800/563-9859** or 780/852-3386. Fax 780/852-4955. 61 units (39 with private bathroom). TV TEL. C$135 (U.S.$88) double with private bathroom, C$89 (U.S.$58) double with shared bathroom. AE, DC, MC, V.

This hotel's lobby is like a hunting lodge, with a stone fireplace, rows of trophy heads of deer and elk, and a great bar with its own huge fireplace. A gray-stone corner building with a homey, old-fashioned air, the Athabasca was built in 1929 as a destination hotel. Each of the guest rooms offers a mountain view, although only half have private bathrooms. The rooms are of fair size, the furnishings simple and tasteful. The Athabasca has an attractive dining room and a small and trim coffee shop. The place is really quite pleasant and one of the few good values in Jasper.

✪ **Becker's Chalets.** Hwy. 95, 3 miles (5km) south of Jasper (P.O. Box 579), Jasper, AB, T0E 1E0. ☎ **780/852-3779.** Fax 780/852-7202. 96 chalets. TV. C$75–C$150 (U.S.$49–U.S.$98) 1-bedroom cabin, C$130–C$205 (U.S.$85–U.S.$133) 2-bedroom cabin, C$180–C$325 (U.S.$117–U.S.$211) 3-bedroom cabin. MC, V.

This attractive log-cabin resort offers a variety of lodging options in freestanding chalets, set in a glade of trees along the Athabasca River. While the resort dates from the 1940s and retains the feel and atmosphere of an old-fashioned mountain retreat, most of the chalets have been built in the last 5 years, and thus are thoroughly modernized. Accommodations come with river-stone fireplaces and full kitchens. The dining room here, open for breakfast and dinner, is one of Jasper's best.

✪ **Tekarra Lodge.** 1 mile (1.6km) east of Jasper off Hwy. 93A (P.O. Box 669), Jasper AB, T0E 1E0. ☎ **888/404-4540** or 780/852-3058. Fax 780/852-4636. www.tekarralodge.com. 52 units. C$139 (U.S.$90) lodge room; C$139–C$189 (U.S.$90–U.S.$123) cabin double. 2-night minimum for cabins in summer. Extra person C$10 (U.S.$7). Rates for lodge rooms include continental breakfast. AE, DC, MC, V.

This charming log-cabin resort is just east of Jasper, situated above the confluence of the Miette and Athabasca rivers. Accommodations are in the lodge or in freestanding cabins (with kitchenette or full kitchen) that can sleep from two to seven people. The cabins are rustic-looking and nicely furnished, but it's the location that really sets Tekarra Lodge apart. Just far enough from the bustle of Jasper, off a quiet road in the forest, it offers the kind of venerable charm that you dream of in a mountain cabin resort. To make the isolation more complete, none of the rooms have private phones or televisions. One of Jasper's best restaurants is located in the lodge, making this a great place for a family seeking solitude and access to good food.

Inexpensive

Two **Hostelling International** hostels, both reachable at P.O. Box 387, Jasper, AB, T0E 1E0 (☎ 780/852-3215; e-mail: jihostel@telusplanet.net), are the best alternatives for the budget traveler. Advance reservations are strongly advised in summer. The 80-bed **Jasper International Hostel,** on Skytram Road 4 miles (6km) west of Jasper, charges C$15 (U.S.$10) for members and C$20 (U.S.$13) for nonmembers. The closest hostel to Jasper, it's open year-round. Two family rooms, a barbecue area, indoor plumbing, hot showers, and bike rentals are available. In winter, ask about ski packages. The **Maligne Canyon Hostel,** off Maligne Lake Road 11 miles (18km) east of Jasper, sleeps 24; rates are C$9 (U.S.$6) for members and C$14 (U.S.$9) for nonmembers. This convenient hostel is just above the astonishing Maligne Canyon. Facilities include a self-catering kitchen and dining area.

In & Around Hinton

Just east of the park gate in and near Hinton are a number of options that offer high-quality accommodations at significantly lower prices than you'll find in Jasper. Downtown Jasper is a 30- to 45-minute drive away from the choices listed below.

Hinton has a number of motel complexes with standard, no-nonsense rooms. The **Best Western Motor Inn,** 828 Carmichael Lane (☎ 800/220-7870 in Canada, or 780/865-7777), has 42 air-conditioned rooms, most with kitchenettes. The **Black Bear Inn,** 571 Gregg Ave. (☎ 888/817-2888 or 780/817-2000), features an exercise room, hot tub, and restaurant. The **Crestwood Hotel,** 678 Carmichael Lane (☎ 800/262-9428 or 780/865-4001), has a pool and restaurant. Doubles at these motels cost between C$79 and C$89 (U.S.$51 and U.S.$58).

A Local Guest Ranch

The **Black Cat Guest Ranch,** P.O. Box 6267, Hinton, AB, T7V 1X6 (☎ 800/859-6840 or 780/865-3084; fax 780/865-1924; www.telusplanet.net/public/bcranch; e-mail: bcranch@telusplanet.net), is a historic wilderness retreat located 35 miles (56km) northeast of Jasper. Established in 1935 by the Brewsters, the ranch boasts a superb mountain setting. The rustic two-story lodge, built in 1978—guests don't stay in the original old cabins—offers 16 unfussy units, each with private bathroom, large windows, and an unspoiled view of the crags in Jasper Park across a pasture filled with horses and chattering birds. There's a large central fireplace room with couches, easy chairs, and game tables scattered about. Lodging rates (C$82 to C$85/U.S.$53 to U.S.$55 per person, double-occupancy, in high season) include three home-cooked meals, served family-style by the friendly, welcoming staff. Activities include hiking, horseback riding (C$16/U.S.$10 per hr. for guided trips), canoe rentals, murder-mystery weekends, and fishing. The ranch staff will meet your train or bus at Hinton.

Mountain Splendour Bed & Breakfast. P.O. Box 6544, 17 Folding Mountain Village, Jasper East, AB, T7V 1X8. ☎ **780/866-2116.** Fax 780/866-2117. 2 units. TV. C$85 (U.S.$55) double. Rates include breakfast. V.

The spacious rooms at this large, modern home are outfitted with private bathrooms, tables and chairs, and English-theme decor. The larger of the two rooms is the English Garden Suite, a comfortable space with a private deck, fireplace, and large bathroom with Jacuzzi, separate shower, and cathedral ceilings. Guests can lounge by the fireplace or watch TV in the light, airy living room, which has picture windows framing a view of Jasper Park. There's an outdoor hot tub as well.

✪ **Overlander Mountain Lodge.** half a mile (1km) from Jasper Park East Gate (Box 6118), Jasper East, AB, T7V 1X5. ☎ **780/866-2330.** Fax 780/866-2332. E-mail: overland@telusplanet.net. 29 units. C$150–C$175 (U.S.$98–U.S.$114) lodge rm, C$100 (U.S.$65) cabin rm, C$250 (U.S.$163) 2-bedroom chalet, C$300 (U.S.$195) 4-bedroom chalet. AE, ER, MC, V.

The Overlander is a historic lodge on the edge of Jasper Park. The original lodge building houses a rustic and evocative dining room and bar with tremendous views of the Rockies, plus cozy guest rooms with queen or twin beds. A newer wing features rooms with gas fireplaces, queen beds, and jetted tubs. The fourplex cabins have sitting rooms and separate bedrooms. Most of the chalets, which are scattered in the forest behind the lodge, contain a fireplace or wood-burning stove, full kitchen, washer/dryer, and patio. Accommodations throughout have private bathrooms and are handsomely furnished with rustic furniture. The dining room serves good Northwest cuisine, with specialties of rack of lamb, venison, and fish. The Overlander's staff is friendly and helpful. This property offers excellent value and makes a charming base for exploring the park.

Suite Dreams B&B. Box 6145 (Lot 3134 Maskuta Estates), Hinton, AB, T7V 1X5. ☎ **780/865-8855.** Fax 780/865-2199. www.suitedream.com. E-mail: sdreams@telusplanet.net. 3 units. TV. From C$60 (U.S.$39) double. Extra person C$20 (U.S.$13). Rates include full breakfast. V.

A modern, wheelchair-accessible home built as a B&B, Suite Dreams offers large, comfortable rooms with lots of natural light in a quiet, forested setting. Each room is decorated according to a horticultural theme and features art from several generations of the owner's talented family. All units have private bathrooms and fridges, and one can sleep up to four. The spacious living room has a fireplace, TV, and VCR. The backyard features 100 yards of golf greens. The hostess is happy to make specialty breakfasts for guests with dietary restrictions.

Wyndswept Bed & Breakfast. 2^1/$_2$ miles (4km) east of Jasper Park gates (Box 2683), Hinton, AB, T7V 1Y2. ☎ **888/996-3793** or 780/866-3950. Fax 780/866-3951. www.wyndswept.com. E-mail: hosts@wyndswept.com. 3 units. TV. C$75 (U.S.$49) double. Extra person C$10 (U.S.$7). MC, V.

This excellent B&B has a hostess who will make you feel like family. The main-floor guest rooms have private bathrooms, robes, hair dryers, handmade soaps, kettles, and other extras. The suite, which gives out onto a deck, measures 1,200 square feet and has a full kitchen, large bathroom, and sitting area; it can sleep up to five. Guests have access to a computer and fax machine. Breakfast is delicious and substantial—there's even a dessert course. Chances are good you'll see wildlife while here: Bears, coyotes, wolves, and deer have all been spotted from the deck.

CAMPING

There are 10 campgrounds in Jasper National Park. You need a special permit to camp anywhere in the parks outside the regular campgrounds—a regulation necessary due to fire hazards. Contact the **parks information office** (☎ 780/852-6176) for permits. The campgrounds range from completely unserviced sites to those providing water, power, sewer connections, laundry facilities, gas, and groceries. The closest to Jasper Townsite is the **Whistlers,** up the road toward the gondola, providing a total of some 700 campsites.

WHERE TO DINE
Expensive
Beauvallon Dining Room. In the Chateau Jasper, 96 Geike St. ☎ **780/852-5644.** Reservations recommended. Main courses C$17–C$32 (U.S.$11–U.S.$21); table d'hôte C$34 (U.S.$22); Sun brunch C$16 (U.S.$10) adults, C$10 (U.S.$7) seniors and youths. AE, DC, ER, MC, V. Daily 6:30am–2pm and 5:30–11pm. CANADIAN.

Offering one of the most ambitious menus in Jasper, the Beauvallon specializes in classic European preparations of Canadian meats, fish, and game. The menu changes seasonally, but might include dishes like Caribou Normandy—caribou loin grilled and served with calvados sauce—or braised venison with chanterelle mushrooms and a creamy red-wine sauce. Other choices, such as northern Pacific seafood fricassee or gingered breast of duck, are equally eclectic. Service is excellent, and the dining room is cozy. The wine list is extensive and well priced.

Becker's Gourmet Restaurant. Hwy. 93, 3 miles (5km) south of Jasper. ☎ **780/852-3779.** Reservations required. Main courses C$12–C$25 (U.S.$8–U.S.$16). MC, V. Daily 8am–2pm and 5:30–10pm. CANADIAN.

Although the name's not very elegant, it's highly descriptive. This high-quality, inventive restaurant serves what could only be termed gourmet food, at Becker's Chalets, one of the nicest log-cabin resorts in Jasper. The dining room is an intimate log-and-glass affair that overlooks the Athabasca River. The menu reads like a novel: four-nut crusted lamb chops, chèvre Mornay sauce and dill on grilled chicken breast, and grilled venison loin with Saskatoonberry compote.

Moose's Nook Dining Room. In the Jasper Park Lodge, 5 miles (8km) east of Jasper. ☎ **780/852-6052.** Reservations recommended. Main courses C$17–$26 (U.S.$11–U.S.$17). AE, CB, DISC, ER, JCB, MC, V. Daily 6–10pm. CANADIAN.

This new restaurant off the great room of the Jasper Park Lodge features "Canadiana" specialties. With equal parts tradition and innovation, the Moose's Nook offers hearty presentations of native meats, fish, and game. Pheasant breast is grilled and served with a compote of local Saskatoonberry, while buffalo steak is prepared with a wild-mushroom, shallot, and whiskey sauce. Lighter appetites will enjoy the seafood hot pot and vegetarian cabbage rolls. The charming, wood-beamed room could double as a hunting lodge.

Moderate
✪ **Fiddle River.** 620 Connaught Dr. ☎ **780/852-3032.** Reservations required. Main courses C$13–C$23 (U.S.$8–U.S.$15). AE, MC, V. Daily 5pm–midnight. SEAFOOD.

This rustic-looking retreat has panoramic windows facing the Jasper railroad station and the mountains beyond. The specialty here is fresh fish, though a number of pasta dishes and red-meat entrees will complicate your decision-making process. While there are plenty of good selections on the menu, Fiddle River offers as many daily specials. One grilled salmon special was served with red-bell-pepper purée and dill cream sauce, while the Caribbean chicken breast was breaded in crushed banana chips and coconut and served with mango and yogurt. The wine list is short but interesting.

Trailhead, follow the main trail a mile up the canyon to see rust-red cliffs. From the same trailhead, turn south and follow Blackiston Creek to Blackiston Falls, a short half-mile (1km) leg-stretcher.

The most famous day hike in the park is to **Crypt Lake.** This 10.6-mile (17km) round-trip hike is moderately strenuous but worth the effort for those in shape. The hike begins with a boat ride to the trailhead, then a steep climb past four waterfalls up the side of Vimy Ride. The trail drops down onto snow-ringed Crypt Lake, right on the international border. The Shoreline International Cruises tour boat to Goat Haunt (see above) makes eight stops daily going both ways at the trailhead.

Long-distance hiking trails skirt the edge of Upper Waterton Lake and link to the trail system in Glacier National Park.

MOUNTAIN BIKING   Unusual in a national park, mountain biking is allowed on a number of trails. Cameron Lake is a good trailhead, offering three different trails. Two short but steep trails climb up to Wall and Forum lakes, while the long-distance Akimina Creek Trail follows an old forestry road 9 miles (14km) up Akimina Creek. For bike rentals, contact **Pat's Cycle Rental** (☎ **403/859-2266**).

GOLF   The ✪ **Waterton Park Golf Course** (☎ **403/859-2114**) is one of the oldest courses in Alberta. An original Stanley Thompson design (he designed the famed courses at Banff and Jasper), the first nine holes were constructed in 1929, the second nine holes 10 years later. Hazards include incredible Rocky Mountain vistas and meandering elk, bear, and moose. Greens fees are C$18 (U.S.$12) for 18 holes.

HORSEBACK RIDING   **Alpine Stables,** across from the golf course on Entrance Road, offers a variety of guided horseback rides on more than 155 miles (250km) of trails. Call ☎ **403/859-2462** to find out which rides are scheduled during your visit.

WHERE TO STAY

All lodgings in the park are in Waterton Townsite, a tiny settlement beside Waterton Lake. No matter where you stay, you won't be more than a 5-minute stroll from the lake.

Aspen Village Inn. P.O. Box 100, Waterton Lake, AB, T0K 2M0. ☎ **403/859-2255.** Fax 403/859-2033. www.telusplanet.net/public/kilmorey/waterton.aspen.html. E-mail: kilmorey@telusplanet.net. 51 units. TV. C$122–C$135 (U.S.$79–U.S.$88) double. Extra person $10 (U.S.$7). Children under 16 stay free in parents' room. AE, DISC, ER, MC, V. Closed mid-Oct to Apr.

You have a choice of three kinds of lodging at Aspen Village: regular motel rooms in the Wildflower building, suite-style rooms in the Aspen building, and duplex cottages. The suites are the newest, and can accommodate up to eight persons each. The entire complex, located 2 blocks from the lake, is hung with flower boxes and is well maintained.

Crandel Mountain Lodge. P.O. Box 114, Waterton Lake, AB, T0K 2M0. ☎ and fax **403/859-2288.** E-mail: crandell@telusplanet.net. 17 units. TV. C$118–C$159 (U.S.$77–U.S.$103) double. Extra person C$10 (U.S.$7). AE, DC, ER, MC, V.

A Bavarian guest house look-alike, the Crandel is one of the original lodges in the park. It has the feel of a country inn, with individually decorated rooms of differing sizes, ranging from small units under the eaves to large, three-room suites. Two wheelchair-accessible units are available as well. Very well maintained and charming, the inn is noted for its friendly staff.

Kilmorey Lodge. P.O. Box 100, Waterton Park, AB, T0K 2M0. ☎ **888/859-8669** or 403/859-2334. Fax 403/859-2342. www.agt.net/public/kilmorey/waterton.html. E-mail:

kilmorey@telusplanet.net. 25 units. C$86–C$133 (U.S.$56–U.S.$86) double. Extra person C$10 (U.S.$7). Children under 16 stay free in parents' room. AE, DC, ER, MC, V.

Beloved by oft-returning guests, the Kilmorey is a rambling old lodge from the park's heyday. One of the few lodgings that has direct lake views, it offers small but elegantly appointed rooms. Expect down comforters, antiques, squeaky floors, and loads of character and charm. The Lamp Post is one of Waterton's most acclaimed restaurants; also on site are the Gazebo Café and the Ram's Head Lounge.

✪ **The Lodge at Waterton Lakes.** P.O. Box 4, Waterton Park, AB, T0K 2M0. ☎ **888/98-LODGE** or 403/859-2151. Fax 403/859-2229. www.watertonresort.com. 80 units. TV. C$135–C$175 (U.S.$88–U.S.$114) double. Extra person C$12 (U.S.$8). Off-season rates available. AE, ER, MC, V.

This brand-new, classy complex sits on 4 acres in the heart of Waterton Townsite. The 80 rooms are in nine separate lodgelike buildings that flank a central courtyard. There are three types of accommodations: large standard rooms with queen beds; deluxe rooms with two queen beds and a sofa bed, a gas fireplace, a two-person shower, and a jetted tub; and kitchenette units with all the features of deluxe rooms plus a dining area and kitchen. All are decorated with an environmental theme and appointed with handsome pine furniture. The Wildflower Dining Room, the Good Earth Deli, and the Wolf's Den Lounge are part of the resort complex. Also on the property are a guest and community sports facility, with a large pool, fitness center, and spa. Winter sports and cross-country ski rentals are available.

Prince of Wales Hotel. Waterton Lakes National Park, AB, T0K 2M0. ☎ **403/226-5551.** In off-season, contact 1225 N. Central Ave., Phoenix, AZ 85077 (☎ 602/207-6000). 87 units. C$175–C$700 (U.S.$114–U.S.$455) double. Extra person C$15 (U.S.$10). Children under 12 stay free in parents' room. MC, V. Closed Sept 27–May 13.

Built in 1927 by the Great Northern Railway, this beautiful mountain lodge, perched on a bluff above Upper Waterton Lake, is reminiscent of the historic resorts in Banff. Rooms have been totally renovated, though many are historically authentic in that they're rather small. Operated by the same dilatory Greyhound/Dial Soap consortium that manages the historic lodges in Glacier National Park in Montana, the Prince of Wales is in need of some serious reinvestment (at these prices, you don't expect water-stained acoustic ceiling tile in the lobby bar). You'll want to at least visit this landmark for the view and perhaps for a meal at the Garden Court restaurant (see below); there's also a pub, lobby bar, and Valerie's Tea Room. Historic-monument status aside, however, there are better places to stay than this handsome doyen.

Waterton Glacier Suites. P.O. Box 51, Waterton Park, AB, T0K 2M0. ☎ **888/527-9555** or 403/859-2004. Fax 403/859-2118. 26 suites. A/C TV TEL. C$159–C$259 (U.S.$103–U.S.$168) double. Extra person C$10 (U.S.$7). AE, MC, V.

These large and attractive suites are some of the nicest lodgings in Waterton, particularly if you're able to step up and pay for a top-end loft suite. All rooms come with satellite TV, refrigerator, microwave, coffeemaker, jetted tub, fireplace, and patio or balcony. The standard units are two-bedroom suites, while the most expensive accommodations are town-house-style suites with good views, two bathrooms, and a two-person Jacuzzi. All are attractively furnished.

WHERE TO DINE

Garden Court. At Prince of Wales Hotel. ☎ **403/859-2231.** Reservations required. Main courses C$18–C$30 (U.S.$12–U.S.$20). MC, V. May 14–Sept 26 daily 6:30–9:30am, 11:30am–2pm, and 5–9pm. PACIFIC NORTHWEST.

Views from this elegant dining room overlook stunningly beautiful Waterton Lake, with the towering peaks of Montana's Glacier National Park incising the southern horizon. By and large, the food is up to the challenge of competing with the vista. Appetizers include warm baked Brie with sliced apples, crostini, and cranberry coulis; and scallops in chives, mushrooms, and cream in a puff-pastry shell. Entrees range from prime rib and buffalo bourguignon to pasta dishes and the house specialty Princess chicken, a spinach-and-feta-stuffed breast with a pine-nut crust, served with Saskatoonberry and onion chutney.

Lamp Post Dining Room. In the Kilmorey Lodge. ☎ **403/859-2334.** Reservations required. Main courses C$14–C$28 (U.S.$9–U.S.$18). AE, DISC, ER, MC, V. Daily 7–9:30am, 11:30am–2pm, and 5–9pm. NORTHWEST REGIONAL.

The dining room at the Kilmorey Lodge has a big regional reputation, and while the food is well prepared and the ambiance pleasant, some of the preparations are a little sketchy. The menu stresses its "mix of cultures," but the most successful dishes are those featuring local beef, regional game and fish, and wild mushrooms and berries. As an appetizer, try the wild-boar pâté. Filet mignon comes with Dijon-mustard glaze, while poached salmon is served with a cucumber-and-yogurt sauce. Alexander the Great Chicken is a grilled breast served with brandied mushroom cream and a grape and Saskatoonberry compote. The wine list is extensive, and the service prompt and friendly despite the busy-ness of the room.

Little Italian Café. Waterton Ave. ☎ **403/859-0003.** Reservations not accepted. Main courses C$7–C$18 (U.S.$4.55–U.S.$12). MC, V. Daily 8am–10pm. ITALIAN.

This friendly little cafe on Waterton's main street is a pleasant place for relatively inexpensive, tasty Italian food. Breakfasts feature egg-rich dishes like eggs Florentine, while the lunch menu specializes in grilled focaccia sandwiches. At night, the menu tilts toward pasta—with more than 20 choices—plus classic Italian preparations of chicken, veal, and beef. The shady patio is a marvelous spot to people-watch.

Kootenai Brown Dining Room. Waterton Ave., in the Bayshore Inn. ☎ **403/859-2211.** Reservations suggested. Main courses C$15–C$22 (U.S.$10–U.S.$14). AE, DISC, ER, MC, V. Apr 1–Oct 15 daily 7–10am, 11am–2:30pm, and 5–9pm. CANADIAN.

The only restaurant in Waterton that's directly on the lake, the food at Kootenai Brown doesn't try to interfere with the view. The dining room has seen some hard use and there hasn't been much in the way of upkeep, but the steaks here are good. The menu is centered on classic western-style cooking, though a few international and fancy dishes appear, like chicken tandoori or stuffed trout with mushroom duxelle. The breakfast buffet is C$8.95 (U.S.$5.80). The Bayshore complex also contains the Koffee Shop (a small cafe with soup, salads, and sandwiches) and a lounge serving a late-night menu of pizza and burgers.

Appendix: British Columbia & the Canadian Rockies in Depth

The more you know about British Columbia and the Canadian Rockies, the more you're likely to enjoy and appreciate everything the region has to offer. The pages that follow include a brief history, a wide range of highly recommended books, a primer on the unique cuisine of the area, and more.

1 British Columbia & the Canadian Rockies Today

Canada's westernmost region has a lot to offer travelers, including dramatic landscapes, a vibrant arts culture, and unparalleled access to outdoor recreation. British Columbia and the Canadian Rockies, which stretch across the provincial border into Alberta, are obviously part of Canada, and have a thoroughly Canadian infrastructure and political system. However, these two giant provinces—British Columbia covers 366,255 square miles (948,600km²), Alberta 255,285 square miles (661,188km²)—are separated from the nation's capital, Ottawa, and the political and cultural centers of eastern Canada by thousands of miles of farmland.

Much closer is the northwestern tier of the United States. While British Columbia and Alberta are definitely part of Canada, they are much closer in spirit to the Pacific Northwest states than to, say, Québec or Nova Scotia. The states of Washington, Oregon, Idaho, and Montana are themselves quite a distance from U.S. power centers, and share their climate, economies, and cultural histories with their northern neighbors. These regions of Canada and the United States have more in common with each other than with the rest of their respective countries—a reality that seems to please everyone in both the Canadian and the American Pacific Northwest.

There's another cultural overlay at work here, not quite at odds with the above observation, but simultaneously true: In the United States, the westering urge—that uniquely North American drive to keep moving west toward unspecified freedom and opportunity—was diffused across a dozen or so states, each of which developed its own culture and institutions. In Canada, there was just British Columbia and Alberta to absorb all the hopes, idealism, and pragmatism of 150 years' worth of western migration.

British Columbia is often called the California of Canada, with Canada's most temperate climate, a vibrant film industry, a visible and powerful gay and lesbian community, and a soft-focus New Age patina. However, British Columbia is also the Idaho of Canada, the Washington State of Canada, and incidentally, the Asia of Canada. In terms of cultural diversity and competing interests, there's a lot going on here.

Likewise, the Alberta of prosperous oil capitals like Edmonton and Calgary may seem like an oil- and agriculture-fueled monoculture, but dozens of its rural communities began as colonies of religious refugees whose stories have a lot in common with the Mormons of Utah. And with its nouveau-riche wealth and well-rehearsed swagger, Alberta is more like Texas than anywhere else on earth.

As if these factors weren't enough to explain the schizoid nature of the two westernmost provinces, the populace is further divided by highly politicized environmental issues. While Canadians in general seem more environmentally conscious than Americans, that doesn't mean that individual Canadians want to lose their salmon-fishing jobs to some vague international treaty, or that they want to close down the mine that's employed their families for generations just because of a little mud in the river. Environmental issues—especially those surrounding logging, agriculture, mining, and fishing—are especially contentious, often pitting urban and rural residents against each other.

It's easy to think of Canada as North America's Scandinavia—well ordered, stable, and culturally just a little sleepy. In fact, during your own travels across British Columbia and the Rocky Mountains, you'll likely find this corner of Canada a fascinating amalgam of cultures, histories, and conflicting interests.

2 History 101

NATIVE WESTERN CANADA According to generally accepted theories, the native peoples of North America arrived on this continent about 15,000 to 20,000 years ago from Asia, crossing a land bridge that spanned the Bering Strait. At the time, much of western Canada was covered with vast glaciers. Successive waves of these proto–American Indians moved south down either the coast or a glacier-free corridor that ran along the east face of the Rockies. As the climate warmed and the glaciers receded, the native people moved north, following ice-age game animals like the woolly mammoth.

The ancestors of the tribes and bands that now live on the prairies of Alberta didn't make their year-round homes here in the pre-Contact era. The early plains Indians wintered in the lake and forest country around present-day Manitoba, where they practiced forms of basic agriculture. In summer and fall, hunting parties headed to the prairies of Alberta and Saskatchewan in search of buffalo. The move to a year-round homeland on the Great Plains was a comparatively recent event, caused by waves of native displacement as the eastern half of North America became increasingly dominated by European colonists. Thus, a number of

Dateline

- **1670** Hudson's Bay Company is established by English King Charles II.
- **1741** Danish sailor Vitus Bering explores northern Pacific coast for Russia.
- **1759** English defeat French at Montréal's Plains of Abraham, ending the French and Indian War; British take control of Upper and Lower Canada.
- **1774** Spaniard Juan Perez sails up British Columbian coast from Mexico, landing in the Queen Charlottes and on Vancouver Island; the first European to explore the coast, he claims all of the Pacific coast for Spain.
- **1776** American colonies declare their independence from Britain; Canada remains royalist.
- **1778** Capt. James Cook of England lands at Nootka Sound, on Vancouver Island,

continues

and trades for otter furs on his way to China, establishing the beginning of the Northwest/China trade triangle. Establishes British claim to Northwest.

- **1778** North West Company establishes Fort Chipewyan on Lake Athabasca, the first European settlement in Alberta.
- **1792** Nootka Accord settles British/Spanish dispute over the Northwest coast; Spain renounces claims to the northern coast.
- **1793** British fur trader Alexander Mackenzie arrives in Bella Coola, becoming the first European to traverse North America.
- **1794** Rocky Mountain House, a North West Company trading post, opens at the juncture of the Peace and Moberly rivers, becoming the first permanent European settlement in British Columbia.
- **1795** Hudson's Bay Company establishes Edmonton House on the banks of the North Saskatchewan River.
- **1804–06** Americans Lewis and Clark journey up the Missouri River and down the Columbia River to the Pacific, then Spanish territory. The journey reveals a great wealth of furs in the Northwest, piquing American settlement interest.
- **1808** Fur trader Simon Fraser floats the Fraser River from the Rocky Mountains to the site of present-day Vancouver.
- **1811** David Thompson floats the entire length of the Columbia River, arriving at the Pacific to find an already-established American trading post, Fort Astoria.
- **1812** Outbreak of War of 1812; British take control of Fort Astoria.

continues

linguistically and culturally unrelated tribes were forced onto the prairies at the same time, competing for food and shelter.

The natives of the prairies relied on the buffalo—actually not a buffalo at all, but an American bison—for almost all their needs. In ways that are difficult to imagine today, the buffalo served as the primary means of life for the early Plains Indians. The hide provided teepee coverings and leather for moccasins; the flesh was eaten fresh in season and also preserved for later consumption. The bones were used to create a number of tools, while dried manure was used in campfires. Before the introduction of horses and firearms, the Indians hunted buffalo with bow and arrow, often using buffalo jumps, or *pishkuns*. The unsuspecting animals were stampeded off cliffs in large herds, after which the tribe harvested the dead and wounded buffalo.

The native Indians along the Northwest coast had a very different culture and lifestyle, and in all likelihood migrated to the continent much later than the Plains Indians. Living at the verge of the Pacific or along the region's mighty rivers, these early people settled in wooden longhouses in year-round villages, fished for salmon and shellfish, and used the canoe as the primary means of transport. The Pacific Northwest coast was one of the most heavily populated areas in Native America, and an extensive trading network developed. Because the temperate coastal climate and abundant wildlife made this a relatively hospitable place to live, the tribes were reasonably well off, and the arts—carving and weaving in particular—flourished. Villages were organized according to clans, and elaborately carved totem poles portrayed ritual clan myths.

EUROPEAN EXPLORATION The first known contact between the natives of western Canada and Europeans came in the last half of the 18th century, as the Pacific Northwest coast became a prize in the colonial dreams of distant nations. Russia, Britain, Spain, and the United States each would assert a claim over parts of what would become British Columbia and Alberta.

The first contacts were along the coast: In 1774, the Spanish explorer Juan Perez landed on the Queen Charlotte Islands and then on the western shores of Vancouver Island, at Nootka Sound. England's James Cook made a pass along the Pacific Northwest coast, spending a couple weeks at Nootka Sound in 1778, where the crew repaired the ship and traded trinkets for sea-otter pelts. Later in the same journey, when Cook visited China, he discovered that the Chinese were willing to pay a high price for otter furs.

Thus was born the Chinese trade triangle that would dominate British economic interests in the northern Pacific for 30 years. Ships entered the waters of the Pacific Northwest, traded cloth and trinkets with natives for pelts of sea otters, and then set sail for China, where the skins were traded for tea and luxury items. After the ships returned to London, the Asian goods were sold.

Since the Spanish and the English had competing claims over the Pacific Northwest coast, these nations sent envoys to the region—the Spaniard Don Juan Francisco de la Bodega y Quadra and the British Captain George Vancouver—to further explore the territory and resolve who controlled it. The expeditions led by these explorers resulted in a complete mapping of the region, though the ownership of the territory wasn't resolved until 1793, when Spain renounced all claims to land along the Northwest coast.

Fur traders also first explored the interior of British Columbia and the Alberta prairies. Two British fur-trading companies, the Hudson's Bay Company (HBC) and the North West Company, began to expand from their bases along the Great Lakes and Hudson's Bay, following mighty prairie rivers to the Rockies. Seeking to gain advantage over the Hudson's Bay Company, the upstart North West Company sent traders and explorers farther inland to open new trading posts and to find routes to the Pacific. Alexander Mackenzie became the first white man to cross the continent when he followed the Peace River across northern Alberta and British Columbia, crossing the Rockies and the Fraser River Plateau to reach Bella Coola, on the Pacific, in 1793. His stone inscriptions still remain on a rock face near the village.

Simon Fraser followed much of Mackenzie's route in 1808, though he floated down the Fraser River to its mouth near present-day Vancouver. Another fur trader and explorer was David Thompson, who crossed the Rockies and established Kootenay House trading post on the upper Columbia River. In 1811, Thompson journeyed to the mouth of the Columbia, where he found Fort Astoria, an American fur-trading

- **1818** Treaty of Ghent ends War of 1812; Spain renounces claim in Pacific Northwest; United States and Britain agree to "joint occupancy" of Pacific Northwest.
- **1821** Hudson's Bay Company and North West Company merge.
- **1825** Hudson's Bay Company's Fort Vancouver is established near present-day Portland, becoming the administrative center over nearly all of the Pacific Northwest.
- **1841** Act of Union creates the United Provinces of Canada.
- **1843** Settlers in Oregon decide to set up American-style government, and British withdraw to north of the Columbia River; Fort Victoria is established on Vancouver Island.
- **1846** U.S.–Canada boundary is established at 49th Parallel.
- **1849** Vancouver Island becomes British colony.
- **1858** Fraser River gold rush begins; the B.C. mainland becomes colony of New Caledonia.
- **1859** First wine grapes are planted along Lake Okanagan by Catholic missionary Father Pandosy.
- **1862** Gold is discovered at Barkerville, beginning the Cariboo gold rush.
- **1866** Colonies of Vancouver Island and New Caledonia combine to form colony of British Columbia.
- **1867** Britain grants further independence to the new Dominion of Canada.
- **1871** British Columbia agrees to join the Dominion of Canada and not the United States, as long as Canada builds the transcontinental railroad.

continues

- **1872** The Dominion Lands Acts, Canada's Homestead Act, opens the prairies to farmers and ranchers.
- **1874** Royal Canadian Mounted Police (RCMP) ride west to establish order on prairies of Ruperts Land (Alberta and Saskatchewan).
- **1875** RCMP establish Fort Calgary at the confluence of the Bow and Elbow rivers.
- **1877** Blackfoot chief Crowfoot signs treaty relegating the tribe, the largest and most powerful of the Canadian Plains tribes, to reservations.
- **1883** Canadian Pacific Railroad reaches Calgary.
- **1885** Canadian Pacific Railroad is completed, and the first train steams from Montréal to Burrard Inlet, on the Pacific near Vancouver; Banff National Park, Canada's first, is proclaimed by Prime Minister John Macdonald.
- **1886** Vancouver, a rail siding near a popular tavern named Gassy's, is established.
- **1896** Gold is discovered in the Yukon; Edmonton becomes a major outfitting center for overland journey to the Klondike.
- **1904** Butchart Gardens open to the public.
- **1905** Alberta becomes a province.
- **1914** Grand Trunk Railroad reaches from Winnipeg to Prince Rupert, becoming Canada's second transcontinental railroad.
- **1914** First ski resort opens at Whistler.
- **1914–18** In World War I, 60,000 Canadian troops die and another 173,000 are wounded.
- **1923** British Columbia restricts immigration by Japanese and Chinese.

continues

post, already in place. Competing American and British interests would dominate events in the Pacific Northwest for the next 2 decades.

By the 1820s, seasonal fur-trading forts were established along the major rivers of Alberta and British Columbia. Cities like Edmonton, Kamloops, Prince George, and Hope all had their beginnings as rough-and-ready trading posts. The primary articles of trade were beaver pelts, which were shipped to Britain to make men's hats. Each of the forts was given an assortment of trade goods to induce the local Indians to trap beaver, otter, fox, wolf, or whatever fur-bearing animals were present. Although the fur companies generally treated the native populations with respect and fairness, there were tragic and unintentional consequences to the relationships that developed. While blankets, beads, and cloth were popular with the natives, nothing was as effective as whiskey: Thousands of gallons of alcohol passed from the trading posts to the natives, corrupting traditional native culture and creating a cycle of dependence that enriched the traders while poisoning the Indians. The white traders also unwittingly introduced European diseases to the natives, who had little or no resistance to such deadly scourges as smallpox and measles. Entire villages of native Indians died of European-introduced plagues.

The Louisiana Purchase, which gave the U.S. control of all the territory along the Missouri River up to the 49th parallel and to the Continental Divide, and the Lewis and Clark Expedition of 1804–06 gave the Americans a toe-hold in the Pacific Northwest. As part of the settlement of the War of 1812, the Pacific Northwest—which included all of today's Oregon, Washington, and much of British Columbia—was open to both British and American exploitation, though neither country was allowed to set up governmental institutions. In fact, Britain had effective control of this entire area through its proxies in the Hudson's Bay Company, which had quasi-governmental powers over its traders and over relations with the native peoples, which included pretty much everyone who lived in the region.

B.C. CONSOLIDATES & JOINS CANADA

From its headquarters at Fort Vancouver, on the north banks of the Columbia River near Portland, Oregon, the Hudson's Bay Company held sway over the river's huge drainage, which extended far into present-day Canada. However, with the advent of the Oregon Trail and settlement in what would become the state of Oregon, the HBC's control over this vast territory began to slip. In 1843, the Oregon settlers voted by a slim majority to form a government based on the American model. The HBC and Britain withdrew to the north of the Columbia River, which included most of Washington and British Columbia.

The U.S.–Canada boundary dispute became increasingly antagonistic. The popular slogan of the U.S. 1844 presidential campaign was "54/40 or fight," which urged the United States to occupy all of the Northwest up to the present Alaskan border, including all of Washington and British Columbia. Finally, in 1846, the British and the Americans agreed to the present border along the 49th parallel. The HBC headquarters withdrew to Fort Victoria on Vancouver Island; many British citizens moved north as well. In order to better protect its interests and citizens, Vancouver Island became a crown colony in 1849—just in case the Americans grew more expansionist-minded. However, population in the Victoria area—then the only settled area of what would become British Columbia—was still small: In 1854, the population counted only 250 white people.

Then, in 1858, gold-rush fever struck this remote area of the British Empire. The discovery of gold along the Fraser River and in 1862 in the Cariboo Mountains brought in a flood of people. By far the vast majority of the estimated 100,000 gold seekers who streamed into the area were Americans who came north from the by-now-spent California goldfields. Fearing domination of mainland Canada by the United States, Britain named the mainland a new colony, New Caledonia, in 1858. In 1866, the two colonies—Vancouver Island and the mainland—merged as the British colony of British Columbia.

As population and trade increased, the need for greater political organization grew. As a colony, British Columbia had little local control, and was largely governed by edict from London. In order for British Columbia and its population to have greater freedom and self-determination, the growing colony had two choices: join the prosperous United States to the

- **1930s** The depression and mass unemployment hit Canada. Prairie farms and ranches are especially hard hit; social unrest rocks Vancouver.
- **1935** Social Credit Party forms in response to the Great Depression; becomes leading political party in much of western Canada until 1980s.
- **1939** Canada declares war on Germany
- **1945** World War II ends; 42,000 Canadians die in the war, another 54,000 are wounded.
- **1947** Native Canadians are granted right to vote in provincial elections; first major oil reserves are discovered in Alberta.
- **1960** Native Canadians are granted right to vote in federal elections.
- **1967** "Vive le Québec Libre": de Gaulle visits Québec, spurring Québec secessionism.
- **1968** The Official Languages Bill declares French and English the two official languages of Canada.
- **1972** Canada bans whaling off the Pacific Coast.
- **1988** Calgary hosts winter Olympic Games.
- **1989** Canada–U.S. Free Trade Agreement eliminates all tariffs on goods of national origin moving between the two countries.
- **1993** Environmentalists, loggers, and law enforcement clash near Clayoquot Sound; 800 logging protesters are arrested.
- **1995** Québec votes narrowly to remain in Canada.
- **1997** Britain hands over Hong Kong to mainland Chinese. Major emigration of Hong Kong Chinese to

continues

Vancouver area precedes the repatriation; Port Hardy fishermen and -women blockade Alaska Marine Highway ferry in protest of Alaskan fishing practices.

■ **1999** Nunavut becomes a standalone territory, splitting off from the Northwest Territories; the first new territory in over a century.

south, with which it shared many historic and commercial ties, or join the new Dominion of Canada far to the east. After Ottawa promised to build a railroad to link eastern and western Canada, B.C. delegates voted in 1871 to join Canada as the province of British Columbia.

THE RAILROADS LINK CANADA Meanwhile, the rule of the HBC over the inland territory known as Ruperts Land relaxed as profits from trapping decreased, and in 1869, the Crown bought back the rights to the entire area. The border between the United States and Canada in the prairie regions was hazy at best, lawless at worst. Although selling whiskey to native people was illegal, in the no-man's-land between Montana and Canada, trade in alcohol was rife.

In response to uprisings and border incursions, the Canadian government created a new national police force, the Royal Canadian Mounted Police. In 1873, a contingent of Mounties began their journey across the Great Plains, establishing Fort Macleod (1874) in southern Alberta along with three other frontier forts, including Fort Calgary at the confluence of the Bow and Elbow rivers. The Mounties succeeded in stopping the illegal whiskey trade and creating conditions favorable for settlement. By 1875, there were 600 residents at Fort Calgary, lured by reports of vast and fertile grasslands.

However, for the prairies and the interior of Canada to support an agrarian economy, these remote areas needed to be linked to the rest of Canada. In 1879, the Canadian Pacific Railroad reached Winnipeg, and in 1883 arrived at Banff. Finding a route over the Rockies proved a major challenge: The grades were very steep, the construction season short, and much of the rail bed had to be hacked out of rock. The section descending the western face of the Rockies near Golden, British Columbia, was particularly challenging; finally, a series of spiral tunnels were drilled through the mountain to achieve a safe gradient.

Canada's transcontinental railway needed a mainland coastal terminus in British Columbia, as the new province's population center and capital, Victoria, was on an island. Railroad engineers set their sites on the sheltered Burrard Inlet, then a sparse settlement of ragtag saloons, lumber mills, and farms. The first train arrived from Montréal in 1886, stopping at a thrown-together, brand-new town called Vancouver. A year later, the first ship docked from China, and Vancouver began its boom as a trading center and transportation hub. Just 4 years after it was founded, Vancouver had already outpaced Victoria in population.

All along the railroad's transcontinental reach, towns, farms, ranches, and other industries sprang up for the first time. In Alberta, huge ranches sprawled along the face of the Rockies, and Calgary boomed as a cow town. The railroads also brought foreign immigration. Entire communities of central and eastern European farmers appeared on the prairies overnight, the result of the railroads' extensive promotional campaign in places like the Ukraine. Other settlers came to western Canada seeking religious tolerance; many small towns on the prairies began as utopian colonies for Hutterites, Mennonites, and Doukhobors. Alberta became a province in 1905, and in 1914 the Grand Trunk Railroad, Canada's second transcontinental railroad, opened up the more northerly prairies, linking Saskatoon and Edmonton to Prince George and Prince Rupert. By 1920, Alberta was Canada's leading agricultural exporter.

427

British Columbia & the
Canadian Rockies in Depth

All this development demanded lumber for construction, and in Canada, lumber—then as now—meant British Columbia. In return for building the transcontinental railroad, the CPR was granted vast tracts of land along its route. As the demand for lumber skyrocketed, these ancient forests met the saw.

As the population, industry, logging, farming, and shipping all increased in western Canada, it was not just the local ecosystem that took a hit. The natives had at first reasonably cooperative relations with the HBC trappers and traders. Although European diseases wiped out enormous numbers of Indians, these early whites did little to overtly disturb the traditional life and culture of the natives.

That awaited the arrival of agriculture, town settlements, and Christian missionaries. After the HBC lost its long-standing role in Indian relations, authority was wielded by a federal agency in Ottawa. The natives received no compensation for the land deeded over to the CPR, and increased contact with the whites who were flooding the region simply increased contact with alcohol, trade goods, and disease. The key social and religious ritual of the coastal Indians—the potlatch, a feast and gift-giving ceremony—was banned in 1884 by the provincial government under the influence of Episcopal missionaries. The massive buffalo herds of the open prairies were slaughtered to near-extinction in the 1860s and 1870s, leaving the once proud Plains Indians little choice but to accept confinement on reservations.

THE 20TH CENTURY The building of the Panama Canal, which was completed in 1914, meant easier access to markets in Europe and along North America's east coast, bringing about a boom for the western Canadian economy. As big business grew, so did big unions. In Vancouver in the 1910s, workers in great numbers organized into labor unions to protest working conditions and pay rates. A number of strikes hit key industries, and in several instances resulted in armed confrontations between union members and soldiers. However, one area where the unions, the government, and business could all agree was racism: The growing Chinese and Japanese populations were a problem they felt only punitive legislation and violence could solve. Large numbers of Chinese had moved to the province and were instrumental in building the CPR; they were also important members of hard-rock mining communities and ran small businesses such as laundries. Japanese settlers came slightly later, establishing truck farms and becoming the area's principal commercial fishermen. On several occasions, Vancouver's Chinatown and Little Tokyo were the scene of white mob violence, and in the 1920s, British Columbia passed legislation that effectively closed its borders to nonwhite immigration.

The period of the World Wars was turbulent on many fronts. Settlers with British roots from all across Canada returned to Europe to fight the Germans in World War I, dying in great numbers and destabilizing the families and communities they left behind. Following the war, Canada experienced an economic downturn, which led to further industrial unrest and unemployment. After a brief recovery, the Wall Street crash of 1929 brought severe economic depression and hardship. Vancouver, with its comparatively mild climate, became a kind of magnet for young Canadian men—hungry, desperate, and out of work. The city, however, held no easy answers for these problems, and soon the streets were filled with demonstrations, the occupation of public buildings, and riots. Vancouver was in the grip of wide-spread poverty.

Anti-German riots took hold of the streets of Vancouver and German-owned businesses were burned. The war years were also hard times for non-white immigrants. In 1941, Japanese-Canadians were removed from their land and their fishing boats and interned by the government on farms and work camps in inland British Columbia, Alberta, and Saskatchewan.

Prosperity only returned with the advent of World War II: the unemployed enlisting as foot soldiers against the Axis nations, and the shipbuilding and armaments-manufacturing industries bolstering the region's traditional farming, ranching, and lumbering.

Alberta's wild oil boom began in 1947, when drillers struck black gold near Leduc and a period of tremendous economic growth ensued. By the 1960s, Alberta was supplying most of Canada's crude oil and natural gas. In the 1970s, as oil-producing nations joined together to form the Organization of Petroleum Exporting Countries (OPEC) and oil shortages hit North America, Alberta was left holding the hose. The value of the province's petroleum resources tripled almost overnight; by the end of the 1970s, its value had quadrupled again, allowing for a period of nearly unlimited building and infrastructure development. Calgary morphed from a sleepy ranchers' town into a brand-new city of soaring office towers, the financial and business center of Canada's oil industry. Throughout this period, Calgary was also the fastest-growing city in Canada. Edmonton, the capital of Alberta, boomed as the center of oil technology and refining. Much of Edmonton's city center was raised and totally rebuilt in the early 1970s boom years.

Since the war years, British Columbia generally boomed economically as well, especially under the leadership of the Social Credit Party, supposedly the party of small business. Father and son premiers, W.A.C. and Bill Bennett, effectively ruled the Social Credit Party and the province from 1952 until 1986. With close ties between government ministers and the resources they oversaw, business—especially manufacturing, mining, and logging—certainly boomed, but along with prosperity came significant governmental scandals, opportunistic financial shenanigans, and major resource mismanagement. Social Credit Premier Bill Vander Zalm was forced to resign in 1991. Reform-minded governments have been in place in Victoria since, although Chicago-style corruption still seems rampant in both government and business.

The 1990s saw a vast influx of Hong Kong Chinese to the Vancouver area, the result of fears accompanying the British hand-over of Hong Kong to the mainland Chinese in 1997. Unlike earlier migrations of Chinese to North America, these Hong Kong Chinese were wealthy middle- and upper-class merchants and business leaders. Vancouver real-estate prices shot through the roof, and entire neighborhoods—like Richmond, south of Vancouver—became Chinese enclaves. Currently, Vancouver has the world's largest Chinese population outside of Asia.

Asians are not the only people bolstering western Canada's fast-growing population. Canada has relatively open emigration laws, resulting in a steady flow of immigrants from the Middle East, the Indian subcontinent, and Europe. Additionally, many young Canadians from the economically depressed eastern provinces see a brighter future in the west. With their strong economies and big-as-all-outdoors setting, Vancouver, Edmonton, and Calgary serve as magnets for many seeking new lives and opportunities.

3 A Taste of British Columbia & the Canadian Rockies

Not that long ago, food in this part of the world was little known, except for the high quality and size of beef steaks and the freshness of salmon from coastal rivers.

Times have really changed. Western Canada is now home to an excellent and evolving regional cuisine that relies on fresh local fruits and vegetables, farm-raised game, grass-fed beef and lamb, and fresh-caught fish and shellfish. These high-quality ingredients are matched with inventive sauces and accompaniments, often based on native berries and wild mushrooms. In attempting to capture what the French call the *terroir,* or the native taste of the Northwest, chefs from Edmonton and Calgary to Victoria and Vancouver are producing a delicious school of cooking with distinctive regional characteristics.

One of the hallmarks of Northwest cuisine is freshness. In places like Vancouver Island, chefs meet fishing boats early in the day to select the finest of the day's catch. The lower Fraser Valley and the interior of British Columbia are filled with small specialty farms and orchards, often organic. Visit Vancouver's Granville Island Market or stop at a roadside farmer's stand to have a look at the incredible bounty of the land.

Cooks in the Northwest are also very particular about where the food comes from. On the one hand, there's a good chance that locally produced fruits and vegetables will be fresher than the same foods shipped in from California. On a different level, however, a food's home address means something else entirely to the serious Northwest cook. Menus often tell you exactly what bay your oysters came from, what farm grew your asparagus, what ranch your beef was raised on, which orchard harvested your peaches. To capture the distinct flavor of the Northwest—its *terroir*—means using only those products that swam in the waters or grew in or on the soil of the Northwest.

Once you've assembled your extra-fresh, locally produced foodstuffs, you need to cook it according to some kind of esthetic. This is where Northwest cooks get inventive. While many chefs marry the region's superior meat, fish, and produce to traditional French or Italian cooking techniques, other cooks turn elsewhere for inspiration. One popular school of Northwest cooking looks west across the Pacific to Asia. Pacific Rim or Pan Pacific cuisine, as this style of cooking is often called, matches the North American Pacific coast's excellent fish and seafood with the flavors of Pacific Asia. The results can be subtle—the delicate taste of lemongrass or nori—or intense, with lashings of red curry or wasabi. However, don't expect Pacific Rim cuisine to follow the rules of Asian cooking: One memorable meal at Calgary's Belvedere restaurant (see chapter 13) matched grilled Pacific salmon with a sauce of Japanese seaweed and reduced red wine, served with heirloom potato cakes.

Other attempts to find the authentic roots of Northwest cooking look back to frontier times or to Native American cooking techniques. There's no better way to experience salmon than at a traditional salmon bake at a native village—most First Nations communities have an annual festival open to the general public—and many restaurants replicate this method by baking salmon on a cedar plank. Several restaurants in Vancouver and on Vancouver Island specialize in full Northwest native feasts. Similarly, Buzzards Cowboy Cuisine in Calgary takes the search for the authentic regional cuisine back to the days of the Open Range. Focusing on foods and ingredients available during the early Canadian west, the restaurant manages to make stylish and delicious food from chuck-wagon staples. For many, the restaurant's specialty meats—like "prairie oysters" (calf testicles)—will either intrigue or repel.

FRUITS OF THE FIELD & FOREST

While there's nothing exotic about the varieties of vegetables available in western Canada, what will seem remarkable to visitors from distant urban areas is the freshness and quality of the produce here. Many fine restaurants contract directly with small, often organic, farms to make daily deliveries of the freshest and most flavorful fruits and vegetables. Heirloom varieties— old-fashioned strains that are often full of flavor but don't ship or keep well— are frequently highlighted.

Fruit trees do particularly well in the hot central valleys of British Columbia, and apples, peaches, apricots, plums, and pears do more than grace the fruit basket. One of the hallmarks of Northwest cuisine is its mixing of fruit with savory meat and chicken dishes. And as long as the chef is slicing apricots to go with sautéed chicken and thyme, she might as well chop up a few hazelnuts (filberts) to toss in: These nuts thrive in the Pacific Northwest, and the presence of a few crunchy hazelnuts in unlikely dishes is a sure sign of Northwest cooking.

Berries of all kinds do well in the milder coastal regions. Cranberries grow in low-lying coastal plains and find their way into a bewildering array of dishes. The blueberry, along with its wild cousin, the huckleberry, are both commonly used in all manner of cooking, from breads and pastries to savory chutneys. In Alberta, another wild cousin, the Saskatoonberry, appears on menus to validate regional cooking aspirations. The astringent wild chokecherry, once used to make pemmican (a sort of Native American energy bar), is also finding its way into fine-dining restaurants.

Wild mushrooms grow throughout western Canada, and harvesting wild mushrooms—like chantrelles, morels, porcinis, and myriad other varieties—is big business. Many are exported to Japan and Europe, but many stay here. Chain grocery stores throughout western Canada now carry a selection of fresh wild mushrooms that only a decade ago would have been seen only in French specialty grocers. Expect to find forest mushrooms in pasta, alongside a steak, in savory bread puddings, or braised with fish.

MEATS & SEAFOOD

Easily the most iconic of the Northwest's staples is the salmon. For thousands of years, the native people have followed the cycles of the salmon, netting or spearing the fish, then smoking and preserving it for later use. The delicious and abundant salmon became the mainstay of settlers and early European residents as well. Although salmon fishing is now highly restricted and some salmon species are endangered, salmon is still very available and easily the most popular fish in the region. Expect to find a salmon dish on practically every fine-dining menu in the Northwest.

However, there are other fish in the sea. The fisheries along Vancouver Island and the Pacific Coast are rich in bottom fish like sole, flounder, and halibut, which grows to enormous size here. Fresh-caught rock and black cod are also delectable, and the Pacific is rich in tuna, especially ahi and albacore.

Although shellfish and seafood are abundant in the Pacific, it is only recently that many of the varieties have appeared on the dinner table. Oysters grow in a number of bays on Vancouver Island, and while wild mussels blanket rocks the length of the coast (and can be harvested for home use), only a few sea farms grow mussels commercially. Fanny Bay, north of Qualicum Beach on Vancouver Island, is noted for both its oysters and mussels, which are available throughout the province. Another shellfish delicacy of the Northwest is the razor clam, a long thin bivalve with a shell that does indeed look like an old-fashioned switchblade razor. The flavor is nutty and rich, and thoroughly delicious. Shrimp of all sizes thrive off the coast of British Columbia, and one of the clichés of Northwest cooking is the unstinting use of local shrimp on nearly everything, from pizza to stews to polenta. Local squid and octopus are beginning to appear on menus, while sea urchin—abundant along the coast—is harvested mostly for export to Japan.

Both British Columbia and Alberta have excellent ranch-raised beef and lamb. Steaks are a staple throughout the region, as is prime rib. You'll see lamb on menus more often in western Canada than in many areas of the United States. Game meats are increasingly popular, especially in restaurants dedicated to Northwest cuisine. Buffalo and venison are offered frequently enough to no longer seem unusual, and farm-raised pheasant is easily available. You'll look harder to find meats like caribou or elk, however. Savor it when you can.

FRUITS OF THE VINEYARDS

British Columbia wines remain one of western Canada's greatest secrets. Scarcely anyone outside of the region has ever heard of these wines, yet many are delicious and, while not exactly cheap, still less expensive than comparable wines from California. There are wineries on Vancouver and Saturna islands and in the Fraser Valley, but the real center of British Columbia's wine making is the Okanagan Valley. In this hot and arid climate, noble grapes like cabernet sauvignon, merlot, and chardonnay thrive when irrigated. You'll also find other more unusual varietals, like gewürztraminer and sangiovese. More than 3 dozen wineries in the Okanagan Valley are open for tastings; when combined with excellent restaurants in Kelowna and Penticton, this region becomes an excellent vacation choice for the serious gastronome.

British Columbia wines are readily available in regional restaurants; in fact, some restaurants offer only local wines. Don't hesitate to ask your server for help in making a selection. There's definitely a range of quality (wine making is still in its adolescence here), and price doesn't always confer quality.

DINING IN RESTAURANTS

Canadians enjoy eating out, and you'll find excellent restaurants throughout British Columbia and Alberta. Many of the restaurants recommended in this guide serve Northwest regional cuisine, the qualities of which are outlined above. These restaurants do their best to serve fresh local produce with preparations that reflect the history or the natural qualities of the region.

However, there is also a wealth of other kinds of restaurants available. If you're a meat eater, it's worth visiting a traditional steak house in Calgary or Edmonton. For reasons that aren't clear, in many smaller centers, Greek restaurants double as the local steak house. Don't be surprised when you see a sign for, say, Dimitri's Steakhouse; both the steaks and the souvlaki will probably be excellent.

Vancouver is one of the most ethnically diverse places on earth, and the selection of restaurants is mind-boggling. You'll find some of the best Chinese food this side of Hong Kong, as well as the cooking of Russia, Mongolia, Ghana, and Sri Lanka, along with every other country and ethnic group in between.

British Columbia in Television & Film

British Columbia is one of the centers of film in Canada, and many Canadian features are set in Vancouver. Numerous Hollywood films have also been shot in the province: *Legends of the Fall, Little Women, Jumanji,* and *Rambo: First Blood* give an idea of the range of films done here. One of the few recent films to feature Vancouver as Vancouver (not as somewhere else) is *Intersection,* with Sharon Stone and Richard Gere. Bill Forsyth's *Housekeeping* was shot in southeastern British Columbia, though the film is meant to portray life in early-20th-century Idaho.

The most noted recent production in the Vancouver area is television's *The X-Files,* which for its first 4 years was shot in and around the city (Vancouver doubles as many American cities, notably Washington, D.C.).

Several Canadian chain restaurants are handy to know about and to keep in reserve. White Spot restaurants are found throughout Canada, and serve basic but good-quality North American cooking. Often open 24 hours, these are good places for an eggs-and-hash browns breakfast. Tim Horton's is *the* place to go for coffee and donuts, plus light snacks. Earl's is a western Canadian chain that serves a wide menu and frequently has a lively and youthful bar scene. Expect grilled ribs and chicken, steaks, and gourmet burgers. The Keg is another western Canadian favorite, and is a bit more sedate than Earl's, with more of a steak-house atmosphere.

4 Recommended Reading

In addition to the specialized volumes listed below, we recommend two excellent books as great adjuncts to this guide, especially if you're on a road trip. The *Big New B.C. Travel Guide* is published by Beautiful British Columbia Magazine—an arm of the provincial tourism office—and is an amazing kilometer-by-kilometer guide to the natural and human history of the province, along with all sorts of curious facts and insights. The *Canadian Rockies,* by Graeme Pole (Altitude), has a similarly encyclopedic approach to western Alberta and eastern British Columbia, with lots of history and nature writing, accompanied by attractive photos. It's also a good source of information on hikes and other outdoor adventures.

CANADIAN HISTORY

If you're planning a trip to Canada, it's a good idea to get a handle on the country's complex history. A basic primer on Canada's historic saga is *The Penguin History of Canada,* by Kenneth McNaught. *The Canadians,* by Andrew H. Malcolm (St. Martin's Press), is an insightful and highly readable rumination on what it is to be Canadian, written by the former *New York Times* Canada bureau chief.

Peter C. Newman writes on Canadian business but has also produced an intriguing history of the Hudson's Bay Company, *Caesars of the Wilderness,* beginning with the early fur-trading days. *The Great Adventure,* by David Cruise and Alison Griffiths (St. Martin's Press), tells the story of the Mounties and their role in the subduing of the Canadian west.

For a specific history of British Columbia, try *British Columbia: An Illustrated History,* by Geoffrey Molyneux (Polestar Books), or *The West Beyond the West: A History of British Columbia,* by Jean Borman (University of Toronto Press). Review Vancouver's past with *Vancouver: A History in Photographs,* by Aynsley Wyse and Dana Wyse (Altitude Publishing).

Alberta: A History in Photographs, by Faye Reinebert Holt (Altitude Publications), is a good introduction to the history of that province, though the engaging *Alberta History Along the Highway: A Traveler's Guide to the Fascinating Facts, Intriguing Incidents and Lively Legends in Alberta's Remarkable Past,* by Ted Stone (Orca Books), is the book you'll want to take along in the car (the same author has a companion volume on British Columbia).

For information on Canada's native peoples, read *Native Peoples and Cultures of Canada,* by Alan D. McMillan (Douglas & McIntyre), which includes both history and current issues. The classic book on Canada's indigenous peoples, *The Indians of Canada* (University of Toronto Press), was written in 1932 by Diamond Jenness. Originally from New Zealand, the author's life is an amazing story in its own right, as he spent years living with various indigenous peoples across the country.

NATURAL HISTORY

Two good general guides to the natural world in western Canada are the Audubon Society's *Pacific Coast,* by Evelyn McConnaghey, and *Western Forests,* by Stephen Whitney (both published by Knopf).

British Columbia: A Natural History, by Richard Cannings (Douglas & McIntyre), is an in-depth guide to the province's plants, animals, and geography. *Plants and Animals of the Pacific Northwest: An Illustrated Guide to the Natural History of Western Oregon, Washington, and British Columbia,* by Eugene N. Kozloff (University of Washington Press), is another good general resource.

For information on the natural history of Alberta's southern prairies, pick up *From Grasslands to Rockland: An Explorers Guide to the Ecosystems of Southernmost Alberta,* by Peter Douglas Elias (Rocky Mountain Books).

Bird watchers might want to dig up a copy of *Familiar Birds of the Northwest,* by Harry B. Nehls (Audubon Society of Portland). Flower enthusiasts should check out *Wayside Wildflowers of the Pacific Northwest,* by Dr. Dee Strickler (Falcon). Explore the gardening scene with *Garden Touring in the Pacific Northwest: A Guide to Gardens and Specialty Nurseries in Oregon, Washington, and British Columbia,* by Jan Kowalczewski Whitner (Alaska Northwest Books).

Read about the natural history of extinct wildlife in *Wonderful Life: The Burgess Shale and the Nature of History,* by Stephan Jay Gould (Norton), which details the discovery and scientific ramifications of the fossil beds found in Yoho National Park.

OUTDOOR PURSUITS

Edward Weber's *Diving and Snorkeling Guide to the Pacific Northwest: Includes Puget Sound, San Juan Islands, and Vancouver Island* (Pisces) is a good place to start if you're planning a diving holiday in the Northwest.

Mountain Bike Adventures in Southwest British Columbia, by Greg Maurer and Tomas Vrba (Mountaineers), is just one of a cascade of books on off-road biking in western Canada.

A good hiking guide to western British Columbia is *Don't Waste Your Time in the B.C. Coast Mountains: An Opinionated Hiking Guide to Help you Get the*

Most from this Magnificent Wilderness, by Kathy Copeland. The *Guide to Climbing and Hiking in Southwestern British Columbia,* by Bruce Fairley, also includes Vancouver Island.

Hiking Alberta, by Will Harmon (Falcon), covers 75 hikes along the eastern face of the Rockies. Chris Dawson's *Due North of Montana: A Guide to Fly-fishing in Alberta* (Johnson Books) will point you toward favorite fishing holes.

FICTION & MEMOIR

Alice Munro's short fiction captures the soul of what it is to be Canadian in brief, though often wrenching, prose. Some of the stories in her recent collection *The Love of a Good Woman* take place in Vancouver. Another good selection of short stories as well as poetry is *Fresh Tracks: Writing the Western Landscape* (Pamela Banting, editor), a collection of writings by western Canadian authors.

The frontier-era conflicts in southern Alberta form the backdrop for the award-winning *The Englishman's Boy,* by Guy Vanderhaeghe (Picador), an atmospheric western with a story that travels from Fort Macleod to Hollywood.

Richard P. Hobson, Jr. writes of his experiences as a modern-day cowboy on the grasslands of central British Columbia in an acclaimed series of memoirs titled *Grass Beyond the Mountains: Discovering the Last Great Cattle Frontier on the North American Continent, The Rancher Takes a Wife,* and *Nothing Too Good for a Cowboy* (McClelland and Stewart).

Vancouver and southwestern British Columbia are home to a number of noted international authors. *Generation X* chronicler Douglas Coupland lives here, as does Jane Rule, author of *Desert of the Heart.* Science-fiction writer William Gibson's dark vision of the cyber-future attracts a large young audience. W. P. Kinsella (*Shoeless Joe*) and mystery writer Laurali R. Wright also make their homes here. Wright's Karl Alberg mystery series usually take place in and around Vancouver.

Index

Index

Index

Index

FROMMER'S® COMPLETE TRAVEL GUIDES

Alaska
Amsterdam
Arizona
Atlanta
Australia
Austria
Bahamas
Barcelona, Madrid &
  Seville
Beijing
Belgium, Holland &
  Luxembourg
Bermuda
Boston
British Columbia & the
  Canadian Rockies
Budapest & the Best of
  Hungary
California
Canada
Cancún, Cozumel &
  the Yucatán
Cape Cod, Nantucket &
  Martha's Vineyard
Caribbean
Caribbean Cruises & Ports
  of Call
Caribbean Ports of Call
Carolinas & Georgia
Chicago
China
Colorado
Costa Rica
Denmark
Denver, Boulder & Colorado
  Springs
England
Europe

European Cruises & Ports
  of Call
Florida
France
Germany
Greece
Greek Islands
Hawaii
Hong Kong
Honolulu, Waikiki &
  Oahu
Ireland
Israel
Italy
Jamaica
Japan
Las Vegas
London
Los Angeles
Maryland & Delaware
Maui
Mexico
Miami & the Keys
Montana & Wyoming
Montréal & Québec City
Munich & the Bavarian
  Alps
Nashville & Memphis
Nepal
New England
New Mexico
New Orleans
New York City
New Zealand
Nova Scotia, New Brunswick
  & Prince Edward Island
Oregon
Paris

Philadelphia & the
  Amish Country
Portugal
Prague & the Best of the
  Czech Republic
Provence & the Riviera
Puerto Rico
Rome
San Antonio & Austin
San Diego
San Francisco
Santa Fe, Taos & Albuquerque
Scandinavia
Scotland
Seattle & Portland
Singapore & Malaysia
South Africa
Southeast Asia
South Pacific
Spain
Sweden
Switzerland
Thailand
Tokyo
Toronto
Tuscany & Umbria
USA
Utah
Vancouver & Victoria
Vermont, New Hampshire
  & Maine
Vienna & the Danube Valley
Virgin Islands
Virginia
Walt Disney World &
  Orlando
Washington, D.C.
Washington State

FROMMER'S® DOLLAR-A-DAY GUIDES

Australia from $50 a Day
California from $60 a Day
Caribbean from $70 a Day
England from $70 a Day
Europe from $60 a Day

Florida from $60 a Day
Hawaii from $70 a Day
Ireland from $60 a Day
Italy from $70 a Day
London from $85 a Day

New York from $80 a Day
Paris from $85 a Day
San Francisco from $60 a Day
Washington, D.C.,
  from $60 a Day

FROMMER'S® PORTABLE GUIDES

Acapulco, Ixtapa &
  Zihuatanejo
Alaska Cruises & Ports of Call
Bahamas
Baja & Los Cabos
Berlin
California Wine Country
Charleston & Savannah
Chicago

Dublin
Hawaii: The Big Island
Las Vegas
London
Maine Coast
Maui
New Orleans
New York City
Paris

Puerto Vallarta, Manzanillo
  & Guadalajara
San Diego
San Francisco
Sydney
Tampa & St. Petersburg
Venice
Washington, D.C.

FROMMER'S® NATIONAL PARK GUIDES

Family Vacations in the
  National Parks
Grand Canyon

National Parks of the
  American West
Rocky Mountain

Yellowstone & Grand Teton
Yosemite & Sequoia/
  Kings Canyon
Zion & Bryce Canyon

FROMMER'S® MEMORABLE WALKS

Chicago
London

New York
Paris

San Francisco
Washington, D.C.

FROMMER'S® GREAT OUTDOOR GUIDES

New England
Northern California

Southern California & Baja
Southern New England

Washington & Oregon

FROMMER'S® BORN TO SHOP GUIDES

Born to Shop: China
Born to Shop: France

Born to Shop: Italy
Born to Shop: London

Born to Shop: New York
Born to Shop: Paris

FROMMER'S® IRREVERENT GUIDES

Amsterdam
Boston
Chicago
Las Vegas

London
Los Angeles
Manhattan
New Orleans

Paris
San Francisco
Seattle & Portland
Vancouver

Walt Disney World
Washington, D.C.

FROMMER'S® BEST-LOVED DRIVING TOURS

America
Britain
California

Florida
France
Germany

Ireland
Italy
New England

Scotland
Spain
Western Europe

THE UNOFFICIAL GUIDES®

Bed & Breakfasts in
  California
Bed & Breakfasts in
  New England
Bed & Breakfasts in
  the Northwest
Beyond Disney
Branson, Missouri
California with Kids
Chicago

Cruises
Disneyland
Florida with Kids
Golf Vacations in the
  Eastern U.S.
The Great Smoky &
  Blue Ridge
  Mountains
Inside Disney

Hawaii
Las Vegas
London
Miami & the Keys
Mini Las Vegas
Mini-Mickey
New Orleans
New York City
Paris

Safaris
San Francisco
Skiing in the West
Walt Disney World
Walt Disney World
  for Grown-ups
Walt Disney World
  for Kids
Washington, D.C.

SPECIAL-INTEREST TITLES

Frommer's Britain's Best Bed & Breakfasts and
  Country Inns
Frommer's Britain's Best Bike Rides
The Civil War Trust's Official Guide
  to the Civil War Discovery Trail
Frommer's Caribbean Hideaways
Frommer's Food Lover's Companion to France
Frommer's Food Lover's Companion to Italy
Frommer's Gay & Lesbian Europe
Frommer's Exploring America by RV
Hanging Out in Europe
Israel Past & Present

Mad Monks' Guide to California
Mad Monks' Guide to New York City
Frommer's The Moon
Frommer's New York City with Kids
The New York Times' Unforgettable
  Weekends
Places Rated Almanac
Retirement Places Rated
Frommer's Road Atlas Britain
Frommer's Road Atlas Europe
Frommer's Washington, D.C., with Kids
Frommer's What the Airlines Never Tell You